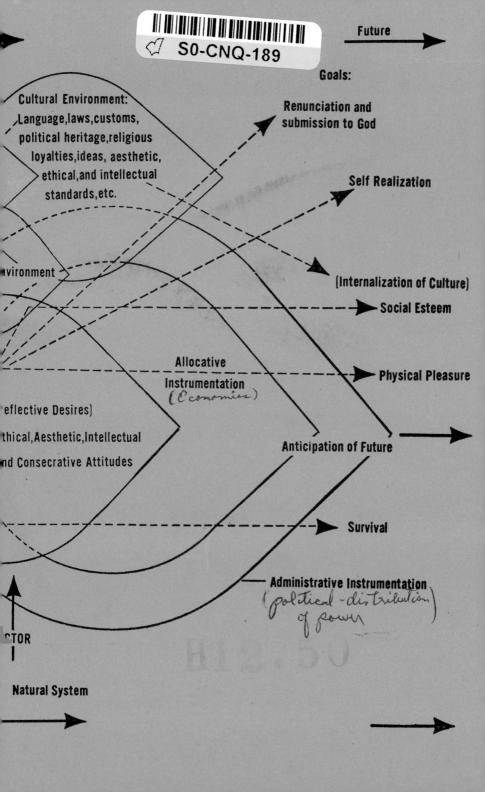

The Problem of Social-Scientific Knowledge

The Problem of Social -

Scientific Knowledge

WILLIAM P. McEWEN

 The Bedminster Press, Totowa, New Jersey, 1963

Readers of this book are invited to send
name and address to The Bedminster Press,
Vreeland Avenue, Totowa, New Jersey, U.S.A.,
to receive announcements and literature about
other books in the social sciences
published by The Bedminster Press.

TO MARJORIE

Preface

When a book bears such an ambitious title as *The Problem of Social-Scientific Knowledge*, its scope and aim should be clarified at the outset. A social scientist who has been arduously engaged in the difficult search for knowledge within the limited area of his own discipline, may protest that it is meaningless for a philosopher to discuss the problem of knowledge for the social-scientific enterprise as a whole. Now he would be right, if it were my intention to present a conglomeration of the research problems of psychology, sociology, anthropology, economics, political science, and history. Since I am not an expert in any one of these fields, it should be clearly understood that at no point in this study shall I presume to pose or solve the specialist's research problems.

It is to another dimension of the problem of obtaining reliable knowledge about human behavior, that this book directs attention. In an attempt to answer the basic question of what kind of social-scientific knowledge is meaningful, I shall suggest an epistemological pattern of reflective inquiry from which I believe the techniques of behavioral research and the categories of behavioral theory are derived. To be sure, some theoreticians among social scientists have been interested in this aspect of the problem of knowledge at a higher level of abstraction. If they are thorough, however, are they not eventually confronted by the persisting epistemological questions for which philosophers are seeking answers?

The aim of this book is to contribute toward the formulation of a philosophical theory of knowledge which emerges out of the context of social-scientific inquiry, in order to provide an epistemological perspective for behavioral research and theory. A precedent for such a philosophical approach can be found in *The Problem of Historical Knowledge* in which Mandelbaum, in a somewhat similar way, applies epistemological principles to the more restricted study of the record of past human actions.

Usually when psychologists, sociologists, anthropologists, economists, political scientists, and historians discuss the problem of knowledge in their respective fields, they are not explicitly considering this more abstract level of an epistemological pattern. This does not mean, however, that social-scientific theories and philosophical theories are mutually exclusive. On the one hand, philosophers such as Cohen, Hempel, Nagel, Northrop, and others have been concerned with some of the epistemological issues which are involved in social-scientific inquiry. Although Dewey, in his *Logic*, seemed to be rejecting epistemology in favor of methodology, I shall later justify my claim that his pattern of inquiry is an essential ingredient in a reconstructed epistemological approach to the social scientist's way of knowing. I endorse Dewey's rejection of those traditional theories of knowledge which were arbitrarily imposed on the actual process of inquiry. Accordingly, I suggest that social scientists who feel that traditional theories of knowledge are fruitless, should study Werkmeister's *The Basis and Structure of Knowledge*. He deals more extensively with an epistemology for the natural sciences than with one for the social sciences. Nevertheless, he makes a most significant contribution to the clarification of behavioral research and theory, when he emphasizes the need for correlating the meaning-issues and the knowledge-issues. For, as we shall subsequently show, it is upon this correlation that a sound epistemological perspective for social-scientific inquiry depends. On the other hand, when a social scientist presses his analysis of human transactions to the cognitive level of "social causation," as MacIver does, or to the cognitive level of "social system," as Parsons does, then he has invoked some basic epistemological presuppositions of behavioral theory and research. If we can make this implicit convergence explicit, we shall discern an important dimension of the problem of social-scientific knowledge, which some research specialists may not be fully aware of.

Although the epistemological principles developed here will be general enough to be applicable to all of the behavioral areas, methodological problems which have been raised by the representatives of specific disciplines will also be taken into account. In fact, there would be no justification for formulating this synoptic system of philosophical generalizations, if it were not designed to compare and clarify the cognitive questions which arise in each of the disciplines.

By committing myself to an examination of the relevant literature in each of the social-scientific disciplines, I have been caught in a dilemma. Despite the fact that I have spent many years in reading journal articles and books by representatives of each of the behavioral fields, I cannot be sure that I have not inadvertently missed some important contributions. If this should be the case, I hope that the authors of such articles or books will understand my predicament. To postpone publication until I could be sure that all relevant writings were included would virtually mean never completing this book.

This book is primarily a monograph which I would have written even if it could not be used as a textbook. My main concern is to direct the attention of the behavioral scientists themselves to the epistemological principles which the problem of social-scientific knowledge entails. I have felt compelled to share with other philosophers the obligation to provide the social sciences with something like the epistemological foundation that Whitehead has formulated for the natural sciences.

While I am chiefly interested in eliciting the response of scholars in support of this objective, perhaps this study can also be used by teachers who need a text for such a course as "Methodology of the Social Sciences." There is a considerable amount of philosophical and social-scientific material available in journals and anthologies, as well as in several books which deal with specific behavioral disciplines. But these widely-ranging ideas need to be coordinated and interpreted in terms of the total problem of social-scientific knowledge as a branch of epistemology.

For several years I have been using the manuscript of this book as a text in my undergraduate course, "The Methodology of the Social Sciences." During the past year, when Mr. Frank Wekerle taught the course, he found that this book could be used effectively without the author as the teacher. Both of us have been able to complete this course in one semester. When I have used the book in graduate courses, I have extended it to two semesters by expanding assignments to include more detailed analyses of the relevant social-scientific sources. A number of philosophers and social scientists from other colleges have indicated that they, too, would like to offer such courses, if they could find a suitable text. Perhaps this book may serve that need.

Teachers who use this book will undoubtedly find that they can refine the discussion of many points which it raises, and add to it other points which have been neglected or insufficiently developed. I do not offer it as a definitive work. If my book helps to establish this new field of study, and provokes another philosopher to write a more advanced approach, it will have served its purpose.

A caveat is required in order to avoid a serious misunderstanding about the use of this book. Neither this book, nor the kind of course for which it can be used as a text, should be considered as a substitute for books or courses which present the substantive content of specific research techniques of the individual behavioral disciplines. If, however, I were not convinced that philosophy can furnish social-scientific inquiry with significant guidance, I would not have spent the time and effort which this book has demanded. I recognize, nevertheless, that no philosopher can actually solve the problem of social-scientific knowledge at the level of generality on which he must operate. If the philosopher can perform the necessary task of clarifying the underlying assumptions about what kind of knowledge is meaningful, then it is up to the experts who are well informed and trained in their specific disciplines to work toward solving their own knowledge problems; for creative research can only be carried out within the delimited scope of a specific area of inquiry. But those research findings can lose their significance as an integral part of cumulative knowledge, if they cannot be related to other results in terms of the broad-gauged principles which concern the epistemologist.

How does one thank the many people who directly or indirectly have helped him in the preparation of such a project as this? In producing this book I was fortunate to have the benefit of the critical assistance of Mrs. Margaret Rowlinson and Dr. Bertram Brettschneider. Without the guidance and suggestions of many of my colleagues in the Division of Social Sciences, I would have found it much more difficult, if not impossible, to become acquainted with the literature of their respective disciplines. Without the questions and constructive criticism of succeeding generations of my undergraduate and graduate students in *The Methodology of the Social Sciences* this work would have been far more inadequate. It seems best not to name these colleagues and students. Since there have been so many throughout the years the list would be long and I fear I might forget to mention some.

Through the considerate offices of President John Cranford Adams, Hofstra University provided released time and facilities for which I am most grateful.

What I owe professionally to the writings of Professor Gordon Allport of Harvard will be quite evident throughout my discussion of psychology; but, beyond that, I am personally obligated to him for his constructive criticisms and encouraging comments in the light of which I revised the entire manuscript.

Rather than to try to tell my wife how much I appreciate her gracious forebearance throughout such an undertaking, I dedicate this book to her.

William P. McEwen
Hofstra University

ACKNOWLEDGMENTS

I am grateful to the following publishers for permitting me to use quotations from works published by them as indicated below:

ADDISON-WESLEY PUBLISHING COMPANY, INC.:
  Handbook of Social Psychology (Vol. I) edited by Gardner Lindzey. Copyright 1954 by Addison-Wesley Publishing Company, Inc. and used with their permission.
GEORGE ALLEN & UNWIN LTD.:
  Philosophy of Physics by Max Planck. Copyright 1936 by George Allen & Unwin Ltd. and used with their permission.
  The Universe in the Light of Modern Physics by Max Planck. Copyright 1937 by George Allen & Unwin Ltd. and used with their permission.
  Where Is Science Going by Max Planck. Copyright 1932 by George Allen & Unwin Ltd. and used with their permission.
THE AMERICAN JOURNAL OF PSYCHOLOGY:
  "The Functional Autonomy of Motives," *The American Journal of Psychology*, Vol. 50, 1937, by Gordon Allport. Reprinted in *The Nature of Personality* by Gordon Allport and used with the permission of *The American Journal of Psychology*.
THE AMERICAN PSYCHOLOGICAL ASSOCIATION:
  "Motivation in Personality: Reply to Mr. Bertocci," by Gordon Allport,

Psychological Review, 47, No. 6, November 1940. Copyright 1940 by the *Psychological Review* and used with their permission.

"The Operational Analysis of Psychological Terms," by B. F. Skinner, *Psychological Review*, Vol. 52, 1945. Copyright 1945 by the *Psychological Review* and used with their permission.

APPLETON-CENTURY-CROFTS, INC.:

Illustrations of Universal Progress by Herbert Spencer. Copyright 1875 by Appleton-Century-Crofts, Inc. and used with their permission.

The Cultural Background of Personality by Ralph Linton. Copyright 1945 by Appleton-Century-Crofts, Inc. and used with their permission.

Readings in the Philosophy of Science edited by H. Feigl and M. Brodbeck. Copyright 1953 by Appleton-Century-Crofts, Inc. and used with their permission.

BASIC BOOKS, INC.:

Toward a Unified Theory of Human Behavior edited by Roy Grinker. Copyright 1956 by Basic Books, Inc. and used with their permission.

THE BEDMINSTER PRESS:

On Theory and Verification in Sociology by Hans Zetterberg. Copyright 1954 by The Bedminster Press and used with their permission.

BLACKIE & SON LIMITED:

Atomic Physics by Max Born. Copyright 1951 by Blackie & Son Limited and used with their permission.

BOLLINGEN FOUNDATION:

Integration of the Personality by Carl G. Jung. Copyright 1939 by Bollingen Foundation and used with their permission.

GEORGE BRAZILLER, INC.:

Present Philosophical Tendencies by Ralph B. Perry. Copyright 1955 by George Braziller, Inc. and used with their permission.

WM. C. BROWN COMPANY PUBLISHERS:

Values and Policy in American Society edited by Grimes-Clark. Copyright 1954 by Wm. C. Brown Company Publishers and used with their permission.

UNIVERSITY OF CALIFORNIA PRESS:

Behavior and Psychological Man by Edward Tolman. Copyright 1958 by University of California Press and used with their permission.

Business Cycles by Wesley Clair Mitchell. Copyright 1913 by the University of California Press and used with their permission.

Culture, Language, and Personality by Edward Sapir. Copyright 1949 by the University of California Press and used with their permission.

Philosophic Foundations of Quantum Mechanics by Hans Reichenbach. Copyright 1944 by the University of California Press and used with their permission.

THE UNIVERSITY OF CHICAGO PRESS:

"The Operation Called Verstehen" by Theodore Abel. Originally published in the *American Journal of Sociology*, 54, 1948, published by The University of Chicago Press. Copyright 1948 by the University of Chicago.

The Physical Principles of the Quantum Theory by Werner Heisenberg.

Published by The University of Chicago Press. Copyright 1930 by the University of Chicago.
The Rules of Sociological Method by Emile Durkeim. Published by The University of Chicago Press. Copyright 1938 by the University of Chicago.
Essays in Positive Economics by Milton Friedman. Published by The University of Chicago Press. Copyright 1953 by the University of Chicago.
Theory of Valuation by John Dewey. Published by The University of Chicago Press. Copyright 1939 by the University of Chicago.
Studies in the Economics of Overhead Costs by John M. Clark. Published by The University of Chicago Press. Copyright 1923 by the University of Chicago.
The Economic Organization by Frank Knight. Published by The University of Chicago Press. Copyright 1948 by the University of Chicago.
Systematic Politics by Charles Merriam. Published by The University of Chicago Press. Copyright 1945 by the University of Chicago.
Procedures of Empirical Science by Victor F. Lenzen. Published by The University of Chicago Press. Copyright 1938 by the University of Chicago.
Anthropology Today by Alfred L. Kroeber. Published by The University of Chicago Press. Copyright 1953 by the University of Chicago.
The Nature of Culture by A. L. Kroeber. Published by The University of Chicago Press. Copyright 1952 by the University of Chicago.
The State of the Social Sciences by Leonard White (ed.) Published by The University of Chicago Press. Copyright 1955 by the University of Chicago.
An Appraisal of Anthropology Today by Sol Tax. Published by The University of Chicago Press. Copyright 1953 by the University of Chicago.
Current Anthropology by William L. Thomas (ed.) Published by The University of Chicago Press. Copyright 1952 by the University of Chicago.
THE CLARENDON PRESS:
The Nature of Historical Explanation by Patrick Gardiner. Copyright 1952 by The Clarendon Press and used with their permission.
The Idea of History by Robin G. Collingwood. Copyright 1946 by The Clarendon Press and used with their permission.
Laws and Explanation in History by William Dray. Copyright 1957 by The Clarendon Press and used with their permission.
COLUMBIA UNIVERSITY PRESS:
The Science of Man in the World Crisis by Ralph Linton. Copyright 1945 by the Columbia University Press and used with their permission.
Naturalism and the Human Spirit by Vervant Krikorian. Copyright 1944 by the Columbia University Press and used with their permission.
Economic Essays in Honor of Wesley Clair Mitchell edited by Taylor. Copyright 1935 by the Columbia University Press and used with their permission.
Nature and Judgment by Justus Buchler. Copyright 1955 by the Columbia University Press and used with their permission.
Theoretical Anthropology by David Bidney. Copyright 1953 by the Columbia University Press and used with their permission.
Research Project in the Origins of Economic History by Karl Polanyi. Copy-

right by the Council for Research in the Social Sciences, Columbia University and used with their permission.

THOMAS Y. CROWELL COMPANY:
Politics, Parties, and Pressure Groups by V. O. Key, Jr. 3rd Edition. Copyright 1950 by Thomas Y. Crowell Company and used with their permission.

THE JOHN DAY COMPANY INC.:
The Spirit of American Economics by J. F. Normano. Copyright 1943 by The John Day Company Inc. and used with their permission.

DOVER PUBLICATIONS, INC.:
The Idea of Progress by John B. Bury. Copyright 1955 by Dover Publications, Inc. and used with their permission.

DUKE UNIVERSITY PRESS:
Theoretical Models and Personality Theory by David Krech and George S. Klein. Copyright 1952 by the Duke University Press and used with their permission.

E. P. DUTTON & CO. INC.:
Critique of Pure Reason by Immanuel Kant (tr. J. M. D. Meiklejohn). Published 1934 by Everyman's Library, E. P. Dutton & Co. Inc. and used with their permission.

FARRAR, STRAUS & CUDAHY, INC.:
The Science of Culture by Leslie A. White. Copyright 1949 by Farrar, Straus & Cudahy, Inc. and used with their permission.

THE FOUNDATION FOR INTEGRATIVE EDUCATION, INC.:
"The Methodology for Integration in the Physical Sciences," in *The Nature of Concepts* by Henry Margenau. Copyright 1950 by The Foundation for Integrative Education, Inc. and used with their permission.

THE FREE PRESS OF GLENCOE, INC.:
Reason and Nature by Morris R. Cohen. Copyright 1953 by The Free Press of Glencoe, Inc. and used with their permission.
The Language of Social Research by Paul F. Lazarsfeld and M. Rosenberg. Copyright 1955 by The Free Press of Glencoe, Inc. and used with their permission.
Evidence and Inference by Daniel Lerner. Copyright 1958 by The Free Press of Glencoe, Inc. and used with their permission.
Human Nature and the Social Order by Charles H. Cooley. Copyright 1955 by The Free Press of Glencoe, Inc. and used with their permission.
Foundations of Social Anthropology by Siefried Nadel. Copyright 1953 by The Free Press of Glencoe, Inc. and used with their permission.
The Theory of Social & Economic Organization by Max Weber (Henderson & Parsons). Copyright 1957 by The Free Press of Glencoe, Inc. and used with their permission.
Methodology of the Social Sciences by Max Weber (Shils & Finch). Copyright 1949 by The Free Press of Glencoe, Inc. and used with their permission.
The Social System by Talcott Parsons. Copyright 1951 by The Free Press of Glencoe, Inc. and used with their permission.
Essays in Sociological Theory, Pure and Applied by Talcott Parsons. Copy-

Constitutional Government and Democracy by Carl J. Friedrich. Copyright 1937 by Harper and Brothers and used with their permission.

The Meaning of Philosophy by Joseph G. Brennan. Copyright 1953 by Harper and Brothers and used with their permission.

The Basis and Structure of Knowledge by William Werkmeister. Copyright 1948 by Harper and Brothers and used with their permission.

HARVARD UNIVERSITY PRESS:

The Foundations of Economic Analysis by Paul Samuelson. Copyright 1937 by Harvard University Press and used with their permission.

Historian and Scientist by Gaetano Salvemini. Copyright 1939 by Harvard University Press and used with their permission.

Toward a General Theory of Action edited by T. Parsons and E. Shils.

Collected Papers of Charles Peirce by Charles Hartshorne and Paul Weiss. Copyright 1931 by Harvard University Press and used with their permission.

D. C. HEATH AND COMPANY:

The Gateway to History by Allan Nevins. Copyright 1938 by D. C. Heath and Company and used with their permission.

HOLT, RINEHART AND WINSTON, INC.:

Social Psychology by Theodore Newcomb. Copyright 1950 by Holt, Rinehart and Winston and used with their permission.

Logic, The Theory of Inquiry by John Dewey. Copyright 1938 by Holt, Rinehart and Winston and used with their permission.

The Method of Sociology by Florian Zaniecki. Copyright 1934 by Holt, Rinehart and Winston, Inc. and used with their permission.

A History of Political Theory by George H. Sabine. Copyright 1950 by Holt, Rinehart and Winston, Inc. and used with their permission.

Society by Robert MacIver and Charles Page. Copyright 1949 by Holt, Rinehart and Winston, Inc. and used with their permission.

Personality by Gordon Allport. Copyright 1937 by Holt, Rinehart and Winston, Inc. and used with their permission.

Man for Himself by Eric Fromm. Copyright 1947 by Holt, Rinehart and Winston, Inc. and used with their permission.

The Assessment of Human Motives by Gardner Lindzey. Copyright 1958 by Holt, Rinehart and Winston, Inc. and used with their permission.

HOUGHTON MIFFLIN COMPANY:

Patterns of Culture by Ruth Benedict. Copyright 1934 by Houghton Mifflin Company and used with their permission.

HUMANITIES PRESS INC.:

The Hero in History by Sidney Hook. Copyright 1943 by Humanities Press Inc. and used with their permission.

RICHARD D. IRWIN, INC.:

A Survey of Contemporary Economics, Volume I, edited by Howard S. Ellis. Copyright 1948 by Richard D. Irwin, Inc. and used with the permission of the American Economic Association.

A Survey of Contemporary Economics, Volume II, edited by Bernard F. Haley. Copyright 1952 by Richard D. Irwin, Inc. and used with the permission of the American Economic Association.

Enterprise and Secular Change edited by Lane and Riemersma. Copyright 1953 by Richard D. Irwin, Inc. and used with the permission of the American Economic Association.

THE JOURNAL OF PHILOSOPHY:

"The Function of General Laws in History," *The Journal of Philosophy*, 39, 1942; which was reproduced in *Readings in Philosophical Analysis*, by Feigl, Sellars, and Hempel, and used with their personal permission.

THE CALVIN K. KAZANJIAN ECONOMICS FOUNDATION, INC.:

The Ethical Basis of Economic Freedom by John M. Clark. Copyright 1955 by The Calvin K. Kazanjian Economic Foundation, Inc. and used with their permission.

KELLEY AND MILLMAN, INC.:

Memorials of Alfred Marshall edited by A. C. Pigou. Copyright 1956 by Kelley and Millman, Inc. and used with their permission.

ALFRED A. KNOPF INCORPORATED:

Understanding History by Louis Gottschalk. Copyright 1950 by Alfred A. Knopf Incorporated and used with their permission.

The Political System by David Easton. Copyright 1953 by Alfred A. Knopf Incorporated and used with their permission.

Personality in Nature, Society, and Culture by C. Klupckhohn, H. Murray, and D. Schneider. Copyright 1955 by Alfred A. Knopf Incorporated and used with their permission.

LIVERIGHT PUBLISHING CORPORATION:

Dynamics in Psychology by Wolfgang Kohler. Copyright 1940 by Liveright Publishing Corporation and used with their permission.

Problem of Historical Knowledge by Maurice Mandelbaum. Copyright 1938 by Liveright Publishing Corporation and used with their permission.

The Place of Value in a World of Facts by Wolfgang Kohler. Copyright 1938 by Liveright Publishing Corporation and used with their permission.

THE MACMILLAN COMPANY:

Encyclopedia of the Social Sciences, Vols. II, IV, V, VII, and XII, edited by Seligman and Johnson. Copyright 1931 by The Macmillan Company and used with their permission.

Psychological Theory by Melvin Marx. Copyright 1951 by The Macmillan Company and used with their permission.

Social Structure by George Murdock. Copyright 1949 by the Macmillan Company and used with their permission.

The Logic of the Social Sciences and the Humanities by Filmer Northrop. Copyright 1947 by the Macmillan Company and used with their permission.

Foundations of Sociology by George Lundberg. Copyright 1953 by The Macmillan Company and used with their permission.

Modes of Thought by Alfred N. Whitehead. Copyright 1938 by The Macmillan Company and used with their permission.

Process and Reality by Alfred N. Whitehead. Copyright 1930 by The Macmillan Company and used with their permission.

Adventures of Ideas by Alfred N. Whitehead. Copyright 1933 by The Macmillan Company and used with their permission.

THE OPEN COURT PUBLISHING COMPANY:
 The Meaning of Human History by Morris R. Cohen. Copyright 1947 by
 The Open Court Publishing Company and used with their permission.
 The Revolt Against Dualism by Arthur Lovejoy. Copyright 1930 by The
 Open Court Publishing Company and used with their permission.

OXFORD UNIVERSITY PRESS, INC.:
 Essays Concerning Human Understanding by John Locke. Copyright 1894
 by Oxford University Press and used with their permission.
 Essays on Sociology and Social Psychology by Karl Mannheim. Copyright
 1953 by Oxford University Press and used with their permission.
 The Uses of the Past by Herbert Muller. Copyright 1952 by Oxford
 University Press and used with their permission.
 History of Economic Analysis by Joseph Schumpeter. Copyright 1954 by
 Oxford University Press, Inc. and used with their permission.
 The Modern State by Robert MacIver. Copyright 1926 by Oxford University
 Press, Inc. and used with their permission.

A. D. PETERS:
 History and Human Relations by Herbert Butterfield. Copyright 1951 by
 A. D. Peters and used with permission of Herbert Butterfield.

THE PHILOSOPHICAL LIBRARY:
 Essays in Science and Philosophy by Alfred N. Whitehead. Copyright 1947
 by The Philosophical Library and used with their permission.
 Existentialism by Sartre (tr. Frechtman). Copyright 1947 by The Philosophical Library and used with their permission.

PHILOSOPHY OF SCIENCE:
 "On Some Methodological Problems of Psychology," *Philosophy of Science*,
 Vol. 7, 1940, by Gustav Bergmann. Copyright 1940 by the *Philosophy of
 Science* and used with their permission.
 "Physics and the Problem of Historico-Sociological Laws," *Philosophy of
 Science*, Vol. 8, 1941, by Edgar Zilsel. Copyright 1941 by the *Philosophy of
 Science* and used with their permission.
 "The Logic of Explanation," *Philosophy of Science*, Vol. 15, 1948 by Carl
 G. Hempel and Paul Oppenheim. Copyright 1948 by the *Philosophy of
 Science* and used with their permission.

PRENTICE-HALL INC.:
 Signs, Language, and Behavior by Charles W. Morris. Copyright 1946 by
 Prentice-Hall, Inc. and used with their permission.
 Modern Economic Thought: The American Contribution, by Allan G.
 Gruchy. Copyright 1947 by Prentice-Hall, Inc. and used with their permission.
 Social Psychology by Solomon E. Asch. Copyright 1952 by Prentice-Hall,
 Inc. and used with their permission.
 Western Political Heritage by William Elliott and Neil McDonald. Copy-
 right 1949 by Prentice-Hall, Inc. and used with their permission.
 The Social Theories of Talcott Parsons edited by Max Black. Copyright
 1961 by Prentice-Hall, Inc. and used with their permission.

PRINCETON UNIVERSITY PRESS:
The Nature of Physical Theory by Percy W. Bridgman. Copyright 1936 by the Princeton University Press and used with their permission.

THE PRINCIPIA PRESS, INC.:
The Logic of Modern Science by Jacob Kantor. Copyright 1953 by The Principia Press, Inc.

RANDOM HOUSE, INC.:
Sociological Perspective by Ely Chinoy. Copyright 1954 by Random House, Inc. Reprinted by permission.
Man In Society by George Simpson. Copyright 1954 by Random House, Inc. Reprinted by permission.

REVIEW OF ECONOMIC STUDIES:
"The Scope and Method of Economics," *Review of Economic Studies*, 13, 1945-6, by Oscar Lange. Copyright 1945-6 by the *Review of Economic Studies* and used with their permission.

ROW, PETERSON & COMPANY:
Symposium on Sociological Theory edited by Llewellyn Gross. Copyright 1959 by Row, Peterson & Company and used with their permission.

SCIENTIFIC MONTHLY:
"The Logic of Historical Analysis," by Ernest Nagel, *Scientific Monthly*, 74, 1952. Copyright 1952 by *Scientific Monthly* and reprinted by permission.

SIMON AND SCHUSTER:
The Evolution of Physics by Albert Einstein and Leopold Infeld. Copyright 1938 by Simon and Schuster and used with the permission of the Estate of Albert Einstein.

SOCIAL SCIENCE RESEARCH COUNCIL:
Bulletin 54, 1946, *Theory and Practice in Historical Study: A Report of the Committee on Historiography*. Copyright 1946 by the Social Science Research Council and used with their permission.
Bulletin 64, 1954, *The Social Sciences in Historical Study*. Copyright 1954 by the Social Science Research Council and used with their permission.

THE SOCIETY FOR THE ADVANCEMENT OF EDUCATION, INC.:
School and Society, Vol. 45—No. 1162, 1937. Copyright 1937 by The Society for the Advancement of Education, Inc. and used with their permission.

ST MARTIN'S PRESS INCORPORATED:
The Condition of Economic Progress by Colin Clark. Copyright 1957 by St Martin's Press, Inc. and Macmillan & Company Ltd. and used with their permission.

STANFORD UNIVERSITY PRESS:
The Policy Sciences by Daniel Lerner and Harold D. Lasswell. Copyright 1951 by the Stanford University Press and used with their permission.

REXFORD G. TUGWELL:
The Trend of Economics by Rexford G. Tugwell, 1924, and used with personal permission.

UNITED NATIONS EDUCATIONAL, SCIENTIFIC
AND CULTURAL ORGANIZATION:
Political Science in the U.S.A. by Dwight Waldo. Copyright 1956 by
United Nations Educational, Scientific, and Cultural Organization and used
with their permission.
UNIVERSITY OF MINNESOTA PRESS:
*Method and Perspective in Anthropology: Papers in Honor of Wilson D.
Wallis* edited by Robert F. Spencer. University of Minnesota Press,
Minneapolis. Copyright 1954 by the University of Minnesota and used
with their permission.
Theory and Method in the Social Sciences by Arnold M. Rose. University
of Minnesota Press, Minneapolis. Copyright 1954 by the University of
Minnesota and used with their permission.
THE UNIVERSITY OF NORTH CAROLINA PRESS:
Scientific Theory of Culture by Bronislaw Malinowski. Copyright 1944 by
the University of North Carolina Press and used with their permission.
UNIVERSITY OF NOTRE DAME PRESS:
Ethics and the Social Sciences edited by Leo R. Ward. Copyright 1959 by
the University of Notre Dame Press and used with their permission.
UNIVERSITY OF PITTSBURGH PRESS:
A Grammar of Human Values by Otto von Mering. Copyright 1961 by the
University of Pittsburgh Press and used with their permission.
JOHN WILEY & SONS, INC.:
Methods of Psychology by Tom G. Andrews. Copyright 1948 by John Wiley
& Sons, Inc. and reprinted with their permission.
Foundations of Physics by Robert S. Lindsay and Henry Margenau. Copyright
1936 by John Wiley & Sons, Inc. and reprinted with their permission.
THE UNIVERSITY OF WISCONSIN PRESS:
Institutional Economics by John H. Commons. Copyright 1959 by the
University of Wisconsin Press and reprinted with permission of the Regents
of the University of Wisconsin.
YALE UNIVERSITY PRESS:
Essay on Man by Ernst Cassirer. Copyright 1944 by the Yale University
Press and used with their permission.
Becoming by Gordon Allport. Copyright 1955 by the Yale University Press
and used with their permission.
The Writing of History by F. M. Fling. Copyright 1920 by the Yale
University Press and used with their permission.
Human Action by Ludwig von Mises. Copyright 1949 by the Yale University
Press and used with their permission.
The Dynamics of Cultural Change by Bronislaw Malinowski. Copyright 1945
by the Yale University Press and used with their permission.
Power and Society by Harold D. Lasswell. Copyright 1950 by the Yale
University Press and used with their permission.

CONTENTS

PART ONE *Prolegomena*

Chapter 1   The Scope of This Book   3

A. *The Aims of This Study*
B. *Epistemology and Methodology*
   1. WHAT IS EPISTEMOLOGY?
   2. EPISTEMOLOGICAL DUALISM
   3. THE EPISTEMOLOGICALLY DUALISTIC CHARACTER OF THE SCIEN-
      TIFIC CONCEPTION OF CONSTRUCTED KNOWLEDGE
   4. WHAT DO SOCIAL SCIENTISTS MEAN BY METHODOLOGY AND HOW
      IS IT RELATED TO EPISTEMOLOGY?

Chapter 2   The Subject Matter of Social Science   20

A. *The Behavioral Process*
   1. THE TEMPORAL DIMENSION OF HUMAN BEHAVIOR
   2. RECIPROCAL COLLECTIVE-INDIVIDUAL FOCI
   3. A TWO FOLD IDENTIFICATION OF THE BEHAVIORAL PROCESS
B. *The Subject Matter of Each of the Behavioral Disciplines*

Chapter 3 The Value-Centric Predicament 29

A. *The Evaluational Dilemma*
1. THE VALUE-MOTIVATION OF BOTH NATURAL SCIENTISTS AND SOCIAL SCIENTISTS
2. THE HUMAN VALUE-SITUATION AS BEHAVIORAL DATA
3. THE SOCIAL SCIENTIST'S PARTICIPATION IN THE VALUE-SITUATION
4. THE CONCERN OF SOCIAL SCIENTISTS ABOUT POLICY RECOMMENDATIONS

B. *Should Social Scientists Render Normative Judgments?*

Chapter 4 Situational Relativism 55

A. *Radical Relativism*
B. *Situational Relativism*
C. *The Relativistic Function of the Meaning-Situation in the Cognitive Process*
D. *The Epistemological Perspective of Representative Ways of Knowing*
1. THE EPISTEMOLOGICAL PERSPECTIVE
2. WAYS OF KNOWING
  a. UNCRITICAL NON-OPERATIONALISM:
    i. DOGMATIC AUTHORITARIANISM
    ii. MYSTICISM
    iii. NAÏVE PRAGMATISM
    iv. NAÏVE SENSE-IMPRESSIONISM
  b. CRITICAL NON-OPERATIONALISM:
    i. PURE RATIONALISM
    ii. PURE EMPIRICISM

E. *The Positive Scepticism of a Situational Relativist*
1. NEGATIVE SCEPTICISM
2. POSITIVE SCEPTICISM

F. *Conclusion to this Prolegomena*

PART TWO *Toward a Definition of Social-Scientific Knowledge*

Chapter 1 Broader Operationalism 91

A. *Is Narrower Operationalism Adequate for Social Science?*
B. *Toward the Requirements of Broader Operational Knowledge*

Chapter 2   The Conceptual Orientation of Behavioral
Data   133

A. *The Nature and Function of a Conceptual Model*
B. *Recognition of the Need for a Conceptual Model*

Chapter 3   A Synoptic Model   146

A. *The Presentation of a Synoptic Model*
B. *The Elaboration of This Synoptic Model*
1. THE INDEPENDENT VARIABLES
   a. THE NATURAL SITUATION
   b. THE CULTURAL SITUATION
   c. THE SOCIAL SITUATION
   d. THE PERSONALITY SITUATION
      i. THE INDEPENDENT VARIABLES OF THE PERSONALITY SITUA-
         TION
         (a) PSYCHODYNAMIC MOTIVATIONAL SITUATION
         (b) INTERPERSONAL MOTIVATIONAL SITUATION
      ii. CONSCIOUS GOAL-SEEKING MOTIVATION AS AN INTERVENING
         VARIABLE OF THE PERSONALITY SITUATION
2. CONSCIOUS GOAL-SEEKING AS THE INTERVENING VARIABLE IN A
   SYNOPTIC MODEL

Chapter 4   Further Elaboration of a Synoptic Model   184

A. *The Diachronic Process*
B. *The Technological Order*
1. ADMINISTRATIVE INSTRUMENTATION
2. ALLOCATIVE INSTRUMENTATION
C. *Broadly Operational Modes of Analysis Required by the Synoptic
   Model*
1. INTEGRATION WITH RELATIVE AUTONOMY
2. THE MOLAR-MOLECULAR DISTINCTION
3. NOMOTHETIC-IDIOGRAPHIC SYNCHRONIZATION
4. FUNCTIONAL-STRUCTURAL SYNCHRONIZATION

PART THREE   *The Epistemological Pattern of
Reflective Inquiry*

Chapter 1   The Epistemological Perspective of Reflective
Inquiry   213

A. *The Value-Situation of Reflective Inquiry*

B. *The Meaning-Situation of Reflective Inquiry*
  1. WHAT KIND OF KNOWLEDGE IS ACQUIRED THROUGH REFLECTIVE INQUIRY?
  2. THE POSTULATIONAL CHARACTER OF THE MEANING-SITUATION
  3. THE EPISTEMOLOGICAL NECESSITY FOR MEANING-POSTULATES
C. *The Knowledge-Situation of Reflective Inquiry*
  1. BY WHAT METHOD AND CRITERION IS BROADLY OPERATIONAL KNOWLEDGE ACQUIRED?
  2. THE HYPOTHETICAL-DEDUCTIVE METHOD AS AN ORGANIZATION OF DIVERSE OBSERVATIONAL AND VERIFICATIVE TECHNIQUES
  3. THE ACKNOWLEDGMENT OF THE HYPOTHETICAL-DEDUCTIVE METHOD BY SOCIAL SCIENTISTS
  4. THE CONSTRUCTIVE CHARACTER OF THE OBSERVATIONAL DATA IN HYPOTHETICAL-DEDUCTIVE INQUIRY

Chapter 2   The Meaning-Situation of Social-Scientific Inquiry   237
A. *A Proposed Answer to the Meaning-Question*
B. *Social-Scientific Endorsement of the Need for Epistemological Postulates*

Chapter 3   The First Postulate of the Meaning-Situation of Reflective Inquiry (Reality)   242
A. *The General Significance of the First Postulate*
B. *The Significance of the First Postulate for Individual Psychology*
C. *The Significance of the First Postulate for Social Psychology*
D. *The Significance of the First Postulate for Sociology*
E. *The Significance of the First Postulate for Anthropology*
F. *The Significance of the First Postulate for Economics*
G. *The Significance of the First Postulate for Political Science*
H. *The Significance of the First Postulate for History*

Chapter 4   The Second Postulate of the Meaning-Situation of Reflective Inquiry (Probability)   269
A. *The General Significance of the Second Postulate*
B. *The Significance of the Second Postulate for Individual Psychology*
C. *The Significance of the Second Postulate for Social Psychology*

D. *The Significance of the Second Postulate for Sociology*
E. *The Significance of the Second Postulate for Anthropology*
F. *The Significance of the Second Postulate for Economics*
G. *The Significance of the Second Postulate for Political Science*
H. *The Significance of the Second Postulate for History*

Chapter 5   The Third Postulate of the Meaning-Situation of Reflective Inquiry (System)   283

A. *The General Significance of the Third Postulate*
   1. SYSTEMATIZATION VS. FRAGMENTATION
   2. SYSTEMATIC HARMONY
   3. LAW-LIKE GENERALIZATIONS
B. *The Significance of the Third Postulate for Individual Psychology*
C. *The Significance of the Third Postulate for Social Psychology*
D. *The Significance of the Third Postulate for Sociology*
E. *The Significance of the Third Postulate for Anthropology*
F. *The Significance of the Third Postulate for Economics*
G. *The Significance of the Third Postulate for Political Science*
H. *The Significance of the Third Postulate for History*

Chapter 6   The Fourth Postulate of the Meaning-Situation of Reflective Inquiry (Causality)   328

A. *The General Significance of the Fourth Postulate*
   1. THE RECONSTRUCTION OF THE CONCEPT OF CAUSATION IN NATURAL SCIENCE
   2. TOWARD A DEFINITION OF CAUSALITY
   3. THE POSTULATE OF BEHAVIORAL CAUSATION
B. *The Significance of the Fourth Postulate for Individual Psychology*
C. *The Significance of the Fourth Postulate for Social Psychology*
D. *The Significance of the Fourth Postulate for Sociology*
E. *The Significance of the Fourth Postulate for Anthropology*
   1. THE PROBLEMS OF SOCIOCULTURAL CAUSATION
   2. DETERMINISTIC VS. RELATIVELY SELF-DETERMINISTIC CONCEPTIONS OF SOCIOCULTURAL CAUSATION
      a. DETERMINISTIC CAUSATION
      b. RELATIVE SELF-DETERMINISTIC CAUSATION
F. *The Significance of the Fourth Postulate for Economics*
G. *The Significance of the Fourth Postulate for Political Science*
H. *The Significance of the Fourth Postulate for History*

Chapter 7   The Fifth Postulate of the Meaning-Situation of Reflective Inquiry (Coherence)   389

A. *The General Significance of the Fifth Postulate*
B. *The Significance of the Fifth Postulate for Individual Psychology*
C. *The Significance of the Fifth Postulate for Social-Psychology*
D. *The Significance of the Fifth Postulate for Sociology*
E. *The Significance of the Fifth Postulate for Anthropology*
F. *The Significance of the Fifth Postulate for Economics*
G. *The Significance of the Fifth Postulate for Political Science*
H. *The Significance of the Fifth Postulate for History*

PART FOUR   *The Methodological Pattern of Reflective Inquiry*

Chapter 1   An Elaboration of the Hypothetical-Deductive Method in the Knowledge-Situation of Reflective Inquiry   425

A. *The Aim of This Elaboration*
B. *The First Stage of Hypothetical-Deductive Inquiry*

Chapter 2   The Second Stage of Hypothetical-Deductive Inquiry   437

Chapter 3   The Third Stage of Hypothetical-Deductive Inquiry   449

A. *The Generic Criterion of Coherence*
B. *The Technique of Deducing Implications*
C. *Techniques for Empirical Testing*
  1. EXPERIMENTAL TESTING
  2. EXPERIENTIAL TESTING
    a. COMPARATIVE CASE ANALYSIS
    b. INTROSPECTIVE PROJECTION

Chapter 4   The Fourth Stage of Hypothetical-Deductive Inquiry   478

A. *The Emergence of the Knowledge-Questions from the Meaning-Questions*
  1. FORMAL AND SUBSTANTIVE LAWS
  2. THE PROBLEM OF SPECIFYING THE LIMITING CONDITIONS OF BEHAVIORAL LAWS

B. *Toward the Construction of Law-Like Generalizations About the Behavioral Process*
   1. THE LIMITED AIM OF LAW-LIKE GENERALIZING
   2. TO WHAT DEGREE DO THE SPECIFIC BEHAVIORIAL DISCIPLINES AIM AT LAW-LIKE GENERALIZATIONS?
      a. THE LAW-LIKE AIMS OF INDIVIDUAL PSYCHOLOGY
      b. THE LAW-LIKE AIMS OF SOCIAL PSYCHOLOGY
      c. THE LAW-LIKE AIMS OF SOCIOLOGY
      d. THE LAW-LIKE AIMS OF ANTHROPOLOGY
      e. THE LAW-LIKE AIMS OF ECONOMICS
      f. THE LAW-LIKE AIMS OF POLITICAL SCIENCE
      g. THE LAW-LIKE AIMS OF HISTORY

CONCLUSION 514
Conversations between a Critic and the Author

BIBLIOGRAPHY 549

INDEX 575

PART ONE *Prolegomena*

1 *The Scope of This Book*

This is a philosophical approach to the problem of acquiring reliable knowledge in the social sciences. When a philosopher trespasses onto the properties of psychology, sociology, anthropology, economics, political science, and history, the guardians of each of these behavioral disciplines have every right to command: "Halt and state your business." Before he proceeds, therefore, the philosopher must clarify his intentions. As he does so, however, the philosopher is equally justified in emphasizing this assumption: When social scientists attempt to construct reasonably acceptable generalizations about human behavior, they are implicitly, if not explicitly, invoking the more general principles of intellectual analysis which are entailed in a philosophical theory of knowledge. The philosopher does not insist that all social scientists be interested in the philosophical presuppositions of their research techniques. But, he does contend that without this assumption, there is no common ground for any significant progress toward resolving the fundamental problems which any thoroughgoing interpretation of behavioral processes involves.

A. The Aims of This Study

It is not the aim of this study to answer the question: Is social-scientific knowledge possible? Psychologists, sociologists, anthropologists, economists, political scientists, and historians have already shown that it is. Instead, we are asking: What is meant by social-scientific knowledge and how is it acquired? Internal criticism will be presented when the means some social scientists select seem to contradict their own aims. But it should be understood that there is no presumption here that a philosopher is placing the behavioral disciplines on trial. What is needed is a mirror in which the practitioners of the various behavioral disciplines can see themselves in order to ascertain whether or not they are operating in accordance with the rules by which the scientific game is played. Accordingly, we shall attempt to show that social-scientific analyses and natural-scientific analyses are separable but congruent modes of reflective inquiry. In no sense should this be taken to be an effort to force social-scientific inquiry to imitate natural-scientific inquiry.

A deliberate effort will be made to avoid arbitrarily imposing philosophical theories on behavioral analyses. Philosophy has no prescription by which the problems of social-scientific knowledge can be readily solved. It aims to provide, however, a comprehensive framework of epistemological principles which may help to correlate and clarify some of the crucial methodological questions which concern a great many social scientists. It is hoped that my proposal regarding behavioral inquiry might correspond to Whitehead's conception of the aim of philosophy with respect to natural-scientific inquiry: "Its search for a rationalistic scheme is the search for more adequate criticism, and for more adequate justification, of the interpretations which we perforce employ." [1]

If such a philosophical synthesis is to serve its appropriate purpose it must be recognized that it is directly applicable to only the more abstract of the several dimensions of the problems of social-scientific knowledge. In no way, therefore, is it a substitute for the substantive inquiry which must be carried on within each discipline. Creative research requires a delimited field of analysis which demands the specialized training in a particular discipline. This study does not pretend to throw much light on the details of day-to-day decisions about research problems which confront the practitioners who are engaged in the specialized work in their own fields. Moreover, there are some dimensions of social-scientific knowledge at the interdisciplinary level which may not be dealt with directly in this study. A philosopher finds, however, that often when his colleagues in the social sciences are dealing with their specialized problems, they are helped by a philosophical analysis of the fundamental presuppositions of scientific inquiry. We are convinced that without a philosophical elaboration and correlation of the epistemological issues the problem of social-scientific knowledge cannot be fully understood. We must acknowledge, however, that it can actually be solved only by the social scientists themselves. It is hoped that this book may encourage them to probe deeper and further in order to work out their own epistemological salvation.

The usefulness of a philosophical framework for the behavioral disciplines becomes most evident when it provides a broader perspective by which interdisciplinary, as well as intradisciplinary, disputes might be resolved. Even when they cannot be completely eliminated, philosophical analysis can at least help the social scientist to distinguish between meaningful and meaningless issues.

There are two respects in which the social scientists' involvements in value considerations have created a need for a philosophical perspective. First, any social scientist who prizes knowledge as an intrinsic value will be motivated by his curiosity to explore the broader cognitive implications of the data, concepts, and techniques he uses in his research. Secondly, any social scientist who cannot completely eliminate normative recommendations from his enterprise is confronted by the question of whether or not such interests invalidate the objectivity of his knowledge claims. It is a primary aim of this study to contribute to meeting both these needs.

In order to make these general statements about the aims and limitations of this study more intelligible, let us attempt to clarify what is meant by philosophical epistemology and by social-scientific methodology. It is on the coordination of these two modes of the process of inquiry that attention will be primarily focused.

B. *Epistemology and Methodology*

1. WHAT IS EPISTEMOLOGY?

Epistemology is that branch of philosophy which aims to ascertain to what degree knowledge is possible, and to examine the structure and function of all ways of knowing. It should not be confused with logic, which is confined to the formulation of principles for valid reasoning, nor with a psychological description and interpretation of some of the psychosomatic functions involved in the process of thinking. Neither the logician nor the psychologist deals with the subjective-objective relation of the perceptual and ideational content which a knower experiences to a substantive referent. The epistemologist, however, is primarily concerned with this crucial question: *How are the perceptions and ideas which the knower has constructed related to the reality to which they supposedly refer?*

The scope of an epistemological analysis of knowledge-claims has been indicated by Werkmeister in terms of "three distinct but related types of problems" which reveal the basis and structure of knowledge: "(1) Who is the knower and how does he acquire knowledge? (2) What does or can he know? (3) When is his belief warranted?" [2] Regardless of how divergent the various epistemological theories may be, each must implicitly, if not explicitly, attempt to justify its answers to these questions.

The epistemological approach of this book will be unlike those traditional theories of knowledge which would arbitrarily impose upon the social sciences a preconceived scheme of categories. Here, we shall be concerned only with those epistemological principles which emerge out of inquiry into human behavior. This reconstructed epistemological approach is, of course, what Dewey advocated, when he condemned one-sided and arbitrary epistemologies which are "guilty of selective abstraction of some conditions and some factors out of the actual pattern of controlled inquiry." The "theory of inquiry" which Dewey presents only appears to replace all epistemology with scientific methodology. What he really has done most effectively, is to reveal the inadequacies of many traditional epistemologies, and to present a more adequate epistemological approach of his own. It will become increasingly evident that the theory of knowledge developed in the present study is based on Dewey's premise that the reliability of knowledge depends upon the "operations by which, in the continuum of experiential inquiry, stable beliefs are progressively obtained and utilized." [3]

2. EPISTEMOLOGICAL DUALISM

In order to provide a meaningful framework for social-scientific inquiry, a theory of knowledge must entail epistemological dualism rather than epistemological monism. Before we justify this claim, let us note what is meant by each of these divergent philosophical assumptions about the relation of ideas to reality. On the one hand, Perry states the assumption of epistemological monism: "When things are known, they are identical, element for element with the idea or content of the knowing state." [4] On the other hand, Lovejoy states the assumption of epistemological dualism: "Whatever knowledge we have of real objects is indirect or representative, the datum whereby you know any such object is not identical with the object known." [5] Neither of these claims can be empirically confirmed or disconfirmed. But the more fruitful of these alternative epistemological premises must be adopted before an investigation in terms of empirically testable hypotheses about either physical events or behavioral events can be undertaken.

Epistemological *dualism is adopted here* on the grounds that it is more fruitful for interpreting the cognitive process of scientific inquiry than is epistemological monism. Yet, we should somehow justify what might appear to be an arbitrary rejection of the conception of immediate knowledge through direct acquaintance with data which epistemological monism requires. There are forms of human expression other than the assertive aspect of inferential generalizations which the natural and social scientist exemplify when they construct descriptions, classifications, explanations, and predictions about observable data. Non-scientific modes of judging include the intuitive experiences of the artist's creative insight, the prophet's revelation, the moral person's conviction about what he ought to do, and one's sensation of, let us say, a toothache. Immediate experiences like these do yield an intimate involvement which might be taken to be direct knowledge by acquaintance.

Such experiences, however, must be clearly distinguished from the scientific assertions with which we are concerned here. If a mystic claims that he has immediately experienced intimate communion with God, we are not presuming to dismiss this kind of knowing as nonsense. But if he insists that his ineffable feeling is evidence for making assertive judgments, we find that we cannot use his conception of what kind of knowledge is meaningful. A work of art that is aesthetically effective elicits a creative response which might reveal emotional depths that could be plumbed in no other way. Consequently, Keats' claim that "truth is beauty, and beauty is truth" is significant. But, for the purpose of any intellectual analysis which demands that all knowledgeable claims must be asserted in examinable statements, his declaration is inapplicable.

In a brilliant analysis of the total process of human judgment Buchler has shown us that "making" and "doing" are modes of human judgment just as much as "asserting." Moreover, such exhibitive and contriving functions fall outside of the categories of either mediate or immediate knowledge. The position we have taken here is not a denial of his view. We simply insist that such non-assertive modes of judgment are not involved in what social scientists are seeking when they attempt to acquire knowledge.[6]

Regardless of how important these issues may be in other contexts the only kind of knowledge that is meaningful for social scientists is that which is inferentially constructed. Do any social scientists assume, as the epistemological monists must, that their constructs can be known to be identical with the reality to which they refer? On the contrary, it seems that they all assume that even though reality (whatever it may be) exists independently of their ideas about it, nevertheless, they themselves cumulatively construct any knowledge they may acquire about that reality. In a subsequent section an entire chapter will be devoted to the elaboration of this fundamental assumption. Consequently, for the present preliminary discussion let us hope that Werkmeister's broader conception of the structure of meaning will suffice to clarify this point: "All concrete situations reveal that the experiential context in which meanings are found is a triadic relation, involving (a) a 'mind' which interprets (b) some specific given experience or 'sign' as standing for or designating (c) some (actual or imagined) object, condition, situation, or process—the 'referent'." [7]

When a scientist adopts epistemological dualism, he abandons absolute truth as the objective of reflective inquiry. What the epistemological dualist does seek through cumulative analysis, however, is an emendable system of reasonably acceptable constructs about his referent. Before we attempt to show how this epistemological assumption underlies social-scientific inquiry, let us briefly note how it is presupposed by natural-scientific inquiry.

3. THE EPISTEMOLOGICALLY DUALISTIC CHARACTER OF THE SCIENTIFIC CONCEPTION OF CONSTRUCTED KNOWLEDGE

According to several *natural scientists* who have critically analyzed their epistemological assumptions, their generalizations about physical events are inferences which they themselves construct out of observable sense-data. This is what we take Einstein and Infeld to mean when they claim that "physical concepts are free creations of the human mind, and are not, however it may seem, uniquely determined by the external world" and that "the scientist must collect the unordered facts available and make them coherent by creative thought." [8] Margenau has extended this constructive principle even beyond the conceptually inferred generalization of natural scientific analysis to the perceptual knowledge of the data themselves: Since "a sense datum is in fact an idealization" and "there is nothing we can point to, saying this is a pure perceptual datum," therefore, "even the most primitive kind of cognition involves a slight degree of conceptualization, involves an investiture of a bare datum with some rational context." Although Margenau cautions that "this admission is not to be interpreted as meaning that external objects are pure inventions," he concludes that "logically much of modern physics is incomprehensible unless the essentially constructed character of physical objects is granted at the very beginning." [9]

This constructive activity characterizes the perceptual as well as the conceptual process of knowing physical events. In order to explain how the gap is bridged between raw sense-data (Werkmeister's "intuitive-sensory basis of first-person experience") and scientific sense-constructs (Werkmeister's "perceptions quantitatively fixed and transformed"), Margenau suggests rules of correspondence between the "perceptory plane (P-plane)" and "the sum total of constructs (C-field)." Insisting that "science finds it necessary to place the data of experience in correspondence with constructs that subject themselves to rational operation," Margenau describes the perceptual process as a "reification" through which there is an almost unnoticed gradual, and continuous passage from the P-plane to the adjacent aspects of the C-field so that "constructs and data shade into each other in our complete experience." For some purposes it is not necessary to emphasize the distinction between "external objects" and the "deliverances of immediate sensation," since "the P-plane may well be regarded as possessing a neighborhood of constructs that partake of the pictorialness of immediate experience." But constructive mental activity must be acknowledged in accounting for the production of perceptual data (table), as well as in the use of such "inferred states" as electrons, phase waves, fields of force, genes, etc., which, as Werkmeister declares, "in the interest of precision, go far beyond the intuitive-sensory basis of first-person experience." [10] Moreover, as Bergmann and Spence have emphasized, "the language of any science contains a whole hierarchy of interlocked empirical constructs—mass, acceleration, momentum, energy, or stimulus trace, excitatory potential, and so on," which are not observable but which are "just as empirical as length, duration, weight stimulus and all other such terms as are sometimes exclusively thought of as being operationally defined." [11]

To what extent do *social scientists* similarly recognize the constructive character of their knowledge-claims about behavioral events? At least some representatives from each of the social-scientific disciplines emphasize this inferential nature of their indirect knowledge. It is important to note their commitment to this conception of mediate knowledge that epistemological dualism entails. For, unlike physical events, behavioral events involve experienced emotions and purposive goal-seeking actions which might seem to beget the direct knowledge by immediate acquaintance that is entailed in epistemological monism.

Let us direct attention to some of the statements by *the practitioners of the specific disciplines* which reveal that they *take the con-*

structive activity of the mind of the investigator to be an essential characteristic of behavioral knowledge.

The conception of *psychological* knowledge in terms of inferential generalizations which the psychologist himself constructs is explicitly acknowledged by Marx: "Symbolic or logical constructs are inferred on the observed relationships between objects and events." [12] Accordingly, when Boring compares behavioral events with physical events as the respective referents of psychology and physics, he claims that the former like the latter "must deal with existential reals which are similarly mediate to experience," for "there is no way of getting at 'direct experience' because experience gives itself up to science indirectly, inferentially, by the experimental method." [13] Similarly, Tolman distinguishes between "immediate experience as the actually given, rich, qualitied, diffuse matrix" from which both psychology and physics have evolved and the logical constructs "by which the psychologist attempts to explain it—to help in predicting and controlling it." [14]

The *sociologist's* predominant interest in the "generic forms, types, and manifold interconnections" of collective phenomena (Sorokin) [15] commits him to a conception of mediate knowledge. Lundberg makes this point even more explicit, when he postulates the independent existence of the external world but identifies sociological knowledge in terms of the sociologist's constructive response to that referent: "All propositions or postulates regarding the more ultimate 'realities' must always consist of inference, generalizations, or abstractions from these symbols and the responses which they represent." [16]

When Kroeber and Kluckhohn critically reviewed concepts and definitions used in *anthropology*, they emphasized that the "patterns of implicit culture" are "purely inferential constructs." The initial observation of the given data and the subsequent validation of the anthropologist's interpretations "unquestionably rest upon systematic extrapolation" in which "he necessarily puts something into the data." Anthropological inquiry would not be possible, therefore, without the "thematic principles which the investigator introduces to explain connections among a wide range of cultural content and form that are not obvious in the world of direct observation." [17]

The highly refined product of *economic* generalizations might disguise the economist's constructive activity by which he produces them. In order to eliminate this misinterpretation, however, Schumpeter directs attention to the "process by which we grind out what we call scientific propositions." In an analysis of economic phenomena, therefore, the economist who attempts to formulate "a more or less orderly schema or picture must not only assemble facts," but he must also be aware that "the very work of constructing the schema or picture will add further relations and concepts to, and in general also eliminate others from, the original stock." [18]

Those *political scientists* who have become concerned about refining their analytical principles agree with Easton that a "fact is a particular ordering of reality in terms of a theoretical interest." [19] Instead of assuming that political facts "speak for themselves," Key declares that "knowledge of an isolated 'act' can be useless erudition." [20] In order that specific political phenomena might be meaningfully organized Herring exhorts his colleagues to aim at "a conceptual scheme for the analysis and ordering of empirical data." [21]

Apart from the reconstructive activity of the *historian's* critical intellect and imagination no meaningful explanations of past events could be formulated. For, as the Committee on Historiography in Bulletin 54 insist, "every fact which the historian establishes presupposes some theoretical construction." [22] It is only an appropriate question which a historian puts to the authenticated testimony that revitalizes some dead event. Moreover, as Gottschalk points out, not only are the initial data unavailable but even the raw records "have to be assayed against an imaginative re-creation, a re-enactment in the mind, of the historical reality." [23]

Parsons has explicitly advocated epistemological dualism as the philosophical theory of knowledge for social-scientific inquiry. Parsons goes further than the behavioral scientists cited above. They have merely indicated that they must rely on the constructive activity of the investigator which epistemological dualism implies. But he insists that "the legitimacy of theoretical abstraction is denied" by the epistemologically monistic premise that "there is an immediate correspondence between concrete experienceable reality and scientific propositions, and only in so far as this exists can there be valid knowledge." In dualistic terms Parsons emphasizes that the external world as the referent of scientific constructs "is not the creation of the individual human mind." But Parsons just as strongly insists that "its order must be of a character which is, in some sense, congruent with the order of human logic." [24]

4. WHAT DO SOCIAL SCIENTISTS MEAN BY METHODOLOGY AND HOW IS IT RELATED TO EPISTEMOLOGY?

If Parsons is right when he holds that "every system of scientific theory involves philosophical assumptions," then a social-scientific methodology is not intelligible apart from its epistemological presuppositions. Defining methodology as "the consideration of the general grounds for the validity of scientific propositions and systems of them" Parsons distinguishes it, on the one hand, from the consideration of specific observational and verificative techniques which it scrutinizes, and, on the other hand, from the consideration of the even broader epistemological questions under which its own questions are subsumed. With respect to the former, i.e., "scientific theory proper," Parsons declares: "Methodological considerations enter in when we go behind this to inquire whether the procedures by which this observation and verification have been carried out—including the formulation of propositions and the concepts involved in them, and the modes of drawing conclusions from them—are legitimate." Among the types of questions this involves, Parsons distinguishes between those which pertain to the general grounds of validity "irrespective of the particular class or kind of empirical facts involved" and those which "arise in connection with judging the validity of propositions about particular kinds of empirical facts and the particular kind of theoretical systems involved in these propositions *as distinguished from others.*" When methodology undertakes both levels of analysis, it "finally, will lead into philosophical considerations." With respect to "the philosophical consideration of the grounds of validity of science," Parsons acknowledges that both types of methodological questions are derived from Kant's more generic epistemological question: How is it possible that we have such valid knowledge? This question must be differentiated, of course, from the older epistemological question: "What philosophical grounds do we have for believing that we have valid empirical knowledge of the external world"? In this book, as was previously noted, we share with

Kant and Parsons the premise that there is some kind of social-scientific knowledge.[25]

Among other social scientists there is not always a clear consensus about what is meant by social-scientific methodology. Before considering some of these various conceptions, we should recognize that all social scientists do not attribute the same significance to methodological considerations. Mills, for example, warns the student that preoccupation with methodology may do more harm than good, if he "loses firm connection with the kinds of problems for which given methods have been devised, and, in the end, makes quite formal, and often even useless, his examination of methods." [26] Since Mills grants that this is "not necessarily the case," but, that "this is surely a very real danger," we can heed his timely warning without abandoning our task. Sjoberg, on the other hand, does not have Mills' reservations. Quite the contrary, he opposes those who want to "bury methodological controversies": "But there is good reason for the social scientist's concern with methodological questions: it is methodology which provides one prime justification for the view that the social sciences are scientific in nature." [27] Moreover, there is wide acceptance among psychologists of the judgment of Krech and Klein that "now is the time for conceptual stocktaking, theory weaving and integration" with respect to the analysis of human personality.[28] Although Friedman is more specifically concerned about "the methodology of positive economics," he declares that "more than other scientists, social scientists need to be self-conscious about their methodology." [29]

Methodology is more directly related to empirical research than to epistemological formulations by Lazarsfeld and Rosenberg when they identify methodology "as a bent of mind rather than as a system of organized principles and procedures." Consequently, they advocate description, rather than prescription, in such an analytical approach. This means that when a methodologist "tells other scholars what they have done, or might do," he does not recommend "what they should do." In other words, "he tells them what order of finding has emerged from their research, not what kind of result is or is not preferable." [30]

Methodology is more congruent with epistemology in Merton's conception of methodology as "the logic of scientific procedure."

For, Merton insists upon distinguishing between the problems of substantive sociological theory proper and the problems of methodology, which "transcend those found in any one discipline, dealing either with those common to groups of disciplines or, in more generalized form, with those common to all scientific inquiry." Merton contends that such methodological knowledge "does not contain or imply the *particular* content of sociological theory" which deals with "certain aspects of the interaction of men." He declares, nevertheless, that methodological knowledge is indispensable: "Sociologists, in company with all others who essay scientific work must be methodologically wise; they must be aware of the design of investigation, the nature of inference, the requirements of a theoretic system." [31]

If Simpson's definition of social-scientific methodology is adopted, it is not clear how we could distinguish between it and epistemology: "Methodology refers to the principles which determine how we look at data, what we look for in data, and what the data are considered to be." Simpson does say, however, that "methodology here signifies the logic of method and not merely the techniques and instruments which make it possible for us to get at the data or observe them more closely." [32]

Rose seems to include epistemology within methodologies when he claims that methodology ranges from "a consideration of assumptions underlying research to a presentation of specific research tools that may or must be used to acquire knowledge." [33]

In the final analysis, however, the interrelatedness of methodological and epistemological problems is more important than the distinction between these two approaches. For purposes of this preliminary chapter, we have been attempting to delineate the separable fields of social-scientific methodology and philosophical epistemology. When we get into the discussion of the problem of social-scientific knowledge, however, we shall be dealing with many cognitive issues which involve concepts such as the following which social scientists in a symposium on sociological theory take to be methodological: "postulates, explanations, models, types, levels, dispositions, transactions, functional relations, processes, probability causality, verification, confirmation, and normative propositions." [34]

When we discuss these and other concepts and techniques with which both the social scientist and the philosopher are concerned,

*we shall treat their methodological aspects in terms of the knowledge-
situation and their epistemological aspects in terms of the meaning-
situation.*

In order to cope with the complex methodological-epistemological
aspects of the problem of social-scientific knowledge, we must translate them into its manageable dimensions. For this purpose the following four questions are proposed:

1. How can social-scientific knowledge be operationally defined?
2. What is the predominant motivation of the person who seeks
   social-scientific knowledge?
3. What kind of knowledge does the social scientist take to be
   meaningful?
4. By what method and criterion can the social scientist coordinate his specific observational, inferential, and verificative techniques for constructing reliable generalizations?

Out of the answers to these questions we shall attempt to formulate
an epistemological perspective for coordinating and clarifying the
methodological issues which behavioral inquiry entails. It is not required or even expected that a consensus will be found with respect
to the answers for all of these questions. What these questions are
designed to provide, however, is a basis for critically understanding
the crucial controversies as well as the significant agreements.

The philosopher's function in this approach to the problem of
social-scientific knowledge should be further clarified. In fact, since
some philosophers seem to object to this division of labor between
the social scientist and the philosopher, it may stand in need of
justification. Couldn't we agree that in the community of reflective
minds the philosopher plays various roles? Locke characterized the
role that might appear to be assigned here as that of an "underlabourer in clearing the ground a little, and removing some of the
rubbish that lies in the way of knowledge." [35] When Winch examines "the idea of a social science and its relation to society," he
objects to this "underlabourer conception" on the grounds that it
implies that "philosophy cannot contribute any positive understanding of the world on its own account" so that "it is parasitic on other
disciplines." Now, it might seem that we have presupposed such a
conception according to which "philosophy has no problems of its

own but is a technique for solving problems thrown up in the course of non-philosophical investigations." In order to eliminate any impression that the present writer would so confine the function of philosophy, he hastens to agree with Winch that the philosopher's "aim is not merely the negative one of removing obstacles from the path of the acquisition of further scientific knowledge, but the positive one of an increased philosophical understanding of what is involved in the concept of intelligibility." [36]

A philosopher does not deny the greater autonomy of philosophy in other areas, when he confines his attention in a particular study like this one to the epistemological interpretation of the issues which arise out of social-scientific methodology. It can be anticipated that in some parts of this study the philosopher will be more of an "underlabourer" than he is in other parts, or than he is in other philosophical pursuits of knowledge. But, even out of those discussions, there will emerge some of the ingredients which would be required if we were engaged here in the development of a more fully autonomous philosophical analysis. In other words, the philosopher does not become merely a handyman for other disciplines, when he applies his analytical tools to their problems. It is impossible for the philosopher to operate in vacuum. He can find out to what degree his epistemological principles are justified, and in what respects they need correction, modification, or abandonment through using these principles in dealing with the cognitive problems that confront the substantive inquiry of the social sciences. This, of course, is what Whitehead did with respect to natural-scientific inquiry. Can anyone who has read Whitehead's works conclude that he made philosophy parasitic?

It will be the aim of the subsequent chapters to carry out Whitehead's recommendation that "the task of philosophy is to recover the totality that is obscured by the selection." [37] The "totality" will be taken here to mean the generic process which characterizes all philosophical-scientific inquiry; the "selection" is the segmentation of this synoptic way of knowing through an overemphasis upon discrete research techniques. Such delimitation is necessary for acquiring substantive knowledge within the specific disciplines of psychology, sociology, anthropology, economics, political science, and history. However, it does obscure some of the essential dimensions of the problem of social-scientific knowledge. Accordingly, in the pages to follow we hope to contribute to the "recovery" of a more comprehensive perspective for understanding the cognitive process by which reliable generalizations about human behavior can be acquired.

Footnotes to Chapter 1 of Part One

1 Whitehead, *Process and Reality*, 22.
2 Werkmeister, *The Basis and Structure of Knowledge*. 4 See the *Dictionary of Philosophy* (Runes), 94-96, for a concise summary by Wood of what is meant by epistemology. Cf. Montague, *Ways of Knowing*, Blanshard, *The Nature of Thought*, Brightman, *An Introduction to Philosophy*, Chapter IV.
3 Dewey, *Logic, The Theory of Inquiry*, 514, 534. For a survey of specific theories of knowledge, see Wood, "Recent Epistemological Schools," in *A History of Philosophical Systems* (Ferm), 516-539.
4 Perry, *Present Philosophical Tendencies*, 126.
5 Lovejoy, *The Revolt Against Dualism*, 303.
6 Buchler, *Nature and Judgment*, 37-41.
7 Werkmeister, *The Basis and Structure of Knowledge*, 7.
8 Einstein and Infeld, *The Evolution of Physics*, 5, 33.
9 Margenau, *The Nature of Concepts* (Proceedings of the Stillwater Conference), 47-50.
10 Werkmeister, *The Basis and Structure of Knowledge*, 341-343.
11 Bergmann and Spence, "Operationism and Theory," *Psychological Theory* (Marx), 59.
12 Marx, *Psychological Theory* (Marx), 9. Cf. Pratt, *The Logic of Modern Psychology*.
13 Boring, *The Physical Dimensions of Consciousness*, 6.
14 Tolman, *Behavior and Psychological Man*, 97.
15 Sorokin, *Society, Culture, and Personality*, 16.
16 Lundberg, *Foundations of Sociology*, 8-9.
17 Kroeber and Kluckhohn, "General Features of Culture," in *Culture, A Critical Review of Concepts and Definitions* (Papers of the Peabody Museum of American Archeology and Ethnology, Harvard University, Vol. XLVII, No. 1, 1952), p. 161-162.
18 Schumpeter, *History of Economic Analysis*, 42.
19 Easton, *The Political System*, 53.
20 Key, *Politics, Political Parties, and Pressure Groups*, 21.
21 Herring, *American Political Science Review*, December 1953, 968-969.
22 *Theory and Practice in Historical Study*, Bulletin 54, 123-124. Hereafter referred to as Bulletin 54.

23 Gottschalk, *Understanding History,* 47, 139-140, and "The Historian's Use of Generalizations," *The State of the Social Sciences* (White), 442-443.
24 Parsons, *The Structure of Social Action,* 23, 753.
25 *Ibid.,* 22-25.
26 Mills, "On Intellectual Craftsmanship," *Symposium on Sociological Theory* (Gross), 26.
27 Sjoberg, "Operationalism and Social Research," *Symposium on Sociological Theory* (Gross), 603.
28 Krech and Klein, *Theoretical Models and Personality Theory,* 2.
29 Friedman, *Essays in Positive Economics,* 40.
30 Lazarsfeld and Rosenberg, *The Language of Social Research,* 4.
31 Merton, *Social Theory and Social Structure,* 84-85.
32 Simpson, *Man in Society,* 48.
33 Rose, *Theory and Method in Social Sciences,* VI.
34 Gross, *Symposium on Sociological Theory* (Gross), 3.
35 Locke, *Essay Concerning Human Understanding,* Preface.
36 Winch, *The Idea of a Social Science,* 4, 20.
37 Whitehead, *Process and Reality,* 22.

2 *The Subject Matter of Social Science*

Social scientists have an understandable reluctance about offering initial definitions of the distinctive subject matter of their respective fields. In many cases, a representative of a discipline would prefer to declare (somewhat in jest) that this discipline is whatever its practitioners are doing. Some have attributed this situation to the immaturity of the social sciences. This is questionable, however, since the assertion is made by those in the most established disciplines as well as by those in the disciplines which have more recently developed. It seems more likely that the difficulty stems largely from the complexity of the interrelated dimensions of human behavior. Regardless of what is the source of the difficulty, social scientists are justified in preferring to define their subject matter at the conclusion rather than at the beginning of the discussion of their fields.

Despite the difficulty of providing an adequate definition of substantive content at the outset, we must have some kind of preliminary identification of the subject matter of the separate disciplines. Consequently, we shall attempt here at least to point to the distinctive dimension of the respective disciplines with the understanding that this will be elaborated in terms of more refined concepts in subsequent chapters. For this purpose we first need a conceptual identification of the social-scientific enterprise as a whole, to which as a conceptual frame of reference, the separable but interconnected fields of each discipline can be related.

A. *The Behavioral Process*

Let us consider the concept of the behavioral process as the orienting concept for identifying the common subject matter of all of the social sciences. A general endorsement for this orienting concept is clearly reflected in the increasing use of the term behavioral science as a synonym for social science. The behavioral process here includes both the sociocultural and motivational aspects of the interaction of groups, as well as of the interpersonal transactions of individuals who are somewhat similarly motivated to satisfy psychic needs and physiological drives by somewhat similar responses to socioculturally begotten goals. Parsons has indentified this datum as a "system of behavior or action" which "is not the physical organism nor the object of physical perception." Rather, it is a new system which "comes into being when there is interaction or transaction . . . between two or more behaving organisms." [1]

When social scientists confine their inquiries to the action of human organisms, as they are related to the goals by which they are motivated and to the sociocultural situations by which they are conditioned, they assume that such behavioral events are just as real as biological and physico-chemical events. Consequently, they do not reduce their behavioral data to the physical properties of these spatio-temporal things out of which human organisms emerge. On the contrary, they take as their distinctive subject matter this actually interrelated, but analytically separable, level among the other levels of existence. Just as organic events have emerged out of inorganic events, so behavioral events have emerged as superorganic phenomena (Sorokin). [2] With respect to them, Bierstedt insists, "there is nothing artificial, preternatural, or supernatural about social phenomena" which are just as "natural as the phenomena of magnetism, gravitation, and electricity." [3] That some biologists endorse this characterization of the emergence of a distinctive behavioral level out of organic processes, is indicated by Emerson's statement that "symbolic communication produces almost a qualitative difference from animals." This is elaborated by Grinker when he emphasizes that "the evolution and ontogenesis of psychological and social systems add new processes which must be considered in their own right and dealt with as if they had their own laws and regulations." [4]

Two basic features of the *behavioral process* are presupposed when it is adopted as the orienting concept for identifying the superorganic subject matter of social-scientific inquiry: (1) its temporal dimension, and (2) its reciprocal collective-individual foci. By showing what each of the presuppositions means, we shall be able to restate more fully what is meant by the behavioral process.

1. THE TEMPORAL DIMENSION OF HUMAN BEHAVIOR

In order to understand what most social scientists mean by the behavioral level of existence, we must recognize that they presuppose that it is a constantly changing temporal process of becoming, rather than a static order of being. Whitehead expressed the corresponding premise with respect to a cosmological conception of the physical level of existence. Instead of adopting the Newtonian premise of "the great all-prevailing passive relationships of the natural world," Whitehead presupposed that "there is no nature at an instance" but that "all the interrelations of matters of fact must involve transition in their essence." In other words, as Whitehead declares, "for the modern view process, activity, and change are the matter of fact." [5] Similarly, Toman assumes that social systems of interpersonal beings "have developed and are continually changing in accelerated fashion"; and Thompson presupposes that "in order to understand the societal system as an ongoing life process, created by and arising from the needs of its human component, we must view it in its total relevant environment extending backward and forward in time and inward and outward in space." [6]

The temporal dimension of the behavioral process is such a basic consideration that this brief reference to it here will be more fully elaborated later in a chapter devoted to a discussion of the diachronic process.

2. RECIPROCAL COLLECTIVE-INDIVIDUAL FOCI

The *behavioral process* fails to serve adequately as an orienting concept, if those who use it do not fully acknowledge the interpenetrating functions of both the collective and the individual aspects of the concrete reality of human action. Either of the alternative presuppositions that the individual is real and the group is an abstraction, or that the group is real and the individual is an abstraction, distorts the experiential data and closes the significant channels of inquiry. On the one hand, where is there to be found a completely isolated individual person whose behavior is entirely uninfluenced by other persons and cultural conditioning? On the other hand, what could be meant by a social group without individual members who influence and are influenced by each other, or a cultural pattern without persons who are its products and its producers?

To recognize this correlation of these two foci does not preclude the abstraction of either the sociocultural factors or the motivational factors for purposes of substantive analysis. At the one extreme, psychologists have learned a great deal about the neurophysiological mechanisms without much reference to institutional and cultural influences. At the other extreme, sociologists and anthropologists have provided much valuable information about institutional and cultural patterns of group relationships through an "empty organism approach" which ignores any given individual actors.

Though it may be legitimate to confine delimited research to one or the other of these two foci, such bifurcation can distort the identification of the behavioral process itself. This is what has happened in the fruitless controversy between some individual-minded and some collective-minded social scientists. Such a person, who mistakes his abstraction as the only significant reality, should recall Cooley's insight that the real referent of behavioral analysis is "human life which may be considered either in an individual aspect or in a social, that is to say, general aspect." [7] With the sophistication of the behavioral disciplines there has been an increasing acknowledgment of this assumption.[8]

3. A TWOFOLD IDENTIFICATION OF THE BEHAVIORIAL PROCESS

In the light of these considerations we can now more fully identify the *behavioral process* in terms of its correlative sociocultural-motivational aspects. When social scientists are concerned about the sociocultural dimension of the behavioral process from the collective aspect, they concentrate their attention on the externalized actualization of a complex cultural pattern in the institutional structure of the interacting role positions of human persons. Such persons are associated in accordance with the role expectancies which characterize family, economic, political, educational, religious, and similarly organized groups. When social scientists are concerned about the motivational dimension of the behavioral process from the individual aspect, they concentrate their attention on the dynamic system of interpersonal attitudes and role behaviors among goaloriented persons. While all human organisms need security as the *means* to realize the biologically-begotten *end* of survival, some reflective persons have the additional desire for freedom as the *means* to realize the socioculturally-begotten *ends* which are prized as intrinsic values that make survival worthwhile.[9]

B. *The Subject Matter of Each of the Behavioral Disciplines*

If we think of the ends-means continuum of the behavioral process as a pie, we can think of the total subject matter of the behavioral disciplines in terms of six pieces into which it has been cut. In this epistemological analysis more emphasis will be placed upon the problems of the social-scientific enterprise as a whole than upon those of specific disciplines. It must be recognized, nevertheless, that since the pie has been cut into six pieces, it has no substantive content apart from those pieces. Consequently, some identification of these separable but interrelated fields of psychology, sociology, anthropology, economics, political science, and history is required. Since the practitioners in each of these disciplines often disagree with each other, when they identify their subject matter, it would be too much to expect that they will completely endorse all of the following statements. But, if they provide nothing more than road signs which indicate the direction of these specific avenues of inquiry, they will have served some useful purpose.

General *psychology* is a heterogenous field which deals with the behavior of human organisms as they are motivated by their conscious and unconscious goal-oriented responses to physical and sociocultural situations. On the one hand, the individual psychologist aims at an explanatory and/or predictive understanding of the actions of particular human organisms. Accordingly, he generalizes from observations of somatic and psychic data in terms of such functions as sensory-motor mechanisms, perceptions, learning, and psychodynamisms, as well as the personological assessments of abnormal and normal motivation. On the other hand, the *social psychologist* deals with such motive-patterns, attitudes, sentiments, and role-behaviors which are involved in the interpersonal transactions of individuals as they stimulate and are stimulated by the other members of an enculturalized group. Although individual psychology and social psychology are interconnected branches of general psychology, throughout this study each will be treated as a separate discipline.

Sociology aims at constructing generalizations about the interaction between human collectivities. For the most part, it is concerned with generic categories that designate the recurrent institutional patterns in the systematic structure and the interrelated functions of the sociocultural process. These categories are abstracted from the totality of a wide variety of specific human relationships.

All *anthropologists* do not yet agree on the best designation for the non-physical branch of their discipline, which is an integral part of the social-scientific enterprise. Should it be known as cultural anthropology or as social anthropology? When Tax considered the fruitless arguments about this issue, he concluded that anthropologists "ought to use the words 'culture' and 'social' interchangeably and forget about the question of terminology and deal with the problems involved." [10] If it were not so awkward, we might designate the social-scientific branch of anthropology as cultural-social anthropology. But for the sake of more facile expression, we shall refer simply to *anthropology* with the understanding that it is both cultural and social in contrast to the more strictly physical branch of anthropology with which we are not directly concerned.

Anthropology depicts man's ways of feeling, believing, and acting by reference to *culture* as a humanly created, transmitted, learned, and modified symbolic pattern. Accordingly, the anthropologist attempts to discover how this cultural pattern is externalized in social institutions, and is internalized in the value-orientations of persons, who, as both products and producers of culture, are motivated by the striving for culturally begotten goals.

Economics has been generally identified as the analysis of the allocation of scarce resources among alternative courses for meeting human needs for material goods and services. On the one hand, the neo-classical economists have treated profit-seeking within the market processes of production, distribution, consumption, and exchange in isolation from other motivational and sociocultural factors. On the other hand, when the institutional economists analyze economic behavior as a selective adjustment of means to ends, they take into account the impingement upon economic actions of other motivational and sociocultural factors. Regardless, of how orthodox or unorthodox an economist's approach may be, his primary subject matter remains the same as that of all other economists, i.e., the allocation of scarce resources.

When *political scientists* attempt to identify the distinctive characteristics of political phenomena they have not achieved a consensus below the broadest level. At that level they generally agree that they are interested in the over-all *authoritative* allocation of opportunities and responsibilities in human communities, i.e., "Who gets What, When, and How" (Lasswell). This involves the policy-making operations of governments under quasi-governmental influences. In an effort to develop a more precise orienting concept than that of the state, some political scientists focus on *power* (e.g., Key), while others focus on the *allocation of values* (e.g., Easton). Is the core of political life to be found in the power-relation of the ruler and ruled which determines the distribution of rights and duties? Or does it lie in the values which those who are empowered use their authority to allocate? Despite the growing interest in such a conceptual orientation of political data, many political scientists seem to be satisfied if governmental activities are somehow involved in the topic to which they are giving attention.[11]

History-as-recorded-and-interpreted is the historian's reconstruction of what he infers about past human actions on the basis of authenticated testimony. If historical inquiry were not so indispensable to the social-sciences, the problem of social-scientific knowledge would be mitigated by leaving it out of account, since its initial data are not open to contemporary observations. Moreover, unlike other behavioral scientists who take abstract generalizations to be an intrinsic end, the historian usually takes abstract generalizations to be only instrumental as the means for his intrinsic end of understanding the concrete whole of specific situations.

The purpose of these sketchy identifications should be borne in mind. They merely indicate the area of the total behavioral process with which each of the specific disciplines is designed to deal. Before we can conceptually organize these interrelated motivational-sociocultural data, however, it will be necessary for us to amplify these preliminary clues in the elaboration of a synoptic model of behavioral transactions.[12]

A word about our subsequent agenda is required. In presenting the problem of social-scientific knowledge, the procedure would be more clean cut if we could move directly from this conception of subject matter, to the conception of what kind of knowledge about it will be considered meaningful. For example, this is what Lenzen does when he proposes that the aim of natural science "is the acquisition and systematization of knowledge concerning the things and phenomena experienced in observation." He assumes that "the initial objects of [natural] science are the things experienced in perception, and their utmost general characters are positions in space and time." [13]

The behavioral transactions of naturalized, socioculturalized, and goal-seeking individuals, however, do not allow such a direct derivation of the kind of knowledge sought from the kind of experiences that is taken to constitute the initial behavioral data. Whereas human emotions and purposes can be excluded from physical data, they are ineradicable aspects of the ends-means actions which constitute behavioral data. It is on the grounds of this value-centric predicament that the objectivity of social-scientific knowledge has been most seriously questioned. Consequently, we cannot adequately formulate a meaningful conception of the requirements for objective social-scientific knowledge until we have understood what this value-centric predicament entails.

Footnotes to Chapter 2 of Part One

1 Parsons, "The Social System: A General Theory of Action," *Toward a Unified Theory of Human Behavior* (Grinker), 56.
2 Sorokin, *Society, Culture, and Personality*, 3-6.
3 Bierstedt, *The Social Order*, 6, 111-113.
4 Emerson and Grinker in *Toward a Unified Theory of Human Behavior* (Grinker), 147, 151, 367.
5 Whitehead, *Modes of Thought*, 200.
6 Toman and Thompson in *Toward a Unified Theory of Human Behavior* (Grinker), 71 and 263.
7 Cooley, *Human Nature and the Social Order*, 1.
8 See Nadel, *Foundations of Social Anthropology*, 92; Smith in *For a Science of Social Man* (Gillin), 64; Newcomb, *Social Psychology*, 333; Murphy, *Personality*, 891; Tolman in *Toward a General Theory of Action* (Parsons and Shils), 339; MacIver, *Social Causation*, 236; Linton, *The Cultural Background of Personality*, 5; Bidney, *Theoretical Anthropology*, 51-53, 70, 105, 117, 334; Kluckhohn and Murray, *Personality in Nature, Society and Culture*, 35-48.
9 See Spiegel in *Toward a Unified Theory of Human Behavior* (Grinker), 167 for a technically elaborated paradigm comparing "psyche with group foci," which substantiates our identification of the behavioral process. Cf. *Personality, Work Community* (Calhoun, Naftalin, Nelson, Papandreou, Sibley), Book 3, pages 3-24, for a less technical discussion which emphasizes the threefold relationship of the symbiotic community, the moral community, and the quality of personal experience.
10 Tax, *An Appraisal of Anthropology Today* (Tax), 225. See Bidney, *Theoretical Anthropology*, 97-103 for an analysis of the genuine issues on which social and cultural anthropologists in the past have had more than merely verbal differences. But note that Bidney's conclusion justifies our proposed usage: "In the future, a unified discipline of anthropology, comprising social anthropology and cultural anthropology, is bound to replace the segmented pseudo-sciences of social anthropology and culturology."
11 See Easton, *The Political System*, 131-134; Key, *Politics, Parties, and Pressure Groups*, 4-7; Waldo, *Political Science in the United States of America*, 18-19.
12 For a survey of these disciplines, see Hoselitz, *A Reader's Guide to the Social Sciences*.
13 Lenzen, *Procedures of Empirical Science*, from *International Encyclopedia of Unified Science: Foundations of the Unity of Science*, Vol. 1, No. 5, pages 1-3.

3 *The Value-Centric Predicament*

A. *The Evaluational Dilemma*

"Two souls, alas, within my breast abide." A social scientist who feels that he is torn between his conflicting loyalties to both truth and justice shares Faust's dilemma. Consider his dual role. On the one hand, he is intellectually obligated to maintain a completely disinterested attitude for the purposes of scientific analysis. However, on the other hand, he is morally obligated to maintain an enlightened good will by providing administrators with intelligent guidance in the making and implementation of public policy decisions. Consider for example, the thesis of the Harvard Research Center in Creative Altruism: "the moral transformation of man and the man-made universe is the most important item on today's agenda of history." [1]

Dedicated as he is to describing the actual sociocultural and/or motivational conditions of human behavior, the social scientist's concern about human welfare drives him to an "agonizing re-appraisal." This desire to resolve frustrations in the sociocultural situation of which he is a participant is understandable enough. Human goal-seeking constitutes his behavioral data. Not only did the social-scientific enterprise emerge in response to practical needs, but his own inquiry probably was instigated in response to some tensions within that human situation. As Bowers testifies, "Practical problems have often—perhaps usually—been the prime impetus to research." [2]

Orientation to practical application raises peculiar value-problems for the social scientist. A natural scientist and a social reformer do not face this dilemma. Since the natural scientist can eliminate human emotion and purpose from his data, he can largely ignore moral issues in his single-minded pursuit of truth. Value repercussions like those triggered by the Copernican and Darwinian theories are exceptions which prove the rule. Since the reformer can largely ignore intellectual issues, he can passionately devote himself to that program which he feels is the only guarantee of social justice. Unlike either of these, however, the social scientist who finds himself in a value-centric predicament is confronted by the difficult task of co-ordinating his intellectual curiosity and his enlightened good will without weakening either of his two commitments.

Some social scientists seem to have grown so tired of facing this dilemma that they have dismissed it as outmoded. To be sure the question about the value-centric predicament was central for German social scientists in the latter part of the nineteenth century. But, if those who consider the problem out of date have found the answers to the questions it entails, they have not shared them with American teachers and students of the social sciences. Moreover, it is hard to dispel the suspicion that those who ignore this dilemma are pretending it is not there, since they do not know what to do about it. Neither this, nor any other genuine problem can be satisfactorily handled simply by branding it as unfashionable.

Others agree with Lundberg, that the only way out of this value-centric predicament is for social scientists to eliminate all concern about values and policy recommendations so that their disciplines might achieve a natural-scientific status by substituting quantitative for qualitative generalizations. Moreover, any deliberative actions which exhibit the reflective decision and obligation of purposive goal-seeking are explained away by reducing these given data to neuro-physiological and psychodynamic and/or institutional, and/or cultural determinants. The desire to be "value-free" is itself a subjective preference which weakens the position of the person who demands that his colleagues transcend their personal preferences. Fashionable as such an aim seems to be, it will be shown that the valuational nature of the social-scientific data precludes its realization, and also, that the cost of such an artificial cloak of scientific respectability is too high. Instead of slavishly imitating the techniques of the natural scientist, the social scientist may find a genuine kinship with the established members of the scientific family in discovering the deeper bonds of shared motivations and a common conception of what kind of knowledge is meaningful.

What considerations demand the attention of the social scientist who, on the one hand, acknowledges his value-centric predicament, but, on the other hand, believes that his approach and that of the natural scientist are separable but congruent modes of reflective inquiry? We submit that there are four: 1. The value-motivation of both natural scientists and social scientists. 2. The human value-situation as behavioral data. 3. The social scientist's participation in the value-situation. 4. The concern of social scientists about policy recommendations. In the light of our subsequent discussions of each of these points we shall then be in a position to ascertain what requirements the social scientists must meet in order to achieve objective knowledge despite the valuational characteristics of his data.

1. THE VALUE-MOTIVATION OF BOTH NATURAL SCIENTISTS AND SOCIAL SCIENTISTS

The social scientist shares with the natural scientist the same reflective attitude toward persisting inquiry which is generated by the desire for knowledge as an intrinsic value. Thus both are motivated to become engaged in a critical but open-minded exploration of experience in terms of verifiable hypotheses that are always subject to correction, modification, or even abandonment, if carefully examined evidence or more logical reasoning demands a more adequate interpretation. Each has as his objective the Faustian satisfaction of never completely satisfying his intellectual curiosity for increasingly more reliable knowledge. Since the social scientist prefers the pursuit to the final achievement of truth, he morally obligates himself to make every possible effort to curb any prejudice, arbitrariness, dogmatism, or emotional bias which might obscure the evidence or distort his interpretations. Although his unwillingness to accept his own or any other knowledge-claim as absolute truth makes him a sceptic, nevertheless, he is a positive sceptic for whom the endlessness of his quest does not stifle his passion for truth. In fact, if he can make some significant progress toward his goal, its very unattainableness adds zest to his intellectual adventure.

Even those social scientists who agree with Lundberg that they should be "value-free" cannot deny that they are "value-bound" by this preference for the pursuit of truth. Isn't their attempt to eliminate all other desires designed to conserve and increase this desire for knowledge? No genuine social scientist can disagree with this aim. He may find, however, that his ideal value of justice is always subordinated to his desire for objective knowledge. Two points which this statement entails need to be elaborated, i.e., the intrinsic nature of intellectual curiosity, and what is meant by the objectivity of scientific knowledge.

What is the relation of the intrinsic and instrumental functions of inquiry? The emphasis upon the intrinsic nature of the social scientist's desire for knowledge as an end in itself should not be misconstrued as minimizing the importance of knowledge for practical use. Philosophers, mathematicians and natural scientists have, for centuries, sought knowledge for both its instrumental and intrinsic value. They have discovered, however, that the utility of information must be held as secondary to the satisfaction of one's intellectual curiosity in order that the former can have the significance which is derived from its having been established as reasonably acceptable by theoretical standards. For example, when Einstein formulated the theory of relativity, he was motivated solely by his intellectual curiosity, even though the practical knowledge about atomic energy was derived from his conclusions. The lesson that the social scientist must learn from these older disciplines is this: No matter how important practical knowledge for policy recommendations may be, the social scientist must not demand that there be practical use for his knowledge beyond the satisfaction of his own intellectual curiosity.

Instead of assuming that he must completely transcend all value preferences in order to be objective, the social scientist might better assume that "objectivity" is determined by the initial intellectual value which motivates his inquiry. Accordingly, *scientific objectivity* would not be necessarily identified by reference to just one of various techniques, e.g., laboratory experimentation, or by reference to just one of various kinds of subject matter, e.g., physical objects with spatio-temporal dimensions. Contrary to these widespread presumptions, it will be the presumption of this study that, irrespective of techniques and data, *scientific objectivity* should be identified by reference to the reflective attitude of the investigator himself who is dominantly mo-tivated by the desire to know.[3]

2. THE HUMAN VALUE-SITUATION AS BEHAVIORAL DATA

When we turn from the common value-motivation of all scientists to their respective subject matters we find that value data are necessarily involved in behavioral events. Whereas the natural scientist must exclude human emotions and purposes of goal-seeking actions from his physical data, the social scientist must include the desires of persons for satisfaction-yielding objectives among their behavioral data. Most social-scientific disciplines are also concerned about the natural, and/or sociocultural, and/or psychodynamic conditions that shape the individual person's actions. However, for these findings to have significance as behavioral data, they must have some bearing upon the value-impregnated motivations of purposive goal-seeking orientations. Consequently, even if a social scientist proclaims that he has no interest in what human relations ought to be, he is not "value-free." For, unless he adopts what will be described later as the "empty organism" approach, he is forced to take the human value-situation as given in the empirical data to which his generalizations apply.

Among social scientists there is wide acceptance of Werkmeister's claim that they are "concerned with a subject matter of which values, and valuations are essential ingredients." [4] This is explicit in Köhler's *The Place of Value in a World of Facts*. With respect to the motivational dimension of the behavioral process, Allport, for example, insists that "the healthy adult, we know, develops under the influence of value schemata whose fulfillment he regards as desirable even though it may never be completely attained." [5] With respect to the sociocultural dimension of the behavioral process, Kluckhohn, for example, insists that the existence and orderliness of social life depends upon the reciprocal process in which, on one side, goal-seeking persons strive to realize culturally produced values, and on the other side, cultural values are creatively modified by such persons: "Any given act is seen as a compromise between motivation, situational conditions, available means, and the means and goals as interpreted in value terms." [6]

In order to clarify the value-centric characteristics of behavioral data we must identify and elaborate what we shall mean by the human value situation. The human value situation shall mean any experience in which a person is aware that he desires some goal and strives to realize that objective in order to satisfy a felt need. This exhibits a correlative subjective-objective pattern in which *desiring* is the subjective aspect and the *desirableness* of the satisfaction-yielding goal is the objective aspect. When a person aims at some goal, his present awareness of desire is linked to the past through conscious memory of past enjoyments, as well as through unconscious psychodynamic functions; and this awareness is linked to future expectations by the anticipation of satisfactory experience.

When Dewey proposed that the human value-situation be conceived in terms of a "continuum of ends-means," he provided social scientists with the significant insight that the prizing of ends and the appraisal of means are inseparably connected. In such a continuum, the means are an instrumental value and the end is an intrinsic value. Throughout this study it should be understood that "intrinsic" does not signify that a value is final, definitive, unchangeable, or supernatural. A value will be taken to be *intrinsic* when in a particular situation it is desired for its own sake, whereas in another situation that same value might be instrumental, i.e., that which is desired as the indispensable condition for realizing some other intrinsic value. This relationship within the "ends-means continuum" is determined by the specific motivation of the goal-seeking person in a given situation. Moreover, an "intrinsic end" which is never completely achieved is always, as Dewey says, "a moving condition of further consequences." [7]

In order to understand the valuational character of behavioral data, it is also necessary to distinguish between what we shall designate as unreflective values and reflective values.

An unreflective value is whatever a naturalized and socioculturalized actor (a mere self) desires without any deliberation about whether or not he ought to desire that satisfaction. Accordingly, *unreflective desires* for such goals as self-preservation, physical pleasure, and social esteem are an individual's antecedently predetermined behavioral responses to the drives of his complex and interrelated physical, biological, physiological, psychological, and sociocultural environment. Examples of such unreflective desires are hunger, thirst, sexual impulses, and will-to-power compulsions. The allegation that this kind of motivation is amoral should not be taken to be an evaluative sanction or condemnation. If and when these desires are experienced along with desires that entail moral, aesthetic, intellectual, or religious significance, the former may become a part of a reflective value-situation that is no longer amoral. But the reference here is to those instances which do not become involved in this way.

A *reflective value is whatever a naturalized and socioculturalized actor* (*who is more than a mere self*) *desires after he deliberates about conflicting unreflective desires and then decides in the light of his own previously acknowledged ideals that he ought to desire that satisfaction.* Accordingly, *reflective desires* such as intellectual curiosity, an enlightened good will, aesthetic appreciation, or a consecration to a sacred cause, which refer to an ideal goal like self-realization, exemplify a relative self-determination. This partially autonomous motivation exhibits individual initiative and responsibility which motivation by unreflective desires does not exhibit. However the person who makes this kind of deliberative decision does not transcend the influences of his antecedent environment. Whatever degree of self-determination he may achieve through this self-restraint, it is always relative, on the one hand, to his complex and interrelated physical, biological, physiological, psychological, and social environment and, on the other hand, to the system of values which he has adopted from among the culturally-begotten ideals for regulating his thought, conduct, and imagination. Nevertheless, when a person does things to himself under these conditions, and within these limitations of what is done to him, then by his own self-creative efforts to realize an ideal goal, he is participating along with the natural, sociocultural, and psychological determinants in the process of producing the kind of person he is becoming.[8]

3. THE SOCIAL SCIENTIST'S PARTICIPATION IN THE VALUE
SITUATION

Most, if not all, social scientists are participants in the human
value situation which they are investigating. It is conceivable that a
historian might not be concerned with the value-orientation of past
human situations which he interprets; a social anthropologist might
feel the same way about a primitive community whose cultural patterns he is attempting to discern. But, even in these disciplines, the
investigator finds it difficult, if not impossible, to avoid projecting
some of his own value preferences when he reconstructs what he
takes these historical or cultural patterns to be. How many, if any,
economists or political scientists can be completely impartial to what
is going on about them with respect to the allocation of economic resources and political opportunities in the communities of which they
are members? Psychologists and sociologists are rarely indifferent to
the improvement of the behavioral or institutional processes with
which they are dealing. Detached as these social scientists may sometimes be in the formulation of their conclusions, it seems unlikely
that the kind of problems they attempt to solve, and the kind of
questions which guide their empirical research, as well as their theoretical constructions, are entirely free from implicit ethical premises.
Like a person who must live in a house while he is remodeling it, the
social scientist is a member of the community in which he plays non-
academic roles in the very institutions he is examining. What Bierstedt has said of sociologists applies as well to other social scientists:
"He himself is a product of his society, and conforms, consciously or
unconsciously to its folkways and mores, its institutions and laws, its
customs and ideologies, its canons of evidence." [9] How can a social
scientist be completely indifferent to changing the sociocultural process of which he is an integral part, when the need for knowledge for
use in the reorganization of human relations instigates his inquiry,
sustains it, and gives it a market value? The astronomer dealing with
the relations among planets or the biologist dealing with the relations
among biological species are not thus inextricably involved in this aspect of the value-centric predicament.

4. THE CONCERN OF SOCIAL SCIENTISTS ABOUT POLICY
RECOMMENDATIONS

Many social scientists who are motivated by an enlightened good
will to work for the realization of ideal goals feel morally obligated
to provide intelligent guidance with respect to the means and the
consequences that are involved in the making and implementation of
public policy decisions. When the social scientist *qua* behavioral analyst formulates and verifies his generalizations about human action *as
it is*, he assumes that his reliable constructs refer to an already actual
sociocultural-motivational dimension of the objective process of existence. In so far as he is not concerned with what human actions and
relations *ought to be*, he assumes that his referent is no more influenced by his thoughts about it than the natural world is affected
by the constructs formulated by the natural scientist. However,
when the social scientist *qua* policy scientist draws theoretical knowledge from specific behavioral disciplines, and aims toward providing
practical knowledge about the conditions that are required as the
means for the conservation and increase of human welfare, then he
presupposes that intelligent intervention in the sociocultural process
may influence what the future of that objective referent may become. According to Rothwell, this means that by his social planning,
the policy scientist systematically attempts "to shape the future by
exerting influence upon trends that flow from the past into the present." If, as Rothwell suggests, "policy" is taken to designate "a body
of principles to guide action," then its application to the human
value-situation can be viewed as "a calculated choice—a decision to
pursue specific goals by doing specific things." The "formulation and
execution of policy" has been described by Rothwell in four steps:
"(1) the clarification of goals, (2) an exhaustive evaluation of the
situation to be met, (3) the selection of the course of action by
weighing the probable consequences of various alternatives, and (4)
the determination of optimum means for carrying out the action decided upon." [10]
It might seem that the social scientist can avoid the prescrip-
tive aspect of the value-centric predicament by establishing a division
of labor between this emerging study of "policy science," and the

various already "existent specializations" (psychology, sociology, anthropology, economics, political science, history) from which it draws much of its content. This is something like Kant's dichotomy of the pure practical reason and the pure theoretical reason. It has been held that this practical application of the social scientist's knowledge is related to his theoretical analysis in the same manner that applied science is related to the natural scientist's theoretical analysis.[11]

Although this distinction may be useful for some purposes, it does not eliminate the value-centric predicament for all social scientists; within each of the specific disciplines there are representatives who are concerned about normative prescriptions which are integral principles of the behavioral processes in each of these special fields. In these cases the moral commitment of the investigator has a direct bearing on his cognitive process of inquiry, i.e., the kind of data in which he is interested, his selection of the specific data which are most pertinent to his inquiry, as well as his procedures in formulating and verifying his theoretical interpretations.

Let us now consider some statements by social scientists which pertain to the function of normative judgments.

How do normative judgments function in *psychology*? As long as psychologists focus their attention on the neuropsychological responses which motivate human behavior they can, for the most part, avoid normative judgments. But, when they take into account psychodynamic and sociocultural responses as essential ingredients of conscious motivation, then normative judgments are of major concern. This is clearly reflected in the declaration by Gordon Allport with respect to the establishment of the Division of Personality and Social Psychology of the American Psychological Association: "We believe that we have a contribution to make in remedying some of the serious social dislocations of today." [12] It is with the same normative aim that Fromm diagnoses the needs rooted in the special conditions of human existence, and prescribes that "our knowledge of these conditions, that is, of the 'human situation,' leads us to establishing values which have objective validity." Goldstein specifies this normative judgment in terms of self-actualization: "Existence means the realization of the individual, of the individual's *intrinsic nature*, the fulfillment of all his capacities in harmony with each other." When Maslow endorses this ideal of self-actualizing growth, he emphasizes that it is not merely an externally-imposed prescription, but rather, it embodies "the values of the best human beings." [13]

Sociologists have been especially concerned about the function of normative prescriptions in their judgments. Since their discipline emerged out of social reform movements, they are understandably anxious to emphasize their disinterestedness when they analyze the structures and functions of communities. Yet when Furfey indicates the current opinion of most sociologists, he does not preclude normative involvement: "Sociology is essentially a pure science," but they agree that sociology "also partakes to some extent of the nature of an applied science," i.e., "to aid the amelioration of society." [14] Some sociologists might not find this acceptable. At one extreme, Lynd advocates a "value-charged" sociology, and, at the other extreme, Lundberg, as previously noted, declares that sociology along with all other social sciences should be "value-free." Most sociologists do not agree with Lundberg that "ethical neutrality" requires them to ignore the purposive goal-seeking which characterizes their behavioral data. Mac-Iver and Page, for example, insist that sociologists should seek "to comprehend the operative significance of the values they embody." [15] However, most do agree that the sociologist should make every effort to curb his personal preferences when he is engaged in an objective analysis. Bierstedt designates such "ethical neutrality" as an essential attitude of mind for the sociologist: "As a scientist he is interested not in what is right or wrong or good or evil, but only in what is true or false." [16]

Objectivity, however, does not preclude all normative concern, for, as Simpson has indicated, "equality of opportunity is for the sociologist a basic value." Accordingly, the sociologist has an ethical commitment when he objectively analyzes such social conditions as crime, juvenile delinquency, social discrimination: "He may observe with detachment the irrationalities of men; but this detachment is itself a value since he knows that if all men could see themselves as he sees them, they would act with less absurdity, cruelty, and ignorance." [17]

Normative judgments seem to be inextricably involved in *anthropological* studies. Not only does the value-orientation of an anthropologist's subjects constitute his behavioral data; but it is unlikely that he can avoid projecting some of his own value preferences when he attempts to depict a cultural pattern. This seems inescapable in the anthropologist's approach which Kroeber describes when he says that "values evidently are intimately associated with the most basic and implicit patterning of the phenomena of culture," and "I think one has to live himself into values to know what they really are." [18]

From the conception of cultural relativity anthropologists have drawn diverse inferences. On the one hand, Benedict emphasizes "the coexisting and equally valid patterns of life which mankind has carved for itself from the raw materials of existence." [19] On the other hand, Kluckhohn finds enough "cross-cultural dimensions" of "thematic value-emphases" to justify what he calls an "objective relativism" which challenges "untrammeled cultural relativity." By this he means that despite the ethnocentric values of each culture, there are some basic disvalues which "are as much givens in human life as the fact that bodies of certain densities fall under certain specified conditions: suffering as intrinsic good, killing, lying, stealing, raping." Accordingly, Kluckhohn concludes that "the human parade has many floats, but, when one strips off the cultural symbolism, the ethical standards represented are akin." [20]

When anthropologists become engaged in the transformation of the societies they are studying, an ethical concern about normative prescription grows out of their scientific interest in values as behavioral data. Redfield reveals this when he explains why it seems unlikely that anthropology can be a pure science: "In advising men of action, in participating in social change—indeed in being themselves agents of social change in acculturated societies—anthropologists come to entertain the question: What, then, is the good life?" [21] A considerable number of anthropologists seem to welcome a justification of this normative concern from Huxley's biologically-oriented examination of cultural evolution. In discussing anthropologists, he concludes: "By clarifying the role of man's ideas of destiny in cultural evolution, they would make it easier for man to achieve his destiny by fuller realization of his possibilities." [22] It is possible that a great many anthropologists would also be receptive to Bidney's philosophically-oriented conclusion to his study of cultural evolution. He exhorts anthropologists to "show their respect for human reason and science by cooperating with other social scientists and scholars with a view to envisaging practical, progressive, rational ideals worthy of winning a measure of universal recognition in the future." [23]

Further attention should be given to Bidney's anthropological-ethical conceptions of a normative science of culture designed to formulate "cultural ideals as possible means and ends of sociocultural life." His dedication to "the pursuit of normative truths capable of producing a universal, cultural unity based on a common core of rational values" is derived from a critical estimate of cultural relativism. Bidney fully appreciates the service both to truth and to justice that has been rendered by the comparative study of cultures in exposing the "dangers of uncritical ethnocentricism." By this Bidney means "an attitude of mind and a mode of conduct characterized by the adherence to *false* absolute values," e.g., "the primitive distinction between in-group *versus* out-group." But, Bidney insists, it does not necessarily follow that all ethical preferences are so ethnocentric that an anthropologist must adopt a moral relativism. For he can discover not only that "the fact of common cultural values provides a basis for mutual understanding between diverse societies," but also that "the Golden Rule is a moral principle which in one form or another has been proclaimed in all civilized societies and transcends the limitations of any one historic culture." [24]

The *political scientist* would seem to be unavoidably involved in the value-centric predicament. Even if he doesn't recommend what ought to be in terms of his own value preferences, he is interested in the ways in which policy-makers allocate the conditions which are required for the realization of human goals. Consequently, he must take as his behavioral data the humanly devised ways by which specific means are selected from alternative means for realizing alternative ends. Recall Lasswell's *Who Gets What, When, and How?* as a title which reveals the allocative nature of the political process.

Most political scientists probably would agree with Lasswell that they are dealing with "the shape and composition of the value patterns of society." [25] That this desire for the means to realize satisfaction-yielding ends in an essential characteristic of the political process is emphasized today by David Easton, when he identifies it as "the authoritative allocation of values for the whole society." [26] It was similarly identified by Aristotle: "As the state was formed to make life possible, so it exists to make life good."

It might not be apparent that those political scientists who use either the "state" or "power" as their orienting concept, consider their data to have a value-dimension; however, their data are no less valuational than Easton's. Elliott, for example, focuses attention upon the "state." But he declares that "no study of politics which is viewed only in behavioristic terms—that is, in terms that rule out the working of a moral conscience in humanity—will ever do justice to the fundamental problems of political organization." [27] The ingredients of causal analysis and the ingredients of normative prescriptions do not seem sharply differentiated here. Odegard's comment on this is instructive: "To be concerned with ethics does not mean that the student of politics must abandon the objectivity of the scientist, yield to wishful thinking or substitute rationalization and revelation for objective observation, measurement, and analysis"; but "it does mean that he cannot be indifferent to the ends for which political power is to be used." [28]

Those political scientists who identify the political process in terms of power relations, aim to eliminate normative questions from their causal analysis and to include some extragovernmental activities within the political process. Key, for example, finds the common denominator of all of the areas of political science to be "the reciprocal relations of governors and governed, which are relations of power." However, the value-dimension of the political data are not eliminated by Key's effort to avoid normative prescriptions. The political process involves the instrumental "use of power" which Key recognizes as the means to the realization of more intrinsic social values: "Yet, by and large, power is a means, an indispensable means to other ends," and "these ends find expression in public policy, notably in legislation." [29] Lasswell's shift of emphasis, from a completely value-free analysis of the empowering responses between those who hold power and those who empower them, to a concern about "the ultimate social goals" of the political process, has led him to a position which attempts to include both causal power analysis and a normative concern about its aims: "I assume it to be obvious that our strong preference for democratic values need not, and ought not, interfere with the objectivity with which we apply ourselves to the task of describing and analyzing facts." For, Lasswell maintains, "the 'non-objectivity' is in our declaration of fundamental preferences." [30]

The fundamental dispute among political scientists does not stem from the valuational character of its data; but, rather, it arises out of conflicting convictions about the part that the political scientist's own moral judgments should play, when he analyzes and interprets political behavior. Now it is doubtful that any political scientist would ever deliberately allow his own normative prescriptions to distort his causal analysis, nor would he ever intentionally substitute his preference for what ought to be for what a given political situation actually is. On one side of the argument, it is feared, nevertheless, that unless the political scientist completely eliminates all of his own ethical evaluations, he will so project them into his generalizations that he will preclude the reasonable acceptability of his analytical descriptions and/or causal interpretations. On the other side of the argument, it is contended that, whether he admits it or not, the political scientist always presupposes certain ethical principles about rights, duties, freedom security and equality, as well as a preference for a democratic or a totalitarian ideology. It is more objective, therefore, for the political scientist to make his conception of political justice explicit.

After discussing this schism in political science, Herring condemns the "footless disputes that can arise from confusing the distinctive purposes of political philosophy and systematic political analysis." Herring maintains that "to argue their relative merits is to ask which leg is better." Accordingly, he concludes that "those studying politics and government, by the very nature of their subject matter, employ both normative and analytical approaches." [31] Sound as Herring's balanced perspective seems to be, it does not provide an easy escape from the political scientist's value-centric predicament. At least one point seems quite clear, however, political scientists must clearly distinguish between causal analysis and normative analysis. Sabine emphasizes this when he insists that "any clearheaded theory of politics requires discrimination between states of facts, causal connections, formal implications, and the values or ends that a policy is designed to achieve." Sabine declares, nevertheless, that he "is also convinced that there is in intelligence and good will a power of discrimination and of intellectual honesty that is not wholly limited by either nationality or by social class." [32]

A *historian* does not transcend the value-centric predicament by rejecting absolute value standards. Regardless of how effective he is in controlling his personal bias (religious, political, racial, etc.), a historian's preference for what is significant determines his selection of specific human events from the totality of past human events. It would be unusual indeed, if such selective decisions were completely uncolored by the historian's own intellectual, ethical, aesthetic, and religious values. Accordingly, Gottschalk has said this about himself and his fellow historians: "If their values have not entered explicitly into their judgments, they have been implicit or unconscious." [33]

When the historian reconstructs the temporal process of past events in terms of a causal pattern, he can hardly avoid a normative referent which reflects his own evaluations. Few, if any, simply record changes. Rather, historians aim at depicting the progressive development of a cumulative course of events, which as Hook insists, is taken to be "a development favorably evaluated from the standpoint of a human interest, end, or ideal." [34] What the historian means by *progress* is always relative, therefore, to what he prizes as the intrinsic value toward which progressive development provides the requisite conditions for realization. Brockunier and Loewenberg acknowledge that the historian's own value-preferences extend even further. "Even the simplest terms in the historian's vocabulary carry value overtones: civilization, rise, fall, decadence, stability, progress, aggression, defense, cruelty, magnanimity." [35] Moreover, in his *Historical Inevitability*, Berlin argues that historians should *not* attempt to maintain complete neutrality with respect to moral standards when they interpret the course of human events.

Economists seem to have been less concerned about their value-centric predicament than any of the other social scientists. Perhaps the more sophisticated status of their discipline has made them less value-shy. Then, of course, their behavioral data of transactions for allocating the means to maximize the satisfaction of scarce material wants, leads directly to normative prescriptions about human welfare. Recommendations about what ought to be, have been the shared objective of the more philosophically-oriented economists such as Smith, Bentham, Mill, and Marx despite the disparity in other respects. But *welfare economics* has been no less important for the neo-classical economists and for their institutionalistic critics as well. Before examining these views more closely, however, we should note that there have been some advocates of ethical neutrality.

Robbins contends that economists should confine themselves to causal and/or statistical analysis, and make no assertions about what the ends of the economic process ought to be. He must recognize, of course, that "human beings have ends in the sense that they have tendencies to conduct which can be defined and understood." But, Robbins insists that the economist should ask no more than "how their progress toward their objectives is conditioned by the scarcity of means—how the disposal of scarce means is contingent on these ultimate valuations." [36]

Welfare economists do not share Robbins' fear that normative prescriptions about social policy would embody personal biases and ideological propaganda which would preclude objective analysis. According to Scitovsky, without this welfare objective the economist would be little more than "a politician's handyman, who has to wait for the latter to state his aims and can merely advise him on how to go about achieving those aims." Since most economists are unwilling to play this role, they attempt to formulate welfare aims for themselves. Scitovsky frankly acknowledges, however, the value-centric predicament of the economist when he assesses the present prospects of formulating a constructive welfare theory: "If he wants to maintain strict objectivity, he becomes a technician; if he wants to advise on policy, he in most cases relinquishes his claim to the objectivity of a natural scientist." [37] Arrow's analysis reveals further complications in the economist's value-centric predicament. Although theoretical economics has always attempted to conceive what the optimum state of welfare would be and how to attain it, welfare economics still needs to clarify its basic principles and to answer some serious questions, "principally revolving about the problems of comparing the welfare of differing individuals in arriving at a social optimum." [38]

A brief glance back over the history of economic thought strengthens the argument that the ethical neutralists have little chance of eliminating the value-centric predicament by abandoning all normative prescriptions. Even when the mercantilists sought to enhance national power through regimenting all economic transactions, they claimed that they were trying to guarantee the self-preservation of each individual person. In the initial classical stage of economic liberalism, Adam Smith's revolt against this regimentation was designed to provide each person with the right to possess private property and to compete freely in an economic process which automatically adjusted itself—if the government did not interfere with it. Under the beneficent guidance of the "invisible hand," however, the person motivated by enlightened self-interest will "prefer that employment which is most advantageous to society." Bentham attempted to prescribe a quantitative goal for the classical welfare view in terms of the "greatest good for the greatest number." It was Mill, however, who contributed a qualitative non-economic welfare prescription for evaluating economic operations, when he called for government legislation, though it should be infrequent, if it were required for "some great good," i.e., the moral and intellectual development of persons.

Among neo-classical economists, Marshall maintained that economic maximization in a market system is morally justified by its enhancement of the extra-economic values of physical health and moral autonomy: but he considered the elimination of poverty as a primary objective of the economic process. Pigou did not seem interested in non-economic welfare standards when he related all welfare to money measure; but he did declare that the economist should attempt to alleviate the deplorable situation in which the "lives of many are harder than they need be."

Keynes' advocacy of the stabilization of mass employment by the fiscal operations of the government not only radically challenged the classical and neo-classical conception of *laissez faire* capitalism; but it also added a new dimension to capitalistic welfare economics, i.e., the social problem of finding work for everyone. Moreover, he related economic operations to extra-market considerations of ethical and religious values.

The ideological revolt by the Marxians and by the Fabian sociologists against *laissez faire* capitalism was so obviously motivated by normative judgments about social justice that no elaboration is needed. But the rebellion against the neo-classical tradition by the institutional economists (Veblen, Commons, Mitchell, Clark, Tugwell, Means) does require closer examination. For its revision of the capitalistic welfare standards stemmed more from theoretical than from ideological principles. With the exception of Veblen who, like Marx, opposed capitalism, the other institutionalists have tried to reconstruct it in the direction of a planned capitalism which has more "faith in social management and the accommodativeness of the individual to circumstances" (Tugwell).[39] Thus, normative prescriptions about the social implications of economic policies which, in a democratic community, aim at freedom under law and equality of consideration, were shifted from the periphery to the center of economic analysis.

Institutionalists have much yet to do in the development of their welfare theory; but the direction in which they are moving is pointed out by J. M. Clark in his *The Ethical Basis of Economic Freedom.* Clark is searching for "a balanced economic system, including a sector of private enterprise with enough size, freedom and vigor to give tone to the whole," which, "in whatever specific form, will stand or fall by a double test: not only whether it can organize the productive powers which modern science makes possible, but whether it can direct them to meet the rapidly-rising standards of human welfare to which science and education are making people increasingly aware." To achieve this welfare aim the authoritative allocation of economic opportunities through governmental legislation is necessary; but, it is not sufficient. In addition, the intellectual initiative and moral responsibility of reflective persons must be exerted through "a creative process of experimental exploration, by the joint efforts of men of good will." Accordingly, economic freedom and equality of opportunity under law, as well as the mutual respect for the dignity of persons as a personal attitude, are the essential ideal means for maximizing human welfare. But, the intrinsic end for which these instrumental values are prerequisites is "self-realization without which life loses its chief meaning." [40]

While this brief survey of the development of welfare principles as an integral part of the evolution of economic theory seems to indicate that the ethical neutralist is swimming against the mainstream of this discipline, the most serious problem of the value-centric predicament has not been solved. The ethical neutralist serves his colleagues well, nevertheless, when he warns against the danger of impairing the objectivity of causal and/or statistical analysis by normative prescriptions. To avoid this real danger, the welfare economist must coordinate his theoretical judgments and value judgments in accordance with a common pattern of reflective inquiry. Otherwise, the intrinsic ends for which economic operations serve as the means might be determined either by dictatorial politicians or by an inexpert public. Welfare economists such as Arrow, Scitovsky, Tugwell, and others insist that they must "lead rather than interpret" public opinion about intrinsic ends. Mitchell disagrees somewhat when he assigns to the public the determination of ends and to the economist the dual responsibility of enlightening the public about ends and of prescribing the most effective means. Mitchell also recognizes that the public's normative judgment about ends may be capricious and emotionally biased; but he adopts the faith that they can become increasingly guided by reason, if scientifically acquired insight provides relatively objective criteria for measuring economic welfare. In support of Mitchell's position Gruchy has declared that "it would never be possible to objectify the entire content of human welfare, but the economic portion of this welfare appears to be amenable to some objectification." [41] Thus it appears that the economists are slightly ahead of other social scientists in pointing out the direction by which a reasonably acceptable welfare theory might be found. But even the economists, no less than the other social scientists, have not yet worked their way out of the value-centric predicament.

B. *Should Social Scientists Render Normative Judgments?*

Weber's thought about ethical neutrality and the normative function of social-scientific disciplines provides a springboard for a contemporary analysis of the issue. He recommends a division of labor in which social scientists cooperate with philosophers. With respect to ideal ends, the social scientists for their part, should confine themselves to deliberative evaluations of "(1) the indispensable means, and (2) the inevitable repercussions, and (3) the thus conditioned competition of numerous evaluations in their *practical* consequences." For his part, the philosopher should go further in order "to lay bare the 'meaning' of evaluations, i.e., their ultimate meaningful structure and their meaningful consequences." Thus far, Weber's allocation seems to be sound. But, who has the responsibility of formulating the conception of the ideal ends for which the means are selected? Weber's answer to this crucial question does not seem to be adequate. "Even such simple questions as the extent to which the end should be taken into consideration, or how conflicts between several conflicting ends are to be arbitrated, are entirely matters of choice and compromise" by each individual person.[42] Here, it seems, Weber makes no distinction between the normative judgment of incompetent and competent persons. This means that the selection of the intrinsic end is purely an arbitrary or capricious preference in which one person's taste is just as good as another's. If this is the case, then there seems to be no way out of the social scientist's value-centric predicament.

Instead of capitulating without a struggle, the social scientist should demand that the philosopher provide him with reasonably acceptable conceptions of such intrinsic life goals. Werkmeister is right when he contends that since "a concern for means only is obviously not sufficient to entail more than a spurious objectivity," therefore, "some ultimate standard must be established." [43] Weber's faith notwithstanding, the subjective preferences of uncritical individual persons are not adequate for this task. Why, then, shouldn't social scientists turn to the philosophical axiologist for his normative judgment about an intrinsic value for which their policy recommendations are the instrumental values?

What does such a cooperative division of labor entail? *On the one hand, the philosophical axiologist should construct the normative generalizations about the intrinsic end for reflective living which define the ultimate good in the value system toward which sociocultural processes ought to be directed. On the other hand, the behavioral scientist who is concerned with policy recommendations should construct the equally significant generalizations about the most effective means for realizing that intrinsic end in the light of the reliable knowledge he has acquired about the consequences of particular decisions with respect to alternative courses of action.* Although this platform for a cooperative normative enterprise does not preclude the possibility of one and the same person functioning in both roles, it is primarily intended as a basis for the coordination of specialized techniques which are applicable to these separable though interpenetrating dimensions of the total "ends-means continuum" of goal-seeking behavior. Some illustration of this crucial point is in order.

Consider, for example the policy recommendation of the normative political theorist that "we ought to have a democratic constitutional government of law rather than a totalitarian nonconstitutional government of men." How does he justify this claim? Only under a constitutional government is freedom under law guaranteed, i.e., an authoritative allocation of rights and duties whereby the freedom of each person is congruent with the equal freedom of all other persons with respect to due process of law. The political scientist can then confirm or disconfirm the implications of this hypothesis or the implications of the totalitarian alternative hypothesis by empirical evidence. But why should people have equal freedom? The political scientists might say that without it and the opportunity to participate in their own policy making decisions (at least through empowering those who do make and execute policies), the individuals cannot develop their own initiative and responsibility. But why should the individual have the right and the duty to develop his intellectual initiative and moral responsibility? For this answer, the political scientist must look beyond the boundaries of his own discipline to the philosophical axiologist. The latter might answer that the ideal goal of "self-realization" as an intrinsic value requires the political opportunity to develop intellectual initiative and moral responsibility. This the political scientist could accept; but he is not methodologically equipped to verify claims about the intrinsic value for reasonable persons. Such is the task to which only the philosophical axiologist's analytical tools are applicable.

Welfare economics provides a corresponding case when a policy-minded economist claims that planned capitalism is preferable to either unplanned capitalism or socialism on the grounds that it better provides for an "equality of economic opportunity." But why is this desirable? If, like Mill and Clark, he insists that only thus can one avoid the undesirable market exploitation of persons and the government monopolizing of persons, then he is assuming that the self-development of persons is an intrinsic value. Knight has reflected this when, in his analysis of "social economic organization," he acknowledges that "living intelligently includes more than the intelligent use of means in realizing ends; it is fully as important to select the ends intelligently." [44]

Instead of denying the right of the social scientist to make any value judgments, this proposal for a division of labor is designed to provide him with an indispensable function in the general normative enterprise, without jeopardizing his scientific status when he deals with the non-normative aspects of the behavioral process. The techniques which he uses for analyzing motivational and sociocultural data are not applicable to the kind of data of reflective value experience which intrinsic values involve. The social scientist is equipped to provide the philosopher with knowledge about human capabilities, about the most effective means to achieve given ends, and about the consequences of alternative courses of action. Such knowledge about instrumental values is required for the making of enlightened policy decisions. But the social scientist is not equipped to deal with the questions about "oughtness" which are involved in the relatively self-determined conduct of reflectively motivated persons.

This question about the normative judgments by social scientists about instrumental values demands some consideration of how a philosopher would proceed in obtaining reliable knowledge about intrinsic ends. Yet, to elaborate a pattern of axiological inquiry here would carry us beyond the limits of our present study. Consequently, a philosophical approach which aims at providing reliable knowledge about intrinsic goals is suggested in the final chapter. There we shall elaborate this procedure for axiological analysis as a mode of the logical pattern of reflective inquiry: (a) Critical inspection of the relevant data of reflective goal-seeking. (b) Formulation of normative hypotheses which function as principles of classification, of explanation, and of purposive control. (c) Coherent verification of the deduced implications of a generic hypothesis in terms of derivative hypothetical claims which must be tested experientially by reflective persons. It is hoped that this philosophical formulation will be of some help to social scientists who are concerned about making reliable normative judgments.

The social scientist who becomes fully aware of his value-centric predicament is confronted, however, by another question which is even more basic to the problem of social-scientific knowledge: *Is his treatment of behavioral data so relative to his own motivational-sociocultural situation that his generalizations about the behavioral process are subjective rationalizations rather than objective judgments?* To deal with this question we must turn to what is generally referred to as the sociology of knowledge.

Footnotes to Chapter 3 of Part One

[1] Sorokin, "The Powers of Creative Unselfish Love," *New Knowledge in Human Values* (Maslow), 3.

[2] Bowers, "Research Methodology in Sociology," *Method and Perspective in Anthropology* (Spencer), 251-252.

[3] Werkmeister supports this principle when he distinguishes this "value for science" from "value of science" and "value in science": "Objectivity is achieved not by denying these valuations but by acknowledging them and

stating them explicitly as integral parts of the projected research," so that "the value premises themselves may be evaluated in the light of criteria which increase the chances of achieving objectivity." (Werkmeister, "Theory Construction and the Problem of Objectivity," *Symposium in Sociological Theory* (Gross) 501, 503. For discussions which bear on this point, see Dewey, "Unity of Science as a Social Problem," *Foundations of the Unity of Science in the International Encyclopedia of Unified Science*, Vol. 1, p. 31; Lewis, *An Analysis of Knowledge and Valuation*, 257, 441-442; Einstein, "Our Debt to Other Men; the Lure of the Mysterious," *Living Philosophies*, pp. 3-7; Flewelling, *Things that Matter Most*, Chapter 13; Russell, *Mysticism and Logic*, 44; Lundberg, *Foundations of Sociology*, 4, 29-31; and Easton, *The Political System*, 225-227.

[4] Werkmeister, "Theory Construction and the Problem of Objectivity," *Symposium of Sociological Theory* (Gross), 495.

[5] Allport, *Becoming*, 75-76. Cf. Murphy, *Personality*, Chapter 41.

[6] Kluckhohn, "Values and Value-Orientation in the Theory of Action," *Toward a General Theory of Action* (Parsons and Shils), 403. All the contributors to this volume presuppose that motivation always involves value activity, when they adopt the premise of "cathectic behavior." Cf. Kluckhohn, "Toward a Comparison of Value-Emphases in Different Cultures," *The State of the Social Sciences* (White), 116-132.

[7] Dewey, *Theory of Valuation*, 27, 35, 44, 53.

[8] In the psychological literature this concept of reflective valuing is most explicitly supported by Allport in his *Becoming* when he explains his concept of "propriate striving" as the process through which a person becomes a more unified personality: "The possession of long-range goals, regarded as central to one's personal existence distinguishes the human being from the animal, the adult from the child, and in many cases the healthy personality from the sick." (50-51) For relevant discussions of "self-actualization," see *New Knowledge in Human Values* (Maslow), pp. 125-128, for Maslow's view; p. 151 for Fromm's view; and p. 179 for Goldstein's view.

[9] Bierstedt, *The Social Order*, 22-23. Cf. Easton, *The Political System*, 225; and Northrop, *The Logic of the Sciences and Humanities*, 225-256.

[10] Rothwell, "Foreword," *The Policy Sciences* (Lerner and Lasswell), ix. In this volume Lasswell clarifies what is meant by the policy orientation within the social-scientific enterprise: "A policy orientation has been developing that cuts across the existing specializations. The orientation is two-fold. In part it is directed toward the policy process, and in part toward the intelligence needs of policy. The first task, which is the development of a science of policy forming and execution, uses the methods of social and psychological inquiry. The second task, which is the improving of the concrete content of the information and the interpretations available to policy-makers, typically goes outside the boundaries of social science and psychology." (3)

A most significant contribution toward the utilization of social-scientific knowledge for the guidance of policy recommendations has been made by the Ohio Wesleyan Associates (Bayliff, Clark, Easton, Grimes, Jennings, Leonard) in their *Values and Policy in American Society*. For a basic criterion the philosopher (Easton) offers the *welfare standard*, i.e., "the maximum harmonious satisfaction of the desires of men as social beings," (41) and he shows why it requires the *social ends* of material well-being, stability, security, equality, justice, and freedom. Accordingly, the economist, political scientist, sociologist, and historian identify and elaborate the distinctive *social objectives* of their own respective disciplines which bear on these *social ends*. They all adopt the following three basic steps as a common procedure for the deliberative evaluation of social policies: (1) Identification of the valued objective. (2) Organization of scientific knowledge that is relevant for understanding the problem and for understanding the means for realizing the valued objective. (3) Evaluation of policies and objectives which relate the broad social ends of the entire society to the narrower social objectives of the specific disciplines which are cooperating in the enterprise.

11 See Loyd Easton, *Values and Policy in American Society*, for a clear statement of this division of labor in which the instrumental judgments in policy prescriptions are taken to correspond to instrumental judgments in applied science: "In the field of the natural sciences, for example, there is the physiologist and the physician, the physicist and the engineer. In the social sciences there is the sociologist and the social worker, the economist and the business administrator." (29) Cf. Ruesch, *Toward a Theory of Behavior* (Grinker), for illustrations of how "science distinctly has become involved in the manipulative aspects of social organization." (x)

12 Allport in *Psychological Theory* (Marx), 156.

13 See *New Knowledge in Human Values* (Maslow), 151 for Fromm; 179 for Goldstein; 125-126, 128 for Maslow.

14 Furfey, "Sociological Science and the Problem of Values," *Symposium on Sociological Theory* (Gross), 526-527. Cf. Lynd, *Knowledge for What*.

15 MacIver and Page, *Society*, 616.

16 Bierstedt, *The Social Order*, 20.

17 Simpson, *Man in Society*, 80.

18 Kroeber in *An Appraisal of Anthropology Today* (Tax), 373.

19 Benedict, *Patterns of Culture*, 287.

20 Kluckhohn, "Values and Value-Orientation in the Theory of Action," *Toward a General Theory of Action* (Parsons and Shils), 418; and "Ethical Relativity: Sic et Non," *The Journal of Philosophy*, Vol. LII, No. 23, Nov. 1955, page 673. See *Appraisal of Anthropology Today* (Tax), 322-341 for an indication of the diversity of the conceptions of value among anthropologists.

21 Redfield in *Anthropology Today* (Kroeber), 738.

22 Huxley, "Evolution, Cultural and Biological," *Current Anthropology* (Thomas), 24

23 Bidney, "The Concept of Value in Modern Anthropology," *Anthropology Today* (Kroeber), 698.

24 Bidney, "The Philosophical Presuppositions of Cultural Relativism and Cultural Absolutism," *Ethics and Social Science* (Ward), 69, 75, 63, 65.

25 Lasswell, *Power and Society*, XVIII.

26 Easton, *The Political System*, 128, 134.

27 Elliott, *Western Political Heritage*, 4-5.

28 Odegard, "A New Look at Leviathan," *Frontiers of Knowledge* (White), 114-115.

29 Key, *Politics, Parties, and Pressure Groups*, 3-7, 15-21.

30 Lasswell, *American Political Science Review*, Vol. 45, 1951, pp. 134-135.

31 Herring, "On the Study of Government," *American Political Science Review*, December 1953, page 969.

32 Sabine, *History of Political Theory* (Rev. 1950), ix. For a recent report about the function of normative judgments in political-scientific analysis, see Waldo, *Political Science in the United States of America*, 15-16, 30-33, 60-61.

33 Gottschalk, *Understanding History*, 244-245.

34 Hook, Bulletin 54, 116-117.

35 Brockunier and Loewenberg, Bulletin 64, *The Social Sciences in Historical Study*, 144. Hereafter referred to as Bulletin 64. Cf. Cohen and Nagel, *An Introduction to Logic and Scientific Method*, 356; and Nagel, "The Logic of Historical Analysis," *Readings in the Philosophy of Science* (Feigl and Brodbeck), 696.

36 Robbins, *An Essay on the Nature and Significance of Economic Science*, 2.

37 Scitovsky, "The State of Welfare Economics," *American Economic Review*, June 1951, pp. 314-315.

38 Arrow, "Mathematical Models in the Social Sciences," *The Policy Sciences* (Lerner and Lasswell), 137-138. For further discussions of welfare economics see Samuelson, *Foundations of Economics Analysis*, Chapter VIII; Reder, *Studies in the Theory of Welfare Economics*, Parts I, III; Arrow, "Social Choice and Individual Value."

39 Tugwell, *The New Republic*, Oct. 6, 1937, pages 239-240.

40 Clark, *The Ethical Basis of Economic Freedom* (The Kanzanjian Foundation of 1955), pages 5, 9. Cf. Mitchell, *The Backward Art of Spending Money*; Kapp, *The Social Cost of Private Enterprise*; Gruchy, *Modern Economic Thought*; Levin, "Standards of Welfare in Economic Thought," *Quarterly Journal of Economics*, Vol. LXX, Feb. 1956.

41 Gruchy, *Modern Economic Thought*, 317. (See 315, 458-459 for his elaboration of Mitchell's and Tugwell's views.) Cf. Scitovsky, "The State of Welfare Economy," *American Economic Review*, June 1951, pages 314-315; Tugwell, *Redirecting Education*, 75; Mitchell, "Intelligence and the Guidance of Economic Evolution," *Scientific Monthly*, Nov. 1936, Vol. XLIII, page 465.

42 Weber, *The Methodology of the Social Sciences*, 18-19. Cf. Northrop, *The Logic of the Sciences and Humanities*, 255-256; Easton, *The Political System*, 241-256; McIlwain, *The Growth of Political Thought in the West*, 369.

43 Werkmeister, "Theory Construction and the Problem of Objectivity," *Symposium on Sociological Theory* (Gross), 504.

44 Knight, *The Economic Organization*, 153-154.

4 *Situational Relativism*

A relativistic conception of social-scientific knowledge is necessarily entailed by the value-centric predicament. Since no social scientist is likely to turn back the clock to an absolute conception of Truth, let us explore the possibility that there is a kind of relativism which, despite the value-centric predicament, does not preclude the construction of objective social-scientific knowledge. Of these kinds of relativism there are two alternatives which demand serious attention: radical relativism and situational relativism. Much of the confusion in discussions of the "sociology of knowledge" might be mitigated, if these positions were more clearly distinguished.

A. *Radical Relativism*

The radical relativist claims that the social-scientific enterprise can not achieve objective knowledge on the grounds that the personal preferences and the sociocultural environment of the investigator predetermine the conclusions he reaches. Usually, the radical relativist exempts the natural scientist from this value-centric and ethnocentric predicament. For, as Pareto insists in *The Mind and Society*, the natural scientist uses the "logico-experimental method" which is not influenced by the "sentimental residues" which distort social-scientific interpretations of human emotions and purposes. For the radical relativist, therefore, the behavioral interpretations by psychologists, sociologists, anthropologists, economists, political scientists, and historians, as well as philosophers, are not distinguishable from folklore, myths, or the arbitrary and dogmatic rationalizations of political, racial, or religious fanatics. The objectivity of all of these claims is indiscriminately challenged on the grounds of the "existential basis of mental production."

The value-centric and ethnocentric predicament, which this phrase from Mannheim expresses, has been taken by some to be the key to radical relativism. It will soon be shown, however, that Mannheim actually advocates "situational relativism," regardless of what is advocated with respect to the "sociology of knowledge" by those who have been influenced by Marx, Durkheim, and Scheler.[1]

There are two internal contradictions in the position of radical relativism which should be noted. In the first place, on what grounds can the radical relativist make an exception of his own assertion about the subjectivity of all claims to knowledge about human affairs? If what he contends about other claims is true, then his own generalization should be included on the condemned list. Wouldn't his own conclusion be just as value-centrically and ethno-centrically predetermined? Consequently, as Nagel has cogently emphasized, if the radical relativists' "claim is peculiarly exempt from what it asserts so that its meaning and truth are not logically dependent upon the social status of those who assert it," then "there is no clear reason why there may not be others" which might be objectively valid.[2]

In the second place, why should it be held that the ideas of the natural scientist are peculiarly exempt from the influence of the motivational and sociocultural factors in his own particular environment? We have already seen how he is motivated by the subjective preference of his "desire to know." Moreover, the way he proceeds to investigate and the availability of the techniques he can use are relative to his sociocultural situation. Can we deny that the high prestige of natural science today is an ethnocentric bias? It would be ironic if this should be the only ground on which the radical relativist could justify his assumption that natural-scientific generalizations transcend the "existential basis of mental production." Moreover, it detracts from the significance of the aim of those social scientists who in their desire to imitate natural scientists attempt to eliminate all goal-seeking actions from their data and all policy-recommendations from their conclusions.

Radical relativism has contributed significantly to the diagnosis of the problem of social-scientific knowledge despite the extravagance and inconsistency of some of its claims. If it had done nothing else, its exposé of the fruitlessness of dogmatic claims about unchangeable values and definitive truths would have made it directly worthwhile. But indirectly it has done even more. From a study of its claims a social scientist should realize that to slavishly imitate the natural-scientific treatment of data may be prompted more by the desire for prestige than by the desire to obtain reliable knowledge. This seems to be what Wirth, for example, has learned: "Whatever may be the possibility of complete detachment in dealing with physical things, in social life we cannot afford to disregard the values and goals of acts without missing the significance of many of the facts involved." But it must also be recognized that our interpretations, as well as our data, are not value-free: "In our choice of areas for research, in our selection of data, in our method of investigation, in our organization of materials, not to speak of the formulation of our hypotheses and conclusions, there is always manifest some more or less clear, explicit or implicit assumption or scheme of evaluation." [3]

Let us now attempt to reconstruct these significant insights of *radical relativism* in terms of a *situational relativism* which avoids the former's self-contradictions and which does not arbitrarily preclude the objectivity of social-scientific knowledge.

B. *Situational Relativism*

Situational relativism in this study will designate the premise of a social scientist who rejects the assumption that he can establish definitive conceptions of truth and justice, but who assumes, nevertheless, that he can make cumulative progress toward the realization of these ideal aims through the construction of hypotheses which are sufficiently objective to be reasonably acceptable. The situational relativist acknowledges the influence of the scientist's subjective preferences and sociocultural environment upon his conception of what kind of knowledge is meaningful. We shall soon see, however, that this is a significant modification of the radical relativist's contention that each substantive conclusion about human affairs is predetermined by the investigator's personal bias. In order to distinguish his value-charged generalizations about human affairs from those of the fanatic and the dogmatist, the social scientist who adopts the premise of situational relativism must construct his generalizations through a reflective process that conforms to the requirements imposed by his conception of what kind of knowledge is meaningful. Moreover, the situational relativist insists that the natural scientist's conception of meaningful knowledge is similarly influenced by motivational and environmental factors, even though human emotions and purposes are excluded from his data. Since the situational relativist does not deem it feasible or desirable for the social scientists to imitate natural scientists, how does he propose to show that social-scientific conclusions are more objective than dogmatic claims of political, social, or religious fanatics who are motivated only by uncritical emotional prejudices? To answer this crucial question, *he must formulate a system of intellectual requirements to which both the natural-scientific and the social-scientific modes of inquiry must conform.*

It is a premise of situational relativism that all ways of knowing exhibit a similar epistemological perspective which for each investigator is relative to his own specific psychological and sociocultural situation. Presently, we shall examine the variety of ways of knowing in order to show that there is considerable diversity among the methods of dogmatic authoritarianism, mysticism, naïve sense-impressionism, naïve pragmatism, pure empiricism, pure rationalism, and the reflective inquiry which has its natural-scientific and its social-scientific modes. Each approach, however, has some method for acquiring beliefs and some criterion for verifying them which we shall call the *knowledge-situation*. But this procedure is not spontaneously generated. Rather, each method and corresponding criterion is relative to some specific *meaning-situation*. Such a *meaning-situation* is constituted by those assumptions which reveal the investigator's presuppositions about what kind of knowledge is meaningful. These postulates, of course, can not be verified in accordance with a criterion which must presuppose them. But, taken together as a system which is more fruitful than alternative postulates, such postulates constitute a culturally-begotten *symbolic frame of reference*. This *meaning-situation*, in turn, is derived from the investigator's *value-situation*, i.e., the investigator's predominant desire which motivates him to adopt one from among other conceptions of what kind of knowledge is meaningful.

Students of Weber's methodology of the social sciences will recognize that his aim to preserve some objectivity despite relativity qualifies him as a "founding father" of what we are calling situational relativism. Parsons makes this clear: "Thus Weber's principle of value relevance, while it does introduce an element of relativity into scientific methodology . . . does not involve the skepticism that is the inevitable consequence of any really radical relativity." [4]

What essentially differentiates *situational relativism* from *radical relativism?* It was mentioned previously that whereas the latter maintained that the *knowledge-situation* is determined by motivational and sociocultural conditions, the former maintains that it is the *meaning-situation* which is so determined. But now that we have recognized that the method and criterion is determined by the conception of what kind of knowledge is meaningful, it might seem that there is little or no significant modification. Slight as it might appear, it is upon this difference that the chances for establishing the objectivity of social-scientific inquiry depends. Although this entire study will be an elaboration of this modification, the two interrelated aspects of it should be noted here. First, *according to situational relativism, the environmental-motivational determination does not preclude the investigator's relatively self-determined capacity for choosing from among culturally-begotten alternatives.* In other words, it is presupposed that a reflective person has some freedom of selection under the conditions and within the limitations which his total existential environment impose upon him. Secondly, *the situational relativist assumes that within the specifiable limits and in accordance with the specific requirements of a given epistemological perspective testable claims can be constructed and verified as reasonably acceptable to a community of reflective minds.* For there to be such a community for reflective consensus, however, the social scientists, natural scientists, and philosophers who share the same general epistemolog-

ical perspective must be motivated by the same intellectual preferences and must share the same conception of what kind of knowledge
is meaningful.

The subsequent elaboration of the epistemological perspective of
situational relativism will be more intelligible, if first we consider
briefly Mannheim's conception of the relativity of social-scientific
knowledge. Instead of supporting radical relativism, as is often supposed, Mannheim, for the most part, advocates situational relativism,
when he analyzes the "existential basis of mental production." Moreover, we can use this opportunity to show that Mannheim is actually
dealing with the psychological and sociocultural conditions to which
the *meaning-situation* rather than the *knowledge-situation* is relative.
Despite the designation "sociology of knowledge," Mannheim himself insists that the solution to the problem of knowledge is to be
found through "the structural analysis of epistemology." He deliberately aims to balance the extreme of a one-sided psychological
analysis of behavioral determinants, with the other extreme of a one-
sided sociological analysis of institutions. Accordingly, Mannheim
declares that he is just as anxious to avoid the "vague ill-considered
and sterile form of relativism with regard to scientific knowledge
which is so prevalent today," as he is to refute the absolutistic theories of knowledge which assume that the "genesis of a proposition is
under all circumstances irrelevant to its truth."

Mannheim's concept of "relationism" conveys nearly the same
meaning as "situational relativism" which is used here. Some of
his ambiguous and confusing statements about the "domains of
knowledge" might appear to support the radical relativists. But
he explicitly rejects the radical relativistic conception of mechanical
predeterminism which does not take into account the range and
degree of variations in the "correlation between life-situation and
thought process." The keynote of Mannheim's "relationism" which
distinguishes it from radical relativism is what he calls the "perspective" of the investigator. Since it is the investigator's "perspective,"
rather than his answer to a particular question, that is the product
of the psychological and sociocultural background, this principle of
Mannheim's "relationism" needs special attention.

By a "perspective," Mannheim means *"the orienting concept
which determines how one views an object, what one perceives in
it, and how one construes it in his thinking."* In other words, "per-

spective" entails "the meaning of the concepts used; the phenomena of the counter-concept; the absence of certain concepts; the structure of the categorical apparatus; dominant models of thought; level of abstraction; and the ontology that is presupposed." Although "perspective" precludes absolute knowledge, it does not preclude "criteria of rightness and wrongness in a discussion," as the radical relativist claims. Thus, a "relational type of objectivity" may be achieved by competent thinkers who have a common conception of the "perspective" to which their assertions are relative. Consequently, Mannheim rejects any mode of thought which neglects the data of the purposive goal-seeking orientation that characterizes all human behavior, i.e., saying "nothing concerning the meaningful goal of conduct." Accordingly, *"a new type of objectivity in the social sciences is attainable not through the exclusion of evaluations but through the critical awareness and control of them."* [5]

C. *The Relativistic Function of the Meaning-Situation in the Cognitive Process*

The persistent and pervasive function of the meaning-situation as a behavioral response of all human organisms to their total natural, sociocultural and psychological environment, has been succinctly and aptly described by Werkmeister: "All concrete situations reveal that the experiential context in which meanings are found is a triadic relation, involving (a) a 'mind' which interprets (b) some specific given experience or 'sign' as standing for or designating (c) some (actual or imagined) object, condition, situation, or process—the 'referent'." The behavioral anticipation which the rudimentary aspect of the meaning-situation involves, is probably experienced by many non-human animals in their various sensory responses to the physical stimuli of environmental conditions. Moreover, meaning-situations characterize innummerable human experiences in which a sense-impression is taken as a sign of an objective referent that has little or no significance for a theory of knowledge beyond the 'constructive functioning' which they exemplify. When communication is limited to the initial sensory-intuitive level of language such signs designate only particular referents. When reflective analysis is not involved, the purely descriptive function of signs may be expressed through gestures or through words that are emotionally laden with magical significance. With the development of the human capability to generalize in response to abstract symbols, however, there has emerged, out of this more extensively shared meaning-situation, the specific kind of meaning-situation which reflective analysis presupposes. This shift of emphasis from mere communication to refined analysis, i.e., "the use of language in the search for truth," has been thus described by Werkmeister: "A rationalization or intellectualization of thought takes place, and gradually there emerge thought-forms which we may designate as modern; and with them come a new conception of language and its function and a new use of words." [6]

The meaning-situation of the cognitive process of abstract analysis is distinguishable from, even though it is interconnected with, the sense meanings which characterize communication among non-human and among human animals. Cassirer, more clearly than any one else, has recognized this unique capability of man to respond to symbols which distinguishes him from those whose reactions to signs are confined to sense-meanings. Cassirer does not deny that some animal behavior is symbolic in the sense that it may exhibit indirect reactions; since he agrees with Yerkes that experimentation with anthropoid apes discloses "antecedents of human symbolic processes." Despite this interconnection of symbolic response with sign reaction, Cassirer maintains that there is a significant difference between the "propositional language" of man, the symbolic animal, and the "emotional language" to which animal expression is confined: "One element, which is characteristic of and indispensable to all human language, is missing; we find no signs which have an objective reference as meaning." Accordingly, Cassirer assigns to "two different universes of discourse" the *signals*, which, as "a part of the physical world" are "operators," and the *symbols*, which as "a part of the human world of meaning" are "designators." Thus, Cassirer concludes "that the animal possesses a practical imagination and intelligence whereas man alone has developed a new form: a symbolic imagination and intelligence." [7]

D. *The Epistemological Perspective of Representative Ways of Knowing*

1. THE EPISTEMOLOGICAL PERSPECTIVE

According to situational relativism, the objectivity of any claim to knowledge is relative to three situations which, taken together, constitute the claimant's epistemological prespective: (i) his value-situation, i.e., the primary preference which motivates him, (ii) his meaning-situation, i.e., the kind of knowledge that he takes to be acquirable; (iii) his knowledge-situation, i.e., the method by which he constructs his knowledge and the criterion by which he attempts to verify it. Within such an epistemological perspective the *knowledge-situation* (methodological) is derived from the *meaning-situation* (epistemological). It is the *meaning-situation*, rather than the *knowledge-situation*, however, that is relative to the claimant's own *value-situation* (motivational) and to the symbolic frame of reference which is an integral part of the cultural pattern that the claimant shares with others as a universe of discourse.

2. WAYS OF KNOWING

A "way of knowing" is taken here to mean a cognitive procedure for substantiating a belief which is justified by its advocate on the grounds that it is more productive of objective knowledge than any other cognitive procedure. As Lewis has wisely said, "knowledge is belief which not only is true but also is justified in its believing attitude." [8] As we shall soon see, different "ways of knowing" exhibit diverse sources for data, techniques, and criteria by which the philosopher or scientist who adopts a given "way of knowing" attempts to formulate human beliefs. It will soon be shown, nevertheless, that all "ways of knowing" exhibit a common pattern or epistemological perspective.

The consideration of representative "ways of knowing" in terms of this epistemological perspective is designed to serve two purposes. First, it aims to show how each of the diverse proposed cognitive procedures is relative to its own motivational and sociocultural context. Secondly, it aims to indicate what is meant by non-operational conceptions of knowledge, of which some are uncritical and some critical. This paves the way for the operational conception of social-scientific knowledge which will be identified and elaborated in the next chapter.

a) Uncritical Non-Operationalism

i) DOGMATIC AUTHORITARIANISM

The dogmatic appeal to authority in order to substantiate a belief precludes any opportunity to examine the grounds that are alleged to support it. Both the authorities and those who accept their dictates may acknowledge the non-logical character of their justification for this way of knowing. But, they usually justify it by emphasizing the limitations of most minds which compel them to depend upon the one absolute source of Truth. The psychological strength of this claim to those who want certainty is the most obvious reason for the widespread adoption of the dogmatic appeal to authority. There is an important difference, however, between the tentative reliance on an expert in whose reflective attitude one has well-founded confidence, and an unquestioning acceptance of arbitrary decrees which are not subject to critical reflection. Even if the dogmatic authority is indifferent to the fact that he thwarts objective inquiry, his Achilles' heel is exposed, when he is asked: "Why should I accept your authority rather than that of another who uses the same justification for dictating a diametrically opposed belief?" As Montague has emphasized, when any one authority attempts to demonstrate his superiority over other equally dogmatic authorities by appeals to reason, mystical institutions, or practical consequences, then he has abandoned authoritarianism as the final court of appeal. In order that the intellectual suicide of all forms of dogmatism might be recognized in our subsequent analyses, it should be emphasized here that when traditional ideas have not been constructively criticized it is just as dogmatic to reject them arrogantly as it is to accept them blindly.

The justification that its advocates have offered for this way of knowing can be categorized by questions of our epistemological perspective which refer to its psychological and epistemological presuppositions:

Value-Situation:	*What is the dominant motivation of those who dogmatically appeal to authority?* They are motivated by the desire for emotional security which generates an unquestioning acceptance of those beliefs which provide this satisfaction or which generates an arrogant rejection of those beliefs which would thwart this satisfaction.
Meaning-Situation:	*What kind of knowledge is acquirable?* It is assumed that absolutely certain Truth is the only genuine knowledge in order to satisfy the desire which determines this conception of what kind of knowledge is meaningful.
Knowledge-Situation:	*By what method and criterion is warranted belief acquired?* Apart from the insistence upon the supernatural source of ideas that should be blindly accepted, or the superior insight of the iconoclast who demands the arrogant rejection of traditional beliefs there seem to be no specified techniques for the pursuit of truth, since it is already obtained by the authority who demands its acceptance.

Several points should be noted in order to avoid misunderstanding: (a) Nothing stated here should be taken to deny that all of us are to a great extent dependent upon the testimony of others. In this unalterable situation the crucial question is that of determining the way in which this testimony from others will be treated. (b) Just because a belief has usually been blindly accepted on the basis of dogmatic authority, this does not mean that the person who rejects this way of knowing must *always* refuse to accept this belief, if he can find warrant for it in an acceptable way of knowing. (c) In the light of this understanding that a value-situation predetermines a meaning-situation, it should be recognized that when a religious leader appeals to dogmatic authority in order to provide his followers the emotional satisfaction of certainty, and, when a reflective person (whether a scientist or philosopher) appeals to reason in order to satisfy the intellectual curiosity that motivates him and his audience, these disparate appeals exhibit divergent commitments to completely different enterprises. It is not presumed that this statement reconciles the conflict that stems from these different motivations; but it may help to clarify the genuine issue which is psychological rather than logical.

(d) This criticism of the use of dogmatic authority does not apply to the person who does not claim that what he believes is warranted by this way of knowing, but instead simply accepts the belief on faith.

Closely related to this appeal to dogmatic authority are the appeals to common agreement and to custom. Their non-operational character is clearly demonstrated by subjecting them to the same kind of analysis that has been applied above to the appeal to dogmatic authority.

ii) MYSTICISM

For this specific purpose of illustrating a non-operational way of knowing by referring to the mystical appeal to intuitive feeling, we must so limit the discussion that it will not include a satisfactory evaluation of the contribution of the positive mystics who have provided a significant source of insight and inspiration for human endeavors. If one accepts Montague's distinction between "positive mystics" and "negative mystics," he can recognize that the former's claims are not necessarily incongruent with operational inquiry which treats them as data that stand in need of reflective interpretation. For, when the positive mystic claims that he has a significant insight, he does not insist that others should accept it simply because he feels that it is true. It is the negative mystic, however, who is completely non-operational when he claims that the warrant for a belief is his own incommunicable feeling that convinces him and should convince others. With respect to the imaginative intuitions of the artist, who has an aesthetic rather than a religious orientation, the creative insights which he "discovers" and symbolically communicates are usually like those of the positive rather than the negative mystic.[9]

The justification that its advocates have offered for mysticism as a way of knowing can be categorized by the questions of our epistemological perspective which refer to its psychological and epistemological presuppositions:

Value-Situation: *What is the dominant motivation of the mystic?* The desire for a *personal* communion with God from which he derives a first-hand divine communication of what is absolutely certain Truth.

Meaning-Situation: *What kind of knowledge is acquirable?*
Since human perceptions are sometimes illusory and human ideas change, the only genuine knowledge that could satisfy the mystic's desire for personal certainty is that of a super-perceptual and super-conceptual revelation by God of His purpose. For the mystic the meaningfulness and the truth of this divine communication are absolutely certified by his own strong, private, ineffable feeling.

Knowledge-Situation: *By what method and criterion is warranted belief acquired?*
By cultivating a susceptible state of mind which ranges in its intensity from meditative contemplation to the ecstatic trance that requires specific techniques for self-hypnosis. In any case, the mystic can strive for an intuitive insight for only so long, after which the revelation must come to him "from without."

iii) NAIVE PRAGMATISM

At first, the claim that a belief is true if it has practical consequences, may appear to be a simple and direct solution to the problem of establishing the warrant for a belief. Actually, scrutiny will reveal that it is complicated considerably by a variety of interpretations of what these terms themselves mean. By designating this way of knowing as "naïve pragmatism," we are completely excluding from this position the views of Peirce and Dewey who have contributed so extensively to the broader operational conception of knowledge. Although they would not subscribe to the conception of verification which will be critically analyzed here, they have this much of a connection with it. From them we shall learn that unless a belief has consequences in the sense of testable implications, then it is not meaningful for operational inquiry. This is not what the naïve pragmatist is saying. James qualified his endorsement of the appeal to practical consequences, when he declared that such a principle could be applied in behalf of the will to believe, if there were no conclusive arguments to the contrary. But what constitutes a contrary conclusive argument? Despite this ambiguity, James' many significant contributions to empirical investigation precludes classifying him in this non-operational group. Perhaps Schiller's emphasis upon the vindication of a belief by the satisfactions it yields for spiritual aspirations qualifies him as a spokesman for this way of knowing. A more likely person for this role, however, is Emerson, even though he never used the term "pragmatism" and his literary sophistication might seem to make it unreasonable to characterize his conception of the cognitive process as "naïve." But we have his own statements to support our selection of him as an advocate of this approach to knowledge.

Emerson's proposal for solving the problem of knowledge by justifying the acceptance of a belief on the grounds that it is "that view which is most desirable to the mind," would eliminate the possibility of objective knowledge. There would be no distinction between an idea which had desirable consequences for the knower and the reality to which his ideas refer. Instead of eliminating the ambiguity about the meaning of "truth" he eliminates the knowledge-situation itself, when he insists that the belief which he desires to be true "carries upon its face the highest certificate of truth, because it animates me to create my own world through the purification of my soul." This reduces "what is true" to "what is valuable to me." This affords no standard for deciding which of two conflicting beliefs is true, when each has practical consequences. Moreover, isn't it possible for a belief to be true which has no other practical consequence than that of satisfying a person's intellectual curiosity? But no genuine solution can be expected from a person who rejects the principle that the warrant for a belief must be founded on observable evidence: "I know against all appearance." Truth not only becomes a matter of whatever opinions are held by different persons, but in order to satisfy a person's changing moods, even the self-contradictory opinions of one person must be accepted as coeval truths, since "with consistency a great soul has nothing to do." Instead of trying to subordinate all other desire to the desire for objective knowledge, Emerson prefers to surrender completely to an emotional bias which he makes no effort to curb. In short, he reduces the knowledge-situation and the meaning-situation to the investigator's personal value-situation.[10]

It might seem superfluous to bring Emerson's view into this account, since it obviously renders all reflective inquiry meaningless; however, it serves a two-fold purpose here. First, it implies that the appeal to practical consequences is equated with verification. This implication, under a milder guise, might seem attractive to social scientists who despair of achieving the objectivity of the physical sciences and consider this approach an alternative. In the second place, when we come to the discussion of the use of critical introspection, we can use Emerson as an example of what must be avoided in order that critical introspection might properly be incorporated within an operational approach to reliable knowledge.

The justification which Emerson (and to some degree James and Schiller) have offered for 'naïve pragmatism' as a way of knowing can be categorized by the questions of our epistemological perspective which refer to its psychological and epistemological presuppositions:

Value-Situation: *What is the dominant motive of the 'naïve pragmatist'?* The desire for an experienced certainty about personal satisfaction.

Meaning-Situation: *What kind of knowledge is acquirable?* Any belief which is fruitful for meeting the need of a more satisfactory life.

Knowledge-Situation: *By what method and criterion are warranted beliefs acquired?* Ascertaining the practical consequences of rival beliefs on the assumption that whichever yields the greater personal satisfaction is true.

iv) NAÏVE SENSE-IMPRESSIONISM

The person who determines the truth or falsity of a belief by comparing it with his sense-impressions has presupposed that knowledge can be *immediately experienced*. The widespread acceptance of this unexamined appeal to what appears to be self-evident for those who are blessed with "common sense" is reflected in the clichés: "Seeing is believing." "The facts speak for themselves." Despite the substantive differences which distinguish sense-claims from the value-claims of the mystic and the naïve pragmatist, the naïve sense-impressionist shares their formal identification of knowledge in terms of *direct acquaintance with* the data of experience. And like them, he refuses to identify the objective of the cognitive process as *mediate generalizations about experiences* which are inferred as constructs by the investigator. Unlike them, however, he appeals exclusively to *perceptions*, whereby his five senses of seeing, and/or hearing, and/or tasting, and/or smelling, and/or touching directly reveal this or that distinct particular thing which appears to have its own spatial and temporal location in the objective physical world. (The degree to which any one or combination of these five senses is involved depends upon the specific perceptual situation.) Even more important for our subsequent analysis of operational knowing, is the point that the naïve sense-impressionist rules out the process of *conception*. In conception thought is not confined to particular sense objects when it constructs general ideas about unperceived as well as perceived data in terms of the generalized relations among them.

Why do we call the radical sense-impressionist 'naïve'? When he attempts to ascertain whether his immediately experienced sense-impression is true, he assumes reasonably, that the data which constitute the content of his sense experiences are produced by an external objective world. His naïveté is exhibited, however, when he insists that no mental activity is required for structurally organizing these data and for functionally constructing perceptions as well as conceptions. Accordingly, when he claims that he has true knowledge because his statement corresponds to the actual fact, he has illogically presupposed that he already knows by direct acquaintance not only his private sense-impressions, but also the actual physical reality which he will expect to discover. If he objects that he doesn't already know what that reality is until after he has compared his sense-impression with it, then we must ask: How can a sense-impression be directly compared with a reality which is, as yet, unknown? Moreover, if it is assumed that all sense-impressions are veridical, how can error in factual judgments be accounted for? If he objects that some are and some are not, how does he determine which of these *sui generis* self-verifying immediate experiences are true and which are false? In a later section of this study it will be shown how false knowledge-claims can be accounted for by reference to the mental activity which all sense perceptions, as well as conceptions, entail. Pending that more advanced analysis, however, it is easy enough to discredit the claim that sense-perceptions are self-evident revelations of reality by simply calling attention to our common experiences in which our sense-impressions are either unclear or actually misleading, i.e., the straight stick which appears bent under water, converging railroad tracks, the light from a star that has burned out of existence, mirages, etc.

Although factual judgments are an essential part of the process of practical identification of the things in the world about us, as well as in the initial and terminal stages of scientific inquiry, this naïve criterion for the verification of knowledge-claims in terms of the correspondence between sense-impressions and objective reality completely distorts the cognitive process. First, it arbitrarily excludes human value-experiences from the factual situation, since the desiring of a satisfaction-yielding objective which motivates all human actions, can not be seen, heard, tasted, smelled, or touched. Second, it precludes a postulational conception of what kind of knowledge is scientifically meaningful. Third, it precludes the theoretical construction of a co-herent system of causal generalizations about physical events, as well as the mathematical-logical formulation of universal and necessary abstractions for deductions in terms of the relation of implication. *Upon this all scientific inquiry depends. All of these ideational proc-esses transcend sense-impressions.*[11]

The unscientific nature of the purely factual judgments of the naïve sense-impressionist can be illustrated by asking him the fol-lowing question: Does the sun move from the east to the west or from the west to the east? Probably he would claim on the basis of his sense perceptions that it moves from the east to the west. But if the Copernican theory is true, as all modern scientists maintain, the sun doesn't move at all. Our earth moves around the sun. Moreover, this heliocentric theory is a conception which contradicts our percep-tions. For practical purposes, nevertheless, we can go on speaking of the sunset and the sunrise.

The justification that has been offered for "naïve sense-impression-ism" as a way of knowing can be categorized by the questions of our epistemological perspective which refer to its psychological and epis-temological presuppositions:

Value-Situation:	*What is the dominant motivation of the naïve sense-im-pressionist?* The desire for indisputable information that is self-evident to everyone.
Meaning-Situation:	*What kind of knowledge is acquirable?* Whatever is self-evident through sense-perceptions.
Knowledge-Situation:	*By what method and criterion is warranted belief acquired?* By comparing the belief with what one sees, and/or hears, and/or tastes, and/or smells, and/or touches, which assumes that, if the statement corresponds with the per-ceived fact, the statement is true.

b) *Critical Non-Operationalism*

Philosophers have not been satisfied with the justifications for the uncritical ways of knowing. Just as Montague asked the authoritarian why should one accept his authority rather than someone else's authority, so the philosopher can direct a corresponding question to the mystic, to the naïve pragmatist, and to the naïve sense-impressionist. Indeed, none of these positions can be defended against the charge of internal self-contradiction which this question entails. Moreover, some contradictory beliefs can both be substantiated by two equally dogmatic authorities, by two equally mystical intuitions, by two equally practical consequences, and by two equally self-evident sense impressions. In order to transcend this uncritical situation, there have developed in the history of philosophical thought two representative ways of knowing, *pure rationalism* and *pure empiricism*, as well as the denial that any way of knowing is feasible, i.e., *pure scepticism*. A careful scrutiny of the history of philosophy will probably convince others, as it has the present writer, that there have been no philosophers who were simon-pure rationalists, empiricists, or sceptics. But, by selecting phases of the writings of those who have professed to hold these positions, we can discover the logical implications of each of these approaches. Moreover, one suspects, at times, that some of the natural scientists and social scientists who seem to think that they are conforming to the demands of one of these radical positions, might well avoid rehashing the traditional controversies if they were more cognizant of those ways of knowing which we are about to summarize. At the conclusion of this subsection we shall find that Kant's critical conception of the cognitive process will serve as an epistemological bridge to an operational perspective for the reflective inquiry of both the natural and the social sciences.

i) PURE RATIONALISM

In order to obtain knowledge that "springs from the light of reason alone," a pure rationalist (e.g., Descartes) seeks to escape from the "fluctuating testimony of the senses," as well as "the blundering constructions of the imagination," by assuming the ontological status of *universals* as the referent of thought. According to this Platonic doctrine, in addition to *particulars* that are actual in the realm of existence, reality includes a harmonious order of qualities and relationships that are potential in the realm of subsistence. Examples of these subsisting universals are the spatial dimensions of highness, wideness, and deepness, the temporal dimensions of beforeness and afterness, the principle of causality, mathematical relations like the properties of a triangle, logical relations of implications in terms of consistency, and qualities like roundness or redness, etc. Universals *qua* universals do not exist in the realm of actuality along with particulars. But a particular thing is *what* it is by virtue of the fact that it is a complex combination of universals. The particular thing is distinguished from universal relations and qualities by its specific spatiotemporal position, and its causal interaction with similarly constituted and specifically located particulars within the total system of existence. Thus the pure rationalist's point in making his basic postulate about the ontological status of subsisting universals would be lost, if he were taken to mean that these universal conceptions were nothing more than the thoughts in his mind. On the contrary, he contends that they are discovered by the mind in order to understand not only particular entities but also the relations among them. This assumption about the ontological-logical priority of universals, however, does not preclude recognizing that in the psychological process of knowing the mind begins with the particulars from which it infers generalizations. But such contingent propositions are not genuine knowledge, even though as opinions they may serve the practical purpose of providing useful information. To obtain genuine knowledge, the mind must begin with the subsistent universal and necessary principles of an *a priori* system, i.e., conceptions which are not dependent upon sense perceptions, but which must be accepted as unquestionably true by all other rational minds.

In addition to the postulation of the ontological status of universals, three other aspects of the pure rationalist's conception of mediate knowledge about reality distinguish it from the naïve sense-impressionist's conception of knowledge by immediate acquaintance with reality. First, the pure rationalist has to show that there is a mind to formulate ideas about the subsisting referents. Descartes sought to establish the self-evident existence of such an active universalizing agent in his, "I think, therefore I am." Even here, however, he did not appeal as much to the immediate experience of the psychological process of thinking, as he did to the logical necessity which demands that thinking implies a thinker. Moreover, the cognitive activity of the mind itself had to be distinguished from its sense content. Accordingly, Leibnitz was willing to grant that the content of experience was derived from the senses as long as this was not taken to include the purposive activity of "the intellect itself."

Second, the pure rationalist sought to identify the referent of pure thought in terms of the analytic principles that expressed the formal relations of implication to which mathematical and logical thinking is confined. In the formulation of the abstract relations of propositions the mathematician and logician are not required to be concerned about whether or not their purely formal statements are factually or materially *true*. In order that their analytic conceptions might be *valid*, however, their reasoning in accordance with the general conditions of formally correct inferences must conform to the criterion of *consistency*, which Aristotle expressed in his Laws of Thought (Laws of Identity, Non-Contradiction, and Excluded Middle). As mathematicians pure rationalists could be sure that the tautological propositions of their formal analytic systems could be absolutely demonstrated as valid. The fact that there can be more than one such internally consistent system does not destroy the validity of any one of them, e.g., Euclidian and non-Euclidian geometrical systems. But the pure rationalists as philosophers went further in their efforts to conceive of the structure of reality in terms of a universal pattern of implicative relations. Such allegedly absolutely certain and genuine knowledge, rather than mere opinion, was not obtainable in terms of the *synthetic principles* which were contingent upon their uncertain and never definitive confirmation in the changing sense-content of experience. But, as we shall soon see, the pure empiricists have charged that for all of its validity the inapplicability of a purely analytic system to experience renders it sterile as a conception of knowledge about experience.

Third, the pure rationalists sought to replace the naïve sense-impressionist's method of perceptual observation with a rigorous method of deductions of consistent and inevitable conclusions from self-evident axioms. The pattern of this deductive procedure for inferring valid conclusions that are necessarily implied by a given premise, was determined by Aristotelian "categorical syllogisms" (Since . . . then . . .). Referring to these processes of logically self-evident intuitions which provide the axioms and the deductive inferences from them, Descartes declared: "These two methods are the most certain routes to knowledge, and the mind should admit no others. All the rest should be rejected as suspect of error and dangerous." [12]

The justification that has been offered for pure rationalism as a way of knowing, can be categorized by the questions of our epistemological perspective which refer to its psychological and epistemological presuppositions:

Value-Situation: *What is the dominant motive of the pure rationalist?*
                       The desire for clear and distinct knowledge that is absolutely true.

Meaning-Situation: *What kind of knowledge is acquirable?*
                       An a *priori* system of universal and necessary principles which are not dependent upon sense perceptions.

Knowledge-Situation: *By what method and what criterion is warranted belief acquired?*
                       By formal mathematical-logical deductions from self-evident axioms in accordance with the requirements of consistency that guarantee validity with respect to the relation of implication.

ii) PURE EMPIRICISM

"Pure Empiricism" is used here to designate that more sophisticated refinement of naïve sense-impressionism which was diametrically opposed to the apriorism of pure rationalism. As with the latter, however, in discussing pure empiricism we shall also be referring to the extreme procedures of a way of knowing which no actual philosopher, as far as we can ascertain, ever completely followed. (Some natural-scientific experimentalists and a considerable number of social scientists who are engaged in nothing but piecemeal research seem to presume that they are pure empiricists.) In a general sense, of course, all operational inquiry is empirical. This will be explained after sufficient qualifications of pure empiricism have been clarified. Despite the significance of the empirical approach, this sketch of pure empiricism can be abbreviated. For, its primitive orientation as naïve sense-impression is still fresh in mind; and its more advanced form of logical positivism will be considered presently. But let us now focus attention on this somewhat artificial but none the less useful representation of pure empiricism as a critical non-operational way of knowing.

The chief objection of the pure empiricists to the aprioristic conception of knowledge in terms of a formally valid system of universal and necessary principles has been that this purely analytical scheme of relations of implication is substantively sterile, for it yields no synthetic hypotheses that can be tested by observation of actual occurrences. The validity of a consistent system of abstract principles can be deductively established without any regard for the existential testimony of experience. Locke's opposition to the rationalistic notion of the mind with an inherent reasoning faculty was too drastic when he pictured the mind as a "blank tablet" on which particular facts made their impressions. Locke could not keep the mind passive in this straitjacket even within his own account of the cognitive process. Moreover, Hume's supremely valiant effort to push pure empiricism to its ultimate conclusion by reducing the mind to a stream of impressions, landed him in a scepticism which would undermine empiricism itself along with rationalism. These shortcomings notwithstanding, Locke and Hume significantly branded a purely formalistic mode of the cognitive process as fruitless for understanding the actual world of people and things.

As a protest against the pure rationalist's ontological conception of the transcendent harmonious system of subsisting universals, the pure empiricist identified the referents of his ideas as an aggregate of particulars. Minimizing, though not quite eliminating, the active agency of the mind, he attempted to let perceptions "speak for themselves" as much as possible. His psychological sophistication compelled him to reject his sense-impressionistic progenitor's naïve presumption that the unvarnished facts of the external world were able to "speak for themselves." The pure empiricist, no less than the pure rationalist, wanted to distinguish absolutely certain knowledge from mere opinion. But since indisputable information about particular perceivable occurrences was not provided by the consistent deductions from self-evident axioms, the pure empiricist adopted the method of induction whereby the cognitive process begins with the observable particulars from which tentative generalizations are inferred. Unlike the pure rationalist's equally valid, but conflicting systems of relations of implication, these generalizations are held to be susceptible to further examination with a view to ascertaining which of rival claims is true and which is false.

In order to verify their inductive judgments the pure empiricists adopted the seventeenth-century scientific movement's technique of experimental testing. Although this is still a correspondence theory of truth, it is a most sophisticated refinement of the naïve sense-impressionist's appeal to the raw perceptual referent with which the impression was compared. Whereas the latter procedure could not account for error, the pure empiricist could attribute it to inadequacies of observation, of inference in drawing his generalization or to inept manipulation of the supposedly controlled factors in the experimentation. The inductive logic which Mill formulated for experimentation can be summarized as follows: "If this fact *a* is really the cause of this event *b*, then we must attempt to ascertain if whenever *a* occurs *b* inevitably also occurs, and whenever *a* is absent, *b* inevitably also is absent."

Significant as this *synthetic* procedure for testing claims about existence was in its advancement beyond the purely *analytic* procedure by which the pure rationalist could achieve only validity, the pure empiricist had a lopsided picture of the natural-scientific approach. Like Bacon before him, who proclaimed that science was entirely inductive, the pure empiricist overlooked the deductive procedure and theoretical postulates which the mathematical side of the physicist's pattern of inquiry involved. Consider, for example, the conceptual framework which a crucial laboratory experiment presupposes. When the scientist claims that he has verified his hypotheses by a crucial experiment, i.e., a laboratory test that could be performed with the same results at any time or in any place, provided that the same controlled conditions prevailed, he assumes that nature operates in an orderly manner so that events occur in uniform and invariable causal sequences. Apart from this assumption about a harmonious pattern of events, the scientist's appeal to the causal formula for experimental testing would be meaningless. Although the empiricist might reasonably object that he cannot prove that causation is true (Hume), he is forced to assume that it is more likely than pure chance. Similarly, he assumes that mathematical relations are objective, when he counts, weighs, and measures. None of his assertions can be dependably communicated unless he assumes the principle of consistency as the presupposition of intelligibility. Moreover, unless the investigator's mind is purposively engaged in the process of experimentation, how does he deductively elaborate the implications of hypotheses in accordance with the hypothetical syllogism (If . . . then . . .) in order to know what he is looking for. Just as his mental activity is operating in his initial observations which are relevant to the questions he has in mind, so also he must conceptually design the experimental pattern of variables so that his perceptual observations under controlled conditions might be meaningful.

Postitivists in the nineteenth and twentieth centuries have tried to get around recognizing this conceptual aspect of the cognitive process by insisting that pure empiricists should accept as genuine knowledge only the findings of direct observation under controlled conditions. When they arbitrarily confine themselves to recording, classifying, and describing such quantitatively measurable data, they have over-looked the theoretical aspect of the scientific pattern of inquiry. In the following passage Einstein and Infeld aim to correct this serious omission: "To obtain even a partial solution the scientist must collect the unordered facts available and make them coherent and under-standable by creative thought." [13]

The justification that has been offered for pure empiricism as a way of knowing can be categorized by the questions of our epistemo-logical perspective which refer to its psychological and epistemological presuppositions:

Value-Situation:	*What is the dominant motive of the pure empiricist?* The desire for indisputable information about particular factual situations without reference to any *a priori* system of universal and necessary principles.
Meaning-Situation:	*What kind of knowledge is acquirable?* Quantitatively analyzed sense perceptions of particular occurrence.
Knowledge-Situation:	*By what method and criterion is warranted belief acquired?* By inductive inferences from observations of sense-data which are verified by experimentally testing their corre-spondence with facts under controlled conditions.

E. *The Positive Scepticism of a Situational Relativist*

When Kant declared that the scepticism of Hume "awakened him from his dogmatic slumbers" he acknowledged the significant pur-pose which a sceptic serves when he stimulates reflective thinkers to re-examine their objectives and remodel their procedures with respect to the cognitive process. The sceptic's contribution to the operational perspective of reflective inquiry can be better clarified and critically evaluated, if we distinguish between negative scepticism and posi-tive scepticism. *The former reveals the basic weakness of all non-operational ways of knowing; the latter reveals the basic strength of the reflective attitude of operational inquiry.* (This terminological distinction was suggested by Montague's corresponding dichotomy of negative and positive mysticism.)

1. NEGATIVE SCEPTICISM

The negative sceptic denies the possibility of obtaining the absolutely certain knowledge which was the objective of both the uncritical and the critical non-operational ways of knowing. The most convincing vindication for his position has already been elaborated in our sketch of the justifications that have been offered for dogmatic authoritarianism, mysticism, naïve pragmatism, naïve sense-impressionism, pure rationalism, and pure empiricism. Each of these defined knowledge in terms of absolute Truth, of which one could be certain if he followed its prescribed method and criterion. But, as we have shown in the questions of the methodological perspective, the knowledge-situation of each was determined by its meaning-situation which defined for it what kind of knowledge was acquirable. And each meaning-situation was itself determined by the value-situation of the person engaged in each of these ways of knowing, i.e., his dominant motivation for desiring knowledge. In other words, conceptions of what kind of knowledge is meaningful and the prescriptions for acquiring truth are subjective derivatives of each one's own personal preferences. If we may postpone the consideration of how broadly operational inquiry fares in this respect, we are compelled by the results of this examination of traditional ways of knowing in the interrogatory terms of our epistemological perspective to support the claim of the negative sceptic that no definitive knowledge can ever be expected.

This already sufficiently discouraging situation is complicated further by the dilemma of the negative sceptic himself, since he has exposed himself to his own artillery. When he claims that he has definitive knowledge that there is no definitive knowledge, his logically self-contradictory predicament is obvious. If he pleads that his own claim should be treated as a special exception, then he has weakened the alleged universality and necessity of his proposition, even if his adversaries were willing to grant this privilege. If he presumes to abandon the logical principle of consistency, then he eliminates the possibility of intelligible communication including that of his own assertion. Tempting as it is to liquidate the sceptic by his own argument, it does not seem quite sporting to do so, especially since what he cannot consistently assert as true, does seem to be meaningful. Both the non-operational advocates of certain knowledge and the negative sceptic have inextricably embrangled themselves in this predicament because they have treated the question of the identification of genuine knowledge as an issue in the knowledge-situation. There is some hope for solving this problem, if it is reallocated in the meaning-situation. The first step toward this solution has been taken by the positive sceptic who abandons what Dewey has called the "quest for certainty."

For the obvious reason that the negative sceptic denies the justification of any way of knowing on the basis of the categorization of the questions of our methodological perspective, which link the knowledge, meaning, and value-situations of each, we cannot apply this principle of interpretation to the justification of his position.

2. POSITIVE SCEPTICISM

The positive sceptic proceeds on *the assumption* that some reliable knowledge can be acquired, if reasonable acceptability is determined in terms of a high degree of probability rather than absolute certainty. If knowledge must be definitive, then the positive sceptic agrees with the negative sceptic that it cannot be achieved; but his conclusion is based on considerations entailed in the meaning-situation rather than those in the knowledge-situation which confounded the negative sceptic. In short, the positive sceptic does not presume to *prove* the possibility or impossibility of acquiring genuine knowledge. In view of the testimony of historical and contemporary efforts to establish the warrant for beliefs beyond any possible doubt the positive sceptic simply assumes that it is pragmatically more fruitful to aim for a lower target which may be within his range. This commits him to the principle that the apparently most established conclusion must be treated as a hypothesis which is always subject to correction, modification, or abandonment, if evidence or reason so demand. But his value-situation which predetermines his meaning-situation is such that any reasonable degree of success will be sufficient encouragement. For his critical but open-minded exploration of experience in terms of postulates and hypotheses is dominantly motivated by his intellectual curiosity for knowledge for its own sake which is nourished more by the pursuit than it is by achievement of his objective. His is the Faustian satisfaction of never being satisfied.

By means of a constructively critical correlation of the most fruitful principles of pure rationalism and pure empiricism, which in isolation are fruitless, the positive sceptic strives to realize his objective of reasonably acceptable knowledge. By Hume he has been convinced that neither rationalism nor empiricism can provide certainty so that, if such must be his objective, with Hume he "must plead the privilege of the sceptic." But evolution rather than revolution is possible, if he is allowed his less ambitious objective. For then he can seek to implement the policy for the pursuit of knowledge which Kant made articulate when he declared: "Concepts without percepts are empty, and percepts without concepts are blind."

Kant's critical correlation of rationalism and empiricism would not have been possible, if he had not adopted the principle of the constructive activity of thought in the organization and interpretation of a person's experience through perception and conception. We may criticize the inadequacies of some of his presuppositions, e.g., his dichotomy of the noumenal reality of unknowable things-in-themselves and the phenomenal world of appearances, or his bifurcation of the theoretical reason for the natural order from the practical reason for the moral order. We may object to his excessive preoccupation with the formal consistency of ideas. However, by emphasizing the constructive activity of reflective thinking, he provided the key to the solution for these problems which he passed on to the others. This may be the key to the solution of many of the epistemological problems of contemporary scientists who are attempting to formulate an adequate conceptual framework for broadly operational inquiry. For, as Margenau and Einstein testify, *constructs* are the constituent elements of the cognitive process as it is conceived today by those scientists who seek to coordinate systematic theory and controlled observations.

The principle of the constructive activity of reflective thinking presupposes the postulate of epistemological dualism, i.e., ideas always refer to reality, rather than epistemological monism, i.e., ideas can be identical with reality. From the previous discussion of epistemological dualism it will be recalled that this means that the reality itself (whatever it is) exists independently of any mind's thought about it; but any genuine knowledge about that reality must be *constructed* by that mind and other minds through the cognitive process of reflective inquiry. To use Kant's own words: "Thus the order and the regularity in the appearance, which we may entitle *nature*, we ourselves introduce." Accordingly, Kant agrees with the pure empiricist that the data which constitute the content of experience are produced by an objective situation that is external to the mind; but with the pure rationalist Kant agrees that the mind must act on these sense-data in order to construct perceptions and conceptions. The perceptual experiences presuppose a spatio-temporal structure which Kant with partial success attempted to explain in terms of the mind's inherent forms of space and time. The conceptual experiences presuppose a system of categories which are principles of objective reference. Among these categories that of causality best illustrates for our purpose this pattern in accordance with which the mind constructs its knowledge about the independently existing world. To use Kant's own words again: "This is the sole possible ground of proof; for the event, in being represented, has objective validity, that is truth only in so far as an object is determined for the concept by means of the laws of causality." [14]

What is required by the reorientation of positive scepticism for the correlation of the empirical and rationalistic approaches in accordance with the Kantian principle of the constructive activity of reflective inquiry? In the first place, the pure rationalist must recognize that what they have claimed to be *a priori* and self-evident truths in their knowledge-situation, e.g., consistency and causality are neither true nor false. Instead of being definitive conclusions, they are initial postulates in their meaning-situation. In the second place, the pure empiricist must recognize that even observations under controlled conditions do not "speak for themselves." A purely factual judgment may be acceptable as an indication that something has occurred, but, neither it, nor the immediately experienced sense-impressions on which it is based, constitute a scientific assertion. For this, an interpretation with a conceptual system of referents is needed, otherwise, there can be no accounting for errors or different conclusions, excepting faulty observations. In the third place, induction and deduction must be combined in a coordinated method of inquiry which incorporates the techniques of each. In the fourth place, a criterion for verification must be postulated, from which the rationalistic standard of logical consistency and the empirical standard of experimental testing can be derived as coordinated requirements for determining the warrant of reasonably acceptable assertions. To meet these demands is the aim for which an operational perspective of reflective inquiry is formulated.

At this point no justification for positive scepticism as a way of knowing will be categorized in terms of the questions of our epistemological perspective which refer to its psychological and epistemological presuppositions. The clues in this regard which have been presented throughout this subsection will now be organized and elaborated in the next chapter at length in terms of what we shall call a broadly operational conception of knowledge. By way of a preview it can be said, however, that the positive sceptic aims at the operational construction of reliable hypotheses about observable data in terms of a coherent system of explanatory and/or predictive generalizations which have causal implications that can be verified to various degrees of probability.

F. *Conclusion to this Prolegomena*

The objectivity of social-scientific knowledge must be established within the limitations imposed by the value-centric predicament. There seem to be no grounds for justifying any absolutistic claim that the way in which a social scientist selects and treats behavioral data (knowledge-situation) can ever transcend all of his own personal preferences (value-situation) or the culturally-begotten conception of what kind of knowledge is significant (meaning-situation). What could be more uncritically ethnocentric than for a social scientist to presume that the relativistic conditions which characterize other ways of knowing do not characterize the epistemological perspective of his own procedure of reflective inquiry? This does not mean, however, that the social scientist must resign himself to the negative scepticism of radical relativism, for this does not preclude the possibility that he might acquire reasonably acceptable knowledge, if the latter is reconceived in terms of the positive scepticism of situational relativism.

From these preliminary considerations we conclude, therefore, that a significant kind of objectivity can be achieved in the social sciences, if each of the members of this community of reflective minds proceeds in accordance with the same rules of inquiry.

It must be acknowledged that the rules themselves are emendable, as well as relative to the motivation and cultural pattern of the players. Consequently, expectations about objective knowledge must be limited to the conditions of the social scientists' epistemological perspective.

It is the aim of Parts Two, Three, and Four of this study to clarify the conditions which are involved in the epistemological perspective of behavioral inquiry. There are, of course, other dimensions of the total problem of social-scientific knowledge with which only the social scientists themselves are equipped to deal. This does not detract from the importance of confronting the complications at the more abstract epistemological level. Accordingly, as an effort to contribute to the clarification of these broad-gauged conditions, we shall direct attention to these topics: Toward a Definition of Social Scientific Knowledge (Part Two); The Meaning-Situation of Social-Scientific Inquiry (Part Three); The Knowledge-Situation of Social-Scientific Inquiry (Part Four).

Footnotes to Chapter 4 of Part One

1 For an informative review of the development of radical relativism, see Wolff, "Sociology of Knowledge," *Symposium on Sociological Theory* (Gross) 567-592. See Merton, *Social Theory and Social Structure*, 258-264, for a most instructive exposition and critical analysis of radical relativism. Cf. Kaufmann, *Methodology of the Social Sciences*, 187-198.

2 Nagel, "The Logic of Historical Analysis," originally published in the Scientific Monthly, 74, 1952, page 167. *Readings in the Philosophy of Science* (Feigl and Brodbeck), 696. Cf. Easton, *The Political System*, 241-265; Mandelbaum, *The Problem of Historical Knowledge;* and Bidney in *Anthropology Today* (Kroeber), 689-698.

3 Wirth, "Preface," to Mannheim's *Ideology and Utopia*, xxii.

4 Parsons, *The Structure of Social Action*, 601. The following statement from Weber's *The Methodology of the Social Sciences* should be noted. "We cannot

discover, however, what is meaningful to us by means of a presuppositionless investigation of empirical data. Rather perception of its meaningfulness to us is the pre-supposition of its becoming an *object* of investigation." (76).

5 Mannheim, *Ideology and Utopia*, 4-5, 17, 73, 239, 244, 254, 256, 274, and *Essays on Sociology and Social Psychology*, 73, 240. Cf. Lavine, "Sociology of Knowledge," *Naturalism and the Human Spirit* (Krikorian), 193, 196-197.

6 Werkmeister, *The Basis and Structure of Knowledge*, 7 and 17, for a more detailed account of the different stages of the meaning-situation which have evolved with the development of language.

For a more positivistic account, see Morris, "Foundation of the Theory of Signs," *International Encyclopedia of Unified Science*, I, 1938. In his more recent *Signs, Language, and Behavior* (1946) Morris is compelled to recognize a distinction between an animal response to environmentally-begotten signs or physically identifiable signals and a human response to the humanly-begotten "propositional symbols": "non-human beings seldom produce the signs which influence their behavior, while human individuals in their language and post-language symbols characteristically do this and to a surprising degree. Here is a basic difference between men and animals, and until behavioral theory develops a semiotic adequate to this difference it will remain what it is today: a careful study of animals and a pious hope for a science of the human person." (198) Also see Ogden and Richards, *The Meaning of Meaning*, 53, 57.

7 Cassirer, *An Essay on Man*, 23-41. For experimental evidence which supports Cassirer's distinctions between sign reactions and symbolic responses, see Yerkes, *Chimpanzees: A Laboratory*. Colony, 189, and Thorndike, *Animal Intelligence*, 119. Cf. *Psychological Theory* (Marx), 166-168, for Allport's review of some of the relevant empirical findings.

8 Lewis, *An Analysis of Knowledge and Valuation*, 9. The phraseology here clearly reflects the title of Montague's classical volume, *Ways of Knowing*. Elucidating elaboration of many of the points that will be made throughout the subsequent parts of this section can be found in this book. For similar assistance, see Blanshard's *The Nature of Thought* (Vol. II). Shorter but helpful accounts are available in various introductory philosophy textbooks; e.g., Brightman, *An Introduction to Philosophy*; Brennan, *The Meaning of Philosophy*; Titus, *Living Issues in Philosophy*.

9 For epistemological analyses of mysticism, see Montague, *Ways of Knowing*, Chapter II, and Blanshard, *The Nature of Thought* (II), 221-225. For a psychological analysis, see Pratt, *The Religious Consciousness*, Chapters, XVI-XX. For a philosophical evaluation, see Hocking, *The Meaning of God in Human Experience*, 341-441.

10 Emerson, *Nature*, parts i and iv. This antirationalism is clearly Emerson's position in the following passage from his *Self-Reliance*: "In your metaphysics you have denied personality to the Deity, yet when the devout motions of the soul come, yield to them heart and life, though they should clothe God with shape and color . . . a foolish consistency is the hobgoblin of little minds, adored by statesman, and philosophers, and divines. With consistency a great soul has nothing to do."

11 The nature and significance of this postulational, constructive, and deductive

procedure in scientific inquiry will be explained fully in our analysis of an operational way of knowing. Until this is offered, may we cite the following passage from Margenau which explicitly supports the basis for our critical analysis: "A sense datum is in fact an idealization. There is nothing we can point to, saying this is a pure perceptual datum. Even the most primitive kind of cognition involves a slight degree of conceptualization, involves an investiture of a bare datum with some rational context . . . It is presumed to be present at times when it is not seen and carries all sorts of expectations with respect to future experiences, which as a datum, it could not possible convey . . . In fact, if modern physics is correct, it is in the highly curious condition of being made up of elementary particles which can never themselves be seen, heard, or touched, although the object is supposed to have all these sensory qualities. If we say that this table is wholly defined by sensory experiences, the assertion that it contains invisible electrons makes no sense at all. Logically, much of modern physics is incomprehensible unless the essentially constructed character of physical objects is granted in the very beginning. ( ) This admission is not to be interpreted as meaning that external objects are pure inventions." (*The Nature of Concepts* [Proceedings of the Stillwater Conference], 47-48. Cf. Margenau, *The Nature of Physical Reality*.) For a philosophical analysis of the correspondence criterion which the naïve sense-impressionist adopts, see Blanshard, *The Nature of Thought* (II), 225-237.

12 Descartes, *Rules for the Direction of the Mind*. The purity of Leibnitz' rationalism was somewhat more adulterated with a recognition of the need for synthetic as well as analytic reasoning. In his *Monodology* (par. 31-36), Leibnitz maintained that in the sphere of pure thought, e.g., mathematics, the criteria are the principles of identity and non-contradiction—which define *formal consistency*; but in the sphere of experience any interpretation must meet the requirements of sufficient reason—which defines *substantive adequacy*.

The distinction between analytic judgments and synthetic judgments that has been used in our discussion was actually not made so explicit until Kant enunciated them as indispensable terms for interpreting these divergent modes of reasoning. Even most anti-metaphysical thinkers today employ this distinction, although they refer to analytic and synthetic propositions rather than to the ontological principles which the pure rationalists postulated as the referent of thought. This analytic-synthetic distinction is especially significant for economic inquiry.

Since the deductive method is so essential for the pure rationalist, it is probably more relevant here than later on to offer a clear definition of what it means. Brennan's definition of strict deduction well serves our purpose: "When from a given statement or statements another statement or statements necessarily follows, the first is said to imply the second, and inference from the first to the second is said to be deductive." (*The Meaning of Philosophy*, 20-21.)

Although the pure rationalist used deduction in terms of the categorical syllogism (Since. . . . then. . . .) in order to demonstrate the absolute truth of his analytic assertions, it will be shown later that deduction is an essential procedure in the hypothetical-deductive method or reflective inquiry in terms of the hypothetical syllogism (If. . . . then) in order to elaborate the implications of hypotheses so that they might be synthetically confirmed or refuted by empirical testing.

13 Einstein and Infeld, *The Evolution of Physics,* 5.

14 See Kant, *Critique of Pure Theoretical Reason,* B815, for this passage, and A126, for the first quotation in this paragraph. Kant's notion of the privately experienced forms of space and time requires more analysis than space allows here. It will have to suffice here to point out that he views them as essential ingredients of experience rather than as subsistent dimensions (pure rationalism) or existential entities (pure empiricism). Kant's contribution to Einstein's reconception of the space-time continuum which replaced the absolute Time and Space of Newton is discussed by the present writer in his *Enduring Satisfaction,* 166-186. See *Enduring Satisfaction,* 136-140, for our criticism of Kant's approach which, however, does not detract from the significance of his principle of the constructive activity of thought.

P A R T T W O *Toward a Definition of*
Social-Scientific Knowledge

1 Broader Operationalism

Operational knowledge might be taken to be the objective of social-scientific inquiry, if we can decide on what it signifies. Most social scientists seem to agree that behavioral knowledge should be identified as operational in the sense that it is a system of reasonably acceptable constructs *about* observable experience. Consequently, they, for the most part, explicitly reject all of the non-operational ways of knowing, even though some social scientists may inadvertently slip into one or the other of them. The basic divergence, therefore, seems to revolve around whether operationalism should be narrower or broader. Advocates of each of these types of operationalism insist upon specific demands which must be met before a proposed hypothesis can be accepted as reliable. On some points these demands are the same; but on other points they differ significantly. It is the aim of this chapter to compare these respective sets of requirements and to show why there is need for a broader operational conception of social-scientific knowledge. In the next chapter we shall attempt to identify and correlate the various fields of behavioral data in terms of a conceptual framework which we shall call a synoptic model. We shall first be concerned with the comparison of narrower and broader operationalism.

A. *Is Narrower Operationalism Adequate for Social Science?*

Throughout this study, *narrower operationalism* will be taken to mean that conception of knowledge in which concepts are reduced to the physical manipulations of the investigator, and the acceptability of knowledge claims depends upon the investigator's ability to verify them through the quantitative measuring of observable data under controlled laboratory conditions. This reductive identification of knowledge was initiated by Bridgman, a physicist, and this verificative requirement was developed by logical positivists as a philosophical criterion of truth.

Although Bridgman has modified his initial premise for identifying scientific knowledge, which has exerted such a tremendous influence on contemporary thought, it is to this initial assumption about the "operational character of concepts" that we should direct our attention: "In general, we mean by any concept nothing more than a set of operations; *the concept is synonymous with the corresponding set of operations.*" This means that a thing is defined by the operations required to construct or observe it. Bridgman distinguishes between a mental concept such as mathematical continuity, which is reducible to the mental operations "by which we determine whether a given aggregate of magnitudes is continuous," and a physical concept such as length, which is reducible to the physical operations "by which length is measured." Instead of using "theoretical constructions" in terms of "fundamental ideas," which, according to Einstein, "play the most essential role in forming a physical theory," and instead of using "intellectual experiment," which, according to Planck, "carries the mind of the investigator beyond actually measuring instruments," Bridgman's operationism confines concepts to only the "range of actual experiment." Accordingly, he insists that concepts are "undefined and meaningless in regions as yet untouched by experiment." [1]

As Bridgman elaborates his epistemological theory based on the premise of "operationism" he seems to move away from the purely empirical conception of direct knowledge by immediate acquaintance. He first indicated this when he claimed that "if experience is always described in terms of experience, there must always be correspondence between experience and our description of it." He seems to reject all inferential construction of generalizations. He takes explanation to mean only "discovering familiar correlations between the phenomena of which the situation is composed . . . to analyze nature into correlations, without, however, any assumption whatever as to the character of these correlations." But, unlike the pure empiricists, Bridgman does not expect definitive knowledge. Like the positive sceptic, he recognizes that experimental knowledge "is often hazy," that "all our experience is surrounded by . . . a penumbra of uncertainty which we have not yet penetrated" and that "we never have a perfectly clean-cut knowledge of anything." This means that even "operationism" cannot guarantee certainty: "It is a general consequence of the approximate character of all measurements that no empirical science can ever make exact statements." Accordingly, Bridgman does not insist that the reduction of physical concepts to physical operations is "a necessity of thought"; and he acknowledges that "other sorts of concepts may be applicable." He justifies his operational definition of knowledge on the pragmatic grounds that he and other physicists find it to be "a useful one."

Most significant for this study is Bridgman's insistence that the behavioral data with which the psychologist deals are so "qualitatively different" from those of the physicist that not only psychology but also sociology, politics, and economics will be revolutionized when "new techniques have been forged to meet the redefinition of more than predominantly verbal thinking." The technique of controlled experiment is more applicable to the "simpler situations of science" than it is to "the more complicated situations of economics or society." "Operationism" thus comes to mean nothing more than that "a solution has to be checked before it can be accepted." [2]

Logical positivism emphasizes the verificative aspect of the conception of knowledge which we are calling narrower operationalism. Bridgman's initial premise of reducing concepts to physical manipulations, it will be recalled, pertained to the identification of usable knowledge rather than to its verification. We do not claim that there was any deliberate collaboration between this laboratory-trained physicist and these logically sophisticated analysts. The appeal to the quantitative measuring of observable data under the controlled conditions of laboratory testing seems to have been enhanced in the minds of some social scientists by Bridgman's prestige. Since Bridgman did not maintain the stringent adherence to pure empiricism which narrower operationalism requires, it is to the methodological perspective of logical positivism that we must turn for a clear-cut expression of its psychological and epistemological presuppositions:

Value-Situation: *What is the dominant motivation of the logical positivist?*
To unify all human knowledge by limiting warranted beliefs to those which can be scientifically demonstrated.

Meaning-Situation: *What kind of knowledge is acquirable?*
The consistent systematization of linguistic propositions constitutes *formal truth*; but only propositions pertaining to sense data that can be observed under controlled laboratory conditions with quantitative results, which can be expressed in the physicalistic language of mathematical equations, constitute *substantive truth*.

Knowledge-Situation: *By what method and criterion is warranted belief acquired?*
By the quantitative operations of observing, measuring, and recording sense data under controlled laboratory conditions.

By this definition of what kind of knowledge is meaningful the logical positivist eliminates as "nonsense" the goal-seeking actions which appear to many social scientists to be motivating factors that must be taken into account in a causal explanation of behavioral transactions. The logical positivist is compelled to disregard these value-data, i.e., human desires for satisfaction-yielding objectives, by his logically prior commitment in his meaning-situation to deal only with those sense-data that can be analyzed by quantitative techniques.

The significant contributions which logical positivism has made with respect to the formal analysis of linguistic propositions (which pertains to one aspect of what they consider meaningful), are not equally balanced by contributions to the improvement of ways for acquiring substantive knowledge. After all, the quantitative techniques of experimental testing had, for a long time, been included among the scientist's intellectual tools. The clarification of linguistic ambiguity, however, has greatly facilitated interdisciplinary communication through translatable, if not always transferable, terminology. The formal gains notwithstanding, logical positivism actually, on the substantive side, has advanced very little beyond pure empiricism. If, as it appears, a thoroughgoing logical positivist rejects all conceptual referents in his substantive verification, which is confined to sense-data, then he must contradict his own meaning-situation. For, like the pure empiricist, he must assume the conceptual postulate of logical consistency in order to communicate intelligibly. Moreover, he must assume the conceptual postulate of causality in order to have a principle of objective reference. Otherwise, his manipulations and calculations would be nothing more than manual and mental gymnastics.[3]

To what extent have social scientists adopted this narrower conception of operationalism?

Among *psychologists*, those who have followed the general lines of Watsonian behaviorism have been so closely allied to the methodological perspective of logical positivism that Hempel has called the application of the latter to the former "logical behaviorism." Although logical behaviorism is not identical with a behavioristic or any other psychological school, as Bergmann has pointed out, it does provide logical criteria and a methodological scheme which behavioristic psychologists have attempted to apply in their empirical research: "1. The principles of operationism to the terms used in psychology and the laws connecting them, 2. Logical (language) analysis of the theoretical systems in which these terms and laws occur." [4] According to Skinner, this narrower operationalistic conception of knowledge is reflected in the claims of psychologists that a concept must be defined "in terms of certain operations" or "that propositions are based upon operations" or "a term denotes something only when there are concrete criteria for its applicability" or "any concept must be referred for its definition to concrete operations." Skinner has been quite sympathetic to the idea of "operationism" for equating explanation and observed correlations in psychological inquiry. Nevertheless, when he reviews such "roundabout expressions" as these, he finds that Bridgman's equating of concepts with a corresponding set of operations "cannot be taken literally, and no similarly explicit but satisfactory statement of the relation is available." Skinner grants that these "roundabout expressions" outline a program; but he insists that "they do not provide a general scheme of definition, much less an explicit statement of the relation between concept and operation." He defines "operationism" as "the practice of talking about (1) one's observations, (2) the manipulative and calculational procedures involved in making them, (3) the logical and mathematical steps which intervene between earlier and later statements, and (4) *nothing else.*" But, he contends, with respect to the first three points, nothing significant has yet been done, since most effort has been directed at showing only what references are meaningless because they are not operational, i.e., point four.[5] As Pratt has indicated, an extreme operationalistic definition in psychology amounts to nothing more enlightening than that "intelligence is what intelligence tests test." [6]

When we look for *sociologists* who have adopted a narrower operationalism for identifying knowledge, we find that it is partially represented by Lundberg. Unlike those narrower operationalists who attempt to eliminate all theorizing, Lundberg emphasizes the necessity for adopting a conceptual framework of postulates for scientific inquiry. He does insist, however, upon a technique-centered, rather than problem-centered, approach in which only quantitatively measurable data are admissible in an operational sociological analysis. Accordingly, against those sociologists who maintain "that in order to measure, we must first define, describe or 'know' what we are measuring," Lundberg argues that "measurement *is* a way of defining, describing, and 'knowing.'" All sociologists would probably endorse Lundberg's exhortation to his colleagues to define their terms for sociological generalizing in a language that is sufficiently operational to indicate "(1) under *what conditions* these generalizations are true, and (2) to *what degree* they are true under these conditions." But they do not all accept Lundberg's claim that sociologists who include unquantifiable purposive goal-seeking actions among their data are appealing to "mysterious intuitive revelations" and that their problem-centered approach has "only a little more objectivity than folklore." [7]

When Sjoberg, for example, refers to the efforts of Lundberg, as well as those of Bain and others, to establish "rigid operationalism," he provides this instructive comment about its feasibility in sociology: "Though rigid operationalism receives wide acceptance, it is viewed with skepticism in a number of quarters." Moreover, Sjoberg anticipates that "the schism between the physical operationalists (with their concern for particulars) and the generalizers is likely to be maintained in sociology for a long time to come." Strongly as Sjoberg himself advocates rigorous measuring techniques, nevertheless, he recognizes that "many segments of social systems do not permit the ready use of some of the precise techniques which rigid operational-

ists idealize." Consequently, he concludes that "these should not be
allowed to dictate the choice of project." [8]

The subsequent discussion of the problem of social-scientific knowledge will proceed on the assumption that it cannot be adequately defined solely in the narrower operational terms of the quantitative
measuring of observable data. This should not be taken to mean
that the significance of such manipulation is impugned as a technique in the process of inquiry. It should be emphasized that much
of the success of natural-scientific inquiry can be attributed to Kepler's premise that "only measurable data are real," i.e., investigatable.
Moreover, observing and recording constitute a procedure which can
be reproduced by other scientists in the same generation or successive generations, despite the divergence in some of their concepts. It
is unlikely that any reflective person would ever question the worth
of this procedure for communication through specifying the instrumental steps by which a conclusion is reached; it is just as unlikely
that he would refrain from using controlled laboratory testing, if and
whenever such precision techniques are applicable. The narrower operationalist fails to recognize, however, that these techniques are only
the instrumental *means* to be used, in some cases, along with other
analytical tools in order to reach the intrinsic *end* of reliable knowledge. Instead of discounting concepts as meaningless, the scientist
must include them among the means he uses. But, the social scientist
must have an operational conception of knowledge which is sufficiently flexible to include meaningful references to behavioral data
that may not always be quantitatively measurable.[9]

Social scientists seem to be looking for a re-evaluation, rather than
a complete rejection, of narrower operationalism. In order to make
operationalism applicable to all behavioral data, there is a need to
restate its principles in such a way that the identifiability and verifiability of reasonably acceptable social-scientific constructs can be established.

As a contribution toward this end the defining principles of a
broadly operational conception of social-scientific knowledge will now
be proposed and elaborated. If the broadly operational conception of
social-scientific knowledge can be shown to be usable, then the psychologist, sociologist, anthropologist, economist, political scientist,
and historian are not compelled to accept the narrower operationalism of logical positivism as the only cloak of scientific respectabil-

ity. When the student of human behavior is liberated thereby from the superficial bondage of imitating natural scientists through using inapplicable techniques, then he may discover his genuine kinship with the acknowledged members of the scientific family in the deeper bonds of a shared motivation and a mutually acceptable conception of what kind of knowledge is meaningful. If and when such a broadly operational conception of knowledge is adopted, then it is pointless to argue about whether or not behavioral analyses can be "scientific." For then, both behavioral *and* natural-scientific analyses would be considered as separable but congruent modes of reflective inquiry.[10]

To what extent have social scientists expressed the need for reconstructing a broader operationalism?

Among both *individual and social psychologists* this need has been emphasized by those who question the sovereignty of experimentation as the one and only technique for empirical testing. When Andrews considers the complexity of the subject matter of individual psychology and the diversity of the techniques "in its heterogeneous domain," he contends that "psychological science is founded upon but not limited by the experimental method." Accordingly, Andrews rejects the identification of psychological knowledge in terms of factual observations alone, on the grounds that "knowledge of facts without knowledge of the procedures to discover the facts does not constitute science." [11] Similarly, social psychologists acknowledge the need for a conception of knowledge which is not exclusively identified by experimentation, "which comes after the problem has been defined and its salient characteristics so well formulated that we know what can be controlled and measured." [12]

Among *sociologists*, there are those like Sjoberg (cited above) who have doubts about the complete applicability of narrower operationalism; and there are those who oppose even aiming at defining sociocultural phenomena in terms of quantitative measurements. MacIver, for example, is just as concerned about empirically testing sociological constructs as is Lundberg. Nevertheless, MacIver insists upon including in his behavioral data those purposive, goal-seeking actions experienced by anyone which "no operational defining can charm away." Accordingly, he calls for an operationalism which can "be understood in a less absolute and more defensible sense." [13]

Among *anthropologists*, there seems to have been very little concern about any kind of operational knowledge; but Murdock reflects a growing interest on the part of some of them for developing a more scientifically sophisticated conception of anthropological knowledge: "When it comes to the formulation and testing of hypotheses, anthropologists reveal little comprehension of the requisites of a viable scientific theory and even less of the methods which science has devised for putting such a theory to the test." [14] Since it is obvious that concepts about the pattern of the relation of the cultural process to social structure and personality cannot be reduced to physical manipulations and quantitative measurements, anthropologists who are not anti-scientific stand in need of some broadly operational definition of knowledge. This seems to be implied in Kroeber's discussion of the aims of anthropology in which he sees future anthropology extending scientific method derived from the natural sciences to the field usually covered by the humanities. But, it should be noted, that "understanding of complex cultural phenomena can be made intelligible only by a method somewhat different from those of established science." [15]

Among *economists*, there are some who are looking for a broader operationalistic definition of knowledge which will avoid the two extremes of the neo-classical formalism and the statistical inventories of piecemeal research. Samuelson, for example, contends that "our theory is meaningless in the operational sense unless it does imply some restriction upon empirically observable quantities." [16] When Gordon attempts to translate Bridgman's "operationism" into economic theory in order to distinguish testable from non-testable economic generalizations, he assumes that "an operational proposition is one that implies or states an operation that could, in principle, be performed, the result of which tests the proposition." Although Gordon indicates that the analytic propositions of neo-classical theory do not constitute this kind of knowledge, he does recognize that they "may be highly useful in finding operationalistic propositions." A strictly positivistic conception of economic knowledge is not adequate, according to Gordon, since an operational definition "does not exclude introspection as a possible method for developing operational propositions." [17] Although Lane hopes that economists can develop for operational *verification* "the rigorous standards of verification developed by natural scientists," he recognizes that for *discovering hypotheses* it is difficult but necessary for the economist to "know by inner experience something about the human nature which is the subject of our generalizations." [18]

Although Friedman calls for a "positive economics" which aims at the same kind of knowledge that is sought by the natural sciences, he is forced to recognize that the economist cannot conduct controlled crucial experiments. He insists, nevertheless that instead of "a retreat into purely formal or tautological analysis," the economist should operationally construct and verify his hypotheses by less rigorous, but equally significant, requirements of empirical testing: "Evidence cast up by experience is abundant and frequently as conclusive as that from contrived experiments." [19]

Political scientists are not uniformly committed to any definition of operational knowledge; and those who are seeking to develop such a conception recognize that it is largely programmatic. At one extreme, those who take as their objective the collection and inventory of governmental and quasi-governmental phenomena might seem to favor a narrower operationalism. At the other extreme, those who take their study to be an application of intelligent insight and creative imagination deny that it is a science and feel free to employ nonoperational principles. Seeking to avoid either of these extremes there are some political scientists who agree with Easton that "political science today is confronted with the need to recognize that scientific understanding of political life is ultimately possible only by clarifying the broad theoretical premises of research." [20] In order that political scientists might refine their definition of knowledge for this purpose, Driscoll and Hyneman urge their colleagues to formulate basic conceptions which "will set the framework within which further methodological problems must be considered—problems of abstraction, significance, tests of validity, and the inter-relationships of empirical data, generalizations, and theory." [21] Leiserson explicitly opposes any attempt to make the propositions of political science as narrowly operational as chemical formulae or engineering specifications; but he does insist that "political scientists cannot escape the problem of identifying and specifying relationships between the variables involved in analyzing human behavior." [22]

The need for an operational definition of *historical* knowledge is not felt by all historians; but there are those who, like Brockunier and Loewenberg, do hope to reduce methodological errors "by defining procedures in operational terms" so that "historical scholarship can demonstrate a significant degree of cumulative analysis." But this requires a commitment by the historian to this principle: "Concepts must be made scientific in the sense that they demand explicit statement and restatement; they must be made open to repeated challenge which is the basic test of hypothecation." [23]

There are some historians who are not interested in the cumulative analysis which requires operational knowledge. First, there are the document-centered historians, who are so exclusively concerned about the authentication of testimony that they refrain from constructing any causal generalizations. Secondly, there are the drama-centered historians, who are so concerned about building up to a climax in the narration of their entertaining chronicles, that they prize aesthetic effectiveness over the depth and breadth of their imaginative reconstructions. Thirdly, there are the cycle-centered philosophers of history, who are so concerned about demonstrating that there is a universal and necessary pattern which embodies *the* transcendent meaning of human history, that they treat ascertainable causal relations among temporal events as mere symptoms of a predetermined cyclical or dialectical scheme. When Cough, as an operational historian, claims that the "chief task of the historian is to ascertain what has happened, to identify events in sequence, and to discover how and why they occurred in a given order," he is not denying the necessity for establishing the authenticity of documents, nor is he minimizing the desirability of literary quality in historical narrative, nor is he precluding the possibility of obtaining significant insights from an overarching philosophy of history. He and like-minded historians do insist, however, that in order to engage in cumulative analysis of "human activity through time" beyond these procedures the operational historian "requires criteria to guide him both in the selection of problems for investigation and in the development of valid concepts and analytical methods." [24] Gottschalk uses the term "historicable" to identify those constructs that can be shown to be "subject to inquiry as to credibility," prior to substantive analyses, which aim at establishing them as "true, reliable, or probable." [25]

B. *Toward the Requirements of Broader Operational Knowledge*

A conception of broader operational knowledge will now be presented in terms of five salient principles. These have been formulated with a view to examining the requirements for determining the identifiability and the verifiability of social-scientific constructs. Like the terms of any definition they are arbitrary in the sense that the principles themselves can neither be confirmed nor denied. The broader operationalist must take his defining principles to be rules which he pragmatically adopts in preference to other rules that are not as fruitful for defining the kind of reasonably acceptable knowledge he is seeking. All social scientists who adopt the rules we are about to consider will not necessarily arrive at the same substantive conclusions with respect to specific claims about human behavior. But when they differ, they will have a common set of rules by which they can regulate their attempt to reconcile their differences in dealing with evidence. Non-operationalists and narrower operationalists simply have different sets of rules.

The manner in which the subsequent principles of broader operationalism are *a priori* must be clearly understood. They are not *a priori* in the sense meant by the pure rationalist when he claimed that he had established Absolute Truth in terms of an *a priori* system of universal and necessary principles. On the contrary, they are *a priori* only in the sense that they express what the broader operationalist means when he endorses a knowledge-claim as a legitimate contender for reasonable acceptance. Thus, as a set of principles, they are *a priori* only in that sense characterizing any definition adopted at the outset of a discussion.

> 1. First, for a belief to be verifiable as a knowledge-claim, it must be stated in a proposition that has implications which can be communicated to other persons in such a way that they can examine, compare, and test the implications of the hypothesis in the light of logical reasoning and observable evidence.

The primary condition of all operational knowledge, as Peirce so forcefully emphasized, is this ability of one person to communicate a belief to another. If scientists did not have the opportunity to check each other's ideas and observations, as well as those of past scientists, there could not be any "community of minds." Such a corroboration has created an atmosphere in which a challenge to an established theory can be a milestone for progress rather than a tombstone signalizing its demise.

The necessity for adopting this requirement can perhaps best be shown by showing the consequences when it is disregarded. The person who appeals to dogmatic authority obviously violates this regulatory principle, when, in order to authenticate the infallibility of his alleged source of absolute truth, he declares that the communication, the examination, and the testing of his definitive doctrines are entirely irrelevant to the vindication of their acceptability. Although the mystic may invite others to strive to realize divine inspiration, if not an ecstatic trance, in order that other persons might discover for themselves what the mystic has intuitively experienced, he spurns all logical reasoning and observable evidence in his yearning for a divine revelation. His private self-validating feeling of the divine presence may be a supernatural communication; but since it is ineffable, it yields no observable and testable implications in the form of assertions that can be humanly communicated. The other uncritical nonoperationalists, the naïve sense-impressionists and the naïve pragmatists, insist on some communication. In the case of the former, there is the demand for corroborating sense-impressions which can be checked by anyone "with eyes in his head." In the case of the latter, there is the demand for corroborating the realization of the satisfaction of desires by anyone who can calculate the practical consequences of a contemplated decision. But, in both cases, the full demands of this first requirement are not met. On the one hand, the naïve sense-impressionist is so completely absorbed with sense data that he is oblivious, not only to "the essentially constructed character of physical objects," [26] but also to the necessity for the inferential construction of generalizations by which sense perception must be interpreted by reasoning. On the other hand, the naïve pragmatist disregards the demands of logical reasoning and observable evidence, which this requirement makes imperative, when he realizes that they would compel his acceptance of a belief that is contrary to what he desires to be true.

This requirement for individual *psychologists* was explicitly acknowledged by Tolman, when he declares that "an operational psychology will be one which seeks to define its concepts in such a manner that they can be stated and tested in terms of concrete repeatable operations by independent observers." [27] Marx testifies to the widespread acceptance by individual psychologists of this principle of *"operational validity,"* which, as the "most essential characteristic of construct formation," demands "the open and clearly stated relationship of the construct to its empirical basis in operations producing the data." [28]

Social *psychologists* acknowledge that it is more difficult for them to meet this requirement than it is for the individual psychologists whose data are more manageable under controlled laboratory conditions. Several of them insist, nevertheless, that the kind of knowledge they seek should be operationally definable and verifiable. Newcomb, for example, recognizes that "methods of observing response and of controlling stimulation are by no means perfected" and that "there are many social-psychological problems to which the methods of hypotheses and controlled observation have scarcely been applied." Hence "too few social psychologists have made more than casual use of the genuinely operational concepts which Professor Parsons demands." Newcomb urges his colleagues to make a greater effort in this direction despite the complexity of their data: "If we really believe, for example, that group memberships determine roles which determine motive which in turn determine vast segments of behavior, why don't we put our belief to the test instead of relying upon anecdotal evidence?" [29]

Among *sociologists* there is considerable disagreement between those who are narrower operationalists and those who are broader operationalists; but they all agree that their constructs should meet this first requirement in the sense that Lundberg, Schrag, and Larsen have expressed it: "To formulate a problem we need, first, to ask a clear and answerable question and, second, to state a tentative solution that can be proved or disproved on the basis of empirical evidence." [30] Bowers has emphasized this principle in terms of what he designates as the demand for "methodological explicitness," i.e., "increasing recognition that it is necessary to record as explicitly as possible all operations involved in executing research that have a bearing on the outcome." [31] Despite the general acceptance of this operational requirement for identifying sociological knowledge, sociological inquiry has not yet gone as far as many sociologists would like to go in meeting its demands. Since no sociologist is more concerned about clarifying and using a theory of "functional analysis" which would exemplify this principle than Merton, his estimate in this matter is especially instructive: "A large part of what is now called sociological theory consists of general orientations toward data, suggesting types of variables which need somehow to be taken into account, rather than clear, verifiable statements of relationships between specified variables." [32]

Anthropologists do not seem to have reached a consensus on this principle. As Spencer has revealed, it is with respect to "the formulation of a particular hypothesis to be tested" that "many cultural anthropologists are in a quandary." [33] Even those who may not go so far as Evans-Pritchard in identifying their study as a branch of the humanities, do hesitate to define anthropological knowledge in such a way that it would exclude "the intuition and experiential background of the investigator" from which he develops "the same kinds of perception utilized by the literary critic or the artist" so that he can "get the feel" of the culture he is studying. For some anthropologists, however, this imaginative response must be incorporated within an operational conception of anthropological knowledge in terms of what Nadel calls "variations found and asked for in the data of observation" which are so correlated that "from them general regularities may emerge." [34] This seems to be what Lesser has in mind when he insists that "the functional relation or relations asserted of any delimited aspect of culture must be such as to explain the nature and character of the delimited aspect under defined conditions." [35]

This first operational requirement is taken to be the basis for defining knowledge by those *economists* who are not satisfied with either the neo-classical conception of purely analytic knowledge or the positivistic conception of purely synthetic knowledge. In order that economists might test alternative generalizations about relevant observational constructs in terms of a broader operational conception of knowledge, Machlup calls for "a procedure designed to find out whether a set of data of observations about a class of phenomena is obtainable and can be reconciled with a particular set of hypothetical generalizations about this class of phenomena." [36] When Gordon suggests the anaylsis of the functional relations of incomes, prices, and the demand curve with increasing or decreasing quality, rather than with tastes, he explicitly acknowledges this operational requirement: "The operational test for the stability of a function is always in its ability to predict changes in the dependent variable from changes in the independent variable." [37]

Leiserson, who is among those *political scientists* who are attempting to redefine the political scientist's conception of knowledge in operational terms, has insisted that "the political scientist cannot escape the problem of identifying and specifying relationships between the variables involved in analyzing political behavior." For only then can he be guided throughout his investigations by this operational question: "Under what conditions do these relationships hold good?" Without this principle for identifying the kind of knowledge for which they are looking, there is no opportunity to correlate "explanatory theoretical configurations and the relatively miniscular research operations of testing limited hypothetical formulations." [38]

No *historian* claims that he or any other historian has ever fully complied with this first requirement of operational knowledge; but there are those who agree with Brockunier and Loewenberg that "various processes in human affairs can be and have been subjected to very considerable analysis of a cumulative kind." Accordingly, they aim at the kind of knowledge which is characterized by this operational principle, i.e., "testable hypotheses and factual support for them are essential for warrantable conclusions." [39] When Aitken and Loewenberg distinguish the kind of historical knowledge for which they are striving, from the broad generalizations of Spengler and Toynbee, they explicitly advocate an operational conception in which a historical interpretation "is stated in such a way that it can conceivably be proved false by reference to empirical evidence." [40]

Reliable historical knowledge must be defined in terms of this requirement that out of available authenticated testimony the historian must imaginatively reconstruct communicable hypotheses with testable implications. Otherwise, a historical judgment would be little more than the unquestioning acceptance of the authority of that past testimony which the historian would select because it would be more pleasing to him. This is the "scissors and paste" procedure that does not require a critical examination of the evidence which might confirm or disconfirm past testimony. Collingwood condemns this when he insists that genuine historical knowledge is always inferential rather than reports which stem from someone's personal memory or from some authority whose claims are not constructively criticized: "History has this in common with every other science: that the historian is not allowed to claim any single piece of knowledge, except where he can justify his claim by exhibiting to himself in the first place, and secondly to any one else who is both able and willing to follow his demonstration, the grounds upon which it is based." [41]

2. Secondly, a verifiable knowledge-claim must be actually verified in accordance with a justified criterion before the assertion as a sufficiently tested hypothesis becomes genuinely operational knowledge.

This demand that a belief must be tested and found to be true rather than false in accordance with a verificative technique that competent persons can use in a similar way distinguishes the critical from the uncritical non-operational approaches to knowledge. Unlike the dogmatic authoritarian, the mystic, the naïve sense-impressionist, and the naïve pragmatist (none of whom found it necessary to state their beliefs in propositions that had implications which could be tested by objective techniques), the pure rationalist acknowledges the requirement of logical consistency and the pure empiricist acknowledges the requirement of experimental testing. Disagreement arises over what constitutes the sufficiency of the objective criterion for substantiating a belief. Each fears that the criterion of the other will not guarantee certainty. But when the positive sceptic revises this objective in terms of reasonable acceptability, rather than definitive truth, he opens the door for the operational use of both the rational and the empirical criteria, if they are used in conjunction with each other. In this new light, logical reasoning is not worthless simply because it allows more than one valid, i.e., internally consistent, explanation. Correspondingly, empirical testing is not worthless simply because the implications of a hypothesis can never be proven absolutely by experimental testing, which, at best, can only show that the evidence examined under controlled conditions did not refute them. By coordinating these deductive and inductive procedures into a two-fold requirement, the positive sceptic makes logical consistency-empirical adequacy sufficient grounds for ascertaining that one belief is more highly probable than alternative claims insofar as available evidence at the time so indicates.

It is clear that psychologists, sociologists, and economists assume that they can meet this demand sufficiently to incorporate it in their conception of knowledge. Some anthropologists, political scientists, and historians, however, have raised some doubts about their fields in this respect.

Anthropologists may agree that there has been little or no verifications of their constructs; but they do not always agree why this is so. According to Bennett and Wolff, some contend that " 'proof' is irrelevant in the sense that man is man wherever found; the grasp of a single instance of the 'unique' itself is knowledge." [42] Others agree with Nadel that they are moving in the direction of testing their constructs, even though there is yet much to be done before such is possible: "In anthropology we are only just beginning to marshal our facts for analysis; we are still operating with limited regularities established for narrow and disconnected collections of cases examined." [43]

All *political scientists* do not seem to agree that the studies of political phenomena are sufficiently unified to provide for adequate testing of their constructs. Some consider their discipline to be more of an art than a science; but others are calling for the development of a methodological perspective which will lead away from the mere collection of "facts" and the premature application of them to practical affairs. Instead of undertaking "the necessary task of developing verifiable theory," Easton says of political science, "as a discipline it has misconstrued the nature of the tools required for the attainment of reliable, generalized knowledge." [44] Easton himself, however, is a good example of those political scientists who are seeking to change this situation by working toward the development of testing techniques. Slow as this movement might seem to be, Driscoll and Hyneman have detected some promising signs: "The lack of elaborate statement about underlying assumptions, guiding conceptualizations, and other methodological considerations cannot conceal the evidence that in recent years there has been both a rapid growth in output of American political scientists which is based upon a conscious regard for sound methodological foundations and a steady rise in the sophistication with which methodological demands are met." [45]

Any *historian* who would not attempt to test the implications of his hypotheses is not actually engaged in the process of inquiry. Grandiose speculations, purely dramatic expositions, and purely narrative chronicles which blindly accept the infallible authority of specific sources have been produced by men who do not accept the responsibility of testing the implications of their assertions; but they are more likely to fall in the class of propaganda than in the class of knowledgeable statements. To produce knowledgeable statements the document-centered historian must authenticate his testimony and the more theoretical historian must confirm the implications of his generalizations about the causal connections among events before either can maintain that his assertion is warranted. When we come to the examination of the verificative techniques in the discussion of the hypothetical-deductive method of historical inquiry, we shall find that several are employed sometimes separately and sometimes in conjunction with each other, e.g., observation of continuous configurations, imaginative reconstruction of alternative hypotheses, comparative case studies, introspective projection. The historians who use these techniques do not always agree about their relative significance. But they do agree with Aitken and Lowenberg that any historical hypothesis must be "tested against the evidence," if it is to become "a generalization which holds with a certain degree of probability and which can serve as a provisional explanation." Moreover, an operational historian is committed to recognize that "if the test is unsuccessful, then our hypothesis and perhaps the whole conceptual structure from which our hypothesis was derived must be questioned." [46]

Although the major emphasis here has been upon the testing of the implications of historical constructs, it must be acknowledged that sometimes historians are compelled to include in their interpretations "summary generalizations" or "imaginative insights" which are reasonably acceptable impressions, rather than hypotheses, from which testable implications can be derived. Brockunier and Loewenberg recognize this, but they contend that this use of "expert guesses is neither peculiar to historical inquiry nor is it a flagrant incongruity in a reflective analysis." For, they contend, "theory that runs beyond the established data is the source of fertility in cumulative scientific analysis." [47]

3. Third, regardless of how firmly established a theory may be, it is operational only so long as those who hold it keep open the door for further inquiry which might necessitate a re-examination of the grounds for its acceptability.

Upon this demand of positive scepticism is based the crucial distinction between the aim of non-operational cognitive processes, which seek definitive conclusions, and the aim of operational cognitive processes, which seeks to avoid making any conclusion definitive. It is obvious to any critical investigator that his initial hypothesis may be no more than an inspired guess, a hunch, an imaginative leap, a supposition, a tentative principle, a provisional statement, or a heuristic device. But, more than this is required with respect to the recognition of the revocability of every kind of operational construct. Even though an assertion is so warranted by verification that it has become a natural law or a theory which conceptually integrates an entire discipline, e.g., the biological theory of evolution; nevertheless, the evidence and reasoning that are sufficient to make it acceptable at one time, are not necessarily sufficient to make it definitive for all time. Any conclusion which is not capable of being revised, expanded, or rescinded fails to meet this demand of operational knowing for a persistent continuity of inquiry. Peirce emphasized this conception of approximate truth, when he justified probable conclusions on the grounds "that though the conclusions at any given state of the investigation may be more or less erroneous, yet the further application of the same method must correct the error." [48]

Most *psychologists* seem to agree with Kelly that an acceptable "theory is frankly designed to contribute effectively to its own eventual overthrow and displacement." In other words, the psychologist offers half-truths rather than infallibility, i.e., "the hope that he may have hit upon some partial truth that may serve as a clue to inventing something better and he invites others to follow this clue to see what they can make of it." [49] Andrews, for example, endorses this principle when he points out that, since the inductive analysis of empirical evidence can diminish error but can never be exhaustive, generalizations about human behavior "are thus of necessity made on the basis of partial evidence, and so they are made only as probable inferences." [50] Similarly, Bergmann and Spence declare that "there is no methodological principle, no 'operational recipe' which guarantees that no relevant factor has been overlooked." [51] Lambert insists that *social psychologists* as well can develop their discipline only so long as they are fully aware of "vulnerability of formulation." [52]

Sociologists are reminded by Zetterberg that none of their generalizations can be verified to the extent that they become inflexible, "since we always run the risk that new observations will disqualify our prediction or that alternative hypotheses will predict observations equally well." [53] Similarly, Rose warns his colleagues that "sociological techniques of acquiring data may not be delicate and precise enough to isolate the basic elements of human behavior and social organization." [54]

As *anthropologists* extend their interest beyond the mere description of a specific culture they are becoming more concerned about constructing generalizations that open up avenues for further inquiry. This seems to be what Nadel has in mind when he declares that "any extension of our knowledge over wider and wider domains will add to the complexity of phenomena, of whose immensity we are already aware." [55]

Economists seem to be divided somewhat on this principle of revisability. On the one hand, it may not be acceptable to those who adopt the rationalistic view of von Mises that "the ultimate yardstick of an economic theorem's correctness or incorrectness is solely reason unaided by experience." [56] On the other hand, it is an essential characteristic of what is meant by economic knowledge for those who adopt the empirical view of knowing in terms of "confirmation till next time," which Machlup compares with a sports elimination: "No empirical hypothesis is safe forever; it can always be challenged for another test and may be knocked out at any time." [57] Since there seems to be a fairly widespread impression that all neo-classical economists have defined economic knowledge entirely in the non-operational terms of unrevisable formal truth, it is instructive to note the following statement by Marshall which reflects this operational principle: "For the actions of men are so various and uncertain, that the best statement of tendencies, which we can make in a science of conduct, must needs be inexact and faulty." [58]

While all *political scientists* seem to agree with Easton that any generalization they make "is a statement of relationship which is only probably, not certainly and finally, true," they have divergent grounds for their common conclusion. On the one hand, there are those who reject absolutism in favor of a relative historicism. On the other hand, there are broader operationalists who would endorse Easton's rejection of this "flight from reason" and his faith in the possibility that, through reflective political inquiry, there can be an identification and cumulative analysis of "the major properties of the political aspects of social life." [59]

The conception of *historical* knowledge as the product of a cumulative process of continuing inquiry presupposes this principle. The historian who adopts it must constructively criticize his past authorities as well as invite contemporary and future historians to correct, modify, or abandon his own inferential generalizations. This is what we take Collingwood to mean by "the idea of history" as an emendable enterprise in which "no achievement is final" and, with respect to which, no historian can "say that his picture of the past is at any point adequate to what his idea of it ought to be." Accordingly, Collingwood opposes any who blindly accept the testimony of past authorities, because they have never been challenged or for political, religious, or similar reasons. Although the historian must rely on past authorities for information, nevertheless, Collingwood contends, the genuine historian must re-interpret those reports in such a way that "he is relying on his own powers and constituting himself his own authority" with the result that "his so-called authorities are now not authorities at all but only evidence." [60]

4. Fourth, operational verification requires that empirical testing must be regulated by conceptual principles.

This insistence upon ideational operations is diametrically opposed to the narrower operational demand initially stated by Bridgman that "we shall no longer permit ourselves to use as tools in our thinking concepts for which we cannot give an adequate account in terms of operations," i.e., *physical manipulations*. The importance of empirical testing is not minimized by this principle. Rather, it is given significance by the operational concepts which suggest how the manipulation of experimental variables might be designed, controlled, and correlated. How does an experimenter know what he is attempting to confirm or deny apart from ideational operations which regulate his investigation? How can an experiment be crucial, i.e., repeatable anywhere and anytime with the same results, if it is not assumed that the conceptual principle of a causal uniformity of events has, does, and always will hold? For all of their precision and accessibility how can purely manipulatory operations answer the question:

evidence for what? When Dewey discussed the indispensability of such ideational operations for the pattern of scientific inquiry in terms of "the operational character of facts-meanings," he measured the immaturity of social-scientific inquiry "by the extent to which these operations of fact-finding and of setting up theoretical ends are carried on independently of each other, with the consequence that factual propositions on one side and conceptual or theoretical structures on the other are regarded each as final and complete in itself by one or another school." [61] Accurate as this characterization of some social-scientific approaches seems to be, there are representatives of each of the behavioral disciplines who are calling upon their colleagues to reconceive the process of verification in accordance with this broader operational correlation of ideational and observational procedures.

The problem of defining what is meant by genuine *psychological* knowledge revolves largely around the question of the relation of its empirical and its theoretical components which this principle entails. Bergmann and Spence consider it to be unfortunate that "there has not always been a proper appreciation of the incompleteness of an approach which neglects either one of these supplementary procedures in science." [62] If psychological knowledge is to be anything more than "mere descriptions and mere correlations of facts," according to Köhler, the demand which this principle imposes must be met: "Mere psychological research gives us a number of rules but no sufficiently coherent framework in which these rules can be combined into a body of systematic knowledge." [63]

This requirement of broader operationalism is designed to expose the fruitlessness of the conflict between those psychologists who call for more theory and less fact. For, as Marx has cogently discerned, the real difficulty is that "we have too little relationship between facts and theories." Consequently, he contends that it is a "major contemporary problem" for psychologists "to stimulate critical evaluation of the relationship between logical constructs and their supporting empirical data." [64]

Social psychologists for the most part have apparently been so overwhelmed by the complexity of their data that much of their research has been on an *ad hoc* basis; but operationalism is precluded by the very nature of their subject matter, i.e., the "thought, feeling, and behavior of individuals" as they "are influenced by the actual, imagined, or implied presence of other human beings" (Allport). Despite the fact that, as Allport reminds us, "theory building in social psychology is still in its infancy," [65] there is, nevertheless, an increasing awareness that ideational principles for regulating empirical testing are needed. At least, this is what Newcomb means when he declares that "too few social psychologists have made more than casual use of the genuinely operational concepts which Professor Parsons demands." [66]

The regulation of empirical testing by conceptual principles for verification is a crucial issue on which *sociologists* are divided. A survey of contemporary sociological studies seems to reveal the predominance of fragmentary research. There is much more concern about the refinement of quantitative techniques for the empirical testing of isolated hypotheses through statistical correlations, than there is for operational concepts. Some sociologists, nevertheless, hold to an ideal conception of sociological knowledge in terms of the long term goal of the *empirical-theoretical system* for guiding observational operations which Parsons and Shils have made explicit: "We speak of an empirical-theoretical system whenever a sufficient number of relevant variables can be brought together in a single (theoretical) system of interdependence adequate for a high level of precision in predicting changes in empirical systems outside special experimental conditions." [67] Parsons and Shils recognize that knowledge of sociological laws today is "too vague and fragmentary" to expect any immediate acquisition of such empirical-theoretical knowledge; but such ideationally operational verification is their aim.

When Merton proposed a "middle range" approach which was designed to maintain a balance between such a theoretical level of verification and the *ad hoc* level of fragmentary research, he insisted not only that research and theory must be joined but also that "their reciprocal roles must be clearly defined." In emphasizing the regulation of empirical testing by conceptual principles, however, we should not overlook this important point made by Merton: Not only does research test the implications of theories but the former shapes the latter, when "it initiates, it reformulates, it deflects and it clarifies theory." [68] Although Stouffer has confined his work primarily to empirical research, he acknowledges, nevertheless, that sociologists may develop conceptual principles that will provide empirical verification with "logical interconnections." [69]

As long as *anthropologists* merely describe and/or imaginatively interpret the cultural traits of a specific community they need not be concerned about the relation of ideational and observational operations in a process of verification; but an awareness of an intellectual obligation in this respect seems to be emerging. When Kroeber, for example, calls for a conception of anthropological knowledge in terms of scientific, rather than of aesthetic, comprehension, he explicitly states this principle of broadly operational verification: "Such a comprehension would be intellectual, aiming at an intelligible concord with reality, resting both on specific evidence and on broad coherent theory." [70] Herskovits seems to have this same principle in mind when he emphasizes that "the relation between research design and theoretical terms of reference in shaping ethnographic studies . . . has not had full recognition." For he expects from anthropological inquiry something more than "research guided by no principle other than to describe a given way of life," which he takes to be "a relatively low level of scientific analysis." [71]

The sophistication of *economic* inquiry can probably be attributed to its persistent identification of economic knowledge in terms of a verificative process which always regulates empirical testing by some system of conceptual principles. As Lange points out, an economic question can be answered only in terms of a procedure of *verification* (testing) which establishes rules according to which hypotheses are accepted as "empirically verified" or rejected as "empirically unverified" or "empirically refuted." [72] Few economists today would agree with Jevons that since economics cannot be experimental, it should be considered "a mathematical science . . . comparatively abstract and general, treating mankind from a simple point of view." [73] Most, however, would agree with Marshall's declaration that "the most reckless and treacherous of all theorists is he who professes to let facts and figures speak for themselves." [74] Even those economists who have modified or rejected the neo-classical, purely deductive conception of knowledge as too formal, assume with Machlup that "the strength of a belief in a hypothesis depends, even more than on any direct empirical tests that it may have survived, on the place it holds within a hierarchical system of inter-related hypotheses." [75] To consider one example, institutional economists have sought to replace analytical theories with synthetic substantive hypotheses about the sociocultural and motivational factors involved in the economic proc-

ess. They share Mitchell's aim, nevertheless, to conceptualize inductively acquired descriptions and statistical correlations as a means of
"conceiving the subject as a whole." [76] Another example is found in
the position of Spiethoff who even more radically opposes the nomothetic generalizations of neo-classical theorizing. But, despite his emphasis upon unique economic phenomena, he concludes that "it is
the task of economic Gestalt theory to make theoretically conceivable
the latter kind of uniformities, though they lack timelessness and
ubiquity." [77]

Political science as a discipline does not exhibit as much clear cut
commitment to ideational operations as does economics. There are
some political scientists, however, who contend that there should be
developed a system of conceptual principles for regulating the empirical testing of hypotheses about the political process. Easton, for example, insists that if political scientists are exclusively preoccupied
with fact-gathering without reference to any ideational principles for
verifying their hypotheses, "then the ultimate value of factual research itself may well be lost." [78] Similarly, Leiserson contends that
instead of relying upon a "lazy epistemological eclecticism" political
scientists should aim at an "intellectual synthesis" which provides
"the basis for deriving hypotheses about behavior that can be tested
empirically . . . and logically related." [79]

Apart from conceptualization there could be no verification of *historical* constructs, for a historian's data pertaining to past human
actions are not accessible through his own observation. This does not
mean, however, that all historians would accept everything that this
principle of ideational operations entails. Exception might be taken
by extremely document-centered chroniclers, as well as by historians
who attempt to avoid all generalizations in their exclusive preoccupation with the uniqueness of historical situations. But Loewenberg
and Brockunier speak for those historians who aim at going beyond
such "simple proof by the documentary method of quoting testimony" toward cumulative analysis. This presupposes that "fundamental coherence of established facts and theories is the test of
objective scientific knowledge in any field." Consequently, they insist that "criteria for any extended judgments of conceptions of history should be explicit and subject to the logic of relevance and
coherence." [80] Gottschalk answers the objections against the generalizing which this principle requires, by acknowledging that "his-

torians study and should study the unique," but by also reminding his colleagues that they cannot avoid all generalizing when they use names, for dating, identifying, and comparing periods of past events. Moreover, Gottschalk takes conceptual principles to be indispensable for regulating the reconstruction and testing of "the generalization about types of human affairs of the past and the generalization assumed to have universal validity for past, present, and future." [81]

5. Fifth, for any discipline to be broadly operational it must take into account the limitations of its specific subject matter in order to determine for its own mode of analysis (a) what observational techniques are applicable to data relevant to the problem of the inquiry, and (b) what testing techniques are applicable for confirming or refuting the implications deduced from the hypothetical constructs which are supposed to classify, explain, or make predictions about those specific data.

Meaningful questions must be appropriate to the context to which they refer. Aristotle's caveat that any given science can only be as precise and as accurate as its subject matter will permit, anticipates this broader operationalistic demand that the mode of analysis must be adapted to the specific problem which the investigator aims at solving, and that the verificative techniques must be pertinent both to the relevant data and to his stage of inquiry. The problem referred to here is a social-scientific question rather than a social need requiring practical action. Failure to distinguish between these two kinds of problems often confuses discussions among social scientists.

This problem-centric orientation for identifying broadly operational social-scientific knowledge is the crucial point of its divergence from the technique-centric orientation of narrower operationalism. It is the technique-centered approach which precludes the inclusion of purposive goal-seeking in narrower operationalistic portraits of human nature. But only by accepting the responsibilities which this broadly operationalistic requirement imposes can a social scientist analyze human behavior in terms of the *relatively* controlled observation of *relatively* manageable variables. Accordingly, he is not compelled to engage in the futile effort to duplicate the precise quantitative experimental testing of isolable factors which the more exact natural scientist aims for when he deals with much more invariant processes.

It should be noted that even within the natural-scientific enterprise the adjustment of techniques to subject matter cannot be entirely ignored. Obviously the manipulation of variables in crucial laboratory experimentation by physicists and chemists cannot be reduplicated by geologists, astronomers, and biologists who along with social scientists confront limitations imposed by their data. Kantor clearly speaks to this point: "Invoking the golden rule of science that the methods and procedures of investigation should be those best adapted to the data and problems, we find that considerable similarity may exist between anthropic and non-anthropic research." [82]

Some clarification of what is meant and implied by the "repeatability of physical events" may be in order. No physical event ever actually recurs; but another physical event with similar characteristics may recur. Nevertheless, physical processes which recur in this sense exhibit more similar elements of much more fully identified events than are exhibited in behavioral processes.

Those social scientists who adopt this data-orientation in their identification of behavioral knowledge, do not minimize the importance of quantitative measurement, controlled observation, statistical correlations, or crucial laboratory experimentation as techniques for testing hypotheses, if such precision tools can be applied without distorting any of the relevant data. The exact procedure which these techniques provide is the ideal sought by the broader operationalist; however, he refuses to accept it as the *sine qua non* for defining behavioral knowledge. This precision of controlled experimental testing, for example, has been approximately realized only by those psychologists who deal with the neurophysiological segment of behavioral data. *With respect to the many other equally essential aspects of the human situation, however, social scientists must use comparative techniques which serve as equivalently as possible to organize and compare variables under conditions that are controlled as much as their specific data allow.*

This crucial point will be elaborated in the next section. There it will be shown how some social scientists hold that in order to treat actual human actions, in addition to the dependent variable of the behavioral response and the independent variable of the environmental stimuli, they must include the intervening variable of purposive goal-seeking. The broader operationalist cannot bring himself to exclude this qualitative dimension of behavioral data in favor of preserving the pristine purity of purely quantitative and physicalistic techniques. In other words, this principle demands that the social scientist's selection of a technique must be motivated more by the desire for a genuine portrait of human behavior than by the desire for the prestige which he may think imitating natural-scientific techniques would confer.[83]

Psychologists are tending to re-examine the technique-centered approach to which they had so strongly committed themselves. An increasing number agree with Marx that they should attempt to eliminate "the various *a priori* biases which in actual practice account for much of the polemic and invective generated in psychological controversies." [84] Allport appeals to the first part of the principle enunciated above which pertains to the data-centering of observational techniques, when he emphasizes the shortcomings of "the preference of positivism for externals rather than internals, for elements rather than patterns, for geneticism, and for a passive or reactive organism rather than for one that is spontaneous and active." Fruitful as the stringent requirements of such "operationism" are for animal and mathematical psychologies, they eliminate an "interest in the existential richness of life" when they discourage "the investigation of consciousness as datum, as well as of personality as a complex structure." For, when the positivist "holds that the devices employed in experimentation or measurement shall be specified in the definition of every concept," he precludes the consideration of "problems having to do with complex motives, high level integration, with conscience, freedom, selfhood." [85] Murphy emphasizes the need for adopting the second part of this principle which pertains to testing techniques, when he declares that "serious doubt has arisen in recent years as to whether experimentation is adequate—even as adequate as the genetic or comparative method—with regard to most of the fundamental issues in the psychology of personality." Instead of confining his data to "the inert, nonsentient attributes described by physics," so that his generalizations are too narrowly restricted, the psychologist studying personality should acknowledge that he is "confronted with a thinking and feeling entity." Accordingly, he must use those empirical testing techniques which are applicable to such data, rather than experimentation regardless of whether or not it is applicable: "Empirical procedure is necessary, an empiricism willing to learn not only regarding the methods of inquiry that will be most fruitful, but regarding the postulates that do least violence to firsthand experience and provide clarity without the arrogance of offering any ultimate classification of man." [86]

Social psychologists dealing with interpersonal relations are bound to find that most of their data, e.g., motives, attitudes, and value preferences, cannot be treated exclusively with experimental and/or statistical techniques. Murphy and Lewin agree that it is necessary to link constructs operationally with observational data, but they claim that systematic observation must be substituted for the more precise techniques.[87] Similarly, Allport declares that "while the experimental method approaches the ideal design for social research, it is not adapted to all of the problems with which social psychology must wrestle." [88] Even if and when more control of the conditions of interpersonal influences is achieved, there are social psychologists (Murphy, Murphy, Newcomb) who insist that this kind of experimentation must be oriented not only to the data but also to the stage of analysis, i.e., "after the problem has been defined and its salient characteristics so well formulated that we know what can be controlled and measured." [89] Statistical techniques employed by sociologists are useful in some comparative case analysis of a system of role relations; but they would distort the distinctive subject matter of social psychology if they were forced upon the "role behavior" in which, as Newcomb contends, the person with *"his own* characteristics . . . cannot help expressing them as he takes his roles in his own, individual way." [90]

Among *sociologists* there is a controversy about whether or not their observational and verificative techniques should be oriented to their problems and data. On the one hand, Lundberg, it will be recalled, advocates the exclusive use of statistical techniques in order that sociology might be "a body of generalizations about social behavior arrived at by the methods of natural science." [91] On the other hand, while Sorokin declares that "in essence the methods and referential principles of sociology are the same as those of the sciences generally," he insists that "sociology has its own modifications of the principles and procedures demanded by the peculiar nature of sociological phenomena, especially by their components of meaning-value-norm." He contends that such modification of techniques is required to some degree in every scientific discipline. But the sociologist who combines the following techniques must make a "considerable modification of each of these methods and techniques, so as to adjust to the specific character of superorganic phenomena": logical-mathematical deductions, corroborated intuitive insights, empirical observation, induction, statistical analysis, case or clinical observation, even experiment.[92]

When Rose deals with the technique-centric or problem-centric controversy, he deplores the exclusive consideration of experimentation and contends that "no technique developed to investigate one set of problems may be borrowed without modification and applied automatically without adjustment to another set of problems." Although he acknowledges the contributions of experimental and statistical techniques, especially as a "wholesome reaction to the anti-empiricism and sloppy 'theorizing' of the earlier sociologist," he contends, nevertheless, "to continue it at this stage of the development of our science is a mark of immaturity." [93] Hart has recently claimed that the development of social theory depends upon a procedure which is "intermediate between causal, common-sense generalizations and rigorously verified conclusions from controlled experiments." He distinguishes this procedure, which "recognizes that mental as well as sensory-motor observations and operations are verifiable and are indispensable in social science" from "behavioristic operationism" which "would rule out all private experience, and hence would exclude all values and all meaning." In other words, a verifiable definition is required, but it must be "applicable to private experience, and to purposes, values, and meanings." [94]

Among *anthropologists* there seems to be general acceptance of the problem-centered principle as it has been expressed by Washburn: "A successful scientific strategy depends on theories and techniques adequate to solve problems and not as ends in themselves." [95] Drawing as it does from the humanities, the natural sciences, and the other social sciences anthropology has been forced to be eclectic with respect to its approaches and techniques. For, as Spencer has pointed out, "in line with the goal of understanding cultural behavior, whether holistically, comparatively, or in diachronic or in synchronic terms, anthropology must remain an empirical discipline and utilize all methods which come to hand." But the anthropologist is frequently faced by "the difficult task of somehow reconciling a scientific approach with data which do not lend themselves to scientific scrutiny." [96] Kroeber and Kluckhohn have identified these data to which analytical techniques must be adapted as the person's culturally-begotten but individually-internalized value experiences that "provide foci for patterns of organization of the material of cultures." Techniques designed to identify observational data only in terms of the organism's response to his environmental stimuli are not applicable to this "intervening variable, unseen but powerful." However, the anthropologist cannot dispense with these value data; for they "provide the only basis for the fully intelligible comprehension of culture, because the actual organization of all cultures is primarily in terms of their values." These subjectively experienced values through collective participation "find objective expression in observable forms of culture and their relations." But, there can be no public observation of the values which reside "in individual persons and nowhere else." This means that while "evidence and the analysis of evidence are indispensable," the qualitatively describable observational data are accessible only through the investigator's intuitive insight. For, "in the collection of information on culture, the inquirer must proceed with empathy in order to perceive the cardinal values as points of crystallization." [97]

The division of *economists* into the orthodox and unorthodox has stemmed from this technique-centric vs. problem-centric identification of their observational data, i.e., the processes which are required for allocating scarce resources among alternative uses to meet the human needs for material goods and services. On the one hand, the orthodox neo-classical economists restricted their motivational data to the profit-seeking desire of "economic man" to realize the greatest satisfaction with the least possible effort. Moreover, they have limited their sociocultural data to a closed economic system that is so regulated by the law of supply and demand that it maintains an equilibrium in which minor deviations cancel each other out. By this delimitation of the behavioral and environmental variables the neo-classical economists could confine their observational and testing techniques to mathematical-logical deductions for making predictions about such uniformly modified economic phenomena as production, distribution, employment, prices, and exchange. Marshall takes this to be the only scientific procedure for economic analysis: "Almost every scientific doctrine, where carefully and formally stated, will be found to contain some proviso to the effect that other things are equal: the action of the causes in question is supposed to be iso-

lated; certain effects are attributed to them, but only on the hypothesis that no cause is permitted to enter except those distinctly
allowed for." [98]

On the other hand, the unorthodox institutional economists contend that the neo-classical concept of "rational activity" ignores too
many other factors of psychological motivation. Moreover, by discounting governmental, technological, ideational and other aspects
of the total sociocultural process the orthodox economist distorts the
actual economic process of producing, distributing, and consuming
scarce goods and services. Even though it means reliance on less precise predictive techniques, the unorthodox economists agree with
Kapp that substantive economic analysis starts from "actual human
needs and places man's dependence upon their interaction with his
natural and social environment in the center of its investigation." [99]
Since the institutionalists have reconceived their data to include more
than a competitive market system, they have a less distinctive subject
matter. But they do have the opportunity to incorporate the techniques of other behavioral sciences in their broader analysis of
economic actions that are conditioned by the psychological and sociocultural factors which the neo-classical economists ignored.

Political science has been, is, and probably always will be problem-
centric rather than technique-centric regardless of whether its orienting concept is "the state," "power relations," or Easton's "authoritative allocation of values." Easton, on the one hand, deplores the
"flight from reason"; but, on the other hand, he opposes a "slavish
imitation of the physical sciences." Despite his aim to make the analysis of political behavior scientific, Easton declares that "if political
science were to insist upon universal adherence to technical rigor, at
the present time, as the only kind of adequate research, there is little
doubt that, in attending so mechanically to form, all life and wisdom
would be squeezed from even the existing insights into political
life." [100] Similarly, when Leiserson suggests a "systematic-empirical
method" for coordinating the political-scientific procedures, i.e., "historical, comparative, statistical, psychological, or descriptive-analytical
case studies," he acknowledges that these observational and verificative techniques are limited by the nature of the data. Accordingly, he
adopts this programmatic principle for refining a broadly operational
inquiry: "If experimental situations approximating the laboratory or
clinic are rarely, if ever, possible for the analyst of political behavior,

he may nevertheless hope to contribute toward a science of political behavior by: (a) intellectual clarification of the objectives and postulates of inquiry, (b) unrelenting effort to relate his limited empirical generalizations to higher-order propositions of functional relations between variables, and (c) through constant professional and personal criticism to deepen his understanding under the conditions under which uniformities of political behavior occur or may be modified." [101]

Historical inquiry is for the most part data-centric rather than technique-centric. Among other possible exceptions would be the scholar who so confines the study of history to the establishment of the authenticity of documents that he rejects any testimony to which his certifying techniques are not applicable. All historians recognize that authentic testimony is necessary. But those who aim at cumulative analysis go further when they inferentially construct explanatory interpretations about the causal relations of past human actions. Since all historians take their distinctive subject matter to be unique events or series of events which, as total situations, have specific locations in an ongoing temporal process, the cumulative analysts face this dilemma. A nomothetic technique of statistical correlations is used by other scientific disciplines for constructing causal generalizations about the universal and uniformly recurring segments that are abstracted from the totalities of unique situations. If historians use this technique, then their data would not be properly historical. If they should use the idiographic technique of *Verstehen*, which Dilthey advocated for intuitively understanding each unique historical situation in itself, then they would not be able to generalize sufficiently about the similarities of past events at the level of abstraction which cumulative analysis requires. In order to escape from this dilemma, the historians who aim at cumulative analysis are required by their data and their stage of inquiry to work out some coordination of nomothetic and idiographic techniques. Otherwise, they could not use the abstract social-scientific generalization as a means to understanding the unique wholes of specific past situations as the end.

Aitken and Loewenberg face this dilemma when they declare that "greater use by historians of the concepts of other social sciences entails not a redefinition of the purposes of history, but a reorientation of interest, a reconsideration of what is possible, and a re-examination of procedure." Historians, however, must always critically adapt their own distinctive data; for "the value of the use of social science in history is to be judged entirely by the fruitfulness of its results when applied intelligently to suitable material." [102]

Broader operationalism as a definition of social-scientific knowledge entails a system of principles that both characterizes meaningful constructs and correlates the areas of behavioral data which social-scientific constructs are designed to explain. Now that we have considered the principles, let us direct our attention to the behavioral data in terms of a synoptic model.

Footnotes to Chapter 1 of Part Two

[1] Bridgman, *The Logic of Modern Physics*, 5-7, 31. Cf. Einstein and Infeld, *The Evolution of Physics*, 312-313, 291, 63, 235, 259-260; and Planck, *Philosophy of Physics*, 27-28.

[2] Bridgman, *The Logic of Modern Physics*, 3, 6, 25, 33, 34, 27; and *The Nature of Physical Theory*, 10, 14. In his "Remarks on the Present State of Operationalism," *Scientific Monthly*, 79 (Oct., 1954), Bridgman says that he feels that he has "created a Frankenstein which has certainly got away from me." (244) For this application of operationalism to behavioral data, see Bridgman, "The Potential Intelligent Society," *Ideological Differences and World Order* (Northrop), 233-234, 239-240; and "Rejoinder and Second Thoughts," *Psychological Review*, 1945, 52, pages 231-234. Cf. Sjoberg, "Operationalism and Social Research," *Symposium on Sociological Theory* (Gross), 603-624.

[3] See Ayer, *Language, Truth and Logic*, for a non-technical elaboration and defense of logical positivism, which more recently has also been called "logical empiricism." Cf. Carnap in the *International Encyclopedia of Unified Science*, Vol. I, No. 3, page 59. See Stevens, "Psychology and the Science of Science," *Psychological Theory* (Marx), 21-51, for an excellent constructively critical discussion of the relation of logical positivism to Bridgman's "operationalism".

[4] Bergmann, "On Some Methodological Problems of Psychology," *Readings in the Philosophy of Science* (Feigl and Brodbeck), 627-629. Originally published *The Philosophy of Science*, 7, 1940.

[5] Skinner, "The Operational Analysis of Psychological Terms," *Readings in the Philosophy of Science* (Feigl and Brodbeck), 585-586. Originally published in the *Psychological Review*, 52, 1945, page 270.

[6] See Pratt, *The Logic of Modern Psychology*, 92, for bibliographical references which indicate the influence of logical positivism and operationism on the many psychologists who have turned to this narrower operationalistic concep-

tion of knowledge in the hope that through such a logical device they could precisely define their subject matter. Although Pratt is referred to by others as an advocate of "operationism," Pratt explicitly recognizes the limitations of this logical device, when an attempt is made to use it in defining psychological concepts: "Extreme operationists would undoubtedly like to wipe out about ninety percent of all psychological concepts, and then start all over again. But to start over again would involve the construction of a whole vocabulary of artificial symbols and the assignment to them of exact meanings, only to discover that after being in circulation for a short time the symbols had acquired quite different meanings." Instead of the "ruthless ostracism" of ordinary words in favor of operational definitions, which the extreme operationist demands, Pratt concludes that both can be retained "by the exercise of compromise and tolerance." (80)

7 Lundberg, *Foundations of Sociology*, 12-13, 60, 64-65, 68, 73. Although Lundberg aims at making sociology a natural science, it is only fair to call attention to this statement in his *Foundations of Sociology*: "No one proposes to put a specimen of society in a test tube for analysis or to measure sociological phenomena with the instruments of the physics laboratory." (100. Cf. his *Sociology*, 8.) In his "The Thoughtways of Contemporary Sociology," however, Lundberg does approve the definition of intelligence as that which intelligence tests test on the apparent grounds that behavioral analysis can thus emulate operationistic physical analysis in which "space *is* that which is measured with a ruler; time *is* that which is measured by a clock; force *is* that which makes pointers move across dials." (*American Sociological Review*, 1936, Vol. I, page 711.)

8 Sjoberg, "Operationalism and Social Research," *Symposium on Sociological Theory* (Gross), 609, 623-624.

9 Marx seems to substantiate in principle this critical estimate of operationism in his *Psychological Theory*: "A more serious misunderstanding of the demands of operationism has apparently resulted from an overly literal interpretation, encouraged perhaps by the somewhat uncritical acceptance of the principle in the early days of its formalization. In answer to criticism of operationism on the ground that too much is demanded, it should be emphasized that operationism is primarily a more or less formal attempt to *stimulate critical evaluation* of the relationship between logical constructs and their supporting empirical data. All concepts do not need to be defined literally in terms of the precise physical operations involved. But it is fair to ask that the observational basis of any concept be made as explicit as possible." (13) Cf. Israel and Goldstein, "Operationism in Psychology," *Psychological Review*, 1944, 51, 177-188.

10 Support for the present writer's distinction between narrower and broader operationalism is to be found in Peter's *Brett's History of Psychology*: "There is thus a wider and a narrower interpretation of 'operationism.' The wider doctrine is accepted by all scientists who make careful attempts to test hypotheses; the narrower doctrine is accepted only by those who assume an observationalistic view of scientific method." (667) Although the present writer did not discover this passage until long after he had used this distinction, he is encouraged by it. For some of his colleagues have objected that the term

"operationalism" should be used only in its restricted positivistic meaning. Support for our basic criticism of narrower operationalism is to be found in Margenau and Werkmeister, whose views merit out attention. Margenau makes these significant comments: "On the basis of purely operational definitions, all concepts are strictly empirical and isolated." This means that operationism "cannot be tolerated as a general directive. For, it would, if carried to its consequences, dissolve the world into an unmanageable variety of discrete concepts without logical coherence." (See Lindsay and Margenau, *Foundations of Physics,* 412 and Margenau, "Causality in Modern Physics," *Monist,* 1931, 41, 1-36.)

More recently Margenau has suggested a more critical reconstruction of the operational definition of scientific quantities: "Every scientific quantity must be defined in two ways: operationally and constitutively. ( ) I regard this matter as very important, for unless the vital interplay between these two procedures leading to concept formation is clearly recognized, we shall not understand why science is the progressing, self-correcting enterprise which in fact it is. Without operational definitions it fails to be applicable. The union of both makes it a going concern." (Margenau, *The Nature of Concepts* [Proceeding of the Stillwater Conference], 54-55.)

Since Bridgman does not recognize constitutive definitions, he is forced to an extreme nominalism which provides no systematic generalization. "In principle the operations by which length is measured should be uniquely specified. In that we have more than one set of operations, we have more than one concept, and strictly there should be a separate name to correspond to each different set of operations." (Bridgman, *Logic of Modern Physics,* 10. Cf. page 16). Margenau contends, however, that if length (which Bridgman uses to illustrate his definition) is also defined constitutively, then the various measuring devices (e.g., yardsticks, traveling microscopes, light signals, etc.) can be brought under one conceptual construct, but they "cannot be joined by reference to immediate experience alone." (*Nature of Concepts,* 56.) Consequently, when deductive science refers to the total field of constructs (C-field) different operational measurements of time can similarly be given a "rational connection." (56)

Werkmeister agrees with Margenau that a literal application of "operationism" (which would make a concept like length synonymous with the physical operations of measuring it) "entails a complete distortion of the meaning and function of concepts." When an object is measured, knowledge about its specific length is acquired, but it does not determine what is meant by the concept of length. This must already be conceptually known by the scientist in order that he can select the appropriate device for measuring a specific object. "It simply is not the case that the concept is synonymous with operations." Werkmeister attributes this mistaken notion chiefly to the "confusion of 'exploratory' experimentation and of concept formation in science." (See Werkmeister, *The Basis and Structure of Knowledge,* 316-317.)

Although Werkmeister has gone to the core of this problem, it should be noted that Bridgman does recognize that physics is full of constructs that, like mental models, are useful, unavoidable, but dangerous: "There are many sorts of constructs: those in which we are interested are made by us to enable us to deal with physical situations which we cannot directly experience through our sense, but with which we have contact indirectly and by inference. Such constructs usually involve the element of invention to a greater or less degree." (*Logic of Modern Physics*, 53. Cf. 54 and 59-60.) But this recognition of the use of constructs in physics does not answer Werkmeister's criticism; for Bridgman seems to have in mind only observational constructs and not the explanatory constructs which are conceptions in the sense that Einstein, Planck, and Margenau have in mind.

11 Andrews, *Methods of Psychology*, 1-2, 4-5.
12 Murphy, Murphy, Newcomb, *Experimental Social Psychology*, 15.
13 MacIver, *Social Causation*, 158.
14 Murdock, "Sociology and Anthropology," *For a Science of Social Man* (Gillin), 27.
15 Kroeber, *Appraisal of Anthropology Today* (Tax), 361.
16 Samuelson, *The Foundations of Economic Analysis*, 7.
17 Gordon, "Operational Propositions in Economic Theory," *The Journal of Political Economy*, Vol. LXIII, April 1955. No. 2, pages 150-151 and 160-161.
18 Lane, *Enterprise and Secular Change*, 526.
19 Friedman, *Essays in Positive Economics*, 10-11.
20 Easton, *The Political System*, 63.
21 Driscoll and Hyneman, "Methodology for Political Scientists: Perspectives for Study," *American Political Science Review*, March 1955, page 192.
22 Leiserson, *Political Science Quarterly*, Dec. 1953, pp. 579-580. Cf. Waldo, *Political Science in the United States of America*, 20-23.
23 Brockunier and Loewenberg, Bulletin 64, p. 136; and Loewenberg, "Some Problems Raised by Historical Relativism," *Journal of American History*, Vol. XXI, No. 1, March 1949, page 17.
24 Clough, Bulletin 64, page 106.
25 Gottschalk, *Understanding History*, 59.
26 Margenau, *The Nature of Concepts*, 56.
27 Tolman in *Psychological Theory* (Marx), 87.
28 Marx, "The General Nature of Theory Construction," *Psychological Theory* (Marx), 9.
29 Newcomb, "Studying Social Behavior," *Methods of Psychology* (Andrews), 692; *Social Psychology*, 18; and *American Sociological Review*, April 1948, pages 170-171. Cf. Bonner, *Social Psychology*, 10-20.
30 Lundberg, Schrag, Larsen, *Sociology*, 7.
31 Bowers, "Research Method in Sociology," *Method and Perspective in Anthropology* (Spencer), 258.
32 Merton, *Social Theory and Social Structure*, 9.
33 Spencer, *Methods and Perspective in Anthropology*, 131-132.
34 Nadel, *The Foundations of Social Anthropology*, 222.
35 Lesser, "Functionalism in Social Anthropology," *American Anthropologist*, N.S. 37 (1935), page 392.
36 Machlup, "The Problem of Verification in Economics," *The Southern Economic Journal*, Vol. XXII, No. 1, July 1955, pages 1-2.

37 Gordon, "Operational Principles in Economic Theory," *The Journal of Political Economy*, April 1955, page 152.

38 Leiserson, *Political Science Quarterly*, December 1953, pages 579-580.

39 Brockunier and Loewenberg, Bulletin 64, pages 136-137.

40 Aitkin and Loewenberg, Bulletin 64, page 28.

41 Collingwood, *The Idea of History*, 252, 257.

42 Bennett and Wolff in *Current Anthropology* (Thomas), 336.

43 Nadel, *Foundations of Social Anthropology*, 234.

44 Easton, *The Political System*, 37.

45 Driscol and Hyneman, "Methodology for Political Science," *American Political Science Review*, March 1955, page 210. Cf. Waldo, *Political Science in the United States of America* (UNESCO), 34.

46 Aitken and Loewenberg, Bulletin 64, page 26. Cf. Hook, Bulletin 54, page 113.

47 Brockunier and Loewenberg, Bulletin 64, 137. They elaborate this point as follows: "The ideal of objectivity presupposes that major hypotheses should be tested. Yet it would retard the advance of knowledge were it insisted that no hypothesis should be presented before it had been fully tested and documented. Great theories in the physical sciences are not only presented before verification but in themselves can never be completely verified. Such theories, however, make it possible to predict and draw inferences that can be tested. Hypotheses should be presented if they suggest explanations; and if they do indeed yield fruitful suggestions, there will be those who will test them. Nevertheless, a distinction should be made between an unsupported hypothesis and a tentative hypothesis for which a considerable body of data is presented. We may classify a very tentative hypothesis by saying that 'it goes beyond the data'; but we should bear in mind that any large hypothesis must go beyond immediately available data and is never completely verifiable." (Bulletin 64, p. 150.)

48 Peirce, *Collected Papers*, 90. For the previous reference to Peirce, see the *Dictionary of Philosophy and Psychology*, Vol. 2, page 502. Cf. Dewey, Logic, Chapter XXIII.

All philosophers and scientists do not use the terms "hypothesis" and "theory" (as well as "assumption," "postulate," or "theorem") in exactly the same sense. In a later section we shall elaborate upon how we shall use the terms "assumptions" and "postulates." Up to now we have taken the chance that the context would clarify what meaning is intended. But something should be noted here regarding "hypothesis" and "theory." The following statement by Margenau seems to serve our present purpose: "A hypothesis . . . is . . . a theory which has at present at least, a limited range of application. It is promoted to the status of a theory if and when its range is deemed sufficiently large to justify this more commendatory appellation." (Margenau, "Methodology of Modern Physics," *Philosophy of Science*, Vol. II [Jan. 1935], page 67.)

49 Kelly, "Man's Construction of His Alternatives," *Assessment of Human Motives* (Lindzey), 33-34.

50 Andrews, *Methods of Psychology*, 44.

51 Bergmann and Spence, "Operationism and Theory," *Psychological Theory* (Marx), 56.

[52] Lambert, *Handbook of Social Psychology* (Lindzey), Vol. I, 87.

[53] Zetterberg, *On Theory and Verification in the Social Sciences*, 268.

[54] Rose, *Theory and Method in the Social Sciences*, 268.

[55] Nadel, *Fondations of Social Anthropology*, 255.

[56] von Mises, *Human Action*, 858.

[57] Machlup, "The Problem of Verification in Economics," *The Southern Economic Journal*, Vol. XXII, No. 1, July 1956.

[58] Marshall, *Principles of Economics*, 29-32.

[59] Easton, *The Political System*, 53-55 and 125-126.

[60] Collingwood, *The Idea of History*, 237 and 248-249.

[61] Dewey, *Logic: The Theory of Inquiry*, 112-114, 418, 491, 507.

[62] Bergmann and Spence, "Operationism and Theory Construction," *Psychological Theory* (Marx), 55.

[63] Köhler, *Dynamics in Psychology*, 110, 117-118.

[64] Marx, "The General Nature of Theory Construction," *Psychological Theory* (Marx), 7, 13.

[65] Allport in *Handbook of Social Psychology* (Lindzey), Vol. I, 4-5, 30.

[66] Newcomb, *American Sociological Review*, April 1948, pp. 170-171.

[67] Parsons and Shils, *Toward a General Theory of Action*, 51.

[68] Merton, *American Sociological Review*, April 1948, page 166; and *Social Theory and Social Structure*, 5, 97-98, 111.

[69] Stouffer in *Toward a General Theory of Action* (Parsons and Shils), 479-480.

[70] Kroeber in *An Appraisal of Anthropology Today* (Tax), 358.

[71] Herskovits, "Some Problems of Method in Ethnography," *Method and Perspective in Anthropology* (Spencer), 3.

[72] Lange, "The Scope and Method of Economics," *Readings in the Philosophy of Science* (Feigl and Brodbeck), 746-747. Originally published in the *Review of Economic Studies*, 13, 1945-1946.

[73] Jevons, *The Principles of Science*, 759-761.

[74] Marshall, "The Present Position of Economics (1885)," *Memorials of Alfred Marshall* (Pigou), 168.

[75] Machlup, "The Problem of Verification in Economics," *The Southern Economic Journal*, Vol. XXII, No. 1, July 1955, page 5.

[76] Gruchy, *Modern Economic Thought*, 22-23, 205, 608.

[77] Spiethoff, "The Historical Character of Economic Theories," *The Journal of Economic History*, Spring, 1952, Vol. XII, No. 2, p. 136.

[78] Easton, *The Political System*, 78.

[79] Leiserson, "Problems of Methodology in Political Science," *Political Science Quarterly*, December 1953, p. 569.

[80] Brockunier and Loewenberg, Bulletin 64, pages 134, 136, 143, 145.

[81] Gottschalk, "The Historian's Use of Generalization," *The State of the Social Sciences* (White), 441.

[82] Kantor, *The Logic of Modern Science*, 280-281. Cf. Conant, *On Understanding Science*, 145; Bush, *Science*, May 31, 1946, p. 664; Northrop, *The Logic of the Sciences and Humanities*, ix.

[83] For an explicit criticism of a narrow operationalistic conception of knowledge,

which would not comply with this principle of broader operationalism, see Maslow, "Problem-Centering vs. Means-Centering in Science," *Philosophy of Science*, 13 (October 1936), 326-331. Maslow blames the following mistakes on the purely technique-centric approach which he calls "means-centering": "Emphasis on polish and elegance rather than on vitality, significance, and creativeness. (2) Giving the commanding positions in science to technicians rather than discoverers. (3) Over-valuation of quantification for its own sake. (4) Fitting problems to techniques rather than vice versa. (5) Creation of a false and pernicious hierarchical system among the sciences. (6) Overstrong compartmentalization between the sciences. (7) Emphasis on the differences rather than the similarities between scientists and other truth seekers (poets, novelists, artists, philosophers). (8) Creation of a scientific orthodoxy, which in turn, (a) tends to block the development of new methods, (b) tends to exclude many problems from the jurisdiction of science, and (c) tends to make scientists 'safe' rather than daring. (9) Neglect of the problem of values, with a consequent blurring of the criteria for judging the worth or importance of an experiment." See Rose, *Theory and Method of the Social Sciences*, 254, for a sociologist's endorsement of this criticism of narrower operationalism.

84 Marx, *Psychological Theory*, 7.

85 Allport, *Becoming*, 11-12.

86 Murphy, *Personality*, 915-917.

87 See Murphy, "The Research Task of Social Psychology," *Journal of Social Psychology*, 1929, 10, pages 107-120; and Lewin, "Field Theory in Social Science." Cf. Deutsch, "Field Theory in Social Psychology" in *Handbook of Social Psychology* (Lindzey), 188, for an instructive discussion of Lewin's view which we are calling broader rather than narrower operationalism. For a discussion of "sociometry," which Moreno introduced in 1934 for "assessing the attractions, or attractions and repulsions within a given group," see Lindzey and Borgatta, *Handbook of Social Psychology* (Lindzey), Chapter 11.

88 Allport, in *Handbook of Social Psychology* (Lindzey), 48.

89 Murphy, Murphy, Newcomb, *Experimental Social Psychology*, 15.

90 Newcomb, *Social Psychology*. 333.

91 Lundberg, *Sociology*, 6; and *Foundations of Sociology*, 20, 60, 76, 100.

92 Sorokin, *Society, Culture and Personality*, 18.

93 Rose, *Theory and Method in the Social Sciences*, vii, 255, 273, 281. Cf. Good and Scates, *Methods of Research*, 697-721.

94 Hart, "Social Theory and Social Change," *Symposium on Sociological Theory* (Gross), 197.

95 Washburn, "The Strategy of Physical Anthropology," *Anthropology Today* (Kroeber), 723.

96 Spencer, *Method and Perspective in Anthropology*, 130-131.

97 Kroeber and Kluckhohn, "General Features of Culture," *Culture, a Critical Review of Concepts and Definitions*.

98 Marshall, *Principles of Economics*, 36-37.

99 Kapp, "Economics and the Behavioral Sciences," *Kyklos*, Vol. VII, 1954, page 223.

100 Easton, *The Political System*, 59-60.

101 Leiserson, "Problems of Methodology in Political Research," *Political Science Quarterly*, Vol. XLVIII, 4, December 1953, page 583.

102 See Aitken and Loewenberg, Bulletin 64, 32-33. They state the basis for an idiographic-nomothetic approach thus: "Each historical event is unique, to be sure, in some respects; but it is also similar in other respects to other historical events." (25) For other discussions which bear on this principle, see Bulletin 64, pages 22-23; Gottschalk, *Understanding History*, 228-229; Danto, "Mere Chronicle and History Proper," *Journal of Philosophy*, March 12, 1953, Vol. 10, No. 6, page 181; Coates, *Journal of Modern History*, Vol. XXI, No. 1 (March 1949), pages 25-27; Beard, Written History as an Act of Faith," *The American Historical Review*, Vol. XXXIX, No. 2 (Jan. 1934), page 226.

2 *The Conceptual Orientation of Behavioral Data*

If broader operationalism is an adequate characterization of social-scientific knowledge, it must provide a conceptual scheme for identifying, classifying, and correlating the relevant behavioral data. These, it will be recalled, include both the motivational and the sociocultural dimensions of the total human situation. Consequently, we shall formulate a synoptic model of goal-oriented behavioral transactions. By this device we shall attempt to present the separable but related observational contexts of the specific disciplines of the social sciences within a comprehensive conceptual framework.

A conceptual orientation of behavioral data is explicitly called for by Parsons when he declares that "it is fundamental that there is no empirical knowledge which is not in some sense and to some degree conceptually formed." Such a conceptual scheme, e.g., the spatio-temporal framework of classical mechanics, "is not merely a reproduction of external reality but a selective ordering of it." Consequently, these schema are "descriptive frames of reference" which function as "modes of general relations of the facts implicit in the descriptive terms employed." [1]

A. *The Nature and Function of a Conceptual Model*

The significance of any conceptual model is always relative to the purpose it is designed to serve. Before we present our synoptic model, we shall consider its nature and function in order to better understand and evaluate it.

First, all scientific inquiry requires a *conceptual framework* for identifying and classifying the relevant observational data which the investigator then can use to construct a *theoretical framework* of verifiable substantive hypotheses by inference. Even the pure empiricist who denies this actually presupposes it.

Second, this construct is only a system of coordinated definitions, which cannot be verified any more than any single definition can be shown to be true or false. For the conceptual framework under discussion here does not contain explanatory and/or predictive constructs such as we shall encounter in the theoretical framework which the second state of hypothetical-deductive inquiry necessitates. The comprehensive conception is no less hypothetical than the more specific observational constructs which it aims to integrate into a complex unity. It is a heuristic device that must be justified pragmatically by its fruitfulness in so organizing the observational data that all channels of inquiry which bear on the "problematic situation" are kept open. As a tentative system of working ideas the conceptual framework, in part or in whole, is always subject to correction, modification, or even abandonment, if a more fruitful classification of the relevant data emerges either from the process of organizing the observations, or from the subsequent *theoretical procedure.* In the latter case, the investigator isolates some aspect of the data in order to construct and verify specific substantive hypotheses.

This emphasis upon the point that the conceptual framework should be adopted or rejected on the grounds of its fecundity rather than on the basis of empirical verification, should not mislead one into underestimating the importance of the conceptual framework for reflective inquiry. Unless an investigator has a question or a set of questions in mind which are germane to his problem, he can hardly determine which observed data are relevant. We might ask: Relevant to what? Furthermore, unless these questions are meaningfully organized, no meaningful answers can be expected. If we may expand Kant's famous statement, we might say: Nature in both its inorganic-organic and in its sociocultural-motivational dimensions must be interrogated. The conceptual framework which organizes the meaningful questions, on the one hand, must provide for the autonomy of each discipline, and, on the other hand, it must offer the opportunity for the coordination of the procedures which deal with these distinct but related avenues of inquiry.

Third, there seems to be a fairly widespread misunderstanding with respect to the alleged apriorism of *conceptual frameworks,* since they are antecedent to the *theoretical frameworks* which depend upon them. (Apriorism, it will be recalled, designates the appeal to universal and necessary principles by which the pure rationalist attempts to establish with mathematical-logical certainty such Truth that does not involve any perceptual reference to observational data.) Indeed it is the case that the *conceptual framework* as a classification of observations has a procedural priority over the *theoretical framework.* Moreover, when thought is purely deductive, as in mathematics or formal logic, a conceptual framework is legitimately *a priori.* We shall encounter the question of whether or not the conceptual framework of neo-classical economics is purely an *a priori* scheme of analytical principles. But we are more concerned here with the conceptual frameworks from which substantive hypotheses are expected to emerge. It is safe to say that most natural scientists and social scientists do not intend to treat their conceptual frameworks as *a priori.* They are formulated after considerable exploratory observations, which have been conducted by previous investigators, if not by themselves. Furthermore, unlike the "pure rationalist" who treats his *a priori* principles as absolute truths of his theoretical framework, the broader operationalist, it will be recalled, holds his conceptual framework provisionally. No apriorist would ever in this manner yield his conceptual system on the grounds that the formulation and empirical verification or substantive hypotheses had disclosed a more fruitful alternative.[2]

Fourth, it should be understood that our synoptic model is designed as a generalized conceptual scheme for systematically organizing the data rather than as an empirical description of actual events. Accordingly, conceptual constructs such as *nature, society, culture, personality* should not be taken as observable entities with particular spatial and temporal location. Rather, these conceptual constructs will be used to identify the patterned contexts of the observational data. As a combination of these constructs, our synoptic model pertains to the actual events of behavioral transaction in the sense that the "time-space continuum" is conceptually designed to identify the contextual pattern of the actual events of physical interaction. The recognition of the correspondence of these generic conceptual constructs, however, does not imply that behavioral events can be reduced to physical events.[3]

Fifth, the purpose which this synoptic model is intended to serve must be differentiated from that of other kinds of models. It is designed to provide a conceptual framework for coordinating the fields of all of the behavioral disciplines without impairing the creative autonomy of any one of them. Accordingly, it should not be confused with conceptual models which aim to organize data for specific research within a discipline, or with those which are intended for conceptually orienting any given discipline. Moreover, it should not be confused with theoretical models, such as that of neo-classical economics which narrowly delimits motivation and the sociocultural factors for purposes of a special kind of analysis. Neither is this synoptic model comparable to a purely mathematical model which has no necessary reference to actual human events. Finally, this synoptic model does not function in the manner of a utopian model which portrays what human relations ought to be. These and other kinds of models serve other purposes; but for conceptually orienting the constructs of behavioral transactions they will not do.[4]

The conceptual orientation which the synoptic model entails is congruent with at least two of the recent interdisciplinary volumes: *Toward a General Theory of Action* (Parsons and Shils) and *Toward a Unified Theory of Human Behavior* (Grinker). With respect to the former, the collaborators agree that "the theory of action is a conceptual scheme for the analysis of the behavior of living organisms."[5] With respect to the latter, the contributors adopt the premise that for behavioral analyses "what we need is a first approximation to a scheme which will enable us to represent physical, psychological, and social events within one system of denotation."[6]

B. *Recognition of the Need for a Conceptual Model*

The need for a conceptual model of behavioral data has been expressed by representatives of each of the social-scientific disciplines, as well as by those who have been engaged in interdisciplinary approaches.

Psychologists who feel that this is time for "conceptual stock-taking" are looking for what Kretch and Klein call "a means of parsimoniously and fruitfully linking all sorts of data" in order to "avoid mere fact gathering." This desire to "build models for the purpose of generating new questions about behavior and gaining new insights and understanding" seems to be shared by "psychiatrists, personologists, perceptionists, learning theoreticians, neurologists, and psychologists." Although some psychologists prefer to conceptualize their data as reducible to underlying neurophysiological mechanisms, Rapaport speaks for those who prefer a purely psychological mode of conation, cognition and affection which is "cast to systematize psychological data—observational and introspective—no matter how remote from neurological or physiological tangible phenomena." [7]

When Murphy presented his "biosocial approach to the origins and structure of personality," he emphasized the need for "a relatively autonomous conceptual framework." It is significant that an experimentalist like Tolman should also be seeking to formulate a *"sui generis* model for identifying the internal workings of the individual actor" on the assumption that "psychology is in large part the study of the internalization of society and culture within the individual human actor." [8]

Gordon Allport's concern about a conceptual model for orienting psychological data has been both critical and constructive. When he criticized the Watsonian S-R model, he contended that "addiction to machines, rats, or infants leads us to overplay those features of human behavior that are peripheral, signal-oriented, or genetic." Consequently, "it causes us to underplay those features that are central, future-oriented, and symbolic." Similarly, the Freudian id-ego-superego model so overemphasizes the irrational and passive aspect of personality that it ignores the active and rational components. Now Allport does not deny the limited usefulness of the neurophysio-

logical models, if those who use them recognize that their respective
approaches are not the only way of orienting motivational data.
Moreover, a multiplicity of theoretical models for specific research
is needed. For conceptually orienting all of the motivational data,
however, Allport maintains that a psychologist "in principle cannot
be satisfied with the segments of persons related to outer coordinates."
On the constructive side, therefore, Allport calls for a conceptual
model which demands that the psychologist "must consider the system as a whole, and show how part systems are related to one another." [9] This does not mean, however, that Allport is minimizing
the influence of the sociocultural process on "the personal impellants
of behavior." For, he shares with Lindzey the conviction that an
adequate conceptual orientation of behavioral data must answer this
question: "In assessing human motives, how important is it to specify
the situational context within which the motives operate?" [10]

The distinctiveness of *social-psychological* knowledge depends
upon the adoption of a model that is sufficiently comprehensive for
conceptually orienting the behavioral data of interpersonal relations.
The social psychologist must do more than observe behavior, on the
one hand, and the sociocultural conditions which influence it, on
the other. He must account for the relationship between these motivational and sociocultural factors. As Newcomb points out, "such
conclusions have to do with *something that happens within the individual* between (1) the impact of social conditions upon him and
(2) his behavior resulting from or reflecting this impact." Since this
"intervening variable" cannot be observed, it can be included among
the observational data only as an inferential construct which a conceptual model requires: "The distinctive feature of social psychology
lies not in the use of intervening variables but rather in the kind of
intervening variables which it uses and in the way in which it relates
them to protoplasm on the one hand and to society on the other." [11]
This recognition of a need for a synoptic model in conceptualized
social-psychological data is endorsed by Bonner when he declares that
"the study of human behavior is the systematic formulation of the
interrelations of the individual, society, and culture." Moreover,
Bonner maintains that social-psychological research and analysis requires this kind of framework for the "ordering of its data" into a
meaningful system: "Without such a conceptual scheme research

becomes mere facts-grubbing, without any discernible pattern or design." [12]

The *sociological* controversies about Weber's "ideal type" reveal that sociological theorists feel the need for some kind of conceptual model for identifying their sociocultural data. Martindale claims that all of the influential contemporary efforts to organize sociological data are adaptations, modifications, or revisions of Weber's mental construct: "An ideal type is formed by the one-sided *accentuation* of one or more points of view and by the synthesis of a great many diffuse, discrete, more or less present and occasionally absent concrete individual phenomena, which are arranged according to those one-sidedly emphasized viewpoints into a unified *analytical* construct." [13] Now Martindale grants that "among contemporary sociological theorists there is by no means equal receptivity to the use of ideal types." But he insists, nevertheless, that "the thinkers who have made basic use of the concept of 'social action' for the analysis of social life have been not only most sympathetic to the use of ideal types but have consciously attempted to improve them." [14]

Zetterberg has shown that the construction and verification of sociological theory requires the prior conceptual orientation of sociological data in terms of a "frame of reference." By this he means "a set of more or less interrelated definitions." He differentiates between such a conceptual model and a "theory" which is a system of definitions and hypotheses of which "the hypotheses of the theories should be capable of empirical verification." [15]

Among those *anthropologists* who are interested in something more than the description of a particular community there is a clearly felt need for some kind of conceptual model. Disagreement arises, however, with respect to what kind of model would best serve to identify the distinctive character of cultural phenomena. On the one hand, White advocates a *sui generis* model when he insists that "the most effective way to study culture scientifically is to proceed as if the human race did not exist." [16] On the other hand, Hallowell advocates a culture-in-personality model when he insists that "the behavioral manifestations upon which we depend for constructing our substantive pictures of cultures are always rooted in the personality structure of individuals." Hallowell does not deny the right of White or any other investigator to delimit the field for purposes of a theoretical investigation. He does contend, however, that a conceptual orientation of anthropological data requires a more comprehensive model of "man as the dynamic center of characteristic modes and processes of adjustment that are central to a human existence in order to emphasize the integral reality of society, culture, and personality structure as human phenomena." [17]

Of all social scientists, the *economist* has been most keenly aware of the need for models by which he might conceptualize the allocation of means to alternative ends. Usually he is less concerned about the literal accuracy and comprehensiveness of his representation than he is about its usefulness as an analytical tool for discerning the means-ends relationships of economic actions. Accordingly, economists have developed what Parsons has called a "distinctive conceptual scheme" for organizing their data in terms of a system of interdependent variables and, thus, to interpret particular phenomena in the light of their interrelations with others in a system." [18]

As long as the neo-classical economists maintained their technique-centered approach, the model of economic man operating in an automatically equilibrating market system served both as a conceptual and as a theoretical model. When the institutional economist sought to reconstruct the data of "economic transactions" [19] in terms of more complex motivational and sociocultural factors, the conceptual scheme became less distinctive. This is evident in J. M. Clark's separation of the conceptual model of interrelated units of a "dynamic social organism" from the traditional theoretical model of "levels of equilibrium." [20]

The most extreme separation of the descriptive conceptual model from the analytic theoretical model is made by Polanyi, when he identifies the empirical economy as "an institutionalized process between men and their natural and social environment, in the course of which they secure their livelihood." Polanyi calls for a model of the economic process which "cannot function apart from the culture, the motivations and valuations of which permeate the society." [21] This is also Kapp's position, when he insists that if economics is to become a substantive science "as an integral part of a science of man and culture," its data must be correlated with the data of other behavioral sciences. Such an approach requires a conceptual model which "starts with actual human needs and places man's dependence upon and interaction with his natural and social environment in the center of its investigation." [22]

To those *political scientists* who are not satisfied with a hit-or-miss approach for interpreting political phenomena Easton recommends the use of an "analytical schema" by which "it would be possible to identify the significant political variables and describe their mutual relations." He has assumed that "when people act, there are various elements in their social, physical and biological environment limiting and determining their activity." Within this more generalized conceptual framework, political scientists need "a guide for selecting the significant variables" in order that they might adequately identify "the major aspects or elements in the political situation." Such a conceptual model should identify and correlate (a) *the situational determinants*, i.e., the physical, non-human organic, and social aspects of the environment which shape and limit the activity of individual participants and (b) *the psychological determinants*, i.e., the individual participant's motivation, feelings, attitudes, and "the kind of person he is." According to Easton, political scientists who construct their theoretical hypotheses without the balanced perspective of such a conceptual model have overemphasizd one of these kinds of determinants at the expense of the other. Especially significant is Easton's insight that, since such a conceptual model is not used by many of the political scientists who set out to deal with motivational determinants, they actually treat "the psychological effect of the situation, rather than the effect of psychology, that is of motivation, on the situation." [23]

Although Easton has offered the most extensive analysis of the need for a conceptual model for political inquiry, his position is endorsed by several other political scientists. Leiserson seeks common concepts "to integrate the data of interpersonal and institutional behavior." [24] Garceau insists that political behavior research be "concerned with the total pattern of social relations." [25] Herring contends that the development of sound political analysis rather than unsupported prescriptions requires a conceptual scheme "which points to certain questions as crucial and thereby offers standards of relevance." [26]

Broadly operational *historians* are urging their somewhat reluctant colleagues to use a conceptual model for identifying and relating their data. Cochran, for example, contends that the historical analysis of "concrete physical, political, or social changes or events" requires a "comprehensive and meaningful syntheses." This means that historical events "should be assigned place and importance on the basis of their estimated relation to underlying forces." For making such an estimate the historian would need some social-scientific model of motivational and sociocultural operations.[27] Similarly, Brockunier and Loewenberg recommend that "a tentative frame of reference or conceptual scheme," which "directs attention to appropriate types of data," should be "set up for exploratory purposes." [28] What are the respective grounds on which some historians advocate and other historians oppose the use of social-scientific models for conceptually orienting historical data?

Among the advocates of such a device for coordinating behavioral and historical constructs, Clough claims that using motivational and sociocultural concepts would help the historian more adequately "to describe changes in the past, to analyze the forces that caused them, and to measure their more important effects." [29] Strong is more specific, when he insists that such a social-scientific conceptual framework is needed by the historian to furnish him with the "empirical equivalents" and "continuant configurations" which are required "for reconstructing movements and forces in the past." [30] Similarly, Watkins contends that "we can apprehend an unobservable social system only by reconstructing it theoretically from what is known of individual disposition." [31]

Why are some historians apprehensive about a model which is constructed in terms of social-scientific concepts? One reason is perhaps that conceptual generalizations about universal segments of human behavior might minimize, if not preclude, the recognition of the uniqueness and wholeness of specific historical situations, as well as the actions of individual persons. Another reason is that a synchronic comparison of similarities among contemporary sociocultural and motivational factors might de-emphasize the diachronic development of events in a temporally successive process.

Broader operationalists must take these reservations seriously, for they point up one of the most difficult problems that complicates the construction of a fruitful synoptic model. This is the difficulty of conceptually representing the uniform characteristics of motivational and sociocultural data without discounting or distorting the uniqueness, wholeness, and temporal character of specific human actions. If such a conceptual model fulfills its proper function, it should render as meaningless the shopworn controversy over the "great man theory" in which historians and sociocultural determinists have been so fruitlessly embrangled.

From this sampling of opinion it is evident that broader operationalists in each of the social-scientific disciplines feel an urgent need for a synoptic model. It should subsume the inexhaustible multiplicity of data under generic concepts which direct attention to persistent and pervasive elements in all human behavior. A significant contribution toward this end of a "balanced consideration of personality in nature, society, and culture" has been presented by Kluckhohn and Murray "within the framework of a complex conceptual scheme which explicitly recognizes, instead of tacitly excluding, a number of types of determinants." In order "to understand in what ways every man is like all other men, like some other men, like no other man," they distinguish four classes of determinants and their interactions: "constitutional, group-membership, role, and situations." But they remind us that "any classification of personality determinants is, at best, a convenient abstraction." Thus they summarize their conceptual orientation of goal-oriented action: "There is (1) the organism moving through a field which is structural both by culture and by the physical and social world in a relatively uniform manner, but which is subject to endless variation within the general patterning due to the organism's constitutionally-determined peculiarities of reaction and to the occurrence of special situations." [32]

We shall now undertake the presentation of and elaboration of our own synoptic model. Although it will modify and add to the concepts of the Kluckhohn-Murray model, it will be at least in principle congruent with their conceptual orientation of behavioral data.

Footnotes to Chapter 2 of Part Two

[1] Parsons, *The Structure of Social Action*, 28. Parsons elaborates his premise as follows: "These underlying features of the action schema which are here called

the 'frame of reference' do not constitute 'data' of any empirical problem; they are not 'components' of any concrete system of action. They are in this respect analogous to the space-time framework of physics. Every physical phenomena must involve processes in time, which happen to particles which can be located in space. It is impossible to talk about physical processes in any other terms, at least so long as the conceptual scheme of the classical physics is employed. Similarly, it is impossible even to talk about action in terms that do not involve a means-end relationship with all the implications just discussed. This is the common conceptual framework in which all change and process in the action field is grasped." This action frame of reference, however, "is not a phenomena in the empirical sense. It is the indispensable logical framework in which we describe and think about the phenomena of action. ( ) This is not true of the components of concrete action systems, or of the values of analytical elements, the specific content of ends and the like. They are of the empirical order of existence and are subject to analyses in terms of causality and concrete empirical process. The distinction between the action frame of reference and the concrete data is vital." (*The Structure of Social Action*, 733)

2 See Cattell in *Assessment of Human Motives*, 206-208, 218, and 231 for an elaboration of a theoretical model for purposes of actual investigation.

3 It should be noted, however, that some social scientists do seem to treat behavioral transaction so mechanistically that such a physical reduction may be intended. Consider, for example, the following statement by Miller, "Toward a General Theory for the Behavioral Sciences," *The State of the Social Sciences* (White), 41: "So the 'goals' which 'impel' the rat to run the maze, the woman to marry, and the candidate to file for public office can be interpreted as internal strains which elicit efforts to achieve inputs of energy and information that will reduce the strains toward an equilibrium point. And no matter whether he is nurtured at court to become Pharaoh or cast away in the bulrushes, a man will search until he finds an environment with inputs capable of diminishing the particular drives within him—strains established by his genetic inputs as modified by later inputs of energy and information, by learning or acculturation."

4 See Simon and Newell, "Models: Their Uses and Limitations," *The State of the Social Sciences* (White), 66-83. Cf. Arrow, "Mathematical Models in the Social Sciences," *The Policy Sciences* (Lerner and Lasswell), 129 ff. The kind of theoretical model that can be used for actual psychological investigation is discussed by Klein and Krech in their *Theoretical Models and Personality Theory*, Preface, 82-83, 88-99, 101-116.

5 Parsons and Shils, *Toward a General Theory of Action*, 53. Cf. 7, 16-27, 30-34, 42, 50-51.

6 Ruesch, "Introduction," *Toward a Unified Theory of Human Behavior* (Grinker), xi.

7 Krech and Klein, *Theoretical Models and Personality Theory*, 1, 2, 56-57, 79.

8 Tolman, "A Psychological Model," *Toward a General Theory of Action* (Parsons and Shils), 359. Cf. Murphy, *Personality*.

9 Allport, Gordon, "Emphasis upon Molar Problems," *Psychological Theory* (Marx), 168; *Becoming*, 5-6. Cf. *Becoming*, vii, 17-19, 51, 66-67.

[10] Lindzey, *Assessment of Human Motives*, 24. Cf. Allport, *Personality*. In *An Assessment of Human Motives* (Lindzey), Allport declares that "a theoretical task for the future is to relate the intraindividual structure to the recurrent situational patterns which in themselves may be regarded as complex social or cultural structures." (246)

[11] Newcomb, *Social Psychology*, 30-33.

[12] Bonner, *Social Psychology*, 7, 36.

[13] Weber, *The Methodology of Social Science*, 90.

[14] Martindale, "Sociological Theory and the Ideal Type," *Symposium on Sociological Theory* (Gross), 67.

[15] Zetterberg, *On Theory and Verification in Sociology*, 10. To illustrate this distinction as it applies to biology, Zetterberg indicates that Linnaeus furnished a "frame of reference" for classifying biological phenomena; but Darwin formulated a "theory" with verifiable hypotheses. (14)

[16] White, "The Locus of Mathematical Reality: An Anthropological Footnote," *Philosophy of Science*, XIV, 289-303.

[17] Hallowell, "Culture, Personality, and Society," *Anthropology Today* (Kroeber), 611, 600.

[18] Parsons and Shils, *Toward a General Theory of Action*, 28.

[19] Commons, *Institutional Economics*, 733.

[20] Clark, J. M., *Studies in the Economics of Overhead Costs*, ix.

[21] Polanyi, "Semantics of General Economic History," Origins of Economic Institutions (Mimeographed manuscript in the Interdisciplinary Project of Columbia University), 6-7.

[22] Kapp, "Economics and the Behavioral Sciences," *Kyklos*, Vol. VII, 1954, pages 219-224.

[23] Easton, *The Political System*, 61-62, 149-150, 155, 193-196, 201, 206, 211.

[24] Leiserson, *Political Science Quarterly*, Dec. 1953, p. 567.

[25] Garceau, *American Political Science Review* (1951), Vol. 45, p. 72.

[26] Herring, *American Political Science Review*, Dec. 1953, pp. 968-969. Cf. Merriam, *Systematic Politics*, Chapter 1 and *Power Politics*, Chapters 1, 2, 4, 7.

[27] Cochran, Bulletin 64, pages 84-85, and 169.

[28] Brockunier and Loewenberg, Bulletin 64, page 131.

[29] Clough, Bulletin 64, page 127.

[30] Strong, "The Materials of Historical Knowledge," *Naturalism and the Human Spirit* (Krikorian), 171.

[31] Watkins, "Ideal Types and Historical Explanation," *Readings in the Philosophy of Science* (Feigl and Brodbeck), 743.

[32] Kluckhohn, Murray, Schneider, *Personality in Nature, Society and Culture*, 63, 56, 65.

3 A Synoptic Model

A. The Presentation of a Synoptic Model

It is the aim of this chapter to present and elaborate a synoptic model of behavioral data. In order to identify and correlate the motivational and sociocultural factors which such human transactions entail, they will be conceptualized in terms of the goal-oriented behavior of human persons when they act under the conditions begotten by the complex whole of their natural-social-cultural-psychological environment. For our analytical purpose of devising an heuristic calculus of determinants, however, we shall abstract from this total behavioral process the following component dimensions: (a) the goal-seeking personality situation with its appended somatic, as well as its private, and its interpersonal, motivations, which comprise psychological data; (b) the social-institutional situation, which identifies sociological data; (c) the cultural situation, which identifies anthropological data; (d) the diachronic process, which identifies historical data; (e) the allocative situation, which identifies economic data, and (f) the administrative situation, which identifies political data.

In order to show how these structurally-identified constructs are functionally-interrelated we shall borrow from Tolman's psychological model the following organization of variables which many broadly operational social scientists have found useful: "(1) independent variables; (2) the dependent variable of behavior or action; (3) postulated intervening variables; and (4) postulated causal connections between the three types of variables." Although Tolman intends this as a formula for distributing explanatory constructs in *theoretical* analysis, we shall find that it is applicable in our conceptual analysis as well. Since Tolman offered this classification of variables for a psychological model, some may wonder whether it is appropriate for conceptually orienting sociocultural as well as motivational data. Actually, this is no problem, especially since Tolman himself has such a synoptic conception of the behavioral process: "Action or behavior of individual human beings practically always takes place *in* and is relative *to*, an environment which typically contains not only 'mere' physical objects but also other persons, collectivities, culturally presented values, and accumulated cultural resources." [1] In fact, Tolman's perspective approximates the comprehensive conceptual orientation of Parsons' general theory of action of which our synoptic model is a modified expansion: "Concrete systems of actions—that is, personalities and social systems—have psychological, social, and cultural aspects." [2]

The remainder of this section will be devoted to elaborating the function of our synoptic model for conceptually orienting behavioral data. It should be kept in mind, as previously explained that it is an heuristic device which is always subject to modification, revision, or abandonment, if a more adequate conceptual scheme is required.

B. *The Elaboration of this Synoptic Model*

1. THE INDEPENDENT VARIABLES

What is signified by each of the constructs which are taken here to be independent variables that provide the stimulus for which the dependent variable of the behavior of an actor and/or actors is the response? They are (a) the natural situation (including the somatic situation), (b) the cultural situation, (c) the social situation, and (d) the unconscious psychodynamic part of the private and interpersonal motivational situation. Each of these conceptual constructs entails some salient points which require the following elaboration.

a) The Natural Situation

This conceptual construct of *nature* is taken here to include the inorganic physico-chemical order of geographical, climatic, atmospheric, planetary and whatever other processes with which physical scientists are concerned, as well as the organic biological order of genetic, racial, subsistential, and whatever other processes of the organism-environment adjustments of sub-human and human species with which the life scientists are concerned. Appended to the organic order of biological processes is the somatic situation which identifies the physiological processes of each human body's muscular, glandular, and neural functions. Rather than to revive the nature-nurture controversy about the predominant influence of heredity *or* environment, the somatic situation is conceived here in terms of the two-fold construct of heredity-environment. This signifies the necessarily reciprocal operations of external inorganic-organic pressures with the internal genetic processes that produce whatever constitutional hereditary predispositions (Allport's "protoplasmic irritability") are taken to be congenital for the human organism.

Dobzhansky seems to speak for most geneticists, when he opposes the "traditional dichotomy of hereditary and environmental traits" on the grounds that "in reality, all traits are both hereditary and environmental." [3] It is this biological generalization which Kluckhohn and Murray adopt, when they claim that organisms "are the product of a long series of interactions between biologically-inherited potentialities and environmental forces." [4] Similarly, Murphy contends that "there develops the paradox that heredity is known only by the liberation of hereditary potentials through *specific environmental forces*; and what is liberated is as much a function of the environing pressures as it is of the latent or potential disposition." [5]

The construct of the natural situation cannot be left out of a synoptic model of human behavior; but its use must be qualified. Nature must be taken into account as an independent variable, not only because the social scientist is dealing with biophysically-begotten human organisms, but also because he conceives of the bodily process "as the source of the viscerogenic drive or energy of action" (Parsons). This through neurophysiological responses (along with psychodynamic and sociocultural responses) is expended in goal-seeking motivation. Moreover, the sociocultural aspect of the behavioral process always operates within an inorganic-organic context in which, for example, climatic, geographical, and racial factors restrictively condition institutions and cultural patterns. It should also be noted that it is the scarcity of natural resources for survival which imposes the inexorable necessity for political administration and economic allocation.

Why must the use of the conceptual construct of nature be qualified? Although the broader operationalist agrees that the human organism cannot be understood apart from the physical heredity-environment which begets it and with which it constantly interacts, he does not agree with the narrow operationalist, such as a radically physiological psychologist, that these biophysical phenomena are his primary data. For, as previously emphasized, he assumes that sociocultural relations constitute a superorganic order which is just as natural as the inorganic and organic orders out of which it has emerged. Accordingly, he assumes that for purposes of social-scientific analysis the motivation of goal-oriented behavior can be taken as given data which are not reducible to the biochemical data of physiological functions required for the biological adjustment of an organism to its physical environment. Relegating other sectors of human actions to physiology and biology, therefore, the social scientist, as Sheldon emphasizes, "is concerned with the activity as related in some manner to things outside the organism itself—activity in terms of *principles of relationship*." [6]

The indirectness of the social scientist's interest in nature as such is brought out by Parsons and Shils when they distinguish the kind of questions the social scientist asks from that which a biological theorist asks with respect to the analysis of goal-oriented motivation. The biological theorist asks: "What does this person have to do in order to survive?" The social scientist, of course, must include survival among the goals which an organism seeks. Since he takes as his more primary concern the actor's selective orientation to internalized cultural values, however, he asks these questions: "What does this

actor strive for?" "On what basis does the actor make his selections?" [7]

b) The Cultural Situation

The conceptual construct of *culture* is taken here to identify the
complex pattern of humanly created and cultivated ways of behaving,
believing, feeling, and tooling which are generally shared by most of
the members of any given community at a particular time. Biological organisms become human when their behavior is motivated by
their responses to such a symbolically communicated design for living which has been transmitted through language and institutions
from previous generations. The ingredients of culture are too in-
exhaustibly various for us to identify, and the hierarchy of the levels
of meaning is too complex for us to attempt to delineate it here. By
a cultural pattern, however, we shall mean a configuration of requirements for organizing human relations (e.g., familial, political,
economic) and for providing ideational orientation (intellectual
standards, ethical commitments, religious loyalties, aesthetic tastes,
political ideologies, etc.). Intangible though it be, this social inheritance is an independent variable which fashions each person's goal-
seeking behavior just as much as does his physical inheritance. In
addition to these intangible organizational and ideational aspects,
there is, of course, the more tangible artifactitious equipment, i.e.,
tooling. This material culture limits the technological potentialities
of a community in its political administration and economic allocation of the means required for the realization of the organizational
and ideational ends.

Since it seems unlikely that we could find or formulate a definition
of culture to which all anthropologists would subscribe, let us attempt to identify the structure of culture as a patterned process which
is functionally exemplified in the concrete behavioral transactions of
the enculturalized members of a community. This means that the
organizational aspect of a cultural pattern is externalized in social
institutions and the ideational aspects of a cultural pattern are internalized in the goal seeking motivation of a person or group of
persons when they select their own ends from among culturally-
begotten symbols. When Parsons insists that "culture does not act—
only human beings act as individuals," he thus succinctly describes

how the structural pattern of a culture is functionally exhibited: "Culture is transmitted, it is shared; it is internalized in the personalities, institutionalized in the social system." [8]

The advantage of this reciprocal conception of the cultural process in a synoptic conceptualization of behavioral data is that it makes it as meaningless for anthropologists, sociologists, and psychologists to argue about the relative priorities of culture, society, and personality as it is to argue about the relative priority of heredity and environment. As Kroeber and Parsons have said of both the former trichotomy and the latter dichotomy, "it is no longer a question of how important each is, but of how each works and how they are interwoven with each other." Kroeber and Parsons do not reduce either the concept of culture to society or the concept of society to culture, when they insist that "they are distinct systems in that they abstract or select two analytically distinct sets of components from the same concrete phenomena." [9] We do not deny their position, therefore, when we emphasize the reciprocity of culture and society in this way. If learning is required for the transmission of a symbolic content, then not only must there be a cultural pattern to be learned, but there must be persons communicating through social institutions (home, school, church) who are teaching and being taught. Moreover, this conception precludes a cultural determinism which would make persons nothing but creatures of culture. To be sure, all people are creatures of their cumulative cultures; but they may also be partial creators of the cultural pattern. Don't some people modify it so that what they transmit to the next generation is not exactly the same as that which they inherited? If a cultural predeterminist discounts all individual initiative and responsibility, how does he account for the changes in the pattern of the institutions and of the goal-seeking orientations in developing human communities? [10]

c) *The Social Situation*

This conceptual construct of *society* is taken here to identify the collective organization of human relationships which exemplify culturally-begotten symbolic norms in distinction to the organization of non-human organisms which seem to be regulated by biological instincts. Consequently, the social situation in which any person acts includes all the other persons who participate with him as members of a community in accordance with patterns of institutionalized role-expectancy. (Although this model focuses attention upon the inter-action of persons in the groups by which individuals are socialized, it is not intended to minimize the significance of macro-sociological analysis of the interaction of groups.)

The notion of a *role* is used here in connection with this predomi-nantly sociological construct to identify the various relational posi-tions which persons play in a collective process, e.g., parent-child, employer-employee, teacher-child. But it is recognized as an abstrac-tion from the actual multiroled transactions which characterize a socialized person's shared goal-seeking experiences. To identify these viable interpersonal responses which motivate specific individuals the social-psychological construct of "role behavior" in Newcomb's sense will be required. At this point, however, we are only concerned with the relational positions themselves. These have developed and will persist in the societal organization of a community regardless of what specific persons happen to fill them. For example, the role of the President of the United States is an integral unit of the structure of our national society regardless of what particular person holds the office and what persons in the role of the electorate empowered him.

While this construct identifies the structure of a society in terms of the generalized pattern by which role positions are organized, it does not determine which collection of groups in the multigrouped social situation is sufficiently inclusive to be identified as a self-contained society. From consideration of sociological and anthropo-logical writings about the scope of a society it may well be inferred that the decision that any specific collectivity is a society rather than a subgroup is largely determined by political or economic or histori-cal or some other purpose for which it is being defined. Useful as such relative definitions are for a specific analysis, it must not be forgotten that in their collective transactions persons play various roles; and that, moreover, the playing of any given group role is only one of any person's many goal-seeking actions.

The institutionalization of culturally-begotten norms for regulating role expectancy through sanctions and punishment as the prerequisite for a social order emerges out of the progressively restrictive process in which folkways, mores, and enactive laws have evolved. Familial, political, economic, religious, and educational, as well as many other types of human relationships, which also entail the prescription of reciprocal rights and duties, become institutionalized when a general formal pattern of such integrated role-expectations is highly stabilized. Now, the generic forms of collective interaction which characterize all institutions can be delimited and theoretically analyzed by the sociologist in terms of generalizations that abstract the recurrent, uniform, and similar elements from the actual sociocultural phenomena without taking into account the unique dissimilarities of each of these sociocultural situations as a whole. For such a delimited and theoretical analysis, the psychological incentives of the actors in these institutionalized sociocultural processes are justifiably assumed to be irrelevant.

It should be remembered, however, that this synoptic model is a conceptual scheme which is primarily designed to correlate as well as identify the sociocultural and motivational data of the behavioral process as a whole. Accordingly, the implication of this construct for the socialization of individuals might be summarized by suggesting that the institutional organization of types of psychological incentives might be classified in terms of three orders of the social situation: (a) *private order*, in which the members of kinship, fraternal, welfare, and recreational associations are predominantly motivated by sympathetic personal concern for each other; (b) *public order*, in which the members of economic, political, and military enterprises are bound by contractual agreements but are predominantly motivated by each member's ambitions for himself; and (c) *normative order*, in which the members of religious, ethical, artistic, and educational movements that have been institutionalized as churches, schools, etc. are predominantly motivated by the respective aspirations they share.

It is through this institutionalized process of socialization that an individual person learns about the alternative culturally-presented values from which he must select those which he internally activates through his purposive goal-seeking. Such sociocultural responses, therefore, must be considered along with neurophysiological and psychodynamic responses in the subsequent constructs which are intended to identify and correlate the factors of human motivation.[11]

d) *The Personality Situation*

Before we elaborate this conceptual construct we must note this warning of Sapir and heed it in our interpretation: "The term personality is too variable in usage to be serviceable, unless its meaning is very carefully defined for a given context." [12] He points out these divergent meanings of *personality*: The subjective awareness of the self, as well as the ideal type of person he is striving to become (philosophical); any given totality of reaction systems (physiological-psychological); the symbolic identification of an individual to differentiate him from other individuals (sociological); and the individual abstracted from a psychophysical whole as a comparatively stable system of reactivity (psychiatric). There are other meanings; but this list indicates the diversity. Needless to say, the conception of personality in a synoptic model must be comprehensive enough to include these and other dimensions. Accepting Sapir's warning, we must try to define what *personality* shall mean in this context.

Personality will be used here to signify a compound conceptual construct which is designed to coordinate the following three dimensions of motivational data: (a) the intervening variable of the *conscious goal-seeking motivation,* which identifies the defining characteristic of a human person's owned experience at any present moment; and (b) the independent variables of two interpenetrating appendages which intimately influence each person's owned present conscious experience: (i) his *private motivational situation,* which consciously and unconsciously generates psychodynamic responses from his own past experiences, and (ii) his *public motivational situation,* which consciously and unconsciously generates attitudes and sentiments out of contemporary interpersonal transactions. With respect to these independent variables, the former pertains to psychoanalytic data, and the latter pertains to social-psychological data.

Psychic bruises from earlier experiences which produce psychodynamic compulsions and interpersonal transactions operate as independent variables which condition the intervening variable, i.e., a person's present goal-oriented decision. In comparison with the natural and sociocultural situations, however, they constitute an internal psychological environment through which the external sociocultural influences must be filtered just as external natural substances must be filtered through the body. The intervening variable (*a* above) of a conscious goal-oriented decision at any given moment will be identified and its function will be explained after the independent variables of the psychodynamic compulsions and interpersonal relations (*b* i and ii above) have been described.

Before either the independent variables or the intervening variables are considered, the meaning of behavioral experience itself must be stated. The concept of personality is abstractly constructed in terms of independent and intervening variables in order to understand concrete experience, the dependent variable. The way a social scientist defines what he means by experience will largely determine the requirements which his construct of personality must fulfil. Accordingly, such a conception of experience must focus attention upon the generic functions of all the motivational data which the social scientist is attempting to conceptualize. The aim of this conceptual construct of personality should be distinguished, of course, from the aims of the personologist's and clinician's *theoretical* constructs. They must specify items such as age, sex, etc. in order to deal with particular cases, but these are not items in a *conceptual* model.

Experience will be taken to mean the temporal process of any person's complex, on-going, unity of consciousness. Despite the irrational impulses and confusing sensations which often disorient conscious awareness, each person's experience exhibits a unique complex order to this extent. His uniquely combined sensations and desires at any present moment not only belong to him alone, so that they cannot be possessed by anyone else, but they are also uniquely connected with the past by his own present memory, and with the future by his own present anticipation of and striving for satisfaction-yielding goals. It is assumed here that there is no point in going behind or beyond this given experiential unity of emotional content and purposive activity in search of a soul-substance. Consequently, if the concept of personality is to serve the aim of this synoptic model as a motivational construct, it must coordinate the somatic and psychodynamic functions which beget a person's consciously experienced drives and needs (emotional content) with his consciously experienced unreflective and reflective goal-seeking (purposive activity) by which the person operates on this content in order to satisfy his desires.[13]

The contemporaneous nature of actually experienced motivational data might be overlooked, if it is not especially noted. Up to this point the major emphasis of this synoptic model has been the correlation of the personality construct with the external situational constructs of nature, culture, and society. Even in the subsequent elaboration of the internal unconscious situation, the ascription of motivation to the psychodynamic responses to antecedent experiences of the person himself refers to conditions that are just as much "outside of" the person's present experience as are the external environmental conditions referred to by neurophysiological and sociocultural responses. In order to balance this situational emphasis which might obscure the significance of the experienced present moment of the individual's private psychological environment let us consider Lewin's emphasis upon the relative autonomy of the contemporary field of motivation.

According to Lewin, the causal influences of past conditions can be ascertained only in terms of their effects in the present "psychological field" or "life space"; for "the psychological past and the psychological future are simultaneous parts of the psychological field existing at a given time." Lewin does not deny that the antecedent constitutional predispositions, neurophysiological maturation, sociocultural learning, and psychodynamic compulsions influence presently experienced drives and needs, when he insists that "any behavior or any other change in a psychological field depends only upon the psychological field *at that time*." For, since the "time perspective is constantly changing," the motivation of "any type of behavior depends upon the total field, including the perspective at that time, but not, in addition, upon any past or future field and its time perspectives." Accordingly, memory of the "psychological past" and anticipation of the "psychological future" are simultaneous aspects of the "psychological field" at any present moment. This means that all experiential processes, e.g., perceiving, desiring, remembering, sensing, anticipating, inferring, feeling, etc., are "derived from the relation of the concrete individual to the concrete situation, and, so far as internal forces are concerned, from the mutual relations of the various functional systems that make up the individual." When motivation involves the arousal of need tensions, the desiring and adoption of goals, the active striving for goals, and the realization of satisfactions that release the tension which instigated this dynamic process, then the need for this satisfaction-yielding goal and the desirability of this objective (positive valence) stems from the experient's own psychological field rather than directly from neurophysiological responses to his biophysical environment. "Instead of linking the need directly to the motoric," Lewin contends, "the need is linked with certain properties of the (psychological) environment" so that "the (psychological) environment then determines the motoric." [14]

i) THE INDEPENDENT VARIABLES OF THE PERSONALITY SITUATION

(A) Psychodynamic Motivational Situation

This conceptual construct identifies the unconscious psychodynamic compulsions which were so significantly specified by Freud in terms of his psychoanalytic model of the id, ego, and superego. For our purpose, the usefulness of Freud's conception of these three interpenetrating strata of personality is not seriously impaired by its shortcomings which have been corrected, modified, and revised by the many social scientists who have adopted them in formulating their own conceptions of psychodynamic (emotional-motivational) data. A detailed exposition of Freud's view is, of course, beyond the limits of this study. The point to be emphasized, however, is that the Freudian formula directs attention to the general kind of psychodynamic motivational data which a synoptic model must include.

The id is the completely unconscious, unorganized, subterranean level of personality which is entirely isolated from the person's external natural and sociocultural environment. The id's phylogenetically and somatically predetermined impulses are utterly amoral and irrational in their one persistent aim of satisfying the all pervasive desire for pleasure. When Freud claims that the id contains only "instinctual cathexes seeking discharge," he means that it is the source and retainer of the dynamic energy of the sexual instincts, i.e., the libido which "is a force of variable quantity by which processes and transformations in the sphere of sexual excitement can be measured." By sexual instincts Freud does not refer only to adult desire for physical relations but also to emotional attachments to persons, objects, and ideals. With respect to the id's determination of the ego and the superego, infantile sexuality is the most important innate impulse in the Oepidus complex. In a child this generates hostility toward the parent of the same sex who is a rival for the love of the other parent.

The ego is the organized level of personality which has partially emerged out of the id. The ego is conscious because it has sensations of its natural and sociocultural environment which modify it. Through perceiving, remembering, learning, and reasoning the ego attempts to regulate the wild pleasure impulses from the id so that they will not jeopardize the ego's self-preservation; but for its energy the ego depends on the id which predisposes limits on what the ego can do. Consequently, when the ego makes a rational effort to govern the pleasure impulses foisted upon it by the id in accordance with the monitoring of the superego in order to meet sociocultural demands, it can achieve only varying degrees of success through postponing, modifying, substituting, and sublimating the irrational impulses. When the ego represses a frustrating desire, it weakens its control of the id which has thereby increased determination of subsequent conscious processes.

The superego which represents parental authority prescriptively punishes the ego by inflicting guilt feelings when the ego responds to the compulsions of the id. Although the superego as an internalized moral code is the conscience of the ego, it is not influenced by any reflective evaluations from the ego, nor by any contemporary sociocultural standards, except those which indirectly come from childhood experiences by way of the parental authority or its later surrogates. More than from socioculturalization, the superego stems from the unconscious guilt feelings of the Oedipus complex which the ego cannot modify regardless of what it consciously learns about sociocultural norms. In short, the monitor for the ego's attempts to control the id is largely determined by the id itself.

The function of the personality within this id-ego-superego structure was conceived by Freud in terms of psychic dynamisms, e.g., repression, regression, reaction-formation, displacement, introjection, identification, projection, symbolization, etc. Repression illustrates the functioning of these mechanisms in abnormal behavior; and sublimation illustrates the functioning of these mechanisms in more normal behavior. (Whether or not sublimation is a defense mechanism like repression is not an important issue for our limited discussion.) When an id-begotten desire is frustrated or is unacceptable to the superego, the conscious ego, in order to avoid pain, represses it back into the id where it causes the libido to "flow back" to points of arrested fixation that have become, as a result of infantile sexuality, established in its development. Although repressed desires are sub-merged in the unconscious id, they continue to influence the con-scious ego by producing neurotic anxieties which are attributable to the accumulation of such psychic bruises. On the constructive side, however, the ego may guard itself from pain through sublimation of an unacceptable gratification, i.e., by diverting the libidinous sexual energy. For the sexual impulse, Freud asserts, "has the power to ex-change its nearest aim for others of higher value which are not sexual." Accordingly, sexual compulsions may function to predeter-mine conscious behavior by the pattern of the personality's ante-cedent experience or they may become the dynamic motivation of such self-creative activities of which a person is capable.[15]

A word about neo-Freudianism is in order. The significance of Freud's contribution to the understanding of both abnormal and normal behavior in terms of the antecedently acquired influence of psychodynamic compulsions is acknowledged by most social scientists. But before such a private motivational situation as an independent variable could be correlated with the sociocultural situation as an independent variable, as well as with the conscious goal-seeking of reflective persons, some crucial revisions were required. That Freud's ideas "stand up under the necessity of being translated into the language of a later day," according to Newcomb, is a tribute to their greatness.[16] Space allows the discussion of only a few of these basic modifications. Fromm and Horney have attempted to eliminate Freud's predominant emphasis upon phylogenetic instinct in the unconscious id which precluded any effective socioculturalization of the conscious ego. Instead of attributing a neurosis to a congenital sexual instinct which motivates the incestuous desire and sexual rivalry of the Oedipus complex, Fromm claims that a neurosis is the result of the child's defeat in his "fight with irrational authority represented by the parents." [17] Horney carries further the sociocul-tural emphasis, when, instead of Freud's sexual instinct, she attributes frustration to "socially induced anxiety compulsion." [18]

The functioning of psychodynamic compulsions in the conscious reflective goal-seeking of normal personalities has been identified by Jung in his construct of the "prospective aim," i.e., the reflective desire for the fulfillment of self-realization. Whereas Adler substituted for Freud's sexuality the will-to-power as the compulsion to com-pensate for an unbearable sense of inferiority, Jung maintained that unconscious compulsion involves both to varying degrees in various situations. Sublimation for Jung, therefore, was not only a technique for curing neuroses but also, in the functioning of the "prospective aim," it was the emergent conscious effort of the reflective person to sublimate his sexual and will-to-power compulsions in accordance with relatively self-imposed ideals. Freud, of course, had taken sublimation to be the diversion of sexual energy to higher and finer goals; but in his *Civilization and Its Discontents* he indicates that his reference to a more qualitatively significant value experience is metaphorical and that he is not sure what he means by a higher goal. In the following statement, however, Jung makes it clear what he means by a higher goal, and he provides a conceptual bridge from the constructs about unconscious motivation to those of conscious motivation (e.g. Allport's "functional autonomy") which Tolman in his model of purposive behavior calls an intervening variable: "Personality can never develop itself unless the individual chooses his own way consciously and with conscious moral decision . . . But a man can make a moral choice of his own way only when he holds it to be the best." [19]

There is an increasing use of modified Freudian constructs by personologists and social psychologists now that they have been revised so that they do not preclude the sociocultural independent variables and the reflective intervening variables which influence conscious goal-seeking behavior. The earlier opposition to Freud by psychologists, as well as by other social scientists, is being replaced by their interest in revised conceptual psychoanalytic models such as that of Rapaport, which aims "to systematize psychological data—observational and introspective—no matter how remote from any neurologically or tangible phenomena." Shakow, for example, makes a good case for his claim that Rapaport's psychoanalytical model in terms of "the need, the need-satisfying object and the need gratification—the pattern of events in that order of time," is an integral part of a more inclusive model of the "constant interchange of transactions" for conceptualizing the motivational data of the entire psychological system. Developments like this bear out the accuracy of Smith's judgment that "psychodynamics having become respectable in psychology, tough-minded psychologists are addressing themselves to motivational problems, and the 'gap' between 'academic' psychology and the more comprehensive but speculative theories of psychoanalysis is at least diminishing." [20]

Further implications of the psychoanalytic principles which are incorporated in this construct of the private motivational situation will emerge in the subsequent discussions about the social-psychological principles of the construct of the public motivational situation and in discussions about the personological principles of the experienced conscious motivation of unreflective and reflective goal-seeking.

(B) Interpersonal Motivational Situation

This conceptual construct, which identifies the data of social psychology, pertains to "the thought, feeling, and behavior of individuals," as Allport says, when they "are influenced by the actual, imagined, or implied presence of other human beings." [21] Parsons has pointed out that within the macroscopic interactive functioning of the large scale social system such a microscopic transactive functioning of the symbolic intercommunication of persons "becomes a special kind of system distinctly different from other types of inter-actions." [22] But, as Ruesch reminds us, this interpersonal context, from which the internal structure of a person is inferred, "is a zone" with "an indefinable boundary." [23] Since an interpersonal transaction is one of the appended dimensions of the compounded personality construct, its functioning interpenetrates with that of the other appended dimensions of neurophysiological and psychodynamic zones. To establish a firm dividing line is difficult, if not impossible.

Murray has made significant efforts to mark off this motivational zone without minimizing this interpretation within the subject's apperceptive experience (Lewin's *beta* situation) and without ignoring the external actuality (Lewin's *alpha* situation). When Murray contends that "an interpersonal proceeding is the psychologist's most significant type of real entity," he assumes that "the unit is not the subject's behavior, but the subject-object interaction." This he takes to be a dyadic proceeding in which "the object (alter, second person) constitutes the everchanging situation for the subject (first person), and the subject constitutes the everchanging situation for the object." Murray declares that for the purpose of identifying and analyzing this interpersonal field "the animal-in-maze model will not serve us." [24]

Kantor also recognizes that a "definite behavioral situation" must be distinguished from neurophysiological functions, "when the individual interbehaves with an object not on the basis of its natural properties, but on the basis of attributed properties, as in social-psychological situations." Accordingly, he rejects the Watsonian S-R model which identifies behavioral data solely in terms of the neurophysiological responses to biological stimuli. Instead, he proposes that "psychological interbehavior may be symbolized as R←⟶S to indicate that it is definitely spontaneous on the basis of previous interactions." [25]

It is even more difficult to mark the boundary between the interpersonal and the psychodynamic aspects of motivation, than it is to distinguish between the interpersonal and the neurophysiological. For all of its neurophysiological concomitants, the symbolic communications of interpersonal motivations pertains to a different level of behavior. But, psychodynamic compulsions infiltrate throughout interpersonal transactions. Doesn't the superego-ego relationship have a direct bearing on the crucial interpersonal transactions of children with parental authority and its surrogates in later life? It is instructive to note Newcomb's acknowledgment that in dealing with the factors of security and insecurity in the "self-other" patterning of interpersonal relations he has discovered that "much of what Freud has to say, and still more of Horney's contributions, might well be stated in these terms for social-psychological purposes." [26] Doesn't this suggest, therefore, that the two-fold motivational situation, in which behavior, if created by goal-seeking correlative functioning of psychodynamic compulsions and interpersonal transactions, corresponds to the two-fold somatic situation in which the biological organism is begotten by the correlative functioning of genetically inherited predispositions and the inorganic-organic environment? For regardless of whatever unconscious desires there may be, they cannot operate as the dynamic stimuli for psychodynamic responses apart from the relational context of interpersonal transactions.

Social psychologists today generally reject McDougall's concept of an innate predisposition and agree with Newcomb that they should "substitute the more distinctive terms 'reflex,' 'drive,' 'motive,' and 'attitude' for the overinclusive term 'instinct,' as applied to human beings." Otherwise, there is no way to account for the modifications of behavior as "energy becomes directed toward selected goals" and for "changes in behavior and motivation which are not accompanied by changes in the person's anatomical structure." But Newcomb is not advocating "nurture" without any recognition of "nature" i.e., congenital genetic and psychic predispositions, for he reconstructs the concept of "degrees of dependability of human motive." [27]

How is the interpersonal motivational situation of the psychological environment differentiated from the sociocultural situation? It is pertinent to note that when socialization and enculturalization are discussed in terms of imitation and suggestions, the social psychologists dealing with interpersonal transactions always ask "by whom and to whom." For the social psychologist is less interested in the similar sociocultural influences on the members of a group than he is, as Newcomb says, "with the influences which play upon individuals as members of various groups." Although the social psychologist agrees with sociologists and anthropologists that "group membership" significantly shapes the common pattern of collective behavior, he, unlike them, is "very much interested in resulting individual differences." The social psychologist, therefore, focuses attention on that aspect of motivation which involves "something that happens within the individual" between the sociocultural impact and his socioculturalized behavior.[28]

In order to distinguish their conception of interpersonal transactions from the earlier conflicting conceptions of motivation in terms of instinct, on the one side, and in terms of habit, on the other, social psychologists are attempting to formulate a revised set of constructs about goal-oriented actions. Newcomb defines *motive* as "a state of the organism in which bodily energy is mobilized and selectively directed toward parts of the environment," and *motive pattern* as a "sequence of behaviors characterized by relative constancy of motivation." Correlative though they be, attitudes and motives are distinguishable in Newcomb's sense that attitudes "represent persistent, general orientations of the individual toward his environment, whereas motives represent orientations which are temporary (though they may be repeated) and relatively specific." [29] Gordon Allport's definition of an *attitude* as a "neuropsychic state of readiness for mental and physical activity" [30] is congruent with this and with Asch's conception of it as a "preconception" growing out of past experience which predisposes the direction of decisions among possible alternatives in new situations.[31] The attitude-sentiment controversy among social psychologists seems to be losing its significance for those who conceive a sentiment to be a complex of emotion-laden attitudes. The older "force of habit" is thus restated in terms of the "persistence of attitudes" which constitute the structure of the interpersonal situation.

The clearest distinction between the interpersonal motivational situation and the sociocultural situation is made by those social psychologists who adopt Newcomb's construct of actual "role-behavior," i.e., "the motive pattern on the part of a specific individual as he takes a role." The role construct of sociologists and anthropologists, it will be recalled, does not refer to the actual behavior of any individual but, rather, to the variety of socially-defined positions which embody the culturally-begotten expectancies that have become institutionalized in terms of reciprocal rights and duties. The role construct serves the aim of formulating a general pattern of sociocultural interaction; but it is not applicable to the motivational data of any specific person's goal-seeking behavior. When Newcomb claims that "role behaviors are unique to each individual," he does not minimize the similarities of behavioral patterns of expectancy that are realized by individuals who through collective consensus and communication act in accordance with shared sociocultural norms. The distinctive feature which he emphasizes is that, "whatever the characteristics he expresses in various roles, they are *his own* characteristics, and he cannot help expressing them as he takes his roles in his own, individual way." By using this construct of role behavior the social psychologist has a concept which can account for the fact that no two people play the same role in exactly the same way. Instead of presenting motivation solely in terms of what others expect of a given person, this construct implies that a person is also significantly motivated by his "self-perception of what others think and expect of him." This seeing oneself as reflected in the eyes of others, which Cooley anticipated in his concept of "the looking-glass self," leads to a distinctively psychological conception of a group "in the sense that individuals perceive it and are motivated in relation to it, and their behavior is thus determined by it."[32] This is what Asch appears to mean when he conceives the dynamic interpersonal relations of individual members of a group as the product of the relatively autonomous activity of the individuals themselves: "The capacity to perceive a situation that includes others and ourselves and to perceive others as referring themselves to the same situation is the first requirement for the formation of a social field, of a *group relation* at the psychological level." [33]

Of all the constructs in the synoptic model, this construct of the interpersonal motivational situation is most necessary in order to correlate the collective aspect and the individual aspect of human goal-seeking behavior. Through its coordination of public sociocultural influences and psychodynamic compulsions it gives meaning to the concepts of a "socialized self" and "personality in culture." Consequently, it renders the following questions meaningless: Which is more real, the self or the society? Which is more objective, the person or the culture? When social scientists adopt this construct, they reject the assumption of the approach which Murphy has called "situationism," i.e., personality "at any given time is a reflection and epitome of specific cultural requirements," in favor of the assumption of the approach which he has called "field theory," i.e., personality is "a flowing continuum of organism-environment events." The constructs which have been used in this synoptic model as independent variables have referred to the organization of both the psychosomatic organism and the physical and sociocultural environment which through their dynamic interaction provide the context of the field of personality structure. Murphy has emphasized why an operational conception of personality structure requires such a recognition of the interdependence of the intervening variables within "the organism-situation field": "We cannot define the situation operationally except in reference to the specific organism which is involved; we cannot define the organism operationally, in such a way as to obtain predictive power for behavior, except in reference to the situation." [34]

Personality must be conceived as both product and producer. Thus far we have been considering only those dimensions of a person which can be identified as independent variables, i.e., his psychodynamic and interpersonal motivations. The persisting characteristics of human personality as the product of its natural and sociocultural environment could not be understood apart from these psychological environments. Necessary as these independent variables of personality are, they are not sufficient for conceptualizing all that the goal-seeking operations of persons entails. A conceptual portrait of personality must also include the correlative functioning of the *intervening variable* through which persons participate to some degree in producing themselves.

For the purpose of elaborating our synoptic model we shall consider the intervening variable of conscious goal-seeking from two aspects. First, we shall present it as the third dimension of the compounded personality construct. Secondly, we shall present it as the intervening variable at the broader level of the entire synoptic model where it can be correlated with the independent variables of the natural, sociocultural, and psychological environments.

ii) CONSCIOUS GOAL-SEEKING MOTIVATION AS AN INTERVENING VARIABLE OF THE PERSONALITY SITUATION

This conceptual construct of conscious goal-seeking is designed to identify the third dimension of the compounded personality structure. Up to this point we have found that when personality is defined without reference to this third dimension, it is conceived to be the product of the total natural and sociocultural environment which shape a person through his neurophysiological, psychodynamic, and interpersonal responses that generate his basic drives and needs. Thus conceived, human personality is taken by Kluckhohn and Murray to be "a compromise function, a dynamic resultant of the conflict between the individual's own impulses (as given by biology and modified by culture and specific situations) and the demands, interests, and impulses of other individuals." [35] There are some social scientists, however, who hold that the two psychodynamic and interpersonal dimensions are necessary but not sufficient for completely identifying the personality structure. In addition to personality as product they focus attention on personality as producer in a relatively self-determined motivational process in which, as Fromm emphasizes, "by far the most important object of productiveness is man himself." [36]

Confronted by the danger and difficulty of including this self-productive dimension within the structure of a personality construct, some social scientists have understandably but arbitrarily refused to take it into account. The danger lies in the possibility that personology might degenerate into existentialism. This deals only with immediate experience in terms of indeterministic self-production which so completely transcends all of the natural, sociocultural, psychodynamic, and interpersonal situational determinants of a person's environment that questions about motivation are rendered meaningless. All social scientists wish to avoid such a "flight from reason," as existentialists themselves declare it to be. But some social scientists feel compelled to take the self-productive aspect of personality into account. Consequently, they must identify it as an intervening variable which, despite its separability, is by definition necessarily interconnected with the independent variables that identify the situational determinants which produce it.

The chief difficulty lies in applying the analytic abstractions, to which all scientific inquiry is committed, to a conscious goal-oriented decision in the concrete fleeting *present moment* of the actor's temporal experience. Those who would exclude this privately owned present moment of conscious decision from their motivational constructs on the grounds that it is inaccessible to public observation, have no answer to the question: Motivation for what? Moreover, only the presently experienced moments are actual. For past moments, though once actual, are no longer themselves actually experienced, except as unconscious or conscious memory-images. Though future moments will at some time be actual, as yet they only subsist as the referent of anticipatory images. Consequently, remembering the past and anticipating the future, as well as the goal-oriented decision which is reactively and proactively in accordance with them, are always themselves presently experienced behavioral actions.

Kelly seems to endorse this way of conceiving an actor's decision-making activity when he analyzes "man's construction of his alternatives" in terms of the principle that "a person's processes are psychologically channelized by the way he anticipates events." Accordingly, the key to a conceptualization of human goal-oriented behavior is "the conjunctive vision" by which man in his "darting present" links his past and future experiences. In order to eliminate the widely held view that antecedently generated motives are imposed upon an inert and static individual, Kelly rejects all motivational constructs as redundant. Kelly's premise that "man lives in the present," which is a point in the ongoing temporal process of his experience, is also the premise on which the functioning of personality is conceptualized here.[37]

An attempt will now be made however to show why Kelly's whole-sale rejection of all motivational constructs is unnecessary in order to take presently experienced decisions into account. Difficult as it is for social scientists to conceptualize the motivation of presently experienced conscious goal-seeking, they are intellectually obligated to include it in a conceptual synoptic model which aims to encompass all of the determinants of the behavioral process. Whether or not an investigator in a specific discipline who is dealing with de-limited data includes or excludes this intervening variable in his *theoretical model* is, of course, another matter.

Let us now consider this third dimension of the compounded personality situation as an intervening variable for the entire synoptic model.

2. CONSCIOUS GOAL-SEEKING AS THE INTERVENING VARIABLE IN A SYNOPTIC MODEL

The *formal identification* of a conscious goal-seeking decision ("cognitive control") as an intervening variable, which intermediates between the stimulus of the independent variables and the response that is observed in the actual behavior, does not resolve the problem of the *substantive identification* of the motives themselves. When Lindzey reviews current assessments of human motives, he concludes that some major issues are not settled. As yet no consensus has been reached about whether one, a few, or many motives should be identified. Most psychologists would probably agree that pure instincts and pure drives are as useless as the previously abandoned concepts of faculties and humors, but, according to Allport, they do not agree about what units of motivation they should use beyond the general notion that such units are "relatively complex structures." Consequently, Allport concludes that "at present, and for some time to come, we must be satisfied to search out the generalized units that define relatively broad forms of organization." [38] Most psychological concepts of such generalized units are no longer confined to the "push of drives," since they also emphasize the "pull of expectations." Accordingly, a conception of behavior which co-ordinates both is needed. Klein has stated quite well what is required in terms of the function of cognitive control in the motivational process: "There needs to be provision for a scheme of regulation that produces structural guarantees of autonomy in a person's behavior; guarantees that ensure that thinking and behavior are products of internal demands, on the one hand, which recruit only certain environmental structures and motor activities for their own requirements; and, on the other, of accommodative processes which are simultaneously responsive to adaptive intentions and to the inherent structural arrangements of things and events." [39]

Tolman's goal-oriented definition of behavior provides a starting point for a reconstruction of such an intraexperiential motivational structure, when he takes behaving to be the operation whereby an organism intends to conquer its environment. "Behavior, which is behavior in our (operational) sense, always seems to have the character of getting-to or getting-from a specific goal-object or goal-situation." Such goal-seeking characterizes the neurophysiological drives and psychodynamic needs out of which conscious purposive operations emerge; but it is only to the kind of behavior that is to some extent immanently determined by what Tolman calls "certain 'inlying' purposes and cognitions" that we are concerned here. When such purposive and cognitive variables are operating, Tolman concludes "they function to produce some sort of modifications or improvements in what were the organism's initially aroused immanent determinants, such that his final behavior, corresponding to these new modified immanent determinants is different from what it otherwise would have been." [40]

If conscious goal-seeking motivation is to be taken as an intervening variable, then a general conception of the complex unity of privately experienced motives is required. Without such a referential context specific motives cannot be identified. This conceptual framework for identifying the persistence of self-identity throughout changing moments of temporal experience is no less a hypothetical construct than is any specified motive that "the psychologist invents in an attempt to explain certain behavior which he observes." [41] To be congruent with the personality construct formulated here, it must presuppose that purposive behavior is "an 'emergent' phenomenon that has descriptive and defining properties of its own" [42] so that it provides a formula for identifying the conscious levels of behavior to which the Watsonian formula of conditioned drives is not applicable. Moreover, the general concept we need here must correlate psychodynamic and learning functions without reducing conscious purposive motivation to nothing but the predetermined effects of unconscious compulsions.

In the contemporary psychological literature there is no concept which is more suitable for this purpose of broadly conceptualizing goal-seeking motivation than Gordon Allport's idea of the "proprium," by which he designates "all the regions of our life that we regard as peculiarly ours." What follows is a paraphrased summary of Allport's "propriate aspects of personality" which as emerging states of awareness constitute the structural context of goal-seeking motivation: (i) *Bodily sense* is not a somatic process but it is one's awareness through organic sensations of one's unity with his own physiological functions which contribute to one's self-awareness. (ii) *Self-identity* is one's awareness of the relation of one's own present experiences with past experience through memory and the awareness of one's self as a result of an awareness of other people which is generated by his interpersonal transaction with them. (iii) *Ego-enhancement* is one's awareness of the self-assertive impulse to satisfy and glorify oneself. (iv) *Ego-extension* is one's awareness of the prizeworthiness of objects, group membership, and ideal causes which he takes to be his very own. (v) *Rational agent* is one's awareness of his own deliberative adjustments in his attempt to solve problems which in a normal personality operates along with the irrational defensive psychodynamisms that generate unconscious compulsions. (vi) *Self-image* is one's awareness both of what his capabilities actually are and of his vision of self-perfection. (vii) As the most distinctive form of reflective goal-seeking motivation, *propriate striving* is one's awareness of his desire for persistently participating in long range enterprises which yields the intrinsic satisfaction of never becoming completely satisfied. (viii) *The knower* is one's experienced awareness of his own cognitive process of making inferences about his own past, his own future, and the external world; but it does not entail the functioning of an unexperienced soul-substance.

Two features of Allport's "proprium" concept should be emphasized. First, though these eight functions have been separated for analysis, no one of them functions independently in the actual experience of goal-seeking behavior; for "at every stage of becoming a fusion of these functions is involved." Secondly, the other seven functions are not strictly motivational but are contributory to the fully motivational variable of *propriate striving*. Consequently, it is with respect to the latter as an intervening variable that Allport's motivational model is most clearly distinguished from the Watsonian and Freudian models in which motivation is conceived in terms of environmentally-created drives or in terms of unconscious compulsions. Instead of conceiving the motivation of conduct that is "ego involved" entirely at the level of a homeostatic process of equilibration for reducing somatic tension or relieving anxiety, Allport concentrates on the higher level of reflective goal-seeking behavior where risk-taking is preferred to stability: "Hence the formula that seems appropriate enough for drive reduction seems to break down when motivation is no longer a matter of segmental drives or of opportunistic adjustment but rather partakes of propriate striving." [43]

The function of a person's goal-oriented conscious motivation in the human value-situation should be more explicitly elaborated in order to distinguish more clearly this intervening variable from the other interpenetrating psychodynamic and interpersonal functions of his personality structure. Conscious motivation is taken here to mean a person's purposive attempt to satisfy emotional desires for some anticipated objective, when that person becomes aware that he desires some goal (cognitive, affective) and strives to realize that objective (conative) in order to satisfy some neurophysiologically-psychodynamically-socioculturally-created drive or need. This common experience of all human individuals can be viewed in terms of its subjective-objective pattern. There is the subjective aspect of *desiring* and the objective aspect of the *desirableness of the goal*. These are necessarily correlative, since a desire always refers to some actual or possible objective and a goal is desirable only if and when some person does (or conceivably could) desire it. Such satisfaction-yielding objectives are, of course, too various to be listed here; but it should be noted that they range from physical objects (apple or cherry pie) to ways of organizing human communities (democracy or totalitarianism) and to states of mind (complacency or persistent striving). When a goal is desired as an end in itself it is called an *intrinsic value*; and when a goal is desired as a means to an end it is called an *instrumental value*. This is a purely functional distinction, however, since the intrinsic or instrumental nature of a goal is relative to a person's desires at a particular time in a specific conjuncture of the "ends-means continuum" (Dewey) which characterizes every human value situation.[44]

Conscious goal-seeking behavior seems to exhibit two general forms of value experiences: *unreflective value experiences*, which are immediate responses to specific stimuli or signs, and *reflective value experiences*, which are delayed responses that are guided by symbols. Since the failure to distinguish between these two separate though interrelated functions is responsible for much needless controversy among social scientists, what each shall mean here needs to be clarified.

An unreflective value is whatever a person desires without any deliberation about whether or not he ought to desire that satisfaction. Unreflective desires for such goals as self-preservation, physical pleasure, or social esteem are a person's responses to the basic drives and needs begotten by his physical-physiological, social-cultural, psychodynamic-interpersonal situations which constitute his complex heredity-environment. Self-preservation (with its associated hunger and thirst compulsions) is, of course, an intrinsic life-goal which all human organisms (with the exception of the pathological suicide) share with every other biological organism. The psychosomatically generated desire for the intrinsic satisfaction of sensual pleasure which is clearly manifested in sexual compulsions is also basic. Similarly, the psychodynamically-interpersonally generated desire for the intrinsic satisfaction of social esteem stems from the will to power as a compensation for an unconscious sense of inferiority. It manifests itself variously in the craving for distinction, or for recognition, or for approval, or for some other kind of appreciation by other people. When a cultural pattern is externalized in the institutions of a religiously and/or politically regimented society, the desires of the socioculturally-determined person are just as unreflective. When a person's behavior is motivated *only* by desires for these intrinsic satisfactions, then it seems reasonable to say that such a person's behavior is predetermined by the independent variables of his complex environment.

A reflective value is whatever a person desires after he deliberates about conflicting unreflective desires and then decides, in the light of his own ideals, that he ought to desire that satisfaction. When a reflective person seeks explanations (intellectual preferences), creatively imagines (aesthetic preferences), acts justly (ethical preferences), and consecrates himself to cooperation with God (religious preferences), the most relevant mental processes are an awareness of better rather than worse, an awareness of commitment to the better, and an awareness of choosing the acknowledged course of action, thought, or feeling. From the motivational side, this construct is endorsed by Allport, when he declares that "in proportion as active schemata for conduct develop they exert a dynamic influence upon specific choices." [45] From the sociocultural side, this construct is endorsed by Kluckhohn when he observes that "it appears to be in the nature of the human animal to strive after ideals as well as mere existence." [46]

Reflective desires for such goals as the intrinsic satisfaction of striving for self-realization or renunciation of one's own effort and submission to the will of God are a person's relatively self-determined responses to socioculturally presented symbols by which he attempts to regulate his thought, conduct, and imagination. This does not imply that a reflectively motivated person is no longer influenced by the independent variables. For whatever may be the degree of autonomy a person achieves by his deliberative selections from among culturally-presented and institutionally-preserved goals, such a reflective decision is always relative to the natural and sociocultural processes that have produced him and the psychological processes that condition his preference for the system of values which he acknowledges as obligating him. The dependence of even the most reflective person's motivation upon these external determinants nothwithstanding, when a reflectively motivated person does things to himself under the conditions and within the limitations of what is done to him, then his own self-creative efforts (intervening variables) participate along with his external determinants (independent variables) in the total process of producing the kind of relatively self-determined person he is becoming.

What is the intrinsic life goal in the purposive striving for which a person might experience an enduring satisfaction of his reflective desires? In western democratic societies the culturally-begotten "design for living" (Kluckhohn) that seems to be most internalized in the goal-seeking orientation of reflective persons is that conception of the highest good which is identified by the axiological construct of self-realization. The person who acknowledges this life plan believes that he finds stimulation and enrichment for himself by cultivating his intellectual curiosity, his enlightened good will, his aesthetic appreciation, and his consecration to a sacred cause (which may be through cooperation with God). Any person, of course, must prize self-preservation; but those who prize self-realization feel that it is required in order to make survival worthwhile. Physical, recreational, familial, and similar enjoyments are prized by the person seeking self-fulfillment just as they are prized by most other people in every culture; but these objectives do not provide a distinctive life style. They do not require the intellectual initiative and moral responsibility in motivating specific decisions which the ideal of self-realization demands. With respect to interpersonal transactions the reflective person's enlightened good will obligates him to help each other person to have the same opportunity for his own self-realization. Accordingly, the ideal aim for the political institutions which externalize this cultural norm is conceived in terms of freedom of opportunity under law and equality of consideration. Competing with self-realization as another culturally-presented alternative life goal in western culture is the concept of the renunciation of human effort and complete submission to the will of God. When a reflective person has mixed loyalties to both of these cultural norms, he is confronted with a basic conflict of intrinsic values. This he must attempt to resolve, if he is to adopt a long-range goal that makes his other reflective value experiences meaningful.

Implicit in this construct of purposive motivation in terms of reflective desiring and striving for the intrinsic satisfaction of self-realization there are two interrelated postulates which should be made explicit: relative self-determinism and "the functional autonomy of motives."

Relative self-determinism is the postulate that a reflectively motivated person may achieve some degree of freedom by making his decisions in accordance with an ideal standard. He has selected it from culturally-presented alternatives and has acknowledged it as more binding on his thought and conduct than any externally imposed obligations. Such autonomy as he may achieve through this self-restraint is always relative both to the somatic, psychological, and sociocultural conditions of his past experience and to the system of values which his conception of an intrinsic life goal entails.

If a social scientist rejects this postulate, he has two alternatives: indeterminism or radical determinism. Since indeterminism means that a person is free to do as he pleases, it renders any conception of motivation meaningless. Since radical determinism means that in some mysterious manner the independent variables make deliberative decisions, it renders meaningless any conception of reflective motivation to select as more reasonably acceptable from alternative hypotheses the one which is best warranted by thought and evidence. Is there one social scientist who would really accept this implication of radical determinism with respect to his own cognitive assertions, even if he professes to have no interest in the concept of self-realization?

By adopting this postulate of relative self-determinism, the social scientist can transcend the fruitless controversy about determinism vs. free will. Murphy speaks for those social scientists who have explicitly recognized the indispensability of this assumption which he calls "soft determinism." Rejecting indeterminism as inapplicable to any conceptual organization of the motivational data which the internal and external pressures on the development of personality involve, Murphy recommends the adoption of "the principle of 'soft' determinism—the participation of the person as cause—as one of the most valuable concepts available." Instead of "hard determinism" which means that "environmental forces can yield only a single result," Murphy assumes that "in the complex interactions which are bound to develop" a person may "slowly develop a relative autonomy, a participation in the causal sequence, based on the influence of his own complex make-up on his conduct." [47]

Without the operation of what Allport has conceptualized as "the functional autonomy of motives" the emergence of reflective motivation in the conscious goal-seeking behavior of relatively self-determined persons would remain a mystery. Consequently, there would be no alternative but to reduce what appears to be some cognitive control by deliberative decision (intervening variable) to the neurophysiological and/or psychodynamic stimuli (independent variables) to which the basic drives and needs of all human organisms are responses. But let us note what Allport's concept means: "The principle of functional autonomy holds (1) that all motives are contemporary, that whatever drives must drive now; that the 'go' of a motive is not bound functionally to its historical origin or to early goals, but to present goals only; (2) that the character of motives alters so radically from infancy to maturity that we may speak of adult motives as supplanting the motives of infancy; (3) that the maturity of personality is measured by the degree of functional auton-omy its motives have achieved; even though in every personality there are archaisms (infantilisms, regressions, reflex responses) still the cultivated and socialized individual shows maturity to the extent he has overcome early forms of motivation; (4) that the differenti-ating course of learning (reflecting ever more diversified environ-mental influence), acting upon divergent temperaments and abilities, creates individualized motives." [48]

In other words, the instrumental values which were previously sought as the means to ends may become intrinsic ends. For, as All-port contends, "people often find that they have lost allegiance to their original aims because of their deliberate preference for the many ways of achieving them." For example, a person who pursues literature in order to satisfy sexual compulsions may come to enjoy it as an intrinsic aesthetic satisfaction "long after the erotic motive has been laid away in lavender." An increasing number of psycholo-gists who have found that a S-R formula about conditioned basic drives is not sufficient for identifying all motivation now agree with Allport that this principle of functional autonomy "helps to account, not for the abstract motivation of an impersonal and therefore non-existent mind-in-general, but for the concrete viable motives of each and every mind-in-particular." [49]

Let us relate this functional autonomy more directly to the goals indicated in our synoptic model. Many instrumental motives which originally served as the means to the satisfaction of unreflective de-sires for survival, physical pleasure, and social esteem (basic drives and needs) may be transformed into intrinsic desires for persons who learn to become more reflective. Consider, for example, the person whose behavior is psychodynamically motivated by a will-to-power compulsion to compensate for an unconscious feeling of inferiority through seeking knowledge as the means of achieving dis-tinction in the eyes of others. If that person becomes more secure, however, he may continue to seek to satisfy his intellectual curiosity as an intrinsic enjoyment.

This discussion of the intervening variable must be concluded with a caveat. All that has been claimed here is that conscious goal-seeking motivation is an essential function in the total behavioral process which the synoptic model is designed to identify. Beyond acknowledging the necessity of such a conceptual construct, however, very little psychological analysis has been done with respect to the operation of reflective thinking on which the purposive realization of ideal values depends. Tolman refers to thinking as "some internal type of process"; but he admits that "satisfactory psychological studies of this *process* are as yet, I would submit, almost nil." [50] Similarly, Murray contends that "we should include *mental needs,* as well as somatic, material, and social needs, in our inventory of human motivation." By this he means "mental aims—say, to observe events and acquire representations of the environment and of cause-and-effect relations, and to make plans," which in the goal-seeking behavior of some people "occupy a superordinate position." But, like Tolman, he concludes that "among the significant variables which await adequate definition is the *phase* of needful, or motivational, activity with which one is dealing, especially the prospective and decision-making phase as contrasted with the phase of actuation or endeavor." [51]

Only if and when psychologists develop adequate constructs for understanding the reflective processes of deliberative decision-making, will the intervening variable of "purposive and cognitive determinants" [52] be taken to function in the manner that this synoptic model conceptualizes. Though it is programmatic, reflective goal-seeking cannot justifiably be omitted in any comprehensive calculus of determinants.

Footnotes to Chapter 3 of Part Two

[1] Tolman, "A Psychological Model," *Toward a General Theory of Action* (Parsons and Shils), 279.

[2] Parsons and Shils, *Toward a General Theory of Action* (Parsons and Shils), 7. Cf. pages 16-26, 27, 30-31, 34, 42, 50-51, 53, 54-61, 247, 279, 359. Our indebtedness to the Parsons-Shils conceptual framework will become obvious. In addition to some modifications to be noted later, our expansion of their account lies chiefly in our development of the areas to which social psychology, economics, political science, and history pertain.

[3] Dobzhansky, "Inside Human Nature," *Frontiers of Knowledge in the Study of Man* (White), 8-9.

4 Kluckhohn and Murray, *Personality in Nature, Society and Culture*, 56.
5 Murphy, *Personality*, 52.
6 Sheldon in *Toward a General Theory of Action* (Parsons and Shils), 30.
7 Parsons and Shils, *Toward a General Theory of Action*, 63. Cf. *Toward a Unified Theory of Human Behavior* (Grinker), Chapters 1, 2, 12, 17, 18, 19.
8 Parsons, "Sociocultural and Personality Systems," *Toward a Unified Theory of Human Behavior* (Grinker), 326.
9 Kroeber and Parsons, "The Concepts of Culture and of Social System," *American Sociological Review*, Oct. 1958.
10 For source materials which are relevant to our elaboration of this conceptual construct of culture, see Linton, *The Cultural Background of Personality*, 20-26, 32, Chapter 5; Bidney, *Theoretical Anthropology*, 62, 75-84, 117, 130, 140, 328, 334; Parsons in *For a Science of Social Man* (Gillin), 71; Kluckhohn in *The Policy Sciences* (Lerner and Lasswell), 86-101; Romero in *Ideological Differences and World Order* (Northrop), 391-392.
11 For source material that amplifies this formulation, see Parsons in *Toward a General Theory of Action* (Parsons and Shils), 191, 197 and in *Toward A Unified Theory of Human Behavior* (Grinker), 325-339; MacIver, *Social Causation*, 273; Lundberg, *Foundations of Sociology*, 375-376; Chapin, *Contemporary American Institutions*, 13-16; Sorokin, *Society, Culture, Personality*, 7; Bierstedt, *The Social Order*, 171-188; Newcomb, *For a Science of Social Man* (Gillin), 253-254; Hocking, *Human Nature and Its Remaking*, 304-321.
   The distinction between the "private order" and the "public order" above corresponds to the common distinction by sociologists between "primary groups" and "secondary groups." Tonnies made this distinction by contrasting "Gemeinschaft" and "Gesellschaft."
12 Sapir, "Personality," *Encyclopedia of the Social Sciences*, Vol. 12, pp. 85-87.
13 Since neither psychologists, nor philosophers, agree about what is meant by experience, all social scientists cannot be expected to agree on the meaning here. However, the *gestalt* and *purposive* features of this conception of experience are becoming increasingly acknowledged. With respect to the *gestalt* feature, note Köhler's claim: "We are aware of definite and very completely organized contexts. There are not separately: a self, an interest, and many things in the field, but, surrounded by many other items a self-interested-in-one-definite-thing." (*The Place of Value in a World of Facts*, 75). With respect to the purposive feature note Gordon Allport's claim: "The most comprehensive units in personality are broad intentional dispositions, future pointed. These characteristics are unique for each person, and tend to attract, guide, inhibit the more elementary units to accord with the major intentions themselves. This proposition is valid in spite of the large amount of unordered, impulsive, and conflictful behavior in every life." (*Becoming*, 92). For philosophical conceptions of experience which emphasize these features of experience, see Whitehead, *Modes of Thought*, 221-222 and *Process and Reality*, 288; Brightman, *Moral Laws*, 79; Lewis, *Mind and the World Order*, 25-26; and McEwen, *Enduring Satisfaction*, 62, 217-218, 245, 247, 255-256.
   This conception of the nature and operational use of the construct of personality for identifying motivational data seems to be justified in the following

statements by social scientists. With respect to the nature of the construct of personality, Kluckhohn and Murray declare: "The *establishments* and processes which constitute personality are out of sight, but their characteristics, relations, and operations can be defined and conceptualized on the basis of the subject's verbal reports (memories of events, introspective judgments, and avowals) and on the basis of observations of his overt behaviors, physical and verbal. Thus the psychologist is directly concerned only with the manifestations of personality, *the facts*. The personality is something that must be inferred from the facts. Hence, in actual practice, the personality is an abstract formulation composed by the psychologist." (*Personality in Nature, Society, and Culture*, 6). With respect to the operational use of the construct, note Kardiner's estimate of "the concept of basic personality structure as an operational tool in the social sciences," when he emphasizes that "the operational value of the concept of basic personality is not only to diagnose the factors which mold the personality but also to furnish some clues about why these influences are what they are." (*The Science of Man in the World Crisis* [Linton], 121).

14 See Lewin, "The Nature of Field Theory," *Psychological Theory* (Marx), 301, 308; A *Dynamic Theory of Personality*, 41; "The Conceptual Representation and Measurement of Psychological Forces." For an excellent analysis of Lewin's view, see Deutsch, "Field Theory in Social Psychology," *Handbook of Social Psychology* (Lindzey), Vol. I, Chapter 5. For discussions which bear on the relevance of Lewin's theory for the concept of a personality construct, see Smith in *For a Science of Social Man* (Gillin), 52-53; Lindzey, *The Assessment of Human Motives*, 24-26; and Kluckhohn and Murray, *Personality in Nature, Society, and Culture*, 14-15; 17, 23, 35, 39. In the latter book Lewin's *vectors*, i.e., action tendencies, are spelled out as: "1) rejection, 2) reception, 3) acquisition, 4) construction, 5) conservation, 6) expression, 7) transmission, 8) elimination, 9) destruction, 10) dependence, 11) avoidance." (23)

For other discussions pertaining to the psychological environment, see Murphy, *Personality*, 18, 30, 714-715; O'Kelly, *An Introduction to Psychopathology*, 465, 554, 459-460; and Tolman in *Toward a General Theory of Action* (Parsons and Shils), 285-302. Tolman's use of *drive*, when the motivation is predominantly psychological, will be followed through this study.

15 For passages quoted from Freud see his *New Introductory Lectures on Psycho-Analysis*, 105; *Three Contributions to the Theory of Sex*, 611; *An Autobiographical Study*, 63; and *Leonardo Da Vinci: A Study in Psycho-Sexuality*, 46. For instructive expositions of Freud's view, see Healy, Bronner, Bowers, *The Structure and Meaning of Psychoanalysis; Handbook of Social Psychology* (Lindzey), Vol. I, Chapter 4 for "Psychoanalytic Theory and its Application in the Social Sciences" by Hall and Lindzey. Among other things, Freud's conception of the "death instinct" has not been included here.

16 Newcomb, *Social Psychology*, 376.

17 Fromm, "Individual and Social Origins of Neuroses," *Personality in Nature, Society, and Culture* (Kluckhohn, Murray, Schneider), 518-519.

18 Horney, *The Neurotic Personality of Our Time*.

19 Jung, *The Integration of Personality*, 269. For a more extended analysis of

Jung's view which was presented above, with further bibliographical references to Jung's works, see McEwen, *Enduring Satisfaction*, 21-31.

20 Smith, "Psychology and Anthropology," *For a Science of Social Man* (Gillin), 38. For Rapaport's "Conceptual Model of Psychoanalysis," see *Theoretical Models and Personality Theory* (Krech and Klein), 56-81. For Shakow's "The Psychological System," see *Toward a Unified Theory of Human Behavior* (Grinker), 27-35. See *The Assessment of Human Motives* (Lindzey); Chapter 5 for Schafer's "Regression in the Service of the Ego: the Relevance of a Psychoanalytic Concept for Personality Assessment"; and Chapter 6 for Janis' "The Psychoanalytic Interview as an Observational Method." Cf. Kluckhohn and Murray, *Personality in Nature, Society, and Culture*, 23-28. Lindzey and Hall survey the influence of psychoanalytical concepts on the social-scientific disciplines other than psychology in *The Handbook of Social Psychology* (Lindzey), Vol. I, 170-175. For further information about the utilization of psychoanalytical concepts, see Murphy, *Historical Introduction to Modern Psychology*, Chapter 22, and *Personality*, 540-593. Cf. O'Kelly, *Introduction to Psychopathology*, 49-54, 488-495, 618-624, 633-640. For critical analyses of the methodological issues which a correlation of psychoanalysis and psychology entails, see *Psychological Theory* (Marx), 332-351 for Kris' "Psychoanalytic Propositions"; 352-370 for Bergmann's "*Psychoanalysis and Experimental Psychology*"; 460-469 for Alexander's "Principles of Psychosomatic Research." For Tolman's utilization of psychodynamic principles, see his "Psychological Model," in *Toward a General Theory of Action* (Parsons and Shils), 307-308; and for Tolman's comparison of "learning" with the "psychological dynamisms," see his *Drives Toward War*, 53-112.

21 Allport in *Handbook of Social Psychology* (Lindzey), Vol. I, 4-5.

22 Parsons in *Toward a Unified Theory of Human Behavior* (Grinker), 190.

23 Ruesch in *Toward a Unified Theory of Human Behavior* (Grinker), 347-348.

24 Murray, "Toward a Classification of Interactions," *Toward a General Theory of Action* (Parsons and Shils), 438; and *Personality in Nature, Society, and Culture* (Kluckhohn, Murray, Schneider), 9-10.

25 Kantor, "Interbehavioral Psychology," *Psychological Theory* (Marx), 321 and 323.

26 Newcomb, *Social Psychology*, 407. See Chapter 11 for the psychoanalytical contributions to social psychology.

27 *Ibid.*, *Social Psychology*, 88, 132. See McDougall, *Introduction to Social Psychology*, 30. Cf. Brown, *Social Psychology*, 12.

28 *Ibid.*, *Social Psychology*, 26-27, 30. Cf. Dewey and Humber, *The Development of Human Behavior*, 9.

29 *Ibid.*, *Social Psychology*, 80, 97, 119-120, 197.

30 Allport in *Handbook of Social Psychology* (Lindzey), Vol. I, 43.

31 Asch, *Social Psychology*, 5, 563-571, 584. Asch claims that social psychologists have not yet been entirely successful in transcending the instinct-habit dichotomy. (75)

32 Newcomb, *Social Psychology*, 328, 330, 332-333, 629; and in *For a Science of Social Man* (Gillin), 247-254. Cf. Sarbin in *Handbook of Social Psychology* (Lindzey), Vol. I, 56.

A Synoptic Model   (181

33 Asch, *Social Psychology*, 162-163.
34 Murphy, *Personality*, 8, 9, 20-21, and 891. Cf. Newcomb, *Social Psychology*, 337, 339-346, 411, 482-483, 629-630; Asch, *Social Psychology*, Ch. 13; Allport, *The Nature of Personality*, 115, 122, 136-137; Sarbin in *Handbook of Social Psychology* (Lindzey), Vol. I, 223-253.
35 Kluckhohn, Murray, Schneider, *Personality in Nature Society, and Culture*, 46.
36 Fromm, *Man for Himself*, 9-91.
37 Kelly, "Man's Construction of His Alternatives," *Assessment of Human Motives* Lindzey), 56.
38 Allport, "What Units Shall We Employ," *Assessment of Human Motives* (Lindzey), 242.
39 Klein, "Cognitive Control and Motivation," *Assessment of Human Motives* (Lindzey), 91.
40 Tolman, "Molar and Purposive Behaviorism," *Psychological Theory* (Marx), 87, 413-416, 418, 424-425. See Tolman, "A Psychological Model," *Toward a General Theory of Action* (Parsons and Shils), 343, 346, for a discussion of the cognitive and purposive determinants in terms of intellectual, aesthetic, and moral values which, when activated, become a part of a person's motivation.
A terminological point should be noted here. MacCorquodale and Meehl have insisted that there should be a distinction between "intervening variable" (as having no factual reference) and "hypothetical construct" (as having a factual reference). For purposes of this synoptic model this distinction does not seem important, especially since Tolman, as well as other psychologists to whom reference is made in connection with this motivational construct, do not follow it. (See *Psychological Theory* (Marx), 110-11. Cf. Tolman, *Toward a General Theory of Action* (Parsons and Shils), 281, 283, 288, 334-335. Also cf. Lindzey, *Assessment of Human Motives*, 22-24.)
41 See Festinger, "The Motivating Effect of Cognitive Dissonance," *Assessment of Human Motives* (Lindzey), 66.
42 Tolman, "Molar and Purposive Behaviorism," *Psychological Theory* (Marx), 413-414.
43 See Allport, *Becoming*, 40-54, 56, 66-67. See Allport in *Psychological Theory* (Marx), 161-166, for his earlier expression of dissatisfaction with "a stimulus-expectancy need-cathexis" principle for reducing tension as a characterization of goal-oriented motivation, e.g., Hull's "anticipatory goal reactions." Tolman's rejection of a conception of behavior in neurophysiological terms and his correlation of psychodynamisms with conscious learning processes seems to make his conception of motivation similar to Allport's. (See Tolman, "A Psychological Model" in *Toward a General Theory of Action* (Parsons and Shils), 279 ff., and Tolman, *Drives Toward War*, 53-69, 95-112.) This general consensus about motivation notwithstanding, Allport is not quite satisfied that Tolman's concept of "expectancy" is strong enough to bring out all that is required for "propriate striving."
For an ingenious philosophical concept of the "procept" which seems to correspond to Allport's psychological concept of the "proprium" see Buchler, *Nature and Judgment*, 122-123.
44 It is likely that most, if not all, social scientists would endorse this conception

of conscious motivation in terms of value experience. In his most instructive analysis of the views of many social scientists about the function of values and value-orientation in human behavior, Kluckhohn concludes that "any given act is seen as a compromise between motivation, situational conditions, available means, and the means and goals as interpreted in value terms." (*Toward a General Theory of Action*, [Parsons and Shils], 403.) Kluckhohn's findings support Murphy's earlier conclusion that "throughout the study of motives and the learning process we have been finding out not only that individuals want different things, but that they set up complex personal systems of wants which are relatively enduring and are maintained in the absence of external reminders; they carry around with themselves personal systems of values" so that "personality is in large measure the personal value system." (*Personality*, 270.)

A considerable number of psychologists who subscribe to this goal-oriented conception of motivation might hesitate to endorse the word "satisfaction," since it is more fashionable to use the negative terms expressing the reduction of drive compulsions, the release of tensions, the relief from anxieties, etc. This kind of terminology more accurately expresses what is discovered through experimentation which applies only to value situations in which the "push" of drives but not the "pull" of intrinsic satisfaction-yielding goals can be manipulated. Although Murray himself contends that intrinsic satisfactions are "as real as determining as anything that numbers can express," he attributes the contemporary reluctance to use these terms to the influence of the Puritan ethic to prize effort for reward and "because it appears to be impossible to translate the formal determinants of intrinsic satisfactions into numbers and equations." (*Assessment of Human Motives* [Lindzey], 195-196.)

45 Allport, *Becoming*, 75-76. Cf. page 22 for Allport's concept of man's distinctive desire for "life style."

46 Kluckhohn, "Values and Value-Orientations," *Toward a General Theory of Action* (Parsons and Shils), 432. See pages 388-433. In *The Policy Sciences* (Lerner and Lasswell), 87, Kluckhohn analyzes the culture-in-personality factors involved here.

47 Murphy, *Personality*, 645. For representatives from each of the other social sciences who also subscribe to this principle of relative self-determinism, see MacIver, *Social Causation*, Chapter 8; Bidney, *Theoretical Anthropology*, 9-14; Clark, *The Ethical Basis of Economic Freedom*, 4; Garceau, *American Political Science Review*, Vol. 45, 1951, pp. 69-70; Tapp, "Historical Causation," *Journal of Philosophy*, Vol. 49, Jan. 3, 1952, pp. 73-74.

48 Allport, *The Nature of Personality*, 104. Originally published in *Psychological Review*, 47, No. 6, Nov. 1940, page 545.

49 Allport, *Personality*, 197 and *The Nature of Personality*, 89-91. Allport's principle of functional autonomy is explicitly referred to by Tolman, when he relates the functions of learning to psychic dynamisms. (*Drives Toward War*, 95 ff.) The same idea is expressed by Klein when he claims that through the cognitive control of motivation "the organism's behavior moves toward achieving freedom from the selective tyranny of drive aims." Recognizing that "autonomy from drive aims and from stimulation can be only relative," Klein

insists, nevertheless, that "drive aims always implicate instrumental and accommodative structures of thought." (*Assessment of Human Motives* [Lindzey], 100.) Murray similarly endorses Allport's principle of functional autonomy and adds what he calls "the principle of subsidation." This means that with a person's development with age of a larger system of needs "motives which were once autonomous become subordinated to a few major purposes." (*Assessment of Human Motives* [Lindzey], 185-186.) Cf. Murray in *Toward a General Theory of Action* (Parsons and Shils), 443. Tolman refers to these acquired functionally autonomous motives as "tertiary needs for culturally provided goals" which as "the product of learning" are distinguishable from "primary needs, i.e., basic hungers and avoidance" and from "secondary or socio-relational needs, such as affiliation (need for love and approval), dominance, dependence, submission and the like." Primary viscerogenic hungers, as well as fear and aggression, and the secondary needs "are either innate or acquired so early in life that they do not reflect enculturalization." (Tolman, "A Psychological Model," *Toward a General Theory of Action* [Parsons and Shils], 321, 335-336. Originally published in the *American Journal of Psychology*, 50, 1937, page 156.)

50 Tolman, "A Psychological Model," *Toward a General Theory of Action* (Parsons and Shils), 357.
51 Murray, "Drive, Time, Strategy, Measurement, and Our Way of Life," *Assessment of Human Motives* (Lindzey), 184. Cf. Kluckhohn and Murray, *Personality in Nature, Society, and Culture*, 11-21.
52 Tolman, "Molar and Purposive Behaviorism," *Psychological Theory* (Marx), 418.

4 *Further Elaboration of a Synoptic Model*

It is necessary, but not sufficient, to identify the behavioral process in terms of the independent and intervening variables we have discussed. Thus far, we have confined ourselves to sociocultural and motivational factors, with which the sociologist, anthropologist, and psychologist are concerned. We must now consider the diachronic process and the technological order, with which the historian, the economist, and the political scientist are concerned.

A. *The Diachronic Process*

This conceptual construct is designed to identify the temporal continuity or duration of human events as the broadest constant factor which encompasses all the situational independent variables, as well as the intervening variable of a reflective person's relatively self-determined motivation in which his present self-creative decision emerges out of antecedent experience and anticipates the realization of future goals. MacIver explicitly acknowledges this defining characteristic of behavioral data: "the universe is a changeful scheme of events and processes," and he explains that "when it changes gradually we call it process" but "when it changes with seeming abruptness . . . we call it event." [1] Without this double-edged reference of contemporary events to their past and to their future, the data of history, political science, and economics could not be identified or correlated within the conceptual framework of a synoptic model. History is unintelligible apart from the concept of antecedent processes through time; and the political and economic manipulation of the means for implementing policy decisions necessarily refers to ends that are projected in anticipation of future states of human affairs.

Before we undertake an elaboration of the construct of the diachronic process as a conceptual characterization of historiographical data, let us first show why this concept of the temporal passage of events is also presupposed in the conceptual framework of the motivational-sociocultural data for psychology, sociology, and anthropology. Thus far their constructs have been predominantly presented in a synchronic perspective as if they were generalizations about simultaneous interactions without temporal dimensions. At this point, however, it is most emphatically maintained that a diachronic-synchronic continuum is essential for a synoptic model of the behavioral process. It is just as indispensable as Einstein's time-space continuum is for the physical model in accordance with which "the concepts of empirical science are reducible to the properties of the spatio-temporal things." [2] Regardless of whether or not sociocultural-motivational events have spatial dimensions, they all are characterized by development through time.

With respect to motivation, Kelly takes the temporal directionality of motion to be the defining characteristic of human experience. In fact, he recommends that psychology abandon its efforts to construct human motives, if the diachronic process is not taken to be a constant factor: "If we want to know why man does what he does, then the terms of our why should extend themselves in time rather than in space; they should be events rather than things; they should be mileposts rather than destinations." [3]

Despite the sociological emphasis upon synchronic structures that can be analyzed without their temporal discussions, sociologists do not ignore the diachronic nature of the sociocultural process. Parsons, a theoretician, insists that the "means-ends schema of action" must be taken to be "non-spatial but temporal." [4] Lazarsfeld, an empirical researcher, contends that "the formation of variables, the study of their interrelations, and the analysis of their change through time form the backbone of all social research." [5]

Anthropologists are more concerned about diachronic development than they appear to be. Social functionalists may agree with Malinowski that "until the nature of the various cultural phenomena, their function and their form are understood and described more fully, it seems premature to speculate on possible origins and stages." [6] However, many more anthropologists today seem to take the temporal dimension of the sociocultural process to be a constant factor. Herskovits, for example, insists that "changes constantly take place as generation succeeds generation, and new ideas, new alignments, new techniques come into the thinking of its members." [7] Nadel makes the diachronic factor even more explicit, when he reminds anthropologists that "nothing in the sphere of social facts is really static and 'regularity' in behavior is only visible over a period of time." [8]

Whereas it is the backward reference of the diachronic process to completed past actions of a "vanished past" that identifies historical data; it is the forward reference of the diachronic process toward possible future actions of the potential future that identifies the policy-oriented data of political science and economics. In the next section the political administration and the economic allocation of means to ends will be identified in terms of separate but interrelated constructs of the technological operations for regulating the sociocultural-motivational factors in the behavioral process. At this point we merely note how these two disciplines require the construct of the diachronic process in the Parsonian sense of "action time as a mode of relation of means and ends." [9]

Obviously the diachronic process is important for those political scientists who were or still are primarily concerned about the historical development of political institutions and those who emphasize normative ideas about what kind of political organization provides the conditions required for realizing the ethical ideal of what human relations ought to be in the future. With the more recent growth of interest in the sociocultural-motivational factors involved in political behavior and power relations, it would appear that political scientists would become more synchronic in their utilization of the causal and statistical techniques of the other social sciences in order to reach analytical generalizations which are both atemporal and value-free. While this seems to be the case to some extent, some political scientists retain their historical and normative interests along with their analytical interest. Moreover, the political scientist is likely to discover that the temporal dimension is still a factor to be reckoned with in the other disciplines from which he is borrowing concepts and techniques.

The forward reference of the diachronic construct pervades the thinking of those political scientists who have combined their causal and statistical concepts of behavior and power with the axiological concepts of policy planning for the future. According to Lasswell, who himself has skillfully coordinated these analytical and policy approaches in his own research, "the policy orientation carries with it a sharpened sense of time" not only "in the selection of a policy-oriented project" but also in the extrapolation of trends: "No sooner do you become interested in future goals than you look sharply into the present and the past in order to discover the degree in which trends approximate values." [10]

The involvement of the diachronic construct in economics is paradoxical. On the one hand, forward *action time* as "a mode of the relation of means and ends" (Parsons) is the defining characteristic of the operation which all economists accept as their initial datum; i.e., the allocation of scarce resources for alternative uses. In addition to this future-orientation of the contemporary data, every economist would probably agree with J. J. Spengler that the historian's time dimension must be taken into account, since "the milieu within which men behave economically has evolved within the womb of time and is, in effect, the residual deposit of past time." [11] Moreover, that concepts of economic change presuppose the diachronic development of dynamic systems seems to be brought out in Samuelson's statement that "a system is dynamical if its behavior over time is determined by functional equations in which 'variables at different points of time' are involved in an 'essential' way." [12]

On the other hand, the orthodox economist abstracts from the actual behavioral process only those variables which can be dealt with as if their contemporary intercorrelated operations were completely devoid of the temporal dimensions of the actual sociocultural-motivational process. Now probably no economist today accepts literally this neo-classical conception of a closed system of equilibrium in which autonomous economic forces automatically readjusted minor disturbances in accordance with the law of supply and demand. But its resistance to the diachronic factor seems to pervade contemporary economic thought enough to elicit criticism from institutional and quasi-institutional economists who feel that sacrificing the temporal dimension of the changing sociocultural process is too great a price for the analytical precision that the synchronic concept of a static economic system allows. Gruchy emphasizes the need felt by many economists for taking the diachronic process as the basic property of economic data: "Just as an 'event' in the natural order is taken by Alfred N. Whitehead to be something which incorporates the past, present, and future, so likewise economic activity is investigated by the holistic economists from a similar three-dimensional viewpoint." [13] Ruggles agrees when he endorses the "operation through time" [14] of Samuelson's "dynamic process analysis," without which "there is little possibility of presenting a reasonably realistic description of such phenomena as speculation, cyclical fluctuation, and secular growth." [15]

If the synoptic model did not include this diachronic orientation, the field of historiographical data could not be conceptually identified and correlated with the fields of other social scientific disciplines. Since "the fundamental problem of historical study is the anaylsis of change over time," as Aitken and Loewenberg declare it to be, the concept of a continuity in the ongoing process of temporally related events "must be *in* the analysis in the beginning." These historians recognize that events may be related in other ways, but, as historical data, they "are events that are related by their position in time." [16] Such particular actions and situations that occurred at and through specific past times would not be meaningful, if behavioral referents could only be identified synchronically in terms of generalized patterns about similarities which had been abstracted from the concrete continuity of chronologically separated events.

When Clough identifies the historian's data as "human activity through time," then it is meaningful for the historian to use, but to subordinate synchronic consideration of similarities in "the structure of relationships and interactions" to his primary diachronic consideration of continuity in the "process of change," i.e., "to ascertain what has happened, to identify events in sequence, to analyze interrelationships among those events, and to discover how and why they occurred in a given order." [17] Obviously, this requires the historian's search for a causal pattern in the process of past events. But, as Aitken and Loewenberg insist, unlike those social scientists who conceive of causation in terms of static models which "push the problem of time into the background," for the historian "the element of time can never be a somewhat inconvenient and unmanageable 'fourth dimension' to be introduced almost as an afterthought in the final stages of the analysis." [18] For the historian, as for Whitehead, the temporal process of becoming is taken to be the defining characteristic of reality.

This independently operating temporal process of constantly changing events should not be confused with the humanly determined clock-time in terms of which the ongoing passage of past, present, and future happenings is measured. Seconds, minutes, hours, days, weeks, months, years, centuries, epochs, etc. are nothing more than artificial devices for dealing with the actual conformation of events in passage.

B. *The Technological Order*

The conceptual construct of the technological order is designed to identify the operations by which groups of individuals regulate instrumental values. These serve as the means to the ends which predominantly determine the goal-seeking orientation of the members of a community. MacIver's conception of what constitutes these technological operations is adopted here: "Comprising the patterns, interadjustments, and trends of the multiplicity of devices, instruments, and technical skills applied to the achievement of human valuations and goals." According to MacIver, these technological functions are exhibited "in the industrial arts, the arts of engineering and design, economic systems of production and distribution, military systems of attack and defense, political agencies of control and manipulation, and broadly in the cumulative though ever-changing apparatus of civilization." [19]

Of these various operations in the technological order, the administrative interadjustments of the political process and the allocative interadjustments of the economic process are selected as the most relevant constructs for our synoptic model. The nature and significance of the other technological factors which MacIver includes are more relevant for another kind of model which would identify and correlate technological devices which are "primarily designed to control things." Since we are more concerned with those factors which "are primarily designed to control the relationships of men with respect to things," we shall confine our attention to the political and economic operations which aim at regulating "the basic technology." [20]

A political-economic system is both the product and the producer of the sociocultural process which it regulates. With respect to their sociocultural functioning the political and economic operations are independent variables. With respect to their motivational functioning in the means-end continuum of goal-seeking behavior the policy decisions are intervening variables. At least this seems to be the case when these policy decisions are deliberately implemented by the selection of the appropriate means which are required for the realization of consciously sought ends which in turn are selected from among culturally-presented alternatives. This does not mean the complex political-economic process in any community has been completely contrived. But it does mean that apart from some purposive selection there could hardly emerge any administrative and allocative functions.

1. ADMINISTRATIVE INSTRUMENTATION

The conceptual construct of administrative instrumentation is designed to identify the political process by which the instrumental values of goal-seeking transactions are authoritatively distributed throughout an entire community. The crucial ingredients of this political process are power, influence, authority, and the motivation of leading and following, as well as the political parties, public opinion, and pressure groups which affect those who make and administer policy decisions. Lasswell focuses attention on this regulation of means for ends when he identifies the aim of the political process as that of determining "who gets what, when, and how." Easton, it will be recalled, conceptualizes the essence of political behavior as "the authoritative allocation of values for a whole society." These are not the intrinsic values which are symbolized in a cultural pattern which a person internalizes. Rather, these are the instrumental values which provide the opportunity to realize the intrinsic goals. But, as Easton insists, the political scientist must adopt some concept of "what kind of goals ought men to seek" in order that he might know "what steps ought the society to take to put them into effect as an authoritative statement of policy." [21]

The indispensability of administrative instrumentation in the goal-oriented behavior of sociocultural animals was emphasized by Aristotle, when he declared that "as the state was formed to make life possible, so it exists to make life good." In other words, every government aims not only to provide security as the means for survival but also to provide whatever other means are required for the realization of the intrinsic ends which a given community prizes as the goals that make survival worthwhile. To be sure, some non-governmental institutions, such as the home, church, and school, do, in varying degrees, regulate these opportunities. But, as Perry contends, it is the function of the political institutions "to bring order into, or to maintain equilibrium among the lesser institutions and groups." [22]

Does the conceptual construct of administrative instrumentation exhibit the functional interdependence of independent and intervening variables? We have previously indicated that it must be taken this way, if it is to fit congruently in our synoptic model. It seems that some political scientists would say that it does so. Elliot, for one, contends against one-sided determinism that "the purposes that men shape in terms of their ability to compare the results of previous experience with desired goals comes into play in any real political situation." [23] Easton, for another, explicitly seeks to correlate the independent and intervening variables: "To explain the determinants of any particular political act, we need to know not only the various circumstances or objective conditions surrounding it, but also the kind of personality, the improperly called 'subjective conditions' that individuals bring to the activity." [24]

The *situational relativism*, which this coordination of independent and intervening variables entails, is clearly advocated by Merriam, when he rejects the racial, geographical, or economic "determinism of personal and social action." In opposition to radical relativism, therefore, he thus identifies political operations: "All governments are set in social patterns and cultural patterns, in which the aspira-

tions and interests of men are experienced and developed." Although
other sociocultural institutions contribute to providing different degrees of external security, internal order, justice, general welfare and
freedom, it is the aim of the state to strengthen and integrate these
efforts by "making possible the fullest and highest development of
the human personality in the framework of social relations." [25]

The conceptual construct of administrative instrumentation is designed to provide a purpose for coordinating the structural and functional aspects of political power. The structural aspect of political
power refers to its substantive sense of authority; its functional aspect
refers to its relational sense of influence. The latter is what Key has
in mind when he claims that "the common denominator is to be
found in the reciprocal relations of governors and governed, which
are relations of power." The purpose which coordinates such authority and influence is to answer the question: Power for what? If the
political scientist conceives the function of power within the framework of the means-end continuum of action, he can adopt Key's answer: "Yet by and large power is a means, an indispensable means to
other ends" which "find expression in public policy, notably in legislation." [26]

2. ALLOCATIVE INSTRUMENTATION

The conceptual construct of allocative instrumentation is designed
to identify the selective function in the economic aspect of the
means-ends continuum of goal-oriented transactions which pertains
to securing a livelihood. The applicability of such a Parsonian "action frame of reference" in terms of "the *act*, the *agent*, the *end*, and
the *situation*" has been emphasized by Papandreou: "The agent is
engaged in action which maximizes a utility index (an ordinally
structured preference system), given the constraints inherent in the
situation." [27] When we use allocative instrumentation to identify the
economic function of disposing of scarce resources among alternative
means for obtaining material ends, we should heed Parson's warning:
"Allocation is a resultant that is only in part a product of deliberate
decision," since "the total allocation in a social system especially
may be the product of many processes that culminate in a distribu-

tion which no individual or collective actor in the system has sought." [28]

The allocation of scarce means in the public transactions of exchange, production, distribution, and consumption has been the defining characteristic of the economic operations in both the orthodox and unorthodox interpretations. When the neo-classical economist postulates a static equilibrium system that operates in accordance with the law of supply and demand, he must assume that a rational actor, who is always motivated to maximize satisfaction and minimize effort, will select the means required for realizing his preferred ends of survival, and/or pleasure, and/or prestige. Even though Polanyi seeks to transfer attention from these narrowly circumscribed concepts of rational motivation and market exchange to the universal process of an empirical economy, he retains the allocation of instrumental values as his key construct.

Let us look more closely at Polanyi's reconstructed concept of allocative instrumentation in an empirical economy. He defines the latter as "an institutionalized process between men and their natural and social environment in the course of which they secure their livelihood." Accordingly, he assumes that ecological adjustments to the resources of the natural environment, the technological adjustments to the availability of mechanical equipment, and institutional adjustments to a specific social setting are the interdependent functions of natural, sociocultural, and motivational variables. Taken together they relate economic actions to the goal-oriented behavioral process as a whole. But even Polanyi concedes that there could be no separable though interrelated economic dimension of human actions bearing on "material want satisfactions" without an allocation of the means for realizing individual preferences. The alternatives from which individual selections can be made are limited, of course, by the scarcity of natural resources, as well as by the "culture, the motivations and valuations of which permeate the society." [29]

As long as there is any scarcity of the natural resources which are required to meet human needs for food, clothing, and shelter, the technological construct of economic allocation is essential in any synoptic model of the behavioral process. Like other unorthodox economists, Kapp opposes the neo-classicist's abstract conception of allocative instrumentation, when he calls for a "humanization of economics" by "placing the living human being once more in the center of economic analysis" through correlating economic concepts with the motivational and sociocultural construct of other behavioral disciplines. Kapp insists, nevertheless, that social science can not fully identify behavioral data without taking into account the allocation of scarce means to which economists direct attention: "The environment offers the potential means for the gratification of recurrent needs not freely but only at the price of overcoming various resistances by human efforts and improved techniques." [30]

A synoptic conceptualization of behavioral data is incongruent with technological determinism; but, the essential function of allocative instrumentation cannot be left out of account. Technological changes, political legislation, culturally-begotten ideals of justice, and other sociocultural and motivational factors reciprocally influence each other as the conditions of policy decisions. But whatever may be the other specifiable factors in the total goal-orientation of a given community, the inexorable demands imposed by scarce resources for satisfying material wants must always be met by some kind of allocation.

C. *Broadly Operational Modes of Analysis Required by the Synoptic Model*

1. INTEGRATION WITH RELATIVE AUTONOMY

When behavioral data are conceptually identified and correlated synoptically in terms of the interrelated functioning of independent and intervening variables, the broader operationalist is compelled to reject an arbitrary claim that isolates any "one and only one" causal determinant. It precludes, therefore, that cultural patterns and motivations can be reduced to institutions, or that motivation can be considered apart from sociocultural conditions, or that cultural patterns are so autonomous that they operate independently of the persons who create, transmit, learn, and internalize them, or that cultural patterns can be understood apart from the social institutions without which they would have no influence or continuity. Our synoptic model is designed to eliminate oversimplified observational constructs which block the channels of cooperative social-scientific inquiry by arbitrarily delimiting behavioral data. The field of each of the specific disciplines is recognized as a separable but interconnected dimension of the total behavioral process.

This does not mean that overcircumscribed observational constructs have no place in social-scientific inquiry. Indeed, they are useful for limited investigations in which the investigator must concentrate on a narrow aspect of the behavioral process as long as he acknowledges his delimitation. Unfortunately, some social scientists who have thus narrowly circumscribed their data seem to be unaware that they have often precluded by definition what they claim that they have empirically refuted.

It is hoped that this synchronization of interdependent factors might contribute to an interdisciplinary cooperation which in no way threatens the relative autonomy of any one of the specific disciplines. Integration which correlates the various areas can open up new avenues for research and can serve as a framework for coordinating the results of fragmentary research. It should serve equally to prevent the kind of amalgamation of social-scientific disciplines which stifles unique creative scholarship that demands the isolation of specific data for a particular piece of research.

When a behavioral scientist identifies and correlates behavioral data in accordance with this comprehensive conceptual scheme, he commits himself to a molar rather than a molecular approach. In order to deal with data in this synoptic manner, social scientists have attempted to coordinate nomothetic with idiographic and functional with structural modes of analysis. A broadly operational conception of knowledge can not be understood apart from the molar approach and the nomothetic-idiographic and the functional-structural modes of analysis. Like the five requirements of broadly operational knowledge and the synoptic model by which behavioral data are identified, these ways of treating behavioral data are justified or not justified by their fruitfulness for inquiry rather than by any appeal to empirical evidence.

2. THE MOLAR-MOLECULAR DISTINCTION

When an investigator uses a molar approach, he assumes as a relational concept (a) that his data constitute a complex whole of interacting factors which cannot be described apart from each other, (b) that the entire behavioral process cannot be reduced to any of its component parts, and (c) that the organization of the whole-part structure is functionally integrated by the dynamic selection of means to ends of goal-oriented actions. As Littman and Rosen have described it, "the molar unit of description is the behavior episode founded in time by initiation of behavior by the need, and cessation of behavior by assessment of the goal." [31] This organizational concept is antithetical to the molecular approach by which the given goal-oriented total behavioral responses are reduced to neuro-physiological processes (receptor-conductor-effector mechanisms *per se*) or to even more elementary components, e.g., "the action of the ultimate nerve cell, the protoplasmic molecules making up the neurons or perhaps the atoms constituting the molecule, or even the electrons, protons, neutrons, etc. constituting the atom." [32] These and muscle twitches were characterized by Hull as molecular in contrast to the molarity of a total behavioral response. Tolman, it will be recalled, made this qualitative distinction central for psychological theory, when he rejected Watson's molecular conception of behavior "in terms of its strict underlying physical and physiological details." Instead, he presented a molar conception of purposive behavior as "an emergent phenomena that has descriptive and defining properties of its own" which "are to be identified and described irrespective of whatever muscular, glandular, or neural processes underlie them." [33] Tolman grants that Watson's situation-act concepts seem to be molar, but Watson did not integrate sensory and motor segments into any connected whole.

As this molar-molecular distinction is used here, it is an essential way of defining social-scientific data. Its referents, however, are not confined to those which Tolman and Hull have employed. In other words, since Tolman and Hull emphasized this relational conceptual distinction in terms of a contrast between psychological and physical factors, it should not be assumed that all physical processes are molecular and all psychological processes are molar. Lashley, for example, has used this distinction to relate neural mechanisms. Weiss, a biologist, presupposes this relational concept with reference to emerging organizations of inorganic and organic processes when he declares that "we now have to resynthesize the conceptual bonds between those parts which we have cut in the first place." [34] Moreover, with respect to the interpersonal transactions of the individual members of human groups, Asch states the social-psychological assumption that "group action is real, having laws that are often not reducible to those of its components taken singly," and "in the course of interaction new relations and properties arise, which are not identical with the properties of their constituents." [35] In short, any organization of events in the hierarchical system of inorganic, organic, and superorganic phenomena may be taken as molar in relation to some orders and molecular in relation to other orders. This interactional conception of molarity presupposes a continuum in which, as Hull suggests, molar postulates might become molecular theorems. Krech supports this position when he contends that "the unity of science will not be achieved by *reducing* psychological principles to neurological ones, and neurological ones to physical ones." Instead he insists, "what we must seek is to make physical principles *congruent* with neurological ones, neurological ones with psychological ones." [36]

The advantage of a molar over a molecular approach lies in the less arbitrary character of the former. If a purely molecular approach is adopted, any chance for a molar synthesis is precluded. But a molarist must utilize the data obtained through molecular analysis. For, as Smith points out, the scientist who rejects "crude elementarism" in order to conceive of behavior as "dynamically organized phenomena" must recognize that "wholeness . . . cannot be described in ways that can be checked independently without the use of more elementary terms." [37] No molarist, it will be recalled, has more strongly insisted than Gordon Allport that "psychology cannot be satisfied with segments of persons related to outer coordinates," but, rather, it "must consider the system as a whole, and show how part systems are related to one another." When he attempts to determine what motivational units should be employed, however, even Allport declares that "ultimately, of course, our hope is to be able to reduce molar units to molecular and, conversely, to compound molecular units into molar." [38]

The *conceptual* rather than *theoretical* role of the molar-molecular distinction, as it is used here for identifying and correlating all social-scientific data, must be reemphasized. When Littman and Rosen concluded that "the role of the molar-molecular distinction has shifted, perhaps to the point of losing its usefulness," they were referring to it as a *theoretical* principle for psychological investigation. If it is taken as no more than this, they present a strong case by showing the confusion that has arisen from seven different meanings that psychologists have given to molarity: interaction, action-units, levels, construction, phenomenal, urgency, holism.[39] Perhaps they are correct when they claim that psychology has incorporated the needed reorientation which the molarists have achieved. However, the point to be emphasized is that the molar organization of behavioral data is no less essential as one of the central ideas in a *conceptual* identification of social-scientific knowledge.

Now that this molar-molecular distinction is no longer staked down to physiological-psychological dichotomies, it has a free-wheeling function as a mobile classificatory tool which is applicable irrespective of the substantive nature of the data it differentiates. This function in terms of "shifting frames of reference" has been explicitly recognized by Scheerer in his assertion that "the molar-molecular distinction varies with the context of the organizational level selected for study." Consequently, the question stressed by Rosen and Littman with respect to whether molarity was "existential" or "instrumental," according to Scheerer, "has no bearing on the crucial issue of the usefulness of the molar-molecular distinction." [40] Although this distinction is not explicitly mentioned, the idea of molarity pervades the thinking of the contributors to *Toward a Unified Theory of Human Behavior* when they discuss the organism-environment context of behavior, the multiple origins of the uniqueness of human society, homeostasis and comparisons of systems, the relation between the small group and the larger social system, and the various types of boundaries.[41]

Since this synoptic model is so obviously molar, it is well for us to note Spence's defense of a molecular elementarism on the grounds that only "certain features of events are repeated" while "total concrete events are seldom, if ever, repeated." Consequently, Spence insists that only a molecular analysis will provide scientific laws: "However fervently the Gestalt psychologist may claim that he deals only with wholes, with total situations, the fact remains that if he is interested in discovering uniformities of scientific laws, he must, of necessity, fractionate or abstract out certain features of the total events he observes." But even Spence grants that, with respect to the conceptual identification of behavioral data, the applicability of the molar or the molecular "depends upon the interest and purpose of the scientist, the kind of law he expects to find or use." Moreover, he acknowledges that "if the two systems of concepts should each be successful in leading to the discovery and formulation of laws, it should also be possible to discover coordinating definitions which will reveal the interrelations of the two systems." [42]

3. NOMOTHETIC-IDIOGRAPHIC SYNCHRONIZATION

A social scientist who conceptually identifies and correlates behavioral data in accordance with the synoptic model must find some way to synchronize *generalizing* in quantitative terms about the elements of behavioral transactions with *individualizing* in qualitative terms about the totality of each behavioral transaction.

When a generalizing mode of analysis is used exclusively without any regard for the uniqueness in the total organization of singular events, it is said to be *nomothetic*. For the most part scientific analysis aims at the construction of abstract laws under which observed particular events can be subsumed. It aims at the conception of a uniform pattern in the sociocultural and motivational processes comparable to a uniform pattern in natural processes by abstracting from them their universal, recurrent, invariant, and quantifiable characteristic properties. The diachronic dimension of the scientist's conceptual framework precludes his assuming that any physical or human event itself actually ever reoccurs. But it does not preclude the possibility that successive events exhibit properties with such similar characteristics that the nomotheticist can for all practical purposes claim that "uniformities or laws describe ways in which events repeat themselves."

The requirements of a broadly operational conception of knowledge prohibit an exclusively *individualizing* treatment of behavioral data which would be indifferent to the problem of constructing nomothetic generalizations about a patterned process; but they equally demand an *idiographic* consideration of such data that would be distorted by purely nomothetic analysis. *Idiographic* designates a way of treating in singular terms the unique, variant, nonrecurrent organizations of qualitatively distinctive wholes. Many of the inorganic, organic, somatic, psychodynamic, social, and cultural conditions which provide the complex stimuli to which behavioral transactions are a response can be dealt with in terms of nomothetic generalizations. But in order for the behavioral scientist to carry his analysis beyond these independent variables to take into account the intervening variable of each person's owned goal-seeking motivation he must deal idiographically with what Goldstein calls the "holistic dependency" of each person's molar response. Nomothetic analysis of the molecular elements is not applicable to the uniqueness that is exhibited in the total goal-oriented response which is a complex-unity of neurophysiological, psychodynamic, and sociocultural responses in each person's diachronically developing experience.

This need for a nomothetic-idiographic synchronization is brought out by Gordon Allport when he attempts to conceptualize an "individual structural pattern." If a psychologist is purely nomothetic in accordance with "the prevailing conviction that science can not deal with individual cases at all, excepting as they exemplify general laws or display uniform structures," then he can not deal with the empirical situation in which "a baby once started on the road of life, will fashion, out of his unique inheritance and special environment, nodes of accretion, foci of learning, directions of growth, that become increasingly unique as the years roll along." But Allport's concern for "improved idiographic analysis" is not contrary to but rather contributory to a more adequate "nomothetic assessment" of whatever pattern goal-oriented motivation exemplifies: "While we must admit the variabilities of the structures we seek, which are caused by changing situations without and continual growth and change within, we should take this fact into our design and theory, not surrendering our belief that reasonably stable personal and motivational structures exist." [43]

For most social scientists, the problem is to work idiographic considerations into nomothetic assessments; but, for the historian, the problem is to work nomothetic considerations into idiographic assessments. The synchronization of idiographic and nomothetic modes of analysis is an essential, but difficult task for historical inquiry. It is essential because it requires an idiographic focus on the *uniqueness* of the singular concrete whole of specific situations in the past; but it equally requires a nomothetic focus on the *uniformity* of an invariant temporal duration of future becoming present and present becoming past in the diachronic passage of events. The historian is not primarily interested in abstracting the similar characteristics from different historical situations in order to construct the kind of generalizations about either all or a selected class of sociocultural phenomena which the sociologists seek. As Fling declares: "The historian is interested in quality, individuality, uniqueness; the sociologist in quantity, in generality, in repetition." [44]

But how could a distinctive event be recognized if it were so completely unique that it had no characteristics that were similar to other events? Moreover, unless the historian is content with presenting a mere chronological sequence, he must construct a causal chain of events of which each specific situation is an interconnected link. The correlative function of instrumental nomothetic and intrinsic idiographic focuses in the historian's interpretations is determined by his primary individualizing aim. Consequently, when the historian borrows or constructs generalizations, it is to use them as a means for clarifying his end of describing and explaining specific past situations. These as molar units are never exactly like any other configuration of events. The complications involved with respect to the theoretical question about laws and historical analysis will be considered later; but the core of the basic conceptual issue has been clearly pinpointed by Gottschalk, when he justified his claim that the historian must use generalizations in order to study the unique: "The sentiment that 'history deals with the unique' is, to begin with, itself a generalization, and, in addition, it raises the query: How is one to recognize the unique without first having become familiar with the general?" [45]

As long as social scientists include the intervening variable of purposive goal-seeking as an integral factor in their conception of knowledge, they are confronted by what Allport has aptly called "the dilemma of uniqueness." It is not a pressing problem for them when they are engaged in substantive research which does not involve the concrete whole of any actual person's own distinctive functions of goal-oriented behavior. Nomothetic abstraction of "the common analytical elements" from social, cultural, and personal phenomena, which do exhibit universal characteristics, is often sufficient for the construction of causal and/or statistical generalizations about typical sociocultural and motivational processes. But they cannot "find the accident of uniqueness irrelevant to their work," when they are dealing with the distinctive self-creative functions of a person whose relatively self-determined purposive goal-seeking is contributing to his own peculiar "idiomatic pattern of becoming." Although idiographic analysis is required to ascertain how a person develops as "an idiom unto himself," nomothetic generalizations are necessary in order to account for the independent variables of natural, somatic, psycho-dynamic, social, and cultural conditions which beget the character-istic ways of behaving that all human behavior exhibits: "Yet at the same time, idioms are not entirely lawless and arbitrary; indeed they can be known for what they are only by comparing them with the syntax of the species." Instead of a purely nomothetic "postulation of abstract or general motives," it will be recalled, Allport has pro-posed the "principle of functional autonomy." Such a construct idio-graphically takes into account the distinctive reflective motivation of mature persons which has emerged out of the basic motivation that they share with all other people. This nomothetic idea "that tells how uniqueness comes about," Allport insists, "is general enough to meet the needs of science, but particularized enough in its operation to account for the uniqueness of personal conduct." [46]

The necessity for synchronizing nomothetic and idiographic fo-cuses in a conception of social-scientific knowledge has also been emphasized by Kluckhohn, Murray, Newcomb, and MacIver. As their basic premise for interpreting the functioning of persons in na-ture, society, and culture, Kluckhohn and Murray declare: "Every man is in certain respects: a. like all other men, b. like some other men, c. like no other man." [47] Newcomb maintains that adequate social-psychological conceptions of interpersonal behavior can not be constructed in the exclusively nomothetic terms of "role-position" and "consensus," since they leave out of account the uniqueness of each person's private self-perceptions. Accordingly, he suggests the coordination of the sociological concept of a socioculturally deter-mined "role" with the social-psychological concept of personally motivated "role behavior" which is unique to each person: "What-ever the characteristics he expresses in various roles, they are *his own* characteristics, and he cannot help expressing them as he takes his roles in his own, individual way." [48] Macrosociologists, who are con-cerned with the pattern of interaction among groups, may grant that there is such a thing as deviant individualized behavior; but they dis-count it as idiosyncratic and do not include it as an idiographic de-terminant in their purely nomothetic conception of variables. Mac-Iver, however, is a microsociologist in the sense that he does assume that in some cases "the role of the conscious agent is a distinctive one" through which "he envisages a total situation, relates it to his own ends, seems to make it, in whatever measure he can, instrumental, so as to turn its intrinsic dynamics into his own means." Such relatively self-determined purposive action through which he modifies the situation "meshes with the total external situation" that is describable by nomothetic generalizations. But the individual's own "*dynamic assessment*," by which he brings "into a single order of coherent relationships the objectively diverse factors involved in social behavior" is idiographic.[49]

4. FUNCTIONAL-STRUCTURAL SYNCHRONIZATION

The aim and limited scope of this discussion should be clearly understood in order that it will not increase the confusion that has already developed in social-scientific literature with respect to the meanings of "function," of "structure," and of the relation of these two terms. The only aim here is to indicate what is meant by function and by structure and how as implications of the molar approach they are related in our synoptic model. Since such an aim limits the scope of this discussion to purely *conceptual* considerations; *theoretical* questions about the use of these terms in the substantive analysis of specific disciplines will not be treated here. Moreover, there is not space to review the significant contributions by such men as Weber, Durkheim, Malinowski, Mannheim, etc. to the use of these terms.

This delimitation should not be taken as agreement with those who claim that there is no longer any issue with respect to these terms in the research efforts of specific disciplines. Evidence to the contrary is available to anyone who will read the contemporary literature in the light of the questions that Merton posed in the cogent paradigms of functional analysis when he sought to codify "manifest and latent functions" in his *Social Theory and Social Structure*. Perhaps there is less interest in this issue simply because some social scientists are tired of trying to reach a consensus. It is more constructive to hope that Firth is correct when he concludes his thoroughgoing examination of "Function" with this statement: "It does seem that discussion has advanced from the somewhat sterile verbal battles about the meaning of the term function to the formulation of more refined and substantial propositions which use its notions or at least its spirit." [50] In a definition of social-scientific knowledge, however, the meaning of the term must be made explicit regardless of whether or not it is out of fashion in the literature of the specific disciplines.

If as the premise for our search we adopt Merton's conclusion that "structure affects function and function affects structure," then we possess the valuable clue that what is meant by each of these terms cannot be understood apart from what it is taken to signify as a correlative of the other. Instead of getting bogged down in the fruitless either-or controversy between the extreme functionalists and structuralists, we can now attempt to ascertain the meaning of each as it emerges conjointly out of their molar context. For, as Merton insists, the "central orientation of functionalism" is "expressed in the practice of interpreting data by establishing their consequences for larger structures in which they are implicated." This is congruent with Malinowski's identification of functional factors "by the part which they play within the integral system of culture, by the manner in which they are related to each other within the system." [51]

What are the advantages of this synchronized functional-structural approach? First of all, it is applicable to all of the data in the behavioral process. This is what Spiegel seems to assume when he contends that a comparison of the "foci of organization" to be found in "the various systems of levels of abstraction which are obviously in transaction with each other in any situation of human behavior" requires the premise that "structure and function are presumably different aspects of the same process." [52] Secondly, with Radcliffe-Brown we can subsume these correlative aspects of the behavioral process under the more general concept of temporal *continuity*: "It is through and by the continuity of the functioning that the continuity of the structure is preserved." [53] And third, structure can be conceived as the product of function in the sense that Aberle, Cohen, Davis, Levy, and Sutton conceive it: "Though the functional prerequisites of a society logically precede the development of a scheme of structural prerequisites—which tells how the functional prerequisites may be met—in actuality the theoretic development of the two approaches is indivisible." [54]

By using these highly generalized ideas we can now identify "structure" as a synchronic *pattern* that evolves out of the diachronic means-ends *function* identified as an operation of *need-fulfillment*.

Such identification is used by Grinker when he compares biological and psychological systems of organization. Instead of "static morphological structures" he refers to *patterns* or *system determinants* and declares that "in the somatic system the primary functional process subsumed under the term of living organization is characterized by needs and need satisfaction for maintenance of somatic homeostasis." [55]

Now let us attempt to apply these ideas to the sociocultural and motivational factors of the behavioral process. Might we not say that, on the one hand, *structure* is exhibited in the *pattern* of the institutions through which role-positions are organized in accordance with the *pattern* of cultural symbols? If so, then might we not say that, on the other hand, *function* is exhibited in the *goal-seeking selections* of whatever means that are required for realizing the end of survival and, in some cases, the additional ends which are desired to make survival worthwhile? Parsons and Shils seem to endorse such a formulation when they discuss the functional problems of allocation and integration: "The structure of the social system in this respect may be regarded as the cumulative and balanced resultant of many selections of many individuals, stabilized and reinforced by the institutionalization of value patterns, which legitimize commitment to certain directions of selection and mobilize sanctions in the support of the resultant orientations." [56]

The synchronization of the functional and structural aspects of the behavioral process of goal-oriented action which the synoptic model entails has been most extensively developed, of course, by Parsons as the "structural-functional" conception of the *social system*. He and Shils define this as "any system of interactive relationships of a plurality of individual actors." As a type of social system, a society is a self-subsistent system which in addition to its territorial and kinship organization requires "a system for determining functions and allocating facilities and rewards and . . . integrative structures controlling these allocations and regulating conflicts and competitive processes." Such "systems of actions are functional systems" wherein "the imperatives which impose certain adaptations on the components result from the empirical possibilities or necessities of coexistence which we designate as *scarcity*, and from the properties of the actor as an organism." The *pattern* which constitutes the *structure* that is thus functionally produced in a social system is distinguished by Parsons from the pattern which constitutes the structure of cultural systems on the grounds that the latter are "symbolic systems in which the components have logical or meaningful rather than functional relationships with one another." As systems of value-orientation, however, the cultural symbols are externalized in the structural pattern of institutionalized role-expectations and are internalized in the functional need-dispositions of goal-oriented actors.[57]

The influence of Parson's "structural-functional" mode of conceptualizing goal-oriented action upon the synoptic model is obvious; but there is one difference in emphasis which should be noted. When Parsons identifies function in terms of the fulfillment of needs, he carefully distinguishes between "the need-dispositions of the actors" as individuals and the "needs in the systematic sense," i.e., "the resultant of the coexistence in determinate relationships in a situation of a plurality of actors each of whom has a system of need dispositions." For, Parsons insists, "the overtones of teleology must be guarded against particularly in dealing with the social system." [58] In the synoptic model, however, there has been no attempt to eliminate teleological overtones when the functional concepts of motivational constructs have seemed to require a recognition of the purposive character of goal-seeking behavior. Recall, for example, Allport's "propriate striving" to which a non-teleological notion of tension-reduction would not apply. Could this not be the difference? Parsons in an effort to be as nomothetic as possible has conceived of personality largely as the product of the sociocultural system. In our synoptic model, however, personality is conceived both nomothetically and idiographically. For we have aimed to take more into account the relatively self-determined purposes of reflectively-motivated persons when they participate in producing themselves and the structure of the sociocultural process of which they are integral functional parts. It should be noted, nevertheless, that when Parsons in another essay describes the relation of the parts to the "system as a whole," he emphasizes that the "functional significance in this contest is inherently teleological." [59]

Gouldner's discussion of "reciprocity and autonomy in functional theory" bears out this implication of the synoptic model, i.e., the dynamic goal-oriented activity of relatively self-determined persons is as essential as their interdependence which provides the equilibrium of a system. Although Gouldner acknowledges that functionalism necessarily treats data in terms of their implications for a broader context, he emphasizes Merton's focus upon the functioning of the component elements which might be lost sight of by someone considering only Parsons' focus upon the "contextual structure" of the systematic whole. Assuming that there are varying degrees of interdependence and, correspondingly, varying degrees of functional autonomy with respect to the relation of a part to its entire system, Gouldner highlights the crucial issue by this question: "What can be predicated about the functional autonomy of the parts of social systems, and in what ways does the problem of the functional autonomy of the parts enter into the analysis of social systems?" Expecting some tension to stem from the "part's tendency to maintain an existent degree of functional autonomy and the system's pressure to control the part," Gouldner insists that "to fit the data of social behavior, the system model required must be such as to facilitate not only the analysis of the interdependence of the system as a whole, but also the analysis of the functional autonomy of its parts, and the concrete strains which efforts to maintain this autonomy may induce." In other words, "the obligations of an actor to the collectivity of which his role is a part" are never unlimited. But, as Gouldner concludes, there is no inherent obstacle which precludes the correlation of relative autonomy and relative interdependence. This is all that our synoptic model demands.[60]

When one acknowledges the significance of a functional-structural synchronization in our synoptic model for a *conceptual* identification of behavioral data, he does not commit himself to functionalism as a *theoretical* method by which an anthropologist or sociologist deals with substantive problems. Even if there were a general consensus on what structural-functional analysis entails, which seems unlikely, there are social scientists who question its usefulness for substantive research. Davis strongly advocates the abandonment of what he calls "the myth of functional analysis" on the grounds that "it rests on the false assumption that there is a special method or body of theory called functional analysis which can be distinguished from other methods or theories *within* sociology and social anthropology." [61] This is an issue which can be dealt with only by the specialists in the respective disciplines which carry on substantive research. But the point to be emphasized here is this: Even those sociologists and anthropologists who agree with Davis do not necessarily question the need for the synchronization of function and structure in the kind of conceptionalization with which we are here concerned. Further problems which arise in connection with "the logic of functional analysis" [62] will be discussed in the later chapter which deals with the explanatory stage of actual investigations.

Footnotes to Chapter 4 of Part Two

1 MacIver, *Social Causation*, 64, 68. Cf. Benson in *Common Frontiers of the Social Sciences* (Kommarovsky), 16.

2 Lenzen, "Procedures of Empirical Science," *International Encyclopedia of Unified Science*, Vol. I, page 3.

3 Kelly, "Man's Construction of His Alternatives," *Assessment of Human Motives* (Lindzey), 56. Cf. Kluckhohn and Murray, *Personality in Nature, Society, and Culture*, 8-9.

4 Parsons, *The Structure of Social Action*, 763.

5 Lazarsfeld and Rosenberg, *The Language of Social Research*, 6.

6 Malinowski, *Encyclopedia of the Social Sciences*, Vol. 4, pp. 624-625.

7 Herskovits in *The Science of Man in the World Crisis* (Linton), 143-145, 149-150.

8 Nadel, *The Foundations of Social Anthropology*, 100.

9 Parsons, *The Structure of Social Action*, 763.

10 Lasswell, *The Policy Sciences* (Lerner and Lasswell), 10-11.

11 Spengler, "Generalists Versus Specialists in Social Science: An Economic View," *The American Political Science Review*, Vol. XLIV, June 1950, page 373.

12 Samuelson, *Foundations of Economic Analysis*, 314.

13 Gruchy, *Modern Economic Thought*, 602.

14 Ruggles, "Methodological Developments," *A Survey of Contemporary Economics* (Haley), Vol. II, 440.

15 Samuelson, "Dynamic Process Analysis," *A Survey of Contemporary Economics* (Ellis), Vol. I, 374.

16 Aitken and Loewenberg, Bulletin 64, p. 24.

17 Clough, Bulletin 64, p. 106, 110.

18 Aitken and Loewenberg, Bulletin 64, p. 241.

19 MacIver, *Social Causation*, 273.

20 *Ibid.*, 286-287.

21 Easton, *The Political System*, 126, 128, 134.

22 Perry, "The Semantics of Political Science," *The American Political Science Review*, June 1950, page 405. Cf. Aristotle, *Politics*, Bk. I, Chapter 2.

23 Elliott and McDonald, *Western Political Heritage*, 14.

24 Easton, *The Political System* 194-196, 200.

[25] Merriam, *Systematic Politics*, vi, 1, 6, 30, 54, 74, 119.

[26] Key, *Politics, Parties and Pressure Groups*, 3-7. Cf. Lasswell and Others, *Power and Society*, 240; and Catlin, A *Study of the Principles of Politics* and *The Science and Method of Politics*.

[27] Papandreou, "Some Basic Problems in the Theory of the Firm," A *Survey of Contemporary Economics* (Haley), Vol. II, 183.

[28] Parsons and Shils, *Toward a General Theory of Action*, 198.

[29] Polanyi, *Semantics of General Economic History*, Research Project on "Origins of Economic Institutions." Columbia University. Council for Research in the Social Sciences (Mimeographed), pages 1-7.

[30] Kapp, "Economics and the Behavioral Sciences, *Kyklos*, Vol. VII, 1954, page 219.

[31] Littman and Rosen, "The Molar-Molecular Distinction," *Psychological Theory* (Marx), 147.

[32] Hull, "The Problem of Intervening Variables in Molar Behavior Theory," *Psychological Review*, 1943, 50, p. 274.

[33] Tolman, "Molar and Purposive Behaviorism," *Psychological Theory* (Marx), 413-414.

[34] Weiss in *Toward a Unified Theory of Human Behavior* (Grinker), 110. Cf. Lashley, "The Problem of Serial Order in Behavior," *Cerebral Mechanisms and Behavior* (Jeffress), 122.

[35] Asch, *Social Psychology*, 263.

[36] Krech, "Dynamic Systems as Open Neurological Systems," *Psychological Review*, 1950, 57, page 246.

[37] Smith in *For a Science of Social Man* (Gillin), 42.

[38] Allport, *Becoming*, 6; and "What Units Shall We Employ?" *Assessment of Human Motives* (Lindzey), 240-241.

[39] Littman and Rosen, "The Molar-Molecular Distinction," *Psychological Theory* (Marx), 153, 147-150.

[40] Scheerer, "Cognitive Theory," *Handbook of Social Psychology* (Lindzey), Vol. I, 95.

[41] See *Toward a Unified Theory of Human Behavior* (Grinker), pages 119-122, 142-144, 151, 190-191, 340-361.

[42] Spence, in *Psychological Theory* (Marx), 176-177. For other relevant discussions see Goldstein, *The Organism*; Hull, *Psychological Theory* (Marx), 207; Krech and Klein, *Theoretical Models and Personality Theory*, 26, 36; Krech and Crutchfield, *Theories and Problems of Social Psychology*, 31; Woodworth, *Contemporary Schools of Psychology*, 89; Marx, *Psychological Theory*, 14-18. Further bibliographical references are furnished by Littman and Rosen and by Scheerer in their articles cited above.

[43] Allport, "What Units Shall We Employ?" *Assessment of Human Motives* (Lindzey), 257-258. Cf. Goldstein, *The Organism*.

[44] Fling, *The Writing of History*, 17.

[45] Gottschalk, "The Historian's Use of Generalizations," *The State of the Social Sciences* (White), 448. For other relevant discussions see Aitken and Loewenberg, Bulletin 64, p. 25; Mandelbaum, *The Problem of Historical Knowledge*, 6; Danto, "Mere Chronicle and History Proper," *Journal of Philosophy*, March

12, 1953, Vol. 10., No. 6, page 181; Sorokin, *Society, Culture, and Personality,* 7; and Larrabee, *Reliable Knowledge,* 302-313.

[46] Allport, *Becoming,* 19-23; and *The Nature of Personality,* 88-91. Originally published in *The American Journal of Psychology,* 50, 1937, page 154.

[47] Kluckhohn and Murray, *Personality in Nature, Society, and Culture,* 35.

[48] Newcomb, *Social Psychology,* 333.

[49] MacIver, *Social Causation,* 236-237, 306. Cf. Eysenck in *Theoretical Models and Personality Theory* (Krech and Klein), 101, 108-110.

[50] Firth, "Function," *Current Anthropology* (Thomas), 255. See Firth's entire essay for a most instructive survey of the varieties of meaning which have been ascribed to the term in the substantive analyses of anthropology and sociology.

[51] Merton, *Social Theory and Social Structure* (1957), p. 19, and all of Chapter I. See Malinowski, "Anthropology," *Encyclopedia Britannica,* First Sup. Vol., 132-133.

[52] Spiegel in *Toward a Unified Theory of Human Behavior* (Grinker), 164-165.

[53] Radcliffe-Brown, "On the Concept of Function in Social Science," *The American Anthropologist,* 27 (1935), pp. 39-402.

[54] Aberle, Cohen, Davis, Levy, Sutton, "The Functional Prerequisites of a Society," *Ethics,* LX, 101-111.

[55] Grinker, *Toward a Unified Theory of Human Behavior* (Grinker), 136-137.

[56] Parsons and Shils, *Toward a General Theory of Action,* 25. This statement is endorsed by the other contributors to this volume.

[57] *Ibid.,* 26, 173 n. 13. See Nagel, *The Structure of Science,* 425, for a discussion of the dilemma of biologists when they attempt to ascertain "to what extent structures may modify functions or functions structures." Note, however, that they generally agree that "the development of function goes hand in hand with the development of structure."

[58] *Ibid.,* 241.

[59] Parsons, *Essays in Sociological Theory, Pure and Applied,* 21.

[60] Gouldner, "Reciprocity and Autonomy in Functional Theory," *Symposium on Sociological Theory* (Gross), 242-244, 254-258, 265-266.

[61] Davis, "The Myth of Functional Analysis as a Special Method in Sociology and Anthopology," *American Sociological Review,* Vol. 24, No. 6, December 1959, p. 757. See Nagel, *The Structure of Social Science,* 520-525, for Nagel's critical analysis of functionalism as "a distinctive theoretical approach in the study of human affairs." (525)

[62] See Hempel, "The Logic of Functional Analysis," *Symposium on Sociological Theory* (Gross), 271-307.

PART THREE *The Epistemological Pattern of Reflective Inquiry*

1 The Epistemological Perspective of Reflective Inquiry

Reflective inquiry is that way of knowing by which operational knowledge is acquired. Borrowing biological terminology, we may say that natural-scientific analysis and social-scientific analysis are related as two species of this generic cognitive process of reflective inquiry. The pattern of this way of knowing will be elucidated here in terms of (a) the distinctive preference of reflective inquirers, (b) the set of postulates they assume, and (c) the investigative and verificative principles they employ. We shall now take these categories of the generic pattern of reflective inquiry to be a referential framework for an epistemological synthesis of the procedures of each of the behavioral disciplines. Parsons' reference to the "rational unity of cognitive experience" seems to intimate that this notion of an epistemological pattern is essential for the methodology of the social-scientific enterprise.[1]

It is a basic premise of this epistemological synthesis that social-scientific analysis should not be forced into a natural-scientific mold. This point needs special emphasis, since the numerous references to natural-scientific procedures might otherwise be taken to imply that the social scientist must imitate the natural scientist. It is only to clarify what a specific cognitive principle means before we consider its use by social scientists that we shall mention natural-scientific analysis. Each of these enterprises has its own task to perform; neither is inferior to the other so long as it meets the logical demands of their common pattern of reflective inquiry. Accordingly, it is meaningless to ask whether or not behavioral analysis is scientific, for such qualification requires that the behavioral analyst must always proceed as does the analyst of physical events. The reliability of the broadly operational knowledge which social scientists attempt to construct for interpreting their own distinctive data is the only point with which we shall be concerned. Consequently, it is to the appropriate demands of the epistemological pattern of reflective inquiry, rather than to the inappropriate demands of natural-scientific techniques, that we shall turn for assessing the achievements of social-scientific analysis.

The epistemological perspective which we used for elucidating what each of the other ways of knowing entailed, will now be used for making explicit what the pattern of reflective inquiry signifies with respect to its value-situation, its meaning-situation, and its knowledge-situation. The crux of each of these three situations, as they are involved in the social-scientific mode of reflective inquiry, will be disclosed by the answers which representatives of each of the behavioral disciplines offer to what we have called the value-question, the meaning-question, and the knowledge-question. We can compare these answers with those offered by the dogmatic authoritarian, or the mystic, or the naïve pragmatist, or the naïve sense-impressionist, or the pure rationalist, or the pure empiricist, as well as with those of the logical positivist. This should show that, with respect to motivation, postulates, and method, social-scientific inquiry is just as distinguishable from non-operational approaches as is natural-scientific inquiry.

A. *The Value-Situation of Reflective Inquiry*

What is the dominant motivation of the scientist who is engaged in reflective inquiry? It is the Faustian quest for the satisfaction of never completely satisfying his intellectual curiosity for increasingly more reliable knowledge. Since this psychological preference was discussed previously in connection with the value-centric predicament of all scientists, its identification will merely be summarized here. This desire for knowledge as an intrinsic value generates the reflective attitude of persisting inquiry. Such, it will be recalled, is the positive scepticism of the person who critically but open-mindedly explores the area of experience with which he is concerned in terms of verifiable hypotheses which are always subject to correction, modification, or even abandonment, if carefully examined evidence and logical reasoning demand a more adequate interpretation. A scientist should acknowledge that his conception of what kind of knowledge is meaningful and consequently the method he employs are derived from this intellectual preference. Accordingly, *scientific objectivity* is not necessarily determined by reference to some special technique such as laboratory experimentation or to some special kind of subject-matter such as physical objects with spatio-temporal dimensions. Instead, *scientific objectivity* is ascribed to any kind of analysis wherein the generalizations have been constructed by a person who is dominantly motivated by the "desire to know."

B. *The Meaning-Situation of Reflective Inquiry*

1. WHAT KIND OF KNOWLEDGE IS ACQUIRED THROUGH REFLECTIVE INQUIRY?

Two points about the significance of any answer to this meaning-question should be mentioned so that they can be kept in mind while considering the answer which will be suggested below. First, any answer is an outgrowth of the respondent's conception of knowledge, i.e., non-operational, or narrowly operational, or broadly operational. Second, what kind of knowledge the respondent considers acquirable in his meaning-situation is determined by his motivating value-situation, and his meaning-situation determines what general method of investigation he will use in his knowledge-situation.

The following answer is offered in an attempt to find a consensus among both social scientists and natural scientists with regard to what kind of knowledge they consider acquirable: *The reflective in-|*

quirer can operationally construct reliable hypotheses about that dimension of reality with which he is concerned in terms of a coherent system of generalizations which have causal implications that can be verified to various degrees of probability. Now it is to be expected that such a broad and abstract statement will appear to be indigestible to many students, as well as to some social scientists who are very competent in their own fields. But a broad level of abstraction is unavoidable for the purpose of representing a consensus among scientists about what kind of knowledge is meaningful. We must start with a tentative statement which transcends the boundaries that different kinds of subject matter impose. It is necessary, however, to break this general statement down into five postulational principles which it implies in order to bring out what we consider to be the basic epistemological issues of the social-scientific problem of knowledge. At this point we shall merely state these postulates in order to direct attention to what assumptions are entailed. When we turn directly to the social-scientific literature itself in the next chapter, we shall find that it is often the failure of social scientists to recognize and/or to agree on these issues that is responsible for the complications in the meaning-situation within, as well as among, behavioral disciplines.

Our general answer to the question about what kind of knowledge is meaningful entails the following assumptions: (a) There is an objective reality to a specific dimension of which the subjective constructs of the particular disciplines refer. (b) A high degree of probability (reasonable acceptability), rather than absolute certainty, is the most that can be expected in the operational verification of generalizations which never exhaust all that is yet to be known. (c) Knowledge about the objective physical and behavioral universe requires an orderly system of constructs. (d) The category of causality is required as the principle of objective reference for the construction of explanatory and predictive hypotheses about the interaction of physical and behavioral events. (e) Coherence (consistency and adequacy) is the generic logical criterion of verification from which the specific criteria for empirically testing the deduced implications of hypotheses are derived. It remains now for us to ascertain to what extent social scientists themselves acknowledge that they presuppose these epistemological postulates.

2. THE POSTULATIONAL CHARACTER OF THE MEANING-SITUATION

The assumption that any scientist makes with respect to each of these five principles is a postulate expressing what he means, rather than a verifiable assertion of what he knows. Thus, what he presupposes about them is neither true nor false in the sense that his substantive generalizations can be confirmed or denied. Since these postulates about what kind of knowledge can be acquired will determine what kind of method and criterion he will employ, they could hardly be constructed and tested by that very method and criterion. But, if, as Kantor has said, "current scientific reorientation demands that all investigation and systematization be based upon definite and deliberate postulates," [2] how does the scientist justify his adoption of these assumptions which his method and criterion of inquiry presupposes?

The adoption of one postulate rather than another can be justified only on the pragmatic grounds that it is more fruitful than an alternative postulate for expressing what kind of knowledge is meaningful to him. Consequently, these heuristic postulates are *a priori* in the pragmatic sense of what Dewey has designated as "an acknowledgment of that to which the undertaking of inquiry commits us." [3] Since these epistemological assumptions are derived from and can be modified by the process of inquiry, their pragmatic *a priorism* in the meaning-situation must be distinguished from purely rationalistic *a priorism*. In the latter, principles such as consistency and causality were asserted as universal and necessary truths in the rationalist's knowledge-situation.

When these heuristically *a priori* postulates are taken together as a systematic scheme of interpenetrating assumptions, they constitute what Lundberg has called "a symbolic frame of reference or universe of discourse." What Lundberg claims about sociological discussion holds for that of all other natural-scientific and social-scientific disciplines as well: "No orderly discussion is possible without such a framework for it is only by reference to such a framework that individual statements about phenomena have meaning." [4] Andrews has similarly acknowledged that such a conceptual scheme of epistemological assumptions is presupposed by psychological inquiry: "Whenever the scientist poses a hypothesis for investigation, designs an experiment, arranges precision instruments for purposes of recording, statistically analyzes the quantitative results of the investigation, and makes inferences about behavior on the basis of the experimental results, he is making a large number of critical assumptions that are based on some one or another philosophical presupposition." [5]

3. THE EPISTEMOLOGICAL NECESSITY FOR MEANING-POSTULATES

The postulates which comprise the meaning-situation of reflective inquiry are the principles of objective reference which provide an answer to the crucial epistemological question: *How are the ideas in the mind of the scientist related to the reality to which they are supposed to refer?* For clarification let us recall Werkmeister's triadic description of the mind-sign-referent continuum of the meaning-situation out of which this central epistemological problem emerges: "All concrete situations reveal that the experiential context in which meanings are found is a triadic relation, involving (a) a 'mind' which interprets (b) some specific given experience or 'sign' as standing for or designating (c) some (actual or imagined) object, condition, situation, or process—the 'referent.'" This characterizes both the sensory-intuitive level of language for communication and the abstract-ideational level of analysis, i.e., "the use of language in the search for truth." [6] It is only with the latter, however, that we are concerned here. Recalling Cassirer's similar distinction, we can state it in other words by saying that we are not now dealing with the "emotional language" in which "signals are operators" but, rather, we are now dealing with "propositional language" in which "symbols are designators." [7] We are proposing the five epistemological postulates of the meaning-situation as *cognitive symbols* (replacing Werkmeister's "signs") which provide the link between the constructive activity in the *mind* of the scientist, who is inferentially generalizing in terms of his own ideas about the nature of the objective world, and the *referent* of his constructive activity, which is the reality itself. In other words, without these five assumptions as principles of objective reference the ideas which scientists formulate *about* the physical and behavioral world would be nothing more than subjective constructs.

In the epistemologically dualistic meaning-situation there is, as Sapir has noted, the problem of making "a complete divorce between reality and our linguistic symbols of reference to it." [8] Neither these five postulates nor any other postulates are required in an epistemologically monistic meaning-situation in which the symbol of a word is taken to be identical with the referent itself. As a positive sceptic, however, the reflective inquirer must persistently inquire in the hope that these or some more adequate postulates he develops will guide his investigations in the direction of what the independently existing state of physical and behavioral affairs actually is. In short, these postulates are the articles of faith which sustain the enterprise of persisting inquiry to which the reflective inquirer has dedicated his intellectual efforts.

The social scientist who strives for clarity and distinctness in his operational conception of knowledge and in his substantive research must resign himself to some degree of obscurity in his meaning-situation. He must not forget that when the pure rationalists insisted that only clear and distinct ideas are meaningful, they committed themselves to a substantively sterile *a priorism* in terms of purely analytic principles of validity which they mistook for absolutely certain truth. Accordingly, the social scientist who aims at the construction of synthetic generalizations about actually experienced behavioral transactions should heed Whitehead's warning: "In our experience there is always the dim background from which we derive and to which we return," for "we are not enjoying a limited doll's house of clear and distinct things, secluded from all ambiguity." [9] Cunningham's emphasis on this same point should also be heard: "All our reasoning, so far at least as it proceeds through the medium of a referential meaning-situation aims at the clarification of points of view centering around what is occasionally in reference; and this clarification is achieved by exploration of the significance of reference, that is, the contextual relationship of the referential meaning-situation, as it is progressively specified through penetration into the penumbral nature of what is in reference." [10]

Our insistence that the scientific construction of operational generalizations presupposes an epistemological framework of postulates as symbolically mediating principles of objective reference does not imply that all other kinds of human endeavor must presuppose this same kind of meaning-situation. In addition to this assertive mode of human judgment, as Buchler contends, there are active and exhibitive modes of human judgments which presuppose other conceptions of the "meaning of meaning": "A satisfactory conception of meaning cannot limit itself to some supposedly important species of meaning, much less outlaw species which insistently characterize human experience." [11] While we agree with Buchler that an all inclusive conception of meaning should pertain to *making* and *doing,* as well as to *knowing,* it is only with the assumptions of *knowing* that we are concerned here.

It remains for us to consider the extent to which the proponents of the various behavioral disciplines explicitly acknowledge these five postulates as assumptions underlying their substantive inquiries. Before we undertake this task, however, we should specify what is meant by the method of inquiry in the knowledge-situation which presupposes such a meaning-situation.

C. *The Knowledge-Situation of Reflective Inquiry*

1. BY WHAT METHOD AND CRITERION IS BROADLY OPERATIONAL KNOWLEDGE ACQUIRED?

This is the knowledge-question to which the following is offered in order to distinguish the investigative procedure of reflective inquiry from that of the other ways of knowing. *The hypothetical-deductive method and the criterion of coherence logically coordinate the various observational, inferential, and verificative techniques which a specific subject-matter requires.*

The social scientist who adopts this method and criterion for constructing generalizations is sharing Kant's intention to correlate the empirical principles of induction and testing with the rationalistic principles of deduction and consistency within the framework of positive scepticism.

There seems to be a fairly general agreement about the logical requirements of inquiry which must be fulfilled by any scientific investigator before he can claim that the reliability of his substantive conclusions are warranted by evidence and reasoning. As one reads the various presentations of an operational method of inquiry, one notices at first the differences in terminology and in the arrangement of steps; but after comparing them more carefully, one discovers that they all exemplify much the same logical pattern. For, like the following paradigm of this hypothetical-deductive method, these presentations indicate the investigative procedure of both natural-scientific and social-scientific inquiries which are designed to find a solution to what Dewey has called the "problematic situation":

1. Observation and classification of all of the factual data which are relevant to the specific problem which instigated the inquiry.
2. Construction through inferred generalizations of a hypothesis or a system of hypotheses which might serve as a causal explanation, as well as a formula for more precise classification and prediction, with respect to the relevant observational data.
3. Verification of the theoretical hypothesis or system of hypotheses in accordance with the criterion of coherence, i.e., consistency and adequacy:
   a. Deductive elaboration of the implications of the hypothesis by logical-mathematical reasoning in the form of the hypo-thetical syllogism (If . . . then . . .).
   b. Empirical testing of consistently-deduced implications of the hypothesis by techniques which are applicable to the specific data to which the proposed hypothesis refers in order to verify its higher degree of adequacy:
      i. Experimental testing for confirming or refuting the hy-pothesis under controlled laboratory conditions and/or controlled observations in the natural sciences (including experimental psychology).
      ii. Experiential testing for confirming or refuting the hypoth-esis under relatively controlled observational conditions in the social sciences and psychology (excluding experimental psychology).
4. Conceptual integration of each hypothesis that has empirically confirmed implications into a coherent system of descriptive generalizations (laws) which are logically consistent, i.e., ab-solutely *valid*, and, in comparison with alternative theories, more adequate for interpreting the context to which it refers, i.e., relatively *true*.[12]

The sharp distinction between observational data and hypothetical inference in our paradigm might be misleading in those cases where hypotheses are included in the data. This is especially the case in historical reconstruction. It also occurs sometimes in other disciplines. Moreover, some analysis begins with an established theory. Nevertheless, for our purpose this presentation will be most useful.

2. THE HYPOTHETICAL-DEDUCTIVE METHOD AS AN ORGANIZATION OF DIVERSE OBSERVATIONAL AND VERIFICATIVE TECHNIQUES

All scientists who follow the general procedure of the hypothetical-deductive method do not always use the same techniques for observing data and verifying their hypotheses about them. Recall the fifth principle of broadly operational knowledge: *The specific subject matter of any given discipline must be taken into account in order to determine for that particular analysis (a) what observational techniques are applicable to the relevant data, (b) what testing techniques are applicable to the kind of hypotheses a specific inquiry requires.* For example, consider the techniques of extrospective observation and introspective observation. Physical events and overt human behavior can be observed through the senses, but much of goal-seeking behavior involves data which are accessible only through introspective analysis. The techniques differ; but they are both included under the first stage of observation. For a further example, the implications of any operational hypotheses must be empirically tested by reference to evidence that confirms or denies them. In some cases, experimental laboratory testing is possible; but, in other cases, experiential testing through comparative case analysis and other less rigorous techniques, are all that are appropriate for that particular kind of data and the constructs which interpret it. The diversity of the techniques, notwithstanding, each of them is one among other tools for fulfilling the requirements of empirical testing. Other techniques will, of course, be cited in the subsequent elaboration of the steps of the hypothetical-deductive method as they are followed by social scientists in their substantive inquiries.

We agree with Northrop that "there is no one scientific method," since by the latter he means what we are calling a technique such as experimental testing. What we mean by method is what he calls for as a "frame of reference" in accordance with which there can be a "specification of the specific stage of inquiry for a given type of problem." [13]

3. THE ACKNOWLEDGMENT OF THE HYPOTHETICAL-DEDUCTIVE METHOD BY SOCIAL SCIENTISTS

The statements from spokesmen of each of the social-scientific disciplines are presented below in order to show that our paradigm of the hypothetical-deductive method will serve as a device for comparing their investigative procedures. Consideration of the problematic aspects of each stage and the specification of the techniques which particular disciplines must use at each stage are postponed until we discuss them in detail in subsequent chapters. For the purpose of this cross-disciplinary analysis only those statements which indicate an inductive-deductive procedure will be cited. It should be recalled, however, that in some social-scientific analysis, as well as in some natural-scientific analysis, the analyst may begin with established theories rather than with his own independent observations as a basis for his own generalizations.

Psychologists have quite explicitly recognized the logical demands of what Brown has called the "hypothetico-deductive method, or the method of constructs" according to which "hypotheses, are devised to account for the descriptive data and from these hypotheses, predictions are made which may be tested in experiment." [14] Clarification of the same view is furnished by Marx, when to his declaration that "the hypothesis is the backbone of all scientific theory construction" he adds that "establishment of empirical propositions is referred to as *inductive,* in contrast with the complementary development of the logical implications of theories, or the *deductive* phase of scientific investigation." [15] The importance of understanding this empirical-rational method is emphasized by Andrews: "Knowledge of facts without knowledge of the procedures to discover the facts does not constitute science, and this is especially true in psychology." [16]

Social psychologists have not yet used the techniques of the hypothetical-deductive method as thoroughly as individual psychologists do; but they do acknowledge that they should strive to do so. Newcomb grants that "there are many social-psychological problems to which the methods of hypothesis and controlled observation have scarcely been applied," not because they are not applicable, but rather, "because we still have much to learn about the ways and means of applying them." Newcomb frankly states that "by no means all social-psychological investigations have been successful in complying with the conditions of scientific inquiry." The detailed analysis in a subsequent chapter will reveal, however, that the complications which make the use of this procedure difficult have not discouraged social psychologists.[17]

Sociologists adopt this hypothetical-deductive procedure, at least in principle, when, as Merton declares, "the investigator begins with a hunch or hypothesis," from which, "he draws various inferences and these, in turn, are subjected to empirical test which confirms or refutes the hypothesis." [18] Sorokin has emphasized that sociologists must use a variety of techniques and that these must be adapted to the specific subject-matter in a general inductive-deductive procedure.[19] Although Lundberg holds to the contrary that subject matter should be adapted to techniques, he too insists that the formulation of a research problem requires framing a question, observation, constructing a hypothesis, and varifying it through "repetition of the study in order to make further and more conclusive tests of the hypothesis or to test revisions of the original hypothesis." [20]

The use of these stages of the hypothetical-deductive method for the construction of sociological theory is most explicitly recognized by Furfey. He summarizes the procedures of the sociological researcher in terms of: (1) *gathering* "a mass of carefully verified facts concerning some phenomenon or group of phenomena"; (2) *conceiving* "as a hypothesis, some generalization which will account for all these facts"; (3) *deducing* from this hypothesis "certain consequences about hitherto unexamined phenomena"; and (4) *deciding* "whether or not his hypothesis should be accepted as a verified generalization of his science." [21]

Anthropologists until recently have been far more concerned about gathering data from their field studies than they have been about the logical procedures of observation, inference, and verification which the hypothetical-deductive method embodies. Since imaginative intuitions have been relied upon by many anthropologists, especially in dealing with the values of the community under study, some anthropologists feel more closely allied to the humanities than to the natural and social-scientific enterprise. Recall Murdock's claim that "when it comes to the formulation and testing of hypotheses, anthropologists reveal little comprehension of the requisites of a viable scientific theory and even less of the methods which science has devised for putting such a theory to the test." [22]

Spencer has emphasized, however, that the anthropologist's dependence upon "his critical judgments and his own intuitive perceptions and sensibilities" does not prevent him from attempting "to weigh and evaluate the evidence which his respondents and observations give him." From these he formulates a *Gestalt* pattern with respect to "the functional interrelationships within a culture." It is when he undertakes "the formulation of a particular hypothesis to be tested," however, "that many cultural anthropologists are in a quandary." [23] This difficulty notwithstanding, Kroeber declares that, if anthropology is to achieve an intellectual comprehension "resting both on specific evidence and on broad coherent theory," then "it is evidently going to be somebody's business to deal scientifically with these human phenomena: to work at a more than aesthetic comprehension of them." [24] The distinction between a method and research techniques that this task requires has been emphasized by Herskovits, when he insists that "the term *method* implies more than the actual procedures employed in prosecuting a given research project." For, as he reminds his colleagues, "techniques are essentially no more than ways of implementing the testing of hypotheses, and there is no hypothesis which does not arise from a body of theory and concept." [25]

Economic inquiry has undergone some significant revisions which bear directly upon the applicability of a hypothetical-deductive method. Traditional economic theory to a considerable extent could be described in terms of a "deductive ideal type method," in accordance with which theorems or laws were deductively derived from a few assumptions or basic propositions. Jevons, for example, sought to make economics "a mathematical science . . . comparatively abstract and general, treating mankind from simple points of view." [26] A procedure which employed deductive techniques came to be identified as *the economic method*. In order to guarantee the predictive power which justified this technique economic data and problems had to be fashioned to fit it.

Economists are now questioning this technique-centered approach. Ruggles, for one, welcomes the more recent growth of a "wide diversity of economic methodologies which are found in current use as an extremely healthy sign." His advocacy of a problem-centered, rather than technique-centered, approach for economics endorses the premise of the hypothetical-deductive method: "Differences in problems require differences in the accent which is laid upon the various stages of the research process; some may be amenable to particular techniques of analysis, and some to others." Accordingly, he outlines the following four consecutive stages for economic research: "(1) the exploration of the problem; (2) the theoretical development of hypotheses; (3) the empirical testing of hypotheses; and (4) the evaluation of conclusions." This logic of inquiry, Ruggles claims, provides a methodological framework for these approaches: "(1) mathematical economics; (2) statistical methods; (3) econometrics; (4) institutional economics; and (5) speculative economics." Ruggles emphasizes the usefulness of statistical techniques for some economic analysis; but he warns that, "like the use of symbols in mathematical analysis, numerical data can give a false impression of concreteness and accuracies to statistical analysis." While econometrics aims at correlative mathematical and statistical techniques, institutional and speculative analysis is still needed when judgment is required because the more precise techniques are not fully automatic.[27]

Some contemporary economists have presumed that only statistical techniques are justified in the same manner that deductive techniques were previously advocated. Consequently, it is significant to note that in his discussion of econometrics, Leontief concludes that "the further progress of quantitative economic analysis will depend upon successful, essentially non-statistical search for promising analytical insights, as much as upon the final statistical sifting of the empirical 'pay dust.' "[28]

Contrary to the widespread impression that all neo-classical economists were purely deductive, Marshall called for an inductive-deductive approach which, instead of relying on any one technique, sought to combine them: "It is the business of economics, as of almost every other science, to collect facts, to arrange and interpret them, and to draw inferences from them."[29] This is incongruent with von Mises' opposition to induction: "The only way to a cognition of these theorems is logical analysis of our own inherent knowledge of the category of action."[30] Thus, Marshall's approach seems to be much closer to that of an economic historian such as Spiethoff who claims that "actually, theoretical deduction and empirical induction go hand in hand in the task of explanation."[31] Marshall's endorsement of the hypothetical-deductive procedure appears to justify Lange's claim that

"theoretical economics provides hypotheses or models based on generalization of observation and subject to empirical test." [32]

Political scientists with a variety of interests and techniques have
always sought reliable descriptions and interpretations; but not until
recently have they become concerned about a justified method which
might regularize their analyses. Driscoll and Hyneman report that in
the past "method" usually referred "only to procedures for collecting
and examining data," and that even now there is no clear consensus
about what political scientists think it means. There is a growing
interest, however, in the "problems of abstraction, significance,
tests of validity, and the interrelationships of empirical data, generalizations, and theory." [33]

For many political scientists methodological problems are more
implicit than explicit; but there are those who agree with Herring
that "there must be rigorous attention to methodology" to guide
political inquiry "between the data-gathering and the concept building" and in "seeking hypotheses for verification or for discard." [34]
Leiserson more specifically sets forth the hypothetical-deductive requirements which must be met in order to acquire reliable knowledge:
"If truly scientific work in political investigation is taken as the desired goal, it is fair to ask what criteria the researcher should expect
of himself and in others." This, Leiserson contends, necessitates an
intellectual synthesis of inductive and deductive procedures: "If he
starts from the findings of fact—generalizations or uniformities drawn
from empirical data—the test is whether he can formulate statements
of relationships between his empirically based concepts, so that the
behavioral uniformities can be logically deduced or derived." [35]

Historians who are committed to the task of "cumulative analysis"
according to "logical as well as temporal patterns" (Aitken and
Loewenberg) are attempting to work out a modified version of the
hypothetical-deductive method which is used by other social scientists.
Such a logical pattern of historical inquiry is exhibited in the following procedure that coordinates "techniques conducive to cumulative
discovery" which, according to Brockunier and Loewenberg, "historians have already adopted": (i) authenticating testimony, (ii) imaginatively reconstructing explanatory hypotheses, (iii) verifying the deduced implications of such constructs, and (iv) formulating law-like
generalizations about specific situations for coherently integrating historical inferences. The lack of contemporary observations in the first

stage, and the difficulty of generalizing about idiographic situations in the fourth stage, present problems that will be dealt with in the subsequent chapter which examines in detail the social scientist's use of the hypothetical-deductive method. The point to be emphasized here, however, is that some historians feel intellectually obligated to adapt hypothetical-deductive requirements as far as possible to their distinctive kind of inquiry. For, as Brockunier and Loewenberg remind their colleagues who "invariably develop conjectural explanations and interpretative syntheses," such a "synthesis is theory, and it is elaborated by historians both inductively and deductively." They feel that the adoption of such a procedure is urgent since "the logic and methods of science have not generally been considered relevant for historical research" and "notions of inductive and deductive methods often remain fuzzy in students' minds." [36]

The historian's use of induction requires elaboration. When Nevins states the three rules of the historian's inductive method, he does not actually eliminate the kind of deduction which the method of reflective inquiry entails, i.e., the deduction of the implications of a hypothesis in order to know what to look for by way of evidence: "The writer must collect all the evidence that he can find," including "every pertinent fact available, not merely part of the pertinent facts." From among the "hypotheses as likely to explain the problem and afford a solution," which a classification of this evidence suggests, the historian "should formulate the most satisfactory hypothesis; examine all the evidence anew in the light it offers; and test it carefully." [37] Although Nevins assumes here that the inductive method of Mill is the only historical method, he is not supporting the claim of such historical theorists as Adams and Burgess who insisted upon "the direct deliverance of 'facts' " as the only scientific method. For, as Randall and Haines have significantly noted, "if this is indeed the proper procedure in historical investigation, history is the only field of knowledge in which such a pure inductive method without hypotheses or guiding principles obtains." Such a "hyperfactualism" is not the prerequisite for maintaining "the scientific spirit in history" which depends rather upon the historian's "determination to make only such conclusions or inferences as are justified by the evidence." [38]

If it is agreed that the historian who aims at "cumulative analysis" uses the hypothetical-deductive method as a coordination of various techniques, then instead of designating documentary analysis as "the historical method," it should be identified as a technique. This terminological alternation of traditional usage does not question the indispensability of establishing the authenticity of testimony, i.e., the "records and survivals of the past." For, without this technique for assessing the genuineness of sources which the historian must collect, evaluate, and extract from, he could not reconstruct his initial data in the first stage of his hypothetical-deductive procedure. Although documentary analysis can be carried on independently of historiographical synthesis, the historian who adopts the hypothetical-deductive method must assume that the techniques of the former and the techniques of the latter, which deal with the inferential construction and verification of interpretative hypotheses, are interpenetrating. This is what we assume Mandelbaum means when he claims that "in every case the historian must proceed in a manner which is both selective and synthetic." [39] It is also presupposed by Cohen and Nagel when they indicate the logical demands upon historical inquiry in terms of the following questions: "1. Are the data of research *admissible* as evidence; are the sources genuine. . . . 2. What is the *meaning* of the assertions contained in the sources; *what do the remains signify?* . . . 3. Are the assertions elicited from the data *true;* can we rely upon the sources for information concerning the past. . . . 4. What are the *explanations* for the past events; what are the systematic connections between the different assertions established as true, in terms of which we achieve an *understanding* of the past." [40]

In so far as historical inquiry proceeds in accordance with the hypothetical-deductive method it seems meaningless to ask whether it is an art or a science. Like the other social sciences, of course, it cannot imitate the natural sciences. But, regardless of whether history is considered one of the social sciences or intimately associated with the social sciences, it is an intellectual pursuit which aims primarily at the acquisition of reasonably acceptable knowledge rather than at the eliciting of an aesthetically effective response. The historian's creative imagination is essential in the most cognitively-oriented approach, and the aesthetic effectiveness of the historian's literary style is important for the reader. But unless these means are subordinated to his search for reliable knowledge as his intrinsic end, it is doubtful that any narrator should be called a historian.

4. THE CONSTRUCTIVE CHARACTER OF THE OBSERVATIONAL DATA
IN HYPOTHETICAL-DEDUCTIVE INQUIRY

Our claim that hypothetical-deductive inquiry begins with the observation and classification of relevant factual data may need some clarification. Otherwise, the sequential order of its first and second stages in our paradigm might seem to be incompatible with the other accounts of the stages of social-scientific inquiry which indicate that it begins with the formulation of a hypothesis. We indicated that this reflective procedure is instigated by a problematic situation which always entails a question in the mind of the investigator before he observes an event which is bound to influence what he observes and how he observes it. Since there still might be some misunderstanding, let us direct attention to the operation of hypotheses in the observational stage. This point was previously discussed in order to show what was meant by the constructed nature of all broadly operational knowledge.

The relevance of the factual data which the investigator observes and classifies in the first stage of hypothetical-deductive inquiry is always determined by some hypothetical question which he brings to his subject matter. It was Kant, of course, who drove this point home when he declared that "nature must be interrogated." In other words, observations have significance only when they affirm or deny some presumption in the mind of the observer. Exploratory observations may require little or no ideational expectancy. If such questions do not soon arise in the observer's mind, however, he is not engaged in a scientific diagnosis of given data. Moreover, without an interrogatory hypothesis, he would have to spend all of his time and effort in a futile attempt to observe everything that happens within the meshwork of the interconnected physical and behavioral events that constitute the observable world. While observation of the factual evidence is essential for scientific inquiry, no amount of observation per se can compel the "facts to speak for themselves." The weakness of this latter non-operational assumption was exposed in the previous assessment of naïve sense-impressionism. Northrop supports our position, when he declares that "the rule governing the method of analysis used in the first stage of inquiry is that the problematic situation must be reduced to the relevant factual situation." [41] But this raises the perplexing problem about what constitutes a fact.

By adopting the assumption that *reality* is never completely identical with the *perceptions of* and the *ideas about* it the epistemological dualist precludes the direct accessibility of unadulterated *facts*. Since he treats his perceptions and ideas as *constructs* and since these refer to the total context of the dimension of reality he is investigating, he gains nothing but further confusion, if he designates reasonably acceptable hypotheses as "facts." Possibly this designation might have some usefulness, if there were some propositional assertions of which he could be absolutely certain. However, his positive scepticism precludes any such definitive conclusion. He might consider his first-person experience of perceiving and thinking, as well as of remembering, desiring, anticipating, imagining, sensing, striving, etc., as facts, which taken together constitute the complex fact of his own consciousness. Useful as this designation may be for phenomenological analysis, it does not pertain to all of the observational data which natural scientists and social scientists are investigating. The significance of this special usage in the behavioral analysis of motivation will be shown later; but, it is not sufficiently general for the orientation we are seeking now. The unqualified point to be emphasized, however, is that regardless of how verified a generalization may be, it does not become a fact for the epistemological dualist. Accordingly, for him to ask whether or not a "fact" is true is a meaningless question.

Commitment to epistemological dualism allows the use of "facts" to denote separable but interrelated focuses in the cognitive process; but only one of these denotations serves the purpose of the first stage of hypothetical-deductive inquiry. As the permissible but less pertinent meaning, "facts" may denote the physical and behavioral events that go on happening independently of anyone's perception or thought of them, but which are taken as the referents of perceptual and ideational constructs. About these Cohen and Nagel have said: "Facts in this sense are neither true nor false, they simply are." As the more germane meaning, "facts" may denote what the investigator takes to be his initial observational data. Such factual data may be given to him by way of sense perceptions of external objects or by way of his own critical inspection of his own mental processes. These experiences are signified by propositions such as "There is a desk" or "I desire an education." About these Cohen and Nagel have said:

"All inquiry must take for granted a host of propositions of this sort, although we may be led to reject some of them as false as the inquiry progresses." "Facts" sometimes denote "certain discriminated elements in sense perception," for example, "This band of color lies between those two bands." Nevertheless, as Cohen and Nagel point out, "no inquiry *begins* with facts so defined"; but, rather, "such sensory elements are *analytically sought by us*, to test the inferences we make." [42]

Since the factual situation which an investigator takes to be his initial observational data is not completely delivered to him by the independently operating events, Margenau reminds natural scientists of "the essentially constructed character of physical objects," [43] and Easton reminds social scientists that "a fact is a particular ordering of reality in terms of a theoretical interest." [44] This means that the selection from a complex multiplicity of the data which are relevant to the problem of a particular inquiry, as well as the organization of their interrelations, is introduced by the observer himself. For even ordinary perceptions require not only the observer's implicit hypothesis that there is a referent for his sense datum, which usually is reproduced and confirmed by his further sensations, but they also require the hypothesis that predicted perceptions can be experienced by other observers. Lenzen insists that this presupposition underlies the procedures of empirical science: "The defining characteristic of perception is the occurrence of a sense datum and its interpretation as the aspect of an objective thing." Furthermore, as Lenzen reports, the activity of the observer himself in the determination of his initial data is even more obvious in the physicist's analysis of microphysical electrons, protons, neutrons, etc.: "In this field, principles become constructive instruments of interpretation, and so observation is more subject to the uncertainties of hypotheses than in perception of common things." [45] But it is with the observational data in the factual situation with which social-scientific inquiry begins that we are primarily concerned.

For a social scientist, who conceptually organizes sociocultural and motivational data in terms of the goal-oriented actions of the behavioral process, human desires for satisfaction-yielding objectives are taken to be just as factual as sense perceptions. If he has identified and correlated his subject matter in terms such as those of our synoptic model, the refusal to recognize human desiring as a factual aspect of human transactions would render his concept of purposive goal-seeking motivation unintelligible. This hypothetical construct of an intervening variable, it will be recalled, was required as a focal point of experiential evidence for the assessment of the other constructs of the social and cultural, as well as the psychodynamic and interpersonal, factors. For the "factuality" of these independent variables depends upon their being taken as conditions which shape the transactions of desire-motivated individuals.

The social scientist's reduction of the problematic situation to the relevant factual situation of behavioral events involves no more hypothetical construction than that introduced by the natural scientist in determining what he will take to be factual physical events. But the quantitative character of the physical data makes it seem more "factual" than the behavioral data which complete quantification would distort. A physicist may not agree with Kepler that "only measurable data are real"; but he cannot deny what Kepler probably meant, i.e., for the purpose of physical analysis the only data which can be taken as factually relevant are those with quantitatively measurable properties. Since the social scientist, unlike the natural scientist, must include human emotions and purposes among the factors in the ends-means continuum of human actions, he cannot make quantitativeness such a defining characteristic of factuality that he would be compelled to exclude all data which require qualitative assessment. As MacIver has emphasized, "quantitative relations hold of social as of all other facts, but they are quite inadequate to reveal the nature of the former." By way of illustrating the complication of the commensurate and the incommensurate in social-scientific data he points out that "a thousand weak purposes cannot be rolled into one strong purpose as a thousand weak units of force are joined into one strong force." [46] The population and financial resources of a community, as well as many similar aspects of the relevant factual situation, can be quantitatively measured; but the operation of the normative cultural symbols are no more completely accessible through quantitative assessment than is the motivation of any given member or group of members of that community who internalize cultural patterns in their goal-oriented behavior.

Now that we have identified the pattern of reflective inquiry in terms of the value-situation, the meaning-situation, and the knowledge-situation, which taken together constitute its epistemological perspective, we are ready to consider some of the statements by representatives of each of the behavioral disciplines which bear on the detailed applications of these principles. Since the value-situation of social-scientific inquiry was discussed previously, in the subsequent chapters attention will be directed to its meaning-situation and its knowledge-situation. Our aim, it will be recalled, is to use the epistemological perspective developed in this chapter as a framework for a comprehensive synthesis of the epistemological assumptions and the methodological procedures which in varying degrees are actually operating in each of the specific behavioral disciplines.

Footnotes to Chapter 1 of Part Three

1 Parsons, *The Structure of Social Action*, 22.
2 Kantor, "Interbehavioral Psychology," *Psychological Theory* (Marx), 318.
3 Dewey, *Logic*, 17-18.
4 Lundberg, *Foundations of Sociology*, 26.
5 Andrews, *Methods of Psychology*, 3.
6 Werkmeister, *The Basis and Structure of Knowledge*, 7, 17.
7 Cassirer, *An Essay on Man*, 23-41.
8 Sapir, *Culture, Language, and Personality*, 8-9.
9 Whitehead, "The Analysis of Meaning," *Essays in Science and Philosophy*, 122-123.
10 Cunningham, "Meaning, Reference, and Significance," *Philosophical Review*, 47 (1938), p. 175.
11 Buchler, *Nature and Judgment*, 154. For related discussions, see Lewis, *An Analysis of Knowledge and Valuation*, ix, 9-10, 19-20, 35; Morris, *Signs, Language and Behavior*, 198; and Ogden and Richards, *The Meaning of Meaning*, 53, 57.
12 The most famous description of the scientific method "in the broader sense" is, of course, Dewey's in *How We Think*, 107, and *Logic*, Chapter VI, "The Pattern of Inquiry." Although his terminology and his order of the steps differ from ours, our indebtedness to Dewey is obvious. Werkmeister, who uses the terms "hypothetico-deductive," offers an excellent account of the scientific method, as well as of the concepts, laws, and principles it entails, in his *The Basis and Structure of Knowledge*, Part IV. A more elementary but dependable account of this reflective procedure is presented by Larrabee in his *Reliable Knowledge*, Chapters 4-12. Underlying all these variously expressed conceptions of the procedures of inquiry there is the premise which Dewey stated in his

Logic: "Inquiry is the controlled or directed transformation of an indeterminate situation into one that is so determinate in its constituent distinctions and relations as to convert the elements of the original situation into a unified whole." (104-105)

See Hempel and Oppenheim, "The Logic of Explanation" in *Readings in the Philosophy of Science* (Feigl and Brodbeck), 319-352, for an advanced analysis of the basic pattern of scientific explanation which, in principle, corroborates this hypothetical-deductive procedure.

[13] Northrop, *The Logic of the Sciences and Humanities*, viii-ix. Accordingly, we similarly agree with Conant (*On Understanding Science*, 145) and with Bush, (*Science*, 103, 664, May 31, 1946), when they deny that there is only one scientific method.

[14] Brown in *Psychological Theory* (Marx), 235-236.

[15] Marx, *Psychological Theory* (Marx), 8.

[16] Andrews, *Methods of Psychology*, 3-5. Cf. Murphy, *Personality*, 915-916; Good and Scates, *Methods of Research*, 989-991.

[17] Newcomb, "Studying Social Behavior," *Methods of Psychology* (Andrews), 692; and *Social Psychology*, 17-18.

[18] Merton, *Social Theory and Social Structure*, 97-98.

[19] Sorokin, *Society, Culture and Personality*, 18.

[20] Lundberg, Schrag, Larsen, *Sociology*, 7.

[21] Furfey, "Sociological Science and the Problem of Values," *Symposium on Sociological Theory* (Gross), 513-514.

[22] Murdock, "Sociology and Anthropology," *For a Science of Social Man* (Gillin), 27.

[23] Spencer in *Method and Perspective in Anthropology* (Spencer), 133.

[24] Kroeber in *An Appraisal of Anthropology Today* (Tax), 358.

[25] Herskovits in *Method and Perspective in Anthropology* (Spencer), 5.

[26] Jevons, *The Principles of Science*, 759-761.

[27] Ruggles, "Methodological Developments," *A Survey of Contemporary Economics* (Haley), Vol. II, 453.

[28] Leontief, "Econometrics," *A Survey of Contemporary Economics* (Ellis), Vol. I, 393.

[29] Marshall, *Principles of Economics*, 29.

[30] von Mises, *Human Action*, 64. See Kaufmann, *Methodology of the Social Sciences*, 212, 228, 234, 238-239 for a discussion of the importance of distinguishing between analytic and synthetic propositions in economics; and Northrop, "The Method and Limited Predictive Power of Classical Economic Science," *The Logic of the Sciences and the Humanities* for a critical challenge of the traditional assumptions of the deductions of dynamic theory.

[31] Spiethoff, "Pure Theory and Economic Gestalt Theory: Ideal Types and Real Types," *Enterprise and Secular Change* (Lane and Riemersma), 450.

[32] Lange, "The Scope and Method of Economics," *Readings in the Philosophy of Science* (Feigl and Brodbeck), 746-749. Originally published in the *Review of Economic Studies*, 13, 1945-1946.

[33] Driscoll and Hyneman, "Methodology for Political Scientists," *American Political Science Review*, March 1955, p. 192.

34 Herring, *American Political Science Review*, December 1953, pp. 968-969.

35 Leiserson, "Problems of Methodology in Political Science," *Political Science Quarterly*, December 1953, pp. 562-563.

36 Brockunier and Loewenberg, Bulletin 64, pp. 139-140. Cf. Aitken and Loewenberg, Bulletin 64, p. 25.

37 Nevins, *The Gateway to History*, 212.

38 Randall, Haines, and others, Bulletin 54, pp. 31-32, 134.

39 Mandelbaum, *The Problem of Historical Knowledge*, 8-9, 246-247.

40 Cohen and Nagel, *An Introduction to Logic and Scientific Method*, 326. Cf. Gottschalk, *Understanding History*, 48-52; and Dewey, *Logic*, 231-233.

41 Northrop, *The Logic of the Sciences and the Humanities*, 34.

42 Cohen and Nagel, *An Introduction to Logic and Scientific Method*, 217-218.

43 Margenau, *The Nature of Concepts*, 48-50.

44 Easton, *The Political System*, 53.

45 Lenzen, "Procedures of Empirical Science," *International Encyclopedia of Unified Science*, Vol. I, No. 5, pp. 4-5, 26.

46 MacIver, *The Elements of Social Science*, 17-18.

2 The Meaning-Situation of Social-Scientific Inquiry

A. A Proposed Answer to the Meaning-Question

By the meaning-situation, it will be recalled, we refer to an investigator's epistemological assumption about what kind of knowledge can be acquired. This prescribes the method and criterion the investigator will use in the construction and verification of generalizations. Any pronouncement about what kind of knowledge is meaningful to all social scientists, as well as to all natural scientists, is indeed presumptuous. There is a reluctance to tell experts what they really presuppose or to give the false impression that one is prescribing to competent specialists what they ought to assume. It is unlikely, moreover, that any statement to cover all disciplines could express a complete consensus. Despite these reservations, some such general tentative statement is required, if we are going to make any attempt to ascertain the mutual epistemological assumptions underlying social-scientific inquiry. For this purpose, the following answer to the meaning-question was proposed in the preceding chapter: *The social scientist, as well as the natural scientist, can operationally construct reliable hypotheses about that dimension of reality with which he is concerned, in terms of a coherent system of generalizations which have causal implications that can be verified to various degrees of probability.*

In order to ascertain what this highly generalized proposal entails, it will be further recalled, we have stated the following five epistemological postulates:

(1) There is an objective reality to a specific dimension of which the subjective constructs of the particular discipline refer. (2) A high degree of probability (reasonable acceptability), rather than absolute certainty, is the most that can be expected in the operational verification of generalizations which never exhaust all that is yet to be known. (3) Knowledge about the objective physical and behavioral universe requires an orderly system of constructs. (4) The category of causality is required as the principle of objective reference for the construction of explanatory and predictive hypotheses about the interaction of physical and behavioral events. (5) Coherence (consistency and adequacy) is the generic logical criterion of verification from which the specific criteria for empirically testing the deduced implications of hypotheses are derived.

To what extent have social scientists themselves presupposed these epistemological assumptions? In this chapter, let us note what representatives from each of the behavioral disciplines have said about the necessity for recognizing this kind of epistemological postulation. Then in the five subsequent chapters we shall consider what some psychologists, sociologists, anthropologists, economists, political scientists, and historians have explicitly acknowledged about each of these five assumptions. Throughout these discussions the following question should be kept in mind: To what extent are the complications within each of these disciplines attributable to the lack of a clear understanding of these postulates which constitute its meaning-situation?

B. *Social-Scientific Endorsement of the Need for Epistemological Postulates*

The need for acknowledging the functioning of epistemological presuppositions in *psychological* analysis is emphasized by Murphy when he writes in the role of a positive sceptic. He contends that "psychology might well appear to be a science of negations," since "the growth of those confident 'schools of psychology' has been largely due to a series of dialectical protests." The selections of data and techniques have been guided by arbitrarily preferred "principles that define the narrow limits beyond which generalizations cannot be made." Murphy warns his colleagues that any kind of psychological inquiry is predetermined by the investigator's presupposition about what kind of objective referent for his constructs is meaningful. Consequently, he calls for more critical awareness on the part of the investigators in the adoption of the postulates in their meaning-situation, for these postulates determine what kind of empirical data and techniques the psychologists will employ in their knowledge-situation: "Empirical procedure is necessary, an empiricism willing to learn not only regarding the methods of inquiry that will be most fruitful, but regarding the postulates that do least violence to firsthand experience and which provide clarity without the arrogance of offering any ultimate classification of man." [1]

When Lundberg critically evaluates the results of *sociological* research, he concludes that its weakness does not lie in its knowledge-situation, in which sociologists seek to construct and verify generalizations. Rather, its chief weakness lies in the lack of an adequate conception of its meaning-situation: "There is no workable set of postulates to guide and organize research." Consequently, Lundberg urges that sociologists should more fully recognize "the basic postulates regarding the nature of 'reality' and 'knowledge' upon which all science proceeds." [2]

In an effort to clarify the meaning-situation of *anthropological* inquiry, Bidney is seeking to develop what he calls metaanthropology: "An ontological, metascientific theory is an attempt to explain why phenomena are related in a given manner by referring to some aspect of reality which provides an intelligible ground for their occurrence and interrelation." Bidney points out to anthropologists who may be indifferent about epistemological assumptions that "ontological postulates constitute an indispensable element in every one of the sciences." Moreover, he does not claim that these postulates can be confirmed in the knowledge-situation. Rather, such epistemological assumptions are justified by their pragmatic fruitfulness in defining what kind of anthropological knowledge is meaningful. He makes this explicit in connection with the first of these epistemological assumptions: "The postulate of objective reality, independent of the observer, is a fruitful one, since it serves as a normative guide to research and presents an intelligible goal for the scientist to approximate." [3]

The importance of making explicit the unverifiable postulates of an *economist's* intellectual orientation has been emphasized by Gruchy. He declares that such a "framework of interpretation" not only provides the economist with a "point of departure" and "establishes the borders within which his theorizing is carried on," but it also "influences the manner in which the scientist goes about selecting and organizing his data, and determines how far he will go in abstracting from the facts of concrete experience. Although the observational, explanatory-predictive, and verificative procedures of economic analysis are derived from the meaning-situation, i.e., a "general framework of interpretation," this set of epistemological assumptions "is not something that the scientist subjects to verification by any inductive procedure." [4]

Political scientists in the past have not been very much concerned about their epistemological assumptions. But Driscoll and Hyneman detect the emergence of an interest in the meaning-situation of political science: "The lack of elaborate statement about underlying assumptions, guiding conceptualizations, and other methodological considerations cannot conceal the evidence that in recent years there has been both a rapid growth in output of American political scientists which is based on a conscious regard for sound methodological foundations and a steady rise in the sophistication with which methodological demands are met." [5]

Historians are becoming more concerned about their epistemological assumptions, though it would be inaccurate to say that all of them have explicitly acknowledged the meaning postulates which their narrative presentation presupposes. The members of a Committee on Historiography who lament that the majority of historians have not "been very critically aware of their own presuppositions" [6] would seem to agree with the epistemological claim by Werkmeister that imaginatively reconstructed historical knowledge "is, and always must be, relative to certain presuppositions on integration." [7] The need for recognizing the influence of the historian's meaning-postulates in his imaginative reconstruction was stressed by Beard when he insisted that "written history is an act of faith" in which "any selection and arrangement of facts pertaining to any large area of history, either local or world, is controlled inexorably by the frame of reference in the mind of the selector and arranger." [8]

Let us now consider in detail the implications of each of these five postulates in the meaning-situations of psychology, sociology, anthropology, economics, political science, and history. Before we cite the statements by representatives of each of these disciplines we shall first state the general significance of each postulate.

Footnotes to Chapter 2 of Part Three

[1] Murphy, *Personality*, 915-917. Cf. Spence, "The Postulates and Methods of Behaviorism," *Readings in the Philosophy of Science* (Feigl and Brodbeck), 571-583.

[2] Lundberg, *Foundations of Sociology*, 8-9, 100-101.

[3] Bidney, *Theoretical Anthropology*, 164, 419.

[4] Gruchy, *Modern Economic Thought*, 9-10.

[5] Driscoll and Hyneman, "Methodology for Political Science," *American Political Science Review*, March 1955, page 210. See Cook, "The Political System: The Stubborn Search for a Science of Politics," *Journal of Philosophy*, LI, 4, Feb. 18, 1954, pages 128-137.

[6] Bulletin 54, page 27.

[7] Werkmeister, *The Basis and Structure of Knowledge*, 328-329.

[8] Beard, "Written History as an Act of Faith," *The American Historical Review*, Jan. 1934, Vol. XXXIX, 227-228. Mandelbaum's *The Problem of Historical Knowledge* is an outstanding contribution to an examination of epistemological presuppositions. A number of his significant points will be considered in connection with specific postulates.

3 The First Postulate of the Meaning-Situation of Reflective Inquiry (Reality)

There is an objective reality to a specific dimension of which the subjective constructs of the given discipline refer.

A. The General Significance of the First Postulate

It is hard to think of any reason why all scientists would not agree that, regardless of *what* reality might be, it is "out there" to be discovered. What would the investigator be investigating, if he did not believe *that* there was an independently existing state of affairs to which his constructs refer. This was expressed by Planck as the metaphysical premise that "the real world—in other words, objective nature—stands behind everything explorable." [1] Similarly, Einstein and Infeld refer to the "existence of the ideal limit of knowledge" which is "approached by the human mind." [2]

Indispensable as this belief in an independent reality appears to be, it cannot be known as a true generalization by a scientist. For his method of constructing hypotheses and his criterion for confirming or refuting their implications must presuppose this belief. He can not disprove the solipsistic claim that there is no objective referent for the constructs in the mind of the scientist. This may be the case. Moreover, how can scientists disprove the alternative phenomenological assumption which Husserl adopts when he declares that "everything which is there for me in the world of things is on the grounds of principle only a *presumptive reality*," whereas "I myself or my experience in its actuality is *absolute Reality*." Husserl does not deny the existence of an objective referent, as does the solipsist; but, as he insists, this phenomenological premise "completely bars me from using any judgment that concerns spatio-temporal existence." In short, Husserl is indifferent about the nature of the objective reality and its relation to the constructs which presuppose it as its referent.[3]

How then does the scientist justify his affirmation that there is an objective reality to which his subjective constructs refer? He justifies his affirmation of this belief on the pragmatic grounds that it is more fruitful for inquiry than the solipsist's denial of it or the phenomenologist's neutrality with regard to it. It is presupposed by his definition of knowledge in terms of inferred generalizations *about* their referents and by his epistemological dualism, i.e., the construct is never considered identifiable with its referent. By now it should be clear, however, that this belief is a postulate in his conception of what is meaningful rather than a substantive hypothesis that is subject to confirmation or refutation by empirical evidence in his knowledge-situation. In other words, he adopts this assumption because of the sterility of the alternative assumptions.

When the epistemological dualist presupposes that there is an objective reality which scientific generalizing does not create, then he can assume along with Kant that whatever knowledge the scientist has about that independently existing reality he constructs himself. Thus he can agree with Einstein and Infeld that "physical concepts are free creations of the human mind, and are not, however they seem, uniquely determined by the external world" as long as he agrees with Planck that "we feel inevitably compelled to postulate the existence of a real world." If this postulate were not included in his meaning-situation, then, for example, he would have to assume in astronomy that the actual relation of the sun and the earth was once geocentric but became heliocentric when the theory of Ptolemy was supplanted by the theory of Copernicus. This no scientist would ever presuppose.[4]

It will be recalled from the previous identification of the behavioral process in terms of the synoptic model that a social scientist formulates *conceptual* constructs simply for identifying some motivational and/or sociocultural aspect of his behavorial data. When he does this, he assumes that his referent is a separable but interrelated dimension of the total objective existential process in which his super-organic data are just as real as are the inorganic and organic data of natural-scientific inquiry. At this point, however, we want to find out what epistemological assumptions he adopts when hc formulates *theoretical* constructs for substantive investigations in his specific discipline. To determine this let us now turn to statements by representatives of each of the social-scientific disciplines.

B. *The Significance of the First Postulate for Individual Psychology*

The broadest dimension of the objcctive reality to which psychological constructs refer is the behavior of human organisms as they are motivated by their conscious and unconscious goal-oriented responses to physical and sociocultural situations. Within this heterogeneous field of general psychology, it will be recalled, we found that individual psychology deals with the assessment of such somatic-psychogenic processes as sensory-motor perceptions and learning, as well as with abnormal and normal motivation. (The corresponding subject matter of social psychology will be identified in the next section.)

The historical development of individual psychology might be depicted in terms of the different concepts which psychologists have successively adopted for identifying their referent. The concept of a soul-substance with inherent faculties was abandoned as a referent, since its unknowability precluded any kind of empirical observations. Similarly, the concept of "private mental processes" was rejected as a referent, since only introspective observations could be used. For a while the concept of a neurophysiological organism was widely adopted as the referent for the stimulus-response constructs of behavioristic psychology. By confining his dimension of reality to muscular, glandular, and neural data which he could extrospectively observe the behaviorist could aim at the same kind of experimental testing and predictive control that had been achieved in the natural sciences. From the discussion of the psychological constructs that were examined in the elaboration of the synoptic model, however, it should be obvious that many contemporary psychologists are rejecting this purely neurophysiological concept in favor of taking as their referent a goal-oriented behavioral process that is also motivated by psychodynamic, interpersonal, and sociocultural responses. For personologists, therefore, the compound construct of "personality" has a two-sided referent. On one side, it is assumed that there is the individual's experience as it is produced by his total natural, sociocultural, psychodynamic, and interpersonal environment, i.e., personality as product. On the other side it is assumed that there is the individual's experience, as the individual who is shaped by these independent variables does to some degree contribute to the kind of person he is in the process of becoming, i.e., personality as producer. The relatively self-determined selection which the latter kind of reflective goal-seeking behavior requires was identified by Tolman as the intervening variable, and it was described by Allport in terms of propriate striving. Consequently, Allport insists that when the personologist assumes that "integrated individuality" is the objective reality to which his constructs refer, then he must use a two-fold nomothetic-idiographic approach.[5]

Out of this cursory summary of the historical development of individual psychology there emerge several points, acknowledged by some psychologists, which bear directly on this first postulate in its meaning-situation. In the first place, there has been one persisting objective referent of psychological constructs throughout all of the changes of opinion with respect to what orienting concept properly identifies genuine psychological data, whether it be a soul-substance, private mental processes, neurophysiological behavior, or purposive goal-oriented behavior. As Smith has declared, "what runs through an otherwise heterogeneous history is a pervading focus on the individual." While Smith is correct when he claims that "the individual has been the primary reference point," it might be added that all psychologists have also assumed that the behavioral reality is a temporal process in which the observable present moment of an individual's experience is the outgrowth of past experiences and refers to future experiences. This is not a denial of Boring's claim that "psychology must deal with existential reals which are similarly mediate to direct experience," since "there is no way of getting at 'direct experience' because experience gives itself up to science indirectly, inferentially." What is contended here is that these mediate constructs would serve no investigative purpose, unless the psychologist assumes that they have an existentially real referent. This is what Smith seems to be contending when he says that "constructs are grounded in reality to the extent that they are embedded in a maturing theory in constant interplay with data." [6]

In the second place, the fruitless arguments among such psychological schools as Watsonian behaviorists, gestaltists, and psychoanalysts stem from their failure to recognize that each of their conclusions is largely determined by the divergence in their delimitation of what kind of data is meaningful. Delimitation of data is of course required for substantive research; but it is unwarrantedly arbitrary for the researcher to dismiss the claims of other schools because they have begun with another body of data. Such narrowly circumscribed conceptions of the objective referent for an "observational framework" have been criticized by Marx as "a priori biases which in actual practice account for much of the polemic and invective generated in psychological controversies." If psychologists realize that these "a priori biases" are postulates which are neither true nor false but rather are "observational frameworks" in their divergent meaning-situations, then, as Marx recommends, they may "be recognized more clearly and explicitly as just such, and not disguised as the apparent function of purely scientific analysis." No appeal to empirical evidence can resolve these conflicting claims when each of them precludes the admissibility of the kind of evidence which would support the other claims. In other words, as Marx says, "alternative theoretical approaches can be directly compared, scientifically, only if they make scientific predictions within the same observational framework." How could this be done unless psychologists share a sufficiently comprehensive conception of what objective referent is meaningful for a synoptic understanding of human behavior? [7]

C. *The Significance of the First Postulate for*
Social Psychology

As the other branch of general psychology, social psychology deals
with the motive patterns, attitudes, sentiments, and role-behaviors
which characterize the interpersonal transactions of the members of a
community. The social psychologist is aware that the social roles which
define the rights and duties of each member are established by the
institutionalization of cultural patterns of feeling, believing, and acting. Leaving these highly relevant social and cultural aspects of the
behavioral process to the sociologist and the anthropologist, the social psychologist focuses his attention upon the resultant reciprocal
stimulation in so far as it motivates each member's goal-seeking behavior. It is this interpersonal dimension of the behavioral process,
therefore, that constitutes the objective referent of the social psychologist's constructs, when he attempts "to understand and explain
how the thought, feeling, and behavior of individuals are influenced
by the actual, imagined, or implied presence of other human beings." [8]

The social psychologist is aware more explicitly than many individual psychologists that human behavior must be viewed in both
its individual and its sociocultural aspects (Cooley). However, it is
from the individual-psychological conceptions of goal-seeking motivation and of learning that the social psychologist derives the constructs by which he avoids the fallacies of the "group mind," at one
extreme, and the "innate instincts," at the other. Interpersonal transactions, for example, are often analyzed in terms of imitation and
suggestibility which have been developed by sociologists. But the
social psychologist always wants to know "imitation and suggestion
by whom to whom" (Yuker).

How does the social psychologist answer the charges of criticism
like that of Nadel who claims that social psychology is nothing more
than a "borderland of psychology and social enquiry"? [9] The social
psychologist must adopt the postulate that interpersonal transactions
constitute a distinctive dimension of the objective reality of the behavioral process which is not entirely reducible to its other social,
cultural, and motivational dimensions. It is in order to make this
postulate explicit that Newcomb has sought to identify a separable

referent for linking "protoplasm" and "society" in terms of "the intervening variables by which the individual organism relates its behavior to the social field." More than the individual psychologist the social psychologist must be concerned about the membership of an individual in groups; but unlike the sociologist and anthropologist, who are concerned with "the fact that all members of those groups are subject to similar influences," the social psychologist presupposes that "his primary concern is with the influences which play upon individuals as members of various groups," i.e., "in resulting individual differences." [10]

Accordingly, in his meaning-situation the social psychologist must assume that there is an objective referent for his analysis of interpersonal transactions when he formulates constructs about motives and attitudes as "inferred conditions which intervene between behavior on the one hand and organisms and social environment on the other." With respect to this first postulate, Newcomb clarifies what the social psychologist must assume about what he means by the variations of an individual's behavior in response to the stimulation of the other members of a group: "No matter how complex the form of stimulation or how many persons involved, the social psychologist proceeds upon the basis of three assumptions: first, that individuals are responding to some form of social influence, direct or indirect, from one or more individuals; second, that individuals' behaviors are not a matter of caprice or sheer chance, but correspond to certain conditions and vary in orderly manner with them; and third, that these conditions may be discovered if observations are properly made and conclusions properly drawn." [11]

D. *The Significance of the First Postulate for Sociology*

The epistemological correlations of a *referent* and *constructs* which this postulate entails is specifically adopted as a presupposition for sociological analysis by Parsons: "It is a philosophical implication of the position taken here that there is an external world of so-called empirical reality which is not the creation of the individual human mind." Parsons completely endorses this assumption that, though the referent is independent of human thought, any sociological knowledge is constructed by the sociologist himself: "The systems of scientific theory under consideration are obviously not this external reality itself, nor are they a direct and literal representation of it." Accordingly, constructs are always emendable, since they are never "such that one and only one such representation is in any sense valid." This means that the *constructs* stand "in a functional relation to" the *referent* "such that for certain scientific purposes they are adequate representations of it." [12]

In order to establish an epistemologically dualistic "symbolic frame of reference" Lundberg also calls for the adoption of this first postulate. His presupposition is such that whatever objective reality may be, its operations do not depend upon the sociological constructs about it, even though any knowledge the sociologist acquires is limited to the generalizations he inferentially constructs from what is given in his experience. "All data or experience with which man can become concerned consist of the responses of the organism-in-an-environment"; but though "we start with symbolized human responses to the immediate datum," the sociologist's "abstractions from these symbols" require the assumption that they have an objective existential referent. "As a metaphysical necessity we grant *that which* in the universe outside of the responding mechanism precipitates the response." Lundberg justifies the adoption of this postulate about the objective reality to which sociological constructs refer on the pragmatic grounds of its fruitfulness for inquiry rather than on the grounds that it establishes definitive truth about what reality in itself actually is: "Scientists had better confine themselves to a modest postulate of 'x' which precipitates our responses"; but the "justification of even the postulate of the 'x' had better be its demonstrable efficiency in helping us to comprehend our world rather than in vociferous declarations about its 'existence' and 'truth'." [13]

Among other sociologists who have also acknowledged the epistemological demand for this assumption there are some who agree with Lundberg that "the metaphysical position necessary and compatible with science is a postulate conceding the existence of *whatever* precipitates our responses." But they do not agree entirely with Lundberg's additional contention that there should be "no further statements whatever about the absolute nature, characteristics, or temporal-spatial qualities of these postulated entities." [14] It is unlikely that contemporary sociologists would make any assumptions about "the absolute nature" of their objective referent in the manner of Spencer. About its "characteristics" and "temporality," however, Sorokin and MacIver have made further statements which they consider essential for rendering the postulate about the objective referent fruitful for sociological inquiry. When Sorokin distinguishes the "superorganic phenomena," which constitute "the realm of interacting human beings and the products of their interactions," from the organic and inorganic phenomena, he substantively characterizes the objective reality: "As the presence of life distinguishes living structures and processes, so the presence of mind or thought in its developed form, differentiates the superorganic phenomena from the organic." [15] In his idea of the three dynamic levels of physical, organic, and conscious being, MacIver also presupposes that objective reality is a process of emergent evolution. Moreover, he assumes that it is a process of temporal duration: "The universe is a changeful scheme of events and processes in which the living being exists not only in the ever-enduring present; it exists, as it were, *in the time dimension*, embracing at each moment the future and the past with the present." [16] The point to be noted for epistemological purposes is that these metaphysical ideas about both that there *is* some objective reality and *what* characterizes it are not asserted as true. Rather, they are taken as assumptions in the sociologist's meaning-situation which sociological inquiry requires as a referential framework.

E. *The Significance of the First Postulate for Anthropology*

The necessity for adopting this postulate with respect to *culture* as the dimension of reality to which anthropological constructs refer has been emphasized by Bidney: "Our conceptual and empirical knowledge of reality varies with our interests and experiences, but reality as an ontological existent independent of man is an absolute object to which our ideas progressively conform in the course of our pursuit of knowledge by scientific methods." Radical relativists, of course, contend that the referent is nothing but the interpreter's own cultural experience. But Bidney makes his opposition to this view explicit when he contends that "the postulate of objective reality, independent of the observer, is a fruitful one, since it serves as a normative guide to research and presents an intelligible goal for the scientists to approximate." [17]

The complications in the meaning-situation of anthropological inquiry would have been much less acute, if anthropologists had thought about and expressed their ideas about culture in terms of the principle of epistemological dualism which Bidney explicitly adopts: "The conceptual construct of culture and the actual process of culture may correspond epistemically in a scientific theory of culture but they are not identical and must not be confused." As many anthropologists acknowledge, however, there has been much disagreement among them with respect to what they mean by culture. Bidney cites five divergent conceptions: the realistic view of culture as a quality of human behavior; the idealistic view of culture as a continuity of communicated ideas; the ideological view of culture as the product of social forces; the abstractionistic view of culture as a configurational pattern constructed by the anthropologist; and the functionalistic view of culture as the instrument for meeting collective needs. When Kroeber, Kluckhohn, White, and other anthropologists review the various conceptions of culture, their lists do not all correspond exactly with Bidney's. But they all emphasize the diversity of conceptions and probably would agree with Bidney that when anthropologists attempt to determine "in what sense is culture real," they have been seeking an answer to this question: "Is it essentially an autonomous form or level of reality, or is it an abstract pattern and configuration other than human behavior?" [18]

It should be noted that either of these two alternative answers to this question presupposes epistemological monism. The former identifies culture with the idea, and the latter identifies culture with the reality. Consequently, many anthropologists have become embroiled in the irresolvable dispute on the "ontological issue whether culture should be regarded as an abstraction or considered a reality *sui generis*, as of a superorganic level of phenomena."

According to Bidney, White has reified culture as a self-subsistent entity when White in his *Science of Culture* insists that the processes and laws of culture can be better understood as a *sui generis* level of reality without reference to the psychological motivations of people. "Culture must be explained in terms of culture." But White admits that "these cultural events could not have taken place had it not been for human organisms." More recently (April, 1959) White has attempted to clarify his position in the face of this criticism by Bidney, Murdock, Strong, Herrick, and others: "When things and events dependent upon symboling are considered and interpreted in terms of their relationship to human organisms, i.e., in a somatic context, they may properly be called *human behavior*, and the science, *psychology*"; but "when things and events dependent upon symboling are considered and interpreted in terms of their relationships to one another rather than to human organisms, we may call them *culture*, and the science, *culturology*." Despite the general impression that White is an ontological superorganicist, however, it may be that subsequent discussions will substantiate Goldstein's contention that White is presenting only a "methodological orientation." [19]

An explicit recognition of this epistemologically dualistic relation of objective referent and subjective constructs should contribute substantially to the resolving of the conflict between social anthropologists and sociologists, on the one hand, and cultural anthropologists, on the other. Whereas the former often assume that cultural phenomena are derived from social phenomena, the latter often assume that social phenomena are derived from cultural phenomena.

The significance of the first postulate for dealing with this fruitless dichotomy will be better understood if we note the serious concern of some social scientists from each of these groups for its elimination. Parsons claims that the formulation of a unified theory of human behavior is blocked by the fact that "the relation between social systems and culture is the subject of unresolved controversy both within the anthropological profession, and between anthropologists and sociologists." [20] At the International Symposium on Anthropology which discussed "Cultural/Social Anthropology" Tax contended that to avoid this impasse "we ought to use the words 'cultural' and 'social' anthropology interchangeably," and Greenberg insisted that neither kind of anthropology was on a higher level of abstraction than the other. For not only can the anthropologist "abstract patterns of social relationships from the actual culture," but he can equally well abstract "cultural patterns from the social interrelations." All of the participants seemed to have agreed that continuing the controversy was pointless. [21]

In an effort to clarify the confusion about the concepts of culture

and society, Kroeber and Parsons have sought a consensus which assumes that the objective referent of the constructs of cultural anthropologists, social anthropologists, and sociologists is the sociocultural
process in accordance with which human actions occur. Instead of
the "preferential a priori" assumption that society determines culture,
they recommend the "preferential a priori" assumption that "neither
can be directly reduced to terms of the other." On these pragmatic
grounds of its fruitfulness for social-scientific inquiry they postulate
the independent existence of a sociocultural process as the objective
referent for the correlative constructs of culture and society: "They
are distinct systems in that they abstract or select two analytically
distinct sets of components from the same concrete phenomena." If
Kroeber and Parsons did not adopt this first postulate with respect
to the objective reality of the sociocultural process (regardless of how
it is conceived), they could not justify their claim that "the analytical discrimination should be maintained without prejudice to the
question of which is more 'important,' 'correct,' or 'fundamental' if
indeed such questions turn out to be meaningful at all." [22]

There are two other aspects of the dimension of objective reality
to which the constructs of anthropological inquiry refer that must
be included in this first postulate of its meaning-situation. One is the
reciprocal functioning of persons in the sociocultural process. The
other is the multilinear evolution of the sociocultural process. Since
each of these characterizations of the objective referent entails causal
operations, they will be elaborated later under the fourth postulate
which pertains to causality. So that their metacultural significance
as ontological referents might not be overlooked, however, let us note
how some anthropologists have acknowledged them as properties of
the independently existing sociocultural process.

Hallowell clearly postulates the ontological status of socioculturalized persons when he declares that while "personality, culture, and
society form systems of relations that function as integral wholes in
a wider universe of other-than-human reality," nevertheless, "they
have no independent existence apart from the social adjustment of
the individuals involved and the organization of human experience,
in a manner that typifies the human situation." Consequently, Hallowell insists, "society, culture, and personality may, of course, be conceptually differentiated for specialized types of analysis and study,"
as long as it is assumed that "a culture as lived is not something

apart from the individuals who live it or separable from the societal organization through which group living functions." In other words, the objective reality of the sociocultural process is unintelligible apart from the internalization of cultural patterns and social structures in the motivation of goal-oriented persons who are both products and producers of the sociocultural process.[23]

The diachronic character of the sociocultural dimension of objective reality is presupposed by the conception of cultural evolution which, according to Steward, "may be defined broadly as the quest for cultural regularities or laws." Although the nineteenth century conception of a *unilinear evolution* of cultures through parallel stages has been abandoned, some contemporary anthropologists assume that there is a *universal evolution* of culture, and others adopt the postulate that the sociocultural process to which their constructs refer exhibits *multilinear evolution*. Steward characterizes the latter as "a somewhat less ambitious approach than the other two," which "is like unilinear evolution in dealing with a particular culture, but it is distinctive in searching for parallels of limited occurrence instead of universals." Although some anthropologists who do not yet recognize these distinctions may not acknowledge the necessity for assuming something about the historical development of cultures, Steward calls for the adoption of the multilinear conception of evolution as a methodological assumption "that significant regularities in cultural change occur" which is presupposed by "scientific generalizations, whether they deal with synchronic, functional relationships or with diachronic, sequential relationships and whether they embrace few or many cultures."[24]

F. *The Significance of the First Postulate for Economics*

Underlying any economist's particular claim about how scarce resources might best be distributed and used is his assumption that *allocative decisions* with respect to the selection of the means for satisfying human wants for material goods and services are always operating in one way or another. It is this inherent choice from among alternative ways of obtaining a livelihood in the ends-means continuum of human actions, that is the objective referent of the constructs which determines "the scope and method of economics." As

Lange has expressed this point, "men must make decisions which, given the organization and institutions of society, determine the distribution of the scarce resources among the different persons as well as the uses to which the scarce resources are put." [25] The diversities of economic theories arise not from different objective referents but, rather, from different conceptions of the determinant of these economic decisions, e.g., Smith's "invisible hand," Marx's "dialectic," Marshall's "equilibrating law of supply and demand," Keynes' "governmental operations," Ayers' "structure of society." Polanyi has presupposed this distinction between the independently existing dimension of economic reality and the constructs which refer to it when he differentiates between the formal and the substantive meanings of the term *economic*. "The formal meaning derives from the means-ends relationship" and "implies a system of logical terms"; but "the substantive meaning—whether predominantly ecological, technological or institutional—derives from man's causal dependence for his livelihood upon nature and his fellows," and "refers to the empirical relationship in which man, as a part of nature and society, stands to his own natural and social environment, on which he ultimately depends for his physical survival." [26]

Although allocative decisions constitute the economic dimensions of behavioral reality for all economic theories, the neoclassicists, who are predominantly formalistic, and the institutionalists, who are predominantly substantive, presuppose different metaphysical frameworks with respect to this objective referent. On the one hand, a Newtonian cosmology embodies the ontological assumptions of the neo-classical approach. This technique-centered postulate about the referent of allocative decision is narrowly circumscribed in terms of rationality in a market environment that mechanically determines economic man. The constructs are often formal. On the other hand, a conception of cosmology like Whitehead's embodies the ontological assumptions of the institutionalistic problem-centered postulate about the referent of allocative decision in the synoptic terms of the transactions of goal-seeking persons in a sociocultural environment to which substantive constructs refer. Let us now ascertain what each of these metaphysical world-views entails with respect to the objective referent.

Neo-classical economists justified their postulate of absolute predictability in accordance with the law of supply and demand, by assuming that their equilibrium system is a sub-system of the Newtonian cosmology. In the latter view, according to Laplace, the universe of matter in motion operates so automatically in accordance with the mechanical laws of gravitation and motion that in principle all future physical states could be predicted from a knowledge of the position and velocity of particles of matter at any given time. Thus economic laws were taken to be as regulatory as natural laws; and a competitive market system of exchange was conceived as an inherent aspect of the total system of nature in which physical things interacted within a static spatial receptacle. Consequently, as Gruchy has shown, the neo-classical economists derived a "common intellectual orientation" with respect to the "simple and stable mechanisms of equilibrium" (Marshall) from the mechanical gravitational adjustments of the Newtonian cosmology and the "universal laws of economics" (J. B. Clarke) in a closed market system which is automatically self-adjusting. Jevons' conception of theoretical economics as "mathematical science . . . comparatively abstract and general, treating mankind from simple points of view" reveals, however, that the neo-classical concern about logically precise predictions, which were analytically deduced from a formal scheme of mathematical axioms (Senior), was not combined with the concern about empirical observation that characterized Newtonian physicists.

By adopting this cosmological conception of an isolated sphere of economic behavior which operated independently of all extra-economic motivational and sociocultural conditions, the neo-classicists felt justified in making predictions about *allocative decisions* on the basis of the postulate that "all units of economic decision act rationally" (Lange). They were aware, of course, that individuals are motivated by desires other than that of maximizing profit, and that market operations are influenced by governmental policies. Only through discounting these extra-economic factors by assuming "all other things being equal," however, could the neo-classical theorist treat *allocative decisions* as the distinctive objective referent of his formalistic predictive constructs.

Since institutionalists have attempted to reconstruct the objective referent of economic analysis, they need to substitute another underlying cosmology for the Newtonian cosmology of the neo-classical theorists. Sufficient as the Newtonian world view might be for this orthodox formalistic analysis of delimited motivational and environmental factors, the unorthodox economists require a more dynamic metaphysical perspective for the substantive conception of the "empirical economy" as an "institutionalized process between men and their natural and social surroundings, in the course of which they secure their livelihood" (Polanyi). Allocative decisions with respect to the disposal of scarce means must be retained as the objective referent. But a broader sociocultural context must be taken into account in order to explain economic choices from among alternative uses, which, as Polanyi emphasizes, "cannot function apart from the culture, the motivations and valuations of which permeate the society." [27]

When Gruchy interprets the unorthodox economic theories of Veblen, Commons, Mitchell, Clark, Tugwell, and Means, he claims that underlying the dynamic ideas of these institutionalistic or holistic economists are the metaphysical assumptions which Whitehead has made explicit in his conception of the universe as an unbegun and unending creative process of temporal events: "Just as an 'event' in the natural order is taken by Alfred N. Whitehead to be something which incorporates the past, present, and future, so likewise economic activity is investigated by the holistic economists from a similar three-dimensional viewpoint." This means that the substantive empirical economy is conceived as an integral sub-system of the cosmic process of interacting temporal events which, taken together as a complex whole, constitute reality in its most comprehensive meaning.

Contrary to the orthodox assumption that allocative decisions can be viewed in terms of a closed, static, atemporal system of equilibrium, which the Newtonian metaphysics implied, Veblen and the others listed above adopted the "preconception of process." According to this functional assumption, reality is a continuous process of emergent evolution in which the collective efforts of individual persons can influence the complex interrelated totality of contemporary economic operations that are the outcome of past operations and that will condition future developments. As Gruchy concludes, "when these economists look at the existing market mechanism, or the whole economy of which the mechanism is a vital part, they see economic institutions which have come from the past, which now exist, and which are in the process of developing new configurations." [28]

G. *The Significance of the First Postulate for*
Political Science

The need to postulate a political dimension of independently existing behavioral reality has been emphasized by Easton when he proceeds on the assumption that "political life constitutes a concrete
political system which is an aspect of the whole social system." While
it must be presupposed that the constructs developed in political inquiry refer to an objective state of affairs within the toal sociocultural-
motivational process, political scientists have not achieved a consensus
about its identifiable characteristics. Deploring this, Easton declares
that "it is the rule rather than the exception to find difficulty in referring political concepts back to the things to which they presumably
refer." [29]

Some political scientists seem to take "government" as their objective referent, but there are grounds for questioning its adequacy for
this purpose. "There is government," according to Shepard, "whenever a group of human beings actuated by common interests and desires creates an organized institutional mechanism for the furtherance
of the ends and for the adjustment and control of their relationships."
Since this could pertain to a church, a trade union, an industrial corporation, or a university, usually "government" is restricted to the
state as "a community in which membership is not voluntary but imposed upon all individuals within a given territory." [30] Although legis-
lative, executive, and juridical mechanisms for determining "who gets
what, when, and how" (Lasswell) are distinctively governmental functions, there is also that of public service which is not so clearly a defining characteristic of all governmental operations.

Perhaps "government" should be conceived as a construct derived
from the more basic objective referent of administrative instrumentation in the ends-means continuum of the goal-oriented behavioral
transactions of naturalized and socioculturalized individuals as they
always seek security as the means to the end of survival, and sometimes seek freedom as the means to the end of self-realization. In our
synoptic model this was used as a construct for identifying the political operations of the technological process as the observational data;
but now, it might be used for further bringing out the identifiable

characteristics of the dimension of objective reality to which the political scientist's interpretative constructs refer. Aristotle, it will be recalled, directed attention to such an allocative operation, when he contended that it was the function of the state to provide survival and freedom as the necessary prerequisites for survival and self-realization: "As the State was formed to make life possible, so it exists to make life good." That he took it to be an objective referent seems clear in his claim that "the State is a natural institution." [31] Moreover, unlike the neo-classical "economic man" for whom the more restricted economic allocations provide the means for material wants, Aristotle's "political animal" requires opportunities which can be provided only by an authority which can allocate the means to ends within a much broader context of human relationships.

When the political scientist postulates his objective referent in motivational-sociocultural terms, he is confronted by the difficulty of demarcating politically oriented goal-seeking from other kinds of human transactions which it involves, e.g., economic, religious, educational, etc. If he agrees with Easton that his objective referent is "the whole range of human behavior that is concerned with the organization of the community under law," then he has the problem of specifying the distinctively political operation in the total behavioral process. In order to solve this problem, as was previously mentioned, political scientists have focused attention on three divergent orienting concepts: the state, power, and the authoritative allocation of instrumental values. To identify observational data we have, thus far, taken the latter to be most pertinent when we identified political action by the construct of *administrative instrumentation*. But is there any way of conceiving the nature of the objective referent so that the other two aspects of the political process can be included?

Political scientists, by adopting the structural-functional approach, might find it fruitful to take the *state* as the structural pattern of the political process which is functionally produced by *power relations* for the purpose of authoritatively allocating the means required to fulfill the common needs of all the members of a given community. Instead of the supernatural concept of the cultish state like that of Hegel, or Mussolini, etc., however, the structure of the political process must be patterned, as in MacIver's conception of the state; that is, in terms of "law as promulgated by a government endowed to this end with coercive power" and of maintaining "within a community territorially demarcated the universal external conditions of social order." [32] Thus, relationally conceived *power* is the defining characteristic of policy-regulated public interaction in this structural pattern of influencing or being influenced. Substantively conceived, however, is it not the *power* of those who influence the making, and/or of those who make policy decisions that functionally produces the relational structure of the "power-oriented context"? When Key substitutes this connotative *power* for the denotative *state*, he can not eliminate the latter. For, "the reciprocal relations of governors and governed" which characterize political power can be distinguished from social power only by referring to the "machinery of government" which, as he quotes from Neuman, "involves the exercise of authority by the organs of the state itself." Therefore, not only is it necessary to retain the structural concept of the state for demarcating the function of political power, but it is equally necessary to take into account the purpose of power-in-state. Power for what? Perhaps Key himself answers in terms of the allocation of values, when he grants that "power is a means, an indispensable means, to other ends" which "find expression in public policy, notably in legislation." [33] Lasswell also has emphasized the functional concept of power; but he too concludes that "the political act takes its origin in a situation in which the actor strives for the attainment of various values for which power is a necessary (and perhaps also sufficient) condition." [34]

Taking this purpose of the political process as the concept for coordinating its denotative structure (state) and its connotative function (power) aspects, can we not agree with Easton that the objective referent is "the authoritative allocation of values for a whole society." Extra-governmental pressure groups are political only by virtue of their relation to the making and implementation of policies for the entire community. Consequently, just as the function of *power* produces the structure of the *state*, so Easton recognizes that "there could be no *authoritative* allocation of values apart from the distribution and use of power." But, like all other functional concepts, functional political operations are meaningful only in connection with the needs they aim to fulfill. [35]

H. *The Significance of the Postulate for History*

The very meaning of history can not be understood without the adoption of this postulate that the historical dimension of objective reality has happened independently of any historian's reconstruction of it, even though his knowledge about such an objective referent is limited to the framework of his reconstructions. Beard emphasized this epistemological dualism of reality and idea in his distinction between "history-as-actuality" and "written history." By "history-as-actuality" he means "all that has been felt, thought, imagined, said, and done by human beings as such and in relation to one another and to their environment since the beginnings of mankind's operation on this planet." By "written history" he means "a systematic or fragmentary narration or account purporting to deal with all or part of this history-as-actuality." [36] If history-as-actuality is taken to be the referent, and written history is taken to be the subjective construct, then "history-as-record," i.e., the documents and memorials pertaining to history-as-actuality on which written history is or should be based, can be taken to be the "sign" in the "mind-sign-referent continuum" (Werkmeister) of the historian's meaning-situation. Cohen contends that this assumption about the meaning of human history is presupposed by anyone who attempts to understand the world today: "All our assumptions in regard to the continuous nature of the things we deal with in the present—the persons, physical objects, or institutions—are inconsistent with the view that the past is nothing at all." In other words, it must be postulated that "what the historian makes is not the past but findings about it." [37]

The contemporary resurgence of a radical historical relativism makes it urgent to emphasize this postulate that "history-as-actuality" must be taken as an objective referent of the subjectively reconstructed "written history." Do those who declare with Becker that "every man is his own historian" really mean, as is sometimes thought, that there is no independent actuality to which changing perspectives and constructs of historical inquiry refer? If the historian adopts the epistemological dualism of this first postulate, then it is not necessary for him to appear to adopt such solipsism in order to oppose a naïve absolutism which identifies the actual past with what is recorded about it. Nor is it necessary for the historian to identify the past with what substantiates some particular political, racial, religious, or other bias. When the epistemological dualist assumes that *whatever actually happened* is the objective referent for his imaginative reconstructions, he does not claim that he has verified his postulate. But he does claim that this postulate is more fruitful for cumulative investigation than either of the absolutistic or solipsistic postulates which entail the irreconcilable extremes of epistemological monism. For the former deals only with the reality and the latter deals only with the idea.

Probably acceptable to most historians would be Clough's designation of "the totality of human activity through time" as the objective referent of the historian's attempt "to ascertain what happened, to identify events in sequence, to analyze interrelationships among those events, and to discover how and why they occurred in a given order." [38] Let us briefly note what each of these aspects of this postulated objective referent entails: (a) *human activity*, (b) *through time*, and (c) *totality*.

(a) *Human activity*. Most historians seem to confine their attention to past human actions. Some do not go quite as far as Collingwood when he contends that the historian's "main task is to think into this action, to discern the thought of the agent." But few, it seems, would question the distinction between the *inside* and the *outside* of an event which he made in order to delimit "the proper sphere of historical knowledge." By the former he meant "that in it which can only be described in terms of thought"; and by the latter he meant "everything belonging to it which can be described in terms of bodies and their movement." [39] For even when the natural and sociocultural variables in the "structure of relationships and interactions" are emphasized, as they are by Clough, these dynamic factors of change are significant for the historian only in so far as they condition human motivation.

(b) *Through time*. The diachronic orientation of all historical analysis was previously emphasized in connection with the identification of its data through the synoptic model; but now it is re-emphasized that the temporal duration of an ongoing process of successive events is the defining characteristic of the historian's objective referent. Although this actually encompasses all the other dimensions of reality to which the constructs of all the other behavioral disciplines refer, some of the other disciplines may minimize the temporal process when they concentrate on a purely synchronic comparison of sociocultural or motivational similarities. For the historians who are concerned about the concrete whole of specific situations, however, the continuity of changing events in the temporal process is always central, i.e., "their data are events that are related by their position in time, no matter in what other ways they may be related." [40] It should be recalled that this independently operating temporal passage is not the humanly created clocktime by which seconds, minutes, hours, days, weeks, months, years, centuries, epochs, etc. are measured.

(c) *Totality*. The total past is the objective to which the historian's reconstructions refer, even though for the purpose of a specific presentation he must delimit his inquiry to some selected trends which he extracts from the total web of interrelated events. This comprehensive whole of vanished human events is the ideal limit of historical knowledge which no particular inquiry or combination of inquiries are expected to reconstruct completely. As the historian seeks to make his contribution toward that goal, he must assume, nevertheless, that such an objective referent has a reality which is approximately discovered by his cumulative analysis rather than is created by it. Natural scientists and social scientists must make this same assumption about the relation of their constructs to their total referent. Recall Einstein's postulate of the "existence of the ideal limit of knowledge" which "is approached by the human mind." But the historian's adoption of this postulate creates more complications for him than it does for others. For, whereas scientists can abstract a specific contemporary segment from the total temporal process, according to Brockunier and Loewenberg, the historian "must also undertake to appraise larger interrelationships and attempt a general synthesis" in which he "not only strives for an understanding of the total situation *as it is* at any given point of time, but also undertakes to explain how that situation *came to be.*" [41]

When the sceptic claims that the unattainability of the historian's ideal objective of completely reconstructing the total past precludes the reasonable acceptability of any historical interpretation, the sceptic has failed to understand the relation of referent and construct which this postulate entails. Ideally, of course, the historian should trace all the antecedents of all events. But since this is impossible, the historian has the same right to a cut-off point that is granted to all

264)   The Epistemological Pattern of Reflective Inquiry

other scientific inquiries. For, as Nagel insists, "unless an inquiry were selective it would never come near to resolving the specific question by which it is generated." [42] In other words, if the historian has initially clarified the scope of his problem, he is not arbitrary because he does not take into account every one of the multiplicity of inter-related events which constitute the totality of the antecedent temporal process. Mandelbaum rightly insists that it would be arbitrary to deny the historian the right to "successive stopping points" which "represent answers to questions posed." [43] Declaring that "it is a curious logic that would allow us nothing because we cannot have everything," MacIver acknowledges that "there is no phenomenon or event that does not depend on the whole history of the universe." But he insists that the construct of the historian can be limited to a "specific conjuncture of events" even though the historian assumes that it has emerged out of the antecedent totality.[44]

When the historian adopts this postulate that "the totality of past actions through time" is an objective referent for his constructs, he escapes solipsism; but such an assumption is not sufficient for saving him from relativism. He does not suppose, as would the solipsist, that only his own mental processes are real. He can not deny, however, that it is he who inferentially selects his ideas about the kind, relevance, order, and significance of events and their relations which he reconstructively imagines history-as-actuality to have been. To be sure, other social-scientific inferences are selective; but those who make them have the advantage of possessing some data which are accessible for observational confirmation or disconfirmation. Before the historical theorist surrenders to the radical relativist, however, he should consider two proposed alternatives. The first proposal is offered by Mandelbaum; and the second proposal is one which the present writer conceives as emerging out of the broadly operational perspective of a growing number of historiographers.

Mandelbaum seems to adopt epistemological monism in order to deliver historical inquiry from the bondage of all kinds of relativism which stems from the Kantian premise that "whatever traits of structure the objects of our knowledge possess must be attributed to the activity of the human mind." According to Mandelbaum, the relativistic claim that the structure of all historical work "depends upon the valuational interests and attitudes of the historian" is the outcome of such a subjectivistic assumption, since it presumes that "the real events of the world, if we could ever perform the impossible and see them in themselves, would present us with a mere flux, devoid of all order, coherence, and meaning." He wants to get away from the epistemologically dualistic assumption "that the 'interpretation' of facts is to be understood as proceeding from the side of the subject, rather than being forced upon the subject by the nature of the material with which he is dealing." Thus Mandelbaum adopts an epistemologically monistic position: "Rather than to assume that the order and structure to be found in our knowledge is a function of the mind's activity in knowing, we have assumed that events in the real world possess a determinate structure of their own, which is apprehended, but not transformed by the mind." Applying this general cognitive principle to history, Mandelbaum maintains that "events of the historical type possess determinate interconnections which are rooted in the events themselves, and are not addenda contributed by the mind." But, if "the relevance of one statement to another depends upon causal factors which relate the events to which the statements refer," and if "such causal connections . . . are objectively ascertainable in the nature of the events themselves," then how can Mandelbaum account for errors in historical judgments? Moreover, this holds for every instance of historical inquiry, since "the concrete structure and continuity to be found in every historical work is not a product of valuational judgments, but is implicit in the facts themselves." [45]

Instead of Mandelbaum's answer to relativism in terms of an epistemological monism, which presupposes that the historian can somehow apprehend the events themselves, there is another possible answer to relativism in terms of an epistemological dualism: The construct is not identical with the referent. Such assumption seems to be more congruent with the other presuppositions of a broadly operational historical analysis; and, furthermore, it retains the epistemological dualism which we have found presupposed by natural-scientific and social-scientific inquiries. This means that the historian must acknowledge that his subjective interpretation (history-as-written) is his best approximation of its postulated objective referent (history-as-actuality). Mandelbaum would be correct, if he objected that this alternative does not eliminate all relativism. What it does do, however, is to substitute for "radical relativism" the "situational relativism" which characterizes the social-scientific enterprise. Since the historian must selectively reconstruct his observational data, he could hardly expect to be less relativistic than the social scientist. The crucial question which we must answer is whether or not he is so much more relativistic that his way of knowing can not conform to the pattern of reflective inquiry which the broadly operational perspective of "situational relativism" requires. According to "situational relativism," it will be recalled, the symbolic frame of reference, which constitutes the meaning-situation of the investigator (whether he be a natural scientist, a social scientist, or a historian), is *relative* to his motivational-sociocultural *situation*.

How can the historian avoid absolutism at one extreme and radical relativism at the other? Mandelbaum does not intend to advocate an absolutistic conception of historical knowledge when he takes the position that the historian's interpretations "are objectively ascertainable in the nature of the events themselves." But how can the radical relativist be shown that this is not absolutism? The historian who adopts the position of "situational relativism" does not abandon hope of acquiring reliable knowledge. For, within the relativistic symbolic frame of reference, he may have the opportunity and responsibility to achieve objective knowledge in terms of a coherent system of explanatory generalizations which yield causal implications that can be verified as reasonably acceptable. No more than this has been claimed for the natural scientist or the social scientist.

Footnotes to Chapter 3 of Part Three

1 Planck, "The Meaning and Limits of Exact Science," *Science*, 1949, p. 319.
2 Einstein and Infeld, *The Evolution of Physics*, 33.
3 Husserl, *Ideas, General Introduction to Pure Phenomenology*, 110-111, 145.
4 Although we have not discovered any scientist who has actually adopted a solipsistic assumption, Bridman's designation of his epistemological assumption as solipsism emphasizes the significance of this postulate. Actually he is not a solipsist, because he assumes that "in the last resort every individual must be his own judge of what he shall accept to be satisfactory evidence of competence in another." (*The Nature of Physical Theory*, 14-15). Instead, he is presupposing that belief in the existence of the external world is a necessary postulate.
5 Allport, *The Nature of Personality*, 97. Cf. Tolman, "A Psychological Model," *Toward a General Theory of Action* (Parsons and Shils), 279 ff.

[6] Smith in *For a Science of Social Man* (Gillin) 33, 47-48. Cf. Boring, *The Physical Dimensions of Consciousness*, 6.

[7] Marx, *Psychological Theory*, 7.

[8] Allport, "The Historical Background of Modern Social Psychology," *Handbook of Social Psychology* (Lindzey), Vol. I, 4-5.

[9] Nadel, *Foundations of Social Anthropology*, 290-294.

[10] Newcomb, *Social Psychology*, 7, 25-27, 33, 35, 37-38. See Newcomb, *American Sociological Review*, Vol. 13, No. 2, April 1948, page 170.

[11] Newcomb, "Studying Social Behavior," *Methods of Psychology* (Andrews), 664. Cf. Murphy, Murphy, Newcomb, *Experimental Social Psychology*, 15-16; Brown, *Social Psychology*, 12; and Dewey and Humber, *The Development of Human Behavior*, 9.

[12] Parsons, *The Structure of Social Action*, 753.

[13] Lundberg, *Foundations of Sociology*, 14-17.

[14] *Ibid.*, 14.

[15] Sorokin, *Society, Culture, and Personality*, 3-6.

[16] MacIver, *Social Causation*, 272. For a philosophical-biological conception of emergent evolution, see Morgan, *Emergent Evolution*, 297. For a metaphysical conception of temporal duration, see Whitehead, *Modes of Thought*, 200, 221-222.

[17] Bidney, *Theoretical Anthropology*, 419.

[18] *Ibid.*, 174, 374.

[19] White, *Science of Culture*, 99-100, 339; *American Anthropologist*, Vol. 61, No. 2, April 1959, page 231. Cf. same journal, page 294 for Goldstein's statement. See Bidney, *Theoretical Anthropology*, 175, 270.

[20] Parsons in *Toward a Unified Theory of Human Behavior* (Grinker), 325.

[21] Tax, Greenberg, and others in *An Appraisal of Anthropology Today* (Tax), 224-225.

[22] Kroeber and Parsons, "The Concepts of Culture and of Social System," *American Sociological Review*, October, 1958.

[23] Hallowell, "Culture, Personality, and Society," *Anthropology Today* (Kroeber), 600, 610, 615. It is not maintained here that all anthropologists attribute the same significance to this aspect of their objective referent. White, on the one hand, seems to reject it when he contends that "the most effective way to study culture scientifically is to proceed as if the human race did not exist." (*Philosophy of Science*, XIV, 289-303). Bidney, on the other hand, insists on this point: "Culture is an attribute of man, a mode of acting and thinking which we attribute to human enterprise." (*Theoretical Anthropology*, 117).

[24] Steward, "Evolution and Process," *Anthropology Today* (Kroeber), 315, 319.

[25] Lange, "The Scope and Method of Economics," *Readings in the Philosophy of Science* (Feigl and Brodbeck), 744. Originally published in the *Review of Economic Studies*, 13, 1945-46.

[26] Polanyi, *Semantics of General Economic History* (Mimeographed), 1, 6, 7.

[27] Gruchy, *Modern Economic Thought*, 10-15 and 22-23. See Jevons *The Principles of Science*, 759-761; and Polanyi, *Semantics of General Economic History* (Mimeo), 1, 6, 7.

[28] Gruchy, *Modern Economic Thought*, 602.

The following statements substantiate Gruchy's claim that the institutionalistic or holistic view presupposes Whitehead's conception of reality as a creative temporal process:

Underlying J. M. Clark's *Studies in the Economics of Overhead Costs* there is the cosmological assumption that economic reality is a "dynamic social organism, rather than a static mechanism with an endless uniformity of perpetual motion." (ix, 485) When Commons describes economic transactions as a "going concern" in his *Institutional Economics,* he refers to the "uncertain expectations of the future which dominate the activity of human beings in the ever moving present." (733) In his opposition to the neo-classical assumption of a static market system Mitchell in his *Business Cycles* declares that "in fact, if not in theory, a *state of change* in business conditions *is the only* 'normal' state." (86)

Machlup has offered the following warning to those economists who might contend that no metaphysical assumptions are involved in their conception of the objective referent for their analytic constructs: "He who never studies metaphysical questions, and even prides himself on his unconcern with metaphysics, often does not know how much in fact he talks about it." ("The Problem of Verification of Economics" *The Southern Economic Journal,* Vol. XXII, No. 1, July 1955, page 2.) Whitehead's philosophical reconstruction of the Newtonian world view is presented in his *Modes of Thought.* The present writer's interpretation of this "reconstruction of the natural order" is offered in his *Enduring Satisfaction,* Chapter VII.

29 Easton, *The Political System,* 44, 96-97, 117.

30 Shepard, "Government," *Encyclopedia of the Social Sciences,* Vol. 7, page 8.

31 Aristotle, *Politics.*

32 MacIver, *The Modern State,* 22.

33 Key, *Politics, Parties, and Pressure Groups,* 3-7.

34 Lasswell and others, *Power and Society,* 240.

35 Easton, *The Political System,* 128-134 and 146.

36 Beard, "Grounds for a Reconsideration of Historiography," Bulletin 54, page 5. Cf. Werkmeister, *The Basis and Structure of Knowledge,* 7.

37 Cohen, *The Meaning of Human History,* 6, 49.

38 Clough, "Change and History," Bulletin 64, pp. 106-107, 110, 116, 120.

39 Collingwood, *The Idea of History,* 210-217.

40 Aitken and Loewenberg, Bulletin 64, page 24.

41 Brockunier and Loewenberg, Bulletin 64, pages 87-88. Cf. Einstein and Infeld, *The Evolution of Physics,* 33.

42 Nagel, "The Logic of Historical Analysis," *Readings in the Philosophy of Science* (Feigl and Brodbeck), 692-693. Originally published in *The Scientific Monthly,* 74, 1952, page 165.

43 Mandelbaum, *The Problem of Historical Knowledge,* 268.

44 MacIver, *Social Causation,* 64-66, 191-192, 254-255.

45 Mandelbaum, *The Problem of Historical Knowledge,* 84-86, 264-268, 97, 203, 270-271, 239.

4 The Second Postulate of the Meaning-Situation of Reflective Inquiry (Probability)

A high degree of probability (reasonable acceptability), rather than absolute certainty, is the most that can be expected in the operational verification of generalizations which will never exhaust all that is yet to be known.

A. The General Significance of the Second Postulate

All scientists share this subjective expectation that relative confirmation is more fruitful than absolute confirmation when they identify the kind of knowledge that is meaningful for scientific inquiry. This presupposition that the verification of scientific constructs will never be definitive is initially derived from the scientist's preference for persisting inquiry rather than for a final achievement of Truth. The scientist would terminate his Faustian quest for the satisfaction of never completely satisfying his increasingly more reliable knowledge as an intrinsic value. Scientific objectivity was previously identified by this positively sceptical attitude which motivates the value-situation of all scientists who seek broadly operational knowledge. Such, it will be recalled, is a critical but open-minded exploration of experience in terms of verifiable hypotheses that are always subject to modification, correction, or abandonment, if carefully examined evidence and/or more logical reasoning yield an even more highly probable interpretation.

By adopting this more fruitful postulate in his meaning-situation, the scientist as a positive sceptic avoids, on the one extreme, the less fruitful claims of all non-operationalists, who assume that absolute certainty is obtainable, and, on the other extreme, the equally less fruitful claim of the negative sceptic, who assumes that no objective knowledge is obtainable. To the absolutist, the positive sceptic can grant that a knowledge claim might be absolutely true; but as long as he is an operationalist he will never treat any scientific generalization as absolutely true. As Einstein and Infeld declare, "there are no eternal theories in science." [1] To the negative sceptic, the positive sceptic can grant that there is no certain knowledge; but he can share Margenau's faith that reasonably verified knowledge is progressively obtainable through cumulative analysis so long as "science is a dynamic, self-corrective discipline with an ideal limit which it does not presume actually to reach." [2]

The negative sceptic is a greater threat to the positive sceptic than is the dogmatic authoritarian or any of the other non-operationalists who hold that anything less than definitive knowledge is not genuine knowledge. For the positive sceptic and the dogmatic authoritarian are motivated by such divergent initial preferences in their respective value-situations, that they are not thinking in the same language. Between them no issue can actually be joined. It is only from the cover of his meaning-situation, however, that the positive sceptic can defend his position from the attack of the negative sceptic. If the positive sceptic asserted in his knowledge-situation that he proved that there is no absolute knowledge, then he would be no less embrangled in a self-contradictory predicament than is the negative sceptic who asserts that he is certain that there is no certainty. To avoid this, however, the positive sceptic must make it clear that he simply is proceeding on the postulate that his investigations are meaningful only if he assumes that absolute confirmation is beyond his grasp. For as Margenau emphasizes, there is no assurance that "our present set of requirements is true." Moreover, the positive sceptic who agrees with Werkmeister that "all scientific knowledge remains subject to revision" must acknowledge that a finite number of observations can never completely verify any hypothesis, since "verification through observations involves inescapably the logical fallacy of affirming the consequent" and "we can never be sure that only one hypothesis can provide the solution of a scientific problem." [3]

The assumption that the most reasonably acceptable generalizations will never exhaust all that is yet to be known is an essential aspect of this second postulate which precludes the termination of inquiry. It is from Weber that contemporary social scientists have inherited this presupposition that regardless of how much is objectively known at any given time such knowledge is functionally related to a broader context of objective reality about which there is always more to be discovered. This does not mean that any aspects of reality are inherently unknowable. Rather, as Parsons interprets Weber, it means that "the development of scientific knowledge is to be regarded as a process of asymptotic approach to a limit"; but it "does not involve the scepticism that is the inevitable consequence of any really radical relativity." [4]

Before we consider the significance of this postulate for the specific social sciences, we should note that this pragmatic assumption of a "high degree of probability" as the top limit of verifiability, i.e., the maximum adequacy for the warrant for an assertion, does not commit the scientist to any particular statistical theory about probability calculations. Such computations of relative frequency have a significant function in the knowledge-situation of several disciplines in the natural and social sciences for determining the "weight of evidence" in terms of correlational coefficients or other statistical measures of concomitant variation. In considering the meaning-situation, however, we are concerned only with the scientist's way of holding his beliefs in terms of what Werkmeister has called their "truth-probability," i.e., "the degrees of evidence supporting each assertion." [5] Accordingly, this pragmatic postulate pertains only to the "reasonable acceptability" or "reliability" or "rational credibility" of knowledge-claims on the assumption that "empirical knowledge has universally this character of some degree of probability instead of complete theoretical certainty." [6] Although the statistical conception of "probability calculations" is not involved in this postulate, we shall find later that it does have a bearing on the fourth postulate about causality.[7]

B. *The Significance of the Second Postulate for Individual Psychology*

It seems that when individual psychologists stop to think about it, most of them would agree with Hull that "theoretical 'truth' appears in the last analysis to be a matter of greater or less probability." Accordingly, Hull makes this claim about the limits of the most significant aspect of psychological verification: "Though principles are the most important products of scientific effort, apparently the most that can be attained in determining their validity is to build up for them a favorable presumption, or probability of impressive magnitude." [8] With respect to substantive hypotheses, Andrews has emphasized that, since the psychological evidence about all human beings is always so incomplete that generalizations from partial evidence "are made only as probable inferences" which differ in "degree of probability," the testing of behavioral hypotheses can only aim "toward diminishing error in the general process of problem solving." [9] With respect to conceptual principles, Tolman, it will be recalled, said about his own psychological model that "any such model must, of course, be ready to undergo variations and modifications to make it correspond better with new empirical findings." [10] Even though Brunswik is primarily concerned with Reichenbach's statistical kind of "probability laws" about concomitant variations, he acknowledges this postulate of "pragmatic probability" as well.[11]

Psychologists make it clear, however, that this does not entail the despairing attitude of the negative sceptic. Hull's assurance that "it is consoling to know that this probability frequency becomes very high indeed," [12] is underlined by Marx when he insists that, although "no final or absolute theories (or laws) are to be expected in science," psychological analysis can be effective "as a uniquely successful tool for the establishment of objective explanatory propositions of a high degree of empirically-tested probability." [13]

The indispensability of this postulate for cumulative psychological inquiry has recently been acknowledged by Kelly in terms of "half-truths vs. infallibility." When he proposes his theory of "man's construction of his alternatives," he insists that it is "frankly designed to contribute effectively to its own eventual overthrow and displacement." Instead of the assumption that his generalization "has been dictated to him by the real nature of things," Kelly "offers only the hope that he may have hit upon some partial truth that may serve as a clue to inventing something better." Since he "assumes from the outset that ultimate truth is not so readily at hand," Kelly calls upon any colleague who appears to have infallibility built into the structure of his theory to submit it "in terms of whether his proposition seems to lead toward and give way to fresh propositions, propositions which, in turn, may be more true than anything else has been thus far." Accordingly, Kelly warns those who claim infallibility on the grounds of first-hand observation that since "facts themselves are open to reconstruction, such a theory soon becomes a dogmatism that may serve only to blind us to new perceptions of the facts." There is also the danger that the technique of experimentation by which older dogmatisms were dispelled might itself lead to a new dogmatism, if the experimenter does not recognize that "the fact that he has hit upon one such way of predicting outcomes may even blind him to alternatives which might have proved far more productive in the long run." [14]

C. The Significance of the Second Postulate for Social Psychology

When psychologists turn from the analysis of individual behavior to that of interpersonal transactions, they take with them the assumption that they will treat no generalization or system of generalizations as definitive. Since their effort to correlate the constructs of sociology and anthropology with those of individual psychology makes their task more complicated, they are probably more aware than some individual psychologists of the necessity for making this postulate more explicit. Thus Lambert declares that "a tradition is in good hands as long as there remains an active searching for defining data, experimental control, precise thought, and, perhaps above all, vulnerability of formulation." [15] Moreover, social psychologists seem to be more receptive to the reconstruction of previously abandoned ideas than other psychologists as clues for pursuing new avenues of inquiry. For, as Hebb and Thompson contend, "no scientific theory can ever be proved true; nor indeed can we ever be finally sure of having proved one wrong." [16]

D. *The Significance of the Second Postulate for Sociology*

Each sociologist actually does adopt this assumption that no generalization can be so surely established that it is beyond revision; but many seem to suspect that some other sociologists need to be warned against the presumption that their views are definitive. MacIver, for example, makes his own presupposition clear when he declares that "the discovery of the causes of social phenomena is progressive and always approximate, always incomplete." Thus, he insists that "the rejection of partial truth, because it is only partial, is still the rejection of truth." But he takes his positive scepticism to be in opposition to extreme positivists who "are hotfoot for absolute and final certainty, for the whole truth wholly demonstrated." Accordingly, he raises this question: "perhaps the very assumption of potential exactitude is mistaken, or at least irrelevant, for some important aspects of knowledge." As positive sceptics who acknowledge that "complete certitude eludes us" and that "the systems we construct do not integrate all the manifestations we discover within them," according to MacIver, we can only "narrow the margin of error." But MacIver is in no way capitulating to the negative sceptic. The inaccessibility of our goal notwithstanding, "our endeavors can bring us always nearer," and "we gain a widening and deepening knowledge." [17]

Now Lundberg adopts a positivistic approach in so far as he reduces purposive behavior to measurable data for statistical analysis; but he agrees with MacIver that highly reliable knowledge is all that sociology can hope to achieve on the grounds that "changing conditions and changing experiences may therefore require changes in postulates or reasoning or both." Consequently, when he proposes his own theoretical system as no more than a "man-made work within which societal phenomena can be meaningfully arranged, verified, and predicted with economy and objectivity," Lundberg insists that he claims "no revelation in its inception, no absolute or intrinsic 'truth' in its propositions, and no finality in its structure." Moreover, Lundberg insists, no one can claim more than this, since "as times and conditions change, all of . . . the frames of reference, including present science, may be expected to prove inadequate and be abandoned for radically different postulates, and may proceed perhaps, according to different techniques and systems of logic." [18]

Znaniecki explicitly appeals to this postulate in his condemnation of enumerative induction in sociology as an approach which is "dominated by the conception of knowledge which regards truth as the final and unshakable result of research past and done." If the sociologist is to be guided by a "dynamic ideal of knowledge," Znaniecki contends, he must adopt an "attitude toward reality" by which he engages in the "quest for new knowledge more than ready and recognized knowledge, a hypothesis that leads to new problems more than a certainty unshakably connected with other certainties." [19]

Since some sociologists who are interested only in fragmentary research contend that systematizers such as Parsons stifle empirical analysis by formulating static systems, the inaccuracy of this charge should be exposed. That this is not the case is evident to those who read the following statement by Parsons which reveals that he presupposes this second postulate: "It cannot be maintained either that in the formulation attained in the present study this theoretical system is complete, or that it will not, with the further development of the social sciences, be superseded by one as radically different from it as it is from the systems from which it has emerged." [20]

E. *The Significance of the Second Postulate for Anthropology*

The emendable nature of all anthropological constructs is presupposed in discussions of the possibility of achieving a consensus among anthropologists. The strong idiographic bent of individual investigators dealing with the unique configurations of specific cultures is an obvious obstacle. But even if agreement on a nomothetic principle for theoretical analysis at the abstract level of universal generalizations should be achieved, as Nadel has declared, definitive confirmation would be precluded by inherent features of anthropological data: "Any extension of our knowledge over wider and wider domains will add to the complexity of phenomena, of whose immensity we are already fully aware."[21] Moreover, regardless of how broadly and deeply an anthropologist comes to understand a given culture, he can not avoid projecting his own values which, as Redfield acknowledges, are never "removable as factors of consequence in anthropological research."[22] Not only does this hold with respect to substantive interpretations of particular practices; but, as Hallowell has pointed out, "the meaning of culture that emerges for us is a function of *our* background, interests, aims."[23]

Instead of regretting the limitations which prevent complete agreement among anthropologists, Gillin cautions that, if anthropologists should ever achieve a systematically organized consensus, it should not become so dogmatically authoritarian that it would stifle new insights and interpretations. To this end he directly appeals to this postulate: "It is to be expected that the common body of understanding will be modified and revised from time to time by such demonstrations."[24]

F. *The Significance of the Second Postulate for Economics*

The limitation of the verification of economic hypotheses to "reasonable acceptability" has been enunciated by Machlup in terms of this postulate as the presupposition of "methodological doubt." By this he means that "testing an empirical hypothesis results either in its disconfirmation or its non-disconfirmation, never in its definitive confirmation," even though "a majority of reasonable men in the field should be prepared to accept them as conclusive." Comparing the continuing process of testing economic hypotheses with an elimination sports contest in which the winner must meet all challengers, Machlup insists that "no empirical hypothesis is safe forever," since "it can always be challenged for another test and may be knocked out at any time" so that "the test result, at best, is a 'confirmation till next time'." As a positive rather than a negative sceptic, however, Machlup assumes that whatever generalizations are "reasonably acceptable" can be considered reliable knowledge: "Even if definitive confirmation is never possible, the number of tests which a hypothesis has survived in good shape will have a bearing on the confidence people have in its 'correctness'."[25]

Have neo-classical economists actually presupposed that the predictive certainty of their laws was achievable? It seems likely that their provisos ("Everything else being equal" and "in the long run") suggest that they did not presuppose as much absolute confirmation as it might appear. Such claims as these, however, are not exceptions to the second postulate, if they are considered only analytic tautologies which may be formally valid regardless of their substantive truth. It does seem, however, that von Mises is assuming that certainty is attainable when he claims that "the theorems attained by correct praxeological reasoning are not only perfectly certain and incontestable, like the correct mathematical theorems," but they also refer "with the full rigidity of their apodictic certainty and incontestability to the reality of action as it appears in life and history." [26]

Among the institutionalistic economists who have accused the neoclassical school of not adopting this second postulate, Clark claims that the latter's deductively formulated theories were taken to possess "absolute verity or eternal adequacy," [27] and Kapp claims that to them the orthodox theorists ascribed "universal validity and absolute certainty." Instead of using such purely formalistic *a priori* generalizations about narrowly circumscribed data, according to Clark, economic inquiry should proceed on the assumption that the most it can hope to obtain, with respect to actual economic operations in the socio-cultural process as a whole, are substantive generalizations that are "significantly true." When Kapp seeks to replace "a system of economic theorems deductively arrived at from introspected valuations and axioms with a genuinely behavioral economics," he emphasizes that "such a science of economics can never be absolutely certain of the validity of its conclusions since new findings concerning human behavior may invalidate or qualify its basic premises and call for new formulations." [28] That this unorthodox approach in terms of emendable knowledge does not generate a fruitless uncertainty, is attested to by Mitchell, when he invites other economists to enjoy the zest of this kind of scientific adventure: "A chance to share in this work with its exacting demands, its frequent disappointments, but its thrilling possibilities, is open to all who will." [29]

G. *The Significance of the Second Postulate for*
Political Science

The inherent limitation of political-scientific knowledge is recognized by Friedrich when he reminds his colleagues that they should not aim "to produce infallible knowledge." Instead, as positive sceptics, their objective should be to provide "a more comprehensive knowledge, a better understanding of matters politic, than is available to the chance observer or the mere practioner." [30] Similarly, Easton assumes that any political generalization "is a statement of relationship which is only probably, not certainly and finally, true." This is not the radical relativist's "flight from reason," which some political scientists are accused of taking. For, even though Easton assumes with other positive sceptics that definitive knowledge "in principle lies beyond the realm of possibility," nevertheless, he shares the situational relativist's aim at reasonably acceptable knowledge: "Each age is called upon to formulate its own views of the limits of political research, and of necessity such views will reflect the level of the prevailing knowledge." [31]

H. *The Significance of the Second Postulate for History*

In so far as any historian assumes his referent to be the "totality of past human actions through time," it seems safe to say that none would claim that his own constructs or those of any other historian, would ever completely account for all past human actions. Gottschalk takes this assumption to be one of the defining characteristics of the "meaning of history": "The reconstruction of the total past of mankind, although it is the goal of historians, thus becomes a goal they know full well is unattainable." [32] Although Brockunier and Loewenberg agree that "no one now supposes that past history in its totality is recoverable," they indicate another aspect of the issues which this postulate entails when they grant that a "few believe that 'facts speak for themselves'." [33] For some might contend that there were many facts the occurrences of which were beyond question.

Those who might adopt this absolutistic position should be reminded, however, that a historical fact does not necessarily mean what actually happened. Rather, as Gottschalk insists, it is a *verisimilar* reconstruction by the historian that "is as close to what actually happened as we can learn from a critical examination of the best available sources." From this Gottschalk concludes that "the historian establishes *verisimilitude* rather than *objective truth*." [34] When competent historians agree that careful authentication substantiates their claim that some event actually occurred, this postulate does not preclude the possibility that it might be absolutely true. But the point to be emphasized is that a broadly operational historian will never treat any "fact" or interpretation of its relations to other "facts" as beyond modification, correction, or abandonment. Such revisions may be demanded for providing more reliable historical knowledge by the discovery of new testimony or more refined critical understanding of previously accepted testimony. Accordingly, Brockunier and Loewenberg insist that "objectivity requires us to be prepared on the basis of the evidence to abandon our most cherished hypotheses." [35]

When the historian gives up the "quest for certainty" and resolves to "write history with the highest possible degree of credibility," [36] he does not believe that he has surrendered to the radical relativists who claim that the historian's imaginative reconstruction of the past events is completely existentially determined by his personal preferences and sociocultural conditioning. The positive scepticism which this broadly operational postulate requires has been well expressed by Coates: "Once we have stamped finality as the great heresy for scholars, we can see the concept of the relativity of knowledge as a movement in the direction of greater objectivity." [37] Similarly, Muller does not find it depressing that the "historian cannot claim possession of the absolute truth." [38] According to Collingwood, the recognition that "in history, as in all serious matters, no achievement is final . . . is not an argument for historical scepticism." [39] Goethe may well have been correct in his claim that "each age must write history anew." But isn't this a predicament which the historian shares with the natural scientist and the social scientist? Instead of forsaking his task of "recreating a verisimilar image of as much of the past as the evidence makes recoverable" (Gottschalk), the historian can justify his faith in reason by contributing to the improvement of historical knowledge through cumulative analysis.

For this purpose, neither absolutism nor radical relativism is as fruitful as this postulate of situational relativism which the positive sceptic adopts when he commits himself to the Faustian *pursuit* of truth. So long as the historian progressively increases and expands his reasonably acceptable hypotheses, the very inaccessibility of the ideal limit of complete truth only adds zest to his intellectual adventure.

A positive rather than negative scepticism with respect to historical knowledge is exhibited in Cohen's answer to the question: "To what extent is knowledge of the past possible?" He grants that historical records "are relatively scant, partial, and fragmentary" and that instead of taking all fragments into account the historian "is forced to make some selection in which operation subjective considerations cannot be eliminated." Accordingly, he concludes that "an element of uncertainty will always attach to our histories"; but, nevertheless, "it is not practically possible to deny that we have some knowledge of the past and that we can improve it by critical or scientific investigation." For to concede that historical inquiry is relative is not to condemn it as purely subjective in the sense that "the historian creates the events he reports." Since the totality of past human actions is inevitably more comprehensive and concrete than any historical account of it, the historian can not be expected to escape altogether from being partial and abstract. Such objectivity as the historian can achieve, however, depends upon his explicitly adopting this second postulate: "A partial or abstract account of reality is false if it purports to be more than it is, but if it acknowledges its limitations it may be true and the only kind of truth to which the historian can attain." [40]

Footnotes to Chapter 4 of Part Three

[1] Einstein and Infeld, *The Evolution of Physics*, 77.

[2] Margenau, *The Nature of Concepts* (Stillwater Conference), 58.

[3] Werkmeister, *The Basis and Structure of Knowledge*, 297.

[4] Parsons, *The Structure of Social Action*, 600-601. Cf. Weber, *The Methodology of the Social Sciences*.

[5] Werkmeister, *The Basis and Structure of Knowledge*, 300-301.

[6] See Machlup, "The Problem of Verification in Economics," *The Southern Economic Journal*, Vol. XXII, No. 1, July 1955, pages 1-2; Larrabee, *Reliable Knowledge*; Lewis, *Analysis of Knowledge and Valuation*, 265.

[7] Although we are not dealing here with mathematical-logical theories of probability, anyone interested in them should see Keynes, *Treatise on Probability*; Reichenbach, "The Logical Foundations of the Theory of Probability," and Carnap "The Two Concepts of Probability" in *Readings in the Philosophy of Science* (Feigl and Brodbeck), 456-474 and 438-455; Nagel, "Principles of the Theory of Probability," *International Encyclopedia of Unified Science*, I, No. 6, 1939; von Mises, *Probability, Statistics, and Truth*; Werkmeister, *The Basis and Structure of Knowledge*, 287-299; Lewis, *Analysis of Knowledge and Valuation*, Chapter X; Kaufmann, *The Methodology of the Social Sciences*, Chapter VII.

[8] Hull in *Psychological Theory* (Marx), 224.

[9] Andrews, *Methods of Psychology*, 4.

[10] Tolman, "A Psychological Model," *Toward a General Theory of Action* (Parsons and Shils), 283.

[11] Brunswik in *Psychological Theory* (Marx), 137.

[12] Hull in *Psychological Theory* (Marx), 225.

[13] Marx, *Psychological Theory* (Marx), 6, 18.

[14] Kelly, "Man's Construction of His Alternatives," *Assessment of Human Motives* (Lindzey), 33-35.

[15] Lambert in *Handbook of Social Psychology* (Lindzey), Vol. I, 87.

[16] Hebb and Thompson in *Handbook of Social Psychology* (Lindzey), Vol. I, 532.

[17] MacIver, *Social Causation*, 383-384 and 392-393.

[18] Lundberg, *Foundations of Sociology*, 3-4 and 28.

[19] Znaniecki, *The Method of Sociology*, 222 and 229.

[20] Parsons, *The Structure of Social Action*, 756. Cf. Rose, *Theory and Method in the Social Sciences*, 262-268.

[21] Nadel, *The Foundations of Social Anthropology*, 255.

[22] Redfield in *Anthropology Today* (Kroeber), 738.

[23] Hallowell in *Anthropology Today* (Kroeber), 609.

[24] Gillin, *For a Science of Social Man* (Gillin), 261.

[25] Machlup, "The Problem of Verification in Economics," *The Southern Economic Journal*, Vol. XXII, No. 1, July 1955, pages 3-4 and 18-19.

[26] von Mises, *Human Action: A Treatise on Economics*, 39.

[27] Clark, *Studies in the Economics of Overhead Costs*, Preface.

[28] Kapp, "Economics and the Behavioral Sciences," *Kyklos*, Vol. VII, 1954, p. 207.

[29] Mitchell, "The Prospects of Economics," *The Trend of Economics* (Tugwell), 33-34.

[30] Friedrich, *Constitutional Government and Democracy*, 8.

[31] Easton, *The Political System*, 4, 52-53, 55, 125-126.

[32] Gottschalk, *Understanding History*, 42 and 48.

[33] Brockunier and Loewenberg, Bulletin 64, page 142.

34 Gottschalk, *Understanding History*, 139-140.
35 Brockunier and Loewenberg, Bulletin 64, page 142.
36 Bulletin 54, page 138.
37 Coates, "Relativism and the Use of Hypotheses in History," *Journal of Modern History*, 21, 24 (March 1949).
38 Muller, *The Uses of the Past*, 29-30.
39 Collingwood, *The Idea of History*, 248.
40 Cohen, *The Meaning of Human History*, 22-24, 46.
Gottschalk indicates the incompleteness of historical knowledge as follows: "Before the past is set forth by this historian, it is likely to have gone through eight separate steps at each of which some of it has been lost; and there is no guarantee that what remains is the most important, the largest, the most valuable, the most representative or the most enduring part." (*Understanding History*, 45-46). Cf. Mandelbaum, *The Problem of Historical Knowledge*, 297-304, 323 for an analysis of the reasons why "each age must write history anew."

Solvemini also emphasizes that "what actually happened" is limited by "that aspect on which attention is focused and about which we have sufficient information." But he insists, nevertheless, that "ignorance is no ground for scepticism" or else "no science would escape scepticism." (*Historian and Scientist*, 49.)

5 The Third Postulate of the Meaning-Situation of Reflective Inquiry (System)

Knowledge about the objective physical and behavioral universe requires an orderly system of constructs.

A. The General Significance of the Third Postulate

When an epistemological dualist presupposes that he constructs his knowledge about an independently existing reality, he must justify the ideational structure which he assumes that this inferential function produces. Unless a social scientist adopts the epistemologically monistic assumption that his constructs are identical with the behavioral reality itself, he must determine whether or not he agrees with Dewey that "in the practice of inquiry verification of an idea or theory is not a matter of finding an existence which answers to the demands of the idea or theory, but it is a matter of the systematic ordering of a complex set of data by means of the idea or theory as an instrumentality." [1]

The ideational operation of such a "systematic ordering," which this postulate requires, is explicitly called for by Toman when he takes "the idea of the continuity of everything in the universe" as the basis for the construction of a unified theory of behavior. He finds an epistemological monism which implies "reality versus the symbol" to be fruitless, since, on the one hand, it deals with "rules of operation with symbols," and, on the other hand, it deals with "the actual rules of operation of the universe external to the symbols." On the grounds that the symbols "make sense only insofar as they refer to things going on externally," Toman finds no alternative to an epistemological dualism which assumes that the symbols "are representative, not identical with things going on elsewhere, nor are they usually complete," since "our symbols always lag behind what is actually going on." This is an advantage in the sense that symbols "have the persistent quality that they outlast a particular event," so that they "are relevant to something which might happen again." It is important to notice, however, that Toman justifies his adoption of a systematic ordering of symbols on the grounds of its pragmatic fruitfulness as a better instrument for inquiry than alternative approaches, rather than upon its inherent truth: "Our working with symbols and our attempt to work with some system rather than others seems to be determined in part by what is convenient to work with." [2]

The extent to which social scientists presuppose this third postulate in their meaning-situation can be brought out by critically examining their answers to these three questions which this major issue entails: (1) Is a systematic organization of interpretative constructs more likely to approximate the objective referent than an approach which is confined to fragmentary research about isolated problems? (2) Is the reality to which constructs refer itself a harmonious system? (3) Can law-like, if not lawful, generalizations be formulated about behavioral events?

1. SYSTEMATIZATION VS. FRAGMENTATION

Among social scientists there is less consensus than there is among natural scientists with respect to the desirability of aiming at a systematic organization of generalizations about reality. To integrate all constructs within a comprehensive scheme of ideas is an ideal aim

which strongly motivated the contributors to the natural-scientific enterprise. Consider, for example, Einstein's answer to the query about
why he was so anxious to construct systematically his Unified Field
Theory: "The idea that there are two structures of space independent of each other, the metric-gravitational and the electromagnetic,
is intolerable to the theoretical spirit." [3]

The positive sceptic's faith in reason which motivates his "adven-
turous search for knowledge about the physical world" [4] provides the
basic justification for his assumption that his constructs should be
subsumed under systematic generalizations. Such a principle of systematic unification cannot be verified in the process of inquiry which
presupposes it. For before the scientist begins to analyze substantive
data he must adopt the "assumption that action is *ordered*; that there
is a certain regularity which permits of systematic study" (Sheldon).[5]
Even though the scientist agrees with Kant that "we ourselves introduce the order and regularity in nature" when we "interrogate nature," nevertheless, the scientist presupposes that he will obtain more
meaningful answers, if he systematically organizes the questions
which determine his classification, explanation, and prediction of observable data. In other words, apparently unique events cannot be
classified without a systematic grouping in terms of significant similarities; apparently unrelated past and present events cannot be causally explained without presupposing that there is some systematic interconnection; and the anticipated future events cannot be predicted
without the supposition that there is some systematic correlation
among the events which constitute the context that is broad enough
to provide statistical averages. Since the classificatory system is *conceptual*, its constructs are untestable, e.g., the constructs of the synoptic model of the behavioral process or those of the time-space model
of the physical process. The explanatory-predictive system, however,
is *theoretical*, and consequently its constructs have substantive implications that are subject to empirical confirmation or refutation. When
we examine the presupposition underlying such verification in connection with the fifth postulate of the meaning-situation, we shall
find that the formal deduction of consistent implications presupposes
a system of logical-mathematical relations, and that empirical testing
to determine which of alternative hypotheses is more adequate presupposes a substantive system of causal relations. Moreover, new
ideas must be congruent with already established systems of knowl-

edge, or, as in some cases, a new system of hypotheses must be reconstructed which is congruent with the new idea, e.g., the systems of Copernicus, Darwin and Einstein.

In a comprehensive analysis of the systematic approach which this postulate entails Parsons and Shils have instructively described the operation of scientific constructs at four different levels of systematization. This exhibits what Dewey means when he claims that "the intervention of systematic thinking" is the *sine qua non* of "continued and regulated inquiry." At the first level, *ad hoc classificatory systems* provide summary statements about the data in terms of arbitrary classes without any necessary interdependence among the classes. On the second level, *categorial systems* provide for interrelation of different classes of subject matter which have interdependent variables. (Contemporary social scientific knowledge about human action is of this categorical type in which "knowledge of laws is both vague and fragmentary" even though the significance and the relations of the variables are known.) On the third level, *theoretical systems* provide knowledge about the general laws of the system to the extent that the elements can be related under ideal conditions so that predictions can be made within the limits of specified conditions. (Classical mechanics illustrates this theoretical type.) On the fourth level, *empirical-theoretical systems* provide "the long-term goal of scientific endeavor" to coordinate factual observations and theoretical generalizations. Although the behavioral sciences are a long way from realizing this ideal, its depiction by Parsons and Shils further clarifies an essential aspect of what this third postulate implies: "We speak of an empirical-theoretical system whenever a sufficient number of variables can be brought together in a single (theoretical) system of interdependence adequate for a high level of precision in predicting changes in empirical systems outside special experimental conditions." [6] It is pertinent to note that Parsons and Shils proceed in their *structural-functional* analysis of human action, which fairly well meets the categorial requirements on the basis of their reasonable faith that "the progress of knowledge will, however, move it steadily," in the direction of a *theoretical system* and eventually in the direction of an *empirical-theoretical system*.

Despite the case for the systematization of constructs which has been presented thus far, there are many social scientists who reject the approach which this third postulate requires in favor of fragmentary research about relatively isolated practical social problems. Nothing that will be said here should be taken to minimize the importance of the essential contributions they have made to the social-scientific enterprise. All that will be emphasized here is that they are mistaken in their assumption that the systematic approach detracts from empirical research. What some researchers fail to recognize is that the construction of systematic schemes is designed as a means for opening up new avenues of empirical inquiry, and for coordinating the results of specific analyses. This probably does not apply to researchers such as Lazarsfeld, who avoids systematization simply on the grounds that his only interest is in dealing with specific problems. His introduction to *The Language of Social Research* seems to indicate the kind of concern about methodology which is not inherently opposed to the systematized approach, provided that others pursue it. Mills, however, is more clearly opposed to the adoption of the requirements which this third postulate imposes. His *The Sociological Imagination* is designed as an exposé of the "useless height" of such systematic "grand theories" as those which Parsons has proposed. Fearful of the dangers of examining principles of analysis apart from their application to specific problems, Mills strongly advocates that social scientists devote themselves to developing "intellectual craftsmanship" in their delimited research rather than to wasting much time with systematic "crash programs" to codify procedures: "If such accounts are not firmly anchored in the actual working of social study, the sense of a significant problem and the passion to solve it cannot be allowed full play in the mind of the working social scientist." Now Mills is correct when he claims that the systematic elaboration of concepts is a "promise to alert us to distinctions" rather than "the actual work of the social studies" in specific research projects; but he fails to show why these two aspects of the social-scientific enterprise are actually as antithetical as he seems to think. His claim that systematic approaches "are statesmanlike withdrawals from the problems of social science" seems to reveal his failure to distinguish between a social problem and a social-scientific problem. It is Mills' own personal affair if he prefers "one account by a working student of how he is going about his work" rather than a "dozen codifications of procedure" on the grounds that he is "made weary" by "method-and-theory-in-general." But it hardly warrants his charge that usually systematic approaches "are based on some grand model of inquiry with which other people are beaten on the head." What can he mean by his claim that "discussion of it interrupts our proper studies"? [7]

There seems to be a general impression among those who confine themselves to the analysis of piecemeal problems that the formulation of a systematic framework of concepts and theories will stifle empirical research on these grounds. First of all, it is held that systematizing will lead to the merely analytical schemes of purely formal systems which the pure rationalists formulated in terms of universal and necessary principles that were logically valid but substantively sterile. And secondly, there seems to be the fear that a systematic approach will reestablish the closed nineteenth century speculative schemes like that of Spencer which discouraged exploration along new lines of inquiry.

The systematizers in the social-scientific enterprise who have adopted this third postulate are just as opposed to purely rationalistic schemes and closed systems as are the fragmentary researchers. For example, not only has Parsons always ascribed great importance to empirical research, but he also designed his systematic framework in order to make empirical research more meaningful by providing a perspective for coordinating the findings of fragmentary investigations and for stimulating new inquiries. When Parsons attempts to present a logically articulated scheme in *The Social System*, he acknowledges that it "is fragmentary and incomplete"; but, nevertheless, his work establishes the postulate that "the concept of system as a guiding conceptual scheme is of the first importance as an organizing principle and a guide to research." [8] Parsons, therefore, does not assume that his or any other systematic scheme is an end in itself. To the contrary, he insists that no logical scheme is so definitive that it cannot be modified, corrected, or abandoned, if a more fruitful system can be devised: "It is not a justified assumption that reality is exhausted by its congruence with the kind of ideal system accessible to the human mind in its scientific phase, such as we call logic." [9] Moreover, no one is more aware of the dangers of relying on inapplicable and unrevisable grand systems than is Parsons. Although Parsons finds the understanding of the common foundations of special theories by placing each of them "in the framework of its role in a functioning system" to be essential and fruitful; nevertheless, he warns that "there is a danger of the old fallacy of the premature closure of a theoretical system," i.e., "Comte and Spencer all over again." Unlike the pure rationalists who claimed that their systems of universal and necessary principles were absolutely true in their knowledge-situation, Parsons adopts the postulate of a systematic approach in his meaning-situation on the pragmatic grounds of its fruitfulness for empirical research: "The concept of system functions as an heuristic device to guide the formulation and empirical solution of such problems." [10]

Although Merton is not completely convinced that the time is ripe for the construction of an effective conceptual scheme, he fully recognizes the "risk of emerging with *ad hoc,* unrelated speculation consistent within a limited range of observations and inconsistent among themselves." Consequently, Merton advocates the use of a "middle range" approach which is designed to maintain, on the one hand, a balance between the significant "minor working hypotheses evolved in abundance during the day-by-day routines of research" and, on the other hand, the significant "all inclusive speculations comprising a master conceptual scheme from which it is hoped to derive a very large number of empirically observed uniformities of social behavior." [11] It is difficult to understand why some social scientists who accept Merton's approach reject Parsons', when Parsons himself has insisted that the aim of his system is to provide "a necessary basis for the most fruitful program of work in special theories as advocated by Merton." [12] Merton, it should be noted, is not opposed to a comprehensive system, but he claims that it should be built up out of more limited special theories.

Among those social scientists who have been mostly concerned with specific research problems there are some, like Stouffer, who acknowledge the empirical interest of systematizers like Parsons and look toward more coordination of the two approaches as a means of "organizing hitherto disconnected clusters of ideas into a single integrated system" which might serve as a "new context for evaluating the separate parts more critically at a theoretical level." Although Stouffer hopes, as a maximum, that a systematic scheme like the general theory of action might generate "middle-range hypotheses capable of empirical verification," he declares that "as a minimum, it is hoped that the effort to tie together the significant ideas about culture, society, and personality will provide broad orientations which map, as it were, areas for suggested research, even if it does not generate specifically deducible testable propositions at a middle range level." [13] Sheldon seems to speak also for other empirical researchers who recognize the substantive applicability of systems when he declares that the general theory of action "is indeed an all-embracing one, and the potentialities for developing a unified social science theory are high, provided one can give factual meaning to the categories in terms of operations and provided one can derive from these categories relationships subject to empirical test." [14] The desirability for such a coordination has been acknowledged elsewhere by Ruesch who insists that for a unitary approach to man "what we need is a first approximation to a scheme which will enable us to represent physical, psychological, and social events within one system of denotation." [15]

2. SYSTEMATIC HARMONY

In addition to the faith that the systematic unification of constructs better approximates the reality to which they refer, some natural and social scientists have explicitly adopted the assumption that the objective referent, the physical and behavioral universe, is itself an harmonious system. Einstein and Infeld have declared that "without the inner harmony of our world, there could be no science." [16] This does not prove that the universe is not chaotic; but it does reveal that the presupposition that there is an orderly pattern in nature is a necessary postulate for natural-scientific inquiry. Correspondingly, when Parsons, referring to the empirical reality of social action, declares that it "must be of a character which is in some sense congruent with the order of human logic," he too assumes that "events in it cannot occur simply at random in the sense which is the negation of logical order." [17]

3. LAW-LIKE GENERALIZATIONS

Unless a scientist assumes that he can formulate law-like, if not lawful, generalizations about physical and/or behavioral events as the objective of inquiry, then his presuppositions about the systematic character of both his constructs and their referents are not sufficient for defining what kind of knowledge is meaningful. The postulate that constructs should be systematically ordered requires an effort to arrive at a law which conceptually integrates all of the explanatory-predictive hypotheses that apply to the entire dimension of reality to which they all refer, e.g., the astronomical context of the heliocentric theory, or the biological context of the evolutionary theory. As Hempel and Oppenheim have correctly said, "the decisive requirement of every sound explanation remains that it subsume the explanandum under general laws." [18]

Despite the necessity to postulate the principle of lawfulness in human endeavor, i.e., "some measure of regularity or of persistence of recurrence," the idea of law is fraught with ambiguity. Just as theologians have presupposed Divine Law; philosophers have presupposed moral law; dramatists have presupposed fate; so also scientists have presupposed, as Whitehead says, that "apart from a certain smoothness in the nature of things, there can be no knowledge, no useful method, no intelligent purpose." The persistence and pervasiveness of the idea of lawfulness, however, has not generated a consensus. For, as Whitehead adds, "the expression of this notion of Law with due accuracy, and with due regard to what in fact is presupposed in human purposes, is a matter of extreme difficulty." On the one hand, a natural law is designed to express a universal and necessary generalization with complete clarity and distinctness. But, on the other hand, there is the assumption about nature upon which the idea of lawfulness depends, i.e., that "there are a variety of existences and types of existences in the connected universe." Whitehead insists that this lies in the "dim background" of our meaning-situation "from which we derive and to which we return." [19]

In an effort to clarify the conception of natural law in the meaning-situation of the scientific enterprise Whitehead has identified four divergent assumptions which have been respectively presupposed by four different ways of formulating natural laws. *The doctrine of imposed law* is the Newtonian assumption that God imposed the laws of gravitation and motion on the matter-in-space which he had created. When God withdrew he left the universe to operate mechanically in accordance with these laws which as inherent structures of nature itself regulated the causal interaction of all physical things within a unified, uniform, and rigidly deterministic system. Such an all-comprehensive formula conceptually integrated nature in a unitary scheme of mechanical causation, in which "every particle attracts every other particle" in accordance with "the products of their masses." It was, of course, a mathematical ideal, but the nineteenth-century materialists applied it to the real world of spatial objects which the natural laws regulate, even though scientific knowledge of matter-in-motion was incomplete. Assuming that the Newtonian laws governed nature, Laplace, for example, declared that if one could know the disposition of all matter and energy, as well as the direction of every particle's motion, at any given time, then with an infinite mathematical formula and the laws of gravitation and motion he could *predict with absolute certainty* the precise disposition of matter at all future times.

The development of the quantum and relativity theories required a re-evaluation of the Newtonian concept of nature. Then the idea of natural laws as inherent in reality itself, and the idea that natural laws embody causation as predictive certainty, were challenged by those who reconstructed their conception of natural laws. Whitehead has designated these as *mere description, conventional interpretation,* and *immanence.* By the doctrine of *law as mere description,* Whitehead means that the scientist describes the persistent pattern which he observes in the succession of natural events. Charles' law of temperature-volume relationship is such an empirical law: "The volume of a gas varies directly with the temperature, other conditions remaining constant." This and similar laws such as "friction produces heat" meet the demands of Bridgman's narrower operationalism. By the doctrine of *law as conventional interpretation* it is meant that statistical correlations about groups of events are more meaningful as laws than are causal generalizations about the interconnections among specified conditions. Actuarial predictions and similar computations of relative frequency in accordance with "probability calculations" presuppose this conception of law.

Whitehead adopts an immanental conception of natural law as the basis of his own reconstruction of the Newtonian cosmology in terms of the interrelated whole of a constantly changing temporal process, to which the quantum and the relativity constructs refer. Accordingly, each particular event is what it is becoming by virtue of its causal interaction with each of the other events which share "some partial identity of pattern." Taken together this plurality of reciprocally interacting events constitute the temporal process of the total universe as a unified whole. By the doctrine of *law as immanent,* therefore, Whitehead means that "these identities of pattern in the mutual relations are the Laws of Nature," and "conversely, a Law is explanatory of some community in character pervading the things which constitute Nature." Further consideration of Whitehead's cosmology would take us beyond the limits of this study; however his statement that "the only intelligible doctrine of causation is founded on the doctrine of immanence" entails two aspects of the immanental assumption about natural law which have a direct bearing on the meaning-situation of scientific inquiry: (a) a law is not inherent in reality itself; but is constructed by the scientist as a comprehensive formula for conceptually integrating the system of generalizations about the entire context of the dimension of reality to which the law refers. (b) As causal generalizations, natural laws are not required to provide predictive certainty. The latter point will be developed in the discussion of the fourth postulate about causality; but the former point needs some elaboration here.[19]

The constructed character of natural laws is more readily recognized in the case of speculative generalizations than in the case of empirical laws such as Charles' law of temperature-volume relationship. About the law of inertia, for example, Einstein and Infeld declare "this law cannot be derived directly from experiment, but only by speculative thinking consistent with observation." Though it is a construct which represents an "idealized experiment" that "can never be actually performed," nevertheless, "it leads to a profound understanding of real experiments." Whereas the law of inertia simply defines "force" and "motion," other speculative generalizations are substantive constructs, e.g., the Newtonian law of gravitation ("the attraction between two objects is directly proportional to the product of their masses, and inversely proportional to the square of the distances between them"), or the heliocentric generalization of Copernicus ("all planets revolve around the sun"), or the evolutionary generalization of Darwin ("all life develops from the less complex to the more complex"). In order to emphasize that these, and similar generalizations for conceptually integrating hypotheses about a given dimension of nature, are not regulatory features inherent in nature, Einstein and Infeld declare that "physical concepts are free creations of the human mind, and are not, however it may seem, uniquely determined by the external world." Whatever the scientist may, at a given time, find the persistently uniform pattern in the changing process of events to be, he must assume, of course, that the actual pattern of events to which the constructed law refers does not depend upon the scientist's thinking and does not change with the modification of the scientist's constructs. Whatever may be the relation of our planet to the sun, it didn't change when the heliocentric theory replaced the geocentric theory. But, as Einstein and Infeld point out, the scientists need laws as "mental structures" to link their observations and objective referent when they "try to form a picture of reality and to establish its connection with the wide world of sense impression." [20]

Lachman similarly characterizes these comprehensive generalizations as constructed principles for conceptual integration when he distinguishes them from "empirical laws" by calling them "scientific theories," e.g., Dalton's atomic theory, Morgan's gene theory, Pasteur's microbe theory, Planck's quantum theory, in addition to the Copernican and Darwinian theories cited above: "A scientific theory is an explicit and objective statement of surmise or speculation which integrates isolated bodies of data into a coherent and consistent framework, which permits the specification of relationships between islands of empirical data, and which permits logical extrapolation from the obtained relationships to hitherto uninvestigated phenomena." [21]

We shall subsequently discuss the formulation of behavioral laws as the fourth stage of the hypothetical-deductive method of inquiry; but, at this point, we should note the problems which will then confront us. (a) How can law be defined so that it applies to both physical and behavioral events? For this purpose we shall assume that *a natural or behavioral law is a causal and/or statistical generalization about the uniform pattern in the processes of a given system of events; and, the applicability of such an integrating concept is limited to the specifically stated conditions.* (b) Is it necessary for social scientists to aim at lawful generalizations? Our answer to this will be the same as that of Hempel and Oppenheim: "In the social no less than the physical sciences, subsumption under general regularities is indispensable for the explanation and the theoretical understanding of any phenomena." [22] (c) Can behavioral laws be formulated? In an effort to ascertain the accuracy of Kantor's claim that "anthropic laws possess as much stability and rigor as are required by anthropic events," [23] we shall show why *law-like* rather than *lawful* generalizations are all that behavioral sciences can hope to achieve.

In that later discussion, attention will be focused particularly on the difficulties of specifying the limiting conditions which the formulation of law-like generalizations requires.

B. *The Significance of the Third Postulate for Individual Psychology*

The evidence seems to justify Lindzey's claim that "contemporary psychologists display for the most part a boundless respect for the importance of systematic theory." [24] Among those comparatively few who object to systematization there are some who contend that the time is not ripe until there has been more fragmentary experimental research, and there are others who, like Marx, warn that the "premature development of an overly-rigid systematic position" incurs great risk, "especially if there is a concomitant attempt to stifle off continued exploratory efforts at other levels of explanation." [25] To the former objection Hull answers that in individual psychology "the conditions for the development of systematic theory are definitely favorable," and "the time is ripe for the attempt whenever someone has the impulse to make it." [26]

Those psychologists who might be classified as systematizers are fully aware of the danger against which Marx cautions. Unlike those psychologists of the recent past who, as Brunswik charges, arbitrarily advocated using as an objective their own systematic theory as the basis for polemical attacks on other systems, the psychologists who today adopt this third postulate use systematizing as a *tool* for understanding general relationships between apparently unrelated phenomena (Hull) [27] and for "specifying the precise form of the interrelations between the variables" (Spence).[28] This shift of interest from "school systems" to "functional relations and systematization" [29] contributes to the attainment of the generalizing aim of all science. Moreover, the use of a systematic theory as an emendable device serves rather than hinders the purpose of research by "unifying or making congruent known empirical findings, and suggesting new empirical relations to be explored and verified." [30]

The postulate that psychological constructs should be organized systematically for use, rather than as an objective, is an assumption underlying three different, though not incompatible, approaches.

Hull advocates the systematization of deductive principles in order to provide a logical design for experimentation. Brunswik advocates a correlational system with a view to the formulation of statistical relationships that do not directly depend upon the empirical observation of a given organism's behavior. Tolman advocates the conceptual systematization of human motivation for the purpose of coordinating it with a conceptual systematization of sociocultural conditions in an integrated social-scientific inquiry. Since Tolman's assumption about a causal system has been previously considered at length in connection with the synoptic model, and will be further examined under the next postulate, it will not be developed here; but his explicit postulation of a systematic causal interconnection of dependent, independent, and intervening variables should be noted. Let us examine, however, the deductive systematizing of Hull and the statistical systematizing of Brunswik.

According to Hull, psychological inquiry will not become a mature science until its experimental observations are logically-empirically systematized: "The orderly arrangement of the observations constitutes the empirical components of science, and the logical systematization of the ideas concerning these observations constitutes the theoretical component." Hull distinguishes three separable but interrelated aspects of the kind of theoretical system which he advocates for psychological analysis. It should include (a) a set of definitions of the essential terms to be used; (b) a set of postulates about what the relations among the natural phenomena are found to be, and (c) "a hierarchy of interlocking theorems ultimately derived from the postulates by a rigorous logical process." Since such "scientific theorems are 'if-then' statements, i.e., they ordinarily state in effect that *if* such and such antecedent conditions exist, *then* such and such consequences will follow," the logical systematizing provides the questions which an experiment is designed to answer. The points to be emphasized here are that this "intimate interaction between observations and ideas" would not be meaningful, if Hull did not presuppose that the phenomena themselves "in the relevant part of nature which the system concerns" constitute a harmonious system and if he did not presuppose that "the postulates of a theoretical system, if valid, are presumptive natural laws." [31]

In order to redirect psychological inquiry away "from the fragmentary molecular" approach to a systematic molar analysis Brunswik has proposed his "objective functional approach" in which the technique of correlational statistics is prescribed as the most effective tool for the formulation of a systematic "distal account of the stimulus situation" and behavioral description "in terms of gross achievement." As a "deliberate lump treatment," which is designed as a purely descriptive "way of registering and conceptually looking at gross correlations in their straightforward actuality," it not only transcends the mediational and physiological analyses of conditioned reflexes, but it requires an "empty organism" approach as well. A system of constant relationships about "what" rather than "how" can thus be conceptually represented "in purely objective and quantitative fashion merely by indicating its success in establishing far-reaching couplings between types of means-objects available in the environment and types of final biological goal effects." The point to be emphasized for this discussion of the third postulate, is that Brunswik does not seem to share Tolman's and Hull's assumption that the behavioral events themselves are harmoniously systematic and can be explained in terms of causal laws. Nevertheless, his statistical analysis none the less requires the postulate of a systematic framework.[32]

C. *The Significance of the Third Postulate for* *Social Psychology*

Social psychologists for the most part seem to have adopted the postulate that knowledge about interpersonal transactions is more meaningful if the constructs about it are systematically organized, even though they do not claim to have as yet established such a system. Much social-psychological research is conducted on an *ad hoc* basis. Nevertheless, many of his colleagues agree with Gordon Allport that "theories that transcend the specific instances are necessary," even though, "theory building in social psychology is still in its infancy." [33] Moreover, systematic frameworks have been imported from various general psychological views into social psychology, e.g., McDougall's "hormic," Floyd Allport's "behavioristic," Brown's "field theory," Sherif's "culturalistic," Krech and Crutchfield's "phenomenological." Asch furnishes an example of the application of a *Gestalt* system to social-psychological subject matter. He declares that the "time does not seem ripe for such an undertaking" as formulating a "system of social psychology." Nevertheless, when he analyzes an attitude as a cognitive structure, he finds it "a structure of a hierarchical order, the parts of which function in accordance with their position in the whole." Asch also takes an attitude to be a "dependent part of a wider system" which functions in the person's scheme of things.[34]

Newcomb explicitly refers to the other two assumptions which we have found that a systematic approach entails. That the social-psychological referent is itself a harmonious system is presupposed by Newcomb in his claim that "order and regularity are to be found not only at the level of the organism but also at the level of collectivities." Moreover, when Newcomb proposes "three possible answers to the problem of the interrelatedness of lawfulness at different levels," he deals with the other aspect of the third postulate. The first assumption that "it is pure chance" he rejects "on the grounds of scientific faith." The second assumption that "lawfulness at the more inclusive level is required by the nature of lawfulness at the less inclusive level" he accepts hypothetically but doubts its adequacy, since "alternate forms of social organization seem equally compatible with given forms of individual organization." The third assumption that "lawfulness at less inclusive levels is required by the nature of lawfulness at more inclusive levels" he thinks should be explored in order to ascertain the likely possibility that "whole-organizations limit and selectively influence various aspects of part-organization." Upon the clarification of this meaning of lawfulness, "psychological theory itself will have been improved." [35]

Although Lewin was sceptical about any abstract systems for social psychologists who faced "the task of developing a general approach which offers specific conceptual tools for solving the concrete problems of a vast and diversified area," he assumed that "the properties of any event are determined by its relations to the system of events of which it is a component and that changes here and now depend on changes in the immediate neighborhood at a time just past." Accordingly, his claim that "the meaning of any concept is determined by its relation to other concepts in the system of concepts of which it is a part" leaves no room to doubt that the systematic organization of constructs is presupposed as a postulate of his "field theory." In this theory, the "field" is that "part of a totality of coexisting facts which are conceived of as mutually interdependent." [36]

While, as Gordon Allport reports, social psychology has no master chart but rather a number of maps available, there are some basic constructs which social psychologists aim to systematize as tools for analysis. Constructs about interpersonal transactions such as the following have been developed recently (around the last ten years) as reconstructions of the earlier conflicting concepts of more specific schools. (a) *Motive* and *motive pattern*. Whereas, a motive is "a state of the organism in which bodily energy is mobilized and selectively directed toward parts of the environment," a *motive pattern* means "a sequence of behaviors characterized by relative constancy of motivation." In this correlative conception the divergent concepts of motive as "drive" and as "direction of behavior" are reconciled.[37]

(b) *Attitude*. If Gordon Allport's definition of an attitude as a "neuropsychic state of readiness for mental and physical activity" is adopted, social-psychological inquiry can avoid the extremes of exclusively instinctivistic and exclusively environmentalistic approaches. As such an enduring factor in behavior an attitude toward another person provides the continuity for the predisposed motives which intermittently recur in response to some specific situation. This distinction is brought out by Newcomb, when he differentiates between the goal-referring motive and the object-referring attitude: "Attitudes thus represent persistent, general orientations of the individual toward his environment, whereas motives are temporary (though they may be repeated) and relatively specific." [38] There is not yet, however, sufficient consensus about the construct of *attitude* as a substitute for older constructs to formulate a systematic scheme. Even if one is willing to consider sentiment as another name for a complex of emotion-laden attitudes, according to Asch, "the category of attitude has remained unclear, and its systematic relation to other psychological functions has been unresolved, partly because the traditional dichotomy of instinct and habit has not been abandoned." [39]

(c) *Role-Behavior*. Without the construct of *role-behavior*, the interpersonal transactions with which social psychologists are concerned could not be sufficiently distinguished from the impersonal functional components of the sociocultural process which the sociologists and anthropologists identify as *role-positions*. For, as Newcomb has formulated it, the former refers to "the actual behavior of specific individuals as they take roles," whereas the latter refers to multi-person "patterns of expectancies" at a collective level of institutional uniformity. It is this construct of *role-behavior* which may make it possible for social psychologists to provide the social-scientific enterprise with a situationally-relative, rather than a radically-relative, conception of the behavioral process. Although the sociocultural situation determines the nature of the role in which any given person performs, perceives, feels, and thinks; still, that person's own desires for the satisfaction which shared goals yield must be considered in a diagnosis of motivation. On the one hand, there is sufficient uniformity for prediction in the sense of reasonable anticipations "because they are behaviors whose meaning is provided by shared frames of reference." On the other hand, as Newcomb insists, "whatever the characteristics he expresses in various roles, they are *his own* characteristics, and he cannot help expressing them as he takes his roles in his own, individual way." [40]

(d) *Psychological Field.* This construct identifies the complex unity of all the mental processes and all the environmental influences which determine any given person's behavior at any given moment. It is essential for any systematic conception of interpersonal transactions. In connection with the synoptic model, it will be recalled, this construct was discussed with special emphasis upon Lewin's idea of the "life space" as a "dynamic whole" of interdependent parts. Newcomb's point to be noted here is that communication and consensus produce the psychological group, but that without the individual's "unique experience of communication and unique perceptions of consensus," the psychological field could not emerge as the intersection of the dynamic process through which a person is both the product and the producer of the group which is psychologically real because "individuals perceive it and are motivated in relation to it." [41] Asch also insists that a "group relation at the psychological level" requires that each participant retains his perspective and asserts his individuality so that "this relation between psychological events in each of the participants makes possible the sharing of actions, feelings, ideas, and mutual acknowledgment." [42]

If social psychologists can systematically correlate such constructs as motive and motive-pattern, attitudes, role-behavior, and the psychological field, they may hold the key to the correlative social-scientific conceptions of the self-in-society and personality-in-culture which require systematization at a more inclusive sociocultural-motivational level. This seems to be the direction in which Newcomb is heading when he assumes that "the behavior of group members whose frames of reference are shared can be understood only as mutually interdependent 'behaviors' which constitute a system" that "social psychology cannot ignore." [43] That this is still programmatic is clearly brought out by Lambert in his analysis of the problems which are involved in the construction of an empirical-theoretical system by social psychologists. Lambert just as strongly emphasizes, however, the necessity for adopting this third postulate in the meaning-situation of social-psychological inquiry: "Much of the theory which has grown from the study of social phenomena in the 'natural' setting still suffers from the fact that it is a happenstance result of the descriptive method, rather than having been systematically constructed on a general basis." [44]

D. *The Significance of the Third Postulate for Sociology*

The assumption that sociological inquiry requires a systematic scheme of generalizations as an *analytical tool*, has functioned paradoxically in its meaning-situation. On the one hand, it is necessarily presupposed by those like Sorokin, who distinguish its nomothetic approach from the idiographic approach of history: "Sociology is a generalizing science of socio-cultural phenomena viewed in their generic forms, types, and manifold interconnections." [45] The systematic interpenetration of constructs is similarly deemed essential if they agree with Simpson that "one of the fundamental lessons sociology teaches is the unity of society and the necessity to understand any particular problem in any one field of sociology within the total context of human relationships." [46] This, of course, was the basic premise of the nineteenth-century founders of sociology who took their all-inclusive systems to be their unalterable ultimate objectives rather than as one among other analytical tools in the way that Parsons has been shown to do. (Recall the discussion above of Parsons' emendable system which guides and coordinates the implications of empirical research.) On the other hand, there are the radically empirical sociologists who are either indifferent about the construction of comprehensive systems of generalizations or else they fear that it will stifle the small-scale research which is directly confirmed or disconfirmed as long as it is fragmentary. Evidently these radical empiricists, who feel no compunction to justify theoretically their choice of observations or to relate what they find, are not aware of the important differences between Spencerian and Parsonian systematizing.

Merton's conception of the "bearing of sociological theory on empirical research" is especially instructive, since his "middle range" approach seems to be the most likely meeting ground for the systematizers and the fragmentary researchers. With some exaggeration, which is justifiable for his purpose, he has attributed as the motto for the former: "We do not know whether what we say is true but it is at least significant." For the latter it is: "This is demonstrably so, but we cannot indicate its significance." Since Merton appeals to Whitehead's wisdom in other discussions, it is likely that he would agree with him here that it is just as important for an idea to be significant as it is for it to be true. At any rate, Merton declares that "there is no logical basis for their being ranged *against* each other." Even though Merton believes that sociology is not yet mature enough "to deal *fruitfully* with abstractions of a high order" in the same way that physics and biology do, nevertheless, contemporary sociological research must presuppose this systematizing in principle in order that ultimately it might "meet the canons of scientific method." [47]

Merton's position is substantially endorsed by Bowers when he reviews this century's "notable progress in the field of research design" which was possible because sociologists corrected the scientific imbalance of "a grand concern over large topics in which the end far overshadowed the means for attaining it." But now that systematic knowledge as an end is often neglected or ignored in favor of the means of research techniques, Bowers concludes that "it is now time that we place as much emphasis on our research objectives and on the outcome of our research as on the methods by which the objectives are implemented and the outcome reached." [48]

Lundberg's insistence that it is necessary for sociology to adopt this third postulate should show that he is an exception to Simpson's generally accurate report that on this issue the conflict is between "those who look forward in the next fifty years mainly to the development of refined statistical and investigatory techniques and those who look forward to the forging of certain grand hypotheses which would illumine the structure and functioning of society and culture." [49] In spite of Lundberg's commitment to statistical techniques, he assumes that they require systematization just as much as Parsons presupposes a systematic framework for his conception of human action. Lundberg makes this explicit when he justifies his premise that "only within a carefully formulated system can cooperative effort as well as orderly verification or refutation take place." With respect to the three aspects of this third postulate mentioned at the outset of our elaboration, Lundberg is noncommital only about the presupposition that the behavioral reality itself is a "harmonious system." He insists that a systematic approach rather than a fragmentary one should be used by sociologists: "A system is needed for the correlation of research so as to make it bear directly and with greatest economy of effort upon the problems (hypotheses) the field presents." Moreover, Lundberg endorses the requirement that to be lawful, generalizations must be formulated as systematically as possible. He insists that in order to formulate "relevant, verifiable, consistent generalizations called principles, or laws" a sociologist must make his system as comprehensive as possible: "The measuring generally of scientific laws requires that they be organized into a system compatible with each other and in terms of which all the behavior within the field can be described." [50]

E. *The Significance of the Third Postulate for Anthropology*

There seems to be an ever-widening awareness among anthropologists that they need to develop a more systematic perspective for guiding their research and correlating their findings. Kroeber, for one example, lauds Slotkin's attempt to work out a systematic scheme of anthropological generalizations in his *Social Anthropology: The Science of Human Society,* despite the fact that Kroeber admits that he and most anthropologists have been partial to "the concrete and pluralistic tradition." [51] A pluralistic approach prevails during the anthropologist's actual field work when he is dealing with the variety of explicit behaviors. Kroeber and Kluckhohn report, however, that now anthropologists "are trying to go deeper to reduce the wide range of regularities in a culture to a relatively few 'premises,' 'categories,' and 'thematic principles' of the inferred or implicit culture." For they not only assume that "the study of culture is the study of regularities," but they also adopt the scientific postulate that "one attempts to understand, explain, or predict a system by reference to a relatively few organizing principles of that system." [52]

While a considerable number of anthropologists may be less concerned about a systematic analysis of culture as a total process than they are about describing the cultural phenomena which they find in the manner of a historical depiction, let us note here what other anthropologists have to say that bears on the three aspects in terms of which we have been elaborating the significance of this third postulate for the other disciplines. Qualifying declarations will be mentioned later.

A systematic rather than a fragmentary approach is proposed by Bidney as the only way in which anthropologists can utilize the reliable findings of other behavioral disciplines without committing neither the *culturalistic fallacy* of taking culture to be "an autonomous level of reality independent of man and society"; nor the *naturalistic fallacy* of taking culture to be merely a derivation from "an *a priori* analysis of human nature in society"; nor the *ethnologistic fallacy* of presupposing that "history *per se* is a sufficient cause or condition of cuture"; nor the *psychologistic fallacy* of presupposing that "psychology alone is the sufficient condition of cultural phenomena"; nor the *sociologistic fallacy* of assuming that "society is the ultimate entity *sui generis* and that all cultural processes and institutions are to be explained by reference to their functions in relation to this self-intelligible reality." When anthropologists do not aim at a systematic approach they either limit themselves to describing isolated phenomena or they adopt as their approach either what Bidney calls "a non-historical functionalism" or "a non-functional historicism." What is needed, according to Bidney, is a system for "combining both approaches into a ethnohistorical functionalism which evaluates cultural functions in the perspective of history and historical cultures as functional wholes." [53]

Do any anthropologists assume that the cultural phenomena themselves constitute a *harmonious system?* An affirmative answer would be offered by those who agree with Kluckhohn and Kelly that "a culture is an historically created system of explicit and implicit designs for living, which tends to be shared by all or specifically designated members of a group at a specified point in time." [54] This is reaffirmed by Kluckhohn and Kroeber, when they insist that "every culture is a structure—not just a haphazard collection of all the different physically possible and functionally effective patterns of belief and action but an interdependent system with its forms segregated and arranged in a manner which is *felt* as appropriate." [55] According to Bidney, anthropologists have "begun to view cultural phenomena as interrelated wholes which are more than the sum of their parts." [56] Moreover, as Kluckhohn insists, it is necessary for them to presuppose that this reality to which their constructs refer exhibits "uniformities of elements and uniformities of patterns." For, "without the discovery of uniformities there can be no concepts, no classifications, no formulations, no principles, no laws; and without these there can be no science." [57]

These anthropologists, who maintain that they must presuppose that cultural phenomena themselves are patterned as a harmonious system, do not imply that there is a consensus with respect to its organization and content. Linton makes this point when he declares that "we all recognize the importance of pattern but none of us has a very clear picture of how to deal with this as something distinct from the elements which are patterned and organized." [58] It is instructive to note, however, that despite the divergent conceptions of the nature of the pattern in culture itself, i.e., functional, structural, or structural-functional, it is presupposed by all that the pattern is systematic.

Among the functionalists, Boas did not reject the idea of the systematic nature of each culture, when he started with the premise that "each culture has its own unique history, dependent partly upon the peculiar inner development of the social group, and partly upon the foreign influence to which it has been subjected." [59] What he did reject was the specific systematization in the universal scheme of parallel sequences through identical stages which the unilinear evolutionists had conceived as inherent in the cultural process itself. Although Malinowski similarly opposed the universal scheme that yielded nomothetic generalizations, when he identified culture idiographically, he not only conceived of it as "an integral in which the various elements are interdependent," but he identified an institution as "an organized, purposeful system of human effort and achievement." [60] Speaking for the structuralists, Murdock claims that "differences of emphasis and some basic cleavages" are not as significant as an agreement among anthropologists about a "system of cultural theory" which refers to the interrelated areas about cultural dynamics, social structure, culture, and personality. Accordingly, he declares that "the present conditions of social-structure studies" is such that the anthropological data can be analyzed comparatively within a systematic framework.[61]

When anthropologists have attempted to use the structural-functional mode of analysis which Parsons has applied so effectively to a wide range of behavioral data, they are committed to a Parsonian conception of the necessity for assuming that the sociocultural process is a harmonious system. Since, as Firth has observed, Parsons has used "the concept of function with more flexibility and more richness of content than anthropologists have done," he has "related it more positively to structural concepts" and he "has faced the difficulties inherent in its implications." [62] The assumption about the systematic nature of the sociocultural referent, however, is required no less by Radcliffe-Brown, when he accounts for "the necessary conditions of existence" by presupposing that "it is through and by the continuity of the functioning that the continuity of the structure is preserved." [63] It is similarly postulated by Bennett and Wolff in terms of a "conceptual scheme which differentiates among levels of meaning," when they look to the development of "structural-functional research and theory" as promising a rapprochement between anthropological and sociological analyses of "structural systems in which behavior is explored in respect to its meaning or function." [64]

Do anthropologists assume that, to be law-like, their generalizations must be systematically constructed? Goldstein indicates an essential feature of such a systematic construction: "If anthropology ever produces a system of laws, I presume that such laws will be of the kind that group together certain specific phenomena which may be shown to have certain determinate relations to each other." [65] An anthropologist could share this assumption without endorsing Wissler's aim to formulate a "universal cultural pattern" for comparatively analyzing all cultures.[66] The majority of anthropologists reject the idea of any universal and necessary unilinear law of cultural evolution in accordance with which all societies develop through the same successive stages. But this does not preclude their aiming at law-like principles for understanding and depictively integrating a specific culture, e.g., Kroeber's "configurations" or Opler's "themes." For example, Steward presupposes the possibility of constructing a system of law-like generalizations about the regularities in the multilinear evolution of cultures through more limited comparisons: "The most fruitful course of investigation would seem to be the search for laws which formulate particular phenomena with reference to particular circumstances." [67]

Is Steward's underlying assumption incongruent with that of those anthropologists who have been strongly influenced by Malinowski's functional approach? Despite one's first impression to the contrary, these assumptions are not mutually exclusive. To be sure, Malinowski was de-emphasizing any system of law-like generalizations when he identified culture as "the body of commodities and instruments as well as of customs and bodily or mental habits which work directly for the satisfaction of human needs." But he did admit that "the cultural process is subject to laws and that the laws are to be found in the function of the real elements of culture." [68] Goldenweiser insists that anthropologists "without aiming at the logical orderliness of evolutionary schemes have renewed their search for relatively stable tendencies and regularities in history and in society." [69]

Special attention should be directed to the basic divergence between those who assume that an idiographic-nomothetic system is required in order to analyze "personality in culture" and those who assume that a purely nomothetic system is required in order to analyze culture as a *sui generis* entity without any reference to motivational factors.

Despite the difficulty of formulating law-like generalizations under which the motivational factors of individual persons could be subsumed, anthropologists like Kluckhohn aim at systematizing all of the motivational and sociocultural factors which are involved in the reciprocal process in which persons are shaped by their culture, and the culture is shaped by the persons who, in some cases, are its self-creative participants. Thus, he postulates that "a balanced consideration of personality in nature, society, and culture must be carried on within the framework of a complex conceptual scheme which explicitly recognizes, instead of tacitly excluding, a number of types of determinants." [70]

In order to provide anthropology with a nomothetic system of lawful generalizations for a "science of culture," White assumes that *for purposes of anthropological analysis* all motivational "types of determinants" must be excluded. In this *methodological superor-*

ganicism he adopts the premise that "cultural phenomena behave in accordance with their own principles and laws," and as such "must be studied and interpreted in terms of culture." By refusing to include any correlation "between particular peoples and particular cultures" he presupposes that culture "constitutes a distinct order of reality in our conceptual scheme of analysis and interpretation." From the vantage point of this broad level of abstraction, White has conceived of culture as a complex totality of interrelated diachronic and synchronic aspects: "The culture of mankind as a whole may be considered temporally as a flowing stream, or nontemporally as a system, or as both, i.e., as a system in a temporal continuum."

How can White completely discount the psychodynamic, interpersonal, and sociocultural responses of the goal-seeking persons who internalize cultural ways of feeling, believing, and acting in the motivational process? As was emphasized under the first postulate, White does not deny the existence of the concrete ends-means continuum; for he acknowledges that culture "has its origin in the organisms of human beings," and he grants that "it could not exist or be perpetuated without the existence and action of human beings." But in strictly anthropological analysis he can limit the meaning of culture to *only* the "extrasomatic, temporal continuum of things and events" because he thinks of motivation only in terms of the somatic processes which he relegates to psychology. Accordingly, by his initial definition of motivation in Watsonian terms he precludes the consideration of the psychodynamic, social-psychological, and sociological data upon which the "personality-in-culture" anthropologist depends.

Regardless of how unjustifiably arbitrary one may take White's exclusion of all idiographic modes of motivation to be when he reduces man to a constant biological factor, nevertheless, it must be recognized that he is thoroughgoing in his adoption of this third postulate. He clearly assumes that the ideological, sociological, technological, and attitudinal components of cultural evolution are meaningful only if it is presupposed that they are systematically interconnected constructs: "The interrelationship of these elements and classes of elements and their integration into a single, coherent whole comprise the functions, or processes, of the cultural system." [71]

In concluding this section, accuracy requires us to note that not all anthropologists fully share the feelings about the significance of this third postulate which has been shown by those we have quoted. Tax is a spokesman for those who understand that the "tradition of science demands rationality," i.e., the systematic "demand that anthropology be justified by showing the logical interrelations of all of its ideas and operations." But they seem to agree with Tax that "it has little to do with the problem of whether anthropology will maintain itself as a subculture." Moreover, Tax goes on to insist even further that "incongruencies and logical inconsistencies are necessary characteristics of a living branch of science." [72] Levi-Strauss, for another example, seems to agree in principle that anthropological constructs should be systematically organized, when he declares that "to adjust our techniques of observation to a theoretical framework . . . is the challenge to modern anthropology." Standing in the way of such a systematic interpretation, however, is the situation in which "the facts themselves are lacking, either not numerous enough or not collected under conditions insuring their comparability." [73]

A most instructive insight into the significance of the third postulate for anthropological inquiry has been provided by Thompson, when she emphasizes that in order for "anthropology to emerge out of the primarily descriptive, natural history phase of scientific development to a more mature, postulational phase" it must use a systematic approach for analyzing "the entire system of interpersonal relations, both formal and informal, which comprise the interaction pattern of society." Otherwise, anthropologists will not be able to participate effectively in multi-disciplinary research. Although "anthropologists have found difficulty in developing a new concept of culture" which is sufficient for this purpose, Thompson insists that an unsystematic conception of culture as an aggregate will not do: "The traditional definition of culture as a sum-total or aggregation of elements, traits or patterns has of course become outmoded." Instead of accepting the depersonalized conception of culture as proposed by White, Thompson agrees with Kluckhohn, Hallowell, and other anthropologists that the construct of personality-in-culture is essential in the systematic conception of the cultural process: "An adequate theory of personality had to be evolved which would account for the growth, development, organization and integration of personality in total relevant setting and under changing pressure from within the human organism and outside it; which would account for the decisive role of culture in the development of personality; and which would account for the creative, purposive role of personality in the building, integration and regeneration of cultures." [74]

F. *The Significance of the Third Postulate for Economics*

The sophisticated refinement of economic theory can be largely attributed to its presupposition that its explanatory-predictive constructs must be systematically related. As Parsons and Shils have acknowledged, economists were "by far the earliest to conceive of the relevant phenomena in terms of a system of interdependent variables and thus to interpret particular phenomena in the light of their interrelations with others in a system." [75] The distinctiveness of such a schematic approach is made explicit by Lange: "Theoretical economics puts the patterns of uniformity in a coherent system." [76] Among traditional economists this has been a basic postulate not only for those who, like Jevons, presupposed a purely analytic system of mathematical-logical relations of implication for deduction, but also for those who, like Marshall, presupposed that the deductive-inductive procedures for constructing more substantive hypotheses must be systematically organized. Recall Marshall's declaration that "the most reckless and treacherous of theorists is he who professes to let the facts and figures speak for themselves." [77]

Marshall's warning does not seem to have been heeded by the many contemporary economists who confine themselves to isolated research projects and rely on their statistical correlations of fragmentary data with little, if any, concern about a generic system of generalizations from which their various premises might be derived. When Machlup describes this "large body of economics apart from its theoretical or hypothetico-deductive system," he identifies the strictly empirical hypothesis of the statistical and economic researcher as "a proposition predicting a regular relationship between two or more sets of data of observation that cannot be deduced from the general hypotheses which control the network of interrelated inferences forming the body of theory of the discipline in question." Since these "correlational and other empirical findings" apply only to "particular relationships" they do not presuppose any systematic principle for "the selection, collection, and organization of empirical data." Consequently they have no bearing on the implications deduced from any established conceptual and/or theoretical scheme. Although much of the information that has been thus acquired is important, nevertheless as Machlup points out, such "successive estimates on the basis of new data have usually been seriously divergent." Moreover, since there is no systematic context of principles, "there is no way of telling whether the previous hypotheses were wrong or whether things have changed." Consequently, Machlup concludes that "the strength of a belief in a hypothesis depends, even more than on any direct empirical tests that it may have survived, on the place it holds within a hierarchical system of interrelated hypotheses." [78]

A contrast between two diametrically opposed uses of systematic analyses is furnished by von Mises and by Kapp. Von Mises presents an *a priori* conception of human action which is systematized in terms of "the deduction of praxiological theorems": "The only way to a cognition of these theorems is logical analysis of our own inherent knowledge of the category of action." [79] In this formalistic analysis of self-evident intuitively experienced "essence of human action" all other sources of behavioral knowledge are irrelevant. Kapp explicitly opposes this purely analytical systematization of economic generalizations when he maintains that economics should be a substantive science which "goes beyond the purely formal explication of the logical character of the means-end relationship." If economics "starts from actual human needs and places man's dependence upon an interaction with his natural and social environment in the center of its investigation," then in the construction of its substantive systematic framework "the basic concepts and conclusions of the behavioral sciences cannot be dispensed with." [80]

In addition to presupposing a systematic approach, both the orthodox and unorthodox movements of economic theorizing assume that the economic process itself is a harmonious system. It is obvious that the neo-classical concepts of rational action and the law of supply and demand require the premise of a closed system of equilibrium. Although the institutionalists rejected this conception of the nature of economic reality itself, they presupposed that the open temporal process to which their constructs refer exhibits some systematic pattern. Gruchy makes this point by a specific reference to

Means: "In developing his new economics Means makes no complete break with his nineteenth-century predecessors"; for "like the neo-classical economists, he recognizes the necessity of creating a systematic pattern of economic thought." Reject though he does the orthodox laissez-faire system of equilibrium and the neo-classical formal mode of analysis, in his revision of "assumptions appropriate to an economy dominated by large corporations" Means acknowledged that some systematic framework was indispensable, since "without a basic theoretical pattern economic analysis would be little more than aimless description." [81] Similarly, when Spiethoff rejects the "pure theory arrived at by abstraction from reality" in favor of "a real institutional situation" which "is arrived at by an economic Gestalt theory," he rejects the neo-classical conception of the economic process as an arbitrarily isolated system. Presupposed by his idiographic-nomothetic isolation of "what is uniform and essential in its concrete framework of concatenations," however, there is his postulate of *Kausalzusammenhang*, i.e., a harmonious system of interacting elements.[82]

By the very nature of their more abstract approach the neo-classicists have had a decided advantage over the institutionalists in formulating lawful generalizations about the uniform patterns of the economic process. By virtue of their proviso of "everything else being equal," they can qualify their predictions about the rational activation of profit-seeking economic behavior. Also, by their proviso of equilibrating market operation, they have built-in specifications of the limiting conditions of laws such as that of supply and demand. Natural laws, it will be recalled, are no less qualified by provisional conditions by which predictions are hedged. The institutional economist, however, rejects these arbitrary delimitations when he constructs generalizations about economic transactions as an integral and interpenetrating part of the broader sociocultural-motivational process. Consequently, he is confronted by the difficult task of trying to state provisions for specifying the limiting conditions of his predictive generalizations about the total economic process. Their critics claim that the institutionalists do not expect to produce anything beyond "interesting statistical material" [83] and that they cannot aim at a "logical system but knowledge of facts of economic life." [83] In answer to these criticisms Gruchy insists, however, that "in their economic analysis the holistic economists go far beyond a simple description of the modern economy to create a systematic, orderly interpretation of the whole economic system." On the basis of a claim such as that of Mitchell, when he declares that "the systematically inclined among us are trying out various methods of conceiving the subject as a whole," Gruchy is justified in his claim that for holistic economists "there still remains the possibility of uncovering a logic of development which will throw some light on the role of economic change in the evolution of society." [84] Homan may be correct when he declares that "in the synthetic and creative construction of an adequate organon, which is the present task of economic theorists, the influence of the institutional movement will be large, but the outcome should be something larger, something better equipped methodologically than the institutional approach alone appears to be." [85] But the point to be emphasized is that some kind of systematization is presupposed by the proponents of each of these divergent approaches as well as of any that is developed in fulfillment of Homan's expectation.

G. The Significance of the Third Postulate for Political Science

Political science has not yet developed a systematic perspective for the selection of its data and the organization of its constructs. Although many who engage in political research feel no need to presuppose this postulate in their search for practical information about isolated fragments of the total political process, there are a few who contend that political scientists *ought* to investigate the programmatic possibility of devising a systematic framework. Speaking for this latter group, Easton insists "that the search for reliable knowledge about empirical political phenomena requires ultimately the construction of systematic theory, the name for the highest order of generalization." For, Easton argues, unless the "hyperfactualists" recognize that "the accumulation of data through acceptable techniques does not alone give us adequate knowledge" and begin to relate their findings systematically, they cannot expect to acquire operational knowledge: "Knowledge becomes critical and reliable as it increases in generality and internally consistent organization, when in short, it is cast in the form of systematized generalized statements applicable to large numbers of particular cases." [86]

The possibilities for developing a systematic approach have been examined by Leiserson in terms of the systematic integration of "the more general concepts and principles of political knowledge" to which the researcher should relate his working assumptions, in addition to formulating and testing his hypotheses. Historical, descriptive, and diagnostic treatments of political data become far more significant when they can be synchronized into a systematic approach: "In systematic theory, the conceptual framework consists of organizing ideas and concepts which, expressed in rigorous and orderly statements or relationships between variables, provide the basis for deriving hypotheses about behavior that can be tested empirically." Accordingly, Leiserson advocates something like Merton's recommendation for a middle range approach in sociological inquiry. When it is used by political scientists, "the threshold of systematic empirical inquiry has been crossed, and the process has begun of mutual interaction between explanatory theoretical configurations and the relatively miniscular research operations of testing limited hypothetical formulations." Within this "systematic-empirical method" for "collecting and analyzing data in political science" the various historical, comparative, statistical, psychological, and descriptive-analytical case study techniques can be coordinated into a unified procedure for cumulative analysis. For, as Leiserson recognizes, each of these apparently conflicting techniques "has a contribution to make in getting at the significant variables involved in the understanding of political processes or behavior patterns." But when they are not systematically integrated, "the inadequacy of such categories, for scientific purposes, lies in their ambiguity and noncumulative character, and in their inability to provide a conceptual apparatus capable of dealing with the strategic or limiting factors in the relations of the political scientist to his observational methods and the uniformities or regularities in his data." [87]

Do political scientists assume that the political process to which their constructs refer is itself a harmonious system? Leiserson's allusion above to "the uniformities or regularities in his data" indicates that he does. So also does Easton when he claims that "the development of theory depends upon the way in which we approach political activity viewed as a body of related phenomena" from which it is possible to abstract "from the whole of concrete interrelated social activity an aspect which we can identify as political." If political scientists do not adopt this postulate, Easton contends, "then clearly there would be no basis for probing further into general political theory." [88] Garceau also at least hints about the necessity of this presupposition when he maintains that political behavior research "is concerned with the total patterns of social relations which are involved in relating the citizen to the state at all institutional levels." [89] Although Easton, Garceau, and some other like-minded political scientists assume that the political process itself exhibits systematic interrelations, they agree with Leiserson that "most political scientists, although perhaps a diminishing majority, are skeptical of both the possibility and importance of systematic theory in this sense." Nevertheless, these systematizers hopefully maintain with Leiserson, that there is no "conclusive evidence that common concepts of sufficient generality will not be found to integrate the data of interpersonal and institutional behavior into an inclusive, logically consistent body of theoretical propositions." [90]

Whether or not political scientists explicitly acknowledge the systematic interrelations of the components of the political process itself, it is maintained here that they make this assumption implicitly when they proceed on the premise that they are dealing with an "ends-means continuum of action" in which there is political allocation of Laswell's "who gets what, when, and how." From the previous discussion of this *administrative instrumentation* as an operational variable in the synoptic model, Merriam's goal-oriented conception of the roots of government will be recalled. The roots of government, he declared, lie in "the necessity of adjusting the needs and desires of human beings struggling for forms of association through which human personalities may be adjusted, aided, or advanced toward higher levels of attainment." [91] In terms of such a purposive allocative operation as this, political scientists might be able to conceive the systematic interrelations of the political process to which their many different constructs refer.

Can law-like generalizations be formulated about political events? Michels' "iron law of oligarchy," by which all large-scale organizations are inevitably governed by an elite ruling class, might appear to be such a law-like generalization. Discussion of the question of its substantive accuracy lies beyond the scope of our present study; but it does indicate that some political scientists do seek to formulate a law-like principle by conceptually integrating their explanatory constructs. When Easton compares the generalizations of the political scientist with the "precise formulations" of the natural scientist, he warns that "if political science were to insist upon universal adherence to technical rigor, at the present time, as the only kind of adequate research, there is little doubt that, in attending so mechanically to form, all life and wisdom would be squeezed from the existing insights into political life." [92] This does not mean, however, that the political scientist should not aim at formulating law-like generalizations through what Leiserson recommends as an "unrelenting effort to relate his limited empirical generalizations to high-order propositions of functional relations between variables . . . to deepen his understanding of the conditions under which uniformities of political behavior occur or may be modified." [93]

H. *The Significance of the Third Postulate for History*

The issues which the adoption of this postulate entails are among the most crucial of those which complicate a reorientation of historiographical analysis. On the one hand, traditional historiographers are suspicious that systematizing would destroy the autonomy of their discipline. On the other hand, broadly operational historians are calling for a "systematic (and *really* scientific) study of the uniformities of human behavior." [94] Brockunier and Loewenberg, for example, acknowledge that "delimitation is essential in inquiries that seek answers to specific questions." They insist, nevertheless, that objective knowledge can be obtained only through a systematic integration that provides "cumulative analysis which eventually can deal with larger interrelationships on the basis of knowledge established in earlier, sharply delimited studies." [95] But, even those who adopt this postulate of systematizing their constructs are confronted by a complication peculiar to history, to which Parsons has directed attention. Whereas it is the aim of the other behavioral sciences to "develop logically coherent systems of general analytical theory," the aim of historiography "is to attain the fullest possible understanding of a class of concrete individuals or of one of a class." [96]

In opposition to those who feel no need for a systematic approach, broadly operational historians are convinced that a systematic perspective is required for guiding the selection and organization of their reconstructed data. Otherwise, Aitken and Loewenberg contend, "without adequate use of theory historical study cannot attain its full potential." [97] Although Cochran is aware that there are serious obstacles "in the path of the historian who approaches the problem of systematic analysis and the building of some empirically based hypotheses," nevertheless, Cochran calls upon his colleagues to aim at a "comprehensive and meaningful synthesis." [98] This does not mean that the traditional narrative account should be abandoned or that all historians should interpret their data at the same level of abstraction. In order that different kinds and levels of interpretation might be systematically congruent, however, Brockunier and Loewenberg recommend that the historian should bring to bear "upon the explanation of particular events concepts and hypotheses that are valid in terms of a more general theory." [99] All of the proponents of this systematic unification through cumulative analysis advocate the historian's use of social-scientific ideas wherever they are applicable so long as they do not eliminate the relative autonomy of historical inquiry.

Among those historians who do not adopt this systematic approach there are (i) those who would confine history to the study of "scientific facts," (ii) those who would confine history to the presentation of intuitively acquired insights into the meaning of completely unique past situations, and (iii) those who seek to reveal the ultimate meaning of the historical process.

(i) In order to discover "exactly what happened" and to report these isolated "facts which speak for themselves" in a chronological sequence the German "scientific school" and their American followers (MacMaster, Burgess, Adams), relied exclusively on the inductive procedure of documentary analysis. As Randall and Haines have noted, they were so misled by a Baconian conception of a natural-scientific approach that they rejected the systematic theory which, of course, is actually an essential feature of all scientific inquiry.[100]

(ii) Although the humanistic historiographers rebelled against the "scientific school" of Ranke when they appealed to intuitive feeling, they too rejected a systematic approach. Underlying Dilthey's claim that an insight into the completely unique events of history can be obtained only through the historian's own intuitive experience of empathetic understanding (*Verstehen*) there was his postulate that "life cannot be brought before the judgment seat of reason." [101] Similarly, Troeltsch presupposed that a systematic reconstruction is not applicable to the concrete totality of unique historical situations: "But the unity and meaning of the whole can only be surmised and felt, it cannot be theoretically expressed or theoretically constructed." [102] Contemporary historians who have adopted this appeal to intuitive feeling in order to preserve the uniqueness of specific historical situations as a concrete whole seem to overlook this possibility. Unique though such situations are as concrete wholes, they have some characteristics in common which can be systematically analyzed in terms of abstract generalizations.

(iii) When philosophers of history (Hegel, Marx, Spengler) present schematic formulae for understanding the ultimate meaning of all human history, they are not actually presupposing this third postulate. It might appear that they are, since they formulate broad generalizations rather than singular narratives. But their dialectical and cyclical formulae are not genuinely analytical tools for constructing causal explanations of the specifiable conditions in the historical process. Particular events are not examined with a view to ascertaining their systematic causal interconnections. They are cited only as symptoms which indicate what stage has been reached at a given time in the universal and necessary operation of the underlying principle of the persistently recurrent pattern of the sociocultural process. The significance of these philosophies of history for other purposes is in no way minimized when we insist that this approach through these comprehensive syntheses is quite distinct from that which the third postulate entails, i.e., aiming at a coherent system of causal generalizations from which empirically verifiable implications can be derived. (Despite the similarity of Toynbee's broad cyclical interpretation to these other philosophies of history, unlike them, his generalizations do seem to have some causal implications that are empirically verifiable.)

Do historians assume that Beard's "history-as-actuality" is a harmonious system? Historians seem to be wary of adopting without reservations a postulate which would correspond to the assumption of Einstein and Infeld that "without the belief in the inner harmony of our world there could be no science." [103] Beard warns that "the idea that there was a complete and actual structuralization of events in the past to be discovered through a partial examination of the partial documentation, is pure hypothesis." If Beard means that it is an unverifiable assumption, then of course he is supporting rather than opposing the postulatory conception of these epistemological principles. That this is the case is strongly suggested by his further declaration that "any overarching hypothesis or concept employed to give coherence and structure to past events in written history is an interpretation of some kind, or something transcendent." [104] Although it too is somewhat qualified, the following statement by Brockunier and Loewenberg less ambiguously affirms the necessity for making this assumption: "History is not exclusively chaos or chance: a degree of observable order and pattern, of partially predictable regularity, exists in human behavior." [105]

As it is conceived here, the assumption that historical events themselves constitute a harmonious system does not commit the historian who adopts it to historical monism rather than historical pluralism. According to monism, each historical event, subevent, or constellation of events is, in itself, an interrelated part of a closed system in which all sets of events are necessarily and completely interdependent. Mandelbaum has described pluralism as "the view that the grand sweep of events which we call the historical process is made up of an indefinitely large number of components which do not form a completely interrelated set." Mandelbaum presupposes the harmonious system of historical events in his conception of the "existential dependence of events," when he opposes the relativistic claim that "in themselves historical events are unstructured and discontinuous." He holds, nevertheless, to a historical pluralism "admitting only such interpenetration of events as we in fact uncover in our concrete investigations," even though he must assume that "it is this very interpenetration of events which saves historical inquiries from chaos." Is this a contradiction? If so, it might be resolved if we take his knowledge-situation to be pluralistic but his meaning-situation to be monistic. So conceived Mandelbaum's objection to historical monism on the grounds that it requires that "understanding would rest upon a mastery of the system as a whole" could be reconciled with his claim that "it may be that, in the end, laws of historical development will be discovered, and that these laws will express functional relations between all historical events and the events in some one field of societal life." [106] In other words, the historian can never actually know that there is a harmonious system among the historical situations themselves. Whatever degree of interpenetration of events within and among historical situations he takes there to be, it can never be more than a pragmatic assumption which cumulative analysis presupposes.

Can law-like, if not lawful, generalizations be constructed about historical events? This is an important question for the historian who attempts to construct substantive law-like generalizations under which he might subsume the reasonably acceptable hypotheses which he has imaginatively reconstructed out of authenticated testimony. For he is confronted with three basic problems that are inherent in his distinctive orientation. First, historical generalizations refer to particular wholes of a spatio-temporal situation rather than to universal segments that have been abstracted from concrete wholes in the formulation of natural laws. With respect to this issue Cohen has cogently noted that whereas "the laws of physics are formulated as equations in which there enter indefinitely repeatable time and space intervals but no date or locations . . . the latter are essential ingredients in history." [107]

Second, historical generalizations are always "postdictive" about past events rather than "predictive" in the sense that natural-scientific and social-scientific generalizations refer to future events. Third, historical generalizations are weakened, if not precluded, by the problem of specifying the limiting conditions of any law-like propositions. Since the second and third of these problems with respect to law-like generalizations are methodological rather than epistemological, they will be discussed later in the knowledge-situation when we elaborate the fourth stage of the hypothetical-deductive method. The first problem, however, raises an epistemological issue. Consequently, it will be elaborated now as an aspect of the meaning-situation of historical inquiry.

Since historical generalizations refer to particular wholes of a specific spatio-temporal situation in terms of "singular statements about the occurrence and interrelations of specific actions," [108] they will always differ from the scientific generalizations which functionally correlate the causal and/or statistical relations of abstracted universal characteristics. There is not even a programmatic possibility that the law-like generalizations of cumulative historical inquiry will approximate natural-scientific laws in the manner that other social-scientific generalizations might. The historian may substantially decrease the margin of error in his contemporary generalizations about a vanished past by improving his techniques of comparative analysis. However, this will not equate the significance of law-like generalizations in historical and non-historical inquiries, for two different aims are involved. On the one hand, the scientist aims at a generalization as an intrinsic end, whereas the historian, on the other hand, uses generalizations as a means for describing and explaining a specific past situation as an intrinsic end of his cognitive process.

The historian's distinctive orientation in terms of singular constructs should not be taken to mean that he assumes that each historical situation is so unique in every respect that it has no characteristics which other historical situations exhibit. Are there many, if any, roles played by any person which have not been played by other persons in other places and/or at other times? In any country has its founding, or its development, or its destruction no parallels in any other country? If historians had to give affirmative answers to these and similar questions, then they could not reconstruct interpretations of causal and temporal relations among past human actions and situations. Without presupposing causal and temporal continuity how could the historian even date an event in a chronological sequence? Moreover, the fact that the historian concentrates chiefly upon specific situations in terms of singular statements does not preclude all possibility of generalizing to the degree that his kind of law-like inferences requires, if such comprehensive integration applies to a pattern of similarities among a sufficient number of situations. What the historian must guard against, of course, is an attempt to reduce the concrete whole of interrelated components to any one of its partial segments. In other words, the historian *may* construct generalizations about some of the universal characteristics of any given total situation; but he *must never* substitute such abstract generalizing for his chief aim of describing and explaining particular situations as concrete wholes which have some unique characteristics.

There seems to be no consensus among philosophers who have dealt with this epistemological problem about historical laws. Werkmeister, on the one hand, maintains that the historian's individualizing orientation is attributable to his distinctive subject-matter which precludes anything more than "generalized sketches of relationships" about events which "are too complex to be readily subsumed under specific equations." [109] Gardiner, on the other hand, insists that "the fact that the historian's interest is directed upon particular events rather than upon universal laws is a fact about the purpose of history and not a fact about the type of event with which history deals." [110] Hempel disagrees with both Werkmeister and Gardiner when he claims that "in history no less than in any other branch of empirical inquiry, scientific explanation can be achieved only by means of suitable general hypotheses, or by theories, which are bodies of systematically related hypotheses." [111] It should be noted, however, that Hempel does not insist that such lawful generalizations must be strictly historical, since the historian may borrow them from other disciplines. Strong seems to have in mind a coordination of nomothetic and idiographic constructs for the increasing systematization of law-like "statements of relationship" when he concludes that historical explanation which uses "general characterizations in causal accounting . . . rises above triviality but falls short of being an explanation by scientific law." [112]

Despite the arguments among epistemologists about the possibility or impossibility of formulating historical laws, those historiographers who aim at cumulative analysis assume that they cannot disregard the ideal objective of constructing sufficiently inclusive, logically consistent, and empirically applicable generalizations which integrate more limited hypotheses. They do not expect more than partial success; but they postulate the necessity for striving toward this intellectual goal nonetheless. Consider, for example, the statements by the Committee on Historiography in Bulletin 54. Although they acknowledge that "attempts to discover 'laws' as exact as those now employed in the physical sciences have failed," they maintain, nevertheless, that "to formulate generalizations of limited validity" is "essential if historical work is to rise above a merely empirical level and if it is to serve any other purpose other than propaganda or literary effect." Such conceptual formulations are always emendable, since they "are useful in the interpretation of the past until their modification is called for by new evidence." When these historiographers aim toward "the most comprehensive historical generalizations" in cooperation with specialists in the social science and humanities, are they not assuming the possibility of constructing a law-like generalization? They refer explicitly to "a statement of relationships—one not possessing the exactness of 'laws' in the physical sciences but still having tentative validity and meaningfulness." [113] This more limited objective does not seem to contradict the declaration by Cohen and Nagel that "empirically ascertainable history does not and cannot prove the existence of universal or necessary laws." [114] Not only are law-like generalizations obtained in accordance with less rigorous demands than are universal and necessary laws, but they also function in historical inquiry as assumptions which are presupposed in the historian's meaning-situation rather than as substantive assertions which can be verified in his knowledge-situation.

Footnotes to Chapter 5 of Part Three

[1] Dewey, *Logic*, 418; *Experience and Nature*, 3-4.

[2] Toman in *Toward a Unified Theory of Human Behavior* (Grinker), 360-361.

[3] Quoted by Barnett in *The Universe and Dr. Einstein*, 119.

[4] Einstein and Infeld, *The Evolution of Physics*, 313.

[5] Sheldon in *Toward a General Theory of Action* (Parsons and Shils), 38. See Kant, *Critique of Pure Theoretical Reason*, A126.

[6] Parsons and Shils, *Toward a General Theory of Action* (Parsons and Shils), 50-51.

[7] Mills, "On Intellectual Craftsmanship," *Symposium on Sociological Theory* (Gross), 26-28.

[8] Parsons, *The Social System*, 537-538.

[9] Parsons, *The Structure of Social Action*, 754.

[10] Parsons, *American Sociological Review*, April 1948, page 157.

[11] Merton, *Social Theory and Social Structure*, 5; *American Sociological Review*, April 1948, page 166.

[12] Parsons, *American Sociological Review*, April 1948, page 157.

[13] Stouffer in *Toward a General Theory of Action* (Parsons and Shils), 479-480.

[14] Sheldon in *Toward a General Theory of Action* (Parsons and Shils), 43.

[15] Ruesch in *Toward a Unified Theory of Human Behavior* (Grinker), x-xi.

16 Einstein and Infeld, *The Evolution of Physics*, 313.

17 Parsons, *The Structure of Social Action*, 753-754.

18 Hempel and Oppenheim, "The Logic of Explanation," *Readings in the Philosophy of Science* (Feigl and Brodbeck), 322-323. Originally published in the *Philosophy of Science*, 15, 1948.

19 Whitehead, *Adventures of Ideas*, 139-151; *Modes of Thought*, 226; "Analysis of Meaning," *Essays in Science and Philosophy*, 122-123.

20 Einstein and Infeld, *The Evolution of Physics*, 33, 310. See Nagel, *The Structure of Science*, 81-83, for a relevant discussion of the distinction between experimental laws and theories. Special attention should be given to his claim that "none of the customary examples of experimental laws are in fact about sense data, since they employ notions and involve assumptions that go far beyond anything directly given to sense." (81)

21 Lachman, *The Foundations of Science*, 50-52.
   In order to eliminate some of the ambiguity about natural laws, they have been variously classified in terms of different levels of scientific generalizations. Lachman, for example, suggests that "there may be a hierarchical arrangement of generalizations into echelons" in which "the orders or levels are dependent upon the ranges of applicability, narrow or extended, of the generalized statements." (85-86) Cf. Dingle, *The Scientific Adventure*, 269-270; and Campbell, *Foundations of Science*, 38-158.

22 Hempel and Oppenheim, "The Logic of Explanation," *Readings in the Philosophy of Science* (Feigl and Brodbeck), 331, 326. Originally published in *The Philosophy of Science*, 15, 1948.

23 Kantor, *The Logic of Modern Science*, 281. Cf. Werkmeister, *A Philosophy of Science*, 277.

24 Lindzey, *Assessment of Human Motives*, 6.

25 Marx, *Psychological Theory* (Marx), 6, 122.

26 Hull, "Hypothetico-Deductive Method," *Psychological Theory* (Marx), 231.

27 Hull in *Psychological Theory* (Marx), 218-221.

28 Spence in *Psychological Theory* (Marx), 185.

29 Littman and Rosen in *Psychological Theory* (Marx), 153-154.

30 Lindzey, *Assessment of Human Motives*, 7.

31 Hull in *Psychological Theory* (Marx), 231-232.

32 Brunswik in *Psychological Theory* (Marx), 131-143, 386-391; *The Conceptual Framework of Psychology*, Chapters III, IV.

33 Allport in *Handbook of Social Psychology*, Vol. I (Lindzey), 50.

34 Asch, *Social Psychology*, 580-582.

35 Newcomb in *For a Science of Social Man* (Gillin), 246-250, 253-254.

36 Lewin, *A Dynamic Theory of Personality*, 41. Cf. Deutsch in *Handbook of Social Psychology*, Vol. I (Lindzey), Chapter 5 for an instructive account of Lewin's view.

37 Newcomb, *Social Psychology*, 80, 97. Cf. Allport in *Handbook of Social Psychology*, Vol. I (Lindzey), 43.

38 Newcomb, *Social Psychology*, 119-120.

39 Asch, *Social Psychology*, 75 (footnote).

[40] Newcomb, *Social Psychology*, 332-333. Cf. Sarbin, "Role Theory," *Handbook of Social Psychology*, Vol. I (Lindzey), Chapter 6.

[41] *Ibid.*, 629.

[42] Asch, *Social Psychology*, 163.

[43] Newcomb, *Social Psychology*, 629-630.

[44] Lambert in *Handbook of Social Psychology*, Vol. I (Lindzey), 77-87.

[45] Sorokin, *Society, Culture, and Personality*, 16.

[46] Simpson, *Man in Society*, 72.

[47] Merton, *Social Theory and Social Structure*, 83-84.

[48] Bowers, "Research Methodology in Sociology," *Method and Perspective in Anthropology* (Spencer), 259.

[49] Simpson, *Man in Society*, 83.

[50] Lundberg, *Foundations of Sociology*, 100, 115-116.

[51] Kroeber in *Current Anthropology* (Thomas), 305-307.

[52] Kluckhohn and Kroeber, "General Features of Culture," *Culture, A Critical Review of Concepts and Definitions* (Peabody Museum, Harvard, Vol. XLVII, No. 1, 1952) pages 161-162.

[53] Bidney, *Theoretical Anthropology*, 23, 95, 120, 248-249.

[54] Kluckhohn in *The Policy Sciences* (Lerner and Lasswell), 87.

[55] Kluckhohn and Kroeber, "General Features of Culture," *Culture, A Critical Review of Concepts and Definitions* (Peabody Museum, Harvard, Vol. XLVII, No. 1, 1952) pages 167-179.

[56] Bidney, *Theoretical Anthropology*, 366.

[57] Kluckhohn and Murray, *Personality in Nature, Society, and Culture*, 37-38.

[58] Linton in *An Appraisal of Anthropology Today* (Tax), 317.

[59] Boas, *Race, Language, and Culture*, 286.

[60] Malinowski, *A Scientific Theory of Culture*, 150; and *The Dynamics of Cultural Change*, 51.

[61] Murdock in *For a Science of Social Man* (Gillin), 23.

[62] Firth in *Current Anthropology* (Thomas), 241-242.

[63] Radcliffe-Brown, *The American Anthropologist*, 27 (1935), pages 394-402.

[64] Bennett and Wolff in *Current Anthropology* (Thomas), 338-340.

[65] Goldstein, *The American Anthropologist*, Vol. 61, Number 2 (April 1959), page 295.

[66] See Wissler, *Man and Culture*.

[67] Steward in *Anthropology Today* (Kroeber), 325.

[68] Malinowski in *Encyclopedia of the Social Sciences*, Vol. 4, pp. 624-625.

[69] Goldenweiser in *Encyclopedia of the Social Sciences*, Vol. 5, p. 662.

[70] Kluckhohn and Murray, *Personality in Nature, Society, and Culture*, 44.

[71] White, *The Evolution of Culture*, 3, 9, 10, 14-15, 16-17, 18, 28.

[72] Tax in *Current Anthropology* (Thomas), 315.

[73] Levi-Strauss in *Anthropology Today* (Kroeber), 549-550.

[74] Thompson, "The Societal System, Culture and the Community," *Toward a Unified Theory of Human Behavior* (Grinker), pp. 71-72.

[75] Parsons and Shils, *Toward a General Theory of Action*, 28.

[76] Lange, "The Scope and Method of Economics," *Readings in the Philosophy*

of Science (Feigl and Brodbeck), 746-747. Originally published in the *Review of Economic Studies*, 13, 1945-46.

77 Marshall, "The Present Position of Economics (1885)," *Memorials of Alfred Marshall* (Pigou), 168. Cf. Jevons, *The Principles of Science*, 759-761.

78 Machlup, "The Problem of Verification in Economics," *The Southern Economic Journal*, Vol. XXII, No. 1, July 1955, pp. 5, 19-20.

79 von Mises, *Human Action*, 49.

80 Kapp, "Economics and the Behavioral Sciences," *Kyklos*, Vol. VII, 1954, pp. 207, 219, 223-224

81 Gruchy, *Modern Economic Thought*, 476-477. Cf. Means, *The Structure of the American Economy*, 96 ff.

82 Spiethoff in *Enterprise and Secular Change* (Lane and Riemersma), 446, 451.

83 See Robbins, *An Essay on the Nature and Significance of Economic Science*, 114; Normano, *The Spirit of American Economics*, 186.

84 Gruchy, *Modern Economic Thought*, 608, 556.

85 Homan, "The Institutional School," *Encyclopedia of the Social Sciences*, Vol. 5, p. 392.

86 Easton, *The Political System*, 4-5, 55.

87 Leiserson, *Political Science Quarterly*, Dec. 1953, page 583.

88 Easton, *The Political System*, 318.

89 Garceau, *American Political Science Review* (1951), Vol. 45, p. 72.

90 Leiserson, *Political Science Quarterly*, Dec. 1953, page 567.

91 Merriam, *Systematic Politics*, 1.

92 Easton, *The Political System*, 59-60.

93 Leiserson, *Political Science Quarterly*, Dec. 1953, page 583.

94 Nichols, Bulletin 64, page 12.

95 Brockunier and Loewenberg, Bulletin 64, page 148-149.

96 Parsons, *The Structure of Social Action*, 760.

97 Aitken and Loewenberg, Bulletin 64, page 25.

98 Cochran, Bulletin 64, page 169.

99 Brockunier and Loewenberg, Bulletin 64, page 101.

100 Randall and Haines, Bulletin 54, pages 30-34.

101 Dilthey, *Gesammelte Schriften*, 261.

102 Troeltsch, *Der Historisimus und seine Probleme*, 174.

103 Einstein and Infeld, *The Evolution of Physics*, 313.

104 Beard, "That Noble Dream," *American Historical Review*, Vol. 41, p. 83.

105 Brockunier and Loewenberg, Bulletin 64, page 95.

106 Mandelbaum, *The Problem of Historical Knowledge*, 26-27, 60, 161, 201-202, 274, 276-277, 288.

107 Cohen, *The Meaning of Human History*, 119.

108 Nagel, "The Logic of Historical Analysis," *Readings in the Philosophy of Science* (Feigl and Brodbeck), 689. Originally published in *The Scientific Monthly*, 74, 1952, page 163.

109 Werkmeister, *The Basis and Structure of Knowledge*, 329.

110 Gardiner, *The Nature of Historical Explanation*, 64.

111 Hempel, "The Function of General Laws in History," *Readings in Philosophi-*

cal Analysis (Feigl and Sellers), 467. Originally published in *The Journal of Philosophy*, 39, 1942.

[112] Strong, *Journal of Philosophy*, January 31, 1952, page 63.

[113] Bulletin 54, pages 138-140.

[114] Cohen and Nagel, *An Introduction to Logic and Scientific Method*, 353.

6 *The Fourth Postulate of the Meaning-Situation of Reflective Inquiry (Causality)*

Causality is required as the principle of objective reference for the construction of explanatory and predictive hypotheses about the interaction of physical events and about behavioral transactions.

A. *The General Significance of the Fourth Postulate*

1. THE RECONSTRUCTION OF THE CONCEPT OF CAUSATION IN NATURAL SCIENCE

The significance of this postulate in philosophical-scientific conceptions of what kind of knowledge is meaningful is attested to by the persistence of the idea of causality throughout the development of critical inquiry. It was deeply implanted in western thought by Aristotle who declared that "we cannot feel that we have understood a thing until we give an account of its causes and its *modus operandi*." [1]

Since there is not sufficient space to elaborate fully the various accounts of causation in the history of western thought, we shall merely note a few salient points about its transference from a principle in the knowledge-situation to a postulate in the meaning-situation of philosophical-scientific inquiry. It was misplaced in the knowledge-situation both by the Cartesians and by the Newtonians. According to the Cartesians, causality was a subsisting *a priori* principle which was an absolutely certain universal and necessary Truth. For the Newtonians, causality was an existing relation which was so inherent in the external world that a rigid causal determinism regulated the interaction of physical events. Hume exposed the futility of trying to verify the *a priori* necessity of causation as a substantive assertion in the knowledge-situation. Although Kant agreed with Hume in rejecting causality as inherent in either subsistence or existence, he insisted that as a regulatory category it must be presupposed in the cognitive experience of constructing the natural order. It remained for contemporary epistemologists who agree with Kant about the indispensability of the causal category, to complete the transfer of it from the knowledge-situation to the meaning-situation.

In his epistemological elaboration of the latter position Planck justifies his adoption of causality as a postulated principle of objective reference on the pragmatic grounds of its fruitfulness in an operational conception of what kind of knowledge is meaningful for scientific inquiry: "It is true that the law of causality cannot be demonstrated any more than it can be logically refuted; it is neither correct nor incorrect; it is a heuristic principle; it points the way, and in my opinion it is the most valuable pointer we possess in order to find a path through the confusion of events, and in order to know in what direction scientific investigation must proceed so that it shall reach useful results." Now Planck acknowledges that "it is perfectly conceivable that one fine day Nature should cause an unexpected event to occur that would baffle us all"; but "in such an event the only course open to science would be to declare itself bankrupt." Accordingly, he insists that without beginning with the general assumption of a rule of causal law "no kind of knowledge can be attained." [2] Planck's defense of this postulate against those who would substitute statistical calculations for causality is especially significant, since he has contributed so extensively to the microphysical theory from which the challenge has emerged. Before we note his rebuttal, let us consider the nature of the substitute which has been proposed by those who would not accept this postulate.

As a principle of objective reference the postulate of causality has been challenged by logical positivists, as well as by some logicians, natural scientists, and social scientists, who favor the postulate of statistical calculations. For they assume that it is more fruitful for the scientist to substitute functional equations for causal sequences, to substitute differential equations for cause and effect relations, and to substitute the mathematical correlation of variables and constants for the formula of causal interaction. With the increasing mathematical sophistication of scientific analysis, Frank, for an example, contends that the use of the principle of causation has become nothing more than "an episode in the history of thought." [3] Similarly, Born has declared that quantum analysis is "in the nature of the case indeterministic, and therefore the affair of statistics." [4]

Heisenberg's principle of "uncertainty relations" is, of course, the basis for this appeal to statistical calculations, for, as he has stated, "the interaction between observer and object causes uncontrollable and large changes in the system being observed, because of the discontinuous character of the atomic process." [5] In other words, since the observer's measuring techniques influence the microprocesses he is measuring, he can neither ascertain the simultaneous positions and momenta of electrons nor can he with certainty predictively relate the given present states to future states of the physical system. Consequently, when electromagnetic energy is interpreted in terms of quanta, or the configurations of fields of energy rather than in terms of discrete particles, predictions are limited to statistical probabilities which are comparable to actuarial calculations.

Despite the necessity for using statistical techniques in microphysics, according to Planck, the postulate that physical events operate causally is not itself thereby rendered fruitless: "The most important advances in the study of atomic processes are due to the attempt to look for a strictly causal and dynamic law behind every statistical law." [6] This is congruent with Reichenbach's contention that, on the one hand, "statistical correlations though indicating causal relationships, offer various forms of causal interpretation," while, on the other hand, "a concept of causality unrelated to probability is empty or meaningless." [7] In other words, it is a Laplacian conception of causation in terms of predictive certainty, rather than every conception of causality, which is actually challenged. For, as Planck reminds us, "scientific thought is identical with causal thought, so much so that the last goal of every science is the full and complete application of the causal principle to the object of research." [8]

When a scientist adopts causality as a principle of objective reference for explanations and predictions, he rejects the claim that statistical correlation is the only postulate for identifying meaningful knowledge. But he in no way minimize the importance of using statistical techniques where they are applicable as analytical tools in the knowledge-situation. MacIver, for example, insists that statistical calculations which do not presuppose a causal process merely "render luminous the void" and reflect only "the empty play of mind." But when it is assumed that the variables exhibit a causal pattern by virtue of which they belong together, then, MacIver insists, a "functional equation" can be used as an "admirable device to symbolize certain highly general or universal relationships under hypothetical conditions." [9] Feigl has differentiated between the use of "ordinary cause-effect terminology" at the "qualitative macro-level" and at "those levels of science which deal with gross behavior" and the use of "mathematical formulation in terms of functional relationship" when "measurement is introduced." Nevertheless, Feigl maintains that "the terms 'cause and effect' of ordinary language need not be rejected if proper caution is employed in their application." [10] In order that the probability aggregate in quantum mechanics might not be "in such a state of flux that no prediction could be made" Northrop insists that "this general rule concerning the universality of statistical laws in nature" must be adopted: "If there are certain laws in science which are statistical then there must also be laws in that science which are not statistical." For without the presupposition of underlying causal laws "the concept of theoretical probability essential to the meaning of the statistical law in question cannot be defined." [11]

The grounds for rejecting Laplace's strictly deterministic conception of mechanical causation in terms of predictive certainty do not therefore necessarily invalidate the assumption that "nothing happens without a sufficient cause," which, as Werkmeister emphasizes, has never been denied by quantum physicists when they have weakened the assumption that "whatsoever can be predicted with certainty is causally determined." [12] According to Laplace's comprehensive mathematical conception of a universal and necessary causal pattern, it will be recalled, predictive certainty was guaranteed by Newton's gravitational and inertial laws as inherent determinants of matter in motion. If, instead of this doctrine of imposed law, one agrees with Whitehead that "the only intelligible doctrine of causation is founded on the doctrine of immanence," then the principle of causality as a postulate in the meaning-situation is not even questioned. After all, even though the microphysicist cannot assume that if he knows A, he can with certainty predict B, nevertheless, regardless of whether the effect is C or D or E, it can hardly be denied that whatever the result turned out to be, it was the effect of causal conditions. Uncertain though the predictive relation may be, to what else other than a causal relationship can a statistical calculation in accordance with probability laws refer?[13]

2. TOWARD A DEFINITION OF CAUSALITY

What is the minimum meaning of causality as a postulate of hypothetical-deductive inquiry? It is the assumption that the objective referent of classificatory, explanatory, and predictive constructs is a temporal process of events which are produced effects and producing causes of the other events with which each event interacts. The anthropomorphic conception of compulsive forces pushing and pulling each other about should not be read into this statement. For causal determinants are taken to be operationally specifiable conditions without which the event that is taken to be an effect would not have occurred. When a condition is specified as a sufficient cause, it is presupposed that without it the effect would not have occurred. It is equally presupposed that the occurrences of the other interconnected events were necessary. Cohen's negative statement of this point is instructive: "A circumstance that is not necessary for a given event, i.e., if the event can take place without it, cannot be the cause; and similarly if a circumstance is not sufficient to bring about the given event, i.e., if the former can occur without the latter, it cannot be the cause." [14]

By directing attention to the hypothetical-deductive method, which was outlined in the earlier chapter about the knowledge-situation of reflective inquiry, we note that each of its four stages would be meaningless without this postulate of causality. In the first stage, the initial observational data are taken to be the effects of as yet unascertained causal conditions. Moreover in classification, the correlating idea, in accordance with which relevant observational data are conceptually organized in terms of their significant interconnections, is a causal orientation, e.g., the Newtonian model of classical mechanics, as well as Tolman's psychological model of causally interacting dependent, independent, and intervening variables.

In the second stage, the formulation of theoretical generalizations presupposes a causal inference. What point would there be for constructing explanatory hypotheses, if it were not assumed that they correlated the adduced antecedent causal conditions of which the given relevant data are the effects to be explained? Similarly, what point would there be for the construction of explanatory hypotheses, if it were not assumed that these reasonable expectations referred to the future effects of the past and present causal conditions.

Causation is similarly presupposed in the third stage of verification. The first step for verifying a hypothesis, in which its implications are consistently deduced, is acausal, i.e., it involves only the formal mathematical-logical system of analytical relations of implication. The second step of empirically testing those deduced implications presupposes that the total context of physical and behavioral events exhibits a uniform and invariable sequence of causes and effects in which alterations of the antecedent events is bound to produce alterations in the subsequent events to which they are functionally related. If an experimenter, for example, does not adopt this postulate of an orderly pattern of causal relations, how could he claim to have performed a crucial experiment, i.e., a laboratory test that can be performed with the same results at any time and in any place provided that the same controlled conditions prevail? By proceeding on this assumption the experimenter manipulates the factors in the experimental situation so that the normal course of events is interfered with sufficiently for him to ascertain whether or not the causal factors do function in the manner in which he has been led by his hypothesis to expect. Both this ideational aspect and this manipulatory aspect of experimental testing conform, therefore, to the following causal formula: "If the independent variable a is to be confirmed as the cause of the dependent variable b, then it must be shown that when a occurs b also inevitably occurs, and whenever a is absent *b* always fails to occur." (Although most experimental testing involves more than two such variables, the causal principle is similarly presupposed.)

When in the fourth stage constructs are conceptually integrated in terms of a lawful or law-like generalization the latter is defined as a causal and/or statistical generalization about the uniform pattern in the process of a given system of events. As previously emphasized, the applicability of such a predictive generalization is limited to the specifically stated conditions. Although the postulate of causality might not appear presupposed when statistical laws are formulated, we must ask again: If statistical correlations do not refer to a patterned causal process, what are the generalizations about?

Emerging out of these conceptions of the status and function of causation with respect to hypothetical-deductive inquiry, is an identification of causality as the relation of any event to the conditions under which it occurs. Although no one seems to have formulated a precise definition of causality, MacIver has provided a most instructive identification of what it entails in terms of these three axioms: "(1) Whatever happens has a cause. (2) Where there is a difference in the effect there is a difference in the cause. (3) Every cause is the effect of a prior cause and every effect is the cause of a posterior effect." [15] MacIver's cogent clarification of some of the misunderstandings of what each of these assertions means, merits special notice.

The first of these axioms has been misconstrued by some to mean that changes in the physical or behavioral situation are to be attributed to the agency of some intervening animistic or anthropomorphic force. Instead of referring to some "detachable entity or power," causation in this context means "that every happening is the manifestation of a special causal nexus, that the event or the change is a consequent stage of a specific process." To attempt to discover a cause, therefore, means that the investigator is seeking a "prior conjuncture." According to this axiom, the event which is taken to be the effect "would not have happened had there not been present, within the totality that contained it, a specific conjuncture of conditions such that, wherever this conjuncture occurs, the event or the change also occurs." [16]

The axiom, "where there is difference in the effect there is a difference in the cause," has been misconstrued to mean that causal uniformity is nothing but a uniformity of sequence. Such is the fallacy of *post hoc ergo propter hoc* (after this, therefore on account of this). Experimental testing would be meaningless without the assumption that under the same conditions there would be such an invariant relation between cause and effect that only an alteration of the former would account for an alteration in the latter. Even though there may be different causes of the same effect, a scientific generalization about a specific cause-effect relation entails the assumption that the specified relationship can be reasonably expected to hold without exception. Evidence to the contrary requires a modification, correction, or abandonment of the substantive generalization rather than of the causal postulate itself. If the scientist presupposes nothing more than that events always follow one after the other in a uniform sequence, without presupposing that they are bound to do so, he has failed to recognize the dynamic nature of causal interaction which means that "everything except the inconceivable whole of things, both acts and is acted upon." Although such dynamic causation requires the presumption of a "total cause-effect relationship," those scientists who construct a causal generalization refer to a specific conjuncture of antecedent conditions, rather than to the totality of the "whole antecedent state of the universe." In other words, the scientist is attempting to ascertain the specific conjuncture of events which, in the total process of events, precipitated the specific change that made the difference in what is assumed to be the effect of antecedent conditions. Out of the complex totality of all of the actual causal conditions that have contributed to the occurrence of any given event, therefore, the scientist must limit his search to that recognizable causal condition "which diverts the pre-established direction of affairs." MacIver calls such a specified antecedent causal condition, which brings to a head the difference in the consequent event, the "precipitant cause," i.e., "some factor that is introduced from the outside or else emerges from within, so that it evokes a series of repercussions or reactions significantly changing the total situation." [17]

The axiom that "every cause is the effect of a prior cause and every effect is the cause of a posterior effect," has been misconstrued by some as signifying a temporal continuity which precludes a recognition of the discontinuity and uniqueness of temporal events. There is no necessary incongruity between the idea of the uniqueness of separable events, and the idea of the temporal continuity of their antecedent and consquent causal relations. All that is demanded by this axiom is that the scientific generalizations about those events, discontinuous though they may be, must pertain to the temporal continuity of the patterned process of their causal relations, i.e., what MacIver designates as the "causal nexus." This "nexus" does not connect otherwise temporally disconnected past causes and present effects; but, rather, "the causal relation is itself the nexus of things as they move from present to future." This temporal perspective for causal continuity makes it possible for MacIver to distinguish between the process and the events themselves: "When the continuity changes gradually we call it a process. When it changes with seeming abruptness, either through the acceleration of process or through the introduction of a new factor from without, we call it event." [18]

Although MacIver finds causality indispensable as a principle of objective reference, he acknowledges that it is a postulate in the meaning-situation of reflective inquiry rather than an assertion which can be verified in its knowledge-situation: "Every advance of science may be said to provide additional evidence of its validity, but we accepted it before we could obtain the evidence, and we must continue to accept it so long as we continue to investigate nature or reality." Thus, MacIver recognizes that the justification for the adoption of the causal postulate "remains a faith, the faith on which all science rests" that is vindicated "whenever we find order or law in nature" and that is renewed "whenever we seek to extend the realm of science." [19]

Recalling Feigl's warning that "proper caution" must be employed in the application of causality, we need to direct our attention to the special complications that are involved when causation is presupposed by the social-scientific analysis of the sociocultural-motivational variables in the behavioral process.

3. THE POSTULATE OF BEHAVIORAL CAUSATION

The complications which are generated by a causal analysis of the sociocultural-motivational variables in the behavioral process have driven social scientists in opposite directions. While some have felt compelled to abandon this assumption, others have felt compelled to reconstruct the traditional causal formula, and to justify it as an indispensable postulate of the meaning-situation of social-scientific inquiry. The latter group does realize that a causal formula about behavioral transactions cannot presuppose the regularity, recurrence, and persistence of human events in the same way that the natural scientist can conceptualize physical events *as if* they occurred in a supratemporal realm. Since the variables in the behavioral process are meaningless apart from the temporal context of present events which emerge out of the past and move toward the future, these social scientists are confronted by the complications of the *reciprocity* and *complexity* of sociocultural conditions, as well as the *variability* of motivational factors.

a. By the *reciprocity* of sociocultural conditions which complicates social-scientific explanations and predictions, we mean the reversibility of cause-effect relations. Physical events are relatively free from reciprocal influences; but sociocultural events often mutually determine each other. Although MacIver insists that sociocultural situations exhibit a "special set of conditions that invest our data with their kind of causality," he acknowledges, nevertheless, that "one can reverse with some degree of truth almost any statement of social causation." To illustrate what he means he asks: "Does the kind of education account for the standard of intelligence in a community? True, but does not the standard of intelligence account for the standard of education?" Now MacIver directs attention to this problem of specifying the causal conditions with a view to making social scientists more cautious in the use of causal analysis. Neurath, however, calls this reciprocity "mutual causation" and emphasizes it as his reason for abandoning the postulate of causality on the grounds that this makes sociocultural data too "clumsy and perplexing" to provide sufficient linguistic precision. While no social scientist minimizes the importance of linguistic precision, if and when it can be obtained, we shall soon see that many consider Neurath's asking-price to be too high.[20]

b. The *complexity* of the causal determinants in the behavioral process is recognized by all social scientists who have discovered that multiple causation must be presupposed in order to avoid the distortions of relevant behavioral data which a simple monocausal formula demands. The synoptic model, it will be recalled, was designed to identify and interrelate the multiplicity of independent inorganic, organic, neurophysiological, psychodynamic, social, and cultural vari-

ables, as well as the intervening variable of purposive goal-seeking.
In contrast to such a conception of multiple causation, there are the
monocausal models of Watsonian neurophysiological response to a
physical stimulus, of Freudian sexual compulsions, and of Marxian
economic determinism, etc. As Feigl has reminded us, "in most of
the significant applications we must remember that it is an entire
set of conditions that represents "the cause of an event" and that
what we may abstract "as 'cause' or 'effect' in a complex situation is
usually only some factor, aspect, magnitude, etc., that we select from
a more complex (and possibly inexhaustible) welter of factual details." [21]

Simply acknowledging the complexity of multiple causal conditions is not enough to justify the postulate of behavioral causation.
Some social scientists have, for all practical purposes, abandoned
the causal assumption in favor of statistical correlations on the
grounds that it is impossible to interrelate, to any significant degree,
all of the determinants of a total causal process. MacIver vehemently
opposes the use of "key causes," i.e., one and only one determinant,
which fails to take into account all of the interdependent causal conditions within a dynamic sociocultural process. He also emphasizes
that in a given research analysis, the investigator must concentrate
upon what he has designated as the "precipitant cause." By this he
means "a specific emergent or interjected condition which diverts
the preestablished direction of affairs." [22] For without this concentration upon such a specifically limited precipitant cause the social
scientist could not isolate causal variables as separable though interdependent factors within the interrelated whole of a total causal
process.

On the assumption that causation is pluralistic rather than monistic Hook calls for a "functional theory of causation together with all
the apparatus of statistical inquiry," which he claims is invaluable for
"accumulating data to be interpreted," for establishing "the irrele-
vance of any two elements in the social environment assumed to be
causally connected," and for developing "a theory of measurement
to determine the relative weight of various causal factors considered."
Only a causal theory, he insists, could "offer an explanation of the
correlations found." Within such a causal framework of independent
and dependent variables changes in the sociocultural process can be
analyzed from many different approaches. Thus religion, or law, or

art, or politics, or economics, could each in turn, be the independent variable from which depend the changes in the other institutionalized aspects of a culture. Hook acknowledges that "strictly speaking, neither the one nor the other member of a functional equation can be called cause or effect." It is possible, however, Hook concludes, to "take the functional relationship between any two variables, say religion and law, and try to show that change in the function which relates the two is itself a function of some third variable, say economics." [23]

c. V*ariability* in the sociocultural aspect of the behavioral process seems to be partially attributable to the intervention of reflectively motivated goal-seeking persons. To account for this purposive causation, it is necessary for the social scientist to correlate sociocultural and motivational data in terms of the interaction of independent causal conditions and intervening causal conditions. On the one hand, the independent causal conditions are those antecedent determinants which influence the emergence of a person's present desire to strive for some specific goal. On the other hand, the intervening causal conditions are the present decisions by which a relatively mature person with intellectual initiative and moral responsibility does things to himself and others within the limitations imposed by the complex of antecedent natural, sociocultural, and psychological conditions of his total environment. The possibility that such relative self-determinism may be a causal factor in what appears to be a rigidly deterministic causal system of events, seems to be presupposed by Hook in his *The Hero in History*. In this work, Hook distinguishes between the merely "eventful man" and the "event-making man." Where the former is largely the product of environmental conditions, the causal influence of the decisions and actions of the "event-making" person are "the consequences of his outstanding capacities of intelligence, will, and character rather than the accidents of positions." [24]

It should be carefully noted that this purposiveness which is imputed to the selective response of a relatively self-determined person is not conceived of as an extra-causal factor. Rather, it is assumed that such purposive goal-seeking is one determinant among other determinants as an integral component of the total causal process. MacIver calls this purposive causation a "dynamic assessment" which in reflectively conscious agents emerges out of the "causal factors of another order," i.e., what we have designated as the independent causal conditions: "The causal role of dynamic assessment is to bring into a single order of coherent relationships the objectively diverse factors involved in social behavior." [25]

Although it is necessary for a relatively self-determined person to have some satisfaction-yielding goal as the future referent of his present desiring and striving, his subsisting ideal which he anticipates does not itself have any causal efficacy in the determination of reflective conduct. It is, rather, the person's present activity of aiming and striving toward that ideal goal which constitutes the purposive causation of the actor who selects one course of action from among culturally-presented alternatives. Accordingly, the reflective goal-seeking of the actor constitutes an additional determinant which precipitates the influence of the antecedent causal conditions that are necessary but not sufficient for producing the given effect without the person's reflective decision. But what will that decision be? Even if the investigator had complete knowledge of the natural, sociocultural, and psychological conditions (independent variables), he could not be sure that he had a precise foresight of the reflective person's selective appropriation of the environmentally-presented opportunities as the means to the intrinsic ends toward which he strives (intervening variable). The more the investigator learned about the system of values such a person preferred, then the more accurate would be the investigator's predictions about that person's behavior, especially if the subject was a person of constant moral and intellectual integrity. Anything beyond a reasonable degree of informed expectation, nevertheless, is precluded by this *variability* which the motivational aspect of behavioral causation entails.

What has been said here about the postulate of behavioral causality may be clarified by recalling some of the salient features of purposive causation which were presented in the elaboration of our synoptic model of the goal-oriented behavioral transactions. Relative self-determinism was adopted since it opened up more avenues for the causal investigation of reflective goal-seeking behavior than did either indeterminism or mechanical determinism. Whereas the former assumption, by which all human decisions are completely spontaneous, renders any questions about sociocultural-motivational explanations and predictions meaningless; the latter assumption, which confines causality to independent variables, precludes any reference to intervening variables. Since the partial self-determination of the semi-autonomous person is just as relative to the system of values he prizes as it is to the antecedent environmental conditions that shape him, the variations between the set of causal conditions which pro-duce unreflective value experience and that which generates reflec-tive value experience should be recalled.

On the one hand, an unreflective value is whatever a person de-sires without any deliberation about whether or not he ought to de-sire that satisfaction. Accordingly, unreflective desires for such ideals are a person's behavioral responses to the drives of his complex and interrelated natural, sociocultural, and psychological environment. Such unreflective desires include hunger and thirst drives, sexual im-pulses, and will-to-power compulsions, etc., which uncritically refer to such goals as self-preservation, physical pleasure, and social es-teem. For the purpose of a causal explanation of his behavior, when a person's motivation is limited to these factors, it can be assumed that his actions are predetermined by antecedent natural, sociocul-tural, and psychological conditions.

On the other hand, a reflective value is whatever a person desires after he deliberates about conflicting desires and then decides in the light of his own ideals that he ought to desire that satisfaction. Ac-cordingly, reflective desires are a person's relatively self-determined responses both to the compulsions of his complex natural, sociocul-tural, and psychological environment, and to the purposively selec-tive culturally-begotten ideal goals, by which he attempts to regulate his thought, conduct, and imagination. Thus, a person can never achieve a self-determination that is not relative to the total complex environment which has produced him, and to the system of values which he has adopted. Psychological limitations and natural-sociocultural conditions notwithstanding, when a person strives to satisfy his reflective desires for ideal goals (e.g., intellectual curiosity, an enlightened good will, etc.), then by this self-creative effort he participates in the total causal process out of which emerges the kind of person he is constantly becoming.

The formula for sociocultural-motivational causation requires a molar analysis which does not preclude a molecular analysis but, rather, includes it. A purely molecular analysis which causally ex-plains human behavior by reducing it to muscular, glandular, neural or to biochemical responses provides important information. However, by excluding consideration of psychodynamic and sociocultural responses, it deals with only a partial aspect of the total process of sociocultural-motivational causation. To account for the *reciprocity, complexity,* and *variability,* which the behavioral interaction of naturalized, socioculturalized, and goal-seeking persons involves, the molar social scientist assumes that his causal generalizations refer (a) to a complex whole of interacting factors which cannot be accounted for apart from each other and (b) to the entire behavioral pattern that cannot be reduced to any of its component parts.

B. *The Significance of the Fourth Postulate for Individual Psychology*

Without the postulate that "nothing happens without a sufficient cause" psychological explanations and predictions about human motivation would be meaningless. Gordon Allport seems to speak for the majority of psychologists who deal with motivational aspects of human behavior, when he declares that behavioral analysis "at its present stage of development will be concerned with causation, or else it will be concerned with nothing of consequence." Moreover, Allport adds, "methodologists who banish causation from the front door often admit it surreptitiously at the back" with the exception of those logical positivists who in rejecting this postulate "spin their logic too fine for the needs of social science." [26]

The conceptual basis for this causal assumption upon which psychological explanations and predictions about motivation are theoretically formulated was presented in terms of the personality construct as an integral part of the synoptic model of behavioral transactions. In order to include but not to confine motivation to neurophysiological responses, it will be recalled, the concept of *personality* was suggested as a compound construct which is designed to coordinate sociocultural responses, psychodynamic responses, and interpersonal responses with each other and with reflective goal-seeking. Whereas the latter was identified as an intervening variable, the other four dimensions of motivational data were identified as independent variables. Taken together they constituted the *psychological environment* in which motivational factors as causal conditions range from Watson's "conditioned reflex" to Gordon Allport's "propriate striving."

If we may assume that the reader will review the previous discussion of the "personality construct," then instead of reiterating the substantive views expressed there, we shall confine the following paragraphs to drawing out the salient causal principles which the motivational constructs of the synoptic model entail. The interpersonal responses referred to above will be dealt with in the subsequent section pertaining to social psychology.

Since the psychological model from which we drew most heavily in the conceptual identification of motivational data was the *sui generis* model of Tolman, his acknowledgement of the necessity for presupposing "postulated causal connections" in his meaning-situation has special significance. Whereas descriptive constructs are organized in terms of dependent, independent, and intervening variables, explanatory constructs are meaningless apart from "postulated types of causal (functional) relationships between independent variables, intervening variables (hypothetical constructs), and the dependent variable of behavior." Moreover, Tolman accounts for the difference between the mechanical causality which is presupposed by those psychologists who analyze motivation exclusively in terms of neurophysiological responses, and the purposive causality which he himself presupposes, when he analyzes motivation in terms of sociocultural, psychodynamic, and conscious goal-seeking responses as well: "The type of postulated interconnecting causal functions assumed by the different theories will be intimately connected with the types of assumed intervening variables." [27]

This distinction between a mechanically causal formula and a purposively causal formula is even clearer in Tolman's comparison of his "molar and purposive behaviorism" with the molecular behaviorism of Watson. Whereas Watson accounts for the motivation of behavior "in terms of its strict underlying physical and physiological details," Tolman's causal account of motivation presupposes that "behavior, as such, is an emergent phenomenon that has descriptive and defining properties of its own" which "are to be identified and described irrespective of whatever muscular, glandular, or neural processes underlie them." Accordingly, Watson has no intervening variable operating as a causal factor between the physical stimulus and the neurophysiological response; Tolman however includes "purposes and cognitions" as "functionally defined variables which are the last step in the causal equation determining behavior." These "function to produce some sort of modifications or improvements in what were the organism's initially aroused immanent determinants, such that his final behavior, corresponding to these new modified immanent determinants, is different from what it otherwise would have been." [28]

Just as the postulate of behavioral causality cannot be verified but must be justified by its pragmatic fruitfulness, so also, as Spence emphasizes, the selection of the reductive causation of the molar approach is determined not by any evidence but by the investigator's conception of which kind of knowledge is more meaningful: "The particular alternative chosen, molecular or molar, depends upon the interest and purpose of the scientist, the kind of law he expects to find." Yet, according to Spence, this does not necessarily preclude an integration in the psychologists's meaning-situation of molecular and molar conceptions of causal analysis: "If the two systems of concepts should each be successful in leading to the discovery and formulation of laws, it should also be possible to discover coordinating definitions which will reveal the interrelations of the two systems." [29]

At the risk of oversimplification, we might say that psychologists construct generalizations about motivation pointing toward causal laws at three levels: the nomothetic, the nomothetic-idiographic, and the idiographic-nomothetic. Whether or not this classification is sufficiently inclusive is not too important if it demonstrates that divergent conceptions of causal explanations of motivation are predetermined by divergent assumptions in the meaning-situation of the particular investigator.

The purely nomothetic approach is represented by Skinner when he claims that "from the point of view of scientific method, at least, the description of behavior is adequately embraced by the principle of the reflex." [30] Since only such basic drives as neurophysiological responses are admissible as motivational data for this molecular approach, consideration of purposive intervening variables and the total motivational pattern (*Gestalt*) are precluded. But, as Spence has pointed out, if the psychologist who is causally analyzing motivation "is interested in discovering uniformities or scientific laws, he must, of necessity, fractionate or abstract out certain features of the total events he observes." [31]

The nomothetic-idiographic approach is represented by Tolman who, in addition to accounting for the basic drives that can be reduced to universal neurophysiological and psychodynamic functions, recognizes in some behavior the operation of cognitive and purposive goal-seeking which exhibits uniqueness when it is considered as a whole. Tolman's molar approach and his use of the intervening variable has been discussed at such length previously that it need not be re-examined here. A point to be noted, however, is Gordon Allport's feeling that, despite Tolman's appeal to intervening variables and his purposive-molar emphasis, Tolman does not sufficiently take into account the "long range orientation" which characterizes the future-directed "dynamics of mature human conduct" in accordance with "directive schemata." Therefore, instead of directing attention to the "de-tensioning" of *specific drives* through Tolman's "expectancy" or Hull's "anticipatory goal reactions," Allport refers to the "propriate striving" for the *intrinsic life goals* of reflectively motivated persons. Our reversal of the nomothetic-idiographic designation to the idiographic-nomothetic designation marks this shift in emphasis among psychologists who presuppose purposive causality in their causal analysis of motivation. Allport's more radical departure requires further notice. He wishes to make central what he finds more peripheral in the discussions of Tolman and Hull, namely, that "motives being always contemporary should be studied in their present structure." Consequently, Allport aims to go beyond a "stimulus-expectancy need-cathexis psychology" toward a "model of personality that stresses active intention rather than passive expectation, contemporaneous rather than past motivation, interest rather than reward, and cognitive as well as reactive dynamism." [32]

When Allport calls for a recognition of the idiographic-nomothetic generalization of the "principle of functional autonomy of motives" as a causal explanation of the "dynamics of mature human conduct," he is aware that he is swimming upstream against the current of the predominant nomothetic presumption of most psychologists. But, since the latter are usually concerned only with the segmented basic drives which motivate all human organisms, i.e., "the abstract motivation of an impersonal and therefore non-existent mind-in-general," Allport feels compelled to provide a causal postulate for explaining "the concrete, viable motives of each and every mind-in-particular." Recall the previous illustration of functional autonomy: a person initially desires knowledge as a means toward achieving the basic goal of survival; but after this need is no longer pressing, this value which was previously instrumental may become intrinsic, that is, the intellectual curiosity for knowledge becomes an end in itself. It is pertinent to reiterate Allport's reply to those psychologists who object that there can never be a scientific account of the "concrete impulses that lie at the root of personal behavior" on the grounds that science can not generalize about "the unique and individual forms for personality." Allport agrees that of course science must generalize, but he also reminds these objectors that "it is a manifest error to assume that a general principle of motivation must involve the postulation of abstract or general motives" and that "a general law may be a law that tells how uniqueness comes about." [33]

When Tolman postulates the operation of "tertiary needs" as "wants to get to and from, to manipulate (as ways of getting to and from) certain relatively universal types of culturally provided goals," he notes that this assumption "is contained in Allport's doctrine of 'functional autonomy.'" He recognizes, however, that his view "is perhaps somewhat different from Allport's." [34] To ascertain this difference we must refer again to Allport's notion of the "proprium" and "propriate striving." The self-creative operations of reflectively motivated persons can be adequately explained, according to Allport, only by the construct of "propriate striving" within the context of what he calls the "proprium." By this, it will be recalled, he means "all the regions of our life that we regard as peculiarly ours." Note in reviewing the discussion of the "proprium" that of all of the eight "propriate aspects of personality" only the "propriate striving" is strictly a motivational factor. However, the other interpenetrating conditions contribute to the cultivation and development of intellectual and ethical desires which motivate the goal-seeking actions of reflective persons who persistently participate in long-range enterprises which yield the intrinsic satisfaction of never being completely realized.

It should be understood that Allport is not minimizing the importance of other psychological generalizations for deterministically explaining other types of human behavior. He simply claims that reflective conduct is unintelligible apart from this postulate of relative self-determinism. A causal "formula that seems appropriate enough for drive reduction seems to break down when motivation is no longer a matter of segmental drives or of opportunistic adjustment but rather partakes of propriate striving." [35] What is required is a causal formula which accounts for the process by which a person who does things to himself (intervening variable) under the conditions and within the limitations of what is done to him (independent variables), by virtue of his own intellectual initiative and moral responsibility, creatively participates together with physical, biological, physiological, psychological, and sociocultural determinants in producing the kind of person he is becoming.

It should also be understood that Allport is not adopting the assumption of "indeterminism" which is incongruent with the postulate of behavioral causation, since the indeterminist presupposes that completely spontaneous human actions are unmotivated. For example, although Sartre does emphasize the influence of a person's life-plan, he is indeterministic to the extent that he assumes that a reflective person can transcend the influence of his physical and sociocultural environment: "At heart, what existentialism shows is the connection between the absolute character of free involvement . . . and the relativeness of the cultural ensemble which may result from such a choice." [36]

This does not mean that Allport is adopting the alternative of radical determinism which Watson presupposes when he claims that the trained behaviorist can predict "given the stimulus, what reaction will take place; or given the reaction state what the situation or stimulus is that has caused the reaction." [37] Neither is he denying the operation of such mechanisms to which a rigid determinist confines his causal explanations, nor is he minimizing their importance for explaining non-reflective behavior. But to explain reflective behavior Allport does presuppose the assumption of relative self-determinism which Murphy has called "soft determinism." By this, it will be recalled, Murphy means "determinism from the inner nature of life, not from external pressures alone" by which a person "will slowly develop a relative autonomy, a participation in the causal sequence, based on the influence of his own complex make-up on his conduct." [38]

The necessity for the postulate of behavioral causation (which is presupposed by both determinists and relative self-determinists) is questioned by Brunswik when he recommends an "empty organism" approach which insists that "psychology, as long as it wishes to deal with the vitally relevant molar aspects of adjustment and achievement, has to become statistical throughout." Confronted by the variability in the complex conditions of any individual organism's behavior, the psychologist, according to Brunswik, has no chance of establishing causal laws with sufficient exactitude to be meaningful in terms of "the nomothetic ideals of traditional experimental psychology as far as relationships between geographic stimulus variables and response variables are concerned." Consequently, Brunswik insists, psychology "should be concerned with molar correlations and be satisfied with probability functions of a low degree of exactitude." He does not preclude the possibility that, at some future time, psychologists may be able to isolate variables and predict psychological events in terms of "general cause and effect relationships." But even then, he contends, causal analysis will depend upon "concomitant variation—of greater or lesser relative frequency" rather than upon empirical-theoretical explanations of specifically observed behavioral actions. If psychologists would shift their attention from specific organisms to "wide-spanning relationships" by "deliberately neglecting the details, even if these details should be relevant in connection with one or the other member of the family of processes mediating this achievement," then, through the use of "correlation coefficients and other statistical measures of concomitant variation," they can analyze *achievement*, i.e., "a generic term for the relationships better than chance existing between, and due to an organism and variables in its physical environment." By eliminating their "mechanistic and nomothetic bias," psychologists could abandon their hopeless attempt to establish causal laws about inherently imperfect "potentialities of adjustment on the part of the behaving organism living in a semi-chaotic environmental medium." Moreover, he declares, through a probabilistic statistical approach, the psychologist could construct a conceptual framework which "has even more generality than the 'general' laws of nature which are observed under such meticulously specified conditions." [39]

In his discussion of the "uniformity point of view" Hull explicitly answers Brunswik's denial of the primacy of the postulate of behavioral causation. Hull does acknowledge the importance of "Brunswik's program of empirical correlational determinations" as a useful statistical technique for the psychologist who is constructing causal laws. Yet contrary to Brunswik's presumption that experimentalists seek predictive certainty for their causal laws, Hull maintains that "it is not unreasonable to hope for the isolation of both primary and secondary behavioral laws which will hold within a narrow margin of error for averages secured from carefully controlled empirical conditions." Although Hull agrees with Brunswik that "under the complex conditions of life the behavior of organisms is variable," Hull disagrees when he announces his belief that "isolable uniformities exist in the field of human behavior." Hull finds that variability is not confined to human behavior; and it can be accounted for "without assuming any lack of uniformity in the supposed laws involved, if it is assumed that "the outcome of a dynamic situation depends upon 1) a set of antecedent conditions and 2) one or more rules or laws according to which, given a certain period of time, these conditions evolve into different conditions or events." Consequently, Hull concludes that the "uncertainty of dynamic outcome" does not "necessarily imply that within the causal segment under consideration stable and uniform sequences may not occur"; for it "may lie entirely in the conditions and not at all in the rules or laws."

Hull avoids the radical causal determinism which Brunswik attributes to "mechanistic and nomothetic bias" when Hull acknowledges that "even if the action of the ultimate molecular units of causal segments were absolutely lawful, the molar outcome of the joint action of the numerous internal elements composing a molar causal segment would vary, because the conditions, being unknown, would presumably vary from one molar situation to another." Moreover, whereas the radical determinist deals only with the independent variables which as antecedent causal conditions mechanically predetermine any present behavioral action, Hull not only includes the operation of intervening variables, but he presupposes the relative autonomy of contemporary goal-seeking motivation which Lewin emphasized as the prerequisite of relative self-determinism: "I fully agree with Lewin that all the factors alleged to be causally influential in the determination of any other event must be in existence at the time of such causal action." [40] Lewin adopted the following premise with respect to the continually changing time perspective: "According to field theory, any type of behavior depends upon the field, including the time perspective at that time, but not, in addition, upon any past or future field and its time perspectives." [41]

C. The Significance of the Fourth Postulate for Social Psychology

Without the assumption that all human actions are the effects of a complex variety of ascertainable causal conditions there would be no point to the task which the social psychologist sets for himself when he attempts to discover "the conditions under which individual behavior varies in response to social stimulation." It is this postulate of behavioral causation which Newcomb explicitly elaborates: "No matter how complex the form of stimulation or how many persons are involved, the social psychologist proceeds upon the basis of three assumptions: first, that individuals are responding to some form of social influence, direct or indirect, from one or more other individuals; second, that individuals' behaviors are not a matter of caprice or sheer chance, but correspond to certain conditions and vary in an orderly manner with them; and third, that those conditions may be discovered if observations are properly made and conclusions properly drawn." [42]

Social-psychological analysis of motivation takes into account the individual psychologist's explanation of how the changing conditions in the organism produce changes in behavior; but its main focus is on "the conditions under which an identifiable kind of interaction does or does not take place" in interpersonal transactions which are not reducible to organic process and physical interaction. Sherif identifies these interpersonal relationships as the "experience and behavior of individuals in relation to social stimulus situations." [43] Murray calls them "interpersonal proceedings." [44] Sears designates these "combined actions of two or more persons" as a "dyadic unit" in which "environmental events are only those changes in environment produced by the behavior of the person under consideration." [45] Despite the terminological differences each of these social psychologists must presuppose a causal connection among the dependent, independent, and intervening variables which Newcomb refers to when he claims that "the distinctive feature of social psychology lies not in its use of intervening variables but rather in the kind of intervening variables which it uses and the way in which it relates them to protoplasm on the one hand and to society on the other." With respect to the kind of intervening variables, Newcomb means "such psychological conditions as motives, attitudes, and ways of looking at things and feeling about things." Moreover, they are related not in terms of biological or social influences but, rather, "in the individual as he develops motives and attitudes." [46] In order to deal with the causal motivation of transacting individuals, however, the social psychologist must treat the behavior of each individual in terms of what Krech and Crutchfield designate as a molar unit: "The unity implied in the molar description is not something arbitrarily imposed by the psychologist in viewing the individual as he behaves; the individual is a dynamic unity, a whole person, and it is as such that he takes part in social phenomena." [47]

The complexity of the variables involved in interpersonal transactions has persuaded Gordon Allport to adopt the postulate of *multiple causation*. He illustrates by showing how causal analysis of *prejudice* may be carried on at six levels: "approach via stimulus object, phenomenal approach, approach via personality dynamics and structure, situational approach, sociocultural approach, and historical approach." The social psychologist may confine his research to any one of these six levels just as long as he remains "respectfully aware of the whole etiological sweep." To this end he must assume with Allport that "causation may be proximate, or causation may be ultimate" and "forces may be precipitating or underlying, they may be in the foreground or in the background." [48]

D. *The Significance of the Fourth Postulate for Sociology*

Sociocultural causation is just as essential for defining what kind of sociological knowledge is meaningful as motivational causation is as a presupposition of psychological inquiry. Its postulatory function is acknowledged by Bierstedt, who states that "no one can explain the principle of causality" by an appeal to the knowledge-situation of reason and experience. Nevertheless, he contends, that the category of causation "is a prerequisite of all intellectual inquiry" and that "unless we assume that events have causes . . . we should have to surrender all of our aspirations to sociological knowledge." The alternative assumption is to presuppose that the socio-cultural process is so capricious that "knowledge becomes fortuitous and science impossible." To plead ignorance "of the causal factors involved," in such a way, Bierstedt insists, is not permitted to either the physicist nor to the sociologist.[49]

Since MacIver's classic analysis of social causation has already been discussed at length, we merely note that what he has claimed about this postulate for the entire social-scientific enterprise applies to sociological inquiry as well. Whereas Bierstedt is adopting MacIver's view, Lundberg challenges much of it and Timasheff amends it. Let us consider these in turn.

Among sociologists, Lundberg seems to have presented the most serious challenge to the postulate of sociocultural causation as MacIver has conceived it. Lundberg grants that in so far as sociological inquiry is a "procedure for discovering the conditions under which events occur," it involves a reference to causal conditions in the operational sense that "cause is imputed to the independent variable or combination of variables when it shows a high probability-expectation in its concomitant variations with other factors or combination of factors, still other supposedly relevant conditions held constant." Lundberg agrees with the advocates of causality that "the description of the interaction of all the necessary *factors* involved in an end result constitutes its explanation." Lundberg contends, nevertheless, that "mathematical formulas in quantitative terms are the most accurate way yet devised for describing just such interaction." He has been convinced by Dodd's *Dimensions of Society* that "the time is ripe for the systematizations of the whole field of general sociology in quantitative symbols." Consequently, Lundberg anticipates that sociological analysis can achieve quantitative precision through statistical calculations in which functional equations replace causal sequences; differential equations replace cause and effect relations; and the correlations of variables and constants replace causal interaction.

Although Lundberg recognizes the provisional usefulness of such constructs as *motive* and *purpose* as intellectual crutches, he advocates the abandonment of the explanations of goal-seeking behavior which presuppose purposive causation on the grounds that they are just as anthropomorphic as ascribing purposiveness to the "flying of a paper before the wind." Since Lundberg rejects the assumption that "the telic character or purposiveness which we like to attribute to societal behavior is an intrinsic character of the behavior rather than our way of describing it," he discounts MacIver's "dynamic assessment" by conscious agents. Lundberg equally opposes Parsons' premise that "the means-end schema becomes the central framework for the causal explanation of action." Although Lundberg denies that he ignores "the memories, value-meanings, ideals, ideas" and the "relevance of anticipated social ends as a partial determinant of social action," he relegates such purposive processes to the epiphenomenal status of "echoes and shadows." [50]

Timasheff identifies and justifies the category of causality in terms of its derivation from the postulate of order. Consequently, just as the postulate of order, i.e., the assumption that "there are invariant relations between phenomena," is "the logical pre-requisite of inductive reasoning," which "cannot be demonstrated by induction or deduction," so also the category of causality, i.e., "invariant relations between phenomena succeeding in time" is a presupposition in the meaning-situation rather than a verifiable assertion in the knowledge-situation of those sociologists who conceive of the sociocultural process as a "dynamic order." If, instead of viewing sociocultural relations as causal sequences in time, a sociologist prefers to view "phenomena in the framework of static order," then he presupposes functional relationships among coexisting phenomena rather than sociocultural causation. But, whether he conceives of order as static or dynamic, limited or universal, his premise, in any case, is determined by what he adopts as more meaningful for identifying knowledge, rather than by any empirically ascertainable evidence.

Timasheff contributes to the clarification of multiple causation when he modifies MacIver's conception that "cause is a conjuncture of factors" by distinguishing *causal order* as necessary "invariant relations in time" from *conjuncture*. By this he means that in addition to causal order there is the "copresence" of chains of invariant causal relations: "In the continuous stream of phenomena, order and conjuncture are so closely interwoven that one could not separate the phenomena into two classes, some causally determined and others conjunctural; in concrete phenomena (provided that they stand under the postulate of order; one may analytically distinguish a causally relevant and a conjunctural aspect." Such a *conjuncture* is not the totality of the factors and their invariant relations which constitute the causal order; but rather, "it is intersection, in concrete time and space, of causal chains standing behind each factor, eliciting, in togetherness, the effect." Multiple causation becomes more intelligible in terms of such a conjuncture of various intersecting causal chains. For, although the effect cannot be attributed to the conjuncture as its cause, the totality of *necessary* causal conditions would not be *sufficient* for the effect to emerge out of the various chains of causal events unless they were coordinated in a spatial-temporal conjuncture: "Conjuncture transforms each causal tendency (corresponding to one of the necessary conditions) from a potential into an actual force; this takes place by the very fact that the other tendencies (conditions, factors) are also present." [51]

Generally speaking, sociological analysis of the behavioral process focuses attention upon the sociocultural aspect rather than the motivational aspect of causation. Microsociologists who bridge the gap between macrosociology and social psychology, as well as MacIver when he writes as a general social scientist, are exceptions. For the most part, however, sociologists deal nomothetically with collective role-positions without concerning themselves about the idiographic features of individual goal-seeking motivation. When Parsons, for example, refers to the "means-end schema" as "the central framework for the causal explanation of action," he appears to be dealing with motivation. Actually, however, as Parsons himself emphasizes, when the sociologist analyzes behavior, he is only interested in "the interaction of pluralities of human beings, the forms their relationships take, and a variety of the conditions and determinants of these forms and of changes in them." [52] Accordingly, when the sociologist deals with the problem of social change, as Bierstedt points out, "personality itself is seen to be shaped and formed by patterns of culture and historical circumstance, and sociologists in consequence tend to interpret changes in societies in terms of deeper-lying phenomena, of which great men are only the surface representations." [53]

This does not mean that all sociologists are radically deterministic in their assumption about the causal pattern of sociocultural change. To be sure, some seem to be; but others, like Bierstedt, acknowledge that "all social change occurs because of the actions of men and women" and that "culture is not self-innovating, ideas are not self-creating, and technology is not self-inventing." But even among those sociologists who acknowledge that a nomothetic-idiographic approach to goal-seeking motivation is required for a comprehensive causal analysis of the behavioral process, it is only to the sociocultural determinants which can be causally analyzed in nomothetic generalizations that they limit their inquiries. As Bierstedt declares, "the causal inquiries of sociology, in short are directed to patterns rather than to particulars, to classes of events rather than to the events themselves." [54]

E. The Significance of the Fourth Postulate for Anthropology

1. THE PROBLEMS OF SOCIOCULTURAL CAUSATION

There seems to be an expanding interest in the postulate of causality as a principle of objective reference among anthropologists who have become persuaded that their discipline should not confine its attention to the level of observation and idiographic description of the culture of a specific community. It is this emerging aim which will increase the scope of anthropological analysis to which Kroeber refers: "When we once have enough sound classification and history of cultures, we should be able to take the next step and, with some genuine solidity, to extricate the processes at work, to generalize the story of culture into its causal factors." [55]

Since the twentieth-century anthropologists have not completed their reconstruction of the nineteenth-century unilinear evolutionary scheme which presupposed mechanical causality, they are not all clear about their committment to the principle of sociocultural causation. Unilinear evolutionists assumed causation, in terms of predictive certainty, to be inherent in the universal succession of stages in the sociocultural process. Laplace's causal determinism with respect to physical events was just as rigidly applied to anthropic events by Tylor, for instance, when he claimed that they "can be shown to come within the range of distinct cause and effect as certainly as the facts of mechanics." [56] Now that anthropologists recognize that "anthropological formulations of knowledge do not serve as bases of prediction comparable with those provided for prediction in the natural sciences," [57] their attitudes toward any conception are diverse. Perhaps we can with some measure of accuracy classify these divergent views as (a) those which abandon any principle of causation, (b) those which implicitly presuppose some principle of causation, and (c) those which explicitly adopt sociocultural causation as a postulate in the meaning-situation rather than in the knowledge-situation of anthropological inquiry.

(a) Benedict is representative of those who abandon causal accounts when she presents aesthetic portrayals of the integrated configurations or patterns of culture which can only be understood through an introspective projection of the anthropologist's creative imagination. Her appeal in *Patterns of Culture* to the non-causal approaches of Dilthey and Spengler clearly indicates her rejection of sociocultural causation as a principle of objective reference. Causal generalizations are also eliminated by Warner in his use of "symbolic representations" and by Whorf when he relies entirely on logical deductions from linguistic categories.[58]

(b) Some causal principle is implicitly presupposed by both the functionalists and the structuralists despite their explicit rejection of the mechanical causality of the nineteenth-century evolutionists. When Malinowski in *The Dynamics of Cultural Change* designates "value as the main motive of organized human effort" and identifies an institution as "an organized, purposeful system of human effort and achievement," [59] has he not presupposed the *means-end schema* which, as Parsons has insisted, is the "central framework for the causal explanation of action"? Apart from the deliberate use of causes for the purpose of obtaining effects that fulfill biopsychological needs in goal-oriented actions, what could be meant by a functional analysis of the dynamics of a culture? And although Murdock turns from a deductive analysis of a system of universal causal, relationships to an inductive statistical analysis of interrelated traits, in an effort to deal with social structure, nevertheless, doesn't he have to presuppose some causal interconnection among the components of the structural process? [60]

(c) Nadel clearly advocates the explicit adoption of the postulate of sociocultural causality in the meaning-situation of anthropological inquiry when he declares that it is "the most pervasive intervening concept which social enquiry can apply." Justifying its adoption on the pragmatic grounds that no other assumption serves as fruitfully to "satisfy our desire to understand," he insists that the other kinds "of explanations in terms of logical and purposive connections . . . always imply also the concept of causality, though often in a sense so basic or general that it may simply be taken for granted." Nadel identifies the function of the postulate of causality as a principle of objective reference for the categories of social understanding as "fitness or requiredness" through which empirically discoverable regularities "acquire meaning and explanatory weight." When the investigator presupposes the pervasive operation of causation, he can coordinate the sociocultural and the motivational aspect of the behavioral process: "Social facts exist and arise *because* the actors have had certain intentions or felt the efficacy of certain mental events, and that they have intentions and other mental events *because* certain social facts happen to exist." Without this postulate which correlates mechanical and purposive causation Nadel could not explain the sociocultural as he does when he asserts that "social facts are 'emergents' from the order of things which we call psychological and organic" so that "the mental event-become-action must add to the environment of objects in which all experiences and actions take place." [61]

Kroeber and Kluckhohn also presuppose that a postulate of sociocultural causality is a necessary assumption for anthropological analysis; but they emphasize that "predictive certainty" must not be included among the demands which this postulate imposes upon those cultural anthropologists who "like all scientists are searching for minimal causal chains in the body of the phenomena they investigate." With a view toward making "some aspects of the behavior of individuals in a culture reducible to generalizations that can be stated with increased economy," they recommend "the refinement and elaboration" of such "pervasive general principles in culture" as Opler's *themes,* Herskovits' *focus,* Kroeber's *configurations of cultural growth,* and Kluckhohn's *implicit culture.* But these causal generalizations as principles of objective reference, are not offered as predictive laws in the manner intended by classical physicists and neoclassical economists. The scope of the postulate of causality is limited to the assumption "that nothing happens without a cause." This allows reasonable expectation for the anthropologist who assumes that "the test of the validity of such 'least common denominators' or 'highest common factors' will, of course, be the extent to which they . . . make the phenomena more intelligible" and who confines his expectation to "reasonably accurate predictions of cultural change under specified conditions." [62]

2. DETERMINISTIC VS. RELATIVELY SELF-DETERMINISTIC CONCEPTIONS OF SOCIOCULTURAL CAUSATION

a) Deterministic Causation

In order that anthropology might develop into a nomothetic "science of culture" White has eliminated "the psychosomatic actions of human beings" from the components of culture. Since he is unencumbered by the requirement to synchronize intervening variables with independent variables, he can causally explain the dependent variable of culture as an entity *sui generis* which deterministically evolves in accordance with autonomous laws. When he restricts "scientific explanation to a quest for determinants, for cause and effect relationships, for distinctions between constants and variables, distinctions between dependent and independent variables," [63] White must adopt mechanical causation as a principle for objective reference. Since any human relative self-determinism is precluded, culture as a "superorganic entity" is conceived as "a stream of interacting elements; one trait reacts upon others and is affected by them in return." Consequently, the causal interconnection among the components of the cultural process parallels the deterministic interconnection among the physical events in the space-time continuum to which the physicist's constructs refer.

White's postulate of mechanical causality is most explicitly and ingeniously expressed in his conception of the *technological determination* of the evolution of the "systematic organization of cultural elements." As a cultural system evolves in order to establish and maintain a moving equilibrium "a balance is struck between the technological, social, philosophical, and sentimental factors" through "the technological change or development that produces change or growth in the other cultural sectors" so that "the motive power of a culture, so to speak, lies in its technology, for here it is that energy is harnessed and put to work." When the "technological, sociological, ideological and sentimental, or attitudinal" classes of cultural phenomena are statically analyzed, they may be viewed merely as inter-related "parts of a whole." However, when they are dynamically analyzed, it is found that they all are operating as causal factors, but "the technological factor determines, in a general way at least, the form and content of the social, philosophic, and sentimental sectors." In other words, if the culturologist is not forced to account for "microscopic details" and, if it is understood that he is not denying the "influence exerted upon technology by social, philosophic, and senti-mental factors," then this mechanistically causal formula means that "in the system that is culture, technology is the independent vari-able, the other sectors the dependent variables" [64]

What justification is there for White's elimination of the interven-ing variable of goal-seeking motivation from his causal formula? Up to this point the present writer has defended White's intellectual right to a "methodological superorganicism," i.e., to treat culture "as if it had an existence of its own, independently of the human spe-cies." White grants that "culture traits do not go walking about like disembodied souls interacting with each other" and that culture "has its origin in the organisms of human beings; it could not exist or be perpetuated without the existence and action of human beings." White's immunity to the charge of arbitrary oversimplification comes up for renewal, however, in connection with the postulate of causa-tion. There are many anthropologists who are not willing to extend this immunity to this aspect of the meaning-situation. This unwill-ingness is increased by what appears to be a bit of legerdemain by which White attempts to make psychodynamic and reflective moti-vation disappear right before your eyes. To those who contend that personality is a producer as well as a product of culture he answers that personality is either the function of the neurophysiological sys-tem, which makes it irrelevant, since the cultural process is extraso-matic, or personality is "the product of human social experience, i.e., as culturally determined." Consequently, White argues, "they are saying that culture causes culture through the medium of human biological organisms, which is precisely what we are maintaining here." [65] This, of course, is not all that the personality-in-culture pro-ponent is claiming. The human self-creative effort for goal-seeking which modifies a cultural process is not confined to the somatic func-tions. What this entails will be elaborated in the subsequent discus-sion of relative self-determinism.

What does Hallowell mean when he charges that White has "an inadequate conception of man"? In addition to recognizing that "human behavior is relative to traditional cultural patterns and historical circumstances" Hallowell contends that culture is "relative to unrealized potentialities that inhere in man's human nature and which permits the emergence of novelty in his mode of life." [66] That White's opposition to Hallowell's conception of personality-in-culture stems from something more than a justified methodological distinction, seems clear when he claims that "the individual is in each case merely an organization of cultural forces and elements that have impinged upon him from the outside and which find their overt expression through him" so that "the individual is but the expression of a supra-biological cultural tradition in somatic form." Instead of leaving psychological factors out of account, i.e., "the most effective way to study culture scientifically is to proceed *as if* the human race did not exist," White's conception of the cultural process entails a predeterministic conception of motivational factors: "Relative to the culture process the individual is neither creator nor determinant; he is merely a catalyst and a vehicle of expression." [67]

b) *Relatively Self-Deterministic Causation*

In order to correlate the idiographic and nomothetic approaches, some anthropologists conceive of the postulate of sociocultural causation in terms of relative self-determinism. On the premise that "all cultural phenomena are natural phenomena modified by human effort and interaction," Bidney presupposes this relatively self-deterministic causation when he depicts "the function of man as a self-determining, active agent who is affected by cultural products and patterns, but is, nevertheless, the primary efficient agent of the cultural process itself." Explicitly referring to Aristotle's conceptual framework of the complex conditions of causation, Bidney conceives of this *efficient* causal operation of socioculturalized persons as interrelated with the *material* causal conditions of artifacts, with the *formal* causal conditions of mentifacts, and with the *final* causal conditions of sociofacts. For explaining cultural development all of these material, formal, and final causal conditions are *necessary*, but without the relatively self-determined goal-seeking of individual persons it is not possible to specify a *sufficient* cause. By adopting this principle that "nothing happens without a sufficient cause" Bidney is aware that he is abandoning the nineteenth-century linear conception of causation in terms of predictive certainty: "It is this inherent circularity of the cultural process which makes all long-range prediction so contingent." [68]

Kroeber's claim that "it will be the psychosomatic actions of human beings that contain the immediate causality of cultural phenomena" entails two points which are significant for this discussion. In the first place, it provides the clue for clarifying what is meant by "a powerful system of circular causality" in the cultural process: "While human beings are always the immediate causes of cultural events, these human causes are themselves the result of antecedent culture situations" so that "there is thus a continuity of indirect causation from culture event to culture event through the medium of human intermediaries." In the second place, it reflects the changing of an eminent anthropologist's conception of deterministic causation to a conception of relatively self-deterministic causation. Kroeber reports that the initial difficulty of specifying causal conditions from among such numerous and complex factors led him "to be skeptical of causal explanations." Then he adopted an idealistic "superorganicism" which precluded relatively self-determined human influence on the cultural process just as much as White's materialistic "superorganicism." Now, however, he has been persuaded by Bidney that "the immediately effective causes of cultural phenomena must reside in human beings," even though they are influenced by their culture. He still holds, however, to an "empty organism" approach for linguistics and cultural history: "On this purely cultural level, the personalities who are the immediate causes are not denied, but they are omitted from the operation." Accordingly, he is willing to assert that "culture causes culture, provided that one does not exclude the agency of men also, other than provisionally and operationally." [69] With a view to estimating the extent of Kroeber's conversion, it might be said that, while he would agree with Linton that "the individual, his needs and potentialities, lies at the foundation of all social and cultural phenomena," Kroeber probably would not go so far as Linton when the latter maintains that "the individual is the logical starting point for any investigation of the larger configuration." [70]

The relatively self-determined motivation of enculturalized persons seems to be presupposed in the causal assumptions which the recon-struction of a multilinear theory of sociocultural evolution entail. In their justified revolt against nineteenth-century unilinear evolution-ism the functionalists seemed to have been so opposed to its postu-late of predeterministic causation that they developed a phobia with respect to any conception of causality. Actually, as was previously indicated, they did implicitly presuppose purposive causation in terms of the ends-means continuum in their accounts of the func-tioning of the specific communities with which they were concerned. But their cultural relativism precluded the relatively self-determined influence of persons on the sociocultural process just as much as did the mechanical causality of unilinear evolutionism. Kroeber, however, has been so impressed by Huxley's reconstruction of biolog-ical evolution, in which relatively self-determined human effort makes a causal difference in the emergence of novel sociocultural processes, that he sees it as "a new through-highway bridge-building between biology and the psychology-anthropology-humanities inquir-ies which deal with culture." [71] The implications for anthropology of this emergent evolutionary view are so significant that Huxley's view merits special attention.

In what sense does Huxley presuppose relative self-determinism in his effort to correlate biological and sociocultural evolution? Em-phatically disclaiming that "purely biological concepts and principles can be immediately applied or directly transferred to anthropology," Huxley insists that man's unique organism with unique properties" and "the increased mental specialization" of cultural systems re-quire specifically anthropological concepts. He conceives of the total universe, nevertheless, as a constantly developing evolutionary process toward novelty, variety, and complexity in which its cultural phase, which is symbolic, has emerged out of an organic phase just as this biological evolution has emerged out of the inorganic phase. It is only to the psycho-social dimension of reality that anthropological constructs should refer. When culture "sub specie evolutionis" is taken to be "a self-maintaining system of . . . the results of the in-tercommunication of the minds of human individuals in society," then it cannot be reduced to the psycho-physical processes of the in-dividuals themselves. Huxley maintains, however, that "the behavior of single individuals may offset the course of psycho-social evolu-tion." Consequently, the development of "cultural pattern-systems in psycho-social evolution" which produces "increasingly full, precise and conscious formulation" is only analogous to the "increasing differentiation of functional organic systems in biological evolution." Accordingly, the psycho-social process operates in accordance with "the same broad scheme of evolutionary relatedness" as in the biological sphere. But, with the "cumulative transmission of experience" through cultural inheritance of intellectual, religious, ethical, and aesthetic ideas, the instances of conscious purposive "fulfillment of potentiality" (mentifact system) comes to "constitute the decisive long-term factors in cultural evolution." In this case, "greater knowledge and fuller truth alone permit a correctly directed type of cultural change." Comparable to the critical point in the evolutionary process when the cultural emerged out of the biological "which permitted the emergence of man as a new dominant type" is the development "from mainly unconscious evolution to change consciously directed." This "will permit the emergence of a new and dominant pattern of organization within the cultural process." [72]

F. *The Significance of the Fourth Postulate for Economics*

Regardless of his theoretical commitment any economist who is concerned about the allocative function in the ends-means transactions by which people secure a livelihood must presuppose some conception of behavioral causation as a principle of objective reference. This does not imply that the allocation of alternative means for obtaining material ends is determined solely by some person's deliberative estimate and selection. In the following account of the "ideal uses" of scarce resources it will be noted that the orthodox conception of an automatic allocative process for attaining economic goals presupposes mechanical causality, while the unorthodox conception of a process which requires human intervention presupposes purposive causality. Nevertheless, since the instrumentation which the allocative process entails must involve some relation to an intrinsic end, a brief consideration of *welfare economics* may provide a clue to the divergence among economists with respect to the nature of the causal postulate each has adopted. For, as Lange has said, "the administration of scarce resources empirically observed can be evaluated in terms of certain social objectives." Consequently, "the social objectives being given, rules of use of scarce resources can be found which are most conducive to the attainment of these objectives." [73]

In Pigou's formulation of the neo-classical *welfare economics*, the attainment of the optimum condition, i.e., an abundance of all goods and services that can be exchanged for money, presupposes a mechanically causal process in which only the quantitatively measurable factor of "real national income" operates as an *independent variable* so that any *intervening variables* of purposive goal-seeking are precluded as irrelevant: "Generally speaking, economic causes act upon the welfare of any country, not directly, but through the making and using of that objective counterpart of economic welfare which economists call the national dividend or national income." Although Pigou acknowledges that the welfare of a community is not confined to its economic welfare, he emphasizes that it is only the latter that "is part of the total welfare which can be brought directly or indirectly into relation with a money measure." [74] This seems to reflect the neo-classical faith in the automatic progress of the mechanical process of the equilibrating forces of supply and demand in which the market exchange mechanism operates as independently of human purpose as did Adam Smith's "Invisible Hand" or Spencer's "felicity-pursuing law."

When J. M. Clark decided that "in a modern economy it has become impossible to trust an 'invisible hand' to turn crude self-interest into an efficient engine for meeting every social need," he clearly adopts a postulate of purposive causation in his analysis of the goal-seeking orientation which identifies the scope and aim of unorthodox *welfare economics*: "We must have a sensitive awareness of what the economic machine is doing to them; and we must work with conscious purpose to make the economy meet these needs." Thus, Clark neither appeals to Smith's enlightened self-interest nor to the neo-classical conception of the "rational motivation of economic man." Instead he appeals here to the enlightened good will of relatively self-determined persons, which he identifies as *responsibility* not only with respect to "the decisions one makes for one's self" but also in voluntary "discretion with due regard to the other interests whom his actions affect." When Clark explicitly adopts the postulate that an individual "does have some margin of discretion in deciding how to act," he is not discounting the causal influence of the independent variables of each person's natural, psychological, and sociocultural environment. Obviously, however, he is insisting upon the inclusion of the intervening variable of the intellectual initiative and moral responsibility of relatively self-determined participants in the democratic process in which "voluntary social adaption" is necessitated by the complexity and enormity of our present economic system. Political legislation is required in a planned capitalistic economy to meet this need. But no authoritative allocation of economic opportunities will be effective for this purpose unless such policy decisions are first understood and discussed through "a creative process of experimental exploration, by the joint efforts of men of good will." [75]

By recalling the calculus of determinants in the synoptic model, we can recognize the complexity of the causal factors which the institutional allocation of scarce means for alternative ends entails. The availability of the physical means depends upon the technological-natural environment; the availability of the institutional means depends upon the social environment; the availability of the purposive motivation depends upon the physiological and psychological environment which has instigated the reflective desire; and the availability of the intrinsic goal depends upon the cultural environment that presents the ideal value alternatives from which reflective persons select their conception of the highest good. This does not deny Parsons' claim that "allocation is only in part product of a deliberate decision"; for by equally imputing causal influence to the independent variables, we agree that "the total allocation in a social system especially may be the product of many processes that culminate in a distribution which no individual or collective actor in the system has sought." [76] But in those cases where deliberate decisions are involved in the allocation of scarce resources, the purposive expectations of persons who take advantage of externally-begotten opportunities cannot be left out of a causal account.

The postulate of causality as a principle of objective reference is no less presupposed in the orthodox conception of uniform laws which were qualified by the *ceteris paribus* formula. Consider, for example, Marshall's justification for the limitation of specified conditions: "Almost every scientific doctrine, where carefully and formally stated, will be found to contain some proviso to the effect that other things are equal: the action of the cause in question is supposed to be isolated; certain effects are attributed to them, but only on the hypothesis that no cause is permitted to enter except those distinctly allowed for." [77] Even when Jevons sought to make deductive economic analysis as purely logical as possible, he had to conclude that economics could never be more than a "comparatively formal science." [78] This is because its basic axioms and predictive principles refer to causally related data and no amount of logical refinement of tautological abstractions could preclude its concern with the causal relation of supply and demand. Those contemporary statistical analysts who presume that they do not presuppose causality might well ponder whether they have really been more successful than Jevons, or whether they, too, actually presuppose some sort of actual causal conditions.

The heuristic and postulatory nature of the principle of causality underlying economic analysis has been emphasized by Spiethoff at the same time that he is insisting that "the foremost and principal task of scholars is the search for causes," which in economics involves "objective causality and motivational causality." There would be no basis for inductive investigation "in which uniformities are brought to light" through observation and analysis, if it were not presupposed that the "species of phenomena, considered as effect, has been linked to certain causes and conditions." Spiethoff grants that "in complicated interrelationships, decisive uniformities can be found, and causal analysis applied, only in an indirect fashion." It is, however, only because causation is assumed to hold that "theoretical deduction and empirical induction go hand in hand in the task of explanation," and that "a subject of investigation can be approached with a hypothesis" so that "with its help an overall picture of the possible relations among phenomena under consideration is constructed." [79]

From the previous discussion it should be clear that both the orthodox and the unorthodox economists would agree with Spiethoff's assumption that "nothing happens without a sufficient cause"; but their divergence on what constitutes a sufficient cause stems from the difference in the "overall picture of the possible relations among phenomena" which each constructs. For the neo-classicist it is the mechanical operation of a closed system of equilibrium with only minor and temporary disturbances; while for the institutionalist, for whom such a conception seems too narrowly circumscribed, an explanation does not adequately account for a "sufficient cause" unless it includes a broader range of the sociocultural and motivational factors in the open, modifiable, multidimensional, reciprocal, constantly changing, temporal process of behavioral transactions. This multiplicity of sociocultural causation as a complex of conditions influencing business cycles is thus elaborated by Mitchell as a postulate which he finds more fruitful than the neo-classical postulate of narrowly delimited monocausality: "As our knowledge grows wider and more intimate, our attitude toward the discussion of causes undergoes a subtle change" so that "when we have accounted in causal terms for each stage in a lengthy series of actions and reactions, we find that our analysis deals with many causes each one of which is logically indispensable to the theory we have elaborated." [80]

Kapp has brought forward and elaborated the attack on monocausality. Regarding the behavior of laborers and labor unions he maintains: "To single out wage objectives as the determinants of union action is to fall into the trap of a traditional concept of social causation which attributes causal potency to one isolated factor without seeing the 'field' or intentional character of the causal nexus." Similarly, when he criticizes the orthodox idea that the entrepreneurial decision to invest is automatic, Kapp claims that it can not be explained by simply referring "to any single factor such as the level of interest rate or the demand for finished goods." [81] For psychological factors such as "waves of optimism and urges to action" (Keynes) and "expectations of profits" should be taken into account. Kapp's acknowledgement that "we have as yet no theory of how expectations are formed and transmitted" points up the importance of the spadework which Katona has been doing with respect to a psychological analysis of expectations in economic motivation. Instead of treating expectations as a narrowly circumscribed constant, as in the neo-classical "economic man," Katona takes expectations to be *intervening variables* that are "mediating between changes in the environment and overt behavior" in the making of some economic decisions. He recognizes that some economic decisions are merely habitual and others are determined by antecedent experiences; but there are in addition those economic decisions in which the person's present deliberative appraisal in accordance with what he expects in the future, significantly influence his selection from among alternatives.[82]

The most significant single-handed reconstruction of the neo-classical conception of equilibrating causal forces, of course, has been that of Keynes for whom the causal relation of supply and demand is influenced by the propensity to consume and the volume of investment so that total income depends upon the volume of total employment. Keynes was unwilling to discount governmental intervention and to delimit motivational factors, as did the neo-classical proponents of an automatically self-adjusting *laissez faire* static system of equilibribrium. On the contrary, Keynes emphasized the influence of the fiscal operations of government, as well as the expectations of investors and the demands of workers, upon the economic operations of employment and investment. Accordingly, Keynes assumes that a combination of qualitative and quantitative factors must function effectively for the restoration of employment and market operations in the constantly evolving economic process in which new factors emerge among the causal conditions that determine national income.[83]

It seems unlikely that any contemporary economist would deny that the change from a dominantly competitive economy to a hybrid economy, in which monopoly or oligopoly is more dominant than individual competition, could have occurred, if the only causal conditions had been equilibrating forces. Gailbraith has attempted to adapt the neo-classical conception of competition among "sellers on one side of the market" by a conception of checks and balances created by competition between "big sellers and big buyers on opposite sides of the market" who provide a "countervailing power" in the monopolistic operation of American capitalism. Although Gailbraith does not exclude the need for some governmental support for facilitating the development of this "countervailing power," the institutionalistic economists advocate a more extensive form of governmental intervention through price and production controls. As Gruchy reports, Mitchell, Clark, Tugwell, Commons, and Means do not agree with respect to the extent that government should regulate the private enterprise system. Nevertheless, they would all agree with Means that the coordination of economic and political allocation through "administrative economics" should be "a kind of planning which is a peculiarly American custom, based on an enthusiastic belief in the ability of democracy to utilize intelligence." [84]

Underlying the recommendations of institutional economists for a controlled capitalism there is the assumption that in the evolution of the economic process sociocultural causality is complex and variable by virtue of the emergence of new economic determinants. This complexity and variability has been analyzed by Commons in terms of five reciprocally causal conditions by which he explains "the expected repetition, with variability, of the totality of all human acting and transacting within the limiting and complementary interdependence of the principles of scarcity efficiency, working rules, sovereignty, and futurity." [85] Technological factors are taken by the institutionalists to be emergent causal factors which significantly influence the entire economic process. For the orthodox economists, however, such technological modifications "of the structure and functioning of the market mechanisms" are acknowledged, if at all, only as "sociological penumbra" [86] to which precise causal generalizations are not applicable. Technological innovations may be omitted from delimited analysis of some economic operations. Gruchy grants this but insists that when the unorthodox economist analyzes "the functioning of the economic system over a period of time which reveals how a technology alters the structuring and functioning of the total complex of economic institutions," then he must presuppose that emergent factors function in the sociocultural causality of the temporal process through which the economic system evolves: "When these economists look at the existing markct mechanism, or the whole economy of which this mechanism is a vital part, they see the economic institutions which come from the past, which now exist, and which are in the process of developing new configurations." [87]

This conception of the economic process in terms of emergent evolution also requires a nomothetic-idiographic perspective in which causal generalizations about the independent variables of environmental determinants are correlated with causal generalizations about the intervening variables of relatively self-determined decisions by reflective persons. Purely nomothetic abstractions about an indefinitely uniform and recurrent process suffice for neo-classical generalizations about the delimited referents of a closed system of equilibrium and a narrowly circumscribed rational choice. But if the economist acknowledges the postulate of purposive causation ascribed above to J. M. Clark, then he can not leave out of account the idiographic operations which MacIver has imputed to economic behavior when he claims that "as a device for interpreting social and economic changes, the concept of equilibrium and disturbance is less serviceable than the concept of equilibrium and precipitant." While nomothetic generalizations about such equilibrium as is found accounts for some of the necessary causal conditions, the sufficient causes in some economic operations can not be accounted for without an idiographic treatment of the relatively self-determined decision of goal-seeking persons that, as MacIver insists, "has intervened, has emerged within or thrust itself into the total situation, in such a way as to bring about a state of disequilibrium, a change of directions, or a realignment of forces." [88] Spiethoff recognizes the need to include such "motivational causality" which he identifies as the "totality of mental activities behind human action" in "economic activities as seen as the result or cause by certain motives." [89] But Commons has more explicitly elaborated the implications of the causal principle which MacIver has called for.

Commons advocates a nomothetic-idiographic approach for economic analysis which is "different from that of the exact sciences because its outcome is the concerted but conflicting action of human wills in an historical evolution of determining what is workable within the changing economic, political, and ethical sequence." When he includes the intervening variable of "volitiency" to identify "human-will-in-action," Commons is not presupposing the noncausal indeterminism of a purely idiographic approach: "We recognize that there can be no science of political economy if the will is free, in the sense of being wholly capricious and undetermined." Yet, he does presuppose relative self-determinism when he contends that economists are required "to look for the uniformities in the operation of the will, if we would have an economic science." However, he just as strongly opposes the neoclassical economists' purely nomothetic approach, which ignored the singular, unique, and nonrecurrent factors which exemplify "voluntarity" and "historicity." Since he aimed to replace the neo-classical static principle of mechanical repetition with an explanatory principle of "futurity," he needed a causal "formula for expressing the uncertain expectations of the future which dominate the activity of human beings in the ever moving present. As long as *rationality* was the keynote of causal interaction, the orthodox nomothetic generalization of an inexorable "law of supply and demand" seemed to be a *sufficient cause*. But, when Commons reconstructed the behavioral interactions of naturalized, socioculturalized, and goal-seeking individuals in terms of *the complex transactions of economic power,* then he had to include idiographically conceived variations in "an adequate and therefore complex formula of transactions whose expected repetition, concurrence, and variability is a going concern." [90]

G. *The Significance of the Fourth Postulate for Political Science*

The postulate of behavioral causation is explicitly assumed by those political scientists who agree with Easton that their discipline is an attempt to "explain a factual situation by formulating a system of constructs that correspond to the significant political variables among which causal relations can be ascertained." [91] It is presupposed less explicitly, if not minimized, by those who find political study a "creative art" and by those political scientists who confine their efforts to the objective collection and classification of facts." But, for instance, when Key declares that "the isolated 'fact' must be related to a larger theory of political behavior before the significance of the 'fact' may be perceived," [92] he seems to be assuming that *to explain* means to ascertain the causal implication of a particular happening in the context of the conditions without which the event in question would not have occurred. Now causality could hardly serve as such a principle of objective reference unless political analysis proceeds on Easton's assumption that "the search for recurrent relationships suggests that the elements of political life have some determinate relations." As Easton reminds those who presume that political facts speak for themselves, "no matter how indifferent a research worker may be to causal theory, the logic behind the selection and the accumulation of facts inevitably implies the existence of a theory, even if it is below the level of consciousness." Although Easton staunchly insists upon the necessity for using this principle of causation for the development of political inquiry "towards the attainment of reliable knowledge," he does acknowledge that it is a postulate in the meaning-situation rather than a verifiable generalization in the knowledge-situation of political science: "Causal theory is a device for improving the dependability of our knowledge." [93]

Among those political scientists who proceed on this assumption, there seems to be a consensus that political inquiry presupposes multiple causation, rather than a monocausality which would permit the investigator to explain a political event by reference to only one determinant. Easton's insistence upon "plural rather than upon single factor causation" does not preclude the concentration upon artificially isolated causal variables for the sake of delimited investigations, if the investigator "conceives of political life, not as the product of any one force, such as class, a political structure, or some special group, but as the product of multiple causes." [94]

It is further presupposed by Key that the cause and effect influence between the governor and those governed exhibits reciprocity when it is conceived in terms of a non-unilateral power relationship: "It is a reciprocal relationship, and the subjects may affect the ruler more profoundly than the ruler affects the subjects." [95] This reciprocal relation of the ruler and ruled, which "constitutes the essence of the study of politics," is also acknowledged by Lasswell, when he declares that "power is an interpersonal situation," since those who hold power are empowered "and depend upon and continue only so long as there is a continuing stream of empowering responses." [96] Such reciprocity applies also to non-governmental political processes such as party leaders—party members; pressure groups —those pressured; or propagandists—those propagandized.

When it is assumed that causal analysis and normative analysis are interdependent aspects of political inquiry, it must also be presupposed that goal-seeking motivation is an intervening variable which must be accounted for in a coherent explanation of political behavior. Such normative causation, which pertains to the desiring and striving for a satisfaction-yielding objective, is assumed to be the defining characteristic of political motivation by Lasswell and Kaplan: "The political act takes its origin in a situation in which the actor strives for the attainment of various values for which power is a necessary (and perhaps also sufficient) condition." [97] With respect to the political act some political scientists are attempting so to conceive of causation that decisions motivated by intellectual initiative and moral responsibility can influence the political process without denying as much causal determinism as is required for formulating reasonable expectations about future political outcomes.

Without some such postulate of relative self-determinism there seems no way out of the dilemma which Garceau describes: "A central conceptual controversy, probably inescapable for political scientists because of their disciplinary heritage, is that involved in perceiving uniformities in behavior, describing recurrent patterns, identifying the determinants and yet reconciling this effort and its underlying premises about the roots of behavior with the liberal, democratic faith in man's individual capacity to determine his own ends, to think rationally and to reach individual and creative decisions." [98] When Pennock discusses the possibilities of causal explanation and prediction of political behavior that is reflectively motivated, he contends that the political scientist should not rule out such causal generalizations because they cannot be constructed with mathematic-like certainty. For this does not mean "that we can do nothing to test their plausibility." [99]

It should be understood that a political analyst who takes this intervening variable of the relatively self-determined decisions of morally responsible persons into a causal account, does not assume that political processes always operate in accordance with reflective purposes. As Perry has stated: "It is clear that mass society with its complex and delicate organization, was not consciously contrived by man, was not planned, blueprinted, and then constructed according to specifications." Accordingly, Perry does not deny that "many of its features are the unintended consequences of the actions of men who neither desire nor desired the consequences." Notwithstanding the operation of independent variables in many situations which require no reference to intervening variables, there are some political situations, nevertheless, in which deliberative decisions influence the outcome: "It is equally clear that the construction of advanced societies has involved foresight, inventiveness, and understanding." Thus, according to Perry, the reflective goal-seeking which exemplified purposive motivation must be included in the postulate of causality which the political scientist presupposes as a principle of objective reference: "To describe behavior, is to relate it to reality in terms of the purposive activity involved; and to relate behavior to reality is to describe its purpose in terms of the component activities as guided by appropriate norms." [100]

A conceptual framework for relating the independent variables in a political scientist's causal generalization about a democratic political situation has been identified by Easton as a "constitutional equilibrium." By this he refers to the necessary conditions of consti-

tutional order within or among nations for a relatively equal distribution of power so that no one participating has a preponderant
control of the policy decisions and executions by which the instrumental values of an entire society are authoritatively allocated.
(Easton is not dealing here with the "general equilibrium theory"
in terms of which some political scientists have unsuccessfully
attempted to utilize the quantitative formulae that have been more
fruitful in physics and economics.) What it entails is the "narrow-
gauge generalization" that "there is an invariant relation between
constitutional order and freedom on the one hand, and the mutual
restraint and limitation flowing from a relatively equal distribution
of power, on the other." [101]

So that Easton's causal formula of "constitutional equilibrium"
might be applicable to a democratic political process, it seems necessary to qualify it further in the motivational terms of the intervening
variable exemplified in the responsible initiative of its participating
citizens to which Herring refers: "The mechanism for democratic
self-control is the citizen's inner control." To Easton's nomothetic
formula that "there is an invariant relation between constitutional
order and freedom, on the one hand, and the mutual restraint and
limitation flowing from a relatively equal distribution of power, on
the other," we would add the idiographic qualification *if the participants in the democratic process are on an extensive scale motivated
by intellectual initiative and moral responsibility*. Without this reflective motivation which Herring has presupposed as an idiographically operating intervening variable, there is no genuinely democratic process, if Dewey's conception of democracy is reasonably
acceptable: "The keynote of democracy as a way of life may be expressed, it seems to me, as the necessity for the participation of every
mature human being in the formation of values that regulate the
living of men together: which is necessary from the standpoint of
both the general social welfare and the full development of human
beings as individuals." [102] It should be noted that if this formula is
taken as a causal generalization for guiding research, intellectually
and morally responsible participation is taken to be as empirically
ascertainable as a variable in voting behavior as is the distribution of
power to which some political scientists confine their causal analysis.

H. *The Significance of the Fourth Postulate for History*

Whenever a historian goes beyond the mere description of the chronological sequence of events in order to explain them, he implicitly, if not explicitly, presupposes the postulate of behavioral causation as the principle of objective reference. For, as Brockunier and Loewenberg insist, "when we speak of explaining or understanding a given sequence of events, we mean that we undertake to give reasons for those particular events or, in other words, to explain why they occurred in that particular order," i.e., "to make a statement about causation." [103] Historians who seem to be unaware that questions about causation pertain to the meaning-situation of historical inquiry, rather than to its knowledge-situation, confuse the pertinent issues when they object that causal generalizations preclude the recognition of specific situations and that causal analysis does not guarantee definitive conclusions.

When the broadly operational historian assumes that historical events are causally determined, he acknowledges that the assumption is "supplied by the historian." However it is an essential part of this assumption that the causal interrelationships are operating independently of the historian's construction of the causal generalizations about them. This epistemologically dualistic assumption that the principle of causality is introduced by the historian himself does not seem to be acceptable to Mandelbaum, when he adopts the epistemologically monistic assumption that the "causal relationship" must lie "in the determinate connection which exists between events." [104] But, both he and the epistemological dualist agree that it must at least be presupposed that the specific causal relationships are discovered and not invented. As Cohen has insisted, "every event is an integral part of a larger segment of history and the task of tracing causal connections is the task of discovering those elements that persist through, and despite, the arbitrary cuts by which we mark off the event we are at the moment seeking to explain." [105]

It seems that historians have a great deal of trouble living with the principle of causality; and yet, they have even more trouble trying to live without it. Beard and Vogts advocated abandoning the use of the principle of causation on the grounds that it is so ambiguous and misleading. However, when Tapp, Nagel, Teggart, Hook, Cohen, Gottschalk, and others attempted to dispense with it, they became convinced that Brockunier and Loewenberg were correct when they contended that "one cannot, however, take refuge in explanations that seem, but only seem, to avoid causal imputation." [106] But, since the historian cannot be satisfied with the naïve assumption, *post hoc ergo propter hoc* (after this, therefore on account of this), he must refine his postulate of behavioral causation. To this end it is necessary for him (a) to clarify what he takes to be the minimal meaning of historical causality, and (b) to recognize the complications which are especially entailed in historical causation.

(a) What is the minimal meaning of the postulate of historical causality? Whenever a historian attempts to relate any given event to its context of a wider range of interconnected events, he presupposes that "nothing happens without a sufficient cause." This means that a causal determinant is taken to be a precipitating *specifiable condition* without the occurrence of which along with other necessary *specifiable* conditions the event which is taken to be an effect would not have occurred. In this conception of a causally structured process of changing events these necessary and sufficient causes are correlative. As Cohen has said, "in its most rigorous form causality denotes the sum of the necessary and sufficient conditions for the occurrence of any event." Confronted with a plurality of causes from which he must select the most significant to him, the historian rarely, if ever, strives to meet the most rigorous demands of the postulate negatively designated by Cohen: "A circumstance that is not necessary for a given event, i.e., if the event can take place without it, cannot be the cause; and similarly if a circumstance is not sufficient to bring about the given event, i.e., if the former can occur without the latter, it cannot be the cause." [107] According to Hook, some historians use "cause" as a synonym for the "consequential order of events in process." [108] Simiand, however, distinguishes between "cause" and "conditions": "Among the various antecedents of phenomena, the one which is linked with it by the most general relations is the cause"; but "conditions are those antecedents which can be replaced by others, while the cause is not or is least of all replaceable." [109] Despite these various largely terminological differences, there seems to be general agreement among historians that no more than "partially predictable regularity," rather than "predictive certainty" (Brockunier and Loewenberg), is all that can be expected from any historian's causal generalizations. It seems clear, nevertheless, that without this minimum meaning of causality there could be no principle of objective reference for historical analysis through the critical selection, explanation, and verification which distinguish broadly operational historical inquiry from a mere chronicle or a purely imaginative portrayal of the past.

The manner in which necessary and sufficient causes mutually require each other is illustrated in the interdependence of the natural environmental and motivational aspects of behavioral causation. Recalling Bidney's anthropological generalization that "all cultural phenomena are natural phenomen modified by human effort and interaction," [110] we can understand Cohen's premise that the "elements of the physical environment are necessary but not sufficient conditions of any particular course of human development." Although the inorganic and organic processes limit the scope of human actions, it is to the sociocultural-motivational factors of behavioral causation that the historian must look for the sufficient causes of specific effects. Thus, Cohen concludes, "to say that men are a product of their environments is only a half-truth; it is equally true that men choose, mould, develop and modify the environment in which they live and work." If the historian extends this correlation of necessary and sufficient causes to the behavioral context so that sociocultural causes are taken to be necessary and the motivations of outstanding persons are taken to be sufficient, then he has a formula for escaping the great man-social forces dilemma. This is what we assume Cohen means when he declares that "the real problem is not whether history is to be written as the biography of great men *or* as a tracing of social forces, for great men are precisely the points of intersection of great social forces." [111]

Historical causation is unintelligible apart from the concept of a *temporal continuum* through which each event is systematically linked as the effect of antecedent events and the cause of subsequent events in the system of the *causal chain* which the historian is attempting to explain. This diachronic system must be distinguished, however, from the synchronic system in which the functional relation of the seamless whole to its interlocking parts may be statically conceived. As Brockunier and Loewenberg emphasize, when the historian attempts to "discover and explain change," he assumes that "a continuum in history is not literally 'that which is absolutely continuous and self-same,' " but, "rather, it is a set of phenomena with a fundamental common character continuing in time and space" which must be analyzed in terms of "continuities and discontinuities." [112] As long as there is this provision against such intermeshing that would preclude separable strands of events, most historians would probably accept Cohen's claim that "no event is necessary absolutely or by itself but only if it is connected with other events and is thus a part of a system." [113]

For the broadly operational historian who, like Brockunier and Loewenberg, "not only strives for an understanding of the total situation *as it is* at any given point of time, but also undertakes to explain how that situation *came to be*," [114] merely to ascertain the uniformity of a temporal sequence of events is not enough to impute a causal chain. In order to avoid the meaningless *post hoc ergo propter hoc*, he must include, in his minimal presupposition of sufficient causation, the principle that there must be an ascertainable difference in the effect where there is a difference in the cause. Such a "precipitant cause" which, according to MacIver, "diverts the pre-established direction of affairs" is called for by Clough as a specified antecedent condition when he claims that the problem of historical causation "is that of identifying logical rather than merely temporal patterns." [115] Since it would be impossible for the historian to suppose that he could take into account all antecedent temporal successions, he must be allowed to confine his analysis to only those causal chains which he deems significant so long as he acknowledges that he has abstracted them from a more inclusive causal pattern. Instead of attempting to consider "the totality of past actions through time," therefore, the historian must take as causal conditions a specific conjuncture of past events which exhibits a difference that *precipitates* a change in the subsequent temporal sequence of historical events.

(b) What complications are especially entailed in the broadly operational postulate of historical causation? Historiographers who are attempting to correlate the "historical" and the "social-scientific" modes of causal analysis are confronted with the complications which integrative efforts always seem to entail. Such complications are not involved in the pure historian's idiographic depiction of the past actions of unique individuals in specific non-recurrent situations; or, in the attempt of some social scientists to explain independent variables entirely in terms of their *structure*; or, in the attempt of other social scientists to explain independent variables entirely in terms of *process*. When, however, Brockunier and Loewenberg seek "to penetrate beneath the superficial manifestations of change and to seek an explanation in terms of underlying trends and conditioning factors," they find that "the related concepts of structure and process provide a highly useful guiding thread in the analysis of causation." Identifying *structure* as "the degree and mode of organization in a situation," they suggest that "the concept of structure enables us to build a theoretical bridge between the unique individual, with all his particularities and idiosyncrasies, and the environment in which the individual acts." Identifying *process* as "the fact that these changes follow a pattern which can be described and analyzed" they suggest that it is useful for understanding that "changes in a structure are frequently not random or haphazard but follow definite patterns through time." [116] Similarly, Cochran calls for the use of such a "comprehensive and meaningful synthesis" by historians who utilize the social-scientific approach which "focuses attention on the aspects of the event that reveal the major dynamic of the culture, the uniformities rather than those features that appear to be most colorful or unique." [117] But, when the historian attempts to construct causal generalizations about the specific conjunctures in the structured process of historical events, he finds that diachronic historical causation is even more complicated than synchronic causation by (i) reciprocity, (ii) complexity, and (iii) variability.

(i) *Reciprocity*. In diachronic historical causation, reciprocity is an extension of the reversibility of sociocultural-motivational causes and effects which MacIver acknowledged as a complication in the postulate of causality for synchronic social-scientific analysis, e.g., standard of intelligence and standard of education. This is emphasized by Tapp when he declares that "not only are causes and effects interchangeable, but that it is often extremely difficult to know when a cause becomes an effect." [118] It is also acknowledged by Cohen as that which makes adequate causal general explanations "inherently difficult of attainment." Instead of being able to suppose that all institutions develop in a linear series in which their temporal priority can always be established, the historian must keep in mind that "many institutions are co-existent and continue to modify each other." [119]

(ii) *Complexity of historical causation*. Unless the historian adopts the non-causal approach of highly generalized philosophies of history (e.g., Hegel, Marx, Spengler), or a monocausal explanation of historical events in terms of an over-simplified linear succession, it would seem that he must presuppose the principle of multiple causation. To be sure, most social scientists must also proceed on the assumption of multiple causation; but some social scientists attempt to escape some of the difficulties this presents by resorting to statistical correlations. The historian, however, is not likely to follow this way out of the complications that arise from the complexity of historical causation. For the effective use of such statistical techniques would eliminate, or at least make peripheral, the specific conjunctures of events which the historian takes to be "the unique historical situation" as well as the significance of the consequences of the decisions made by outstanding personalities.

In order to escape from the infinite regress of considering all possible causal conditions back through the "totality of past human actions through time," the historian must be allowed to confine his analysis to a limited number of turning points or crucial changes which have contributed to and precipitated ascertainable conjunctures in the broader course of human events. But, as Gottschalk reminds his colleagues, "the immediate cause is not really a cause; it is merely the point in a chain of events, trends, influences, and forces at which the effect begins to become visible." The complexity of historical causation has similarly been acknowledged by all of the contributors to Bulletin 54: "A cause never operates except as a part of a complex or series." [120] Nagel's recognition of this situation and his elaboration of what it implies with respect to the historian's use of causal explanations is most instructive. Although even the natural sciences are not completely successful in ascertaining all of the necessary and sufficient causes of the effects they aim to explain, historical inquiry is less effective than any other kind of analysis, "since the full circumstances are often quite complex and numerous and are usually not known." Although vagueness and lack of precision "are often legitimate grounds for doubt concerning the validity of specific causal imputations in history," Nagel concludes, "there appears to be no compelling reason for converting such doubt into wholesale skepticism." [121]

Once the complexity of multiple causation has been acknowledged, the historian must realize that to reduce a variety of factors to only one determinant, or to omit all relevant conditions but one, or to underestimate any part of a complex conjuncture of events, is to distort history-as-actuality. Although Brockunier and Loewenberg report that "a prolific source of historical controversy is the problem of assigning weights to factors that have causal influence," nevertheless, if the historian acknowledges that his selection of causal factors is derived from his own estimate of what is most significant, then he is not disavowing this postulate. There are few, if any, historians who actually disagree with Block's claim that "the monism of cause can be for history only an impediment," since "history seeks for causal wave trains and is not afraid, since life shows them to be so, to find them multiple." [122]

(iii) *Variability of historical causation.* A causal analysis of the diachronic relation of past events is especially complicated by the factors of "chance" and uniqueness." If they hold for past human actions, they hold, of course, for the contemporary human situations to which all social-scientific constructs refer. But, whereas most non-historical behavioral analyses discount them or treat them only peripherally, the historian can not use a causal formula which does not fully take them into account. As we now consider each of these features in turn, we should keep in mind that the historian must presuppose a pluralistic conception of serially-determined chains of events. These chains may not be so interdependent that they can be monistically conceived within the context of a unitary scheme of interlocking aspects of a mutually determined whole. Mandelbaum has shown how this "essential pluralism, in which entities stand in partial but not complete relation to each other" is congruent with a molar conception of the unique combinations of events which a historian takes as the referent of his causal generalization in terms of a complex unity of multiple subevents: "The subevents are literally the determinate conditions of there being any event at all, for where there are no fibers there can be no strand of history." [123] Moreover, as Teggart has emphasized, without this pluralistic assumption there would be no basis for the comparative analysis upon which a causal approach depends.[124]

How can a historian refer to "chance" as a part of his causal explanation? Contrary to the assumption that the acknowledgment of contingency precludes causality, the broadly operational historian never implies that any event happened spontaneously or that any human action was ever unmotivated.

He assumes that each situation has been the outcome of its own specific temporal sequence of antecedent causal conditions which has a knowable interconnection with other corresponding causal sequences. When these various trains of events cross with a result that has been anticipated on the basis of what is known about each of them, the effect is explained by a pluralistic causal account in which "chance" is not ascribed. But, if temporal sequences intersect in a manner that was not expected, in the light of what was known about them separately and/or conjointly, then chance is imputed as one factor in the total explanation, along with the specification of the causal conditions within each of the specific chains of events.

Does the attribution to accident decrease with increased comprehension of the causal interconnection among these unilinear sequences? It would seem so, but fortuity with respect to the outcome of conjunctures precludes the possibility of ever eliminating contingencies to the extent that the causal necessity required for strict predictability could ever be established. This judgment is congruent with Cohen's claim that "accidents, like necessity, are thus relative to our system," [125] and with Gardiner's ascription of "chance to the valuable collision of two or more independent chains of causes.[126] It is most instructive to note Hook's definition of a chance event as the unpredictable happening "which has historical effects but not historical causes, e.g., the tidal wave at Lisbon." For this means that "chance events in history are not uncaused events but events, some of whose antecedents or causes are not directly related to determining strands or strands which they twist or snarl in ways that cannot be foretold by a knowledge of the earlier patterns of these strands alone." [127] Although this limitation has discouraged some historians from constructing causal generalizations, there are others like Brockunier and Loewenberg who assume that human behavior sufficiently exhibits "a partially predictable regularity" so that "history is not exclusively chaos or chance." Cochran, for example, acknowledges "chance event"; but he calls upon his colleagues to look for causal uniformities which "reveal the major dynamics of the culture." [128]

By treating each past situation as a unique whole the historian does not preclude causal generalizations even though he complicates their construction. The uniqueness lies in the particular way that the component elements of each specific situation are combined. Among the segments of each situation, however, there are some that are similar to the component segments of past and future situations. Moreover, there seems to be no inherent reason why the general pattern of causal relationships among the sub-events in one specific situation could not be sufficiently like that in another specific situation to make them comparable. Since even physical events do not recur in exactly the same way, it is only to similar properties of subsequent events that his constructs about "recurrent events" refer. Accordingly, when Aitken and Loewenberg emphasize that "no historical events can be utterly and completely unique," [129] they presuppose that the recurrence of similar elements in successive historical situations is sufficient to construct some causal generalizations for explaining why a total situation has occurred as it did.

Purposive causation is an ineradicable part of the historian's postulate of causality. Since past human actions constitute his subject matter, his adoption of either supernaturalistic predeterminism, or naturalistic predeterminism, or indeterminism, or relative self-determinism, is a necessary premise for explaining the deliberative decisions which are involved in the policy-making process to which so much of the historian's attention is directed. The selection of means to achieve preferred ends in the ends-means continuum of human actions would remain a mystery apart from the relatively self-deterministic assumption that persons with hopes, fears, ideas and aspirations do things to themselves under the causal conditions of their environmental factors which limit their alternatives and do things to them. No historian, therefore, can ignore Cohen's question: "Is human volition a verifiable causal element in history, and are there ascertainable causes that history can recognize for the ways in which human beings exercise the volition?" [130] For the historian to presuppose either predeterminism or indeterminism would be to render such a question meaningless.

The function of reflectively motivated decisions in human history has been emphasized by Tapp, when he declares that "intelligence would seem to be true cause in history" in those instances wherein "man has been able to assess more fully the possibilities for certain courses of action" and has acted "with a view to what he would like the future to be." This does not imply that every course of action is primarily determined by rational selection or that sociocultural, psychological, and natural determinants which shape any deliberative decision are ignored. The purposive causation exhibited in relatively self-determined goal-oriented behavior, however, is likely to be of more central concern. Consequently, there is required an idiographic-nomothetic approach such as that which Tapp presupposes, when he insists that a statesman "in being free does not break laws, for he cannot escape them." Instead, "he simply acts in a deliberate and purposive manner within the limits of the law." No indeterminist would agree with Tapp that an accounting for this kind of limited freedom "demands the deepest possible understanding of laws operating in history." [131]

Footnotes to Chapter 6 of Part Three

[1] Aristotle, *The Physics*, 26.

[2] Planck, *The Philosophy of Physics*, 76; *The Universe in the Light of Modern Physics*, 59.

[3] Frank, *Journal of Philosophy*, August, 1934, Vol. 31, pages 421-428.

[4] Born, *Atomic Physics*, 90.

[5] Heisenberg, *The Physical Principles of the Quantum Theory*, 3.

[6] Planck, *The Universe in the Light of Modern Physics*, 83.

[7] Reichenbach, "Probability Method in Social Science" *The Policy Sciences* (Lerner and Lasswell), 121.

[8] Planck, *Where is Science Going*, 158.

[9] MacIver, *Social Causation*, 52, 55, 100-101.

[10] Feigl, "Notes on Causality," *Readings in the Philosophy of Science* (Feigl and Brodbeck), 410-411.

[11] Northrop, *The Logic of the Sciences and the Humanities*, 215-216.

[12] Werkmeister, *A Philosophy of Science*, 277.

[13] Whitehead, *Modes of Thought*, 226. Cf. Nagel, "Causal Character of Modern Physical Theory," *Readings in the Philosophy of Science* (Feigl and Brodbeck), 419-437 and Nagel, *The Structure of Science*, 292-293, 316, 324, 334-335.

[14] Cohen, *The Meaning of Human History*, 112.

[15] MacIver, *Social Causation*, 23, 26, 30.

[16] Ibid., 23.

[17] Ibid., 163.

[18] Ibid., 68.

[19] Ibid., 33-34.

[20] MacIver, *The Elements of Social Science*, 12. Cf. Neurath *Foundations of the*

Unity of Science, International Encyclopedia of Unified Sciences, Vol. III, No. 1, pp. 20-22.

[21] Feigl, "Notes on Causality," *Readings in the Philosophy of Science* (Feigl and Brodbeck), 410.

[22] MacIver, *Social Causation*, 172.

[23] Hook, "Determinism." *Encyclopedia of the Social Sciences*, Vol. 5, page 114.

[24] Hook, *The Hero in History*, 153.

[25] MacIver, *Social Causation*, 306.

[26] Allport, in *Toward a General Theory of Action* (Parsons and Shils), 368, 372, 384-385.

[27] Tolman in *Toward a General Theory of Action* (Parsons and Shils), 284.

[28] Tolman in *Psychological Theory* (Marx), 413-414, 418, 424-425.

[29] Spence in *Psychological Theory* (Marx), 177.

[30] Skinner in *Psychological Theory* (Marx), 448.

[31] Spence in *Psychological Theory* (Marx), 176.

[32] Allport in *Psychological Theory* (Marx), 161-164.

[33] Allport, *The Nature of Personality*, 89-91.

[34] Tolman in *Toward a General Theory of Action* (Parsons and Shils), 321-322.

[35] Allport, *Becoming*, 40-54, 65, 66-67.

[36] Sartre, *Existentialism*, 37-38, 47, 89.

[37] Watson, *Behaviorism*, 11.

[38] Murphy, *Personality*, 644-645.

[39] Brunswik in *Psychological Theory* (Marx), 187-188, 191, 193-197, 199-201.

[40] Hull in *Psychological Theory* (Marx), 204-206, 214.

[41] Lewin in *Psychological Theory* (Marx), 308.

[42] Newcomb, "Studying Social Behavior," *Methods of Psychology* (Andrews), 664.

[43] Sherif, *An Outline of Social Psychology*, 1.

[44] Murray in *Toward a General Theory of Action* (Parsons and Shils), 438.

[45] Sears in *Toward a General Theory of Action* (Parsons and Shils), 469-471.

[46] Newcomb, *Social Psychology*, 32-33.

[47] Krech and Crutchfield, *Theory and Problems of Social Psychology*, 31. Cf. Scheerer, "Cognitive Theory," *Handbook of Social Psychology* (Lindzey), Vol. I, 94-109 for an instructive discussion of molar causality.

[48] Allport in *Toward a General Theory of Action* (Parsons and Shils), 368-372.

[49] Bierstedt, *The Social Order*, 498.

[50] Lundberg, *Sociology*, 7; *Foundations of Sociology*, 20-21, 54, 79-80, 83, 122-123, 222, 260. Cf. MacIver, *Social Causation*, 29.

[51] Timasheff, "Order, Causality, Conjuncture," *Symposium on Sociological Theory* (Gross), 146-147, 153, 155.

[52] Parsons, *The Structure of Social Action*, 750; *For a Science of Social Man* (Gillin), 68.

[53] Bierstedt, *The Social Order*, 508.

[54] Ibid., 508, 502.

[55] Kroeber in *Appraisal of Anthropology Today* (Tax), 367, 371.

[56] Tylor, *Researches into the Early History of Mankind*.

[57] Redfield in *Anthropology Today* (Kroeber), 733-735.

58 Linguistics is a closely allied field which presupposes systematization in its conception of configurational patterns wherein, as Whorf explains, "there are no variables but, instead, abrupt alternations from one configuration to another" much in the manner of quantum phenomena. (Whorf, *Four Articles on Metalinguistics*, 11). The relevance of such a systematic interrelationship of symbols for anthropology has been brought out by Sapir: "Language is felt to be a perfect symbolic system, in a perfectly homogeneous medium, for the handling of all references and meanings that a given culture is capable of, whether these be in the form of actual communications or in that of such ideal substitutes of communication as thinking." (*Culture, Language, and Personality*, 6). Kroeber, however, is not as convinced as some anthropologists about the significance of linguistics as it has been developed to date for understanding culture. (See Kroeber in *An Appraisal of Anthropology Today* [Tax], 368-370.) The present author does not have the competence or space to elaborate here. For pertinent discussions, see *Anthropology Today* (Kroeber) 265 for Greenberg's "Historical Linguistics and Unwritten Language"; and 807 for Hass' "The Application of Linguistics to Language Teaching."
59 Malinowski, *The Dynamics of Cultural Change*, 42-51.
60 See Murdock, *Social Structure*.
61 Nadel, *Foundations of Social Anthropology*, 207, 213, 216-217, 256-258.
62 Kroeber and Kluckhohn, *Culture, a Critical Review of Concepts and Definitions* (Peabody Museum, Harvard) Vol. XLVII, No. 1, 1952, page 161 ff.
63 White, *The Science of Culture*, 144.
64 White, *The Evolution of Culture*, 18-19, 24, 26, 27, 30.
65 Ibid., 14.
66 Hallowell, in *For a Science of Social Man* (Gillin), 200, 204.
67 White, *The Science of Culture*, 167-168. Cf. pages 100, 192.
68 Bidney, *Theoretical Anthropology*, 16-18, 79-82, 105-106, 115-116, 334.
69 Kroeber, *The Nature of Culture*, 132.
70 Linton, *The Cultural Background of Personality*, 5.
71 Kroeber, "History of Anthropological Thought," *Current Anthropology* (Thomas), 294.
72 Huxley, "Evolution, Cultural and Biological," *Current Anthropology* (Thomas), 3, 16, 11-2, 13, 19, 21, 22. For other discussions of cultural evolution, compare *Current Anthropology* (Thomas), pages 31 ff. for Sears, 61 ff. for Eisley, and 277 ff. for Howells.
73 Lange, "The Scope and Method of Economics," *Readings in the Philosophy of Science* (Feigl and Brodbeck), 747-748. Originally published in the *Review of Economic Studies*, 13, 1945-46.
74 Pigou, *Economics of Welfare*, 10-11, 127-130.
75 Clark, J. M., *The Ethical Basis of Economic Freedom*, 9, 20, 30.
76 Parsons in *Toward a General Theory of Action* (Parsons and Shils), 198.
77 Marshall, *Principles of Economics*, Book I, pp. 36-37.
78 Jevons, *The Principles of Science*, 759-761.
79 Spiethoff in *Enterprise and Secular Change* (Lane and Riemersma), 449-450.
80 Mitchell, *Business Cycles, the Problem and Its Setting*, 54.

81 Kapp, "Economics and the Behavioral Sciences," *Kyklos*, Vol. VIII, 1957, pp. 211-212.
82 Katona, "Expectations and Decisions in Economic Behavior," *The Policy Sciences* (Lerner and Lasswell), 221-233.
83 Keynes, *The General Theory of Employment, Interests, and Money.*
84 Means, *Progress Report, National Resources Committee*, 2. See Gruchy, *Modern Economic Thought*, 580-581. Cf. Galbraith, *American Capitalism; The Concept of Countervailing Power.*
85 Commons, *Institutional Economics*, 719.
86 Robbins, *An Essay on the Nature and Significance of Economic Science*, 38.
87 Gruchy, *Modern Economic Thought*, 602.
88 MacIver, *Social Causation*, 169-170.
89 Spiethoff, "Pure Theory and Gestalt Theory," *Enterprise and Secular Change* (Lane and Riemersma), 449-450.
90 Commons, *Institutional Economics*, 723, 738.
91 Easton, *The Political System*, 68, 97-98, 160, 218-219.
92 Key, *Politics, Parties, and Pressure Groups*, 21.
93 Easton, *The Political System*, 53.
94 Ibid., 291.
95 Key, *Politics, Parties, and Pressure Groups*, 5.
96 Lasswell and Kaplan, *Power and Society*, 10.
97 Ibid., 240.
98 Garceau, *American Political Science Review*, Vol. 45, 1951, pp. 69-70.
99 Pennock, *American Political Science Review*, Vol. 45, 1951, pages 1081, 1083.
100 Perry, *American Political Science Review*, June 1950, pages 394, 406.
101 Easton, *The Political System*, 291-292, 302-303.
102 Herring, *American Political Science Review*, Dec. 1953, page 973. See Dewey "Democracy," *Readings in Philosophy* (Randall, Buchler, Shirk), 347.
103 Brockunier and Loewenberg, Bulletin 64, pages 86-87.
104 Mandelbaum, *The Problem of Historical Knowledge*, 239. Cf. page 259.
105 Cohen, "Causation and Its Application to History," *The Journal of the History of Ideas*, Vol. 3, 1942, pages 12, 14.
106 Brockunier and Loewenberg, Bulletin 64, page 146. Cf. Gottschalk, *Understanding History*, 210.
107 Cohen, *The Meaning of Human History*, 112.
108 Hook, Bulletin 54, page 112.
109 Simiand, "Causal Interpretation and Historical Research," *Enterprise and Secular Change* (Lane and Riemersma), 479-480.
110 Bidney, *Theoretical Anthropology*, 334.
111 Cohen, *The Meaning of Human History*, 221.
112 Brockunier and Loewenberg, Bulletin 64, page 95.
113 Cohen, "Causation and Its Application to History," *The Journal of the History of Ideas*, Vol. 2, 1942, pages 10, 14.
114 Brockunier and Loewenberg, Bulletin 64, pages 87-88.
115 Clough, Bulletin 64, page 111. Cf. MacIver, *Social Causation*, 163.
116 Brockunier and Loewenberg, Bulletin 64, pages 95-97.

117 Cochran, Bulletin 64, page 163.
118 Tapp, *The Journal of Philosophy*, XVIX, Jan. 31, 1952, pages 73-77.
119 Cohen, *The Meaning of Human History*, Chapter 8.
120 Bulletin 54, page 137.
121 Nagel, "The Logic of Historical Analysis," *Readings in the Philosophy of Science* (Feigl and Brodbeck), 697, 699-700. Originally published in the *Scientific Monthly*, 74, 1952, page 169.
122 Brockunier and Loewenberg, Bulletin 64, page 147. See Block, *Reflections on the Historian's Craft*, 103.
123 Mandelbaum, *The Problem of Historical Knowledge*, 225, 274.
124 Teggart, "Causation in Historical Events," *The Journal of the History of Ideas*, Vol. 3, 1942, page 6.
125 Cohen, "Causation and Its Application to History," *The Journal of the History of Ideas*, Vol. 2, 1942, pages 10, 14.
126 Gardiner, *The Nature of Historical Explanation*, 111-112.
127 Hook, Bulletin 54, page 116.
128 Cochran, Bulletin 64, page 163.
129 Aitken and Loewenberg, Bulletin 64, page 25.
130 Cohen, *The Meaning of Human History*, 120.
131 Tapp, *The Journal of Philosophy*, XVIX, Jan. 31, 1952, pages 73-77.

7 *The Fifth Postulate of the Meaning-Situation of Reflective Inquiry (Coherence)*

Coherence, i.e., consistency and adequacy is the generic logical criterion of verification from which specific criteria and techniques for empirically testing the deduced implication of hypotheses are derived.

A. *The General Significance of the Fifth Postulate*

As a comprehensive ideational framework the criterion of *coherence* defines the aim of reflective inquiry and provides the standard for verifying the reasonable acceptability of the explanatory and predictive generalization which the scientist constructs. Recall Einstein's declaration that "to obtain even a partial solution the scientist must collect the unordered facts available and make them coherent and understandable by creative thought." [1] This logical criterion is *generic* in the sense that it sets forth the broadly operational requirements for the hypothetical-deductive procedures of (a) the deductive technique by which the implications of explanatory-predictive hypotheses are elaborated and (b) the inductive techniques by which these deduced implications are empirically tested. The nature and function of these techniques, which are derived from this generic criterion, will be examined later in the elaboration of the third stage of the hypothetical-deductive method. Since we are concerned here with the meaning-situation, rather than the knowledge-situation in which such techniques are operative, we shall confine our present discussion to this generic criterion which identifies what kind of broadly operational knowledge is meaningful.

When a broader operationalist appeals to the generic logical criterion of coherence in order to verify a generalization, he must answer two questions: Can the analytical aspects of his hypothetical construct meet the demands of *logical consistency* in order to be formally valid? Can the substantive aspects of his hypothetical construct meet the *causal adequacy* in order to be observationally confirmed? On the one hand, *consistency* is regulated by the mathematical-logical rules of validity to which the scientist must conform in order to avoid contradictory assertions among hypotheses within a system, as well as between his proposed hypothesis and the implications he has deduced from it in accordance with the hypothetical syllogism (If . . . then). On the other hand, *adequacy* is ascertained by the empirical testing of these consistently-deduced implications by such specific techniques as are appropriately applicable to the kind of observational data under analysis. This matter of appropriate applicability needs special emphasis by reference to our earlier distinction between narrower and broader operationalism.

Narrower operational claims about purely observational testing notwithstanding, it is assumed here that the technique or techniques for empirically testing the implications of scientific generalizations must be adapted to the peculiar nature of the subject matter. This broadly operational approach does not minimize the use of laboratory experiments and/or statistical devices wherever they are applicable without distorting the relevant data. But it is not in terms of these physical manipulations and purely quantitative measurements that verification is defined. For this we must use coherence as the comprehensive ideational scheme of logical requirements which designs what techniques the investigator can appropriately apply and what kind of questions he should be seeking to answer. Accordingly, the natural scientist and the experimental psychologist attempt to confirm the comparatively greater adequacy of one hypothesis over alternatives by the techniques of experimental testing and/or controlled observation with such statistical correlations as refine these precise operations. The social scientist, however, is compelled by the nature of his sociocultural and motivational data to use for empirical testing of alternative hypotheses the less precise technique of comparative case analysis, which provides some relatively controlled observation. In dealing with motivational data he may also be required to use introspective projection. In order to distinguish the latter two less precise techniques from the others, we have designated them as *experiential* rather than *experimental* techniques of *empirical* testing.

Regardless of which of these techniques is used in the knowledge-situation, each is justified by its function as a means to the end of a coherent system of constructs which identifies in the meaning-situation what kind of knowledge is *reasonably acceptable*. For *reasonably acceptable* we can use the word *true*, if it is clearly understood that no verified hypothesis is ever so completely confirmed that it is beyond correction, modification, or abandonment when reasoning or evidence so demand. The awareness that a completely coherent system of scientific generalizations is always an unattainable objective does not generate the fruitless uncertainty of negative scepticism. Rather, the appeal to a progressively expanding coherence elicits the positive sceptic's fruitful uncertainty that is necessary for his pursuit of an ideal of truth so infinite that no mind can ever fully reach it.

In order to determine the comparatively *greater adequacy* of one hypothesis over other proposals, its *relevancy, systematic congruency,* and *fruitfulness* must be shown. These three requirements for the empirical testing of the consistently-deduced implications of hypotheses by inductive techniques might be said to be *secondary criteria* which are derived from the generic criterion of coherence. Let us briefly elaborate what each of the secondary criteria demands.

(a) Relevancy means that, to be adequate, the hypothesis must be inferred from a range of observations that is sufficiently wide so that no data which are relevant to the question which instigated the inquiry are arbitrarily excluded.

(b) In order to be adequate, the hypothesis must be a harmonious part of a comprehensive system of generalizations which, to date, is the most congruent conceptual and theoretical integration of the total context of the data to which the inquiry is applicable. There are times, however, when a scientific system of long standing must be re-evaluated (Newtonian by Einstein) or replaced (Ptolmaic by Copernicus) in favor of a more reasonably acceptable system of ideas; one which is congruent with the new hypothesis that does not fit in to the heretofore established system. Since such cases are rare, it is to be expected that incongruent hypotheses which point toward intellectual revolutions should be extensively re-examined by replication.

Although the systematic integration of hypotheses is no substitute for empirical testing, it is often ignored by those pure researchers who unjustifiably fear that the harmonious unification of new and old hypotheses into an integrated system will minimize the importance of observation and will stifle independent inquiry. Social scientists should think, however, of Parson's statement that "the results of analysis on the different levels, in terms of the various frames of reference, etc., are capable of being integrated into a coherent body of knowledge." The process of achieving systematic congruency presupposes the second postulate; that is, regardless of how well established any system of ideas may be, it can always be revised. Since Parsons has led the advance of the social-scientific endeavor toward the fulfilment of this requirement for systematizing as an essential aspect of verification, it is instructive to recall his own acknowledgment that no system is definitive: "It cannot be maintained, either that in the formulation assumed in the present study this theoretical system is complete, or that it will not, with the further development of the social sciences, be superseded by one as radically different from it as it is from the systems from which it has emerged." [2] In short, without this demand for systematic congruency, there would be no grounds for the persistent efforts of successive scientists to contribute to cumulative analysis.

(c) In order to be adequate, the hypothesis must be fruitful for further inquiry, i.e., it should give rise to questions which in turn might lead to a fuller comprehension of the context to which the hypothesis directly refers. At least potentially, if not actually, the hypothesis should also contribute to the cross-fertilization of other related contexts.

It is necessary to emphasize that logical consistency is necessary, but it is not sufficient without empirical adequacy for verifying the coherence of knowledge-claims. The relation between the separable but interdependent requirements of consistency and those of adequacy is taken by Hempel and Oppenheim to be the basic pattern by which scientific explanations are verified in accordance with both their "logical conditions of adequacy" and "empirical conditions of adequacy." [3] Since among philosophers the absolute idealists have used the word "coherence" to mean logical consistency without the empirical requirement of adequacy, it should be understood that *causal adequacy* in terms of relevancy, systematic congruency, and fruitfulness, is also required in this postulate of coherence. A hypothesis that meets only the demand of logical consistency would be formally valid; but there would be no assurance that it was not substantively sterile. Moreover, two contradictory systems of hypotheses might both be equally logically consistent, e.g., the Ptolmaic geocentric theory and the Copernican heliocentric theory; but in order to confirm the implications of one rather than the other, scientists had to undertake empirical testing to ascertain which system was more adequate. Although absolute validity, which means that there is no logical contradiction, can be established, this should not be mistaken for certainty with respect to truth. When substantive truth is identified in terms of a total coherence, as previously shown, it can at best be only approximated by reasonably acceptable but always revisionable hypotheses.

The function of the generic logical criterion of coherence in the scientific process of verification might be likened unto the function of a constitution in the political process of authoritatively allocating rights and duties. Just as the aim of the specific laws of a political community is derived from the constitution which defines the conception of what governmentally-legalized relations between persons should be, so the aim of the specific techniques of the hypothetical-deductive method is derived from the criterion of coherence which defines the conception of what the epistemologically-dualistic relations between constructs and objective referents should be. Neither the juridical procedure nor the reflective procedure ever fully realizes its respective ideal of justice or truth. When those intrinsic ideals are acknowledged as objectives, however, they determine the policies which juridical and reflective decisions aim to implement. Accordingly, the way in which a constitution provides a systematic framework for political legislation and adjudication, corresponds to the way in which the criterion of coherence provides a synoptic pattern for scientific construction and verification.

In concluding the elaboration of the term *coherence*, it might be well for us to re-emphasize that it is a postulate in the meaning-situation of all reflective inquiry which can not be verified in the knowledge-situation of any particular scientific analysis. Unless the scientist adopts this assumption, his observational, inferential, verificative, and integrative techniques have no significance. But no one or more of these techniques can substantively prove the truth of what their hypothetical-deductive combination presupposes. Nor can the truth of coherence be analytically demonstrated beyond the assertion of circular arguments. The assertion that the criterion of coherence rules out incoherent statements as false, is no more convincing than the parallel statement that the criterion of self-evidence is self-evidently true. How can the broader operationalist show that a person forsakes the pursuit of truth, if he adopts a non-operationalistic criterion by appealing to dogmatic authority; or, to mystical intuition; or, to naïve sense impressions; or, to naïve pragmatism; or, only to an *a priori* system of universal and necessary principles; or, only to quantified sense-data? The broader operationalist cannot do so through any amount of reasoning or presentation of evidence. As with constitutions and definitions, the generic criterion of coherence, as well as any other criterion for verification, can also be justified as a postulate only by showing that it is more fruitful than alternative postulates with respect to the purpose of those who adopt it.

B. *The Significance of the Fifth Postulate for Individual Psychology*

All psychologists seem to agree with Marx that "testability is the absolutely essential characteristic of any scientifically useful hypothesis" [4]; but they seem to be divided into narrower and broader operationalism with respect to the requirements for verification. The narrower operationalists are the molecular experimentalists who would confine empirical testing to physical manipulations with the purely quantitative techniques. These were developed by Watson in terms of the neurophysiological response to independent variables. They were logically justified by the logical positivists. The broader operationalists are the molar experimentalists and the personologists who find that such a restrictive mode of empirical testing serves in some cases, but that in others, it so arbitrarily excludes data which are relevant to the hypothesis undergoing verification that it distorts the factual situation of goal-seeking behavior to which the construct refers. As Gordon Allport has characterized this radically empirical criterion of verification, "it is not sufficiently iconic with our subject matter." [5] Not only does the molar approach require the introduction of an intervening variable in order to deal with purposive behavior as "an emergent phenomenon that has descriptive and defining properties of its own" [6]; but it also makes it necessary for the molar psychologist to formulate some ideational framework for verifying his explanatory and predictive generalizations.

Hull has called for a generic logical criterion like coherence: "Actually hardly a detail even of experimental procedure lacks its logical aspect." When the experimentalist manipulates variables, he is seeking to ascertain the relation of antecedent and consequent conditions which are prescribed by the logical relation of implication, i.e., "if such and such antecedent conditions occur, then such and such consequences will follow." In his search for a generic criterion as an ideal "goal or state of things to be striven for and to be approximated as closely as possible," Hull has adopted the formulation of a verificative system of three principles which, with only slight terminological differences, expresses what we have meant by the demands of the generic logical criterion of coherence: "the postulates shall be (1) as *few* as possible, (2) *consistent* with each other, and (3) *sufficient* to mediate the deduction, as theorems, of all the relevant facts." [7] In addition to the rationalistic requirement of *formal consistency* Hull's statement about *sufficiency* pertains to the requirements for ascertaining the greater empirical *adequacy* of one hypothesis over others. This suggests the applicability of the substantive criteria of *relevancy, systematic congruency,* and *fruitfulness.* Let us briefly consider some of the claims of other psychologists as well as Hull who have made the demands of these secondary criteria more explicit.

Relevancy is acknowledged by those psychologists who, as mentioned above, insist that hypotheses must be derived from all of the data that are relevant to the particular problem to be solved. Not only Watsonian behaviorists but also some psychoanalysts, as well as any other proponents of an overly-circumscribed conception of initial data, fail to meet this demand. This is implied in Gordon Allport's declaration that "addiction to machines, rats, or infants leads us to overplay those features of human behavior that are peripheral, signal-oriented, or genetic" so that "it causes us to underplay those features that are central, future-oriented, and symbolic." [8] There is also Maslow's criticism of "means-centered" approaches which foster the arbitrariness of "fitting problems to techniques rather than vice-versa." [9]

Hull himself emphasizes that a hypothesis must be a harmonious part of a comprehensive system of generalizations which to date is the most adequate conceptual integration of the total context to which the specific psychological process of verification is applicable: "The principle of sufficiency is the critical consideration in evaluating the postulates of a scientific system" which "means that the postulates must be sufficient to permit the derivation of the theorems which will state the nature of the outcome of all the dynamic situations possible of combinations from the conditions implicit in the several postulates as those under which each is operative." [10]

There seems to be widespread agreement among psychologists that, in order to be adequate, a hypothesis must be fruitful for further inquiry. Marx, for example, contends that "the only scientific test of any type of theoretical approach is its ability to generate fruitful experiments or other observations and to lead to more satisfactory and more comprehensive theories." [11] Cantril similarly insists that, in order to maintain the "constant flow of one hypothesis from another, with each hypothesis trying to go beyond established formulations in its inclusiveness," it is essential for psychological verification to require that "an hypothesis must be tested both in terms of its ability to predict immediate events and its promise of leading to further, more adequate hypotheses." [12] Krech and Klein designate the requirement of coherence as the "surplus value" which a theory must possess in order to be verified: "An adequate theory is one which encompasses all the known correlations with the most parsimonious scheme of constructs, and allows of new possibilities of correlations." [13]

C. *The Significance of the Fifth Postulate for Social Psychology*

Despite the *ad hoc* character of most present social-psychological inquiry, Newcomb claims that it should aim at a comprehensive, ideational framework within which its explanatory and predictive generalizations might be verified "in terms of a single body of co-herent concepts and principles." [14] Although it is not evident that all social psychologists have explicitly adopted this postulate of co-herence as a generic logical criterion, it does seem to underlie the verificative procedures of those who have been strongly influenced by Lewin's conception of field theory as "a method of analyzing causal relations and building scientific constructs." [15] As Deutsch has shown, "in this constructive approach the meaning of any con-cept is determined by its relation to other concepts in the system of concepts of which it is a part" so that "the reality of specific phe-nomena are derivable or constructable from the relevant constructive elements or constructs." [16] Consistency, on the one hand, and the secondary criteria of relevancy, systematic congruency, and fruitful-ness for determining adequacy, on the other, seem to be clearly im-plied as requirements for verifying such inferences about causal rela-tions as they are meaningfully connected within the context of broader generalizations.

D. *The Significance of the Fifth Postulate for Sociology*

When Zetterberg describes the process of verification in the con-struction of sociological theories as "an attempt to investigate whether a theory is probable or improbable," he designates the re-quirements which we have identified in terms of logical consistency and causal adequacy as the essential modes of the generic criterion of coherence: "We are going to call a theory probable if: (a) its hypotheses are un-contradictory, and (b) its hypotheses are empiri-cally true or probable." [17] Despite the divergence of the theoretical and the research approaches in sociology, the proponents of each agree that only knowledge which is thus coherently verified is meaningful. Speaking for the theoreticians, MacIver declares that sociology should "advance beyond description and classification, and 'measurement' to the coherence and articulation that distinguish every developed science." [18] As researchers, Lazarsfeld and Rosenberg prescribe that "once the matter of these basic units or variables has been dealt with, the next major problem is obviously the interrelationship of such variables in a coherent analysis." [19]

Lundberg acknowledges the necessity for adopting this postulate of a coherent verificative scheme when he accounts for the lack of scientifically significant sociological research: "The main reason appears to be that there exists for sociology no coherent body of scientific theory with reference to which research can be undertaken or evaluated." Only when meaningful knowledge is so conceived can it be maintained that "the backbone of any science is a series of relevant, verifiable, consistent generalizations called principles, or laws," and that "to attain such a set of principles it is necessary first to formulate a set of hypotheses and second to test them empirically." [20]

In connection with his distinction between nominal and real definitions, Bierstedt has emphasized how consistency is necessary, but is not sufficient for verifying the substantive truth about concepts which "have referents in the empirical world." Although it is important to establish the formal validity of a merely conceptual scheme, it "requires only a stipulation" and is "sterile unless it can produce a theory." Nevertheless, Bierstedt acknowledges the significance of such a conceptual system as that of Dodd for correlating "the dimensions of society" in terms of the mathematical equations and symbolic logic of the S-system which is notable for "its precision, its parsimony, its consistency, and its comprehensiveness." [21]

The demand for adequacy beyond formal consistency is called for by both MacIver and Lundberg despite their disagreement about what kind of causal variables are relevant. When MacIver designates causal attribution as the "progressive revision of an hypothesis," he maintains that the "process of revision . . . is also a process of verification" which provides the tests by means of which "we can check the adequacy and the validity of the causal hypothesis." [22] Similarly, Lundberg insists that "the tests of the adequacy (truth) of any system at any given time will in any event be determined by certain empirical tests, notably whether the system affords a rationale of the adjustments that have to be made and whether it aids in planning these adjustments." [23] Other sociologists have pointed out the need for the secondary criteria of relevance, systematic congruency, and fruitfulness which provides such a rationale.

The principle of relevancy, which MacIver presupposes in his assertion that "the causal conjuncture must be seen in its specific relation to the specific environment," is also assumed by Merton, who advocates both precision and logical coherence, i.e., formal consistency. Nonetheless Merton warns that "care must be taken to see that significant problems are not thus inadvertently blotted from view." He declares that "the pressure for logical consistency has at times invited logomachy and sterile 'theorizing' inasmuch as the assumptions contained in the system of analysis are so far removed from empirical referents or involve such high abstractions as not to permit of empirical inquiry." [24]

The principle of systematic congruency is widely acknowledged by sociologists who insist that to be verified a hypothesis must be able to be included as an harmonious part of a comprehensive scheme of generalizations which, to date, is the most adequate theoretical integration of the total context of data to which the inquiry is applicable. As MacIver contends, "to be more understandable a causal explanation of social behavior must be more coherent with what knowledge we already possess regarding the responses of human beings to the conditions under which they live." [25] Merton refers to this criteria as "the internal coherence of a theory" which has "much the same function" as making predictive inferences more precise for "reducing the likelihood that competing theories can adequately account for the same data." This, of course, is no substitute for empirical testing; but, "the integrated theory sustains a larger measure of confirmation than is the case with distinct and unrelated hypotheses, thus accumulating a greater weight of evidence." [26] Without the appeal to this secondary criteria of internal coherence, there would be much less point for sociologists to undertake as much "replication" as they do. For, as Rose says, in this procedure they either repeat "a study of a given problem with research procedures and measuring devices as similar to the original ones as possible, but with a different sample of cases" or they "test the conclusion of a previous study, using any scientifically proper research procedure and measuring devices with the new cases." [27]

Unlike a nineteenth-century systematizer (e.g., Spencer), contemporary sociologists agree that any hypothesis or system of hypotheses must point beyond itself so that it is fruitful for further inquiry. Thus, as MacIver warns, "the systems we construct do not integrate all the manifestations we discover within them," so that "the verification of any significant hypothesis of social causation is never complete, but only approximate." [28] It is necessary for the sociologist to assume that his explanatory-predictive generalizations must lead to the fuller comprehension of a more inclusive generalization about that particular context and must contribute to the understanding of other related contexts. As Merton emphasizes, "it is well known that verified predictions derived from a theory do not 'prove' or 'demonstrate' that theory; they merely supply a measure of confirmation, for it is always possible that alternative hypotheses drawn from different theoretic systems can also account for the predicted phenomena." [29]

E. The Significance of the Fifth Postulate for Anthropology

As an epistemological postulate, coherence is adopted by Bidney as the generic logical criterion of verification which *should* define the objective of anthropological inquiry. In order to construct "a coherent, universal, logical concept which in practice may be verified by the consequences to which it leads" it will be necessary for anthropologists "to acknowledge that an adequate and scientific definition is one that provides a logically coherent, as well as practically verifiable, concept—which connotes the essential properties of an object and at the same time denotes the practical epistemological means of its own verification." [30] For the most part, however, as Murdock reports, anthropologists have not been concerned with formulating and conforming to a logical criterion for verifying explanatory-predictive hypotheses: "When it comes to the formulation and testing of hypotheses, anthropologists reveal little comprehension of the requisites of a viable scientific theory and even less of the methods which science has devised for putting such a theory to the test." [31]

There are growing signs that some anthropologists are moving away from the imaginative depiction of cultural phenomena, which requires only the collection and description of data, to the more intellectual construction of explanatory generalizations which requires coherence as a criterion. Nadel, for example, reports that "in anthropology we are only just beginning to marshal our facts for analysis; we are still operating with limited regularities established for narrow and disconnected collections of 'cases examined.' " He contends, nevertheless, that in order to achieve verifiable assertions "these limited and disconnected regularities must be unified and built into embracing ones, though we cannot as yet foresee the end result." If anthropologists are to advance beyond the description of "simple correlations" to the construction of scientific explanations of "complicated interconnections," Nadel contends, they must "think along new lines" which means we "must not only widen our knowledge but also learn to frame it in a new way." [32] Similarly when Kroeber calls for a new approach, he explicitly advocates the generic logical criterion of coherence. Instead of an "aesthetic comprehension" he recommends an "intellectual comprehension," which "is aiming at an intelligible accord with reality, resting on both specific evidence and on broad coherent theory." [33] Consistency in terms of absence of self-contradictions and adequacy in terms of relevancy, systematic congruency, and fruitfulness are clearly implied. Let us consider some other statements which deal more specifically with each of these secondary criteria.

Anthropologists who are working toward the establishment of the criterion of coherence acknowledge the necessity for achieving the kind of deductive consistency which is exhibited in Whorf's linguistic analysis; but they also insist that it is not sufficient for obtaining substantively true generalizations. Such a demand for going beyond formal consistency to empirical adequacy is expressed by Kroeber and Kluckhohn: "The test of the validity of 'least common denominators' or 'highest common factors' will, of course, be the extent to which they not only make the phenomena more intelligible but also make reasonably accurate predictions of cultural change under specified conditions." [34] In another place Kroeber recognizes that "to take a series of aesthetic judgments and weld them together into an intellectually satisfying coherence," is difficult. Nevertheless, he insists, that "an adequate intellectual theory system has evidently got to conform to the extended reality of nature also." [35]

The requirement that anthropological generalizations must be derived from the specific kind of data that are relevant to the kind of hypotheses the anthropologist is attempting to verify, has been emphasized by Herskovits. He recognizes that "fundamental to scientific procedure is the principle that data must be presented in such a manner that they can be checked by independent observers"; but he also insists that this requirement must be implemented for the purpose of "the sciences that deal with human social life." The use of purely objective techniques that allow public observation is desirable, but it should not be used so exclusively that it distorts the data or excludes some that are pertinent: "For if the need to conduct research so as to enable it to be repeated is accepted as a basic tenet of science, it is just as basic to recognize and admit the limitations of a technique which yields results that, despite their appearance of regularity and accuracy, are, at base, spurious." [36]

Systematic congruency is a verificative principle for anthropologists; but, instead of primarily subsuming their constructs under nomothetic universal generalizations, they usually integrate the cultural phenomena idiographically in terms of the internal congruency of a specific cultural pattern. Redfield points out that the verification of "an account of a culture or system of social institutions" is satisfied "only in part by the correspondences between the more comprehensive propositions and the documentation offered"; for the anthropologist seems to be more persuaded by the "congruence of the parts within a whole conceived." In other words, "it is as if in the establishment of 'truth' about a culture or a personality, a part is played by an act of apprehension of the totality on the part of him who accepts the presentation as true." [37]

The fruitfulness of a hypothesis, among other criteria of its reasonable acceptability, is presupposed by Bidney when he recommends going beyond the merely descriptive stage of formulating constructs in terms of cultural pluralism to comparative analysis which might provide "significant generalizations concerning the conditions of the cultural process and the values of civilization." [38]

F. *The Significance of the Fifth Postulate for Economics*

The postulate of coherence as a generic logical criterion for verifying the generalizations of theoretical economics has been acknowledged by Lange in his previously quoted description of the scope and method of economics: "Theoretical economics puts the pattern of uniformity in a coherent system." It is necessary for the theoretical economist to meet the demand of *formal consistency* when he presents "the laws of economics as a deductive set of propositions derived by the rules of logic (and of mathematics) from a few basic propositions." Although it is necessary to derive such theorems from such assumptions or postulates, nevertheless, it is not sufficient for verifying their substantive truth. For this he must show that his formally valid constructs are *more causally and/or statistically adequate* than alternative explanatory-predictive generalizations: "The theorems, in turn, are subjected to test by empirical observation." But when economic inquiry becomes operational in fulfilling the demands of adequacy, its synthetic propositions cannot be established with the kind of logical certainty which characterizes the purely formal validity of its purely analytical propositions. Consequently, Lange raises this question: "What is to be considered as an acceptable degree of approximation inducing us to accept a hypothesis as 'true' and what degree of approximation is to be judged as insufficient, making us reject the hypothesis as incompatible with the facts?" According to Lange, "the question can be answered only in terms of a procedure of *verification* (testing) which establishes rules according to which hypotheses are accepted as 'empirically verified' or rejected as 'empirically unverified' or 'empirically refuted.' " [39]

Machlup's description of the process of economic verification is more inductive-deductive than Lange's which we have seen to be more deductive-inductive: "The hypothesis is *tested* by a two-step procedure: first deducing from it, and the factual assumptions with which it is combined, all the conclusions that can be inferred, and, second, confronting these conclusions with data obtained from observation of the phenomena concerned." Accordingly, if the deduced implications of a hypothesis are not refuted, i.e., "a reasonable correspondence is found between the deduced and the observed," then "the hypothesis is confirmed." [40]

Whether or not there is any significant difference between Lange's and Machlup's descriptions of the verificative process, they both presuppose the essential requirements of *formal consistency* and *substantive adequacy* as a two-fold postulate which cannot itself be formally or substantively verified. As Schumpeter has emphasized, economic analysis will become more refined with respect to verification to the degree "to which increasingly more rigorous standards of consistency and adequacy will be applied." [41] But, as Hutchison has insisted, this and other logical criteria of verification are postulates which are justified as fulfilling the scientific demands of empirical testability only if we define them as such.[42]

When Gruchy points out the three criteria to which economic doctrines should conform in order to be verified, he designates the component elements of coherence. Although he does not present a unified logical criterion, note that the first of the following questions pertains to *consistency* and the last two pertain to *adequacy:* "Are the doctrines logically consistent? Are they in correspondence or agreement with the actual facts? And, finally, do they work out in actual practice as predicted?"[43] Gruchy contends that all three of these demands *should* be met; but he claims that some economists do not meet all of these requirements in their analyses. It is the neo-classical economist's almost exclusive reliance on formal consistency alone that, according to Gruchy, threatens the neo-classical claims with sterility.

Do any economists actually appeal only to formal consistency for verifying their explanatory-predictive propositions? This seems to be the case when Jevons, as previously mentioned, called on economists to make their discipline "a mathematical science . . . comparatively abstract and general, treating mankind from simple points of view."[44] According to Lane, there are some contemporary theorists who "claim that logical consistency is the one and only test of all generalization," since they are only "concerned with ways of finding the logical consequences of certain assumptions."[45] In his criticism of extreme apriorism, Machlup declares that those who seek to formulate a pure, exact economics "contend that economic science is a system of *a priori* truths, a product of pure reason, an exact science reaching laws like those of mathematics, a purely axiomatic discipline, a system of pure deductions from a series of postulates, not open to any verification or refutation on the grounds of experience."[46] Actually, as both Gruchy and Machlup admit, the neo-classical economists did not always proceed in accordance with this formalistic mode alone. It was a *comparatively* formal science that Jevons advocated. Marshall sought to avoid "long trains of deductive reasoning" even when he was recommending mathematical-logical manipulations of exact terms. Moreover, he held that economic premises should approximate the observable facts as much as possible.[47] Gordon is probably correct when he reports that "many of their critics notwithstanding, the best economists have practically all been concerned with empirically relevant material." [48]

For the most part, therefore, it seems that economists would agree that logical consistency is necessary, but that it is not sufficient for verifying the warrantability of their generalizations. Gordon refers to a purely consistent system of analytic propositions in economics as "formally valid but sterile." [49] Similarly Williams insists that "the striving for logical consistency" makes theory "increasingly remote from reality." [50] Insufficient though formal validation is by itself, a causal and/or statistical analysis cannot dispense with a logical organization of its data. As Mills has said, "the instrument of logical deduction may yield an orderly theoretical structure, the counterpart of which is difficult to find in reality, while a frontal attack on reality may reveal nothing but disorderly and disconnected phenomena." [51]

How have economists viewed the operational demands of empirical adequacy which must be met in order to show that a proposed hypothesis is more reliably confirmed than alternative causal constructs? In our attempt to answer this question let us break it down into three component questions that pertain to the demands of what we have called the secondary verificative criteria which are derived from the generic logical criterion of coherence, namely, relevancy, systematic congruency, and fruitfulness.

(a) *Must a hypothesis be derived from all of the observations that are relevant to the particular question it is intended to answer?* A clear affirmation of this requirement for determining the comparative adequacy of an economic hypothesis is expressed by J. M. Clark: "The core of method lies, not in induction nor in deduction, but in taking account of all relevant facts and excluding none." [52] When institutionalists criticize the neo-classical theorists for ignoring the broader aspects of motivation and the changing sociocultural nature of the economic process in order to isolate the factors of rational choice and a static equilibrium, they, as Hamilton claims, are seeking to "find in relevance and truth a substitute for formal precision in statement." [53] But it will be recalled that Marshall just as strongly acknowledged this criteria of relevancy when he declared that "the most reckless and treacherous of all theorists is he who professes to let the facts and figures speak for themselves." [54]

Unorthodox economists can be just as guilty of violating the rule

406)   The Epistemological Pattern of Reflective Inquiry

of relevancy as the orthodox they attack, if they adopt too narrow an operationalism which arbitrarily excludes all introspectively observed motivational data, or if they become so zealous about statistical analysis that they exclude all but quantitatively measurable factors. For it is the problem which instigates the inquiry, rather than the technique which appeals to the investigator, that should determine what observations are relevant and which hypothetical questions in the mind of the investigator are suitable for classifying the data by which the economists' explanatory-predictive generalizations might be empirically confirmed. Conforming to this requirement seems to be what Lane has in mind when, despite his advocacy of applying to economic testing "the rigorous standards of verification developed by natural scientists," he recognizes the necessity for the economist to adopt introspective techniques in order that he might "know by inner experiences something about the human nature which is the subject of our generalizations." [55]

This principle of relevancy has been recognized by other economists. Knight rejects the logical positivistic criterion which requires that they "deny the relevance of any other categories of interpretation" than physicalism which excludes problem-solving behavioral data. It is in the name of the principle of relevancy that Knight warns those who rely exclusively on statistical correlations that "in the field of human interests and relationships much of our most important knowledge is inherently nonquantitative and could not be put in quantitative form without being destroyed." [56] Extensively as Mitchell has employed statistical techniques, he, nevertheless, warns that "there is a danger that the seductions of statistical techniques may blind enthusiasts to the imperfections and inadequacies of the data." [57] Accordingly, the economist who meets the demands of relevancy can agree with Lane that economic generalizations are not "subject to different criteria of truth, to different logical standards in verification, than those applied in the study of the physical universe" as long as he provides for specifically applicable techniques which do not exclude or distort relevant aspects of man's goal-seeking behavior when he is seeking to satisfy his material wants.[58]

(b) *Must an economic hypothesis be a congruent part of a comprehensive system of generalizations which, to date, is the most adequate conceptual integration of the total context of data to which the inquiry is applicable?*

The sophisticated status of traditional economics among the other social sciences is largely the result of its long commitment to the fulfillment of this requirement for cumulative analysis. Lange's statement that "theoretical economics puts the patterns of uniformity in a coherent system" was previously elaborated enough to show that the basic propositions and the consistently derived theorems constitute a system of generalizations which are designed to integrate conceptually the total context of economic actions. As long as an investigator accepts this ideational scheme as established knowledge, any new hypothesis must fit harmoniously into it. The possibility must always be left open, however, that the established system might have to be modified, corrected, or abandoned in favor of another system of which this hypothesis is an integral part.

When the unorthodox economists challenged the neo-classical approach, they objected to its restrictive formalism, but not to the verificative demand for a congruent system in terms of which the warrant for hypotheses might be ascertained. For, as Gruchy has reported, "in their economic analysis the holistic economists go far beyond a simple description of the modern economy to create a systematic, orderly interpretation of the whole economic system." [59] Similarly, when Spiethoff in order to verify generalizations about the diachronic development of the economic process substitutes substantive, synthetic, and dynamic generalizations for the formal, analytic, and static neo-classical synchronic system of equilibrium, he seeks nevertheless for "what is uniform and essential in this concrete framework of concatenations," i.e., a systematic *Gestalt* of congruently interrelated parts.[60]

Since Machlup seeks to solve the "problem of verification in economics" in the heuristic terms of an inductive procedure in which empirical testing "results, at best, in a confirmation till next time," it might be expected that he would be opposed to the systematization of congruent hypotheses as a part of the process of verification. To the contrary, however, he contends that "the strength of a belief in a hypothesis depends, even more than on any direct empirical tests that it may have survived, on the place it holds within a hierarchical system of inter-related hypotheses." [61]

(c) *Must an economic hypothesis be fruitful for further inquiry?*

Unorthodox economists have been more concerned than orthodox economists about meeting this demand that a hypothesis must lead to a fuller comprehension or a more inclusive insight into the context of economic data, as well as that it must contribute to the understanding of the contexts of other behavioral sciences. Tugwell's declaration that "there has been a drift toward the substitution of consequences for premises in the search for truth in all fields," [62] expresses the exploratory experimentalism of the unorthodox approach which exemplifies this third requirement of coherence. There is considerable justification for identifying this pragmatic appeal to the fruitfulness of economic hypotheses with the institutionalistic approach which is contrasted to the neo-classical appeal to the logical precision of their premises. Despite J. B. Clark's neo-classical emphasis upon the logical analysis of a static equilibrium, his son, J. M. Clark and Gruchy claim that he presents some intimation of the importance of "fruitfulness for further inquiry," when he anticipates the development of a more dynamic perspective even though the cumulative analysis it would require is "so large that the execution of it will occupy generations of workers." [63]

The growing conviction that economic constructs should contribute to, as well as be enlightened by, the constructs of other behavioral sciences is not accepted by all economists; but, for those who advocate interdisciplinary cooperation it has become one credential for the reasonable acceptability of economic hypotheses. Kapp, for example, maintains that "just as the science of economics must build conceptual bridges to the science of man, the emerging science of man and human behavior must never lose sight of one of the most fundamental conditions of all human existence and human behavior; namely . . . that the environment offers the potential means for the gratification of recurrent wants not freely but at the price of overcoming various resistances by human effort and improved techniques." [64] Expressing a completely contrary opinion, however, Colin Clark declares: "Let economists get on with their work, and let the students of the other sciences get on with theirs." [65]

This divergence of opinion reveals that whether or not one accepts the criteria of "fruitfulness in contributing to other contexts" is not a matter that can be determined by an appeal to evidence. Rather, this disagreement stems from different preferences from which there is derived their respective conceptions of what kind of knowledge is meaningful. This, of course, also holds for the other two secondary criteria, i.e., consistency and adequacy, as well as for the generic logical criteria of coherence, from which their significance is derived.

G. *The Significance of the Fifth Postulate for Political Science*

Easton represents one group of political scientists who have explicitly adopted the postulate of the criterion of coherence as a generic logical criterion of verification: "The idea of coherence is an inescapable premise if one seeks to construct a conceptual framework for any area of knowledge." [66] But there are many political scientists who claim that they are interested only in fact-finding rather than in any conceptual framework. Others seem to be suspicious of any logical scheme of verification that might substitute causal analysis for normative analysis. Among political scientists there is no consensus with respect to a criterion for the verification of their different kinds of constructs; for, as Heller reports, "the discipline is lacking in either a clearly delimited set of problems or a definitely prescribed methodology." This does not preclude the more widespread adoption of coherence, however, since Heller indicates that the ideas about power with which many political scientists are dealing are "constructed more or less systematically by a process of abstracting the common elements to be found in a number of concrete states." [67] Consequently, Leiserson hopefully maintains that there is no conclusive evidence that common concepts of sufficient generality will not be found to integrate the data of interpersonal and institutional behavior into an inclusive, logically consistent body of theoretical propositions." [68]

Before such a verificative aim could become more widely acknowledged, however, those political scientists who have confined their study to isolated problems must realize that "the accumulation of data through acceptable techniques does not alone give us adequate knowledge." In making this point, Easton indicates that some criterion like coherence is required to determine what techniques are appropriate and how the research results should be correlated: "Knowledge becomes critical and reliable as it increases in generality and internally consistent organization, when, in short, it is cast in the form of systematic generalized statements applicable to a large number of particular cases." [69]

The "requirements of a good classification system," which Lazarsfeld and Barton devised for the policy sciences, suggest the principles of consistency and adequacy, as well as the secondary criteria of relevancy and systematic congruency. (i) *"Articulation"* of specific phenomena in terms of their general relations suggests the need for a comprehensive ideational perspective in classification and verification. (ii) *"Logical correctness,"* which requires that "in an articulated set of categories those on each step must be exhaustive and mutually exclusive," expresses the demand for *consistency*. (iii) *"Adaptation of the structure of the situation,"* which requires a comprehensive account of the "situation as a whole," expresses the demand for *relevancy*. (iv) *"Adaptation to the respondent's frame of reference,"* which requires the presentation "as clearly as possible of the respondent's own definition of the situation—his focus of attention, his categories of thought" suggests some of the aspects of the demand for *systematic congruency*.[70]

The importance of the principle of relevance for the process of verification in political theory is revealed by Waldo's account of the "confusion and friction" which arises out of the controversy between some political scientists who take into account only those data which pertain to moral inquiry and others who take into account only those data which pertain to causal inquiry.[71] Among the other merits of Easton's approach for political analysis is his insight that causal and moral data are not mutually exclusive but rather must both be accounted for in a reasonably acceptable generalization which includes all of the relevant aspects of political behavior: "Political science has displayed an initial coherence because it has attempted to understand the functioning and determinants of policy." [72]

The importance of systematic congruency has been emphasized by Easton, when he reminds those of his colleagues who do piecemeal testing of the results of their empirical research, that "without systematic theory such matters are necessarily decided in a hit-or-miss way." What is needed, according to Easton, is the effort to construct a "relatively consistent body of concepts" in terms of which the reliability of research findings will be increased by corroboration with other research findings what cumulatively become the established knowledge: "Knowledge becomes more reliable because it becomes part of a web of theory, each strand of which helps to support the other and has, as well, independent bases of proof." Easton recognizes that, as yet, "political science does not seem to possess this systematic coherence." As Easton regretfully reports, "there seem to be no broad variables common to the whole discipline; instead there seems to be a large number of heterogeneous fields." [73]

The importance of fruitfulness as one of the secondary criteria of the generic logical criterion of coherence has been acknowledged by Catlin when he declared that "although the nuclei of sciences can be profitably pointed out, the boundaries are an experimental matter to be determined by the limits of fruitful and coherent investigation." [74] Fruitfulness is also taken by some political scientists to be the demand that the reasonable acceptability of their hypotheses depends to a significant extent upon their applicability to the policy sciences. As Hilgard and Lerner have insisted, to clarify goals, isolate factors, project trends, and specify alternatives of policy is a sequence of activities whose difficulty requires, and whose importance deserves, the best scientific efforts available in the community." [75]

H. *The Significance of the Fifth Postulate for History*

The adoption of the postulate of coherence as a generic logical criterion for verifying historical generalizations is urged by Brockunier and Loewenberg as the aim of cumulative analysis: "Criteria for any extended judgment of conception of history should be explicit and subject to the logic of relevance and coherence." [76] The logicians, Cohen and Nagel, support this historiographical claim, when they declare that "the propositions dealing with the past must be so connected that they form a coherent whole." [77] Like other broader operationalists, Aitken and Loewenberg acknowledge that logical consistency is necessary but not sufficient without causal adequacy, when they declare that "internally consistent" generalizations about historical events must be treated as "tentative working hypotheses which are to be treated for adequacy." [78]

The epistemologically dualistic character of coherence for historical verification in terms of consistency and adequacy is brought out by Donagan when he clarifies what this generic criterion entails as an ideational framework that determines the design of the historian's

412)   **The Epistemological Pattern of Reflective Inquiry**

testing procedure. Since "history begins with an imaginary reconstruction of the past which is designed to account for whatever evidence the historian possesses," he must meet the demands of consistency and adequacy in order to verify his theses: "He supports or
throws doubt on his reconstruction partly by internal criticism— Is it
consistent? Will any alternative equally account for the evidence?—
and partly by deducing from his reconstruction what new evidence
would be pertinent, searching for it, and revising his reconstruction
in the light of what he may find or fail to find." [79] Epistemological
dualism is similarly presupposed by Strong when, as the "criteria of
explanation in history," he designates "reliability, cogency, and ap-
propriateness" as the demands to which a system of constructs must
conform in order to be warranted assertions.[80]

Mandelbaum seems to reject epistemological dualism and the criterion of coherence in *The Problem of Historical Knowledge*. There
he advocates a correspondence criterion on the basis of an epistemologically monistic postulate that systematic relevancy and coherency
are "objectively ascertainable in the nature of the events themselves."
In his journal article "Causal Analysis in History," however, he appears to be more dualistic in his epistemological criterion for determining "the acceptability of any account" in terms of the "sense of the
evidence" to which the historian must appeal "when faced by ascertained facts and alternative interpretations." For here Mandelbaum
seems to be dealing more with the system of inferences which the
historian himself constructs, when he claims that "no hypothesis is
ever verified except to the extent that it affords us a more comprehensive and intelligible account of the facts which fall within its
scope than any alternative hypothesis is able to do." [81]

The secondary criteria of relevancy has been widely acknowledged
by these and other historians who aim at cumulative analysis as one
of the essential demands for greater adequacy. In other words, they
assume that any historical hypothesis must be inferred from a range
of authenticated testimony that is sufficiently wide so that no reconstructed data are arbitrarily excluded which might be pertinent to the
questions that have arisen in the historian's mind about the totality
of the specific situation which he is interpreting. Two kinds of historians probably would not feel compelled to fulfill this requirement.
The purely document-centered historian, for one, would be likely to
reject this verificative demand on the grounds that it requires the his-

torian to formulate conceptual generalizations for the selection and organization of the documentary evidence and theoretical generalizations for the causal interpretation of such critically reconstructed data. Since they assume that the testimony speaks for itself, they assume that the constructive procedure for meeting this requirement introduces the errors of human judgment. It seems naïve, however, for them to assume that there is no subjectivity in the authentication of the documents, just as it seems arbitrary for them to preclude the possibility of emendable causal interpretations. After all, even the authenticated testimony on which they depend is infected with the subjectivity of the past reporters.

The drama-centered historians constitute another group who do not feel compelled to conform to the principle of relevancy, if the inclusion of certain data would spoil the aesthetic effectiveness of the narrative presentation. It is supposed that historical narration is going to be more widely read if it is presented with a creative flair that appeals to the imagination of the reader. It is doubtful, however, that any narrator should really be called an historian, if he neglects pertinent evidence in order to enhance the aesthetic effectiveness of his creative portraits of the past. Creative insight, of course, is required for cognitive processes of introspective projection and imaginative reconstruction. Only if the imaginatively gifted historian regulates his interpretation of authenticated testimony in accordance with the requirements of relevancy and the other demands for intellectual adequacy, can he be sure that his presentation is, as Gottschalk says, distinguished "from fiction, poetry, drama, and fantasy" because "his imagination is directed toward *re-creation* and not creation." [82]

There has been considerable controversy among historians about the requirement of the secondary criteria of systematic congruency. On the one hand, as we have previously noted, traditional historiographers seem to be suspicious of systematizing as too analytical for the historical approach. On the other hand, broadly operational historians recognize that there are serious obstacles "in the path of the historian who approaches the problem of systematic analysis and the building of some empirically based hypotheses." [83] Nevertheless, they agree with Cohen that in history, as well as in any other scientific inquiry, "no fact can be established or made intelligible unless it is already related to other facts or is part of a larger system, which is especially true of complex facts such as the existence of moral or economic movements." [84] Nichols, for example, insists that only a systematic history is scientific.[85] To those historians who argue that they face an impossible task, if they must make each aspect congruent with all others in a total system, Brockunier and Loewenberg reply that "delimitation is essential in inquiries that seek answers to specific questions" but that only through showing the systematic congruence of these answers can historians hope to achieve "cumulative analysis which eventually can deal with larger interrelationships on the basis of knowledge established in earlier, sharply delimited studies." [86]

The secondary criteria of fruitfulness for further inquiry is acknowledged as a verificative demand for showing the greater adequacy of their claims by those historians who agree with Brockunier and Loewenberg that a "revisionary self-corrective process" is a necessary part of verification, since "theory that runs beyond the established data is the source of fertility in cumulative scientific analysis." [87] Similarly, Cohen claims that the world of reality is more than can be reproduced or represented in any intelligible account, and that any such account is necessarily partial and to some extent abstract." For this assumption entails the premise that "a partial or abstract account of reality is false if it purports to be more than it is, but if it acknowledges its limitations it may be true and the only kind of truth to which the historian can attain." [88]

While such intellectual humility should be expected from all historians, just as it is from any other reflective inquirer, those historians who hesitate to emphasize this point have a reason which deserves some extended consideration: To acknowledge the demand for fruitfulness presupposes that historical knowledge is always relative. While this is no less presupposed in other disciplines, historians are especially sensitive to it. It would seem futile to deny the "situational relativism" which admits that any investigator's knowledge-situation is relative to his meaning-situation and value-situation. This has been presupposed throughout this entire analysis. But, does fruitfulness as a secondary criteria necessarily compel the historian to surrender to the radical relativist who claims that all historical interpretations are so entirely relative to the historian's subjective biases, as well as to his sociocultural environment, that none of them has any reasonable acceptability?

In order to maintain the objectivity which is sufficient for constructing reliable historical generalizations, the historian does not have to avoid all value judgments; but, he must make every effort to subordinate his own preferences about the good, the beautiful, and the sacred, to his desire for what is true. It must be strongly emphasized, of course, that objectivity is precluded in the selection and the interpretation of historical data which are deliberately designed as arbitrary justifications of religious dogma, racial prejudice, etc. In such cases the propagandists offer neither authenticated documentary evidence nor any implications that could be confirmed or refuted by other historians. Moreover, it must never be assumed that any account is above revision. Regardless of how unprejudiced and broadly operational a historian may be, nevertheless, he cannot eliminate all valuational and evaluational factors from his verificative judgment about which hypothesis is more fruitful than alternative interpretations. Not only are his data laden with the value experiences of the persons whose past actions he is imaginatively reconstructing in terms of his introspective projection of his own goal-seeking behavior, but the historian's selection of what human events he will interpret is determined by his preference for what is significant enough to be worth reconstructing. His own intellectual standards, aesthetic tastes, and moral convictions emerge out of his participation in his own contemporary sociocultural process. These are bound to influence his selections and interpretations to some degree. As Cohen and Nagel have noted, even when the historian merely wants "to understand the effects of the moral standards of any epoch," he cannot avoid adopting "a point of view somewhat wider than the age itself and must therefore pass judgment on the adequacy of its ideas and standards," that "is itself a moral question which the historian answers on the basis of his own moral assumptions." [89] But, whether or not historians have ever avoided or could avoid all moral, aesthetic, or religious preferences, the point to be emphasized is Gottschalk's declaration that "it is not conceivable that a serious historian will discuss anything without betraying whether he considers it true or untrue." [90] The objective of his judgment depends upon the intellectual integrity which the historian exhibits as he attempts to meet all of the other demands of coherence. As long as this much is assured, it is a matter for those who share his value-meaning-and-knowledge-situations to consider whether or not the evidence he cites confirms the implications of the interpretations he has offered. As Randall and Haines have insisted, "knowledge can be 'objective' only for some determinate context; it is always a knowledge of the relations essential for that context." [91]

If the historian who makes every effort to meet the demands of coherence were expected to eliminate all value referents, he would not be able to interpret the significance of the course of past events. As Brockunier and Loewenberg contend, "even the simplest terms in the historians' vocabulary carry value overtones: civilization, rise, fall, decadence, stability, progress, aggression, defence, cruelty, magnanimity." [92] To insure the relative objectivity of his interpretation, however, the historian must make his value-perspective explicit. The conception of progress serves to illustrate this point.

Whether or not the historian's evaluation of *progress* is relatively subjective or relatively objective depends upon what he takes *progress* to mean. As long as the significance of human actions was judged in terms of the Greek conception of fate or in terms of the Judaic-Christian conception of Divine Providence, no empirically verifiable generalizations about human behavior were possible. To provide a naturalistic rather than supernaturalistic account of human affairs, nineteenth-century thinkers (Marx, Comte, Spencer) developed the conception of *automatic progress*, which Bury in his brilliant analysis has described as follows: "The idea of human progress is a theory which involves a synthesis of the past and a prophecy of the future," that is "based on an interpretation of human history which regards men as slowly advancing—*pedetemti progredientes* in a definite and desirable direction and infers that progress will continue indefinitely." [93] This blind faith in automatic progress, which "must be the necessary outcome of the psychical and social nature of man," is as non-operational as the providential theory it aimed to replace. Consider, for example, Spencer's claim that in the necessary progress of cosmic evolution "it is certain that man must become perfect" so that "always toward perfection is the mighty movement—toward a complete development and a more unmixed good." [94] It is this "illusion of cosmism and futurism" which Nelson has so cogently exposed as an unwarranted faith in the realization of a utopian human community.[95]

For the purpose of ascertaining whether or not a historical hypothesis is more fruitful than alternatives with respect to progress, the latter must be conceived as contingent and situationally relative to human effort rather than as an automatic cosmic necessity. Although the latter is diametrically opposed to radical relativism, it has several serious shortcomings. First, as previously intimated, it yields no causal implications that can be empirically confirmed or refuted. Second, it presupposes that, for the history of human affairs to be meaningful, there must be what Muller in his *The Uses of the Past* has rejected as a "clear pattern or determinate plot"; whereas, historical pluralism is required as a premise for causal analysis. Third, the idea of automatic progress does not distinguish between the conceptions of *change, development,* and the *normative progress* which reflects the historian's own evaluation of what is significant.

For these distinctions let us turn to Hook. He defines *change* as "differences in the behavior of human beings as members of a social group or differences in the behavior and organization of things and institutions which condition changes in human behavior." He defines development as "any series of events in thought, action or institutional arrangements which exhibits a directional, cumulative change that terminates in an event marked off by recognized qualitative novelty or exhibits in its course a perceptible pattern of growth." Moral and/or aesthetic and/or religious and/or intellectual ideals are involved, however, in the normative concept of progress which Hook has defined as "a development favorably evaluated from the standpoint of a human interest, end, or ideal." [96]

The contingent conception of progress is not only congruent with the situational relativism which characterizes the entire scientific enterprise; but it also provides empirically testable causal implications, allows for historical pluralism, and distinguishes between change, development, and progress. What is meant by and implied by the idea of contingent rather than automatic progress? According to the contingent view, progress means the increase of the conditions which are required for realizing whatever the historian prizes as an intrinsic value. In order to be objective, the historian must explicitly acknowledge and formulate his conception of such a life-goal or ideal of what human relations ought to be, to which his conception of progress is relative. Unlike the advocates of Divine Providence and automatic progress, the broadly operational historian is fully aware that his axiological construct can be revised so that he is willing to modify, correct, or abandon it in favor of a more reasonably acceptable ideal norm.

The historian is said to be objective when he internally evaluates the progress of a given past human community in terms of what they accomplished in realizing what mattered most to its members. Why shouldn't this external evaluation of the progressiveness of historical events be considered just as objective as long as he makes known his ideal norm? Any other historian or social scientist has the opportunity to criticize internally the consistency between his premises and his conclusions, and to criticize externally the adequacy of his premises about human capabilities in the light of the reasonably acceptable knowledge about human motivation and sociocultural conditions that the other behavioral sciences provide.

Once the historian has abandoned absolute standards of truth and value, it is difficult to see how he could avoid the subjectivity which the radical relativist ascribes to all interpretations of past human actions, if the historian does not adopt the generic logical criterion of coherence. But, if he makes his imaginative reconstructions conform to the demands of consistency and of adequacy in terms of their relevancy, systematic congruency, and fruitfulness, then the reliability of his knowledge is different only in degree from that of other social scientists who have the advantage of contemporary observational data. Historians can share the same conception of what kind of knowledge is meaningful with other broader operationalists.

Footnotes to Chapter 7 of Part Three

[1] Einstein and Infeld, *The Evolution of Physics*, 8-9.
[2] Parsons, *The Structure of Social Action*, 755-756.
[3] Hempel and Oppenheim, "The Logic of Explanation," *Readings in the Philosophy of Science* (Feigl and Brodbeck), 321-322.
[4] Marx, *Psychological Theory* (Marx), 11.
[5] Allport, *Psychological Theory* (Marx), 168.
[6] Tolman, *Psychological Theory* (Marx), 413-414.
[7] Hull, *Psychological Theory* (Marx), 230-231, 222.
[8] Allport, *Psychological Theory* (Marx), 168.
[9] Maslow, "Problem-Centering vs. Means-Centering in Science," *Philosophy of Science*, 13 (Oct. 1936), 326-331.

[10] Hull in *Psychological Theory* (Marx), 223.

[11] Marx in *Psychological Theory* (Marx), 16.

[12] Cantril and Others, "Psychology and Scientific Research," *Science*, 110, page 491.

[13] Krech and Klein, *Theoretical Models and Personality Theory*, 15.

[14] Newcomb, *Social Psychology*, vii.

[15] Lewin, *Field Theory in Social Science*, 45.

[16] Deutsch in *Handbook of Social Psychology* (Lindzey), Vol. 1, 187.

[17] Zetterberg, *On Theory and Verification in Sociology*, 10.

[18] MacIver, *Social Causation*, 80.

[19] Lazarsfeld and Rosenberg, *The Language of Social Research*, 6.

[20] Lundberg, *Foundations of Sociology*, 100-101.

[21] Bierstedt in *Symposium on Sociological Theory* (Gross), 133-137.

[22] MacIver, *Social Causation*, 385.

[23] Lundberg, *Foundations of Sociology*, 100-101.

[24] Merton, *Social Theory and Social Structure*, 94-95.

[25] MacIver, *Social Causation*, 93.

[26] Merton, *Social Theory and Social Structure*, 94-95.

[27] Rose, *Theory and Method in the Social Sciences*, 262.

[28] MacIver, *Social Causation*, 392.

[29] Merton, *Social Theory and Social Structure*, 94-95.

[30] Bidney, *Theoretical Anthropology*, 341.

[31] Murdock in *Toward a Science of Social Man* (Gillin), 27.

[32] Nadel, *Foundations of Social Anthropology*, 234.

[33] Kroeber in *An Appraisal of Anthropology Today* (Tax), 358-359.

[34] Kroeber and Kluckhohn, "General Features of Culture," *A Critical Review of Concepts and Definitions*, 161-162. Cf. pp. 167-179.

[35] Kroeber in *An Appraisal of Anthropology Today* (Tax), 359.

[36] Herskovits in *Method and Perspective in Anthropology* (Spencer), 21.

[37] Redfield in *Anthropology Today* (Kroeber), 735.

[38] Bidney in *Anthropology Today* (Kroeber), 698.

[39] Lange, "The Scope and Method of Economics," *Readings in the Philosophy of Science* (Feigl and Brodbeck), 746-747. Originally published in the *Review of Economic Studies*, 13, 1945-46.

[40] Machlup, "The Problem of Verification in Economics," *The Southern Economic Journal*, Vol. XXII, No. 1, July 1955, page 4.

[41] Schumpeter, *The History of Economic Analysis*, 42.

[42] See Hutchison, *The Significance and Basic Postulates of Economic Theory*, 157-162.

[43] Gruchy, *Modern Economic Thought*, 421.

[44] Jevons, *The Principles of Science*, 759-761.

[45] Lane, *Enterprise and Secular Change* (Lane and Riemersma), 526.

[46] Machlup, "The Problem of Verification in Economics," *Southern Economic Journal*, Vol. XXII, No. 1, July 1955, pages 4-5, 7.

[47] Marshall, *Principles of Economics*, 781.

[48] Gordon, *The Journal of Political Economy*, Vol. LXIII, April 1955, No. 2, page 160.

49 Gordon, *The Journal of Political Economy*, Vol. LXIII, April 1955, No. 2, page 157.

50 Williams, "An Economist's Confessions," *American Economic Review*, XLIII (March 1952), p. 4. (This is cited by Gordon in *The Journal of Political Economy*, Vol. LXIII (April 1955), No. 2, p. 160.)

51 Mills in *Economic Essays in Honor of Wesley Clair Mitchell*, 358.

52 Clark, "The Socializing of Theoretical Economics," *The Trend of Economics* (Tugwell), 75.

53 Hamilton, "The Institutional Approach to Economic Theory," *The American Economic Review*, March 1919, Vol. ix, page 318.

54 Marshall, "The Present Position of Economics (1885)," *Memorials of Alfred Marshall* (Pigou), 168.

55 Lane, *Enterprise and Secular Change* (Lane and Riemersma), 526.

56 Knight, "What Is Truth in Economics," *The Journal of Political Economy*, XLVIII, Feb. 1940, No. 1, pages 5-6, 27.

57 Mitchell, "Quantitative Analysis in Economic Theory," *The American Economic Review*, Vol. XV, March 1925, page 31.

58 Lane, *Enterprise and Secular Change* (Lane and Riemersma), 526.

59 Gruchy, *Modern Economic Thought*, 608.

60 Spiethoff in *Enterprise and Secular Change* (Lane and Riemersma), 446-447.

61 Machlup, "The Problem of Verification in Economics," *The Southern Economic Journal*, Vol. XXII, No. 1, July 1955, page 5.

62 Tugwell, *The Trend of Economics*, 394.

63 Gruchy, *Modern Economic Thought*, 343-345.

64 Kapp, "Economics and the Behavioral Sciences," *Kyklos*, Vol. VII, 1954, page 219.

65 Clark, Colin, *The Conditions of Economic Progress*, 1.

66 Easton, *The Political System*, 291.

67 Heller in *Encyclopedia of the Social Sciences*, Vol. 12, pages 207-209.

68 Leiserson, *Political Science Quarterly*, December 1953, page 567.

69 Easton, *The Political System*, 55.

70 Lazarsfeld and Barton in *The Policy Sciences* (Lerner and Lasswell), 156-157.

71 Waldo, *Political Science in the United States of America*, 33.

72 Easton, *The Political System*, 142.

73 *Ibid.*, 98.

74 Catlin, *The Science and Method of Politics*, quoted by Easton, *The Political System*, 90.

75 Hilgard and Lerner in *The Policy Sciences* (Lerner and Lasswell), 42-43.

76 Brockunier and Loewenberg, *Bulletin 64*, page 145.

77 Cohen and Nagel, *An Introduction to Logic and Scientific Method*, 340-341.

78 Aitken and Loewenberg, *Bulletin 64*, pages 29-30.

79 Donagan, "Verification of Historical Theses," *The Philosophical Quarterly*, Vol. 6, No. 24, July 1956, page 196.

80 Strong, "Criteria of Explanation in History," *Journal of Philosophy*, Jan. 31, 1952, pages 57-67.

81 Mandelbaum, *The Problem of Historical Knowledge*, 270-271; "Causal Analysis in History," *Journal of the History of Ideas*, Vol. 3, 1942.

[82] Gottschalk, *Understanding History*, 49, 244-245.

[83] Cochran, *Bulletin 64*, pages 62, 69.

[84] Cohen, *The Meaning of Human History*, 33.

[85] Nichols, *Bulletin 64*, page 12.

[86] Brockunier and Loewenberg, *Bulletin 64*, page 149.

[87] Brockunier and Loewenberg, *Bulletin 64*, page 137.

[88] Cohen, *The Meaning of Human History*, 46.

[89] Cohen and Nagel, *An Introduction to Logic and Scientific Method*, 356.

[90] Gottschalk, *Understanding History*, 49, 244-245.

[91] Randall and Haines, *Bulletin 54*, pages 22-23.

[92] Brockunier and Loewenberg, *Bulletin 64*, page 144.

[93] Bury, *The Idea of Progress*, 5.

[94] Spencer, *Illustrations of Universal Progress*, 5.

[95] Nelson, "The Future of Illusions," *Psychoanalysis*, Vol. 2, No. 4 (Spring-Summer 1934), pages 16-37.

[96] Hook, *Bulletin 54*, pages 116-117.

PART FOUR *The Methodological Pattern of Reflective Inquiry*

1 An Elaboration of the Hypothetical-Deductive Method in the Knowledge-Situation of Reflective Inquiry

A. The Aim of this Elaboration

By the hypothetical-deductive method, it will be recalled, we mean the general procedure by which the broader operationalist logically coordinates the various observational, inferential, and verificative techniques which the specific subject matter of a particular discipline requires for constructing reasonably acceptable causal generalizations. We have outlined the hypothetical-deductive method in terms of the following four stages:

1. Observation and classification of all of the factual data which are relevant to the specific problem which instigated his inquiry.
2. Construction through inferred generalizations of a hypothesis

or a system of hypotheses which might serve as a causal explanation, as well as a formula for more precise classification and prediction, with respect to the relevant observational data.

3. Verification of the theoretical hypothesis or system of hypotheses in accordance with the criterion of coherence, i.e., consistency and adequacy:

   a. Deductive elaboration of the consistent implications of the hypothesis by logical-mathematical reasoning in the form of the hypothetical syllogism (If . . . , then . . .).

   b. Empirical testing of consistently-deduced implications of the hypothesis by techniques which are applicable to the specific data to which the proposed hypothesis refers in order to verify its higher degree of adequacy.

      i. Experimental testing for confirming or refuting the hypothesis under controlled laboratory conditions and/or controlled observations in the natural sciences (including experimental psychology).

      ii. Experiential testing for confirming or refuting the hypothesis under relatively controlled observational conditions in the social sciences and psychology (excluding experimental psychology).

4. Conceptual integration of each hypothesis that has empirically confirmed implications into a coherent system of descriptive generalizations (laws) which are logically consistent, i,e., absolutely *valid*, and, in comparison with alternative theories, more adequate for interpreting the context to which it refers, i.e., relatively *true*.

Although we have already indicated the general function of this inductive-deductive procedure in order to show how it synthesizes specific techniques of reflective inquiry, now we need to examine what spokesmen for each of the disciplines have said about the crucial issues that are involved in their application of such techniques. We share Northrop's conviction about "the importance and necessity of any empirical science possessing an explicit logical analysis of its concepts and method, if its principles are not to be misunderstood and misused." [1]

B. *The First Stage of Hypothetical-Deductive Inquiry*

What is entailed in the application of investigative techniques with respect to the observation and classification of all of the factual data which are relevant to the specific problem that instigated a particular inquiry? There is no substitute for careful observation of the physical or behavioral events which occur independently of the observer who must attempt to ascertain the factual situation with the most refined, instruments available. But such a diagnosis is always conceptually regulated! The inspection of perceptual and/or value data serves no scientific purpose unless the observer introduces some significant connection among them which has some bearing upon the question which instigated his inquiry. Only when his inspection of his observational data is thus ideationally designed can he, on the one hand, select from among the great number of observable occurrences only those which are relevant to his problem and, on the other hand, include enough data to provide a range of information that is comprehensive enough to suggest further relevant observations. The social scientist who is reluctant to acknowledge this "reified" nature of his observational data which are not accessible without the "constructive activity of thought" (Kant) should recall Margenau's claim that the sensory experience (P-plane) to which the physicist's generalizations refer is unintelligible "unless the essentially constructed character of physical objects is granted in the very beginning." [2] Or, as Lenzen points out with respect to physical observation, "the defining characteristic of perception is the occurrence of a sense datum and its interpretation as the aspect of an objective thing." [3]

Observational data cannot be used for explanatory-predictive generalizations unless they are classified in terms of generally significant similarities that are determined by a correlating idea in the investigator's mind rather than by chance resemblances in the given data which cannot "speak for themselves." This constructive character of all classificatory schema is exemplified no less in an Einsteinian model of a time-space continuum than it is in the synoptic model of the goal-seeking behavioral transactions of socialized individuals. There are, of course, significant substantive differences between the physical and the behavioral observational data thus classified by these respective models. But the quantitative nature of the former and the qualitative-quantitative nature of the latter stems from differences in the kinds of subject matter. Human emotion and purpose can be excluded from the observational data which the physical scientist classifies; but a purely quantitative classification of motivational and sociocultural data that eliminated emotion and purpose would preclude the most meaningful dimensions of the factual situation of goal-oriented behavior. The synoptic model, it will be recalled, is a conceptual classification of the observational data for behavioral inquiry. To it each specific discipline can add its own theoretical model for classifying those aspects of goal-oriented behavior to which its own particular explanatory-predictive constructs refer.

To what extent, if any, is there justification for *the limited use of critical introspective observation* in the initial inspection of motivational data? This is the most crucial issue which complicates the first stage of the social scientist's inquiry. Purely extrospective observation, which confines him to the observational construct of the "conditioned physiological response to a physical stimulus," does not provide a sufficiently penetrating or comprehensive diagnosis of the most relevant data that are operating in goal-seeking motivation, i.e., present memories of the past, present anticipations of the future, sense-perceptions, emotional responses, desires, compulsions, needs, imaginings, and thinking. Such mental processes are accessible only through the investigator's self-examination. Yet, haven't the most significant developments in scientific psychology been made in recent years by the use of purely extrospective observation which has excluded all data that are not susceptible to public inspection? Nevertheless, as Lerner has pointed out in his *Evidence and Inference*, "introspection helps to close the gap between the body of evidence assembled, and the inference drawn from this evidence." However, in order to be scientifically appropriate, introspection must always be "called into question and subjected to test." [4]

What do some contemporary *psychologists* have to say about this complication with respect to using the technique of introspective inspection at the initial observational stage of inquiry? Contending that critically employed introspection is indispensable, Murray declares that "instead of crippling himself by renouncing this source of valuable information, limiting his data (as some scientists advise) to the behaviors which he himself can observe and faithfully record, the psychologist should discover and correct for all the determinants of error in the communication of memories, plans, valuations, self-estimates, and so forth." [5] According to Alexander, the psychosomatic factors of emotions, ideas, and purposes "can be studied also through introspection or by verbal communication from those in whom these physiological processes take place." Much as advancement of our knowledge about motivation does depend upon improved physically observable data, Alexander insists that "it is hardly conceivable that the different moves of two chess players can ever be more clearly understood in biochemical or neurophysiological than in psychological and logical terms." [6] With respect to the use of introspection in studying perceptual phenomena Gibson has declared that "there is nothing in the least erudite or mysterious in the examination of one's own experience despite the popular belief to the contrary and introspection is as valuable to contemporary students as it ever was." [7] Andrews has instructively noted that all of the subjective techniques involving introspection "can be handled with a considerable degree of objectivity and that all the objective methods have some of the characteristics of subjectivity." [8] Allport justifies his somewhat unorthodox emphasis upon the introspective analysis of propriate striving by pointing out that "people, it seems, are busy leading their lives into the future, whereas psychology, for the most part, is busy tracing them into the past." [9]

Despite the need to use introspective techniques in the observation of goal-seeking data, such findings must be sufficiently corroborated by extrospective observation under reasonably controlled conditions that provide the opportunity for public inspection of expected overt behavior. It is to Watson's credit that he made psychologists (as well as other social scientists) aware of the inaccuracies and distortions of purely introspectional reports. Impressions of one's own mental processes, as such, should not be considered warranted beliefs, any more than sense-impressions, as such, should be considered infallible indices of the external physical reality which they seem to reveal. Both need to be interpreted in terms of constructs that have implications which can be publicly confirmed to a reasonable degree before they can be treated as observational data from which classificatory, explanatory, and predictive hypotheses can be inferred. Without this safeguard of requiring extrospective corroboration, the unlimited and incautious use of uncritical introspective techniques could reduce the diagnosis of purposive motivation to the unreflective level of such non-operational data as the mystic appeals to, when he claims that his self-evident warrant for his intuitively-acquired belief is his own private, ineffable feeling.

It is one thing, however, to guard, as we must, against the misuse of introspection which could lead us back to naïve mysticism, naïve sense-impressionism, or naïve pragmatism; but, it is quite another matter to disregard the desires, emotions and, purposes which an individual experiences privately. Lack of proper caution could reduce behavioral analysis to obscurantism, while the elimination of personally experienced data substitutes neurophysiological functioning for the motivational aspects of behavioral transactions. Consequently, when a broader operationalist selects and classifies the observational data for goal-seeking behavior, his own introspections or the reported introspections of others are applicable to the intrinsic *end* toward which the subject professes to be striving; but extrospective observation must be used for inspecting the overt action the subject engages in as the *means* for realizing such an objective. When George discusses the use of models and theories for behavioral analysis, his conclusion reinforces this point: "For psychology, we have in practice to combine, for many purposes, information from introspective and behavioristic sources, and we are forced into a degree of eclecticism." [10]

Tolman's limited use of introspection within the conceptual framework of his operational behaviorism furnishes a significant clue to how the social scientist might solve this observational problem in those cases where the factual situation demands a critical inspection of the motivational data of purposive actions. Since Tolman's motivational construct of the intervening variable and his psychological model for conceptually classifying behavioral variables has already been extensively discussed, we shall recall here only a few brief passages which bear directly upon the limited use of critical introspection.

First, goal-seeking is the defining characteristic of motivation: "In behaving an organism . . . 'intends' and more or less successfully 'conquers' its environment" so that "behavior, which is behavior in our operational sense, always seems to have the character of getting-to or getting-from a specific goal-object, or goal-situation."

Second, an observational construct which reduces all psychological data to neurophysiological data, arbitrarily distorts the relevant purposive aspects of this factual situation. Watson's observational construct of a "conditioned reflex" does not require introspective inspection, since his stimulus-response formula entails only the extrospectively observable dependent variable (muscular, glandular, neural reactions) and the independent variable (physical and physiological environment). In modifying the behavioristic approach, however, Tolman added the intervening variable between the independent variables (which also include the sociocultural and psychodynamic environments), and the dependent variable (which is the behavioral actions themselves rather than their concomitant neurophysiological functions). Now, it is only through the use of an introspective technique that the psychologist can observe such "inlying purposes and ideas" which "the mentalists would call conscious awareness and ideas . . . which may on certain occasions occur in an organism as a substitute or surrogate for actual behavior."

Despite his acknowledgment of the necessity for using introspection where extrospective techniques are applicable, Tolman warns against its uncritical employment: "Where the intervening variable in question is, as in psychoanalysis and in many personality studies, itself some complicated resultant of the social situation, . . . then such an intervening variable can, and perhaps must, be mirrored by introspection." Yet here, and even more so in experimental research, the introspective technique must not be used alone: "I have denied that introspective behavior provides any *sui generis* type of information concerning the intervening variables"; for "introspection is just one more behavior which in some cases (but in some cases certainly will not) provide a good, standard experimental setup for discovering and studying specific types of intervening variable." Although Tolman anticipates that, if and when *thinking* "is ever adequately explained by a psychologist," he will find that "he cannot study the process itself which produces changes except by asking for introspections." But the investigator should be aware that the "unsatisfactory and unreliable character of introspections, when it comes to reporting on thought processes, is notorious." [11]

Many psychologists, nevertheless, seem to agree with Gordon Allport: "Without forgetting for a moment what we have learned about rationalizing and about the untrustworthiness of introspective

reports on motives, we may safely declare that the opposing of motive and thought-process has gone much too far." [12]

What do some other social scientists have to say about the
limited use of critical introspective observation? With the exception
of a considerable number of *sociologists*, who opposed any egocentric
references, for the most part other behavioral disciplines have relied
upon introspective and extrospective techniques: Since "culture systems are obviously *only* understandable by this method," therefore,
"in the sciences of action we combine both Verstehen and observation of behavior, that is, of the external spatial course of events." [13]
Although Znaniecki opposes observational techniques which preclude "innumerable first-hand experiences without which cultural
life becomes incomprehensible," he believes that the method of
introspective psychology has thus far failed definitely to discover
what the agent's experience of activity 'really is'. Consequently, he
adopts as his observational data the theoretically reconstructed experience of a person, i.e., "it is the dynamic objective manifestation of his activity, the gradual construction in actual empirical
reality of a definite system of values—a poem or musical composition, a religious ceremony, a financial undertaking, an association." [14] MacIver, it will be recalled, more directly uses introspective
analysis in the reconstruction of motivational data, when he declares
that "as human beings we are immersed in the strivings, purposes,
and goals that constitute the peculiar dynamics of this area of reality." [15]

Anthropologists have used introspective techniques much more
than sociologists. For, as Bennett and Wolff emphasize in their comparison of these disciplines, "while the sociologist proposes to stand
away, to perceive man 'objectively', not to involve his own feelings
and reactions, the cultural anthropologist has often striven to know
man *through* his own feelings and reactions, to view the human beings
he studies as 'fellow men', not as 'subjects'." [16] As Redfield has said,
"the anthropologist's own human nature is an instrument of work,"
i.e., "the anthropologist, in understanding a culture or a personality"
is "guided by projection of his own human qualities into the situation
to be understood." [17] Nadel contends that the anthropologist should
not feel apologetic about using introspection, since it is not "so formidable and dubious as it is sometimes made out to be" when it is understood as "the scrutiny of data in our awareness, which proceeds in

precisely the same manner and with the same validity as the empirical scrutiny of the so-called 'objective' data of the physical world or indeed of behaviorist experiments." [18]

Theoretical economists derive their generalizations about motivation by an appeal to introspectively discovered preferences which allegedly are self-evident to all persons. This is Robbins' point when he declares that "the ultimate constituents of our fundamental generalizations are known to us by immediate acquaintance," rather than inferentially as are physical objects with the result that they are "so much the stuff of our every day experiences that they have only to be stated to be recognized as obvious." [19] He refers, of course, to what neo-classical economists have taken to be the universal rational motivation of maximizing satisfaction with a minimum of effort. Unorthodox economists, who challenge this premise as too narrowly circumscribed and limited to a market system, do not eliminate the use of introspection in discovering a wider range of economic motivation. Northrop's comment about theoretical economics, which applies to some extent to unorthodox economics as well, is instructive: "In this manner a science which found its subject matter to be constituted of private, introspected, relativistic, personal valuations nevertheless attained a theory which is publicly valid." [20]

The *historian*, of course, cannot observe the past human actions which he imaginatively reconstructs as accurately as he can out of what seems to him to be the most authentic testimony. As Gottschalk has declared, such is "the extraction of credible particulars from the sources (or parts of sources) proved genuine." [21] We must keep in mind, however, Collingwood's contention that each historian must critically evaluate his "authoritative" sources "when he describes certain historical facts as his data," since, "for the purposes of a particular piece of work there are certain historical problems relevant to that work which for the present he proposes to treat as settled." The point to be noted is this: "If they are settled, it is only because historical thinking has settled them in the past, and they remain settled only until he or someone else decides to reopen them." Consequently, historical facts can never "speak for themselves"; for, "anything is evidence which enables you to answer your question—the question you are asking now." [22] Although this holds for all scientific observation, the historian who is many times removed from the event in question lacks the contemporary referents for checking his reconstructed data which are often available to other social scientists.

The historian's position with respect to his initial data is more vindicated, if, instead of referring to historical facts, he attempts to establish the degree to which his data are verisimilar or factual in the sense of credible beyond plausability. "What is meant by calling a particular event *credible*," Gottschalk explains, "is not that it is actually what happened, but that it is as close to what actually happened as we can learn from a critical examination of the best available sources." [23] It is with the ability, willingness, and accuracy of the primary witness with respect to the truth, as well as corroborating testimony, therefore, that the historian must be concerned. With respect to such evidence in history Aron has declared that the data would no longer be the available documents or monuments, but "past facts hypothetically reconstituted as the initial step of the historical analysis." [24]

The historian must use introspection, since, as Collingwood has claimed, he "must re-enact the past in his own mind." Gottschalk also emphasizes this when he grants that "the raw records may provide our best means of discovering what actually happened if we ever can," but that "the data derived from an analysis of the historical records have to be assayed against an imaginative re-creation, a re-enactment in the mind, of the historical reality." But just as the other social scientists must combine extrospective with introspective observation, so also "the historian must use some more objective techniques to support his subjective process of re-creation." [25]

As a surrogate for extrospective observation some historical theorists suggest an attitude and a procedure for providing reasonably reliable "contemporaneity of evidence." "Historical mindedness" is the attitude which the historian must adopt so that his own preferences will not distort his understanding of what motivated the actions he is imaginatively reconstructing in the "contemporary past." Although Gottschalk recognizes how difficult it is for the historian "to shed his own personality" when he uses his own introspectively acquired emotions and purposes for understanding his subject's motivation; Gottschalk insists, nevertheless, that "the obligation upon him is obvious if he is attempting to understand and impartially judge rather than to criticize others' acts and personalities." [26]

As a procedure for critically checking the introspectively recon-

structed observational data with which the historian begins, Strong
has suggested the "empirical equivalent" of "continuant configurations" or "the reconstruction of past relationships." By this he
means that, when the historian subjectively imagines the motivation
of past actions, he must limit his conception to what can reasonably
be expected in observable contemporary actions under similar circumstances: "The record in documents of actions and production
engaged in by men long since dead is not questioned so long as
these conform to abilities that men could be expected to have from
what is now known of the limits of human capacities and powers." [27]
For this procedure, the usefulness of the synoptic model as a conceptual framework for a portrait of the motivational goal-seeking
under natural and sociocultural conditions should be too obvious to
require elaboration.

Footnotes to Chapter 1 of Part Four

[1] Northrop, *The Logic of the Sciences and Humanities*, 241, 247, 253-254.
[2] Margenau, *The Nature of Concepts* (Proceedings of the Stillwater Conference),
47-48.
[3] Lenzen, "Procedure of Empirical Science," *International Encyclopedia of
Unified Science*, Vol. I, No. 5, pp. 4-5.
[4] Lerner, *Evidence and Inference*, 17.
[5] Murray in *Toward a General Theory of Action* (Parsons and Shils), 440.
[6] Alexander, "Principles of Psychosomatic Research," *Psychological Theory*
(Marx), 461-462.
[7] Gibson, "Studying Perceptual Phenomena," *Methods of Psychology* (Andrews),
162.
[8] Andrews, *Methods of Psychology*, 6.
[9] Allport, *Becoming*, 51.
[10] George in *Symposium on Sociological Theory* (Gross), 338.
[11] Tolman in *Psychological Theory* (Marx), 87, 413-414, 416, 418, 424-425,
101-102; and in *Toward a General Theory of Action* (Parsons and Shils), 357.
[12] Allport in *Psychological Theory* (Marx), 162.
[13] Parsons, *The Structure of Social Action*, 765.
[14] Znaniecki, *The Method of Sociology*, 55-59.
[15] MacIver, *Social Causation*, 262-264.
[16] Bennett and Wolff in *Current Anthropology* (Thomas), 334.

[17] Redfield in *Anthropology Today* (Kroeber), 733.

[18] Nadel, *Foundations of Social Anthropology*, 74.

[19] Robbins, *An Essay on the Nature and Significance of Economic Science*, 90 ff, 105.

[20] Northrop, *The Logic of the Sciences and the Humanities*, 241.

[21] Gottschalk, *Understanding History*, Chapter VII.

[22] Collingwood, *The Idea of History*, 244-245, 281-282.

[23] Gottschalk, *Understanding History*, 139.

[24] Aron, "Evidence and Inference in History," *Evidence and Inference* (Lerner), 21.

[25] Gottschalk, "The Historian's Use of Generalizations," *The State of the Social Sciences* (White), 442-443.

[26] Gottschalk, *Understanding History*, 137.

[27] Strong, "The Materials of Historical Knowledge," *Naturalism and the Human Spirit* (Krikorian), 159.

2 *The Second Stage of Hypothetical-Deductive Inquiry*

What is entailed in the construction through inferred generalizations of a hypothesis or system of hypotheses which might serve as a causal explanation, as well as a formula for prediction and a more precise classification of the relevant observational data?

In order to interpret the relevant data which he has observed and classified, the broader operationalist attempts to construct reliable hypotheses about objective reality in terms of a coherent system of *substantive* explanatory and predictive generalizations. Substantive in this sense means that the explanatory and predictive constructs have causal implications which can be logically deduced and empirically confirmed or refuted in the succeeding verificative stage of hypothetical-deductive inquiry.

Such theoretical constructs, out of which lawful generalizations are formulated, must be distinguished from the conceptual constructs by which observational data are descriptively identified. When Bergmann and Spence describe how the scientific psychologist inductively generalizes from observations in terms of the "functional relationships among variables," they insist that "explanatory work proper starts, and can start, only after the empirical constructs have been laid down." [1] Although social psychologists have not as yet in actual practice refined their explanatory and predictive constructs to the degree that the individual psychologists have, Newcomb acknowledges this in principle: "Methods of accurately observing response to social stimulation and of controlling social stimulation must be subservient to the major problem of explaining the psychological processes which determine behavior." [2]

The scientist not only must use hypothetical investigation; but he must also construct a system of hypothetical principles for the sake of introducing the order or causal connection among the observational data which explanatory and predictive generalizations require. Factual observations will yield no meaningful answers unless they are approached with meaningful questions that are organized in the mind of the investigator in accordance with some tentative principle of interpretation, i.e., a hypothesis. Kant's insight that "nature must be interrogated" means that chance observations have significance as discoveries only when they affirm or deny some presumption in the mind of the investigator which is linked to a system of ideas. Accordingly, observation of data and the formulation of hypotheses go hand in hand mutually supporting and modifying each other. Moreover, in order to be persistently useful such hypotheses must be suggestive for further inquiry with respect to new data and their interrelationships. For, as Cantril has emphasized as a premise of psychological research, "in scientific procedure there is a never ending process of hypothesizing, a constant flow of one hypothesis from another, with each hypothesis trying to go beyond established formulations in its inclusiveness." [3]

Natural scientists and social scientists alike aim at the formulation of inferential generalizations as a primary object of inquiry. As Hempel has said, "Empirical science, in all its major branches, seeks not only to *describe* the phenomena in the world of our experience, but also to *explain* or *understand* their occurrence: it is concerned not just with the "what?", "when?" and "where?", but definitely, and often predominantly, with the "why?" of the phenomena it investigates." [4]

It is generally recognized that *theoretical constructs* function both as *explanations* of present effects by reference to past causes, and as *predictions* of future effects by reference to present causes. For analysis in physics, Reichenbach has used "postdictability" to characterize explanation and "predictability" to characterize predictions.[5] Correspondingly, for sociological analysis, Zetterberg distinguishes between the inferential procedures of the "retrospective design" which "advances from the establishment of effects to the establishment of causes" and the "prospective design" which "goes from the establishment of causes to the establishment of effects." [6]

Although social scientists generally agree that behavioral analysis should proceed from *description* to explanation, there is not complete agreement with respect to the degree that explanatory generalizations must provide *prediction*. An examination of the social-scientific literature substantiates the report by Hempel and Oppenheim that "providing an explanation of the phenomenon it investigates" is "the chief objective of science," but "there exists considerable difference of opinion as to the function and the essential characteristics of scientific explanation." [7] Let us now consider some representative statements that reveal this divergence.

This is a controversial issue among psychologists. On the one hand, many who have been influenced by the Watsonian ideal of the predictive control of human behavior seem to insist that exact predictibility is the *sine qua non* for admissible explanatory hypotheses. On the other hand, Marx contends that "the ultimate aim of all natural science is explanation and understanding and not simply prediction and control in a practical sense, as is often assumed." Just as Brown has shown that seismology is scientifically significant without any predictive control of earthquakes, so also, Marx argues, in dealing with human behavior, that "the causes are too obscure, intricate, and inaccessible for exact prediction." [8]

The controversy about the necessity for predictive certainty has been especially acute in economics. The neo-classical economic theory achieved its pre-eminent status by virtue of the predictive precision which its mathematical-logical deductive system provided. Fashioned in the image of Newtonian mechanism, it aimed at strictly predictive generalizations about future economic states which were deductively derived from presently given economic states. It was this basic assumption which the institutionalists and other unorthodox economists challenged when they criticized the neo-classical theorists' narrowly circumscribed conception of human motivation and the sociocultural process. Consequently, the unorthodox economists do not insist upon the exactness of their predictions. Moreover, as Northrop has pointed out "a theoretical economic dynamics is impossible within the framework of classical economic theory," for these two basic reasons: "(1) The subjective relative character of valuations necessitates the grounding of the public validity of economic theory on their generic properties merely, thereby leaving the state of a system at a given time unprecisely designated theoretically. . . . (2) The failure of the total quantity of valuations to obey a conservation law prevents the prediction of a future state, even if the present state were given specifically." The first failure stems from the economist's abstract conception of human preferences, which in no way corresponds to Newton's designation of the specific properties of the momenta and positions of all masses. The second failure stems from the unavoidable fact that human preferences do not remain constant in time.[9] Nevertheless, prediction remains the crucial principle in what Friedman (following Keynes) has called the "methodology of positive economics": "Viewed as a body of substantive hypotheses, theory is to be judged by its predictive power for the class of phenomena which it is intended to 'explain'." [10]

Among sociologists disagreement about the function of predictive generalizations reflects the divergence of premises with respect to the priority of techniques or the priority of subject matter. On the one hand, narrower operationalists who seek to imitate natural sciences grant that sociological research does not as yet yield exact predictions; but they insist, nevertheless, that sociologists should adopt this objective which will be possible when quantitative techniques are sufficiently refined. Lundberg advocates this approach but warns his colleagues that "only when standardized public instruments for the observation and measurement of these behavior phenomena are developed "can predictive hypotheses" be put to empirical test." [11] On the other hand, broader operationalists insist that, regardless of how much sociological techniques are improved, the subject matter of sociology will never be suitable for more than what Rose has called "informed expectations." [12] For, as Gross has emphasized, "social events, it appears, are tied together occasionally or frequently, but never invariably." [13] This limitation is acknowledged by Frank when he declares that "institutional patterns or prescribed roles can be more or less successfully predicted because we know that a certain number of individuals are going to exhibit these roles and use these institutional patterns with certain recurrent regularities." [14]

By noting how laws bear upon predictive generalizations we may better understand why psychologists, theoretical economists, and sociologists are generally more interested in predictions than are anthropologists, political scientists, and historians. Most psychologists, economists, and sociologists would agree that an explanatory-predictive generalization must entail a general law, such as Hempel has designated as "a statement of universal conditional form which is capable of being confirmed or disconfirmed by suitable empirical findings." [15] The majority of anthropologists, political scientists, and historians, however, seriously doubt that they can ever formulate such "universal conditions." Consequently, they have less confidence that their generalizations could ever have very much predictive significance. This point will be elaborated in the discussion of the fourth stage of the hypothetical deductive method which deals explicitly with the problem of formulating behavioral laws. Despite this basic problem encountered by anthropologists, political scientists, and, in particular, by historians, the subsequent statements of their aims with respect to prediction indicate that they do not altogether abandon the predictive function of their hypotheses.

Even though anthropologists agree that their lack of precision techniques and the complexity of their data preclude exact predictions, some have shown an interest in the possibility of developing predictions about sociocultural processes. When, for example, Kroeber and Kluckhohn assess the use of anthropological generalizations as "least common denominators" or "highest common factors," they assert that their validity will depend upon "the extent to which they not only make the phenomena more intelligible but also make possible reasonably accurate predictions of cultural change under specified conditions." [16]

The political scientist who is interested in constructing predictive generalizations acknowledges that this is only programmatically possible. Taking issue with the many political scientists who are content merely to classify their data, Leiserson insists that an attempt to develop explanatory-predictive constructs can not be avoided by the analyst of political behavior. He becomes engaged in systematic inquiry as soon as he seeks an answer to this crucial question: "Under what conditions do these relationships hold good." Accordingly, when Leiserson advocates the establishment of a "systematic-empirical method" in addition to the traditional approaches which do not involve the predictive function of hypotheses, he is calling for "a conceptual apparatus capable of dealing with the strategic or limiting factors in the relations of the political scientist to his observational methods and the uniformities or regularities in his data." Leiserson recognizes the difficulty of "specifying in advance the data relevant to the hypothesis delimiting the problem under investigation": but he takes this to be necessary if the political scientist is to move beyond the merely diagnostic stage of inquiry.[17]

Since the historian deals primarily with the past, it is obvious why he has more interest in postdictive rather than predictive generalizations. All historians, however, do not ignore the predictive function of an explanatory hypothesis. For instance, Nevins claims that "it enables communities to grasp their relationship with the past, and to chart on general lines their immediate forward course." [18] According to Strong, however, such alleged expectations from the historian's merely narrative presentation of temporal sequences amounts only to "more or less shrewd guesswork." Consequently, Strong contends, "predictions can be made as a probability judgment only by the historian who has reconstructed the past in terms of contemporary empirical equivalents" on the hypothesis that "the continuant configuration which has been holding will continue to hold." [19]

When Gottschalk declares that "it would thus appear that, in many instances, the acceptable historical generalization differs from the social-science concept only in tense," we assume he means that even the soundest of historical explanations should not be expected to be predictive. Since the historical construct always refers to vanished data, even the limited prediction, which the verification of the deduced implications of social-scientific hypotheses requires, cannot be required of historical hypotheses. Nevertheless, mindful of this, some historians simulate the "reasonable expectations" of the social scientist when they prognosticate by drawing analogies involving "historical parallels," or by extrapolating "historical trends." Historians who are fully aware of the complexity, variability, and uniqueness of historical situations with "too many unknowns" can hardly ignore Gottschalk's warning that such historical analogies and trends "present us most often with clues to *possible* rather than probable behavior, with the ability only to *anticipate* rather than to *predict*, to take *precautions* rather than to control." For the historian is confronted with the "unresolved problem of determinism and free-will, the misunderstood, perhaps not understandable, role of accident in history, the highly debatable place to be assigned to personality and leadership, the changing social atmosphere from place to place and from generation to generation." Accordingly, Gottschalk advises, "the careful historian ought to limit himself merely to stressing one among several possible outcomes when a current situation appears analogous to a past one." As he acknowledges, this is essentially the warning of the Committee on Historiography in Bulletin 54 against pretentions by historians that they can predict more than they actually are able to do. But the Committee does claim that at least this much "reasonable expectation" is warranted in historical constructs: "In certain and limited cases, however, by the use of historical knowledge and analogies, the historian may in respect of given situations, indicate various contingencies, one or more of which may be anticipated with a high degree of probability." [20]

The debate about historiographical predictions is an issue which can not be understood apart from the basic question about historical laws. Although this problem of lawful generalizations will be discussed more fully later, it is necessary to make some reference here to those aspects of it which bear directly on historical predictions. A new dimension of the problem of prediction emerges when Popper's and Hempel's "covering law" theory, which implies that the historian's predictions can, in principle, be like the natural scientist's predictions, is challenged by Dray on the premise that there "is, or very well may be, a 'law' with only a single case." It should be kept in mind during the subsequent discussion of Dray's view of prediction in history, that he is not advocating the traditional intuitional approach which opposes any conception of historical laws. For Dray, as for Popper and Hempel, historical knowledge can be obtained only through the inferential process of constructing explanatory-predictive generalizations.

Why does Dray oppose the view of Popper and Hempel that "the logical structure of *explanation* is equivalent to that of *prediction* and *verification*" as long as they are subsumed "under an independently validated general law"? Dray's objection to the strict correlation of explanation and prediction is two-fold. First, he contends that "neither explanation nor prediction need be law-covered in historical cases." Second, he insists that, to refuse to recognize that "there is a logical dissimilarity between explanation and prediction," is to depart from the ordinary meaning of the term 'explanation,' which is also its meaning in history." In support of his challenge he points out that knowledge which is sufficient to predict an event, is not necessarily sufficient to explain that event, even though he does not deny that "the elaboration of a continuous series may often satisfy the condition that what is explained be predictable from the data which the explanation contains." Moreover, he insists, instead of holding with Hempel that "an explanation" is not complete unless it might as well have functioned as a prediction, most historians, as well as some physicists and logicians, adopt the pragmatic meaning of explanation.[21] Bridgman identified this when he claimed that "the essence of an explanation consists in reducing a situation to elements with which we are so familiar that we accept them as a matter of course, so that our curiosity rests." [22] This does not preclude "retrospective foresight" by which, according to Aron, historical reconstruction "seeks to elaborate the system of interpretation which would have made possible a prediction of the actual course of events." [23]

In an effort to find some basis of agreement among these diverse conceptions of the function of predictive generalizations let us ask to what extent behavioral scientists would accept the previously-quoted statement by Hempel and Oppenheim that it is the "potential predictive force which gives scientific explanation its importance." The writers whom we have quoted do not all agree that an explanation must yield predictions to be important; nevertheless, do they not all acknowledge that a satisfactory explanation must have at least some *potential* predictive force? If this is the case, then we should say that, instead of demanding a "strict correlation" between explanation and prediction such that it provides predictive control, there could be a general acceptance of a more flexible correlation of these two interrelated but separable functions of scientific inference. By a more flexible conception we mean this: On the one hand, without explanatory inferences about what has happened there would be no basis for predictive inferences about what will happen. On the other hand, without some predictive inferences, there would be no logical relation of implication (if-then) as a pattern in the verificative procedure of consistently deducing the implications of an explanatory generalization so that they could be confirmed or disconfirmed by empirical evidence.

The modification of precise prediction to "reasonable expectations," as well as the more strict to the more flexible correlation of explanation and prediction, does not mitigate all of the complications which confront the social scientist when he constructs explanatory-predictive generalizations. Most of these additional complications stem from the nature of behavioral events which are not susceptible to the same kind of treatment as natural events. Consequently, the social scientist may agree with Gross that "the best way to find order in social behavior is to work 'as if' the data before them were amenable to devices that resemble those used in natural science." [24] However, they usually agree with Werkmeister that recognition of the "complexities of human relations" should discourage "too hasty emulation of the natural sciences" in the construction of explanatory-predictive generalizations.[25] What Rapoport has said of all social-scientific techniques applies especially to prediction: "Because it is harder to learn to observe in a certain way or to abstract in a certain way than to get consistent results from measurement, the social scientist's concepts are harder to come by than the physical scientist's." [26]

The specification of the limiting conditions of purposive goal-seeking behavior is the most formidable obstacle which stands in the way of isolating and correlating the causal variables that accurate predicting requires. MacIver makes this problem clear when he directs attention to what might be called the reciprocity of sociocultural-motivational causation. Instead of encouraging the futile attempt of establishing rigorous predictions in terms of one way cause and effect relations among behavioral events MacIver exhorts the social scientist to recognize that "one can reverse, with some degree of truth, almost any statement of social causation," e.g., predictions about education and the standards of intelligence, slavery and lack of technological development, severity of criminal code and crime, low wages and poverty, intemperance and destitution.[27] The difficulty of specifying the limiting conditions of purposive behavior is also acknowledged by Merton in terms of the "self-fulfilling prophesy," i.e., in the evolving human situation to which predictive generalizations refer, the actions of the participants may be changed by the reconstruction of their aims on the basis of this knowledge.[28]

A further question arises out of the recognition of this difference between behavioral and physical data. Does functional analysis constitute an approach that is different in kind from the causal approach for which the construction of explanatory-predictive generalizations is designed? According to Hempel, the constructs about human behavior which functional analysis provide are modified teleological explanations, rather than explanatory-predictive generalizations which the natural sciences formulate in terms of testable causal law: "Thus, functional analysis seeks to understand a behavior pattern or a sociocultural institution in terms of the role it plays in keeping the given system in proper working order and thus maintaining it as a going concern." But, unlike the nomological generalizations of the physical sciences, the kind of functional analysis used by psychology, anthropology, and sociology "no more enables us to predict than it enables us to explain the occurrence of a particular one of the items by which a given functional requirement can be met." Despite Hempel's unwillingness to accept the generalizations of functional analysis as theoretical explanatory-predictive constructs, he does grant that as *conceptual* constructs they serve "as a program for research guided by certain heuristic maxims or "working hypotheses." But, to be *theoretically* fruitful "it seems highly desirable and indeed necessary to pursue the investigation of specific relationships to the point where they can be expressed in terms of reasonably precise and objectively testable hypotheses." [29]

Although all social scientists intend that their explanatory-predictive generalizations should be verified, many are confronted with

complications when they attempt to establish the reasonable acceptability of their hypotheses. We now turn to the elaboration of these
aims and problems which social-scientific verification entails.

Footnotes to Chapter 2 of Part Four

[1] Bergmann and Spence in *Psychological Theory* (Marx), 57.
[2] Newcomb in *Methods of Psychology* (Andrews), 665.
[3] Cantril and others, "Psychology and Scientific Research," *Science*, November 1949, page 491.
[4] Hempel, "The Logic of Functional Analysis," *Symposium on Sociological Theory* (Gross), 271.
[5] Reichenbach, *Quantum Mechanics*, 13.
[6] Zetterberg, *On Theory and Verification in Sociology*, 62.
[7] Hempel and Oppenheim, "The Logic of Explanation," *Readings in the Philosophy of Science* (Feigl and Brodbeck), 319, 323, 324. Originally published in *Philosophy of Science*, 15, 1948.
[8] Marx, *Psychological Theory* (Marx), 5.
[9] Northrop, *The Logic of the Sciences and the Humanities*, 245-246.
[10] Friedman, *Essays in Positive Economics*, 8.
[11] Lundberg, *Foundations of Sociology*, 136.
[12] Rose, *Theory and Method in the Social Sciences*, Chapter 14.
[13] Gross, *Symposium on Sociological Theory* (Gross), 535.
[14] Frank in *Toward a Unified Theory of Human Behavior* (Grinker), 331.
[15] Hempel, "The Function of General Laws in History," *Readings in Philosophical Analysis* (Feigl and Sellars), 459. Originally published in *The Journal of Philosophy*, 39, 1942.
[16] Kluckhohn and Kroeber, "General Features of Culture," *Culture, A Critical Review of Concepts and Definitions* (Peabody Papers) Vol. XLVII, No. 1, p. 162.
[17] Leiserson, *Political Science Quarterly*, Dec. 1953, pages 562-563, 575-580, 583.
[18] Nevins, *The Gateway to History*, 3.
[19] Strong, "The Materials of Historical Knowledge," *Naturalism and the Human Spirit* (Krikorian), 178-179.
[20] Gottschalk, *Understanding History*, 259, 263-264, 264-265, 269. See Bulletin 54, page 139.
[21] Dray, *Laws and Explanation in History*, 39, 59-60, 77.
[22] Bridgman, *The Logic of Modern Physics*, 37.
[23] Aron in *Evidence and Inference* (Lerner), 26.
[24] Gross, *Symposium on Sociological Theory*, (Gross), 536.

25 Werkmeister, "Theory Construction and Objectivity," *Symposium on Sociological Theory* (Gross), 490.

26 Rapoport, "Mathematical Models," *Symposium on Sociological Theory* (Gross), 352.

27 MacIver, *The Elements of Social Science*, 12.

28 Merton, *Antioch Review* (1948), 193-210.

29 Hempel, "The Logic of Functional Analysis," *Symposium on Sociological Theory* (Gross), 278, 301, 302.

3 *The Third Stage of Hypothetical-Deductive Inquiry*

A. *The Generic Criterion of Coherence*

> *What is entailed in the verification of a hypothesis or a system of hypotheses in accordance with the criterion of coherence, i.e., consistency and adequacy?*

The justification for the techniques which are used in the verification of social-scientific hypotheses is derived from the fifth postulate of the meaning-situation of reflective inquiry. Accordingly, before examining this verificative procedure let us briefly review what we have assumed when we presupposed that coherence is the generic logical criterion of verification from which specific criteria and techniques for empirical testing of the deduced implications of hypotheses are derived.

The defining principles of this comprehensive ideational framework for determining the reasonable acceptability of the explanatory-predictive generalizations, it will be recalled, are consistency and comparative adequacy. For ascertaining consistency it is necessary to use a mathematical or logical technique for deducing the implications of hypotheses which are to be tested. For ascertaining comparative causal adequacy these specific criteria were presented: relevancy, systematic congruency, and fruitfulness. In order to meet these demands, a hypothesis must be empirically confirmed by either experimental and/or experiential testing. It is with these operational procedures in the knowledge-situation i.e., controlled experiment, controlled observation, statistical correlation, comparative case study, and introspective projection that we are now concerned. These techniques, it will be noted, are the instrumental means by which the social scientist attempts to realize the intrinsic end of a coherent system of reasonably acceptable generalizations.

B. *The Technique of Deducing Implications*

A clear distinction must be made between the aim of the deductive techniques of social scientists, who use them merely to elaborate the valid implications of their hypotheses, and the aim of the pure rationalists, who use them to establish the absolute truth of an *a priori* system of universal and necessary generalizations. When the behavioral scientist adopts the assumption of contemporary mathematicians and logicians that their reasoning is conventional rather than absolutistic, he holds that the relation of implication (if-then) pertains only to the validity of inferences in the consistent formulation of abstract relations regardless of the substantive truth of the hypotheses from which the implications are being deduced. The investigator who uses this hypothetical syllogism, however, needs to establish no more than that the derived proposition follows consistently from the hypothesis which serves as its premise. The investigator seeks to establish the validity of this relation of implication only as a means for deciding what questions he should be seeking to answer when he engages in empirical testing in order to determine which construct is relatively more adequate.[1]

As long as a social scientist assumes that his verificative operations are limited to experimental testing, he will usually not acknowledge that this technique derives its significance from the ideational criterion of coherence. But there is growing recognition in each of the social-scientific disciplines that it is by the questions which the investigator asks in terms of this relation of implication, that his procedure for empirical testing is determined. George, for example, calls attention to this problem of the psychologist who is "working beyond the confines of a narrow Watsonian Behaviorism" in the direction of "the coherence, precision and logical consistency of a scientific theory." Instead of continuing to use "the relatively crude statistical methods of handling groups, attitudes, etc.," he insists that "we should have a flexible framework which would serve as a scientific tool for research to encompass the experimental work in progress, and be precise enough to avoid the pitfalls of ordinary language." [2]

The deductive phase of the process of verification is necessitated and justified by the fact that no scientific generalization in itself can be directly verified. Only derivative hypotheses deduced from it are susceptible to confirmation or refutation by empirical testing. Consider, for example, the evolutionary generalization that "all life has developed from the less complex to the more complex, *then* there should be evidence that the various forms of life are interrelated." Furthermore, "if life has developed from the less complex to the more complex, *then* there should be evidence that the various forms of life are modifiable." With these conceptually designed questions in mind the biologists can proceed with observational research that may lead to negative or affirmative answers. Research in comparative anatomy, genetics, embryology, paleontology, etc. has produced observational data which are more intelligible when they are conceptually integrated in terms of the evolutionary hypotheses than they are when they are so interpreted by alternative generalizations, e.g., the special creation theory of *Genesis*. Consequently, the theory of evolution is accepted as reliable knowledge. Like any other "warranted assertion" it is, of course, subject to modification, correction, or abandonment, if new discoveries can be more reasonably interpreted in accordance with a modified, corrected, or entirely alternative generalization.

Representatives from each of the constitutive disciplines have even more explicitly recognized that without this conceptual directive an investigator would not know what to be looking for. Newcomb advocates this for social psychology even though some social psychologists do not always follow such a procedure: "The steps in the scientific method of verification are, in the brief, (1) outlining a hypothesis, based upon conclusions drawn from previous (but not necessarily systematically controlled) observations, concerning the exact conditions under which a given event will vary in its occurrence; (2) arranging situations in which all conditions known to be relevant, other than those described in the hypothesis, are not allowed to vary, while the hypothetical conditions are varied in known ways." [3]

Merton indicates that the sociologist also "begins with a hunch or hypothesis, from this he draws various inferences and they in turn are subjected to empirical test which confirms or refutes the hypothesis." Merton contends, however, that in addition to confirming or refuting hypotheses, the observation of evidence may also lead to a modification of the hypothesis.[4] When Zetterberg declares that "the best piece of proof we have is that our hypothesis can predict observations," he recognizes the limits which are inherent in this kind of sociological verification: "This is an incomplete proof since we always run the risk that new observations will disqualify our prediction or that alternative hypotheses will predict observations equally well." Disproving the opposite hypothesis, i.e., the "null-hypothesis," is what actually is done. Accordingly, "designs for testing working hypotheses must reveal not only the extent to which our data fall in the direction predicted by the hypothesis," but they must also establish "the certainty with which we have disproved the hypothesis contrary to the working hypothesis," as well as "the certainty and extent to which we have disproved alternative hypotheses to the working hypothesis." [5]

Anthropologists, as previously noted, have not exhibited widespread concern about verification. Nevertheless, when Malinowski describes the aim of his functional analysis to be "taking an individual culture as a coherent whole," he expects it "to produce a number of predictive statements as guides for field-research." [6]

With respect to the verification of economic constructs this more recent use of this hypothetical-deductive technique in the third verificative stage of a predominantly inductive procedure requires special attention. For neo-classical economic theorists were largely deductive in the analytical manner of formalistic logicians and mathematicians. Machlup opposes this *a priori* conception when he describes the two-step procedure by which an economic hypothesis is verified as "first deducing from it and the factual assumptions with which it is combined all the conclusions that can be inferred, and second, confronting these conclusions obtained from observation of the phenomena concerned." Accordingly, Machlup endorses the broadly operational principle that if no implications can be consistently deduced from a hypothesis, there is no way by which it can be empirically tested. Although Machlup agrees with other social scientists that the confirmation of the hypothesis is achieved, if testing shows that "no irreconcilable contradiction is found between the deduced and the observed," he, like Zetterberg, soundly warns that "testing an empirical hypothesis results either in its disconfirmation or its non-disconfirmation, never in its definitive confirmation." But this does not preclude *reasonable acceptability*, since a hypothesis confirmed and reconfirmed any number of times will have a more loyal following than one only rarely exposed to the test of experience." [7] This limitation of the verificative process has similarly been emphasized by Gordon in more negative terms: "For a proposition to be testable by some physical operation, it must predict that certain observations will *not* occur, so that, if they do, the proposition is refuted." [8]

Leiserson calls for this verificative procedure in political science even though "experimental situations approximating the laboratory or clinic are rarely, if ever, possible for the analyst of political behavior. So that political scientists should not "complacently use the facts to justify lazy epistemological eclecticism," Leiserson calls upon his colleagues for an "unrelenting effort to relate his limited empirical generalizations to high-order propositions of functional relations between variables." [9]

In his analysis of the verificative process in historical inquiry, Werkmeister insists that only with respect to the historian who has interpreted and woven his collected facts into "a coherent pattern," can it be said that "the logic of confirming or refuting his hypothesis is then the same as that of testing a hypothesis in any field of science." [10] This is corroborated by Brockunier and Loewenberg when they urge historians to go beyond "simple proof by the documentary method of quoting testimony" in order to develop verificative techniques which might furnish a "more coherent basis for cumulative theory." [11] From Donagan's description of the procedure by which the historian verifies his "imaginary reconstruction of the past," verification appears to require the same correlation of deductive and inductive techniques that is required for each of the other scientific disciplines. In order to determine whether or not his hypothesis is consistent or whether or not any alternative will "equally account for the evidence," the historian "supports or throws doubt on his reconstruction partly by internal criticism . . . and partly by deducing from his reconstruction what new evidence would be pertinent, searching for it, and revising his reconstruction in the light of what he may find or fail to find." [12]

C. *Techniques for Empirical Testing*

What techniques does a broader operationalist use, when he attempts to test his working hypothesis empirically in order to show that such an explanatory-predictive construct has a higher degree of adequacy than that of a contrary hypothesis, as well as that of alternative hypotheses? In order to decide what he should be looking for when he undertakes empirical testing he shares with all other scientists the same deductive procedure for elaborating the substantive implications of his hypotheses. For the actual empirical testing, however, the broader operationalist must use only those techniques which are applicable to the specific kind of data to which his particular construct refers. Accordingly, let us try to classify and clarify the various techniques for empirical testing in terms of the two separate but interrelated modes: *experimental* testing and *experiential* testing. (1) *Experimental testing* is required for confirming or refuting the implications of a hypothesis under controlled laboratory conditions and/or controlled observations in the natural sciences (including experimental psychology). (2) *Experiential testing* is required for confirming or refuting the implications of a hypothesis under relatively controlled observational conditions in the behavioral sciences (excluding experimental psychology).

Let us now consider what each of these verificative techniques entails, and what a representative from each of the behavioral sciences has said about their applicability to his specific data.

1. EXPERIMENTAL TESTING

Experimental testing requires both ideational and manipulatory operations. The ideational operations are based on the investigator's presupposition that the process of physical events is a uniform and invariable sequence of causes and effects. If he did not adopt the postulate that nature operates in an orderly manner, there would be no justification for the preeminence in scientific verification of the crucial experiment, i.e., a laboratory test that can be performed with the same results at any time or in any place provided that the same controlled conditions prevail. Proceeding on this causal assumption, the experimenter manipulates the factors in the experimental situation so that the normal course of events is interfered with sufficiently for him to ascertain whether or not the causal factors actually do function in the manner which he has been led by his hypothesis to expect. Both this ideational aspect and this manipulatory aspect of experimental testing are regulated by a logical pattern which can be expressed in the following symbolic formula: "If the independent variable a is to be established as the cause of the dependent variable b, then it must be shown that whenever a occurs b also inevitably occurs, and whenever a is absent b always fails to occur." Although much actual experimental testing involves more than two variables, this is the basic structure of the performance.

The techniques for observing, measuring, recording, etc. that are used in experimental testing are similar to those which were used in the first stage of inspecting and classifying the initial data. But at this more advanced stage, in which conditions are deliberately manipulated, the results are more meaningful because they are the outcome of the conceptual design which the investigator has in mind. This does not mean that absolute proof is guaranteed in a laboratory experiment in which the previously ascertained conditions can be controlled and manipulated with considerable precision. It does mean, however, that the margin of error is increasingly restricted, when observations under these controlled conditions are so systematically organized that the performance which confirms the implications of a hypothesis can be consistently reduplicated by other investigators.

In the organization of the conditions for experimental testing, some factors are eliminated from consideration or are held constant; but other factors are taken to be relevant to the question in the mind of the investigator in terms of which the performance of the experiment is designed. Among these designed factors, the presumed causes are viewed as *independent variables* and the presumed effects are viewed as *dependent variables.*

Of the various manipulations of these factors that have been used for experimental testing, the following indicate the direction toward increasingly refined precision in the isolation and control of the observational conditions. First, when two experimental set-ups are correlatively designed to be identical with the exception of one factor, the divergence between results from the respective experiments can be attributed to that one factor. Second, this procedure becomes more complicated, when the single independent variable is manipulated at different levels of intensity. The ideal, of course, is to be able to measure quantitatively these gradations of intensity so that the results can be expressed in terms of mathematical equations. Third, by coordinating experimental formulae with statistical formulae some investigators have been able to establish a range of functional relationships that is sufficiently reliable to make it possible to manipulate several independent variables at the same time.

Some economists, sociologists, and psychologists use statistical correlation instead of experimentation for empirically testing their constructs rather than merely as a device for making experimentation more precise. These social scientists see no alternative to this procedure, since their variables cannot be controlled to the degree that experimentation requires. In view of the widespread development of this practice Zetterberg has felt the necessity to warn his colleagues that "the use of statistics is no substitute for theorizing and hypotheses formation" and that it is not "the only acceptable method of evaluating a hypothesis in a theory of nature." For, not only is it the case that "non-quantitative methods under certain circumstances give equally or more plausible results than some quantitative methods," but, moreover, "the main reason for the use of quantified variables treated statistically is that we obtain through them a quantitative expression of the plausability of the null-hypothesis." Zetterberg finds support for his position in Churchman's theory of experimental inference in which he concludes that for statistical tests to be meaningful those who use this technique must assume that "every statistical hypothesis should be a consequence of a formal theory of nature." For it is not enough merely to statistically test distribution hypotheses about a set of data, since "to paraphrase Kant, statistical tests without theory are blind: no general results can be asserted, no predictions made unless one assumes that the statistical hypotheses are consequences of a general theory within which prediction can be made independent of specialized restrictions." [13]

Two points about experimentation should be noted. First, that controlled experimental testing is the ideal technique which all natural scientists and social scientists would prefer to use, if and when it is applicable to their specific data. Nothing that the present writer has said throughout this study is intended to detract from the paramount significance of the experimental techniques by which control, precision, and corroboration through the repetition of manipulations are obtained. The subsequent discussion of other techniques for empirical testing is simply a frank acknowledgment that the use of this more exact technique is not feasible. Secondly, that the experimental testing of rival hypotheses, and the testing of novel constructs to which here we have confined our attention, are not the only experimental procedures. As Werkmeister has explained, among several purposes for which experiments are designed there are also the other aims "to see what is the case" (exploratory); or, to check on "chance observations"; or, to test "accepted or traditional principles or laws"; or, "to re-check generally accepted facts." [14]

The techniques of relatively controlled observations of the natural course of events must be used for empirical testing in those cases where the techniques of laboratory experimentation are not applicable to the data with which the implications of hypothetical constructs must be compared. For, as Lachman has pointed out, even the natural scientist who places his "greatest confidence in the results of experimentation" must recognize that "not all natural phenomena may be investigated experimentally" and thus must acknowledge that "science derives data about certain categories of events by means other than experimentation." Moreover, Lachman insists, not only is it "physically impossible to bring certain phenomena into the laboratory," but also "bringing a phenomenon into the laboratory so distorts the phenomenon that its identity is questionable and the information derived therefrom may be misleading." [15]

It should also be noted that experimental testing itself cannot be significantly designed for the purpose of verification until after there have been extensive observations of untampered-with regularities of causal relations among natural events; for, no experiment would be "crucial" apart from the emendable assumptions it presupposes. In order to emphasize this point, Cohen and Nagel have declared that "every experiment, therefore, tests not an isolated hypothesis but the *whole body* of relevant knowledge logically involved." [16] This non-laboratory kind of empirical testing is required in some physical sciences, some biological verification, and practically all social-scientific verification with the exception of experimental psychology. The astronomer and the geologist, for example, cannot manipulate their independent and dependent variables in a laboratory. But they can achieve considerable precision in their verificative observations. Sociology, anthropology, and social psychology must use the same kind of observational techniques; but they are rarely, if ever, as precise as those of astronomy, geology, and biology. For all of these disciplines, however, simultaneous observations of the same anticipated events by independent observers is sought in lieu of the repetitive manipulations of artificially controlled conditions. Although the deliberate manipulations of laboratory experimentation represent the ideal of precision for empirical testing, in dealing with some natural and behavioral data, the careful observation of the typical course of events has some advantage over observation of a situation in which a considerable degree of artificiality has been the cost for manipulated precision.

Social scientists who attempt to be as experimental as possible recognize that partial success in controlling the conditions and manipulating variables is the most they can expect. This is explicitly acknowledged by Friedman with respect to the verification of economic generalizations: "The necessity of relying on uncontrolled experience rather than on controlled experiment makes it difficult to produce dramatic and clear-cut evidence to justify the acceptance of tentative hypotheses." But this does not deter the economist from empirically testing the deduced implications of his generalizations: "Reliance on uncontrolled experience does not affect the fundamental methodological principle that a hypothesis can be tested only by the conformity of its implications or predictions with observable phenomena; but it does render the task of testing hypotheses more

difficult and gives greater scope for confusion about the methodological principles involved." [17] Consequently, the social scientist attempts to make up the lack of extensive experimental testing with
controlled observations as another tool for empirically testing the implications of his hypotheses. Newcomb, for example, indicates that
"the social psychologist uses experimental and also various other
methods of controlling his observations" by "observing in the most
accurate manner possible the consequences of varying the hypothetical conditions" and by "confirming, revising (for future confirmation), or rejecting the initial hypotheses." [18]

2. EXPERIENTIAL TESTING

What is meant by *experiential testing* for confirming or refuting the
implications of social-scientific hypotheses through relatively controlled observations? *Experiential testing* in this context designates
the verificative process which combines the relatively objective comparative case techniques with the relatively subjective technique of
introspective projection. The necessity and justification for this two-
fold procedure as one mode of empirical testing of behavioral hypotheses will be more evident if we review the complications involved
in social-scientific verification.

Even if the social scientist can show that he has soundly observed
and classified his initial data, he has an even more difficult task in
trying to show that he has genuinely verified his explanatory and/or
predictive hypotheses about behavioral interaction. Crucial laboratory experimental testing of the implications of hypotheses under
controlled laboratory conditions is possible in those physical sciences
where the investigator is dealing with isolable factors which operate as invariant processes that can be manipulated and ascertained
with quantitative precision. The social scientist cannot be sure that
the behavioral interaction of naturalized, socioculturalized, and goal-
seeking individuals exhibits such uniformity when it is observed with
a view toward confirming or refuting explanatory constructs about it.
Furthermore, the interpenetrating environmental and motivational
factors which constitute the interrelated whole of a sociocultural
process are so complex that it does not seem possible for the social
scientist to isolate one variable at a time in order to make successful

predictions that are more precise than "reasonable expectations." Under these circumstances it is difficult, if not impossible, to eliminate all but one of what appear to be several alternative hypotheses. In addition to this complexity, there is the variability of a person's behavior as he plays different roles in different groups.

Since the social scientist cannot ignore the unique and variant aspects of human behavior, he cannot hope to engage in experimental manipulations in which he can keep all but one factor constant while he varies that one. Moreover, he cannot assure all other investigators that the conditions are such that they can get the same results at any place and at any time, if they reproduce the same conditions. His own operations may be influencing the outcome, when he tampers with behavioral interaction. Interfering conditions cannot be removed from the sociocultural-motivational situation in the same way a physical scientist utilizes a vacuum. Although in some physical situations the interfering conditions cannot be removed, still the physical scientist can make allowances for them in his calculations. The social scientist can never be reasonably sure of this in the behavioral situation. Since persons play so many social roles, it is difficult to isolate a causal context of motivational interaction. When the natural scientist compares two distinct alternative physical situations, it is usually possible for him to ascertain the differentiating factor. Rarely, if ever, however, can two sociocultural situations be found which are identical with the exception of the one factor that is present in one and missing in the other. Even if this differentiating factor can be located, the allegedly constant factors often become modified without the investigator's control or knowledge.

Fully recognizing these methodological limitations that are imposed by the nature of their subject matter, some social scientists have lowered their sights. They do not aim at as high a target as experimental testing or observations that lead to the precise mathematical equations which have given verification in the physical sciences its quantitative exactness. These investigators, who recognize that they must settle for less precision and less probability, look, nevertheless, for verification in terms of approximately empirical confirmation of the implications of social-scientific constructs through *experiential testing*. This combines as much relatively controlled observation as possible with such "imaginative reconstruction of alternative hypotheses" (MacIver) as behavioral data demand. By thus adapting the techniques of verification to the nature of their subject matter, they aim at an empirical testing of explanatory hypotheses which is far more reliable than the unexamined conjectures or biased speculations of what Parsons has condemned as a "dangerous irrationalism which lets go of all scientific standards altogether." [19]

Now that we have recognized the inherent complications which confront the social scientist when he attempts to test empirically his explanatory and/or predictive hypotheses, we shall consider, in turn, each of these techniques of his two-fold pattern of experiential testing: (a) the *comparative case analysis*, which is an approximation of experimental testing and controlled observations for dealing with *independent and dependent variables*, and (b) *introspective projection*, which is required by the behavioral data of goal-seeking motivation that is accounted for by the *intervening variable*.

a) *Comparative Case Analysis*

The technique of comparative case analysis seems to be different more in degree, than in kind, from experimental testing. This assumption of a considerable number of behavioral scientists has been made explicit by Parsons, when he declared that "experiment is, in fact, nothing but the comparative method where the cases to be compared are produced to order and under controlled conditions." [20] The necessity for adopting this procedural postulate has been recognized by Rose, when he emphasized that "the social scientist cannot properly take over the experimental method from the older sciences without examining it for its problems and assumptions in relation to his specific topic for research." [21] Since this is a crucial point, let us note what representatives of each of the disciplines have to say about the limitation of empirical testing to the experiential technique of comparative case analysis.

The psychologist uses this technique when, as Newcomb explains, he selects subjects with different experiential backgrounds "to whom such experiences have happened 'naturally,' taking pains to see that the individuals compared are as nearly as possible alike in other respects." [22] Murphy has noted that "serious doubt has arisen in recent years as to whether experimentation is adequate—even as adequate as the genetic or comparative method—with regard to most of the issues in the psychology of personality." [23]

Sociologists, more clearly than psychologists, have acknowledged that their empirical testing is limited to comparative case analysis. The general statements by Parsons and Rose about the need for comparative analysis in all social-scientific testing reflects the sociologist's commitment to this technique. Durkheim established it as a cornerstone of sociological inquiry. He emphasized that it is not possible to directly compare artificially produced phenomena in order to show that they are dependent on each other when their simultaneous presence or absence occurs: "When . . . the production of facts is not within our control and we can only bring them together in the way they have been spontaneously produced, the method employed is that of indirect experiment, or the comparative method." [24] Zetterberg has indicated the more specific controls which sociologists can use in accordance with their "pseudo-experimental design" for testing by comparative analysis: (a) "successive breakdown of available data around the criteria given by the alternative hypothesis," (b) "selective sampling or matching," and (c) "the use of statistical adjustments." [25]

The technique of comparative analysis has been the subject of a rather extended controversy among anthropologists. Those who acknowledge the demand for empirical testing would agree with Herskovits that "data must be presented in such a manner that they can be checked by independent observers." But they also share his conviction that, since the techniques of experimentation and controlled observation are not applicable to their unrepeatable data, they should "recognize and admit the limitation of a technique which yields results that, despite their appearance of regularity and accuracy, are, at best, spurious." [26] In emphasizing this limitation of anthropological data, Linton, for example, insists that "the very nature of the material precludes, in large part the use of experimental methods." [27] Accordingly, Nadel recognizes that "the artificial induction of variations in phenomena is replaced by the observation of variable phenomena," and he calls upon his colleagues to "study variation, found and looked for, in the data of observation, and correlate them so that from them general regularities may emerge." Nadel is fully aware, however, that since the verificative technique for making relatively controlled comparisons of observed situations "as such is only handling the materials which might yield relevant knowledge," such "comparisons need further refinement—planned selection and vigorous checks or controls—to approach the accuracy of a quasi-experimental method." [28]

Whereas some anthropologists disclaim this technique of comparative analysis, others claim that it should be revived, if indeed it was ever abandoned. Since functionalists like Malinowski rejected the evolutionary approach to cultural analysis in order to deal with the unique operations of an isolated community, they abandoned the comparative technique with which 19th century evolutionism had been identified. The historical school under Boas had not actually eliminated comparisons of different cultural forms. Despite the claim of those who have been so influenced by the functionalists that they have abandoned all comparative analysis, Ackerknecht advocates it in some form on the grounds that "one of the great advantages of the comparative method will be that in a field where controlled experiment is impossible, it provided at least some kind of control." Instead of allowing many valuable data to be neglected or to be treated only impressionistically, Ackerknecht looks to the revival of the use of comparative analysis along with the historical and functional techniques: "In whatever form the comparative method may reappear, it will express the growing desire and need in cultural anthropology to find regularities and common denominators behind the apparent diversity and uniqueness of cultural phenomena." [29] Kroeber goes even further than Ackerknecht when he claims that the technique was never given up, but "only changed its tactic." Kroeber insists that, in order to seek the "knowledge of process" which characterizes all scientific inquiry, the anthropologist must begin with the "description of the properties of the form and substance of the phenomena, their ordering or classification upon analysis of their structure, and the tracing of their changes or events." [30] Similarly, Kluckhohn declares that "from the point of view of subject matter, the sole feature which has distinguished every branch of anthropology and which has not been characteristic of any of the other human studies is the use of comparative data." [31]

Lewis disagrees to the extent that "comparison is a generic aspect of human thought rather than a special method of anthropology or of any other discipline." However, Lewis does acknowledge that among other aims "for testing hypotheses or arriving at general principles of societal development," a useful purpose is served by the anthropologists who "in their systematic study of similarities and differences, strive for a greater degree of control by utilizing the methods of correlation and co-variation." [32]

Until recently economists have not discussed the technique of comparative case study as extensively and explicitly as have sociologists and anthropologists. The neo-classical economic theorists who relied upon formalistic deductions felt no need for such a technique for empirically testing the substantive implications of their analytic generalizations. But since Marshall insisted that "economics uses both induction and deduction," he acknowledged the significance of the comparative method in the study of economic history.[33]

The applicability of comparative case analysis to economic data has been clarified and elaborated recently by Goldsmith in his comparative study of economic growth and structure. He presupposes that such a general procedure is not confined to any one technique: "The study of comparative economic growth and structure is not dependent on or even closely linked to any one statistical or analytical technique." The selection of the specific technique must be guided by the nature of the "different problems within the field." Comparative case analysis is exhibited, therefore, in these three approaches: "the national accounting approach, the input-output (inter-industry relations) technique, and the construction of formal economic models." [34] Goldsmith and most of the other participants in the conferences on comparative economic growth and structure (conducted by the National Bureau of Economic Research) seem to have in mind the use of comparison for classifying data and for formulating generalizations about them. Tinbergen, however, refers explicitly to comparison as a technique for empirical testing in the verificative process: "Any attempt at finding empirical evidence on whatever subject has to consist of comparative studies, since it is only by comparing different situations that we can hope to get evidence on the influences exerted by changes in data." [35]

When Abramovitz, Kuznets, and Williamson discuss the development of an economics of growth, they presuppose the use of comparison for both formulating and testing hypotheses.[36] Moreover, Ruggles shows why, in econometrics, statistical research "as the collection and manipulation of numerical observations" requires comparative analysis as a verificative technique: "By designing the economic theory in such a manner that it can be tested by available data, and by simultaneously providing a theoretical framework for the statistical analyst, econometrics is able to overcome many of the difficulties which are normally inherent in the separation of the various stages of research." [37]

Political scientists engage extensively in comparative studies; but they are only beginning to define the testing techniques of comparative analysis which is necessary, if, as Leiserson hopes, they are "to integrate the data of interpersonal and institutional behavior into an inclusive, logically consistent body of theoretical propositions." [38] Even though Heller frankly acknowledges that "the discipline is lacking in either a clearly delimited set of problems or a definitely prescribed methodology," nevertheless, he emphasizes that it is with the kind of data to which the testing technique of comparative analysis is applicable that many political scientists are concerned: "Present day political science revolves primarily around the attainment, consolidation, and distribution of political power whether in an actually existing state or in a hypothetical state, constructed more or less systematically by a process of abstracting the common elements to be found in a number of concrete states." [39]

Broadly operational historians who aim at cumulative generalizations which are not derived from a single instance agree with Brockunier and Loewenberg that comparison and contrast are required as techniques "to develop theory about classes of historical phenomena." [40] Even the purely narrative historian uses some historical comparison, when, as Hook says "he selects a group of relevant or plausible antecedent factors, which appear to be relatively exhaustive, in order to test his hypothesis that one of them or a combination of them is more decisive than the others." [41]

More than this is advocated by Brockunier and Loewenberg, when they go beyond the appeal to documentary evidence alone to the claim that causal generalizations as one kind of historical hypotheses can be empirically tested by this experiential technique as long as a sufficient number of cases can be compared and contrasted in the logical pattern of Mill's concomitant variation. Not only can the historian adopt a working hypothesis about a causal connection, "if one phenomena varies whenever an associated phenomena varies in some particular manner," but, "where several types of phenomena are discovered to coexist over a long period, comparison of their relationships at different points in time may reinforce hypotheses concerning a causal connection between them." [42]

When Gottschalk describes this technique of "comparing and contrasting similar categories of historical developments (such as wars, dictatorships, urban growth, and frontier settlements) in an effort to discover and account for similarities and dissimilarities," he suggests the corroborative techniques of meta-history. According to this contrary-to-documentary-evidence procedure, the historian imaginatively reconstructs what he believed would have happened, if a person had not acted as he did or events had not transpired as they seemed to have done. For assessing "the significance, greatness, or the influence of a person, thing or event," according to Gottschalk, "that is as near as the historian can come to the process of the natural sciences whereby the investigator removes a factor in order to determine its function in an experiment." [43]

Teggart's description of the technique of comparative analysis is especially significant, since he himself actually applied it in his *Rome and China* (*A Study of Correlations in Historical Events*). The two events he seeks to correlate are "the political disturbances in Western China and the Asiatic frontier regions of the Roman empire" and "the barbaric invasions in the regions of the Danube and Rhine." About this comparative analysis he makes this statement which reveals the applicability of such a technique: "The discovery that certain sets of events—wars in Asia and barbaric invasions in Europe—are correlated is a matter of unusual importance, for it demonstrates the existence of a type of order of historical facts which has not hitherto received attention." Teggart explicitly uses Mill's formula of concomitant variation in his empirical testing of the implications of this hypothesis: "I use the word 'correlation' because it has been found, in all cases, that when the first event occurred (in the T'ien or the Roman East), the second occurred (on the Panponian Danube or the lower Danube and the Rhine), and, further, that when the first event did not occur, the second did not occur." [44]

Reactions to Teggart's claim indicate the complications which the use of the verificative techniques in historical analysis entails and point out the direction in which it might be improved. Cohen, on the one hand, emphasizes the complexity of possible influences that preclude an exact estimate of causal relations. He warns that even when a correlation between sets of events is discovered, there is no definite assurance that other factors are not operative or that a "series of coincidences" did not exist. Accordingly, Cohen concludes that since "historical phenomena do not come to us already properly classified," we should recognize that "it is we who classify them in diverse ways according to the purposes of our inquiry." [45] Referring to Teggart's hypothesis for illustrating his point Cohen warns that "the category of 'trade disturbance' may thus include diverse phenomena some of which may and some of which may not be relevant to the invasions of the Roman Empire or to rebellions within it." Zilsel, on the other hand, claims that "Teggart's statistical verification of the correlation between these sets of events is so scientifically accurate that his conclusion can be taken to be a historical law." [46]

Leaving to historians the dispute about the substantive issue, could we draw this inference with respect to the use of the technique of comparative analysis for empirically testing historical hypotheses? The effectiveness of this technique in dealing with the diachronic data of historical inquiry will depend to a considerable degree upon how other social scientists refine this technique of comparative analysis in dealing with synchronic data.

Strong's proposal about "empirically equivalent continuant configurations" may be quite helpful for the historian who needs another analytical tool to refine his comparative technique. By this Strong means that, when the historian subjectively imagines the motivation of past actions, he must have some reasonably acceptable conception of what could be expected which is derived from his knowledge of contemporary human actions: "The record in documents of actions and production engaged in by men long since dead is not questioned so long as those conform to abilities that men could be expected to have from what is now known of the limits of human capacities and powers." [47]

b) Introspective Projection

Among the social scientists who use experiential testing for confirming or disconfirming the implications of their hypotheses there are some who use introspective projection in order to deal with the intervening variable of goal-seeking motivation. By this technique we mean the procedure through which the social scientist interprets the motivation of another person or persons in terms of his estimate of what his own emotions, attitudes, sentiments, and purposes would have been in the situation to which the hypothesis refers.

It should be emphasized, however, that when a broader operationalist uses introspective projection, he always combines it with the other experiential testing technique of comparative case analysis. This precaution corresponds to that which is demanded at the first stage of hypothetical-deductive inquiry wherein extrospective observation of the relevant data of goal-seeking behavior is required along with the introspective inspection of one's own emotions and purposes. MacIver, for example, advocates this "imaginative reconstruction" in "the interpretation of the teleological aspects of social phenomena" on the grounds that, "as human beings we are immersed in the strivings, purposes, and goals that constitute the peculiar dynamics of this area of reality." Even though he claims that such inferences about the distinctive factors of human behavior "are validated as causes by our own experience," he insists, nevertheless, that the use of this technique must be "disciplined and safeguarded by the rigorous use of the more secure methods of scientific inquiry." [48]

This limitation of the use of introspective projection distinguishes this comparative *technique* from the traditional *method* of V*erstehen* which was proposed by Dilthey and others as a substitute for the entire hypothetical-deductive method with its verificative criterion of coherence. According to the proponents of the *Geisteswissenschaften* movement in the latter part of the nineteenth century, through this *empathetic understanding* the social scientists can obtain autonomous insights which are not otherwise available. They adopted the premise that the goal-seeking behavior of reflective persons is completely distinct from the physical processes to which natural-scientific constructs refer. Accordingly, they turned their backs on even what we have called broader operationalism and appealed to introspective intuitions alone. Instead of accounting for intervening variables along with independent variables, as does the social scientist who uses introspective projection, the advocates of V*erstehen* disregard the independent variables. Consequently, on the one hand, Dilthey and his followers conceived of their intuitively acquired knowledge of the "articulation of individuality" as absolutely self-certified by *immediate experience*. On the other hand, broader operationalists from Weber to MacIver acknowledge that introspective projection provides only inferentially-constructed and tentatively-verified hypotheses as reasonably acceptable *knowledge about experience*. Weber makes clear his assumption that the verification of such a revisionable conclusion must be corroborated by other techniques: "More generally, verification of subjective interpretation by comparison with the concrete course of events is, as in the case of all hypotheses, indispensable." [49]

As we now consider the statements by broader operationalists who use introspective projection, we must bear in mind that their approach must be distinguished from the non-operational *Verstehen* just as much as from that of the narrower operationalists who deny that a testing technique must be adapted to a specific subject matter.

Among psychologists those who can help to refine this introspective projection as a technique for experiential testing are those who have been concerned about combining introspective with extrospective observation in the initial stage of critically inspecting the motivational data of purposive behavior. Most relevant in this regard, therefore, are the previously discussed concepts of Tolman, Allport, Newcomb, Murray, Murphy, and others about the "intervening variable" and about the idiographic dimension of persons engaged in reflective goal-seeking behavior. These broader operationalists are fully aware that the critical use of the technique of introspective projection would lead to non-operational criteria such as the naïve-pragmatic appeal to desirable consequences or the mystical appeal to emotional intuitions. In addition to the negative task of guarding against the reduction of imaginative reconstruction to obscurantism, the psychologist has the more positive task of helping other social scientists to cultivate and develop their capacity for critically introspecting and projecting their inferred generalizations about goal-seeking motivation.

The significance of the psychologist's contribution to the improvement of this technique of experiential testing can be brought out by relating it to Abel's cogent criticisms of *Verstehen*, in which he seems to object equally to what we have called introspective projection. Abel acknowledges that "it appears highly probable that the hunches which lead to certain hypotheses concerning human behavior originate from the application of the operation of *Verstehen*." He seriously doubts, however, that any "application of personal experience to observed behavior" is justified as a testing technique. As the grounds for his doubts, he emphasizes that there are formidable obstacles which confront the development of a sufficient "introspective capacity of the interpreter." Not only will the effective verificative use of projecting these estimates "vary with the amount and quality of the personal experience" of the interpreter, but "it will also depend on his ability to generalize his experience" without substituting personal familiarity for objective understanding. Now Abel grants that "in some cases it *may be possible* to secure objective data on the basis of which the verification of an interpretation can be approximated." But he calculates that "owing to the *relative inaccessibility* of emotional experiences, *most* interpretations will remain mere expressions of opinion, subject only to the 'test' of plausibility." [50]

To make emotional experiences relatively more accessible rather than relatively inaccessible, therefore, becomes the responsibility of the psychologist. For, to the degree that psychologists can improve the tools for making emotional experiences more accessible, there will be an increase of the reasonable acceptability of introspectively projected interpretations. Abel seems to be right when he warns that present psychological techniques for attributing feelings to others in specific situations are not precise enough for the interpreter to be sure that he is imputing the actual stimulus and response. But, if these psychological techniques are refined, is it not possible to expect that a competently trained social scientist might functionally correlate the causal dependence of specific feeling stimuli with specific feeling responses?

The direction in which psychologists might move in order to make emotional experiences relatively more accessible has been pointed out by Alexander in terms of what he calls "emotional syllogisms." "Just as the logic of intellectual thinking is based on repeated and accumulated experiences of relations in the external world, the logic of the emotions is based on the accumulated experiences of our own emotional reactions." In opening up this avenue of inquiry, Alexander is presupposing his conception of "psychological factors." This was previously discussed in connection with the psychoanalytic factors of goal-seeking motivation: "The distinctive feature of psychogenic factors such as emotions or ideas and fantasies is that they *can* be studied also psychologically through introspection or by verbal communication from those in whom these physiological processes take place." In opposition to narrower operationalists who would confine research to glandular, muscular, and neural data, it will be recalled, Alexander declared that "it is hardly conceivable that the different moves of two chess players can ever be more clearly understood in biochemical or neuro-physiological than in psychological and logical terms." [51] Despite Abel's reluctance to acknowledge the significance of introspective projection as a testing technique, even he recognizes the possibility of improving psychological tools for this purpose in the manner Alexander describes.

Among sociologists there has been considerable controversy about the legitimacy of introspective projection as a testing technique. Those who have opposed it are usually less open-minded than Abel. This might be expected from those sociologists who largely confine their attention to the structure of the nomothetic interrelations of depersonalized roles and institutions. In addition to Weber and Mac-Iver, however, there are other sociologists who feel compelled to include this verificative technique when it is required by the data to which a more idiographic hypothesis refers. Cooley presupposes this when he maintains that a genuine understanding of other human beings depends upon the interpreter's ability to share their "state of mind." By his "humanistic coefficient" Znaniecki refers to this kind of vicarious experience as a source of intimate insight into some aspects of the motivation of human behavior which the objective techniques of empirical testing leave out of account. Similarly, Sorokin contends that an intuitive "logico-meaningful method" provides a more immediate and readily recognizable knowledge than that which is provided by the "causal functional unities" of the physical techniques.[52]

Anthropologists tend to project their own feelings into their generalizations about human motivation even more than sociologists. When Bennett and Wolff indicate that the anthropologist substitutes "a technically unlimited understanding" for the sociologist's more precise measuring instruments, they conclude that "while the sociologist prepares to stand away, to perceive man 'objectively,' not to involve his own feelings and reactions, the cultural anthropologist has often striven to know man *through* his own feelings and reactions, to view the human beings he studies as 'fellow men,' not as 'subjects.'" [53] When Kroeber declares that "values evidently are intimately associated with the most basic and implicit patterning of the phenomena of culture," he indicates that "it looks as if values must be found, got at, or determined by empathy," i.e., "values have got to be felt, at least vicariously." Carefully distinguishing this "experiencing them in some degree" from any "mystic or supernatural means," Kroeber insists that "one has to live himself into values in order to know what they really are." [54]

Among economists who are concerned with the motivation of purposive behavior, some use of introspective projection seems indispensable. Not only is it implicit in the neo-classical conception of rational man, but, as Spiethoff emphasizes, to *understand* "economic activities as seen as the result or caused by certain motives," requires its explicit use.[55] Perhaps the clearest recognition of the applicability of this testing technique in economic inquiry has been provided by Commons in his discussion of "volitiency": "The subject matter with which an economist deals is not a mechanism or an organism whose notions the investigator cannot *understand*—it is human beings whose activities he can fairly well understand by putting himself 'in their place' and thus constructing the 'reasons,' in the sense of motives or purposes, or values, of their activity under all of the variable conditions of time and place." [56]

There seem to be no political scientists who have explicitly employed introspective projection as a testing technique; but their data are susceptible to it. Merriam reveals in his discussion of the roots of government that the very necessity for the allocative political process stems from this kind of value experiences which would be accessible only through introspective projection: "We shall start by noting that government arises from the necessity of adjusting the needs and desires of human beings struggling for forms of association through which human personalities may be adjusted, aided or advanced toward higher levels of attainment." [57] Comparative case analysis is required for dealing with the sociocultural aspect of political behavior. But, without some use of an imaginative reconstruction of the human emotions and purposes which are involved in "this adaptation of energies, and value systems," by what other technique could the political scientist assess his inferences about the goal-oriented motivation of political behavior?

Among historians, those who acknowledge that they imaginatively reconstruct the past explicitly use the technique of introspective projection for interpreting the goal-seeking motivation of past human actions. As Salvemini has said, when historians look at past human situations not only from without but also from within, "they are able to utilize the analogy between their own personal experience and that of the men who were the authors of the facts under investigation." [58] Purely document-centered historians probably do not feel the need for this technique. Moreover, Popper and Hempel, who are primarily concerned about nomothetically subsuming all historical explanations under general laws, insist that the use of the method of empathy "does not guarantee the soundness of the historical explanation to which it leads," even though "this procedure may sometimes prove heuristically helpful." [59]

Broadly operational historiographers take this nomothetic aspect into account when they engage in comparative analysis of the sociocultural processes; but they attempt to correlate this reference to "covering law" with the idiographic aspect of experiential testing of motivational hypotheses through introspective projection. When Dray, for example, contends that historical understanding must be empathetic on the grounds that "the historian must be able to 'work' the agent's calculation," he draws support from Butterfield's statement that "the only understanding we ever reach in history is but a refinement, more or less subtle and sensitive, of the difficult—and sometimes deceptive—process of imagining oneself in another person's place." Now Butterfield acknowledges that it is not actually possible for the historian so to feel and think in the part of "the doer of the action." But he insists that the historian must attempt to "put himself in the place of the historical personage, must feel his predicament, must think as though he were that man." [60]

If it is necessary for any social scientist, who is dealing with contemporary observational data, to impute the motivation of other persons in accordance with what he discerns through the inspection of his own motives, then the historian, who must imaginatively reconstruct the motivation of past actors, could hardly dispense with this technique. What else other than his own goal-seeking orientation is accessible as an "empirical equivalent" of past goal-seeking orientations? But this does not mean that the historian possesses some special kind of immediate insight which is superior to other testing techniques. As Gardiner has emphasized, such imaginative understanding "is instead seen to be a *way* by which we interpret other people's behavior: it is not knowledge of another order achieved by an identification of our thoughts, feelings, etc., with theirs or by an abstruse technique for looking into their minds." [61]

The use of the experiential technique of introspective projection as one of the techniques for empirically testing the implications of historical hypotheses should not be confused with the non-operationalistic appeal to self-certifying intuitions. Probably no historical theorist has insisted more vigorously than Collingwood that "the historical process is a process in which man creates for himself this or that kind of human nature by re-creating in his own thought the past to which he is heir." This means that ideas about past human actions live in the present by virtue of the historian's imaginative reconstruction which entails inferences from his own emotional and purposive motivations. But it does not mean that the past human actions themselves live in the present experiences of the historian. Those vanished actions themselves are referents about which inferential propositions are constructed. Collingwood clarifies his premise that "immediate experience is not historical thought," when he distinguishes his inferential conception from the intuitional premise that past history "lives in the present's immediate experience of itself." Dilthey presupposed the latter in his advocacy of *Verstehen*: "The living past of history lives in the present; but it lives not in the immediate experience of the present, but only in the self-knowledge of the present." [62]

Gottschalk shows why the historian does not substitute his own subjective feeling for objective interpretation by using introspective projection. When Gottschalk explains how the historian might try "to reach understanding by examining his subject from the vantage point of his own present" through this psychological analogy as an "empirical equivalent," he claims that "only by such an analogy (or contrast) can he understand the setting of the testimony of his sources and the behavior to which it testifies." Gottschalk just as strongly insists that such a projection of one's own introspectively acquired "mental reactions" is justified as a verificative technique only if the investigator himself has cultivated a sufficient degree of historical-mindedness, i.e., "the ability to put oneself in the place of other individuals of other times and to interpret documents, events, and personalities with their eyes, standards, and sympathies (without necessarily surrendering one's own standards)." [63]

In concluding this discussion of introspective projection as an experiential technique for empirically testing behavioral hypotheses we must recognize that it confronts the social scientist with a dilemma. On the one hand, if he does not apply it to internalized purposive goal-seeking, he precludes much of the motivational data that are relevant to the behavioral constructs which are being verified in terms of their consistency and adequacy. On the other hand, to meet these demands of the logical criterion of coherence, the social scientist must also formulate law-like, if not lawful, generalizations with which introspective projection seems to be incongruent. As we now undertake a survey of social-scientific views about behavioral laws, we shall be virtually engaged in an interpretation and critical appraisal of Kantor's claim that "anthropic laws possess as much stability and rigor as are required by anthropic events." [64]

Footnotes to Chapter 3 of Part Four

[1] See Columbia Associates, *An Introduction to Reflective Thinking*, 97-98. Cf. Stabler, *Introduction to Mathematical Thought*, 1-19, for a mathematician's analysis of the relation of mathematics to logic and science, which clearly describes and illustrates the "conventional" rather than "absolutistic" conception of mathematical reasoning. Cf. Richardson, *The Fundamentals of Mathematics*, Chapter I for another explanation of the postulational nature of mathematics and logic. For interpretations which bring out the indispensability of mathematics for the development of the natural sciences, see Whitehead, *Science and the Modern World*, Chapter II; and Werkmeister, *A Philosophy of Science*, Chapter II. A more detailed analysis of the function of logic and mathematics in scientific inquiry is offered by Werkmeister in his *The Basis and Structure of Knowledge*, Part III.

[2] George in *Symposium on Sociological Theory* (Gross), 313, 333-334.

[3] Newcomb, *Social Psychology*, 14.

[4] Merton, *Social Theory and Social Structure*, 97-98, 111.

[5] Zetterberg, *On Theory and Verification in Sociology*, 59.

[6] Malinowski, *A Scientific Theory of Culture*, 67.

[7] Machlup, "The Problem of Verification in Economics," *The Southern Economic Journal*, Vol. XXIX, No. 1, July 1955, pages 4-5.

[8] Gordon, *The Journal of Political Economy*, Vol. LXIII, April 1955, No. 2.

[9] Leiserson, *Political Science Quarterly*, Dec. 1953, pages 563-583.

[10] Werkmeister, *The Basis and Structure of Knowledge*, 326.

[11] Brockunier and Loewenberg, Bulletin 64, pp. 134, 136.

[12] Donagan, "The Verification of Historical Theses," *The Philosophical Quarterly*, Vol. 6, No. 24, July 1956, pages 195-196.

[13] Zetterberg, *On Theory and Verification in Sociology*, 70. See Churchman, *Theory of Experimental Inference*, 218.

14 Werkmeister, *The Basis and Structure of Knowledge*, 309-310.

15 Lachman, *The Foundations of Science*, 96.

16.Cohen and Nagel, *An Introduction to Logic and Scientific Method*, 220-221. See Nagel, *The Structure of Science*, 452-453 for his more recent elaboration of the justification of this broader concept of empirical testing in which "controlled investigation" in some natural sciences (e.g. astronomy, geology) must be used instead of "controlled experimentation."

17 Friedman, "The Methodology of Positive Economics," *Essays in Positive Economics* (Friedman), 40.

18 Newcomb, *Social Psychology*, 14.

19 Parsons, *The Structure of Social Action*, 774.

20 *Ibid.*, 743.

21 Rose, *Theory and Method in the Social Sciences*, 281.

22 Newcomb, "Studying Social Behavior," *Methods of Psychology* (Andrews), 674.

23 Murphy, *Personality*, 915-917.

24 Durkheim, *The Rules of Sociological Method*, (translated by Solovoy and Mueller and edited by Catlin), 125. Merton, *Social Theory and Social Structure*, 54.

25 Zetterberg, *On Theory and Verification in Sociology*, 67-68.

26 Herskovits in *Method and Perspective in Anthropology* (Spencer), 21-22.

27 Linton, *The Cultural Background of Personality*, 1.

28 Nadel, *The Foundations of Social Anthropology*, 222.

29 Ackerknecht in *Method and Perspective in Anthropology* (Spencer), 122-124.

30 Kroeber in *Method and Perspective in Anthropology* (Spencer), 273-274.

31 Kluckhohn, *Mirror for Man*, 223.

32 Lewis in *Current Anthropology* (Thomas), 259-260.

33 Marshall, *Principles of Economics*, 29, 768. Cf. Jevons, *Principles of Science*, 759-761.

34 Goldsmith in *The Comparative Study of Economic Growth and Structure* (National Bureau of Economic Research, 1959), pages 6, 67.

35 Tinbergen in *The Comparative Study of Economic Growth and Structure* (National Bureau of Economic Research, 1959), page 193.

36 Abramovitz, Kuznets and Williamson in *A Survey of Contemporary Economics* (Haley), Vol. II, pages 132, 180, 181.

37 Ruggles in *A Survey of Contemporary Economics* (Haley), Vol. II, pages 417, 423.

38 Leiserson, *Political Science Quarterly*, Vol. LXVIII, Dec. 1953, No. 4, p. 567.

39 Heller in *Encyclopedia of the Social Sciences*, Vol. 12, pages 207, 209.

40 Brockunier and Loewenberg, Bulletin 64, page 151.

41 Hook, Bulletin 54, page 113.

42 Brockunier and Loewenberg, Bulletin 64, pages 151-152.

43 Gottschalk, *Understanding History*, 242, 263.

44 Teggart, "Causation in Historical Events," *Journal of History of Ideas*, Vol. 3, pages 8-9.

45 Cohen, "Causation and Its Application to History," *Journal of History of Ideas*, Vol. 3, 1942, pages 16-17.

[46] Zilsel in *Readings in the Philosophy of Science* (Feigl and Brodbeck), 720.

[47] Strong in *Naturalism and the Human Spirit* (Krikorian), 159.

[48] MacIver, *Social Causation*, 262-264.

[49] Weber, *The Theory of Social and Economic Organization*, 88.

[50] Abel in *Readings in the Philosophy of Science* (Feigl and Brodbeck), 680-685. Originally published in the *American Journal of Sociology*, 54, 1948, pages 216-217.

[51] Alexander, "The Logic of Emotions and Its Dynamic Background," *International Journal of Psychoanalysis*, Vol. XVI, Oct. 1935, page 399. "Principles of Psychosomatic Research," *Psychological Theory* (Marx), 461-462.

[52] See Cooley, *Sociological Theory and Social Research*, 290; Znaniecki, *The Method of Sociology*, 167; Sorokin, *Social and Cultural Dynamics*, 26.

[53] Bennett and Wolff in *Current Anthropology* (Thomas), 334.

[54] Kroeber in *An Appraisal of Anthropology Today* (Tax), 373.

[55] Spiethoff in *Enterprise and Secular Change* (Lane and Riemersma), 449.

[56] Commons, *Institutional Economics*, 723.

[57] Merriam, *Systematic Politics*, 1-2.

[58] Salvemini, *Historian and Scientist*, 69.

[59] Hempel in *Readings in Philosophical Analysis* (Feigl and Sellars), 467. Originally published in *The Journal of Philosophy*, 39, 1942.

[60] Dray, *Laws and Explanation in History*, 119, 121, 126, 144. See Butterfield, *History and Human Relations*, 116-117, 145-146.

[61] Gardiner, *The Nature of Historical Explanation*, 133.

[62] Collingwood, *The Idea of History*, 174.

[63] Gottschalk, *Understanding History*, 136-137, 272-273.

[64] Kantor, *The Logic of Modern Science*, 281.

4 The Fourth Stage of Hypothetical-Deductive Inquiry

What is entailed in the conceptual integration of each verified hypothesis into a coherent system of theoretical generalizations which might be designated as lawful or law-like generalizations?

A. The Emergence of the Knowledge-Questions from the Meaning-Questions

The issues involved in answering this question in the knowledge-situation of the hypothetical-deductive method, with which we are here concerned, emerge out of the ideas in the meaning-situation of reflective inquiry which were dealt with in connection with the third postulate: *Knowledge about the objective physical and behavioral universe requires an orderly system of constructs.* There it was maintained that unless a scientist assumes that he can formulate law-like, if not lawful generalizations, about physical and/or behavioral events as the objective of inquiry, then his presuppositions about the systematic character of both his constructs and their referents are not sufficient for defining what kind of knowledge is meaningful. In other words, as Hempel and Oppenheim contend, "in the social no less than the physical sciences, subsumption under general regularities is indispensable." [1]

Two other salient features of the meaning-postulate should be recalled as presuppositions of the subsequent discussion. In the first place, a law is not inherent in reality itself; but, rather, it is constructed by the scientist himself as a comprehensive formula for conceptually integrating the system of generalizations about the entire context of the dimension of reality to which it refers. In the second place, as causal explanations neither the laws of the natural sciences nor the law-like generalizations of the social sciences are expected to provide predictive certainty.

In the light of these assumptions in the meaning-situation, what in the knowledge-situation can be meant by a physical or behavioral generalization which is law-like, if not lawful? For our purpose we shall take an integrating concept to be a causal and/or statistical generalization about the uniform pattern in the processes of a given system of events, the application of which is limited by the specifically stated conditions. Without this provisional stipulation (if-then) no substantive law could be adequately formulated.

1. FORMAL AND SUBSTANTIVE LAWS

In order to ascertain why the construction and utilization of law-like behavioral generalizations is more complicated than that of lawful natural generalizations, we must distinguish between their formal and their substantive aspects. If a behavioral law is conceived in *purely formal terms,* there seems to be no reason why a behavioral scientist should not be as successful as a natural scientist. While Cohen is correct, when he declares that physical events do "show certain abstract uniformities of repetition which enable us to predict what will happen with greater certainty than in the social realm," nevertheless, we must not forget that even physical events do not themselves recur. Once an event, whether physical or behavioral, has occurred it is never repeated. What is meant, therefore, is that at successive times physical events occur which have characteristics so similar to previous events, that for purposes of constructing lawful generalizations they can be assumed to be recurrent. Although similarity of the characteristics of successive behavioral events is not so clearly evident, this does not preclude the construction of a behavioral law in purely formal terms. Cohen himself composes the law of inertia with the behavioral law of social heredity: "All social institutions will be transmitted by parents to children, or people will believe and act as did their fathers before them, except insofar as certain factors produce changes in our social arrangements and in our ideas and sentiments." [2] In this connection, it should be recalled that the physicist's law of inertia merely defines "force" and "motion." No experimentally testable substantive prediction is provided by the tautological assertion that "every body perseveres in a state of rest, or of uniform motion in a right line, unless it is compelled to change that state by forces impressed thereon."

When the social scientist turns from the formal statement of a behavioral law to its substantive application, he encounters the difficulty of stating the limiting conditions of his law-like generalization without eliminating the distinctiveness of the empirical goal-seeking situation. This difficulty is the result of these three complications which have been encountered separately in connection with various aspects of the meaning-situation: (a) The problem of isolating causal variables in the human situation. (b) The problem of incorporating the normative referents of the intervening variable in goal-seeking behavior. (c) The problem of coordinating the nomothetic with the idiographic constructs about goal-oriented behavior.

2. THE PROBLEM OF SPECIFYING THE LIMITING CONDITIONS OF BEHAVIORAL LAWS

a) *Can the Social Scientist Isolate Causal Variables?*

Exactness has been achieved to a significant degree in the formulation of natural laws because the physical and biological scientists have dealt with the kind of subject matter that allowed them to take into account only a comparatively few variables; but sociocultural-motivational data do not usually yield to such an isolating procedure. In most cases the empirical human situation entails a considerable number of causal factors which are so interdependent that to limit or to dissect them will destroy the actual behavioral interaction of naturalized, socioculturalized, and goal-seeking individuals. The motivational data and sociocultural conditions to which any such meaningful generalization must refer, cannot be divorced from their spatial and temporal contexts. Accordingly, these generalizations cannot be expected to embody the universality of natural-scientific generalizations that can be asserted without any spatio-temporal references. For example, the physical law that "friction produces heat" is so independent of any specific spatio-temporal context that, if it is true anywhere or at any time, it is true everywhere and at all times. The social scientist has a better chance of obtaining this kind of universality and precision when he confines his analysis to data that are subject to predictions which may be justifiably qualified by limiting conditions. Reasonable expectation about population data, for example, is possible on the basis of statistical analyses of recurring demographic patterns. *For this purpose,* most of the motivational and sociocultural factors, which for other social-scientific purposes will not remain constant enough to be isolated, may be delimited or sufficiently accounted for so that they can be considered as constants. But the social scientist cannot expect the same degree of success, when, for example, he is forecasting reasonable expectations about the reactions of individuals to democratic and totalitarian ideologies. In this case the cultural factors of historically acquired values, and the expectations of the individuals who constitute the involved groups, are modifiable by human goal-seeking which defies the precise predictions that abstract generalizing of scientific laws requires. When the social scientist attempts to construct a predictive generalization about what can be reasonably expected as the result of a given set of conditions and actions, provided that no others influence the outcome, he finds that changes in the given set of factors influence and are influenced by changes in other factors which he has not taken into account.

b) *Can the Social Scientist Incorporate the Normative Referents of Goal-Seeking Behavior in a Law-Like Generalization?*

The goal-seeking motivation of the behavioral interaction of naturalized and socioculturalized individuals makes it necessary for the social scientist to formulate generalizations which have both descriptive referents and normative referents, i.e., purposive striving in ac-

482)   The Methodological Pattern of Reflective Inquiry

cordance with relatively self-determined standards. This qualitative
aspect of behavioral events precludes the possibility of the completely quantitative predictions which characterize the mathematical
equations of natural laws. The natural scientists can generalize with
reasonable assurance that the mechanical pattern of independently
real causal connections discovered among physical events will persist
throughout the spatio-temporal process. Even though the natural
scientist constructs his theoretical generalizations about that dimension of reality with which he is concerned, he can assume that his
cognitive process in no way modifies the objective referents of these
natural laws. But the social scientist who is concerned about the
goal-seeking orientation of human behavior cannot make this assumption. Although the social scientist may, in some investigations,
confine his attention to purely descriptive generalizations about actual behavioral interaction; nevertheless, sociocultural causation also
entails those modes of action in which human persons attempt
purposively to control the sociocultural process to which their generalizations refer. Without normative reference to the standards in
accordance with which these efforts are made, the sociocultural laws
will exclude any reference to the factors of thought, imagination,
and conduct by which reflective persons creatively modify the sociocultural process in which they participate.

The difficulty of formulating such sociocultural laws, which include this normative referent to reflective goal-seeking, is not sufficient to justify the social scientist's discounting reflective goal-seeking as a factual aspect of the human value situation. Dewey's insight
on this point is most pertinent: " 'Fact,' physically speaking, is the
ultimate residue after human purposes, desires, emotions, ideas and
ideals have been systematically excluded. A social 'fact,' on the other
hand, is a concretion in external form of precisely these human factors." Accordingly, unlike the natural scientist who is formulating
predictive laws about non-human events, the social scientist who is
attempting to formulate law-like generalizations cannot disregard the
"ends-means continuum" of behavioral transactions in which the
actors are motivated by their present desires for the realization of
future goals. What human persons do or do not do with respect to
the selection of the means for realizing these ends is one of the significant causal factors which must be included in the construction of
predictive generalizations about behavioral actions. In making such

inferences the social scientist uses the same formula that is used by the natural scientist: "If something occurs, then something else happens." But, as Dewey has declared, when the social scientist attempts "to discover the conditions underlying the 'if,' " he finds that "they involve human decisions to do something from which it follows that something else happens." Since "the objective material constituting the 'if' belongs to us, not to something wholly independent of us," therefore, "we are concerned, not with a bare relation of cause and effect, but with one of means and consequences, that is, of courses deliberately used for the sake of producing certain effects." [3]

c) *Can the Social Scientist Coordinate the Nomothetic and the Idiographic Aspects of Behavior in Law-Like Generalizations?*

If the social scientist could disregard the unique and nonrecurrent characteristics of the goal-seeking motivation of behavioral interaction (intervening variables), he would have much less difficulty in establishing abstract general laws about the sociocultural conditions (independent variables). These would correspond to natural laws which causally relate the abstracted universal, recurrent, invariant, and quantifiable characteristics of physical events in terms of uniform patterns. This kind of *generalizing analysis*, which discounts the unique organization of singular events, has been designated as nomothetic. The greatest achievements of natural-scientific inquiry have been made through the use of this kind of nomothetic analysis. Although most social scientists would like to utilize this nomothetic approach exclusively, there are some broader operationalists who cannot bring themselves to disregard those unique aspects of the organization of personalities, societies, cultures, and historical events which are concrete constituents of the motivational and sociocultural dimensions of reality. This kind of individualizing analysis of the unique organization of events, which does not exhibit indefinitely recurrent characteristics that can be brought under a uniform pattern, has been designated as idiographic.

The intellectual responsibilities of the social scientist and the scholar or artist in the humanities are not the same. Since the latter aims at aesthetic effectiveness rather than the lawful or law-like generalizations which reflective inquiry requires, he can deal in exclusively idiographic terms with the qualitative characteristics of a singular person or situation. He has no obligation to verify and conceptually integrate his imaginative insights. But, when the social scientist acknowledges idiographic factors, he must correlate his constructs about them with his nomothetic constructs about the segmented qualities and relations which he has abstracted from the more inclusive context of a concrete situation. For laws or law-like principles must be abstract generalizations about a uniform pattern with which the artist or scholar in the humanities need not be concerned.

What have social scientists themselves said about the possibility of their sufficiently specifying the provisional limitations and conditions which the formulations of law-like generalizations presuppose?

B. *Toward the Construction of Law-Like Generalizations about the Behavioral Process*

1. THE LIMITED AIM OF LAW-LIKE GENERALIZING

What is meant by a law-like generalization can be clarified by reference to this question: Are sociocultural generalizations really laws or are they only statements of tendencies? It would be unreasonable to expect the social scientist to achieve the same degree of probability that the natural scientist can achieve. But the mere plausibility of a social-scientific generalization is not enough to warrant designating it as a law. Yet, as Cohen has reminded us, "one of the most usual ways of generalizing from insufficient instances and ignoring or lightly disposing of contrary facts is to call our generalization a tendency." Similarly, "in the social sciences, where single factors cannot be easily isolated and independently measured, an essential indeterminateness in discussion is inevitably produced by reliance on the notion of 'tendency.'" Since one tendency may be a generalization about only one aspect of the total motivational-sociocultural context, while an opposite tendency may be a generalization about another aspect of the total motivational-sociocultural context, there is no fruitful conceptual integration of the relevant data such as a *law* is required to provide for a given context. In view of this situation Cohen has made the following suggestion: "The way out of such typical sloughs of social science is to recognize that while full description of some of the facts may be needed in the beginning of social science, the ideal end is to attain universal statements about partial aspects of all the phenomena in a given class." [4]

Two conceptions of behavioral laws seem to challenge Cohen's proposed solution. For one thing, Hart claims that the assertion of a tendency about cultural acceleration can have more rigor than Cohen recognizes. For another, Parsons aims at an ideal end of lawful generalizations which pertain more to the totality of the phenomena in a given class rather than, as Cohen proposes, to "the partial aspects of all the phenomena in a given class." Some further consideration of each of these views is justified by their relevance to the basic issue.

Hart proposes that social-scientific inquiry about sociocultural change has been sufficient to justify this *Law of Cultural Acceleration:* "Over the long sweep of time, man's power to carry out his purposes, in the material, biological, psychological, and sociological realms, has tended to increase at an accelerating rate (though with recurrent stagnations and setbacks), and the rate of acceleration has itself tended to accelerate." Hart grants that this law does not conform to a rigorous definition of a scientific law such as "a statement of an order or relation of phenomena which, so far as known, is invariable under the given conditions." But, Hart insists, neither do Gresham's Law and the Law of Diminishing Returns. In the range from merely plausible tendencies (Cohen) to highly probable tendencies (Hart) the law-likeness, if not lawfulness, of behavioral generalizations seems to be a matter of degree. Hart also emphasizes that the comprehensiveness of behavioral laws is not a weakness, as has been charged by some critics, since the Laws of Gravitation and Thermodynamics are similarly general.[5] For the more systematic development of this point, however, let us turn to Parsons.

Parsons has suggested four behavioral laws which might correspond to the laws of motion in classical mechanics, if the "motivational power of an act" is taken to be the counterpart of "mass":

Law I: An action process will continue unchanged in direction and rate unless impeded and neglected by opposing forces.

Law II: If, in a system of action, there is a change in the direction of a process—not rate but direction—it will be balanced by complementary change which is equal in force and opposite in direction.

Law III: An increase in the rate of an action process is a function of the magnitude of the motivational force involved.

Law IV: Any pattern of process in a system of action will tend to be confirmed or eliminated as a function of its place in the integrative balances of the system.[6]

2. TO WHAT DEGREE DO THE SPECIFIC BEHAVIORAL DISCIPLINES AIM AT LAW-LIKE GENERALIZATIONS?

From the statements of some of the representatives of social-scientific disciplines we hope to be able to discover the kind of law-like principles toward which each is working. For, despite the difficulties each acknowledges with respect to the specification of the limiting conditions in the provisional clause in each discipline, there is a concern about constructing predictive generalization regarding a causal and/or statistical pattern in behavioral transactions.

a) *The Law-Like Aims of Individual Psychology*

The psychologists dealing with basic drives seem confident of their ability to construct behavioral laws; and even the personologists who recognize the obstacles in their more complicated motivational data persist in their attempt to formulate law-like generalizations. The following law of conditioning or learning is applicable to the primary level of behavior in which the variables can be sufficiently isolated to allow controlled observations, if not experimentation: "In general, any act which is performed shortly before the reduction of a primary need, like that concerned with food, water, pain, optimal temperature, or sex, will be conditioned in such a way that when the organism is again in that situation or one resembling it, and suffers from that need or one resembling it, that act will tend to be evoked." [7]

It is much more difficult to specify the limiting conditions when more complex motives are included. Cattell, for example, aims at a "dynamic calculus" for the assessment of human motivation in terms of "interests, drives, attitudes, values conflict, defense dynamisms, and such dynamic structure as the ego, superego, and the self sentiment." Instead of a "set of laws," however, he acknowledges that his findings only promise "an avenue to laws and perhaps a firm foundation on which to erect genuine theory in the future." Programmatic as his "dynamic calculus" may be, nevertheless, he insists that "the scientific, theoretical group of dynamic phenomena which we seek requires . . . the discovery of dynamic laws, and this discovery of dynamic laws can be derived from, and only from, *observations dealing with changing strength of motives and changing structure of motives.*" [8]

The problem of coordinating the nomothetic and idiographic aspects of behavior in terms of law-like generalizations has been faced more squarely by Gordon Allport than by any other psychologist. While others have dealt with the other two complications of isolating motivational variables and accounting for the purposive selection of means to ends in goal-oriented behavior, Allport has more thoroughly explored the "dilemma of uniqueness." From our previous discussion of its bearing on the motivational factor in our synoptic model let us now draw out its implications for law-like generalizations.

First, Allport recognizes that for much social-scientific generalizing about average types of people, cultures, and stages of social development, including "many areas of psychology where individuality is of no concern," a purely nomothetic abstraction of similar characteristics with universal dimensions is required. In other words, the unique dynamic structure of each individual personality can be legitimately ignored in the construction of statistical and/or causal laws about universal segments of a person, if the investigator acknowledges that these uniformly persistent and pervasive characteristics are actually his abstractions from the concrete whole of a given person's own unique organization. In the second place, Allport is not concerned with uniqueness as such, but, rather, with man's psychological distinctiveness. He is fully aware that, as we emphasized previously, all natural objects, as well as human persons, have some uniqueness. Nevertheless, when the natural scientists construct and apply universal laws about physical things in terms of "common analytical elements," which they artificially abstract from the particular objects which combine these universal dimensions, they "find the accident of uniqueness irrelevant to their work." For physical objects, which are so purely reactive that their moving requires manipulation, "are incapable of becoming." Behavioral scientists, however, cannot construct sufficiently coherent laws for conceptually integrating all of the relevant functions of human persons, if they assume that each person's uniqueness is irrelevant. When the behavioral scientist makes this purely nomothetic assumption in order to emulate the natural scientist, he arbitrarily ignores the empirical evidence of the psychological distinctiveness of each human person's capacity for "becoming." To this Allport directs our attention: "Man alone has the capacity to vary his biological needs extensively and to add to them countless psychogenic needs reflecting in part his culture (no other creature has a culture), and in part his own style of life (no other creature worries about his life-style)."

While Allport recognizes the usefulness of the nomothetic generalizations by which the psychologist conceptually integrates the "stable features" of personality in terms of the "universal processes common to the species," he insists that behavioral laws must also express "the idiomatic pattern of becoming" which can be constructed only through idiographic analysis. When Allport deals with the "dilemma of uniqueness," he assumes that the idiographic analysis of the unique features of a person's purposive goal-seeking is separable from the nomothetic analysis of the natural, sociocultural, and psychological aspects of the total environment that conditions his distinctive thought, feeling, and conduct. But he also assumes that the integration of these separable constructs about the behavioral interaction of naturalized, socioculturalized, and goal-seeking individuals can be law-like. On the one hand, "each person is an idiom unto himself, an apparent violation of the syntax of the species." Nevertheless, on the other hand, "idioms are not entirely lawless and arbitrary," since "they can be known for what they are only by comparing them with the syntax of the species." Allport's principle of the "functional autonomy of motives" is designed to show that "a general law may be a law that tells how uniqueness comes about" and "to account, not for the abstract motivation of an impersonal and therefore non-existent mind-in-general, but for the concrete, viable motives of each and every mind-in-particular." [9]

b) *The Law-Like Aims of Social Psychology*

Most social psychologists seem to agree with Allport that a "master chart" for analysis "is not yet available";[10] despite this lack those who

are concerned about a theoretical framework take law-like generalizations for empirical research as their ultimate objective. For, as Newcomb reports, "those psychologists who have turned their attention
to theoretical problems of social behavior have repeatedly discovered
that order and regularity are to be found not only at the level of the
organism but also at the level of collectivities." Although this does
not mean that the "interrelatedness of lawfulness at different levels"
has been established as a basis for social-psychological analysis, Newcomb is convinced that the fruitfulness of further social-psychological inquiry depends upon aiming toward a molar conception of law-
like generalizations. Accordingly, rather than to ascribe order and
regularity to chance, or to the determination of the more inclusive
levels by the less inclusive levels, Newcomb recommends the exploration of the possibility that "lawfulness at less inclusive levels is
required by the nature of lawfulness at more inclusive levels." [11]

Without the inclusion of the idiographic aspects of "role behavior"
along with the nomothetic aspects of "role positions" and "consensus," according to Newcomb, no sufficiently coherent law-like generalizations about a person's transactions with others will ever be
attained in social psychology: "Whatever the characteristics he expresses in various roles, they are *his own* characteristics, and he cannot help expressing them as he takes his roles in his own, individual
way." [12]

c) *The Law-Like Aims of Sociology*

Since sociologists are primarily generalizing about the synchronic
patterns of diachronically recurrent phenomena, they would probably
all agree with Lundberg that "unity, coherence, and integration of
generalizations, as well as the multiplicity of their applications, must
be the ideal sought." [13] Moreover, since many sociologists seem to
share Hart's confidence that predictions about social scheduling can
be made "within reasonable margins of error," it seems likely that
they would respond affirmatively to the declaration following from
it: "If sociology is to become a science worthy of the name, the
energies of its practioners might better be directed toward improving
the techniques of prediction rather than toward demonstrations that
prediction is impossible." [14]

A controversial issue has developed with respect to the question of whether or not sociological laws are qualitative or quantitative. On the one hand, MacIver presupposes a difference between quantitative laws about the uniform pattern of natural events and law-like generalizations about the uniform pattern of behavioral events which are qualitative as well as quantitative when he claims that "the differentiation of community is relative to the growth of personality in social individuals." [15] On the other hand, when Lundberg prescribes the formula of sociological laws in quantitative terms, he insists that with respect to such "generalizations about societary phenomena," which sociologists should construct, "the term 'scientific law' can and should mean in the social sciences exactly what it means in any of the other sciences." [16] A closer examination of how Lundberg's attempts to specify the limiting conditions of predictions will disclose how the sociologist might isolate crucial variables, if he is willing to discount the purposive goal-seeking and the idiographic aspects of human behavior.

According to Lundberg, if social scientists are to be like natural scientists, they must also aim at formulating "valid and verifiable principles or laws comprehending with the greatest parsimony all the phenomena of that aspect of the cosmos which is under consideration." In this respect Lundberg is rejecting the narrower operational presumption that *laws* must be strictly empirical statements about observable events. In the following statement, however, Lundberg rules out any anthropic generalizations which apply to goal-seeking behavior that cannot be quantitatively measured in the same way that physical events are precisely measured: "A scientific law is (1) a group of verbal or mathematical symbols (2) designating an unlimited number of defined events in terms of a limited number of reactions (3) so that the performance of specified operations always yields predictable results (4) within measurable limits." Instead of a "double set of axioms" for behavioral laws, on the one hand, and for physical laws, on the other, Lundberg calls for a "quest for axioms from which societal as well as 'physical events' can be deduced," even though such a quest may "call for modification in the theoretical framework of the 'physical' sciences as in the social." [17]

Lundberg is fully cognizant of the difficulties which must be encountered in the formulation of generalizations about sociocultural and behavioral data that could justifiably be designated as *laws*. He wisely recognizes, however, that there is no necessary discrepancy between the "objectivity" of the natural-scientific and the "objectivity" of the social-scientific construction of laws. For "objectivity" does not depend upon the kind of data from which the generalizations are inferred. Rather, it characterizes or does not characterize the attitude of the person who is seeking to construct the *law*, i.e., "man's ways of responding and communicating his responses." With respect to the data, however, there are obstacles in the way of the formulation of sociocultural laws, since the social scientist does not have the "techniques of measurement" by which he can either eliminate or allow for "disturbing influences" in the manner of the natural sciences: "We do not know under what specific conditions they are true and to what degree they are verifiably true under these conditions." Without denying that "sociological laws" are ethnocentric, Lundberg points out that the universality of physical laws is achievable through the artificial and rigidly circumscribed conception of their referents: "The universality of their *practical application* flows from the refined measuring instruments that have been devised for measuring the *degree to which actual natural situations deviate* from the ideal conditions specified in the formal statements of the law." When a physical law is anything more than a tautological statement which defines the terms involved (e.g., the *law of inertia* that merely defines "force" and "motion"), a physical law must depend upon the ability of the scientist to measure the variations which it must either eliminate or allow for: "Except for these measurements, physics would have to have a separate law for every altitude and every wind velocity." When the social scientist cannot find experimental warrant for his sociocultural generalizations, he can use instead the procedure of statistical correlations for acquiring a reasonably reliable check on his generalization. For, as Lundberg contends, "the time is ripe for the systematization of the whole field of sociology in quantitative terms." [18]

Although all sociologists would like to construct nomothetic laws about the interaction of human groups, there are some who feel compelled to include the idiographic functions through which an individual person may conserve and increase his relative autonomy. Thus, Chinoy rejects a radically relativistic determinism which would reduce the intervening variable of a reflective person's motivation to the independent variables of society and/or culture: "The individual must be seen as an active being who is likely to behave in more or less standardized fashion, but who also possesses the capacity for innovation and deviation and can through his actions significantly influence and change the nature of culture and society." [19] This necessity for including the idiographic factor in sociocultural causation, it will be recalled, is forcefully emphasized by MacIver in his conception of the "dynamic assessment" through which a reflective person "envisages a total situation, relates it to his own ends, seems to make it, in whatever measure he can, instrumental, so as to turn its intrinsic dynamism into his own means." Accordingly, MacIver finds that lawful and law-like nomothetic generalizations about the physical, organic, cultural, technological, and social orders are necessary, but they are not sufficient when the decisions of relatively self-determined persons are involved. A purely nomothetic law constructed entirely in terms of mechanical determinism "misapprehends the interactivity of the factors within the causal complex," since "in this interactivity the role of the conscious agent is a distinctive one, to express which the term 'response' is wholly inadequate." [20]

d) *The Law-Like Aims of Anthropology*

It is not clear that all anthropologists are concerned about law-like generalizations about the sociocultural process. Those anthropologists who agree with Lesser that "the functional relation or relations asserted of any delimited aspect of culture must be such as to explain the nature and character of the delimited aspects under defined conditions" [21] seem to be aiming at a law-like formula. Murdock, for example, declares that "cultural forms in the field of social organization reveal a degree of regularity and of conformity to scientific law not significantly inferior to that found in the so-called natural sciences." [22] But many anthropologists seem to be far more interested in the pattern of specific communities which encompass all the traits of that particular group than they are in the segment that must be abstracted from each community which might be similarly abstracted as elements from the life of other communities.

One can not always be sure that a law-like pattern is the objective, even when Opler seeks to generalize about the structure of cultural phenomena in terms of "themes," or Herskovits in terms of "forces," or Kroeber in terms of "configurations of cultural growth," or Kluckhohn in terms of "implicit culture." [23] For, as Bennett and Wolff have reported, since the anthropologist "is more concerned with 'pattern' than 'law,' " anthropological materials "frequently represent instances of human behavior which he seizes and organizes, rather than statistical frequencies which prove or disprove a particular hypothesis." [24] Moreover, as Koppers points out, "there are no fixed laws in diffusion, either in transmission or in acceptance or rejection" and even when culture becomes stable "every case will have to be considered individually." [25]

Could such "highest common factors" (Kroeber and Kluckhohn) as "themes" or "configurations of cultural growth" lead to law-like generalizations? On the one hand, Linton claims that the "ultimate aim of the ethnologist," as with the sociologist, economist, and historian, when seeking to understand cultural change, is "to arrive at certain generalizations, or 'laws,' in common parlance, which will make it possible to predict the course of events and ultimately to control it." [26] A considerable number of anthropologists who associate sociocultural laws with the nineteenth-century evolutionism still share Boas' convictions that "generalizations will be more significant the closer we adhere to definite forms" and that "the attempts to reduce all social phenomena to a closed system of laws applicable to every society and explaining its structure and history do not seem a promising undertaking." Boas grants that a few generalizations like the following may be formulated: "the relation between density of population and increased social regulation; the limiting effect of environment and of economic conditions; and the moulding effect of a pattern in one domain of life over others." But, Boas contends, "these generalizations, unless qualified by an application to specific social conditions, are likely to be so vague that their value for the understanding of definite problems is not great, while the specific cases are so complex that the generalizations are no longer applicable to any considerable number of societies." [27]

More recently, however, Steward has proposed a law-like conception of sociocultural evolution in terms of some parallel developments rather than universal stages. This multilinear interpretation of evolution does not entail the final and absolutely closed system that precludes any divergence among cultures which has made the nineteenth-century unilinear conception of evolutionary law unacceptable. Steward does not expect that "any formulation of cultural regularities provides an ultimate explanation of culture changes," since even "in the physical and biological sciences, formulations are merely approximations of observed regularities and they are valid as working hypotheses despite their failure to deal with ultimate regularities." Emphasizing that such an anthropological generalization is always subject to qualification or reformulation, he insists that "so long as a cultural law formulates recurrences of similar inter-relationships of phenomena, it expresses cause and effect in the same way that the law of gravity formulates but does not ultimately explain the attraction between masses of matter." In his attempt to generalize about the nomothetic aspect of the sociocultural process, however, Steward does not leave out of account the idiographic aspect with which so many anthropologists are primarily concerned: "If the more important institutions of culture can be isolated from their unique setting so as to be typed, classified, and related to recurrent antecedents or functional correlates, it follows that it is possible to consider the institutions in question as the basic and constant ones, whereas the features that lend uniqueness are the secondary or variable ones." Steward acknowledges that the unilinear conception of sociocultural law does not allow for divergence and "universal evolution has yet to provide any very new formulations that will explain any and all cultures." Thus, he calls for a construction of lawlike generalizations about "limited similarities and parallels": "The most fruitful course of investigation would seem to be the search for laws which formulate particular phenomena with reference to particular circumstances." [28]

Goldstein recognizes that anthropologists have not yet established any nomothetic system of law-like generalizations about the sociocultural process; but he contends that if and when they do, they will not necessarily demonstrate a radically causal determinism: "If anthropology ever produces a system of laws, I presume that such laws will be of the kind that group together certain specific phenomena which may be shown to have certain determinate relations to each other." This would mean that "when certain variables take specified forms, then one or another variable dependent upon these will have certain specified characteristics" so that "if we are aware that one or more of these variables are undergoing determinate change, it may be hoped that we will be able to predict the future state of the dependent variables." When Goldstein acknowledges "the logical possibility that there are sociocultural laws," he emphasizes that this would not eliminate the postulate of relative self-determinism, since "the possibility of discovering these laws may enable us to make our freedom of action more effective." [29]

e) The Law-Like Aims of Economics

Probably more than the practitioners of any other behavioral science, economists have been concerned with constructing predictive generalizations that are law-like, if not lawful. With the possible exception of those piecemeal researchers who show no interest in the theoretical foundations of their discipline, most economists seem to agree with Lange that, "like all scientific laws, economic laws are established in order to make successful predictions about the outcome of human actions." This objective has been more significant in economics than in other kinds of behavioral predictions. Lange seems to speak for most economists, when he acknowledges that "most economic laws are thus 'limited historically' to certain given types of social organization and institutions." Moreover, none seem to deny his claim that it is difficult to construct such predictive generalizations because "the number of the conditions circumscribing the validity of economic laws is great, and it is difficult to ascertain whether they are all satisfied in any particular situation." [30] But, if and when these obstacles are surmounted, even the most unorthodox opponent of a substantively sterile rationalism would have to concede to von Mises that, "all theorems of economics are necessarily valid in every instance in which all the assumptions presupposed are given"; for, von Mises grants that "of course they have no practical significance in situations where these conditions are not establablished." [31]

It is instructive to note the implications of the change from the conception of absolute mechanistically invariant economic laws which determine the process of exchange to law-like generalizations in terms of causal and/or statistical constructs about economic transactions. Cairnes enunciated the classical faith in economics as a universal science "founded on invariable laws of nature," when he declared that "alike in the case of the physical and of the economic world, the facts we find existing are the results of causes between which and them the connection is constant and invariable." [32] Say's law of "supply and demand" was accepted as an inherent force in nature that operated just as automatically as Smith's "invisible hand," or Malthus' law that "population (tending to increase in geometric ratios) would always tend to outstrip the means of subsistence (which can increase in no more than arithmetic ratio)."

Tugwell exposes the fruitlessness of this classical conception of a mechanistic economic law as an "inescapable trend of development" on the grounds that it precludes the causal factor of man's own relatively self-determined purpose, i.e., "man can change society in very nearly any respect he cares to; he has only to will it persistently and strongly enough, to formulate his ideals distinctly enough, to go slow enough and to keep close enough to present determinants in transforming his environment into the ideal." [33] Tugwell similarly denies the fruitfulness of the "laws of marginal value" and attacks the neo-classical appeal to the iron "law of wages" and the "law of diminishing returns" for the reason that they can be circumvented by human intelligence. Tugwell's emphasis upon this intervening variable in the ends-means continuum of economic transactions is very significant; but his charge that Marshall took economic laws to be absolute is hard to understand. Even if the deductive conception of economic laws of other neo-classicists renders them as substantively sterile as Tugwell and other institutionalists contend, Marshall's conception is a notable exception.

Committed to the principle that "induction and deduction are both needed for scientific thought," Marshall insisted that economic generalizations are law-like constructions rather than immutable laws in the classical sense. Even though he recognizes that the law of gravitation is a "statement of tendencies," he acknowledges that "there are no laws of economics which can be compared for precision with the law of gravitation." Marshall is fully aware that "the actions of men are so various and uncertain that the best statement of tendencies which we can make in a science of human conduct must needs be inexact and faulty." But he insists, nevertheless, that economists should by "steady patient inquiry" frame "as best we can well thought-out estimates, or provisional laws of the tendencies of human actions." Accordingly, when Marshall assumes that a Social Law is "a statement that a certain course of action may be expected under certain conditions from the members of a social group," he maintains that "economic laws, or statements of economic tendencies, are those social laws which relate to branches of conduct in which the strength of the motive chiefly concerned can be measured by a money price." [34]

Marshall soundly coordinates the formal and the substantive aspects of the law-like generalizations by which the economist attempts to predict economic outcomes. On the formal side, the economist, like any other scientist, can legitimately delimit the causal factors by the proviso that "other things are equal." When Marshall deals with the specification of these limiting conditions, however, he emphasizes the difficulty that arises because "time must be allowed for causes to produce their effects." For, not only the material, but also the causes may change before the tendencies which the laws describe "have a sufficiently 'long run' in which to work themselves out fully." [34]

Marshall goes even beyond this hypothetical status of the law-like predictions which the economist constructs, when he acknowledges that substantive generalizations are actually relative to the specific sociocultural process in which the economic events to which they refer take place: "Though economic analysis and general reasonings are of wide application, yet every age and every country has its own problems; and every change in social conditions is likely to require a new development of economic doctrines." Despite this difficulty in specifying the conditions which limit predictive generalizations about economic actions, Marshall insists that "many of them may rank with the laws of those natural sciences which deal with complex subject matter." [34]

Among contemporary economists, concern about this problem of constructing law-like generalizations for causal explanation and prediction seems to depend upon the gauge of their interests. If an economist has only a narrow-gauged interest in a specific research area, then statistical correlations usually suffice to meet his limited theoretical needs. If, however, an economist has a broad-gauged interest in formulating a theory of economic growth, then he becomes acutely aware of the complications which the construction of economic laws entails. If he has completely reconstructed his conception of the limiting conditions in the dynamic terms of a constantly changing sociocultural process, rather than in the static terms of an equilibrating system, his attempts to isolate the variables and to delimit the contingencies through the provisional clause of his predictive generalization becomes even more difficult than that of Marshall. Abramovitz has clearly formulated this aspect of the problem of constructing law-like generalizations toward which broad-gauged economists must aim: "The study of economic growth also presents in aggravated form that universal problem of economics and of social science, the distillation of dependable uniformities from a process of cumulative change." [35]

Samuelson has developed "dynamic process analysis" on the premise that "this feature of self-generating development over time is the crux of every dynamic process." Without minimizing the "dangers involved in its use," Samuelson insists, nevertheless, that without this approach the economists can not formulate realistic interpretations of "speculation, cyclical fluctuations, and secular growth." Statics is inapplicable, since that approach only "concerns itself with the simultaneous and instantaneous or timeless determination of economic variables by mutually interdependent relations." Samuelson does not deny that static analysis of changing events is possible; but he believes that the economist must do more than treat each "changing position" as "successive states of static equilibrium." Accordingly, it would seem that those economists who aim at law-like generalizations about the actual economic dimension of the sociocultural process should take into account Samuelson's conception of dynamic analysis: "It is the essence of dynamics that economic variables at different points of time are functionally related; or what is the same thing, that there are functional relationships between economic variables, and their rates of change, their 'velocities,' 'accelerations,' or higher 'derivatives of derivatives.' " [36]

f) *The Law-Like Aims of Political Science*

Political scientists do not exhibit a widely-felt, common concern about the formulation of law-like generalizations; however, some are developing the theoretical principles for analysis out of which law-like constructions may emerge. Those who doubt the applicability of rational inquiry to the political process, are indifferent to this objective, as are those who are entirely engrossed in piece-work research about practical issues. An effort to work out some law-like generalizations is traceable, however, in the theoretical development from such ideas as "Natural Law" through the "iron law of oligarchy" to the contemporary notions of a "general equilibrium" and "constitutional equilibrium."

The eighteenth-century conception of "Natural Law" is no more than an abandoned ethical-religious notion which would be irrelevant here, if it did not still implicitly influence even many of those political scientists who have explicitly rejected it. According to this theory, there is a cosmic guarantee of the objectivity of the ideal ends for which the democratic political process allocates the means. For, according to this view, natural rights to security, freedom, and equality were just as divinely imposed as were the Newtonian laws of gravitation and motion. The appeal to the supernatural buttressing has been largely eliminated by those political scientists who seek for an objectively uniform pattern in the political process. There persists, nevertheless, the underlying conviction that a true conception of what human relations ought to be is congruent with what motivational and institutional potentialities actually are. Among political scientists this has been acknowledged by Waldo: "The significance of natural law ideas in American political thinking lies in the fact that regardless of whether the doctrine has been employed for 'conservative' or 'liberal' or 'radical' purposes, its exponents have assumed that there existed no deep cleft between 'what is' and 'what ought to be.' " [37]

The "iron law of oligarchy" has been constructed in terms that are diametrically opposed to the "Natural Law" on which the eighteenth century democratic ideology was based. Michels has formulated this explanatory-predictive generalization or law that "oligarchy is, as it were, a preordained form of the common life of great social aggregates" from "the principle that one dominant class inevitably succeeds to another." [38]

Whether or not a political scientist is convinced that there is sufficient evidence to warrant this inference as a law-like generalization about the political process, he cannot deny that it is more meaningful for analysis than the doctrine of Natural Law. Easton, for example, has acknowledged that "it is a theory, therefore, since it has broader implications than the actual facts which it was designed to draw together." [39] But this does not mean that he and like-minded political scientists are satisfied with it as a law, or with the non-constitutional government of men which it entails.

Instead of the "iron law of oligarchy," Easton suggests the following narrow-gauged generalization as a law-like implication of the concept of a "constitutional equilibrium" in the allocative political process: "There is an invariant relation between constitutional order and freedom, on the one hand, and the mutual restraint and limitation flowing from a relatively equal distribution of power, on the other." [40] In order to understand and evaluate the significance of this law-like generalization, we must ascertain what is meant by the broader concept of "general equilibrium" and by the narrower concept of "constitutional equilibrium" from which Easton's law-like proposition is derived.

What is the broader meaning of political equilibrium? Its molar significance has been indicated by Lowell: "In order to understand the organic laws of a political system, it is necessary to examine it as a whole, and seek to discover not only the true functions of each part, but also its influence upon every other part, and its relation to the equilibrium of the complete organism." [41] What it entails with respect to political regulation has been expressed by Perry: "Political science seems to be concerned with whatever social actions, techniques, and institutions are used by a society or civilization to bring order into, or to maintain equilibrium among, the lesser institutions and groups." [42] While some political scientists seem to conceive of equilibrium in terms of the kind of static balance that the neoclassical economists had in mind, others agree with Friedrich when he refers to "the maintenance of an equilibrium between various rival groups and claims, not a stable equilibrium, but a moving one which continuously adjusts itself to the shifting balance of these groups as they evolve." [43] Easton concludes, however, that the usefulness of the idea of "general equilibrium" as a basis for law-like generalizations is impaired because it does not sufficiently specify whether it refers to "an actual condition" or to "an equilibrating or balancing tendency." Moreover, he contends, it would require more quantification in political-scientific analysis than can be reasonably expected. [44]

Easton hopes to find a much more fruitful conceptual framework for constructing law-like generalizations in the idea of "constitutional equilibrium." This construct refers to the necessary conditions of constitutional order within or among nations for a relatively equal distribution of power so that no one participant has a preponderant control of the policy decisions and executions by which the instrumental values of an entire society are authoritatively allocated. Quantification of the causal variables is not required in this characterization of "either an ideal or an existing democracy as a constitutional equilibrium." But it does specify that "only under conditions where power is spread throughout the system so that each element is restrained by other elements can an equilibrium be achieved." Whereas the "general equilibrium" theorists do not uniformly insist upon this "equal balance," Easton elaborates on this essential feature of "constitutional equilibrium": "In this context, a political system is said to be in equilibrium when there is some kind of equality in the distribution of power, either among social classes, groups, as nations, or in the political structure, so that no one group can use its power without inhibition or limitation." Such, then, is the concept "constitutional equilibrium" from which Easton has derived this law-like generalization that "there is an invariant relation between constitutional order and freedom, on the one hand, and mutual restraint and limitation following from an equal distribution of power, on the other." [45]

The issue about "freedom" in this concept and this law requires further examination. Easton contends that without the "constitutional equilibrium" to which this law-like proposition refers there could be no political freedom: "Equilibrium here means not a state of rest but a condition where power is so widely dispersed that each element must vie with the others to influence policy and in the process the restraint exercised by each upon the other permits the existence of political freedom." [46] But does Easton's law-like generalization sufficiently include among the causal variables the relatively self-determined decisions of reflective persons who exhibit intellectual initiative and moral responsibility? Merriam seems to have this in mind when he insists that "political association begins with the emergence of conscious and purposeful personalities" and that "there will always be a margin of alternatives—a margin where human values and choices will be important and conclusive." [47]

How might this *intervening variable of responsible initiative* be included among the causal variables that are the referents of a law-like generalization about the goal-oriented ends-means continuum of political action? On the one hand, Key contends that "initiative and leadership rest, not in the mass, but in whatever group of leaders it tolerates." [48] On the other hand, after examining the check and balance system of a democratic government, Herring insists that there is no automatic control by which it can be protected against demagoguery or conspiracy. This requires the *responsible initiative* which comes from "the capacity of each citizen to weigh and to judge." For Herring, therefore, the relatively self-determined decisions of individual persons cannot be ignored in an analysis of the distribution of power in a constitutional self-government under law: "The mechanism for democratic self-control is the citizen's inner control: his knowledge of government, his shrewd political judgment, his capacity to turn from emotional appeals and fears to a sensible estimate of the situation." [49] It is this *responsible initiative* of voluntarily cooperative reflective persons which Dewey also took to be the precipitant causal variable in the production of a democratic process: "The keynote of democracy as a way of life may be expressed, it seems to me, as the necessity for the participation of every mature human being in the formulation of values that regulate the living of men together: when it is necessary from the standpoint of both the general social welfare and the full development of human beings as individuals." [50]

Perhaps this factor of the relatively self-determined decisions of persons, which Merriam, Herring, and Dewey emphasize, could be coordinated with the law-like generalization, which Easton's "constitutional equilibrium" concept entails, by specifying the former as the limiting conditions for the uniform operation of the latter: "There is an invariant relation between constitutional order and freedom on the one hand, and the mutual restraint of power on the other," *if the participants in the democratic process are extensively motivated by intellectual initiative and moral responsibility.*

If political action is conceived in terms of an "ends-means continuum," the application and verification of this expanded law-like generalization can be empirically confirmed or disconfirmed by actual observation. It should be noted, by those who might take this to be nothing but a statement of faith in a democratic ideal, that it involves the same kind of "if-then" formula which applies to any other pattern of causal relations. Is there any reason why in principle this predictive statement about reflective motivation could not be empirically checked just as much as predictive generalizations about causally interrelated sociocultural factors could be checked? To be sure, it is more difficult to construct predictive generalizations about political outcomes when the way power is distributed may be contingent upon the event-making decisions of individual persons. Economists or sociologists who are concerned only with nomothetic generalizations may eliminate this problem by means of the provisional clause of his law-like statement. For those political scientists who share the historian's idiographic interests, however, the sacrifice of the intervening variable of *responsible initiative* would be too high a price to pay for a more clean-cut law-like generalization.

g)   *The Law-Like Aims of History*

When the broader operationalist considers the possibility of constructing law-like historical generalizations, he finds himself in the crossfire of two combatants. At one extreme, there is the intuitionist who in the light of his exclusively idiographic predilection for historical insight or a completely unique approach dismisses such an aim as meaningless. At the other extreme, there is the proponent of "general laws in history," who seems to place law-like generalization too far beyond the historian's reach, when he insists that "general laws have quite analogous functions in history and in the natural sciences." [51] This conception of the function of a general law should not be confused with the dialectical or cyclical conception of a predetermined scheme of the invariant succession of events proposed by Hegel, Marx, Spencer, Spengler, and others.

Hempel makes two concessions, however, which open up for the broader operationalist at least an alternative avenue to explore. First, when Hempel claims that a historical explanation requires statements of "universal conditional form," he grants that they may be borrowed from other disciplines: "Many of the universal hypotheses underlying historical explanation, for instance, would commonly be classified as psychological, economical, sociological, and partly perhaps as historical laws; in addition, historical research has frequently to resort to general laws established in physics, chemistry, and biology." Second, Hempel acknowledges the usefulness of an "explanation sketch," i.e., "a more or less vague indication of the laws and initial conditions considered as relevant," even though "it needs 'filling out' in order to turn into a full-fledged explanation." [51]

When Donagan challenges the Hempelian conception of "the

suitability of general hypotheses" on the grounds that explanations of historical actions are, in our present state of knowledge, independent of general laws," he contends that such "law-like statements" are verifiable. For, to a significant degree they meet the demands which Hempel requires of general laws: "They must both admit of scientific substantiation and logically entail what they explain." [52]

Hempel's acknowledgement of the limited usefulness of an "explanation sketch," which we take to mean an increasingly more law-like generalization, is more significant than his concession that historians may and do depend on other disciplines for their laws. Essential as the latter is, it does not relieve the historian from the responsibility to forge out his own law-like generalizations. When the broadly operational historian turns his back on the intuitional approach and moves in the direction toward constructing generalizations which are as law-like as he can make them, he should realize that their significance does not depend upon their being as nomothetic as natural-scientific laws. For, the historian will do well if he can make his general propositions analogous to the law-like behavioral generalizations under which other social-scientific explanations are purportedly subsumed.

Dray contends that the "covering law" theory proposed by Hempel and Popper "commonly leads its advocates into talking about explanations in history in ways that are either radically incorrect or misleading in important respects." For, whereas "covering laws" revolve primarily around universally-holding predictions, most historians are primarily concerned only with particular explanations. They assume that if a previous event had not occurred "in that *particular situation*, if everything else remained the same, (a subsequent event) that which in fact occurred would not have done so; or, at any rate, that it would have been different in important respects." Accordingly, Dray insists, "to give and to defend a causal explanation in history is scarcely ever to bring what is explained under a law, and almost always involves a descriptive account, a narrative of the actual course of events, in order to justify the judgment that the condition was indeed the cause." [53]

The historian can, of course, construct purely analytic generalizations in a "universally conditional form" which are just as formally valid as those of the natural and other social sciences. Recall Newton's law of inertia which simply defines what is meant by force as "that which produces motion" and Cohen's law of social heredity which simply defines what is meant by the persistence of sociocultural transmission, i.e., "people will believe and act as did their fathers before them except in so far as certain factors produce changes in our social arrangements and in our ideas and sentiments." Simply by changing the tense so that this prediction is a post-diction the historian could, without fear of contradiction, assert the following as universally valid: *Throughout the development of all human communities, the children of each generation have behaved, felt, and believed in the same manner as did their parents, if there was nothing to interfere with this way of transmitting sociocultural patterns.* But would any historian be interested in such a substantively sterile generalization? Formally valid as it is, the historian prefers to deal with the actual development of human affairs, even if he has to employ singular constructs.

What happens when the historian undertakes to construct substantive law-like generalizations under which he might subsume his reasonably acceptable explanations of the past human actions that he has imaginatively reconstructed out of authenticated testimony? He is confronted with at least three basic problems which are inherent in his distinctive orientation: (a) Historical generalizations refer to particular wholes of a specific spatio-temporal situation rather than to universal segments that have been abstracted from concrete wholes in the formulation of natural laws. (b) Historical generalizations are always "postdictive" about past events rather than "predictive" in the sense that natural-scientific and social-scientific generalizations refer to future events. (c) Historical generalizations are weakened, if not precluded, by the process of specifying their limiting conditions. The latter problem, it will be recalled, confronts the social scientist as well; but for the historian it is even more serious.

(a) Although the distinctive character of the referent of a historian's generalization was discussed as a postulate in the meaning-situation, in order to clarify this discussion of generalizations in the knowledge-situation let us recall Nagel's statement that they are usually "singular statements about the occurrence and interrelations of specific actions." [54] This precludes the possibility that even the most law-like construct about the vanished past could be equated with those scientific generalizations which functionally correlate the causal and/or statistical relations of abstracted universal characteristics.

Where the scientist takes abstract generalizing to be his intrinsic aim, the historian takes it to be an instrumental aim. In other words, the historian may construct generalizations about some of the universal characteristics of a total situation; but, he must not allow such abstract generalizing to replace his chief aim of describing and explaining particular situations as concrete wholes which include some unique and some universal characteristics. Without the latter there could be no comparison of specific situations upon which explanations depends.

(b) Is there any significant sense of law-likeness in which the historian's postdictive reference to past events can be related to the predictive reference to future events which are constructed by other behavioral and natural scientists? For comparison let us recall the predictive generalizations of the economist as described by Lange: "Like all scientific laws, economic laws are established in order to make successful prediction of the outcome of human actions." In other words, by specifying given limiting conditions the economists can assert that if certain conditions are operating, then certain consequences can be reasonably expected in the future. But historical generalizations have no future referents such as the function of prediction requires. If, however, the historian can be allowed to modify the predictive function so that, instead of referring to future events, it refers to what investigation might reasonably be expected to discover in the comparison of isolated historical situations, then the historian has a surrogate for the usual kind of prediction. This is what we understand Zilsel to mean when he declares that "evidently prediction must not be taken in a temporal meaning only."

Zilsel's discussion merits special attention. Zilsel fully recognizes that there are only a few historical systems that are sufficiently independent for the purposes of this kind of comparative analysis by which the "law-concept" might be applied to historical situations. He maintains, nevertheless, that "if a historical regularity, obtained by comparing certain historical systems, is confirmed in other and independent systems, it may be considered, at least for the present, as verified." When Zilsel cites examples of temporal laws in history, he grants, however, that they "are yet incomplete in so far as only necessary but not sufficient conditions are given." Accordingly, he maintains that these incomplete laws "describe temporal processes in yet rather vague formulations and may be called historical laws in a narrow sense." As an example, Zilsel cites this generalization: "In isolated historical systems tribal organization precedes the beginnings of the state." But Zilsel very soundly advises us to be quite modest "in our expectations regarding historical laws." [55]

(c) To what extent, if any, can the historian specify the limiting conditions of his generalizations which purport to be law-like? Even a broader operationalist such as Werkmeister recognized that the distinctive subject-matter and individualizing orientation of historical interpretation preclude anything more than "generalized sketches of relationships" about events which "are too complex to be readily subsumed under specific equations." Not only is information about crucial initial conditions inaccessible, but it is difficult to obtain a reasonable consensus among historians about the reconstructed data which are accessible in many cases. Consequently, Werkmeister is correct when he declares that "it is impossible to obtain sufficient knowledge of all initial and contributory conditions which determine the course of a historical event." [56] But what is the case, if the historian does not expect to obtain "knowledge of all initial and contributory conditions" which a law requires? Could he not still aim at law-like generalizations for which sufficient knowledge might be available?

Relaxing the demands upon the historian does not relieve him of providing some reasonably acceptable specification of the limiting conditions of a law-like generalization. Consequently, he is confronted by a much more serious problem than is the theoretical economist who can formulate the qualifications by which disturbing factors can be discounted or balanced out. A provisional clause such as "everything else being equal" can be used by theoretical economists, as well as by natural scientists, to specify the ideal conditions, even though they know that they are only artificially circumscribing the initial conditions upon which their predictive generalizations are contingent. It seems unlikely, however, that any historian *qua* historian would be willing to go so far in abstracting the segments of the totality of a historical context for the sake of stating such a qualifying provision in order to safeguard his generalization. The physicist may isolate all the causal variables when he generalizes that "friction produces heat." But the historian cannot so eliminate all but a few of the properties and environmental conditions by an analogous purely synchronic assertion. For, unlike the physicist, as well as the theoretical economist, the thoroughly diachronic historian cannot so transcend specific spatio-temporal contexts.

These serious obstacles, notwithstanding, some historians have law-like aims. Gottschalk reports that "despite persistent and widespread apprehension," historians are increasingly seeking to "shed some light on the causal relationship among historical phenomena" in the three endeavors: "(1) to discover single cases that will illustrate a social-science generalization, (2) to discover single cases that will contradict a social-science generalization, and (3) to apply a social-science generalization to a historical trend or a series of similar events." [57] For example, what are the issues such historians must deal with if they attempt to recast MacIver's law-like sociological generalizations into a historical form? Instead, of: "the differentiation of community is relative to the growth of personality in social individuals," they might generalize that "in the development of sociocultural systems the differentiation of community *has been* relative to the growth of personalities in social individuals."

One of the historian's foremost problems is that of accounting for the causal influence which the decisions of particular persons have upon the sociocultural process to which the purported law-like generalization refers. As we have seen, any social scientist who deals with the intervening variable of goal-seeking motivation is confronted with this problem. In a great many other social-scientific predictions the normative referents of individual ends-means actions can be delimited by the provisional clause. Few historians, however, are willing to dispense with the standards by which deliberative policy decisions are made and implemented. If they did so, they would be required to ignore the thought, imagination, and conduct of those especially equipped persons who creatively modify the sociocultural process of which they are both products and producers. Consequently, even the historian who has law-like aims, when he reconstructs the causal sequence of past human actions, usually recognizes that, in some cases, the course of human affairs would have taken another turn than it did, if some persons had not acted as they did. In other words, what actually happened was precipitated by the use of specific means to achieve ends that some especially gifted persons deliberately sought to realize. Being in the crucial role at the crucial time is a necessary condition. But, to recall Hook's terminology, such an "event-making man is an eventful man whose actions are the consequences of outstanding capacities and intelligence, will and character, rather than the accidents of position." [58] Zilsel similarly notes that historical generalizing cannot discount that "human individuals influence history to different degrees because they differ in their personal gifts and abilities." [59]

Does the recognition of the causal influence of the relatively self-determined decisions of outstanding persons preclude the kind of "reasonable expectations" which law-like generalizations require? Cohen claims that it does not do so, when he considers "intelligent volition" as "a verifiable causal element" among other distinctive traits of causal law in history. Cohen grants that in any judgment there are "insuperable difficulties in finding out in advance, with any high degree of rigor and accuracy, what people will want to do under given conditions." But he insists, nevertheless, that this difficulty does not preclude any degree of prediction: "To deny the possibility of any prediction at all is inconsistent with the practice and postulates of rational science or history." Recognition of the causal influence of human purposes upon the development of human affairs as an intervening variable does not mean that the historian is adapting the one-sided "great man theory," which discounts the independent variables of the natural, psychological, and sociocultural environment. For, as Cohen insists, "this does not mean that pure or disembodied thought is known to be a cause for any event in nature." [60]

When Cohen warns historians against both "pan-logism" and "nominalism," we assume he is referring to the fruitless extremes of a radically nomothetic orientation or of a radically idiographic orientation. The reconstruction of past human actions out of present data logically "must implicitly or explicitly involve laws"; but "it is a demonstrable error to suppose that anything in regard to specific existence can be deduced from purely logical considerations." No explanation logically deduced from a general law and empirically tested can "explain what it was that enabled men of genius to do the unprecedented things which they did." Their actions of course, would not have been possible apart from sociocultural conditions which may be "connected according to laws of an invariant order." But the complexity and number of inorganic, organic, and mental factors make it unlikely that historians will ever "be able to discover the laws or to formulate manageable equations for dealing with the phenomena." Moreover, unlike the consideration of the temporal relations between physical systems in which "the effects of intervening history can be eliminated," in human history for which dates and locations are essential "the effects of age and experience cannot be wiped out." [60]

The historian who aims at law-like generalizations agrees with other broadly operational scientists that his idiographic assertions must be coordinated with nomothetic inferences; but for him this is a more complicated task. Whereas other social scientists have a supply of nomothetic constructs, he has few, if any, of his own. Consequently, the historian must borrow some nomothetic assertions from other disciplines. Although, as Lane points out, "the historian is a consumer, rather than a producer of broad generalizations," nevertheless, the historian has a "consumer's responsibility for the quality of the particular product he uses." [61] Such a responsible coordination of idiographic and borrowed nomothetic constructs is needed by historians, if they use what Strong called "continuant configurations." By this, he means that "the judgments of relation-statements supported by fact-statements inferred from the material of historical reconstruction" are compared with similar "configurational organizations" of contemporary human actions. [62]

Even though the historian cannot construct his own genuinely nomothetic generalizations, is it possible for him, if he is so minded, to construct nomothetic-like generalizations as a means to making his interpretation about the past actions of a specific person, past sociocultural situations, or a causal sequence of human events more comprehensive? Lane suggests that the historian might formulate constructs which exhibit "intermediate degrees of generality" within his own field. These constructs do not exhibit "the maximum possible generality" that the genuinely nomothetic laws are designed to express as the intrinsic goal of strictly scientific inquiry. But, as Lane emphasizes, these "historical generalizations" are "worthwhile because they are ends in themselves, that is, because they satisfy the historical interest," rather than "because they are stepping stones to broader generalizations." [63] Isn't this what the Committee for Bulletin 54 meant when they acknowledged the ideal of "extending historical research and thought as far as possible in the direction of comprehensiveness and synthesis as well as by inquiring more deeply into the particular and the unique?" [64] *Nomothetic-like* though this may be, it must not be confused with the genuinely nomothetic law which Hempel has in mind as the generalization from which idiographic explanations are strictly deduced. Aron seems to express more accurately the aim of most historians when they are dealing with the lives of human actors, with why and how situations happened, with historical configurations, and with patterns of change: "We want to understand the human actors, explain the events, elaborate historical units consistent with the articulation of reality, and discover whether there are great lines of evolution which either humanity as a whole or each historical unit follows." [65]

If this assessment of historical inquiry has been accurate, it seems that, at least in principle, the broadly operational historian aims at the same kind of verification which other social scientists seek. Accordingly, he too attempts to construct reliable hypotheses in terms of a coherent system of generalizations which have causal implications that can be verified to various degrees of probability.

Footnotes to Chapter 4 of Part Four

[1] Hempel and Oppenheim, "The Logic of Explanation," *Readings in the Philosophy of Science* (Feigl and Brodbeck), 326. Originally published in *Philosophy of Science*, 15, 1948.

[2] Cohen in *Readings in the Philosophy of Science* (Feigl and Brodbeck), 669.

[3] Dewey, "Social Science," *New Republic*, July 29, 1931.

[4] Cohen in *Readings in the Philosophy of Science* (Feigl and Brodbeck), 672-673.

[5] Hart in *Symposium on Sociological Theory* (Gross), 200-202.

[6] Parsons in *Toward a Theory of Human Behavior* (Grinker), 66. For a logical analysis of Newton's "laws of motion," see Nagel, *The Structure of Science*, 157-162, 185, 201-202.

[7] See Skinner in *Psychological Theory* (Marx), 439-448. Cf. Miller in *The State of the Social Sciences* (White), 29-65. Cf. Cattell in *Assessment of Human Motives* (Lindzey), 201-223.

[8] Cattell in *Assessment of Human Motives* (Lindzey), 198-199.

[9] Allport, *Becoming*, 19-23; *The Nature of Personality*, 89-90.

[10] Allport in *Handbook of Social Psychology* (Lindzey), Vol. I, 51.

[11] Newcomb in *For a Science of Social Man* (Gillin), 246-247.

[12] Newcomb in *Social Psychology*, 333.

[13] Lundberg, *Foundations of Sociology*, 137.

[14] Hart in *Symposium on Sociological Theory* (Gross), 226.

[15] MacIver, *Community*, 231.

[16] Lundberg, *Foundations of Sociology*, 133, 136-137.

[17] *Ibid.*, 133, 135.

[18] *Ibid.*, 137-142, 122.

[19] Chinoy, *Sociological Perspective*, 53.

[20] MacIver, *Social Causation*, 236-237.

[21] Lesser, "Functionalism in Social Anthropology," *American Anthropologist*, N.S. 37 (1935), page 392.

[22] Murdock, *Social Structure*, 259.

[23] See Kroeber and Kluckhohn, "General Features of Culture," *Culture, A Critical Review of Concepts and Definitions* (Peabody papers), Vol. XLVII, No. 1.

[24] Bennett and Wolff in *Current Anthropology* (Thomas), 336.

[25] Koppers in *Current Anthropology* (Thomas), 179.

[26] Linton in *The Science of Man in the World Crisis*, 12.

[27] Boas in *Encyclopedia of the Social Sciences*, Vol. 2, page 110.

[28] Steward in *Anthropology Today* (Kroeber), 325; "Cultural Causality and Law," *American Anthropologist*, No. 1, pages 1-27.

[29] Goldstein, *American Anthropologist*, Vol. 61, No. 2, April 1959, pages 295-297.

[30] Lange in *Readings in the Philosophy of Science* (Feigl and Brodbeck), 746. Originally published in the *Review of Economic Studies*, 13, 1945-46.

[31] von Mises, *Human Action*, 66.

[32] Cairnes, *The Character and Logical Method of Political Economy*, 19-20. (Quoted by Mills in *The Trend of Economics* [Tugwell], 48.)

[33] Tugwell, *The Trend of Economics*, 390-394.

[34] Marshall, *Principles of Economics*, 31-33, 36-38. Cf. Jevons, *Theory of Political Economy*, 3-4.

[35] Abramovitz in *A Survey of Contemporary Economics* (Haley) Vol. II, 177.

[36] Samuelson in *A Survey of Contemporary Economics* (Ellis), Vol. I, 354, 374-376.

[37] Waldo, *Political Science in the United States of America*, 14.

[38] Michels, *Political Parties*, 377-392.

[39] Easton, *The Political System*, 56-57.

[40] *Ibid.*, 302-303.

[41] Lowell is thus quoted by Easton, *The Political System*, 266.

[42] Perry, *American Political Science Review*, June 1950, page 405.

[43] Friedrich, *Constitutional Government and Democracy*, 136.

[44] Easton, *The Political System*, 274-292.

[45] *Ibid.*, 302-303.

[46] *Ibid.*, 302.

[47] Merriam, *Systematic Politics*, 1, 329.

[48] Key, *Politics, Parties, and Pressure Groups*, 9.

[49] Herring, *American Political Science Review*, Dec. 1953, page 973.

[50] Dewey, "Democracy," *Readings in Philosophy* (Randall, Buchler, Shirk), 347.

[51] Hempel in *Readings in Philosophical Analysis* (Feigl and Sellers), 459, 465, 467, 469, 470. Originally published in *The Journal of Philosophy*, 39, 1942.

[52] Donagan, *Mind*, Vol. LXVI, N.S. No. 262, April 1957, pages 157, 164.

[53] Dray, *Laws and Explanation in History*, 1, 102, 113.

[54] Nagel, "The Logic of Historical Analysis," *Readings in the Philosophy of Science* (Feigl and Brodbeck), 689.

[55] Zilsel in *Readings in the Philosophy of Science* (Feigl and Brodbeck) 715, 718-720. Originally published in *Philosophy of Science*, 8, 1941.

[56] Werkmeister, *The Basis and Structure of Knowledge*, 329.

[57] Gottschalk, *Understanding History*, 252.

[58] Hook, *The Hero in History*, 153-154.

[59] Zilsel in *Readings in the Philosophy of Science* (Feigl and Brodbeck), 717-718.

[60] Cohen, "Causation and Its Application to History," *Journal of the History of Ideas*, Vol. 3, 1942, pages 25-29. See Nagel, *The Structure of Science*, 548-550, for Nagel's support of Cohen's position when Nagel insists that the natural sciences are not exclusively nomothetic and history is not exclusively idiographic.

[61] Lane, *Enterprise and Secular Change* (Lane and Riemersma), 529.

[62] Strong in *Naturalism and the Human Spirit* (Krikorian), 179-182.

[63] Lane, *Enterprise and Secular Change* (Lane and Riemersma), 523-524, 533.

[64] Bulletin 54, page 134.

[65] Aron, "Evidence and Inference in History," *Evidence and Inference* (Lerner), 23. See pages 25-41 for Aron's discussion of the influence of individual persons on historical events.

Conclusion: Conversations Between a Critic and the Author

Critic: After wandering through the byways of all of the disciplines, I feel very much like Ulysses. But after his Odyssey he was more fortunate than I, for at least he returned home; whereas I feel that I am still left at sea. Don't you think you ought to provide me with some specific conclusions?

Author: I know how you feel, but I fear that I am not in a position to eliminate your frustration. You were warned that I could not hope to do any more than some initial spadework toward dealing with the continuing problem of social-scientific knowledge. Instead of my presenting conclusions, therefore, why don't you raise some of the questions that bother you most.

Critic: I would prefer some definite conclusions, but I see your point. Perhaps you will summarize your basic arguments so that I may see how they bear on the purpose of your study. What was your main purpose?

Author: The aim of this philosophical effort has been to suggest a comprehensive framework which might help to correlate and clarify some of the methodological questions for which many social scientists are seeking answers. From the various selections that have been cited, it should be evident that they implicitly, if not explicitly, invoke the more general problems of analysis which are involved in a philosophical theory of knowledge.

Critic: But haven't you made your analysis unduly abstract?

Author: Unless I am mistaken, a philosophical formulation of such a comprehensive perspective must deal with the abstract dimension of the problem of social-scientific knowledge. The philosopher is not equipped with the training and techniques which are required to deal with the many other aspects of the problem of knowledge that confront the practitioner who is engaged in creative research within a delimited area.

Critic: It seems to me that you are prejudiced against the narrow research in which most social scientists are engaged.

Author: But I have insisted quite frequently that substantive knowledge about specific aspects of human behavior can be obtained only by the researcher who applies precision techniques to narrowly circumscribed data.

Critic: Then why don't you emphasize the significance of such specialized inquiries and deal more with their problems?

Author: Since all practicing social scientists are fully aware of the significance of specialized research, there is little need to emphasize its importance. But many researchers seem to be unaware that when they justifiably segment behavioral data and use only one technique, they lose sight of the broader epistemological issues. Consequently, we have directed attention to this more neglected aspect of the problem of knowledge. What are some of the questions you think a research specialist might raise?

Critic: There are at least three questions which need clarification. What does this epistemological approach mean by objectivity? What does it imply about interdisciplinary integration? Why does it imply that with respect to knowledge about values, philosophical analysis is needed in addition to social-scientific analysis?

Author: Let's start with the first question. I have assumed that in order to examine the warranty for objective behavioral knowledge, it has been necessary to delve into the subterranean recesses of the social scientist's value-situation and meaning-situation.

Critic: But why should the social scientist accept your assumption? The researcher who works single-mindedly within a delimited area quickly establishes the objectivity of his facts by simply pointing to the quantitative nature of his data, or to the controlled nature of his experimental techniques.

Author: If that is all the researcher looks for, then I would say that he fails to recognize that his justification, which appears to be so acceptable and objective in his knowledge-situation, is derived from his own motivation and his own underlying assumption about what kind of knowledge is meaningful. Far more essential for objectivity than any precision technique, is that the social scientist subordinate all other desires to his desire to know. Without this compulsive attitude for persisting inquiry, the scientist has no firm ground on which he can make his bid for epistemological objectivity.

Critic: Do you mean to say that good intentions establish the objectivity of behavioral knowledge?

Author: Not at all. In addition, the scientist must guide his search for the reasonable acceptability of a substantive hypothesis by the requirements which his conception of meaningfulness imposes.

Critic: But how does he come by these requirements?

Author: He maintains this epistemological objectivity as long as he is operationally constructing reliable hypotheses about the dimension of reality which he is concerned with, in terms of a coherent system of generalizations which have causal implications that can be verified to various degrees of probability.

Critic: Oh yes, now I recall that you presented the assumptions which this epistemological objectivity entails in terms of the five postulates of the meaning-situation of reflective inquiry. Doesn't his commitment to this meaning-situation presuppose some prior intellectual commitments?

Author: It certainly does. For a scientist to adopt this psychological-epistemological conception of objectivity he must be motivated as a *positive sceptic* to hold his meaning-situation as a *situational relativist* and his knowledge-situation as a *broader operationalist.*

Critic: Do you think that any natural scientist would be satisfied with such a qualified conception of epistemological objectivity?

Author: Well, Margenau claims that some are in an article he wrote on the "Perspectives of Science." [1] He declared that "by recognizing its own need for commitment to postulates and axioms of which it cannot be sure in *a priori* or in final fashion, it made common cause with those disciplines in which commitment to norms, ideals, and values is essential to progress."

Critic: Probably all research specialists would adapt the positive sceptics conception of emendable rather than absolute knowledge.

Author: Since research specialists reject absolutism, I suppose that they accept what I call situational relativism rather than radical relativism.

Critic: Please distinguish between them again.

Author: According to radical relativism, all judgments are subjective, since they are completely determined by psychological and sociocultural conditions. According to situational relativism, a person's meaning-situation is derived from his cultural symbols and psychological nature; but, within a given meaning-situation it is possible to establish principles of inference and verification by which one claim can be shown to be more reasonably acceptable than another.

Critic: Most of us who concentrate on research would probably say that theoretical systems are radically relativistic, but that experimental and/or statistical analyses are situationally relativistic. I know that this doesn't sound very sporting, but the theoretician has no way of escaping his own psychological and cultural bias by empirical testing.

Author: But don't you realize that these empirical testing techniques would not themselves be meaningful apart from the theoretician's criterion of coherence. Moreover, experimental testing and statistical correlations would not be meaningful to people who do not presuppose the framework of reflective inquiry which the theoretician has established in our culture. To examine our differences more specifically, let's consider the principles of broader operationalism. To what extent do you accept its five requirements?

Critic: Well, I would accept the first three principles but would have some reservations about the fourth, and I would reject the fifth. All researchers would agree that a verifiable knowledge claim must be stated in a proposition that has implications which other people can examine and test. Moreover, not only must any hypothesis be tested but it should always be subject to re-examination. Some, but not all, researchers might balk at adopting the requirement that empirical testing must be regulated by conceptual principles. From what I said before about safeguarding objectivity, however, it should be clear that I cannot adopt a problem-centered rather than a technique-centered approach.

Author: Then you do not agree that the social scientist must take into account the limitations of his specific subject matter in order to determine what observational and testing techniques are applicable to his specific data.

Critic: No, I don't. I doubt that an empirical researcher could be significantly productive if he, as investigator, must have an operational conception of knowledge which is so broad that he can include meaningful constructs about behavioral data which inherently are not quantitatively measurable.

Author: It would seem then that you are advocating a narrow operationalism.

Critic: Perhaps I am, but I feel that if we are really aiming at objective knowledge, a broader operationalism which relaxes techniques is too much of a compromise. In other words, to borrow William James' terminology, broader operationalism is too "tender minded." We have to be "tough minded."

Author: I want to make it clear that I do not accuse all of those who aim at "tough mindedness" of being motivated by the desire to attain prestige by imitating the natural scientist. Whether or not this unconsciously persuades some of you to be "tough minded," I still assume that your conscious motivation is to make behavioral knowledge more objective. Now let us try to tie this down more specifically. Would you say that our conceptual orientation of the observable data is too inclusive?

Critic: Yes. I think that a model should simplify rather than complicate the conception of the factors with which an analysis is dealing.

Author: When I suggest a synoptic model for conceptually orienting behavioral data I fully acknowledge that a theoretical model for identifying and classifying the data with which a research specialist is concerned should be narrowly circumscribed. Moreover, I recognize that all of the factors in the total behavioral situation which are not directly relevant to his immediate problem can be disregarded by the researcher. I grant that he should, whenever possible, aim at precision by eliminating data that cannot be dealt with quantitatively. But isn't the price of precision too high when it requires a very limited conceptual orientation? Such a delimited framework will not serve the purpose of identifying the separable but interconnected dimensions of the total behavioral process. Moreover, if the investigator has no comprehensive conceptual model in mind, he may slip back into the unwarranted claim that one isolated factor is the only causal determinant. Such arbitrary delimitation blocks the channels of cooperative interdisciplinary inquiry. I cannot ignore these channels when we are analyzing the problem of knowledge in the social-scientific enterprise as a whole.

Critic: It would appear that we are concerned with two different problems; but I can't see what use such a synoptic model could have for a social scientist who is primarily concerned with empirical research.

Author: Well, first of all, when a social scientist considers such a synoptic model he may become aware of research areas that would not otherwise have occurred to him. And secondly, a synoptic model provides a framework within which the findings of particular research undertakings might be correlated.

Critic: Well, perhaps this is possible, but I'm still not convinced that this justifies the compromise you make when you synthesize the molecular with the molar and the nomothetic with the idiographic models of analysis. After all, most research is molecular and nomothetic.

Author: My justification for this is very much like my justification for the synoptic model itself. Since we are dealing with the problem of knowledge for the entire social-scientific enterprise we cannot allow the successful application of the molecular and nomothetic models of analysis in some areas to become the defining characteristics of objectivity for all areas. As we have shown, each of the disciplines has researchers who are concerned with interdisciplinary data that cannot be dealt with adequately unless we combine the molar with the molecular and the idiographic with the nomothetic. It seems to me that you suggest that such problems be discounted as meaningless. If I did that I would be circumventing, rather than exploring, the problem of social-scientific knowledge. If molar and idiographic situations were completely disallowed, wouldn't we be confining behavioral analyses to a self-contradictory kind of objectivity about what is not actually real? The purely nomothetic molecularist may have precise surgical instruments; but he is operating on skeletons rather than upon living beings.

Critic: Don't you agree that the objectivity of scientific knowledge about uniform patterns requires abstract generalizations about artificially segmented dimensions of actual events? These can be obtained only by way of a molecular and nomothetic approach.

Author: Of course, I agree that molecular and nomothetic analyses are necessary; but I am also insisting that when one is dealing with some behavioral data, molecular and nomothetic analyses are not sufficient. That is why I synchronize the molar-molecular and the nomothetic-idiographic. I am equally opposed to anyone who would advocate a purely idiographic or a purely molar approach. Since the aiming at nomothetic law-like generalizations is so well established in our contemporary intellectual climate, we don't have to belabor its significance here.

Critic: You've revealed quite a molar bias!

Author: I do overemphasize the molar, but I have recognized that in some cases molecular analysis is required. Where a molarist can use molecular analysis, a molecularist cannot use molar analysis. Consequently, I have objected to the delimitation of what can be known about human behavior in terms of molecularism.

Critic: Haven't you felt the need for a molar approach in order to make room for purposive causation? Doesn't this jeopardize scientific description and explanation?

Author: Obviously, I reject any characterization of behavior that eliminates the goal-seeking actions which constitute our given empirical data. But that doesn't make the causal account unscientific. Purpose may be treated as an intrinsic end by a philosopher, but not by a social scientist. As Krech and Klein emphasize: "We raise the question 'why' only to discover 'how' and 'what' answers." [2]

Critic: Maybe we have to take purposive causation into account now, but when a social science outgrows its youth, it must substitute quantitative for qualitative variables in the manner of the natural scientist.

Author: Before I answer the crucial part of your query, let me say that I agree with Hoselitz that the methodological shortcomings of social science should not be blamed simply on its youth. Thoughtful people have been concerned with social questions just about as long as they have been asking questions about the physical world. But what I take to be your crucial claim is substantiated by Hoselitz when he points out why the natural sciences forged ahead of the behavioral sciences. In the seventeenth century the exact formulation of theoretical physics replaced mere speculation in qualitative terms.

Critic: Then why do you object so much to statistical analysis?

Author: I don't object, but since you seem to think so, I should clarify my position. I fully acknowledge the usefulness of statistical calculations as techniques in the observational, classificatory, and testing stages of scientific analysis. For some social scientists to whom the "promised land" of controlled laboratory experimentation is denied, statistical quantification has been a boon. What Reitman has said about psychology holds to a considerable extent for all of the imprecise social sciences "with their large uncontrolled sources of error variance." Since psychology is limited to "probabilistic, best guess knowledge," Reitman accurately emphasizes the "real increase in scientific efficiency which results from the rational utilization of descriptive and test statistics." [3]

Critic: Wait a minute, I'm confused. You seem to have switched horses. Aren't you agreeing with me that social scientists should use statistical quantification in order to increase their objectivity?

Author: Up to this point I have simply acknowledged the importance of statistical techniques in the knowledge-situation of many behavioral investigations. But I haven't switched horses. The point I want to emphasize is that the usefulness of statistical correlation in the knowledge-situation does not justify substituting it for the postulate of causation in the meaning-situation. The increased effectiveness of statistical research doesn't detract from a causal conception of what kind of knowledge is meaningful.

Critic: Haven't some physicists abandoned causality in favor of a statistical conception of knowledge in order to cope with chance occurrences?

Author: While some make this claim, I agree with Nagel's conclusion that "saying an event 'happens by chance' is not in general incompatible with asserting the event to mean that the event has no determining conditions for its occurrence." [4] Now, I doubt that any natural scientist or social scientist would make such an assertion. To assume that the absolute fortuity of events is inherent would preclude statistical as well as causal knowledge. The deleterious consequences of abandoning the postulate of causation when accounting for conscious goal-seeking behavior should be obvious.

Critic: Yes, I can see that the "empty organism" approach which statistical correlation entails would not throw any light on motivation, especially the purposive goal seeking you're interested in. But why shouldn't the sociologists be satisfied with an exclusively statistical conception of knowledge about the actions of collectivities?

Author: Some agree with Lundberg that sociologists should aim at nothing but quantitative knowledge; but others agree with Simpson's more qualified use of statistical techniques. Simpson has emphasized that when sociology "is concerned with trends and tendencies in a mass of cases" it depends upon statistical analysis of quantitative data in order to "seek the typical measure in a mass of cases (the average), the deviations from the typical, and other relevant information." He agrees with Bertrand Russell that this is important knowledge, but that quantification should not be taken therefore as the only kind of significant knowledge. For this would exclude the case-study technique which "communicates and illuminates the dynamic quality of human behavior." Moreover, purely statistical replication may merely perpetuate the error of prior statistical correlations.[5]

Critic: Do you realize that political scientists are increasingly looking to statistical analysis for more reliable knowledge?

Author: Yes, Eulau emphasizes the need for statistical techniques in political science. Nevertheless, in principle, he supports my claim that such techniques derive their significance from the investigators meaning-situation. He warns his colleagues that "there are those who, entranced by interview schedules, scales, indices, and statistical devices, undertake research without being aware of the many epistemological and methodological assumptions they make in using these techniques."[6]

Critic: Let's take up my second question. Whenever you refer to integration at various points you sound very much like Hayek when he laments "the dilemma of specialization." How can any social scientist conduct research without specializing in some limited area?

Author: Of course, substantive research requires delimitation by a competent specialist.

Critic: Then why have you advocated an amalgamation of all the behavioral disciplines?

Author: I am as opposed as you are to an amalgamation which would stifle the specialist's creative scholarship. What the social-scientific enterprise needs is a genuine integration which correlates the new various research findings about human behavior and opens up new avenues for research.

Critic: Why do you so vehemently reject the logical positivist's proposal to unify all human knowledge?

Author: The logical positivist's contribution to clarifying linguistic ambiguity and to facilitating interdisciplinary communication should not be underestimated. But genuine integration of behavioral disciplines requires more conceptual principles than the logical positivist will allow. His quantitative rigor precludes purposive causation, and, without that, our goal-seeking conception of human behavior would be meaningless.

Critic: Would you be satisfied with Miller's proposal for integrating the behavioral sciences through a general systems theory which he takes to be "a series of related definitions, assumptions, and postulates about all levels of systems from atomic particles through atoms, molecules, crystals, viruses, cells, organs, individuals, small groups, societies, planets, solar systems, and galaxies." [7]

Author: While Miller does recognize that living things "are open systems, with important inputs and outputs," so that "laws which apply to them differ from those applying to relatively closed systems," he seems to reduce too much to preserve the emergent superorganic characteristics to which so many behavioral constructs refer.

Critic: But, as Nagel points out in *The Structure of Science,* despite the scepticism of some physicists about "the ideal of a comprehensive theory which will integrate all domains of natural science in terms of a common set of principles," nevertheless, "that ideal continues to leaven current scientific speculation, and, in any case, the phenomenon of a relatively autonomous theory becoming absorbed by, or reduced to, some other more inclusive theory is an undeniable and recurrent feature of the history of modern science." [8]

Author: Yes, but Nagel is referring here to the reduction of thermodynamics to statistical mechanics, and he emphasizes that organic biology, for example, has shown that "the pursuit of mechanistic explanations for vital processes is not a *sine qua non* for valuable and fruitful study of such processes." [9] In other words, the mechanical unity of 17th century physics is not the only objective of integration. Consequently, many social scientists feel that the superorganic level of sociocultural and motivational processes requires nonmechanical principles of integration even more than the organic level does.

Critic: Do you mean you prefer a supernatural referent as a substitute for the material referent of mechanical unification?

Author: Not at all, for, as Weber emphasized, when social scientists adopt the ends-means orientation for behavioral data, their referent is neither supernatural nor material. But it is no less real than those other referents. In fact, when Hoselitz analyzes the development of social sciences during the last two hundred years, he finds that interdisciplinary unification which transcends overspecialization requires this common framework. "But the final barrier to full cooperation in the social sciences will be removed only when all specialists are able to see and appraise their special fields of research in its context within the whole field of the study of man and society." [10]

Critic: But how can there be interdisciplinary integration when there is no intradisciplinary integration?

Author: You have a good point. To cite one illustration, the need for intradisciplinary integration is strongly felt by Krech and Klein when they conclude that "an adequate personality theory must be a thoroughgoing behavior theory and that all theories of behavior must be personality theories." [11] Now, personologists can correlate their constructs with those of anthropologists, for example, in terms of a personality-culture approach. But this does not constitute a genuine correlation of the disciplines of psychology and anthropology.

Critic: Why, then, don't the advocates of interdisciplinary integration hold their fire until each discipline becomes more integrated?

Author: That would be as unfeasible as for one discipline to refrain from drawing upon another discipline until the latter had solved all of its problems. Moreover, attempts at some kind of interdisciplinary cooperation throw considerable light on the intradisciplinary problems.

Critic: Don't you integrators overlook the fact that the division of labor among the different disciplines of the social sciences has evolved in response to the demands of behavioral research?

Author: Well now, all social scientists don't agree that the diversity of subject matters is as inherent as you suggest. When Parsons, for example, claims that "no academic organization of the disciplines can overcome this inherent logical cross-and-interpenetration of the various behavioral fields," he insists that "in which disciplinary category a given empirical field is predominantly placed is usually a matter of

historical accident and pragmatic convenience, not of scientific principle." [12] For another, MacIver characterizes the "various academic
imperialisms" as "an escape from the harder problem of a more inclusive methodology" and condemns "the common tendency to make
the field of one's special interest the inclusive ground within which
the causes of all relevant phenomena are to be sought." [13] When
Gillin analyzes some of the pertinent practical and theoretical problems of interdisciplinary cooperation he concludes: "Apparently the
students of man and his ways must either stop being interested in
such questions, or they must get together to some extent in order to
help each other to provide reliable answers." [14]

Critic: Don't you realize that if an integrated body of social-scientific knowledge should be established, there would be the great danger that it would become a latter-day scholasticism which would appeal to dogmatic authority?

Author: Such academic imperialism is a possibility; but I am
assuming that there would always be enough heretics to enforce critical reconstruction whenever the need for reopening avenues of inquiry demanded. But avenues of inquiry can be blocked just as effectively by the narrowly circumscribed compartmentalization through
which the practitioners in the most fashionable discipline might arbitrarily depreciate the significance of others.

Critic: What do you integrators suggest?

Author: Among other proposals, Smith looks toward the emergence of what he calls "appropriate mutually compatible conceptual
models." [15] Newcomb calls for a conceptual integration of the elements and systems of the social systems: "If each of the several disciplines of human behavior took its neighbor's macrocosm, and its alternative neighbor's microcosm as its own macrocosm, their problems
of articulation would be minor ones." [16]

Critic: It seems to me that you ought to decide which disciplinary
fields might serve as basic foundations for all of the others. Then
you could build up a hierarchy of levels.

Author: But that is not what we mean by integration. I agree
with Parsons that the effort to do this "is only a symptom of the
growing pains of a very young family of scientific disciplines." Instead, Parsons maintains that it will only be when the various disciplines "have come to regard themselves and each other as the formu-

lators of very important special cases relative to a more general theory, that a higher level of theoretical maturity in our fields will have been reached." [17]

Critic: I am strongly persuaded by Black's suspicion that the "elaboration of a conceptual scheme, such as Parsons offers us, would have to await a wealth of well-founded empirical generalizations." [18] On the basis of your own description and analysis of the empirical generalizations in the various disciplines, I should think you'd have to agree that there *is* no wealth of well-founded empirical generalizations about human behavior.

Author: Yes, I agree that most of the behavioral disciplines have not as yet constructed a wealth of well-founded empirical generalizations. But I don't agree that this means that the formulation of conceptual schemes should be postponed. A conceptual system is designed to guide the development of empirical generalizations. Parsons clearly indicates that he is not advocating a closed theoretical system for integrating the various disciplines: "Notwithstanding some statements which I have made on occasion, my present considered opinion is that though it has moved in that direction, my approach is not yet a logico-deductive system, but rather a temporal and historical series of contributions toward the development of such a system." [19] I agree with Parsons that we are not limited to the alternatives of either an integrated deductive system or unrelated generalizations.

Critic: If not these extremes, then what ultimate goal does Parsons seek?

Author: Parsons aims at a "unified conceptual scheme which is taken for granted in the relevant professions and, as a matter of course, used as the base of operations for exploring the problems on the new frontiers of knowledge."

Critic: Is this just his dream of what he thinks ought to be, or does he expect that such integration will eventually emerge?

Author: He indicates the latter when he declares that he is "deeply convinced that the ultimate development of such a scheme is essential and that the general trend of intellectual history is in that direction." [20]

Critic: Since you have dealt with epistemological issues in all of the behavioral disciplines more extensively than has Parsons, would you say that you have advanced beyond Parsons' position?

Author: No, not at all. My indebtedness to Parsons is obvious. But even where I have directed attention to problems with which he is not directly concerned, I am simply spading another part of the garden. Actually, all that I have attempted to do is to raise the questions which must be answered by the social scientists themselves, rather than by a philosopher. Genuine integration must be achieved by those social scientists who are working in their respective substantive fields.

Critic: But how do they go about achieving such a goal?

Author: Perhaps the most fruitful kind of integration is generated when specific scientists coordinate their efforts in dealing with a common problem. Consider, for example *Values and Policy in American Society* by the Ohio Wesleyan Associates. For a basic criterion the philosopher offers the *welfare standard,* i.e., "the maximum harmonious satisfaction of the desires of men as social beings," and he shows why it requires the social ends of material well-being, stability, security, equality, justice, and freedom. Accordingly, the economist, political scientist, sociologist, and historian identify and elaborate the distinctive *social objectives* of their own respective disciplines which bear on these *social ends.* They all adopt the following three basic steps as a common procedure for the deliberative evaluation of social policies: (1) Identification of the valued objective. (2) Organization of scientific knowledge that is relevant for understanding the problem and for understanding the means for realizing the valued objective. (3) Evaluation of policies and objectives which relate the broad social ends of the entire society to the narrower social objectives of the specific disciplines which are cooperating in the enterprise.[21]

Critic: Let's discuss my third question. Why do you claim that in order to acquire adequate knowledge about human values, we must have philosophical as well as social-scientific analyses? Doesn't von Mering in his *A Grammar of Human Values* do a thorough job within a social-scientific framework?

Author: Not only is von Mering's contribution most significant, but it provides a basis for the kind of comparison we need for dealing with this issue. First, I share his basic premise that "knowing and valuing are social facts and, therefore, analyzable within a scheme of social action." This is obvious from the elaboration of my synoptic model as a conceptual orientation of behavioral data. Moreover, in constructing this synoptic model it would not have been necessary for me to introduce the intervening variable of relatively self-determined goal seeking in terms of reflective valuing, if I did not agree with von Mering that, "man is not merely a simple reacting mechanism, but is endowed with interpretive and expressive capacities; he must face the paradox of his essential solitariness within a web of relatedness to others." If you recall my identification of unreflective value experience, you will see that I agree with von Mering that "the biographical situation itself leads the individual into conflicting value commitments." Furthermore, when he claims that "all valuation is a kind of reaching out beyond the immediate present; it is a matter of growth for the individual," he is acknowledging the functioning of what I have identified as reflective value experience. Doesn't von Mering emphasize the relative self-determinism which reflective valuing presupposes when he insists that a person "through the operation of deliberation and judgment tends to attach plus and minus subjective weights to the existing diverse open values." [22]

Critic: I wonder if you and von Mering do agree as much as you suppose. Instead of your unreflective-reflective classification of value motivations, he classifies values as existential, normative, and idiosyncratic and he refers to "three possible valuative directions, the simplistic, restrictive, and comprehensive." [23]

Author: When you take this to be a conflict between von Mering's classification and mine, you have forgotten the distinction between conceptual and theoretical constructs. As a part of my synoptic model my unreflective-reflective classification is designed to do no more than organize the observational data for all of the behavioral disciplines. von Mering, however, has formulated a theoretical classification which is designed to provide explanatory-predicative hypotheses that are verifiable through empirical research. In order to obtain substantive knowledge about "the special impact of social contacts and intercultural living on human valuation" he systematically explains the "patterning of individual and cultural values" in terms of what he takes to be this testable hypothesis: "As breadth, but especially as intensity of personal contact with peoples from other cultures increases, individual and group standards of valuation tend to become less narrow or restricted, less simple in content and more comprehensive." Accordingly, von Mering is concerned about "gathering reliable and quantifiable data" with research instruments "whether a scale, questionnaire, or clinical interview." [24]

Critic: But when von Mering adopts the "empirical deductive" method for dealing with value data rather than the "historical descriptive" and "systematic deductive" methods, he seems to be advocating what you have called the hypothetical-deductive method. When von Mering declares that he "is content to conceive of all scientific knowledge as probable, . . . and as systematic," he seems to share your meaning-situation. Moreover, he, like you, claims that in order to make survival worthwhile, man often discovers that "life has meaning to him only if asserted—if affirmed in terms of self-realization." Now even if there is a distinction between the conceptual classification of values in your synoptic model and von Mering's theoretical classification for purposes of a specific inquiry, I still have this question: Since he adopts the meaning-situation, the knowledge-situation, and the intrinsic goal you approve, what could a philosopher add to his empirical constructions and verification of value hypotheses? [25]

Author: Your question is a crucial one. I do share von Mering's conception of the pattern of inquiry. Moreover, I agree with him that in the value-situation "neither means nor ends have an independent existence of their own," since "they represent a continuum, or they have a unitary existence to the experiencing individual despite what philosophers call the logical priority of ends." But this does not preclude the philosopher's distinctive role in the division of labor which he shares with the social scientist.[25]

Critic: It seems that you have in mind Weber's division of labor between the social scientist who deals with "(1) the indispensable means, (2) the inevitable repercussions, and (3) the thus conditional competition of numerous possible evaluations in their practical consequences" and the philosopher who "can go further and lay bare the 'meaning' of evaluations, i.e., their ultimate meaningful consequences" so that he can indicate their "place" within the totality of all the possible "ultimate evaluations and delimit their spheres of meaningful validity."

Author: Yes, I agree with Weber that the social scientist should confine himself to the means and that the philosopher should elaborate the meaning of evaluations. But I do not agree with Weber that "even such simple questions as the extent to which the end should be taken into consideration, or how conflicts between several concretely conflicting ends are to be arbitrated are entirely matters of choice or compromise by each individual." [26]

Critic: But how can the selection of intrinsic ends be anything more than a matter of each person's own subjective personal preference?

Author: When one is engaged in a descriptive analysis like that of von Mering, ideal ends can be attributed to the personal preferences of the socioculturalized individuals whom he is studying. For he is concerned only with a "statistical analysis of cultural and individual value patterns" with a "major focus on cultural, rather than private value patterns." [27] But when a social scientist makes objective policy recommendations, he can't rely on each person's personal preference about the intrinsic ends. For this he must turn to the philosopher.

Critic: How, then, do you modify Weber's statement of this division of labor?

Author: I suggest that, on the one hand, the philosophical axiologist should construct the normative generalizations about the intrinsic ends which defines the ultimate good in the value system by which the allocation of opportunities ought to be regulated. On the other hand, the policy scientist should construct the equally significant generalizations about the most effective means for realizing that intrinsic end in the light of the reliable knowledge he has acquired about the consequences of particular decisions with respect to alternative courses of action.

Critic: Could you illustrate what you mean?

Author: For example, consider the policy recommendation of the normative political theorist that "we ought to have a democratic constitutional government of law rather than a totalitarian non-constitutional government of men." How does he justify this claim? Only under a constitutional government is freedom under law guaranteed, i.e., an authoritative allocation of rights and duties whereby the freedom of each person is congruent with equal freedom of all other persons with respect to due process of law. The political scientist can then confirm or disconfirm the implications of this hypothesis or of the totalitarian alternative hypothesis by empirical evidence. But why should people have equal freedom? The political scientists might say that without it and the opportunity to participate in their own policy making decisions (at least through empowering those who do make and execute policies) the individuals cannot develop their own initiative and responsibility. But why should the individual have the right and the duty to develop his in-

tellectual initiative and moral responsibility? For this answer the political scientist must look beyond the boundaries of his own discipline
to the philosophical axiologist. The latter might answer that the
ideal goal of "self-realization" as an intrinsic value requires the political opportunity to develop intellectual initiative and moral responsibility. The political scientist could accept this; but he is not
methodologically equipped to verify this normative judgment as an
alternative to other rival normative claims about the intrinsic value
for reasonable persons. The task is such that only the philosophical axiologist's analytical tools are applicable. Similarly, when a
policy-minded economist claims that planned capitalism is preferable to either unplanned capitalism or socialism because it better
provides for the development of persons rather than either ex-
ploitive or governmental power, the economist must turn to the
philosophical axiologist for the justification of the intrinsic value of
personal development.

Critic: But how can a philosophical axiologist provide highly reliable conclusions about the intrinsic ends of reflective desiring?
You have maintained throughout your analysis that the objectivity
of broadly operational knowledge can be achieved only in terms of
the construction and verification of a reasonably acceptable system
of coherent hypotheses. I don't see how a philosopher could achieve
correspondingly objective knowledge about intrinsic goals.

Author: Whether or not he is successful, I think that it is the
philosopher's responsibility to attempt to formulate broadly operational hypotheses about the thought, conduct, and imagination of
reflectively motivated persons which can be used by reflective persons for the purposive control of their deliberative behavior. With
this as his objective, the axiologist must adapt the hypothetical-
deductive method to reflective desiring as his distinctive data. This
means that the logical pattern of inquiry requires that axiological
analysis can yield reliable knowledge about intrinsic life goals only
if its conclusions are operationally acquired: (a) through critical inspection of the relevant data of reflective goal seeking; (b) through
the formulation of normative hypotheses which function as principles of classification, of explanation, and of purposive control; and
(c) through the coherent verification of the deduced implications
of a generic hypothesis in terms of derivative hypothetical claims
which must be tested experientially by reflective persons.

Critic: There are several questions I would like to ask about each of these steps of axiological inquiry. To begin with, how can one be sure that he is critically inspecting the relevant data of reflective goal seeking? As I recall, you identified the value situation entirely in terms of one's private experiences of desiring and striving for one's own subjective satisfaction. Moreover, the most relevant factors by which you distinguish between reflective and unreflective motivation are the awareness of deliberation and the awareness of obligation which cannot be examined.

Author: The critical inspection of reflective value experience requires the use of both introspective and extrospective techniques. Previous discussions have already shown that this kind of observational analysis is needed to deal with the "intervening variables" of goal-seeking behavior with which many psychologists are concerned. Even if one does not agree that this limited use of introspection is admissible in the social-scientific diagnosis of behavioral data, he cannot eliminate it from an axiological analysis of reflective value experience without precluding the possibility that the axiologist can observe any data that are relevant to the kind of questions he is attempting to answer with respect to intrinsic life-goals. For a person's private commitment to these ideal ends is not open to external scrutiny, even though, as Dewey has emphasized, the means he chooses in order to realize the relatively self-imposed objective he professes to desire are observable by others.

An axiologist must use extreme caution in the application of this introspective technique no less than must a broadly operational social scientist who finds that his subject matter requires it. On the one hand, an uncritical reliance on the introspection of conscious processes alone will lead to the non-operational intuitive thinking of a naïve mystic, who fails to account for the influences of the natural, sociocultural, and psychological factors which shape the individual. On the other hand, an uncritical reliance on extrospective techniques alone will lead to the reductive thinking of a naïve behaviorist, who does not account for the experience of a reflective person who is engaged in the purposive process of adjusting his thought, conduct, and imagination to relatively self-imposed norms which cannot be experimentally manipulated or quantitatively counted, weighed, or measured.

When the philosophical axiologist includes introspection among the techniques he uses to obtain the observational data from which he will attempt to construct objective normative judgments, he is compelled by the nature of these data to go even further than the social scientist can safely go in his observational diagnosis. Perhaps the difference lies in the axiologist's more extensive use of introspection, as well as introspective retrospection (memory), and introspective prospection (anticipation), when he discovers that the emotional and purposive ingredients of reflective desiring are practically inaccessible through public observation.

It would seem unreasonable and arbitrary to doubt that a critical inspection of reflective processes discovers that ideal value experience is just as factual as sense experience of the physical world. But normative judgments, like descriptive judgments, require more than the critical inspection of observational data. Accordingly, reflective value experiences must be classified and interpreted in terms of operationally verifiable hypotheses. Otherwise, religious fervor, moral anguish, aesthetic ecstasy, social enthusiasm, pseudo-scientific dogmatism, or fanciful speculation may be mistakenly substituted for sound normative judgment. This requires a coherent conception of ideal value realization which has implications that can be experientially confirmed or disconfirmed to a highly probable degree of "reasonable acceptability."

Critic: I am not sure that I understand what you mean when you claim that in the second stage of axiological inquiry normative hypotheses must serve to classify, to explain, and to control purposively the relevant data of reflective value experience.

Author: Without a normative hypothesis the axiologist would have no correlating idea by which he might select and classify, from all of his many desires, those desires which are relevant. Kant's advice that physical nature must be interrogated applies also to human nature.

Critic: What kind of questions serve as such normative hypotheses?

Author: In the development of western culture there have emerged three such normative questions: First: Does *happiness* or *pleasurable feeling* provide an intrinsic goal for reflective desiring? Second: Does *survival* provide an intrinsic goal for reflective desiring? And third: Does *self-realization* provide an intrinsic goal for reflective desiring? The basic supposition in the mind of the axiologist will be the *correlating idea* with which he classifies particular kinds of desiring as instrumental, intrinsic, and higher or lower intrinsic values. To be sure, such a definition of the *summum bonum* is a leading question, but, as has been shown, no reflective inquiry is free from similar presumptions. It must be obvious from what I've said before that I consider *self-realization* to be the most fruitful *correlating idea* for harmoniously coordinating ethical, aesthetic, intellectual, and religious preferences. Experience has convinced many reflective persons that *happiness* or *pleasurable feeling* is a by-product of progress toward *self-realization* and that mere physical environmental adaptation or *survival* requires some more intrinsic value such as *self-realization* to make it worthwhile. In accordance with this conception of the *summum bonum* any value may in a given situation be *instrumental*, i.e., a *means* to the realization of the *end* which is the *intrinsic* value in that particular situation.

Critic: When such normative constructs are for explanation or purposive control of reflective value experience, can't they be shown to refer to nothing else but neurophysiological, psychodynamic, or sociocultural responses?

Author: If we were concerned here only with the primary values of unreflective desiring, our descriptive hypotheses would refer exclusively to physiological, psychological, and sociocultural drives. But since we are concerned here with the ideal values of reflective desiring, our normative hypotheses will refer to ideal goals. Of course, drives and goal seeking interpenetrate in the concrete experience of even the most reflective persons. This methodological distinction is justified, however, if we do not forget, like the Watsonian behaviorist at the other extreme, that we have so abstracted. Critical inspection and classification of ideal value experiences reveal that when a reflective person seeks explanations (intellectual preferences), creatively imagines (aesthetic preferences), acts justly (ethical preferences), and consecrates himself to cooperation with God (religious preferences), then the most relevant mental processes are an awareness of better rather than worse, an awareness of commitment to the better, and an awareness of choosing the acknowledged course of action, thought, or feeling. Normative judgments about this type of experience must be expressed in terms of a coherent system of normative hypotheses which *explains* how persons have developed such an enlightened, creative, just, and consecrated personality-determining attitude, and which *predicts* (reasonable expectation) how such *self-realization* can be further increased through purposive self-control.

Critic: But in what sense can such an intrinsic value be taken to be objective?

Author: A generic normative hypothesis must be formulated which defines the ultimate intrinsic quality of mind and its relations to other minds which is progressively realizable but beyond complete realization. The *objective* property of this value lies in the rational desirability of this self-imposed ideal to which all reflective subjective desiring refers. As a goal for the organization of all of one's reflective preferences, this generic norm must provide an integrating perspective which gives to otherwise isolated, momentary, and transient enjoyments an enduring satisfaction. The objective character of this goal does not depend upon everyone's pursuit of it. To be objective, however, it must be a potential satisfaction as a rational end for some minds.

Critic: But isn't your generic statement that self-realization is the *summum bonum* simply an analytical proposition?

Author: Right you are! Moreover, as an analytical statement it is not itself verifiable as true or false. It, like a mathematically ideal case of Newton, is too often taken to be an *a priori* truth. After an axiologist thus analytically defines his intrinsic goal, he must then look for empirical confirmation of what he asserts. Accordingly, he must deductively elaborate derivative hypotheses from his analytical conception of the intrinsic goal. These must be *expressed in synthetic propositions.* Not only must they be mutually compatible within a consistent system, they must also be testable for their comparative adequacy. Only thus can the advocates of *self-realization* demonstrate the greater reliability of their normative judgment over that advocated in the hedonistic or the survivalistic theories about the meaning of life. In other words, these derivative norms, which are always subject to modification, correction, or abandonment in favor of more adequate hypotheses, should be experientially verifiable by reflective persons who use them as principles for guiding the purposive development of a harmonious system of discriminating preferences.

Critic: Could you explicitly formulate such derivative hypotheses?

Author: The explicit formulation of derivative hypotheses is an axiological problem which lies beyond the limits of this study. I have confined my attention to the epistemological principles that normative judgments in general value theory involve. For such a substantive analysis an extended separate study is needed. In working out a coherent system of these normative standards for thought and conduct which are implied by the ideal of self-realization there are, however, some general axiological requirements that must be met. The norms must be self-imposed; and intentions must not only be mutually compatible, but they must also provide for a consistent relation between choices of means and ends. The objectives which constitute a person's values must be planned, comprehensive, and harmonious. The objective state of affairs (e.g., social relations) involving specific circumstances and ascertainable consequences must be taken into full account. If self-realization is to yield implications that are more adequate than those derived from hedonistic and survivalistic conception, it is necessary to show how individualism and altruism mutually require each other.

Although the analytic statement of the generic hypothesis which conceptually integrates the total context of ideal value realizations is a necessary step in the cognitive process; taken by itself, it is not verifiable. Verification of a proposed system of normative hypotheses requires an exploration of the implications of the integrating conception in accordance with the logic of the hypothetical syllogism (if-then) which regulates all reflective inquiry.

Critic: I can understand your use of a normative hypothesis for classification and explanation; but I can't see how you could verify an assertion about such subjective desires. When you talk about the verification of normative hypotheses, aren't you referring to the kind of aesthetic truth Keats had in mind when he declared that "beauty is truth"? Or is it what St. Thomas had in mind when he called for a double standard of truths of reason and truths of faith?

Author: That certainly is not what I mean! A belief about the ideal value realizations of reflective minds, like a belief about the causal interaction among physical events, may be true, even if no human mind verifies it. But such a belief is not admissible as reliable knowledge until it meets the requirements of consistency and adequacy which the criterion of coherence entails. Two other related presuppositions should be recalled: (1) It is necessary but not sufficient to demonstrate that the derivative hypotheses are valid implications of the generic hypothesis and that they are mutually consistent. (2) A high degree of probability, rather than the demonstrable validity of a mathematical-logical system, is the most that can be expected.

Critic: But what techniques could ever be used to determine whether or not any normative proposal meets these requirements of verification?

Author: Let us assume that advocates of the hedonistic, survivalistic, and self-realizational theories have each formulated a normative system of a generic and several derivative hypotheses. How can discriminating minds determine which is more coherent? With a view to such verification each reflective person in the light of his own personal and social experiences might answer for himself the following sets of questions:

Is the proposed generic norm sufficiently comprehensive to be adequate as a *referent* for all the relevant processes of reflective desiring? In other words, does it provide an intelligible pattern for integrating and interpreting the anticipated satisfactions of my intellectual, aesthetic, ethical, and religious aspirations? (If his answer is affirmative, is not the adoption of this generic normative hypothesis a *justified assumption?*)

Do the derivative normative hypotheses implicatively follow from the generic norm? Taken together are they mutually compatible in a harmonious system? (If his answers are affirmative, is it not reasonable to conclude that it meets the rational requirement of *consistency?*)

Does this system of derivative normative hypotheses explain any ideal value experiences which have yielded my most enduring satisfactions? When I follow this system of norms, does my life become more meaningful than it did without such a creative purpose? (If his answers are affirmative, is it not reasonable to conclude that this system of a generic norm and its derivative hypotheses meet the empirical requirements of adequacy?)

When the axiologist attempts to confirm the "reasonable acceptability" of a normative hypothesis about an intrinsic goal by experientially ascertaining its greater adequacy over alternative conceptions, he is using one of the various techniques of empirical testing. This conforms, of course, to the fourth requirement of broader operationalism, i.e., the verificative technique must be adapted to the subject matter. Even the social scientist, you will recall, had to make this adjustment when he used "introspective projection."

Critic: The social scientist who used "introspective projection" could at least balance out his experiential testing with comparative case analysis. This doesn't seem to be available to the axiologist.

Author: Since the uniqueness of relatively self-determined decisions requires an idiographic rather than nomothetic analysis, the axiologist cannot be expected to use the more rigorous technique of experimental testing, in which the investigator himself manipulates the causal conditions, or even the technique of controlled observation, in which the data are taken to be devoid of any autonomy. These idiographic limitations notwithstanding, when the axiologist experientially tests the implications of his normative construct, as in all other kinds of empirical testing, he uses his adaptation of Mill's causal formula in terms of which all comparative techniques (including experimentation) proceed: "If this factor *a* (the reflective choice of the appropriate means) is really the cause of this effect *b* (an enduring satisfaction), then when *a* is absent, *b* is absent, and when *a* occurs, *b* also occurs."

Like all other modes of empirical testing, the experiential testing of axiological verification depends for its justification upon the assumption that there is a "community of reflective minds" who are competent in both skill and motivation. A crucial laboratory experiment, for example, would be impossible unless there were appropriately skilled and motivated scientists who could similarly manipulate the causal factors and control the conditions in the same way at any time or place. In the same way, the verification of a normative hypothesis through the experiential testing of its implications in reflective value realizations would be impossible unless there were appropriately skilled and motivated persons who could deliberatively analyze and evaluate their moral, aesthetic, intellectual, and religious desires with a critical attitude that is relatively unfettered by personal and cultural bias. Now, if from the writings of past thinkers and from their own reflective analysis of their own experiences a considerable number of competent persons find, through normative inquiry, that one conception of an intrinsic life goal is more coherent than others for making their existence meaningful, then can it not be said that such experiential testing confirms its reasonable acceptability to a significant, even though limited, degree? The objectivity of such normative judgments does not depend upon the reduction of axiological data and the axiological techniques which are appropriate for the natural-scientific, or even the social-scientific modes of hypothetical-deductive inquiry. Operationally, normative objectivity must be estimated in terms of the reflective attitude of those persons who are dominantly motivated in their analysis of ideal value experiences by the "desire to know." It will be recalled from the previous discussion of the pattern of reflective inquiry, that the objectivity of natural-scientific and social-scientific judgments essentially depends upon this dominant motivation of the investigator. In a less academic sense, the objectivity of the collaborative *community of reflective minds* is like the objectivity which distinguishes the collaborative judgment of nine supreme court justices from the consensus of a lynching mob. Disagreement among the justices does not destroy their objectivity provided that each is so motivated that he is responsive to rational persuasion.

Critic: That sounds like Plato's philosopher kings.

Author: No! The emphasis upon the *collaborative community of reflective minds* should not be taken to mean that individual initiative and responsibility in the deliberative analysis and evaluation of ideal ends is minimized. This is the defining characteristic of reflective normative inquiry which distinguishes it from the absolutistic establishment of life goals by an appeal to dogmatic authority. It is one thing to claim, as some social scientists do, that the choice of the intrinsic end of social action is completely relative to whatever each individual's preference and conscience dictate. It is quite another thing to claim, as we are doing here, that individual persons must provide this conception but that they should conform to the requirements of a mode of reflective inquiry before their conclusions are to be viewed as reasonably acceptable. As in any other mode of reflective analysis, complete agreement about ideal ends should not always be expected; and if and when it is found, such conclusions are always subject to correction, modification, or even abandonment in favor of more reasonably acceptable constructs. In order to conserve and increase a *community of reflective minds,* of positive sceptics, as well as situational relativists, it is necessary to avoid what Mill called a "tyranny of the majority" no less than a "tyranny of the minority." This means that the policy-minded social scientist must act with some degree of faith in human rationality, when he accepts from the philosophical axiologist the conception of a reasonably acceptable intrinsic end to which the social-scientific deliberative evaluations of the most effective instrumental means refer. It should be recognized, however, that without similar acts of faith in human rationality, there can be no dependence of one social-scientific discipline upon any other, or of any upon the disciplines of the natural sciences.

Critic: Your *community of reflective minds* reminds me a great deal of Rousseau's mystical appeal to the "General Will" by which decisions are made without, or contrary to, the decisions of particular individuals.

Author: That is not what I mean by a *community of reflective minds.* The individual's own deliberative appraisal is the heart of this kind of axiological verification through experiential testing.

Critic: When you appeal to one's own private feelings don't you sound like a mystic?

Author: No. The mystic insists that the truth of his claim is certified by its very ineffability, but I am calling for a *community of minds* in order that there might be the communication without which the process of verification could not be operational.

Critic: But aren't you abandoning your epistemological dualism in favor of epistemological monism, when you confirm the implications of your hypotheses in your own immediate experience?

Author: You have called attention to a crucial issue. The confirmatory data are found in a quality of mind which is not an inferred construct but is directly enjoyable. It is at this point that dualistic constructs "touch base" with one's actual experience.

Critic: That sounds very much like mystical feeling.

Author: It is to the extent that a mystic enjoying divine communion, and, let us say, a person making a moral decision, are directly experiencing their referents. But the mystic's experience is completely private, while the person engaged in a moral decision is interacting with other human persons. Consequently, interpersonal transactions among individuals who have first-person experience constitute the defining characteristic of a *community of reflective persons.*

Critic: I am reluctant to accept as the capstone of the verification of normative hypotheses something so tenuous and intangible as a quality of mind, even when it is shared through the interpersonal transactions of a *community of reflective persons.*

Author: Your reaction is quite understandable. But if you stop to think about it, you'll realize that this is also the case for most of the other human enterprises to which we commit our efforts. Consider, for example, the liberal arts aim which binds a college faculty together into a *community of minds.*

Critic: Indeed? Remember that I too am a member of a college faculty. Couldn't you find a better example in the international community of natural scientists who are committed to increasing our technological knowledge? Whether or not their products are destructive or constructive for society, their tangible results clearly verify the implications of their hypotheses. Moreover, despite the tensions of a cold war which has accelerated their achievement, both totalitarian and democratic scientists attempt to break through ideological barriers to share their cumulative research. This collaborative effort to achieve technological knowledge may well transcend ethnocentrism.

Author: I'm the last person to minimize the social importance of the technological knowledge which the community of natural scientists has achieved; but to this social need for such practical knowledge for its usefulness, there is a corresponding social need for the pursuit of knowledge for its own sake. But this is not "useless knowledge." I agree with Whitehead that "education is the cultivation of the art of the utilization of knowledge." [28] Whether or not the general public is fully aware of it, the faculties of liberal arts colleges have the social responsibility to provide their students with the opportunity to liberalize their minds. I grant you that many college faculties are quite vague about what they take a liberal arts aim to be. In his excellent analysis of the purposes of higher education, Huston Smith has wisely reminded us that it is this very diversity in the educational process which stems from cultural diversity that increases its strength and richness. I think he is correct when he claims that despite this culturally-derived disagreement, "it is nevertheless possible for educators to move toward significantly greater agreement on proximate objectives without compromising their final loyalties and basic perspectives." [29] Naturally, the specialist in a given discipline is devoted to his subject. Nevertheless, don't you find that most teachers of liberalizing arts and sciences would agree with Whitehead that "the function of Reason is to promote the art of life," i.e., "(i) to live, (ii) to live well, (iii) to live better." [30]

Critic: Could you specify more clearly what the liberalizing aim entails?

Author: It seems to me that in order for a person to become liberalized he must cultivate a vertical dimension and a horizontal dimension for his conscious experience. He discovers the vertical dimension when he becomes motivated by persistent inquiry for knowledge and the appreciation of beauty as an intrinsic satisfaction. Necessary as this intellectual curiosity is, it is not sufficient. In order to acquire something more than what Whitehead has condemned as inert ideas, he must develop his horizontal dimension in terms of significant ideas that reveal the interconnection and relevancy of factual information. This is what I assume Whitehead meant when he declared that "it is just as important that ideas be significant as it is for them to be true." Not only must the issues involved be vital, but the ideas should serve toward merging separable aspects of knowledge into a meaningful whole.

Critic: I suppose that you have in mind just a few disciplines which contribute toward this liberal arts objective.

Author: No, I agree with Justus Buchler that "any discipline, taught or studied which helps to develop the imagination, which deepens insight, which points the way to further values and further knowledge, and which transforms experience into something richer is liberal because it is liberalizing." [31]

Critic: I can see how individual scholars could have this aim but I can't quite grasp the notion of these scholars being banded together into a community by such an aim. And don't forget the main point of this discussion. Without the corroboration of like-minded people, your principle of normative verification breaks down.

Author: Your last point is well taken. After I clarify the notion of the liberalizing community I will relate it to experiential testing. Robert Oppenheimer, whose characterization of the scientific community of which every scholar is a member may help you to understand what we are talking about, said, that "the receptacle of all the knowledge we have, the agencies to whom this knowledge is entrusted and who create it, are not individual men" but rather "communities of men." Oppenheimer identifies such a community as a "cognitive syndicalism," in which "the true intimate collaboration of men, is best exemplified by groups of specialists who understand each other and help each other." [32]

Critic: But aren't the nature and functions of such an intellectual community culturally determined? Wouldn't Oppenheimer's description of the cognitive community fit the theologically-biased medieval scholastic universities just as well as the scientifically-biased universities in the contemporary democracies? The former would not be possible in our pluralistic culture and the latter would not be possible in the monolithic culture of the Middle Ages.

Author: When I read Ulich's account of the change in philosophies of education from the medieval scholastic universities of Albert of Cologne, Thomas Aquinas, and Duns Scotus, through those which were humanistic, then idealistic and down to contemporary controversies between the generalists and the specialists, sometimes I, too, am almost persuaded by the radical relativist that there is no persistent purpose which transcends the bias of each of the cultural frameworks from which each aim is derived. This ethnocentrism notwithstanding, Ulich emphasizes this important point: "The truly decisive changes and movements in the history of higher education have not been caused by pressure from the outside or by timidity and intellectual disloyalty from the inside" but, to the contrary, "they have been caused by the fact that universities are the living incorporations and symbols of man's insatiable thirst for truth." [33] As long as any faculty conserves and increases the intellectual ideal of its own meaning-situation, it seems to me its conception of a liberalizing education is both product and producer of its cultural symbols. This, of course, is the situational relativism in accordance with which the relatively self-determined intellectual, aesthetic, and moral efforts of collaborating scholars constitute an intervening variable. McKeon's interpretation of the function of universities in the modern world supports situational rather than radical relativism: "The educational theories and practices of peoples and times are determined by prevailing social relations and values and by available knowledge and attitudes toward its use; and educational systems are, in turn, powerful influences in the development of society and the advancement of knowledge." [34]

Critic: Even if such an intellectual élite can themselves achieve some relative self-determinism in the pursuit of their ideal quality of mind, how can they instill this desire for intrinsic aesthetic and intellectual values in students who attend college merely as a means to vocational and/or prestige ends?

Author: Although a few students come to college with the expectation of being liberalized, the majority of them confront each teacher with the challenge to transform his student's values so that they are susceptible to the pursuit of the intellectual, aesthetic, ethical, and perhaps the religious ideas the teacher prizes. In order to prepare the soil for the seeds which he hopes to plant, the teacher might well present the quest for liberalization as the spiritual adventure which Byron called the "eternal spirit of the chainless mind." The student whose imagination is kindled by the physical adventurer who scales a mountain peak, simply because it is there, may be responsive to the spiritual adventuring of artists who seek to elicit his aesthetic appreciation; of the men of God who have sought to kindle his sense of consecration; of the prophets of every generation who have engendered his moral dignity; and the scientists and philosophers who are insatiably compelled in their exploration for an answer to the questions "how" and "why."

Critic: Perhaps the student might respond to this spiritual adventure for a short while, but I have found that if a student can be weaned away from his dependence on dogmatic authority, he ends up as a radical relativist who is sceptical about the significance of all moral convictions and intellectual principles.

Author: In an attempt to surmount this obstacle to liberalization, the teacher must convince his students that instead of blindly accepting or arrogantly rejecting his intellectual, ethical, aesthetic, and religious inheritance, he should maintain an attitude of constructive criticism.

Critic: What can the student expect to realize through this spiritual adventure with an attitude of constructive criticism?

Author: He has the opportunity to achieve the ability to resolve three paradoxes which confront any reflective person. He can learn how to combine conviction with openmindedness, to combine individualism with altruism, and to realize the intrinsic satisfaction of never being satisfied. No one ever perfectly resolves these dilemmas, but when a person successfully does so to an appreciable degree, he has achieved the quality of mind which characterizes a liberalized person.

Critic: When the teacher attempts to induct his students into this community of reflective minds, how can he avoid dictating what they ought to do in a manner that precludes the student's development of his own relative self-determination?

Author: You have hit what is probably the most sensitive point in the process of a liberalizing education, as well as the experiential confirmation of normative principles. Since most students have little or no desire for knowledge, beauty, justice, and consecration as ends in themselves, the teacher must act as an authority until the student develops the intellectual initiative and responsibility to make his own critical assessments and reconstructions. This is similar to the problem which confronts parents who must gradually free their child from their apron strings. When we consider the case of new nations which have just emerged from the yoke of colonialism, we should recognize that even those leaders who want democracy face this same kind of predicament, if their people do not yet have sufficient training for participation in self-government. A teacher is presented no greater challenge than that of leading some of his students from an uncritical dogmatism and others from uncritical relativism into the situational relativism whereby each student can himself become constructively critical and self-creative. Whether or not each student appreciably realizes this liberalized quality of mind, the teacher finds his own deepest satisfaction in the achievement of those who do. In order to elicit the student's relative self-determinism, however, the teacher must often tentatively adopt the role of an authoritarian which he must gradually relinquish as his students develop their initative and responsibility. The teacher thus becomes one of what Huston Smith has called "floor authorities": On the one hand, "authorities involved in overdependence, authoritarianism, and conformity each place a ceiling upon freedom, a kind of lid above which it cannot rise." But, on the other hand, "authority can also provide a floor on which freedom can stand, a solid ground from which it can build with confidence." [35]

Critic: But don't you find that among most students, as Eric Fromm has found among most people, that there is no genuine desire for freedom when a person discovers the hazards of independence without the protection of authority.

Author: Yes, this is a threat to liberalization of which the teacher must be aware. To avoid this "escape from freedom" or its counterpart of cynical relativism, the teacher must constantly remind his students that no one achieves freedom simply by rejecting traditional beliefs and standards. Once the student has acquired the motivation and capacity for reflective inquiry and creative imagination, he must replace the outmoded beliefs and standards with those which he has forged out on his own.

Critic: I should remind you again that we are primarily discussing the role of a *community of reflective minds* in the experiential testing of the implications of normative hypotheses.

Author: Yes, I should now clarify this connection. The membership of the *community of reflective minds* who corroboratively test the implications of value judgments must be drawn from those liberalized teachers and students who participate in the educational enterprise as the wellspring of abundant living. In monolithic cultures, value patterns are established by an appeal to religious and/or political authority. In our pluralistic culture, the growing number of scholars has the responsibility for providing a rational vision. Without this vision, Whitehead warned, "society lapses into riot." In order to achieve such a rational vision one must, among other things, resolve some basic dimensions of the problem of knowledge.

Footnotes to Conclusion

1 Margenau, "Perspectives of Science," *The Key Reporter,* Vol. XXV, No. 1, Autumn 1959.
2 Krech and Klein, *Theoretical Models and Personality,* 11.
3 See *A Reader's Guide to the Social Sciences* (Hoselitz), p. 7 for Hoselitz and p. 238-239 for Reitman.
4 Nagel, *The Structure of Science,* 334-335.
5 Simpson, *Sociologist Abroad,* 41-45.
6 *A Reader's Guide to the Social Sciences* (Hoselitz), 126.
7 Miller, "Toward a General Theory for the Behavior Sciences," *The State of the Social Sciences* (Leonard D. White), 31-32.
8 Nagel, *The Structure of Science,* 336-338.
9 *Ibid.,* 445.
10 Hoselitz, *A Reader's Guide to the Social Sciences,* 16.
11 Krech and Klein, *Theoretical Models and Personality Theory,* 5.

[12] Parsons, *American Sociological Review*, Vol. 13, 60 No. 2, April 1948, p. 164.

[13] MacIver, *Social Causation*, 76-77.

[14] Gillin in *For a Science of Social Man* (Gillin), 271.

[15] Smith, "Anthropology and Psychology" in *For a Science of Social Man* (Gillin), 64.

[16] Newcomb, "Sociology and Psychology," *For a Science of Social Man* (Gillin), 227.

[17] Parsons, "Psychology and Sociology," *For a Science of Social Man* (Gillin), 101.

[18] Black, "Some Questions about Parsons' Theories," *The Social Theories of Talcott Parsons* (Black), 283.

[19] Parsons, "The Point of View of the Author," *The Social Theories of Talcott Parsons* (Black), 321.

[20] Parsons, *The Social Theories of Talcott Parsons* (Black), 359-360.

[21] See Bayliff, Clark, Easton, Grimes, Jennings, Leonard, *Values and Policy in American Society*.

[22] von Mering, *A Grammar of Human Values*, 13, 81, 89, 90.

[23] *Ibid.*, 91.

[24] *Ibid.*, 15, 24.

[25] *Ibid.*, 51-52, 65-66.

[26] Weber, *The Methodology of the Social Sciences*, 18-19. Cf. Northrop, *The Logic of the Sciences and Humanities*, 255-256.

[27] von Mering, *A Grammar of Human Values*, 101-103.

[28] Whitehead, *Aims of Education*, 6.

[29] Smith, *The Purposes of Higher Education*, 3.

[30] Whitehead, *The Function of Reason*, 2, 5.

[31] Buchler, "Reconstruction in the Liberal Arts," *A History of Columbia College on Morningside*, 132.

[32] Oppenheimer, "Science and the Human Community," *Issues in University Education* (Frankel), 55.

[33] Ulich, "The American University and Changing Philosophies," *Issues in University Education* (Frankel), 24-25, 40-41.

[34] McKeon, "University in the Modern World," *Issues in University Education* (Frankel), 1.

[35] Smith, *The Purposes of Higher Education*, 6, 7.

Bibliography

Abel, Theodore. "The Operation Called *Verstehen*," *Readings in the Philosophy of Science* (Herbert Feigl and May Brodbeck). New York: Appleton-Century-Crofts, 1953.

Aberle, D. F., A. K. Cohen, A. K. Davis, M. J. Levy, Jr., and F. X. Sutton. "The Functional Prerequisites of a Society," *Ethics*. Vol. LX, No. 2, January, 1950.

Abramovitz, Moses, Simond Kuznets, and Harold F. Williamson. "Economics of Growth," *A Survey of Contemporary Economics* (Bernard H. F. Haley). Homewood, Ill.: Richard D. Irwin, Inc., 1952, Vol. II.

Ackerknecht, Erwin H. "On the Comparative Method in Anthropology," *Method and Perspective in Anthropology* (Robert F. Spencer). Minneapolis: University of Minnesota Press, 1954.

Aitken, Hugh and Bert J. Loewenberg. "The Process of Historical Research," *The Social Sciences in Historical Study* (Bulletin 64). New York: Social Science Research Council, 1954.

Alexander, Franz. "The Logic of Emotions and Its Dynamic Background," *International Journal of Psychoanalysis*. Vol. XVI, (October 1935).

———. "Principles of Psychosomatic Research," *Psychological Theory* (Melvin H. Marx). New York: The Macmillan Co., 1951.

Allport, Gordon W. *Personality*. New York: Henry Holt, 1937.

————. *The Nature of Personality*. Cambridge: Addison-Wesley Press, Inc., 1950.

————. "The Emphasis of Molar Problems," *Psychological Theory* (Melvin H. Marx). New York; The Macmillan Co., 1951.

————. "The Historical Background of Modern Social Psychology," *Handbook of Social Psychology* (Gardner Lindzey). Cambridge: Addison-Wesley Publishing Co., Inc., 1954, Vol. I.

————. *Becoming*. New Haven: The Yale University Press, 1955.

————. "What Units Shall We Employ," *Assessment of Human Motives* (Gardner Lindzey). New York: Rinehart and Co. Inc., 1958.

————. "Prejudice: A Problem in Psychological and Social Causation," *Toward A General Theory of Action* (Talcott Parsons and Edward A. Shils). Cambridge: Harvard University Press, 1959.

Andrews, Tom Gaylord. "An Introduction to Psychological Methodology," *Methods of Psychology* (T. G. Andrews). New York: J. Wiley and Sons, Inc., 1948.

Aristotle. *The Politics* (Tr. H. Rackham). Cambridge: The Harvard University Press, 1950.

————. *The Physics* (Tr. Philip H. Wilksteed). Cambridge: The Harvard University Press, 1952.

Aron, Raymond. "Evidence and Inference in History," *Evidence and Inference* (Daniel Lerner). Glencoe, Ill.: The Free Press, 1958.

Arrow, Kenneth J. *Social Choice and Individual Values*. New York: John Wiley and Sons, Inc., 1951.

————. "Mathematical Models in the Social Sciences," *The Policy Sciences* (Daniel Lerner and Harold D. Lasswell). Stanford, California: Stanford University Press, 1951.

Asch, Solomon E. *Social Psychology*. New York: Prentice-Hall, Inc., 1952.

Ayer, Alfred J. *Language, Truth, and Logic*. New York: Dover Publications, 1952.

Barnett, Lincoln K. *The Universe and Dr. Einstein*. New York: W. Sloane Associates, 1948.

Barton, Allen H. and Paul R. Lazarsfeld. "Qualitative Measurement in the Social Sciences: Classification, Typologies and Indices," *The Policy Sciences* (Daniel Lerner and Harold D. Lasswell). Stanford, California: Stanford University Press, 1951.

Bayliff, Russell E., Eugene Clark, Loyd Easton, Blaine E. Grimes, David H. Jenning, and Norman H. Leonard. *Values and Policy in American Society* (Blaine E. Grimes and Eugene Clark). Dubuque, Iowa: Wm. C. Brown Co., 1954.

Beard, Charles A. "Written History as an Act of Faith," *The American Historical Review*. Vol. XXXIX, No. 2 (January 1934).

————. "Problems of Terminology in Historical Writing," *Theory and Practice in Historical Study: A Report of the Committee on Historiography* (Bulletin 54). New York: Social Science Research Council, 1946.

————. "That Noble Dream," *American Historical Review*. Vol. 41.

Benedict, Ruth. *Patterns of Culture*. New York: Houghton Mifflin Co., 1934.

Bennet, John W. and Kurt H. Wolff. "Toward Communication Between Sociology and Anthropology," *Current Anthropology* (Wm. L. Thomas). Chicago: University of Chicago Press, 1956.

Benson, Lee. "Research Problems in American Political Historiography," *Common Frontiers of the Social Sciences* (Mirra Komarovsky). Glencoe, Ill.: The Free Press, 1957.

Bergmann, Gustav. "Psychoanalysis and Experimental Psychology," *Psychological Theory* (Melvin H. Marx). New York: The Macmillan Co., 1951.

Bergmann, Gustav and Kenneth W. Spence. "Operationism and Theory Construction," *Psychological Theory* (Melvin H. Marx). New York: The Macmillan Co., 1951.

Bergmann, Gustav and Kenneth W. Spence. "On Some Methodological Problems of Psychology," *Readings in the Philosophy of Science* (Herbert Feigl and May Brodbeck). New York: Appleton-Century-Crofts, Inc., 1953.

Bidney, David. *Theoretical Anthropology.* New York: The Columbia University Press, 1953.

———. "The Concept of Value in Modern Anthropology," *Anthropology Today* (A. L. Kroeber). Chicago: The University of Chicago Press, 1953.

———. "The Philosophical Presuppositions of Cultural Relativism and Cultural Absolutism," *Ethics and the Social Sciences* (Leo Richard Ward). Notre Dame, Indiana: The University of Notre Dame Press, 1959.

Bierstedt, Robert. *The Social Order.* New York: McGraw-Hill Book Co., 1957.

———. "Nominal and Real Definitions in Sociological Theory," *Symposium on Sociological Theory* (Llewellyn Gross). White Plains, New York: Row, Peterson and Co., 1959.

Black, Max. *The Social Theories of Talcott Parsons* (Max Black). Englewood Cliffs, N.J.: Prentice-Hall, Inc., 1961.

Blanshard, Brand. *Nature of Thought.* New York: Macmillan, 1939.

Boas, Franz. "Laws of Cultural Development," *Encyclopedia of the Social Sciences* (Edwin R. A. Seligman and Alvin Johnson). New York: The Macmillan Co., 1931, Vol. II.

———. *Race, Language, and Culture.* New York: The Macmillan Co., 1949.

Bonner, Hubert. *Social Psychology: An Interdisciplinary Approach.* New York: American Book Co., 1953.

Borgatta, Edgar F. and Gardner Lindzey. "Sociometric Measurement," *Handbook of Social Psychology* (Gardner Lindzey). Cambridge: Addison-Wesley Publishing Co., 1954, Vol. I.

Boring, E. G. *The Physical Dimensions of Consciousness.* New York: Century, 1933.

Born, Max. *Atomic Physics.* New York: Hafner Publishing Co., 1951.

Bowers, Anna Mae, William Healy, and Augusta F. Bronner. *Structure and Meaning of Psychoanalysis.* New York: A. A. Knopf, Inc., 1930.

Bowers, Raymond V. "Research Method in Sociology: The First Half Century," *Method and Perspective in Anthropology* (Robert F. Spencer). Minneapolis: University of Minnesota Press, 1954.

Brennan, Joseph G. *The Meaning of Philosophy.* New York: Harper and Brothers, 1953.

Brett, George S. *History of Psychology* (R. S. Peters). New York: The Macmillan Co., 1953.
Bridgman, Percy W. *The Logic of Modern Physics*. New York: The Macmillan Co., 1927.
———. *The Nature of Physical Theory*. Princeton: Princeton University Press, 1936.
———. "Rejoiner and Second Thoughts," *Psychological Review*. Vol. 52, No. 5, (September 1945).
———. "The Potential Intelligent Society," *Ideological Differences and World Order* (Filmer S. Northrop). New Haven: Yale University Press, 1949.
———. "Remarks on the Present State of Operationalism," *Scientific Monthly*. No. 79 (October 1954).
Brightman, Edgar S. *Moral Laws*. New York: The Abingdon Press, 1933.
———. *Introduction to Philosophy*. New York: Holt, Rinehart, and Winston, Inc., 1951.
Brockunier, Samuel H. and Bert J. Loewenberg. "Objectivity, Certainty, and Values," *The Social Sciences in Historical Study* (Bulletin 64). New York: Social Science Research Council, 1954.
Bronner, Augusta F., William Healy, and Anna Mae Bowers. *The Structure and Meaning of Psychoanalysis*. New York: A. A. Knopf, Inc., 1930.
Brown, J. F. "Topology and Hodological Space," *Psychological Theory* (Melvin H. Marx). New York: The Macmillan Co., 1951.
Brown, Lawrence G. *Social Psychology*. New York: McGraw-Hill Book Co., 1934.
Brunswik, Egon. "The Conceptual Focus of Systems," *Psychological Theory* (Melvin H. Marx). New York: The Macmillan Co., 1951.
———. *The Conceptual Framework of Psychology*. Chicago: University of Chicago Press, 1952.
Buchler, Justus. "Reconstruction in the Liberal Arts," *A History of Columbia College on Morningside*. New York: Columbia University Press, 1954.
———. *Nature and Judgment*. New York: Columbia University Press, 1955.
———. *The Concept of Method*. New York: Columbia University Press, 1961.
Bury, John B. *The Idea of Progress*. New York: Dover Publications, 1955.
Bush, Vannevar. "Science and Life in the World," *Science*. Vol. 103, No. 2683, (May 31, 1946).
Butterfield, Herbert. *History and Human Relations*. London: Collins, 1951.
Cairnes, John E. *The Character and Logical Method of Political Economy*. London: Macmillan, 1857.
Calhoun, Don, Arthur Naftalin, Benjamin Nelson, Andreas G. Papandreou, and Mulford Q. Sibley. "The Nature of Community," *Personality, Work, Community*. Chicago, Philadelphia, New York: J. B. Lippincott Co., 1957.
Campell, Norman R. *Foundations of Science*. New York: Dover Publications, 1957.
Cantril, Hadley. "Psychology and Scientific Research," *Science*. Vol. 110, No. 2862 (November 4, 1949).
Carnap, Rudolf. *Foundations of Logic and Mathematics* from *International Encyclopedia of Unified Science* (Volumes I and II: Foundations of the Unity of Science). Chicago: University of Chicago Press, 1938, Vol. I, No. 3.

———. "The Two Concepts of Probability," *Readings in the Philosophy of Science* (Herbert Feigl and May Brodbeck), New York: Appleton-Century-Crofts, Inc., 1953.

Cassirer, Ernest. *Essay on Man.* New Haven: Yale University Press, 1944.

Catlin, G. E. G. *The Science and Method of Politics.* New York: A. A. Knopf, 1927.

———. *A Study of the Principles of Politics.* New York: Macmillan, 1930.

Cattell, Raymond. "The Dynamic Calculus: A System of Concepts Derived from Objective Motivational Measurement," *Assessment of Human Motives* (Gardner Lindzey). New York: Rinehart, 1958.

Chapin, Francis S. *Contemporary American Institutions.* New York: Harper and Brothers, 1935.

Chinoy, Ely. *Sociological Perspective.* Garden City, New York: Doubleday, 1954.

Churchman, Charles W. *Theory of Experimental Inference.* New York: The Macmillan Co., 1948.

Clark, Colin. *The Conditions of Economic Progress.* New York: St. Martin's Press, 1957.

Clark, Eugene, Russell E. Bayliff, Loyd Easton, Blaine E. Grimes, David H. Jenning and Norman H. Leonard. *Values and Policy in American Society* (Blaine E. Grimes and Eugene Clark). Dubuque, Iowa: Wm. C. Brown Co., 1954.

Clark, John M. *Studies in the Economics of Overhead Costs.* Chicago: University of Chicago Press, 1923.

———. "The Socializing of Theoretical Economics," *The Trend of Economics* (Rexford Guy Tugwell). New York: A. A. Knopf, 1924.

———. *The Ethical Basis of Economic Freedom.* Westport: The Calvin K. Kazanjian Economics Foundation, Inc., 1955.

Clough, Shepard. "Change and the Historian," *The Social Sciences in Historical Study* (Bulletin 64). New York: Social Science Research Council, 1954.

———. "Conceptions and Misconceptions," *The Social Sciences in Historical Study* (Bulletin 64). New York: Social Science Research Council, 1954.

Coates, Wilson H. "Relativism and the Use of Hypothesis in History," *Journal of Modern History.* Vol. XXI, No. 1 (March 1949).

Cochran, Thomas C. "The Social Sciences and the Problem of Historical Synthesis," *The Social Sciences in Historical Study* (Bulletin 64). New York: Social Science Research Council, 1954.

———. "A Survey of Concepts and Viewpoints in the Social Sciences," *The Social Sciences in Historical Study* (Bulletin 64). New York: Social Science Research Council, 1954.

Cohen, A. K., D. F. Aberle, A. K. Davis, M. J. Levy Jr., and F. X. Sutton. "The Functional Prerequisites of a Society," *Ethics.* Vol. LX, No. 2 (January 1950).

Cohen, Morris R. and Ernest Nagel. *An Introduction to Logic and Scientific Method.* New York: Harcourt Brace and Co., 1934.

Cohen, Morris R. "Causation and its Application to History," *Journal of the History of Ideas.* Vol. 3 (1942).

————. *The Meaning of Human History*. La Salle, Ill.: Open Court Publishing Co., 1947.

————. "Reason in Social Science," *Readings in the Philosophy of Science* (Herbert Feigl and May Brodbeck). New York: Appleton-Century-Crofts, Inc., 1953.

Collingwood, R. G. *The Idea of History*. Oxford: Clarendon Press, 1946.

Columbia Associates in Philosophy. *An Introduction to Reflective Thinking*. New York: Houghton Mifflin Co., 1923.

Commons, John R. *Institutional Economics*. Madison, Wisconsin: University of Wisconsin Press, 1959.

Conant, James B. *On Understanding Science*. New Haven: Yale University Press, 1947.

Cook, Thomas I. "The Political System: The Stubborn Search for a Science of Politics," *Journal of Philosophy*. Vol. LI, No. 4 (February 18, 1954).

Cooley, Charles H. *Sociological Theory and Social Research*. New York: Henry Holt and Co., 1930.

————. *Human Nature and the Social Order*. Glencoe, Ill.: The Free Press, 1955.

Crutchfield, Richard S. and David Krech. *Theory and Problems of Social Psychology*. New York: McGraw-Hill Book Co., 1948.

Cunningham, G. Watts. "Meaning, Reference, and Significance," *Philosophical Review*. Vol. 47 (1938).

Davis, A. K., D. F. Aberle, A. K. Cohen, M. J. Levy Jr., and F. X. Sutton. "The Functional Prerequisites of a Society," *Ethics*. Vol. LX, No. 2 (January 1959).

Davis, Kingsley. "The Myth of Functional Analysis as a Special Method in Sociology and Anthropology," *American Sociological Review*. Vol. 24, No. 6, (December 1959).

Descartes, Rene. "Rules for the Direction of the Mind," *Descartes Selections* (Ralph M. Eaton). New York: Charles Scribner's Sons, 1955.

Deutsch, Morton. "Field Theory in Social Psychology," *Handbook of Social Psychology* (Gardner Lindzey). Cambridge: Addison-Wesley Publishing Co., 1954, Vol. I.

Dewey, John. *Experience and Nature*. New York: W. W. Norton, 1929.

————. "Unity of Science as a Social Problem," *Encyclopedia and Unified Science* from *International Encyclopedia of Unified Science* (Volumes I and II: Foundations of the Unity of Science). Chicago: University of Chicago Press, 1938, Vol. I, No. 1.

————. *Logic, the Theory of Inquiry*. New York: Henry Holt and Co., 1938.

————. *Theory of Valuation*. Chicago: University of Chicago Press, 1939.

————. "Democracy," *Readings in Philosophy* (John H. Randall, Justus Buchler, and Evelyn U. Shirk). New York: Barnes and Noble, 1950.

Dewey, Richard and Wilbur J. Humber. *The Development of Human Behavior*. New York: The Macmillan Co., 1951.

Dilthey, Wilhelm, *Gesammelte Schriften*. Leipzig: B. G. Teubner, 1959.

Dingle, Herbert. *The Scientific Adventure*. New York: Philosophical Library, 1953.

Dobzhansky, Theodosius. "Inside Human Nature," *Frontiers of Knowledge in the Study of Man* (Lynn White, Jr.). New York: Harper and Brothers, 1956.

Donagan, Alan. "The Verification of Historical Theses," *Philosophical Quarterly*. Vol. 6, No. 24 (July 1956).

———. "Explanation in History," *Mind*. Vol. LXVI, N.S., No. 262 (April 1957).

Dray, William. *Laws and Explanation in History*. London: Oxford University Press, 1957.

Driscoll, Jean M. and Charles S. Hyneman. "Methodology for Political Scientists: Perspectives for Study," *American Political Science Review*. Vol. XLIX, No. 1 (March 1955).

Durhkeim, Emile. *The Rules of Sociological Method* (Tr. Sarah A. Solovay and John H. Mueller, and Edited by George E. G. Catlin). Chicago: University of Chicago Press, 1938.

Easton, David. *The Political System*. New York: A. A. Knopf, 1953.

Easton, Loyd, Russell E. Bayliff, Eugene Clark, Blaine E. Grimes, David H. Jenning, and Norman H. Leonard. *Values and Policy in American Society* (Blaine E. Grimes and Eugene Clark). Dubuque, Iowa: Wm. C. Brown Co., 1954.

Einstein, Albert. "Our Debt to Other Men: The Lure of the Mysterious," *Living Philosophies*. New York: Simon and Schuster, 1937.

Einstein, Albert and Leopold Infeld. *Evolution of Physics*, New York: Simon and Schuster, 1938.

Elliot, William and Neil McDonald. *Western Political Heritage*. New York: Prentice-Hall, Inc., 1949.

Emerson, Alfred E. "Homeostasis and Comparison of Systems," *Toward a Unified Theory of Human Behavior* (Roy R. Grinker). New York: Basic Books Inc., 1956.

Eysenck, H. J. "The Organization of Personality," *Theoretical Models and Personality Theory* (David Krech and George S. Klein). Durham, North Carolina: Duke University Press, 1952.

Feigl, Herbert. "Notes on Causality," *Readings in the Philosophy of Science* (Herbert Feigl and May Brodbeck). New York: Appleton-Century-Crofts, Inc., 1953.

Festinger, Leon. "The Motivating Effect of Cognitive Dissonance," *Assessment of Human Motives* (Gardner Lindzey). New York: Rinehart and Co., Inc., 1958.

Firth, Raymond. "Function," *Current Anthropology* (William L. Thomas, Jr.). Chicago: University of Chicago Press, 1956.

Flewelling, Ralph T. *Things That Matter Most*. New York: The Ronald Press Co., 1946.

Fling, F. M. *The Writing of History*. New Haven: Yale University Press, 1920.

Frank, Lawrence K. "Social Systems and Culture," *Toward a Unified Theory of Human Behavior* (Roy R. Grinker). New York: Basic Books Inc., 1956.

Frank, Philip. "Causation: An Episode in the History of Thought," *Journal of Philosophy*. Vol. 31 (August 1934).

Freud, Sigmund. *New Introductory Lectures on Psychoanalysis*. New York: Norton and Co., Inc., 1933.

———. *An Autobiographical Study* (Translated by James Strachey). London: Hogarth, 1935.

———. "Three Contributions to the Theory of Sex," *The Basic Writings of Sigmund Freud*. New York: Random House, 1938.

———. *Leonardo da Vinci, A Study in Psychosexuality*. New York: Random House, 1947.

Friedman, Milton. "The Methodology of Positive Economics," *Essays in Positive Economics* (Milton Friedman). Chicago: University of Chicago Press, 1953.

Friedrich, Carl J. *Constitutional Government and Democracy*. New York: Harper and Brothers, 1937.

Fromm, Erich. *Man For Himself*. New York: Holt Rinehart and Winston, Inc., 1947.

———. "Individual and Social Origins of Neurosis," *Personality in Nature, Society, and Culture* (Clyde Kluckhohn and Henry A. Murray and David M. Schneider). New York: A. A. Knopf, 1955.

———. "Value, Psychology and Human Existence," *New Knowledge in Human Values* (Abraham H. Maslow). New York: Harper and Brothers, 1959.

Furfey, Paul H. "Sociological Science and the Problem of Values," *Symposium on Sociological Theory* (Llewellyn Gross). White Plains, New York: Row, Peterson and Co., 1959.

Galbraith, John K. *American Capitalism: The Concept of Countervailing Power*. Boston: Houghton Mifflin Co., 1956.

Garceau, Oliver. "Research in the Political Process," *American Political Science Review*. Vol. 45 (1951).

Gardiner, Patrick. *The Nature of Historical Explanation*. London: Oxford University Press, 1952.

George, F. H. "Models and Theories in Social Psychology," *Symposium on Sociological Theory* (Llewellyn Gross). White Plains, New York: Row, Peterson and Co., 1959.

Gibson, James J. "Studying Perceptual Phenomena," *Methods of Psychology* (T. G. Andrews). New York: John Wiley and Sons, Inc., 1948.

Gillin, John. *For a Science of Social Man*. New York: The Macmillan Co., 1954.

Goldenweiser, Alexander. "Social Evolution," *Encyclopedia of the Social Sciences* (Edwin R. A. Seligman and Alvin Johnson). New York: The Macmillan Co., 1931, Vol. V.

Goldsmith, Raymond W. "Exploratory Report," *The Comparative Study of Economic Growth and Structure*. (National Bureau of Economic Research, Inc.). 1959.

Goldstein, Kurt. *The Organism*. New York: American Book Co., 1939.

———. "Health as Value," *New Knowledge in Human Values* (Abraham H. Maslow). New York: Harper and Brothers, 1959.

Goldstein, Leon J. "Laws as Processes," *American Anthropologist*. Vol. 61, No. 2 (April 1959).

Good, Carter V. and Douglass E. Scates. *Methods of Research*. New York: Appleton-Century-Crofts, Inc., 1954.

Gordon, Donald F. "Operational Propositions in Economic Theory," *The Journal of Political Economy*. Vol. LXII, No. 2 (April 1955).

Gottschalk, Louis, *Understanding History*. New York: A. A. Knopf, 1950.

————. "The Historian's Use of Generalizations," *The State of the Social Sciences* (Leonard D. White). Chicago: University of Chicago Press, 1955.

Gouldner, Alvin W. "Reciprocity and Autonomy in Functional Theory," *Symposium on Sociological Theory* (Llewellyn Gross). White Plains, New York: Row, Peterson and Co., 1953.

Greenberg, Joseph H. "Historical Linguistics and Unwritten Languages," *Anthropology Today* (A. L. Kroeber). Chicago: University of Chicago Press, 1953.

Grimes, Blaine E., Russll E. Bayliff, Eugene Clark, Loyd Easton, David H. Jenning and Norman H. Leonard. *Values and Policy in American Society* (Blaine E. Grimes and Eugene Clark). Dubuque, Iowa: Wm. C. Brown Co., 1954.

Grinker, Roy R. "Comparison Between Systems of Organization," *Toward a Unified Theory of Human Behavior* (Roy R. Grinker). New York: Basic Books, Inc., 1956.

Gross, Llewellyn. *Symposium on Sociological Theory* (Llewellyn Gross). White Plains, New York: Row, Peterson and Co., 1959.

Gruchy, Allan G. *Modern Economic Thought.* New York: Prentice-Hall, Inc., 1947.

Haas, Mary R. "The Application of Linguistics to Language Teaching," *Anthropology Today* (A. L. Kroeber). Chicago: University of Chicago Press, 1953.

Haines, IV, George and John H. Randall. "Controlling Assumptions in the Practice of American Historians," *Theory and Practice in Historical Study: A Report of the Committee on Historiography* (Bulletin 54). New York: Social Science Research Council, 1946.

Hall, Calvin S. and Gardner Lindzey. "Psychoanalytic Theory and Its Application in the Social Sciences," *Handbook of Social Psychology* (Gardner Lindzey). Cambridge: Addison-Wesley Publishing Co., Inc., 1954, Vol. I.

Hallowell, A. Irving. "Culture, Personality, and Society," *Anthropology Today* (A. L. Kroeber). Chicago: University of Chicago Press, 1953.

————. "Psychology and Anthropology," *For a Science of Social Man* (John Gillin). New York: The Macmillan Co., 1954.

Hamilton, Warton H. "The Institutional Approach to Economic Theory," *The American Economic Review.* Vol. IX, No. 1 (March 1919).

Hart, Hornell. "Social Theory and Social Change," *Symposium on Sociological Theory* (Llewellyn Gross). White Plains, New York: Row, Peterson and Co., 1959.

Healy, William, Augusta F. Bronner and Anna Mae Bowers. *The Structure and Meaning of Psychoanalysis.* New York: A. A. Knopf, Inc., 1930.

Hebb, D. C. and W. R. Thompson. "The Social Significance of Animal Studies," *Handbook of Social Psychology* (Gardner Lindzey). Cambridge: Addison-Wesley Publishing Co., Inc., 1954, Vol. I.

Heisenberg, Werner. *The Physical Principles of the Quantum Theory* (Tr. Carl Eckart and Frank C. Hoyt). Chicago: University of Chicago Press, 1930.

Heller, Hermann. "Political Sciences: Content and Method," *Encyclopedia of the Social Sciences* (Edwin R. A. Seligman and Alvin Johnson). New York: The Macmillan Co., 1957, Vol. XII.

Hempel, Carl. "The Function of General Laws in History," *Readings in Philosophical Analysis* (Herbert Feigl and Wilfrid Sellars). New York: Appleton-Century-Crofts, 1949.

———. "The Logic of Functional Analysis," *Symposium on Sociological Theory* (Llewellyn Gross). White Plains, New York: Row, Peterson and Co., 1959.

Hempel, Carl and Paul Oppenheim. "The Logic of Explanation," *Readings in the Philosophy of Science* (Herbert Feigl and May Brodbeck). New York: Appleton-Century-Crofts, 1953.

Herring, Pendleton. "On the Study of Government," *American Political Science Review*. Vol. XLVII, No. 4 (December 1953).

Herskovits, Melville J. "The Processes of Cultural Change," *The Science of Man in the World Crisis* (Ralph Linton). New York: Columbia University Press, 1954.

———. "Some Problems of Method in Ethnography," *Method and Perspective in Anthropology* (Robert F. Spencer). Minneapolis: University of Minnesota Press, 1954.

Hilgard, Ernest R. and Daniel Lerner. "The Person: Subject and Object of Science and Policy," *The Policy Sciences* (Daniel Lerner and Harold D. Lasswell). Stanford, California: Stanford University Press, 1951.

Hocking, William E. *The Meaning of God in Human Experience*. New Haven: Yale University Press, 1920.

———. *Human Nature and Its Remaking*. New Haven: Yale University Press, 1923.

Homan, Paul T. "The Institutional School," *Encyclopedia of the Social Sciences* (Edwin R. A. Seligman and Alvin Johnson). New York: The Macmillan Co., 1931, Vol. V.

Hook, Sidney. *The Hero in History*. New York: Humanities Press, 1943.

———. "Illustrations of Problems of Terminology in Historical Writing," *Theory and Practice in Historical Study: A Report of the Committee on Historiography* (Bulletin 54). New York: Social Science Research Council, 1946.

Horney, Karen. *The Neurotic Personality of Our Time*. New York: W. W. Norton and Co., Inc., 1937.

Hoselitz, Bert F. *Reader's Guide to the Social Sciences*. Glencoe, Ill.: The Free Press, 1959.

Hull, Clark L. "The Problem of Intervening Variables in Molar Behavior Theory," *Psychological Review*. Vol. 50, 1951.

Humber, Wilbur and Richard Dewey. *The Development of Human Behavior*. New York: The Macmillan Co., 1951.

Husserl, Edmund. *Ideas, General Introduction to Pure Phenomenology* (Tr., W. R. Boyce Gibson). New York: The Macmillan Co., 1952.

Hutchison, T. W. *The Significance and Basic Postulates of Economic Theory*. London: Macmillan, 1938.

Huxley, Julian S. "Evolution, Cultural and Biological," *Current Anthropology* (William L. Thomas, Jr.). Chicago: University of Chicago Press, 1956.

Hyneman, Charles S. and Jean M. Driscoll. "Methodology For Political Scientists: Perspectives For Study," *American Political Science Review*. Vol. XLIX, No. 1 (March 1955).

Infeld, Leopold and Albert Einstein. *Evolution of Physics*. New York: Simon and Schuster Inc., 1938.

Israel, H. E. and B. Goldstein. "Operationism in Psychology," *Psychological Review* (1944).

Janis, Irving L. "The Psychoanalytic Interview as an Observational Method," *Assessment of Human Motives* (Gardner Lindzey). New York: Rinehart and Co., Inc., 1958.

Jenning, David H., Russell E. Bayliff, Eugene Clark, Loyd Easton, Blaine E. Grimes and Norman H. Leonard. *Values and Policy in American Society* (Blaine E. Grimes and Eugene Clark). Dubuque, Iowa: Wm. C. Brown Co., 1954.

Jevons, William S. *The Theory of Political Economy*. New York: The Macmillan Co., 1879.

————. *The Principles of Science*. London: Macmillan and Co., Ltd., 1924.

Jung, Carl G. *The Integration of Personality*. New York: Farrar and Rinehart Inc., 1939.

Kant, Immanuel. *Critique of Pure Reason*. New York: E. P. Dutton and Co., 1934.

Kantor, Jacob. "Interbehavioral Psychology," *Psychological Theory* (Melvin H. Marx). New York: The Macmillan Co., 1951.

————. *The Logic of Modern Science*. Bloomington, Ind.: Principia Press, 1953.

Kaplan, Abraham and Harold D. Lasswell. *Power and Society*. New Haven: Yale University Press, 1950.

Kapp, Karl W. *The Social Costs of Private Enterprise*. Cambridge: The Harvard University Press, 1950.

————. "Economics and the Behavioral Sciences," *Kyklos*. Vol. VII (1954).

Kardiner, Abram. "The Concept of Basic Personality Structure as an Operational Tool in the Social Sciences," *The Science of Man in the World Crisis* (Ralph Linton). New York: Columbia University Press, 1945.

Katona, George. "Expectations and Decisions in Economic Behavior," *The Policy Sciences* (Daniel Lerner and Harold D. Lasswell). Stanford, California: Stanford University Press, 1951.

Kaufmann, Felix. *Methodology of the Social Sciences*. New York: Oxford University Press, 1944.

Kelly, George A. "Man's Construction of His Alternatives," *Assessment of Human Motives* (Gardner Lindzey). New York: Rinehart and Co., Inc., 1958.

Key, V. O. *Politics, Parties, and Pressure Groups*. New York: Thomas Y. Crowell Co., 1950.

Keynes, John M. *A Treatise on Probability*. London: Macmillan and Co., Ltd., 1921.

————. *The General Theory of Employment, Interest, and Money*. London: Macmillan and Co., Ltd., 1936.

Keyserling, L. H. and R. G. Tugwell. *Redirecting Education*. New York: Columbia University Press, 1934, Vol. I.

Klein, George S. and David Krech. "The Problem of Personality and Its Theory," *Theoretical Models and Personality Theory* (David Krech and George S. Klein). Durham, North Carolina: Duke University Press, 1952.

Klein, George S. "Cognitive Control and Motivation," *Assessment of Human Motives* (Gardner Lindzey). New York: Rinehart and Co., Inc., 1958.

Kluckhohn, Clyde. *Mirror For Man.* New York: Whittlesey Houses, 1949.

————. "Toward a Comparison of Value-Emphases in Different Cultures," *The State of the Social Sciences* (Leonard D. White). Chicago: The University of Chicago Press, 1955.

————. "Ethical Relativity: Sic et Non," *The Journal of Philosophy.* Vol. LII, No. 23 (November 1955).

————. "The Study of Culture," *The Policy Sciences* (Daniel Lerner and Harold D. Lasswell). Stanford, California: Stanford University Press, 1956.

————. "Values and Value-Orientation in the Theory of Action," *Toward a General Theory of Action* (Talcott Parsons and Edward A. Shils). Cambridge: Harvard University Press, 1959.

Kluckhohn, Clyde and A. L. Kroeber. "General Features of Culture," *Culture, A Critical Review of Concepts and Definitions* (Papers of the Peabody Museum of American Archaeology and Ethnology). Harvard University, Vol. XLVII, No. 1, 1952.

Kluckhohn, Clyde, Henry Murray and David Schneider. *Personality in Nature, Society and Culture.* New York: A. A. Knopf, 1955.

Knight, Frank H. "What is Truth in Economics?" *The Journal of Political Economy.* Vol. XLVIII, No. 1 (February 1940).

————. *The Economic Organization.* Chicago: The University of Chicago Press, 1948.

Kohler, Wolfgang. *The Place of Value in a World of Facts.* New York: Liveright Publishing Corporation, 1938.

————. *Dynamics in Psychology.* New York: Liveright Publishing Corporation, 1940.

Koppers, Wilhelm. "Diffusion: Transmission and Acceptance," *Current Anthropology* (Wm. L. Thomas, Jr.). Chicago: The University of Chicago Press, 1956.

Krech, David. "Dynamic Systems as Open Neurological Systems," *Psychological Review.* Vol. 57 (1950).

Krech, David and Richard S. Crutchfield. *Theory and Problems of Social Psychology.* New York: McGraw-Hill Book Co., 1948.

Krech, David and George S. Klein. *Theoretical Models and Personality Theory.* Durham, N. C.: Duke University Press, 1952.

Kris, Ernest. "Psychoanalytic Propositions," *Psychological Theory* (Melvin H. Marx). New York: The Macmillan Co., 1951.

Kroeber, Alfred L. *The Nature of Culture.* Chicago: The University of Chicago Press, 1952.

————. "Concluding Review," *An Appraisal of Anthropology Today* (Sol Tax). Chicago: The University of Chicago Press, 1953.

————. "Critical Summary and Commentary," *Method and Perspective in An-*

thropology (Robert F. Spencer). Minneapolis: The University of Minnesota Press, 1954.

————. "History of Anthropological Thought," *Current Anthropology* (Wm. L. Thomas, Jr.). Chicago: The University of Chicago Press, 1956.

Kroeber, Alfred L. and Talcott Parsons. "The Concepts of Culture and Social System," *American Sociological Review.* (October 1958).

Kroeber, Alfred L. and Clyde Kluckhohn. "General Features of Culture," *Culture, A Critical Review of Concepts and Definitions* (Papers of the Peabody Museum of American Archaeology and Ethnology). Harvard University, Vol. XLVII, No. 1, 1952.

Kuznets, Simon, Moses Abramovitz, Harold F. Williamson. "Economics of Growth," *A Survey of Contemporary Economics* (Bernard F. Haley). Homewood, Ill.: Richard D. Irwin, Inc., 1952, Vol. II.

Lachman, Sheldon J. *The Foundations of Science.* Detroit: The Hamilton Press, 1956.

Lambert, William W. "Stimulus Response Contiguity and Reinforcement Theory in Social Psychology," *Handbook of Social Psychology* (Gardner Lindzey). Cambridge, Mass.: Addison-Wesley Publishing Co., Inc., 1954, Vol. I.

Lane, Frederick C. *Enterprise and Secular Change* (Frederick C. Lane and Jelle C. Riemersma). Homewood, Ill.: Richard D. Irwin, Inc., 1953.

Lange, Oscar. "The Scope and Method of Economics," *Readings in the Philosophy of Science* (Herbert Feigl and May Brodbeck). New York: Appleton-Century-Crofts, Inc., 1953.

Larrabee, Harold A. *Reliable Knowledge.* New York: Houghton-Mifflin Co., 1945.

Larsen, Otto M., George A. Lundberg, and Clarence C. Schrag. *Sociology.* New York: Harper and Brothers, 1954.

Lashley, K. S. "The Problem of Serial Order in Behavior," *Cerebral Mechanisms in Behavior* (Lloyd A. Jeffress). New York: John Wiley and Sons, Inc., 1951.

Lasswell, Harold D. and Abraham Kaplan. *Power and Society.* New Haven: Yale University Press, 1950.

————. "The Policy Orientation," *The Policy Sciences* (Daniel Lerner and Harold D. Lasswell). Stanford, California: Stanford University Press, 1951.

————. *American Political Science Review.* Vol. 45 (1951).

Lavine, Thelma Z. "Naturalism and the Sociological Analysis of Knowledge," *Naturalism and the Human Spirit* (Yervant H. Krikorian). New York: Columbia University Press, 1944.

Lazarsfeld, Paul F. and Allen H. Barton. "Qualitative Measurement in the Social Sciences: Classification, Typologies and Indices," *The Policy Sciences* (Daniel Lerner and Harold D. Lasswell). Stanford, California: Stanford University Press, 1951.

Lazarsfeld, Paul F. and Morris Rosenberg. *The Language of Social Research.* Glencoe, Ill.: The Free Press, 1955.

Leibniz, Gottfried. "The Monodology," *Leibniz Selections* (Philip P. Wiener). New York: Charles Scribner's Sons, 1951.

Leiserson, Avery. "Problems of Methodology in Political Science," *Political Science Quarterly* (December 1953).

Lenzen, Victor F. *Procedures of Empirical Science* from *International Encyclopedia of Unified Science* (Volumes I and II: *Foundations of the Unity of Science*). Chicago: University of Chicago Press, 1938, Vol. I, No. 5.

Leonard, Norman H., Russell E. Bayliff, Eugene Clark, Loyd Easton, Blaine E. Grimes and David H. Jenning. *Value and Policy in American Society* (Blaine E. Grimes and Eugene Clark). Dubuque, Iowa: Wm. C. Brown Co., 1954.

Leontief, Wassily. "Economics," *A Survey of Contemporary Economics* (Howard S. Ellis). Homewood, Ill.: Richard D. Irwin, Inc., 1948, Vol. I.

Lerner, Daniel and Ernest R. Hilgard. "The Person: Subject and Object of Science and Policy," *The Policy Sciences* (Daniel Lerner and Harold D. Lasswell). Stanford, California: Stanford University Press, 1951.

Lerner, Daniel. "Introduction, On Evidence and Inference," *Evidence and Inference* (Daniel Lerner). Glencoe, Ill.: The Free Press, 1958.

Lesser, Alexander. "Functionalism in Social Anthropology," *American Anthropologist*. N.S. 37 (1935).

Levin, Harvey J. "Standards of Welfare in Economic Thought," *Quarterly Journal of Economics*. Vol. LXX (February 1956).

Levi-Strauss, Claude. "Social Structure," *Anthropology Today* (A. L. Kroeber). Chicago: University of Chicago Press, 1953.

Lewin, Kurt. *A Dynamic Theory of Personality*. New York: McGraw-Hill Book Co., 1935.

————. *The Conceptual Representation and the Measurement of Psychological Forces*. Durham, North Carolina: Duke University Press, 1938.

————. *Field Theory in Social Science*. New York: Harper and Brothers, 1951.

————. "The Nature of Field Theory," *Psychological Theory* (Melvin H. Marx). New York: The Macmillan Co., 1951.

Lewis, Clarence I. *Mind and the World Order*. New York: Charles Scribner's Sons, 1929.

————. *An Analysis of Knowledge and Valuation*. LaSalle, Ill.: Open Court Publishing Co., 1947.

Lewis, Oscar. "Comparisons in Cultural Anthropology," *Current Anthropology* (Wm. L. Thomas, Jr.). Chicago: The University of Chicago Press, 1956.

Levy, M. J. Jr., D. F. Aberle, A. K. Cohen, A. K. Davis and F. X. Sutton. "The Functional Prerequisites of a Society," *Ethics*, Vol. LX, No. 2, January 1950.

Lindsay, Robert B. and Henry Margenau. *Foundations of Physics*. New York: J. Wiley and Sons, Inc., 1936.

Lindzey, Gardner. "The Assessment of Human Motives," *Assessment of Human Motives* (Gardner Lindzey). New York: Rinehart and Co., Inc., 1958.

Lindzey, Gardner and Edgar F. Borgatta. "Sociometric Measurement," *Handbook of Social Psychology* (Gardner Lindzey). Cambridge: Addison-Wesley Publishing Co., 1954, Vol. I.

Lindzey, Gardner and Calvin S. Hall. "Psychoanalytic Theory and Its Application in the Social Sciences," *Handbook of Social Psychology* (Gardner Lindzey). Cambridge: Addison-Wesley Publishing Co., Inc., 1954, Vol. I.

Linton, Ralph. *The Cultural Background of Personality*. New York: Appleton-Century-Crofts Inc., 1945.

Mannheim, Karl. *Ideology and Utopia*. New York: Harcourt, Brace and Co., 1936.
────. *Essays on Sociology and Social Psychology* (Paul Kecskemeti). New York: Oxford University Press, 1953.
Margenau, Henry. "Causality in Modern Physics," *Monist*. Vol. 41, 1931.
────. "Methodology of Modern Physics," *Philosophy of Science*. Vol. II, January 1935.
────. *The Nature of Physical Reality*. New York: McGraw-Hill Book Co., Inc., 1950.
────. "The Methodology for Integration in the Physical Sciences," *The Nature of Concepts, Their Inter-Relation and Role in Social Structure* (Proceedings of the Stillwater Conference conducted by the Foundation for Integrated Education, Inc. and Co-Sponsored by Oklahoma A&M College, F. S. C. Northrop and Henry Margenau, Co-Chairmen, June 6, 7, 8, and 9, 1950 at Stillwater, Oklahoma).
Margenau, Henry and Robert S. Lindsay. *Foundations of Physics*. New York: J. Wiley and Sons, Inc., 1936.
Marshall, Alfred. *Principles of Economics*. London: Macmillan and Co., Ltd., 1938.
────. "The Present Position of Economics (1885)," *Memorials of Alfred Marshall* (A. C. Pigou). New York: Kelly and Millman, Inc., 1956.
Martindale, Don. "Sociological Theory and the Ideal Type," *Symposium on Sociological Theory* (Llewellyn Gross). New York: Row, Peterson and Co., 1959.
Marx, Melvin H. "The General Nature of Theory Construction," *Psychological Theory* (Melvin H. Marx). New York: The Macmillan Co., 1951.
Maslow, Abraham H. "Problem-Centering vs. Means-Centering Science," *Philosophy of Science*. Vol. 13, October 1936.
────. "Psychological Data and Value Theory," *New Knowledge in Human Values* (Abraham H. Maslow). New York: Harper and Brothers, 1959.
McDonald, Neil and William Elliot. *Western Political Heritage*. New York: Prentice-Hall, 1949.
McDougall, William. *An Introduction to Social Psychology*. Boston: J. W. Luce and Co., 1921.
McEwen, William P. *Enduring Satisfaction*. New York: Philosophical Library, Inc., 1949.
McIlwain, C. H. *The Growth of Political Thought in the West*. New York: Macmillan, 1932.
McKeon, Richard. "Universities in the Modern World," *Issues in University Education* (Frankel). New York: Harper and Brothers, 1959.
Means, Gardiner C. *Progress Report, National Resources Committee*. Washington: National Resources Committee, 1937.
────. *The Structure of the American Economy*. National Resources Committee, Washington, D. C., U. S. Gov. Printing Office, 1939-40.
Meehl, Paul E. and Kenneth MacCorquodale. "Operational Validity of Intervening Constructs," *Psychological Theory* (Melvin H. Marx). New York: The Macmillan Co., 1951.

———. "Pattern in Cultural Phenomena," *An Appraisal of Anthropology* (Sol Tax). Chicago: The University of Chicago Press, 1953.

Littman, Richard A. and Ephraim Rosen. "The Molar-Molecular Distin *Psychological Theory* (Melvin H. Marx). New York: The Macmilla 1951.

Locke, John. *Essays Concerning Human Understanding*. Oxford: Clarendo 1894.

Loewenberg, Bert J. "Some Problems Raised by Historical Relativism," *of Modern History*. Vol. XXI, No. 1 (March 1949).

Loewenberg, Bert J. and Samuel H. Brockunier. "Objectivity, Certaint Values," *The Social Sciences in Historical Study* (Bulletin 64). New Social Science Research Council, 1954.

Loewenberg, Bert J. and Hugh Aitken. "The Process of Historical Res *The Social Sciences in Historical Study* (Bulletin 64). New York: Science Research Council, 1954.

Lovejoy, Arthur C. *Revolt Against Dualism*. LaSalle, Ill.: Open Court Pub Co., 1930.

Lundberg, George A. "The Thoughtways of Contemporary Sociology," *An Sociological Review*. Vol. I, 1936.

———. *Foundations of Sociology*. New York: Macmillan, 1953.

Lundberg, George A., Clarence C. Schrag, and Otto N. Larsen. *Sociology* York: Harper and Brothers, 1954.

Lynd, Robert S. *Knowledge for What?* Princeton: Princeton University 1939.

MacCorquodale, Kenneth and Paul E. Meehl. "Operational Validity of vening Constructs," *Psychological Theory* (Melvin H. Marx). New The Macmillan Co., 1951.

Machlup, Fritz. "The Problem of Verification in Economics," *The So Economic Journal*. Vol. XXII, No. 1 (July 1955).

MacIver, Robert M. *Community*. London: Macmillan, 1915.

———. *The Modern State*. Oxford: The Clarendon Press, 1926.

———. *Social Causation*. Boston: Ginn and Co., 1942.

———. *The Elements of Social Science*. London: Methuen and Co., Ltd.,

MacIver, Robert M. and Charles H. Page. *Society*. New York: Holt, Ri and Winston Inc., 1949.

Malinowsky, Bronislaw. "Anthropology," *The Encyclopedia Britannica*. York: Encyclopedia Britannica, Inc., 1922, First Sup. Vol.

———. "Culture," *Encyclopedia of the Social Sciences* (Edwin R. A. Sel and Alvin Johnson). New York: The Macmillan Co., 1931, Vol. IV.

———. *A Scientific Theory of Culture*. Chapel Hill: The University of Carolina Press, 1944.

———. *The Dynamics of Cultural Change*. New Haven: Yale University 1945.

Mandelbaum, Maurice H. *The Problem of Historical Knowledge*. New Liveright Publishing Corporation, 1938.

———. "Causal Analysis in History," *Journal of the History of Ideas*. V 1942.

Mering, Otto von. *A Grammar of Human Values*. Pittsburgh: University of Pittsburgh Press, 1961.

Merriam, Charles E. *Political Power*. New York: McGraw-Hill Book Co., Inc., 1934.

———. *Systematic Politics*. Chicago: The University of Chicago Press, 1945.

Merton, Robert K. "Discussion of: The Position of Sociological Theory," *American Sociological Review*. April 1948.

———. "The Self-Fulfilling Prophecy," *Antioch Review*. Vol. 8, 1948.

———. *Social Theory and Social Structure*. Glencoe, Ill.: The Free Press, 1949.

Michels, Robert. *Political Parties* (Tr., Eden and Cedar Paul). New York: Hearst's International Library Co., 1915.

Miller, James G. "Toward a General Theory for the Behavioral Sciences," *The State of the Social Sciences* (Leonard D. White). Chicago: The University of Chicago Press, 1956.

Mills, C. Wright. "On Intellectual Craftsmanship," *Symposium on Sociological Theory* (Llewellyn Gross). White Plains, New York: Row, Peterson and Co., 1959.

Mills, F. C. "On the Changing Structure of Economic Life," *Economic Essays in Honor of Wesley Clair Mitchell*. New York: Columbia University Press, 1935.

Mises, Ludwig von. *Human Action*. New Haven: Yale University Press, 1949.

Mises, Richard von. *Probability, Statistics, and Truth*. New York: The Macmillan Co., 1939.

Mitchell, C. W. "Intelligence and the Guidance of Economic Evolution," *Scientific Monthly*. Vol. XLIII, November 1936.

Mitchell, Wesley Clair. *Business Cycles*. Berkeley: University of California Press, 1913.

———. "The Prospects of Economics," *The Trend of Economics* (Rexford G. Tugwell). New York: A. A. Knopf, 1924.

———. "Quantitative Analysis in Economic Theory," *The American Economic Review*. Vol. XV, March 1925.

———. *The Backward Art of Spending Money*. New York: McGraw-Hill Book Co., Inc., 1937.

Montague, William P. *Ways of Knowing*. New York: Macmillan, 1925.

Morgan, C. Lloyd. *Emergent Evolution*. New York: Henry Holt and Co., 1928.

Morris, Charles W. *Foundations of the Theory of Signs* from *International Encyclopedia of Unified Science* (Volumes I and II: Foundations of the Unity of Science). Chicago: The University of Chicago Press, 1938, Vol. 1, No. 2.

———. *Signs, Language, and Behavior*. New York: Prentice-Hall, Inc., 1946.

Muckler, F. and L. I. O'Kelly. *An Introduction to Psychopathology*. Englewood Cliffs: Prentice-Hall, Inc., 1955.

Muller, Herbert J. *The Uses of the Past*. New York: Oxford University Press, 1952.

Murdock, George P. *Social Structure*. New York: The Macmillan Co., 1949.

———. "Sociology and Anthropology," *For a Science of Social Man* (John P. Gillin). New York: The Macmillan Co., 1954.

Murphy, Gardner. "The Research Task of Social Psychology," *Journal of Social Psychology*. Vol. 10, 1929.
————. *Personality*. New York: Harper and Brothers, 1947.
————. *The Historical Introduction to Modern Psychology*. New York: Harcourt, Brace, and Co., 1949.
Murphy, Gardner, Lois B. Murphy, and Theodore M. Newcomb. *Experimental Social Psychology*. New York: Harper and Brothers, 1937.
Murphy, Lois B., Gardner Murphy, and Theodore M. Newcomb. *Experimental Social Psychology*. New York: Harper and Brothers, 1937.
Murray, Henry A., Clyde Kluckhohn, and David Schneider. *Personality in Nature, Society and Culture*. New York: A. A. Knopf, 1955.
Murray, Henry A. "Drive, Time, Strategy, Measurement, and Our Way of Life," *Assessment of Human Motives* (Gardner Lindzey). New York: Rinehart, 1958.
————. "Toward a Classification of Interaction," *Toward a General Theory of Action* (Talcott Parsons and Edward A. Shils). Cambridge: Harvard University Press, 1959.
Nadel, Siegfried F. *Foundations of Social Anthropology*. Glencoe, Ill.: The Free Press, 1953.
Naftalin, Arthur, Don Calhoun, Benjamin N. Nelson, Andreas G. Papandreou, and Mulford Q. Sibley. "The Nature of Community," *Personality, Work, Community*. Chicago, Philadelphia, New York: J. B. Lippincott Co., 1957.
Nagel, Ernest and Morris R. Cohen. *An Introduction to Logic and Scientific Method*. New York: Harcourt, Brace and Co., 1934.
Nagel, Ernest. *Principles of the Theory of Probability* from *International Encyclopedia of Unified Sciences* (Volumes I and II: Foundations of the Unity of Science). Chicago: The University of Chicago Press, 1939, Vol. I, No. 6.
————. "The Causal Character of Modern Physical Theory," *Readings in the Philosophy of Science* (Herbert Feigl and May Brodbeck). New York: Appleton-Century-Crofts, Inc., 1953.
————. "The Logic of Historical Analysis," *Readings in the Philosophy of Science* (Herbert Feigl and May Brodbeck). New York: Appleton-Century-Crofts, Inc., 1953.
————. *The Structure of Science*. New York: Harcourt, Brace and World, Inc., 1961.
Nelson, Benjamin N. "The Future of Illusions," *Psychoanalysis*. Vol. 2, No. 4 (Spring-Summer 1934).
Nelson, Benjamin N., Don Calhoun, Arthur Naftalin, Andreas G. Papandreou, and Mulford Q. Sibley. "The Nature of Community," *Personality, Work, Community*. Chicago, Philadelphia, New York: J. B. Lippincott Co., 1957.
Neurath, Otto. *Encyclopedia and Unified Science* from *International Encyclopedia of Unified Science* (Volumes I and II: Foundations of the Unity of Science). Chicago: The University of Chicago Press, 1938, Vol. I, No. 1.
Nevins, Allan. *The Gateway to History*. New York: Heath and Co., 1938.
Newcomb, Theodore N., Gardner Murphy, and Lois B. Murphy. *Experimental Social Psychology*. New York: Harper and Brothers, 1937.
Newcomb, Theodore N. "Studying Social Behavior," *Methods of Psychology*

(Tom Gaylord Andrews). New York: J. Wiley and Sons, Inc., 1948.

———. "Discussion of: The Position of Sociological Theory," *American Sociological Review* (April 1948).

———. *Social Psychology.* New York: The Dryden Press, 1950.

———. "Sociology and Psychology," *For a Science of Social Man* (John P. Gillin). New York: The Macmillan Co., 1954.

Newell, Allen and Herbert A. Simon. "Models: Their Uses and Limitations," *The State of the Social Sciences* (Leonard D. White). Chicago: The University of Chicago Press, 1956.

Nichols, Jeannette P. "Reactions to Bulletin 54," *The Social Sciences in Historical Study* (Bulletin 64). New York: The Social Science Research Council, 1954.

Normano, Joao F. *The Spirit of American Economics.* New York: The John Day Co., 1943.

Northrop, Filmer. *The Logic of the Sciences and Humanities.* New York: The Macmillan Co., 1947.

Odegard, Peter H. "A New Look at Leviathan," *Frontiers of Knowledge* (Lynn White). New York: Harper and Brothers, 1956.

Ogden, Charles K. and I. A. Richards. *The Meaning of Meaning.* New York: Harcourt, Brace, and Co., 1956.

O'Kelly, L. I. and F. Muckler. *An Introduction to Psychopathology.* Englewood Cliffs: Prentice-Hall, Inc., 1955.

Oppenheimer, J. Robert. "Science and the Human Community," *Issues in University Education* (Frankel). New York: Harper and Brothers, 1959.

Page, Charles H. and Robert MacIver. *Society.* New York: Holt, Rinehart and Winston, Inc., 1949.

Papandreou, A., Don Calhoun, Arthur Naftalin, Benjamin N. Nelson, and Mulford Q. Sibley. "The Nature of Community," *Personality, Work, Community.* Chicago, Philadelphia, New York: J. P. Lippincott Co., 1957.

Papandreou, A. "Some Basic Problems in the Theory of the Firm," *A Survey of Contemporary Economics* (Bernard Haley). Homewood, Ill.: Richard D. Irwin, Inc., 1952, Vol. II.

Parsons, Talcott. "The Position of Sociological Theory," *American Sociological Review* (April 1948).

———. *The Structure of Social Action.* Glencoe, Ill.: The Free Press, 1948.

———. *Essays in Sociological Theory, Pure and Applied.* Glencoe, Ill.: The Free Press, 1949.

———. *The Social System.* Glencoe, Ill.: The Free Press, 1951.

———. "Psychology and Sociology," *For a Science of Social Man* (John P. Gillin). New York: Macmillan, 1954.

———. "The Social Systems: A General Theory of Action," *Toward a Unified Theory of Human Behavior* (Roy A. Grinker). New York: Basic Books Inc., 1956.

———. "Boundary Relations Between Sociocultural and Personality Systems," *Toward a Unified Theory of Human Behavior* (Roy R. Grinker). New York: Basic Books, Inc., 1956.

Parsons, Talcott and A. L. Kroeber. "The Concepts of Culture and Social System," *American Sociological Review* (October 1958).

Parsons, Talcott and Edward A. Shils. "The Social System," *Toward a General Theory of Action* (Talcott Parsons and Edward A. Shils). Cambridge: Harvard University Press, 1931.

Peirce, Charles S. *Collected Papers* (C. Hartshorne and P. Weiss). Cambridge: Harvard University Press, 1931.

———. "Scientific Method," *Dictionary of Philosophy and Psychology* (J. M. Baldwin). Gloucester, Mass.: Peter Smith, Publisher, 1957.

Pennock, J. Roland. "Political Science and Political Philosophy," *The American Political Science Review*, Vol. 45, 1951.

Perry, Charner. "The Semantics of Political Science," *American Political Science Review*. Vol. 44, No. 2 (June 1950).

Pigou, Arthur C. *The Economics of Welfare*. London: The Macmillan Co., 1952.

Planck, Max. *Where is Science Going?* New York: W. W. Norton and Co., Inc., 1932.

———. *The Philosophy of Physics*. London: George Allen and Unwin, Ltd., 1936.

———. *The Universe in the Light of Modern Physics*. London: G. Allen and Unwin, Ltd., 1937.

———. "The Meaning and Limits of Exact Science," *Science*. Vol. LXXXVIII (1949).

Polanyi, Karl. "Semantics of General Economic History," *Research Project on "Origins of Economic Institutions."* Columbia University Council for Research in the Social Sciences, Mimeograph.

Pratt, Carroll C. *The Logic of Modern Psychology*. New York: The Macmillan Co., 1939.

Pratt, James B. *The Religious Consciousness*. New York: The Macmillan Co., 1920.

Radcliffe-Brown, Alfred R. "On the Concept of Function in Social Science," *The American Anthropologist*. Vol. 27 (1935).

Randall, John H. Jr. and George Haines IV. "Controlling Assumptions in the Practice of American Historians," *Theory and Practice in Historical Study: A Report of the Committee on Historiography* (Bulletin 54). New York: Social Science Research Council, 1946.

Ranke, Leopold von, *Zur Kritik neuerer Geschichtochreiber*. Leipzig, 1874. (*Sämmtliche Werke*, Vol. 34)

Rapaport, David. "The Conceptual Model of Psychoanalysis," *Theoretical Models and Personality Theory* (David Kretch and George S. Klein). Durham, North Carolina: Duke University Press, 1952.

Rapoport, Anatal. "Uses and Limitations of Mathematical Models in Social Sciences," *Symposium on Sociological Theory* (Llewellyn Gross). White Plains, New York: Row, Peterson and Co., 1959.

Reder, Melvin W. *Studies in the Theory of Welfare Economics*. New York: Columbia University Press, 1947.

Redfield, Robert. "Relations of Anthropology to the Social Sciences and to the

Humanities," *Anthropology Today* (A. L. Kroeber). Chicago: The University of Chicago Press, 1953.

Reichenbach, Hans. *Philosophic Foundations of Quantum Mechanics.* Berkeley and Los Angeles: University of California Press, 1944.

———. "Probability Methods in Social Science," *The Policy Sciences* (Daniel Lerner and Harold D. Lasswell). Stanford, California: Stanford University Press, 1951.

———. "The Logical Foundations of the Concept of Probability," *Readings in the Philosophy of Science* (Herbert Feigl and May Brodbeck). New York: Appleton-Century-Crofts, Inc., 1953.

Richards, I. A. and Charles K. Ogden. *The Meaning of Meaning.* New York: Harcourt, Brace, and Co., 1956.

Richardson, Moses. *Fundamentals of Mathematics.* New York: The Macmillan Co., 1941.

Robbins, Lionel. *The Nature and Significance of Economic Science.* London: Macmillan and Co., Ltd., 1935.

Romero, Francisco. "Man and Culture," *Ideological Differences and World Order* (F. S. C. Northrop). New Haven: The Yale University Press, 1949.

Rose, Arnold M. *Theory and Method in Social Sciences.* Minneapolis: University of Minnesota Press, 1954.

Rosen, Ephraim and Richard A. Littman. "The Molar-Molecular Distinction," *Psychological Theory* (Melvin H. Marx). New York: The Macmillan Co., 1951.

Rosenberg, Morris and Paul F. Lazarsfeld. *The Language of Social Research.* Glencoe, Ill.: The Free Press, 1955.

Rothwell, Charles E. "Foreword," *The Policy Sciences* (Daniel Lerner and Harold D. Lasswell). Stanford, California: Stanford University Press, 1951.

Ruesch, Jurgen. "Introduction," *Toward a Unified Theory of Human Behavior* (Roy R. Grinker). New York: Basic Books, Inc., 1956.

———. "The Observer and the Observed: Human Communication Theory," *Toward a Unified Theory of Human Behavior* (Roy R. Grinker). New York: Basic Books Inc., 1956.

Ruggles, Richard. "Methodological Developments," *A Survey of Contemporary Economics* (Bernard F. Haley). Homewood, Ill.: Richard D. Irwin, Inc., Vol. II, 1952.

Runes, Dagobert D. *Dictionary of Philosophy.* Patterson, New Jersey: Littlefield, Adams and Co., 1956.

Russell, Bertrand. *Mysticism and Logic.* New York: Barnes and Noble, 1954.

Sabine, George H. *A History of Political Theory.* New York: Henry Holt and Co., Rev., 1950.

Salvemini, Gaetano. *Historian and Scientist.* Cambridge: Harvard University Press, 1939.

Samuelson, Paul A. *Foundations of Economic Analysis.* Cambridge: Harvard University Press, 1937.

———. "Dynamic Process Analysis," *A Survey of Contemporary Economics* (Howard S. Ellis). Homewood, Ill.: Richard D. Irwin, Inc., 1946, Vol. I.

Sapir, Edward. "Personality," *Encyclopedia of the Social Sciences* (Edwin R. A. Seligman and Alvin Johnson). New York: The Macmillan Co., 1934, Vol. XII.

———. *Culture, Language, and Personality*. Berkeley: University of California Press, 1949.

Sarbin, Theodore R. "Role Theory," *Handbook of Social Psychology* (Gardner Lindzey). Cambridge: Addison-Wesley Publishing Co., Inc., Vol. I, 1954.

Sartre, Jean P. *Existentialism* (Tr., Frechtman). New York: Philosophical Library, 1947.

Scates, Douglas E. and Carter V. Good. *Methods of Research*. New York: Appleton-Century-Crofts, Inc., 1954.

Schafer, Roy. "Regression in the Service of the Ego: The Relevance of a Psychoanalytic Concept for Personality Assessment," *Assessment of Human Motives* (Gardner Lindzey). New York: Rinehart and Co., Inc., 1958.

Scheerer, Martin. "Cognitive Theory," *Handbook of Social Psychology* (Gardner Lindzey). Cambridge: Addison-Wesley Publishing Co., Inc., Vol. I, 1954.

Schrag, Clarence C., George A. Lundberg, and Otto N. Larsen. *Sociology*. New York: Harper and Brothers, 1954.

Schumpeter, E. B. *History of Economic Analysis*. New York: Oxford University Press, 1954.

Schneider, David, Clyde Kluckhohn, and Henry Murray. *Personality in Nature, Society, and Culture*. New York: A. A. Knopf, 1955.

Scitovsky, Tibor. "The State of Welfare Economics," *American Economic Review*, June 1951.

Sears, Robert R. "Social Behavior and Personality Development," *Toward a General Theory of Action* (Talcott Parsons and Edward A. Shils). Cambridge: Harvard University Press, 1959.

Shakow, David. "The Psychological System," *Toward a Unified Theory of Human Behavior* (Roy R. Grinker). New York: Basic Books, Inc., 1956.

Sheldon, Richard C. "Some Observations on Theory in the Social Sciences," *Toward a General Theory of Action* (Talcott Parsons and Edward A. Shils). Cambridge: Harvard University Press, 1959.

Shepard, W. J. "Government," *Encyclopedia of the Social Sciences* (Edwin R. A. Seligman and Alvin Johnson). New York: The Macmillan Co., Inc., Vol. VII, 1937.

Sherif, Muzafer. *An Outline of Social Psychology*. New York: Harper and Brothers, 1956.

Shils, Edward A. and Talcott Parsons. "The Social System," *Toward a General Theory of Action* (Talcott Parsons and Edward A. Shils). Cambridge: Harvard University Press, 1959.

Sibley, Mulford Q., Don Calhoun, Arthur Naftalin, Benjamin N. Nelson, and Andreas G. Papandreou. "The Nature of Community," *Personality, Work, Community*. Chicago, Philadelphia, New York: J. B. Lippincott Co., 1957.

Simiand, Francois. "Causal Interpretation and Historical Research," *Enterprise and Secular Change* (Frederic C. Lane and Jelle C. Riemersma). Homewood, Ill.: Richard D. Irwin, Inc., 1953.

Simon, Herbert A. and Allen Newell. "Models: Their Uses and Limitations,"

The State of the Social Sciences (Leonard D. White). Chicago: The University of Chicago Press, 1956.

Simpson, George. *Man in Society.* Garden City, New York: Doubleday and Co., Inc., 1954.

————. *Sociologist Abroad.* The Hague: Nijhoff, 1959.

Sjoberg, Gideon. "Operationalism and Social Research," *Symposium on Sociological Theory* (Llewellyn Gross). White Plains, New York: Row, Peterson and Co., 1959.

Skinner, B. F. "Descriptive Behaviorism," *Psychological Theory* (Melvin R. Marx). New York: The Macmillan Co., 1951.

————. "The Operational Analysis of Psychological Terms," *Readings in the Philosophy of Science* (Herbert Feigl and May Brodbeck). New York: Appleton-Century-Crofts, Inc., 1953.

Smith, Huston. *The Purposes of Higher Education.* New York: Harper and Brothers, 1955.

Smith, M. Brewster. "Anthropology and Psychology," *For a Science of Social Man* (John P. Gillin). New York: The Macmillan Co., 1954.

Sorokin, Pitirim A. *Society, Culture, and Personality.* New York: Harper and Brothers, 1947.

————. *Social and Cultural Dynamics.* New York: The Bedminster Press, 1962.

————. "The Powers of Creative Unselfish Love," *New Knowledge in Human Values* (Abraham H. Maslow). New York: Harper and Brothers, 1959.

Spence, Kenneth W. "The Emphasis on Basic Functions," *Psychological Theory* (Melvin H. Marx). New York: The Macmillan Co., 1951.

————. "The Postulates and Methods of Behaviorism," *Readings in the Philosophy of Science* (Herbert Feigl and May Brodbeck). New York: The Macmillan Co., 1951.

Spence, Kenneth W. and Gustav Bergmann. "Operationism and Theory Construction," *Psychological Theory* (Melvin H. Marx). New York: The Macmillan Co., 1951.

Spencer, Herbert. *Illustrations of Universal Progress.* New York: D. Appleton, 1875.

Spencer, Robert F. "The Humanities in Cultural Anthropology," *Method and Perspective in Anthropology.* Minneapolis: University of Minnesota Press, 1954.

Spengler, J. J. *The American Political Science Review.* Vol. XLIV (June 1950).

Spiegel, John P. "Comparison of Psychological and Group Foci," *Toward a Unified Theory of Human Behavior* (Roy R. Grinker). New York: Basic Books, Inc., 1956.

Spiethoff, Arthur. "The Historical Character of Economic Theories," *The Journal of Economic History.* New York University Press, Vol. XII, No. 2 (Spring 1952).

————. "Pure Theory and Economic Gestalt Theory: Ideal Types and Real Types," *Enterprise and Secular Change* (Frederick C. Lane and Jelle C. Riemersma). Homewood, Ill.: Richard D. Irwin, 1953.

Stabler, E. Russell. *An Introduction to Mathematical Thought.* Cambridge: Addison-Wesley, 1953.

Stevens, S. S. "Psychology and the Science of Science," *Psychological Theory* (Melvin H. Marx). New York: The Macmillan Co., 1951.

Steward, Julian S. "Evolution and Process," *Anthropology Today* (A. L. Kroeber). Chicago: The University of Chicago Press, 1953.

————. "Cultural Causality and Law: A Trial Formulation of the Development of Early Civilizations," *American Anthropologist*. Vol. 51.

Stouffer, Samuel A. "An Empirical Study of Technical Problems in Analysis of Role Obligation," *Toward a General Theory of Action* (Talcott Parsons and Edward A. Shils). Cambridge: Harvard University Press, 1959.

Strong, Edward W. "Criteria of Warranted Assertability of Explanation in History," *The Journal of Philosophy*. Vol. XLIX, No. 3, January 31, 1952.

————. "The Materials of Historical Knowledge," *Naturalism and the Human Spirit* (Yervant H. Krikorian). New York: Columbia University Press, 1944.

Sutton, F. X., D. F. Aberle, A. K. Cohen, A. K. Davis, and M. J. Levy Jr. "The Functional Prerequisites of a Society," *Ethics*. Vol. LX, No. 2, January, 1950.

Tapp, E. J. "Some Aspects of Causation in History," *Journal of Philosophy*. Vol. 49 (January 31, 1952).

Tax, Sol. *An Appraisal of Anthropology Today* (Sol Tax). Chicago: University of Chicago Press, 1953.

Teggart, Frederick J. "Causation in Historical Events," *The Journal of History of Ideas*. Vol. 3 (1942).

Thompson, Laura. "The Societal System, Culture and the Community," *Toward a Unified Theory of Human Behavior* (Roy R. Grinker). New York: Basic Books, Inc., 1956.

Thompson, W. R. and D. O. Hebb. "The Social Significance of Animal Studies," *Handbook of Social Psychology* (Gardner Lindzey). Cambridge: Addison-Wesley Publishing Co., Inc., 1954, Vol. I.

Thorndike, E. L. *Animal Intelligence*. New York: The Macmillan Co., 1911.

Timasheff, N. S. "Order, Causality, and Conjuncture," *Symposium on Sociological Theory* (Llewellyn Gross). White Plains, New York: Row, Peterson and Co., 1959.

Tinbergen, Jan. "Comparative Studies of Economic Growth," *The Comparative Study of Economic Growth and Structure* (National Bureau of Economic Research, Inc., 1959).

Titus, Harold H. *Living Issues in Philosophy*. New York: The American Book Co., 1946.

Tolman, Edward C. *Drives Toward War*. New York: D. Appleton Century-Crofts, Inc., 1942.

————. "The Intervening Variable," *Psychological Theory* (Melvin H. Marx). New York: The Macmillan Co., 1951.

————. "Molar and Purposive Behaviorism," *Psychological Theory* (Melvin H. Marx). New York: The Macmillan Co., 1951.

————. "A Psychological Model," *Toward a General Theory of Action* (Talcott Parsons and Edward A. Shils). Cambridge: The Harvard University Press, 1959.

Toman, James E. P. "Stability vs. Adaptation," *Toward a Unified Theory of*

Human Behavior (Roy R. Grinker). New York: Basic Books, Inc., 1956.

Troeltsch, Ernest. *Der Historismus and Seine Probleme.* Tuebingen, 1922.

Tugwell, Rexford G. "Experimental Economics," *The Trend of Economics* (Rexford G. Tugwell). New York: A. A. Knopf, 1924.

Tugwell, Rexford G. and L. H. Keyserling. *Redirecting Education.* New York: Columbia University Press, 1934, Vol. I.

Tylor, E. B. *Researches into the Early History of Mankind and the Development of Civilization.* London: John Murray, 1865.

Ulich, Robert. "The American University and Changing Philosophies," *Issues in University Education* (Frankel). New York: Harper and Brothers, 1959.

Waldo, Dwight. *Political Science in the United States of America.* Paris: United Nations Educational, Scientific, and Cultural Organization, 1956.

Washburn, S. L. "The Strategy of Physical Anthropology," *Anthropology Today* (A. L. Kroeber). Chicago: University of Chicago Press, 1953.

Watkins, J. W. N. "Ideal Types and Historical Explanation," *Readings in the Philosophy of Science* (Herbert Feigl and May Brodbeck). New York: Appleton-Century-Crofts, Inc., 1953.

Watson, John Broadus. *Behaviorism.* New York: W. W. Norton and Co. Inc., 1939.

Weber, Max. *The Theory of Social and Economic Organization* (Tr., A. M. Henderson and Talcott Parsons). Glencoe, Ill.: The Free Press, 1957.

———. *Methodology of the Social Sciences* (Translated by and edited by Edward A. Shils and Henry A. Finch). Glencoe, Ill.: The Free Press, 1949.

Weiss, Paul. "General Discussion Terminating the First Conference," *Toward A Unified Theory of Human Behavior* (Roy R. Grinker). New York: Basic Books, Inc., 1956.

Werkmeister, William H. *A Philosophy of Science.* New York: Harper and Brothers, 1940.

———. *The Basis and Structure of Knowledge.* New York: Harper and Brothers, 1948.

———. "Theory Construction and the Problem of Objectivity," *Symposium on Sociological Theory* (Llewellyn Gross). White Plains, New York: Row, Peterson and Co. 1959.

White, Leslie A. "The Locus of Mathematical Reality: An Anthropological Footnote," *Philosophy of Science*, Vol. XIV (1947).

———. *The Science of Culture.* New York: Farrar, Straus, and Cudahy, Inc., 1949.

———. *The Evolution of Culture.* New York: McGraw-Hill Book Co., Inc., 1959.

White, Lynn. *Frontiers of Knowledge in the Study of Man.* New York: Harper and Brothers, 1956.

Whitehead, Alfred North. *The Function of Reason.* Princeton: Princeton University Press, 1929.

———. *The Aims of Education.* New York: The Macmillan Co., 1929.

———. *Process and Reality.* New York: The Macmillan Co., 1930.

———. *Adventures of Ideas.* New York: The Macmillan Co., 1933.

———. *Science and the Modern World.* New York: The Macmillan Co., 1935.

———. *Modes of Thought.* New York: The Macmillan Co., 1938.

————. "The Analysis of Meaning," *Essays in Science and Philosophy*. New York: The Philosophical Library, 1947.

Whorf, B. L. *Four Articles on Metalinguistics*. Washington, D.C.: Department of State, 1950.

Williams, John H. "An Economist's Confessions," *American Economic Review*. XLII (March 1952).

Williamson, Harold F., Moses Abramovitz, and Simon Kuznets. "Economics of Growth," *A Survey of Contemporary Economics* (Barnard H. F. Haley). Homewood, Ill.: Richard D. Irwin Inc., 1952, Vol. II.

Winch, P. *Idea of a Social Science and Its Relationship to Philosophy*. New York: Humanities Press, 1958.

Wirth, Louis. "Preface," *Ideology and Utopia* by Karl Mannheim. New York: Harcourt, Brace and Co., 1936.

Wissler, Clark. *Man and Culture*. New York: Thomas Y. Crowell Co., 1923.

Wolff, Kurt H. "The Sociology of Knowledge and Sociological Theory," *Symposium on Sociological Theory* (Llewellyn Gross). White Plains, New York: Row, Peterson and Co., 1959.

Wolff, Kurt H. and John W. Bennett. "Toward Communication Between Sociology and Anthropology," *Current Anthropology* (Wm. L. Thomas). Chicago: University of Chicago Press, 1956.

Wood, Ledger. "Recent Epistemological Schools," *A History of Philosophical Systems* (Vergilius Ferm). Ames, Iowa: Littlefield, Adams, and Co., 1958.

Woodworth, Robert S. *Contemporary Schools of Psychology*. New York: The Ronald Press Co., 1948.

Yerkes, Robert M. *Chimpanzees: A Laboratory Colony*. New Haven: Yale University Press, 1944.

Zetterberg, Hans L. *On Theory and Verification in Sociology*. New York: The Tressler Press, 1954.

Zilsel, Edgar. "Physics and the Problem of Historico-Sociological Laws," *Readings in the Philosophy of Science* (Herbert Feigl and May Brodbeck). New York: Appleton-Century-Crofts, 1953.

Znaniecki, Florian. *The Method of Sociology*. New York: Farrar and Rinehart, Inc., 1934.

INDEX OF NAMES

Abel, T., 469-471
Aberle, D. F., 204
Abramovitz, M., 464, 498
Ackerknecht, E. H., 463
Adams, H. G., 228, 317
Adler, A., 159
Aitken, H., 106, 109, 124, 131, 188,
    189, 227, 317, 383, 411
Alexander, F., 429, 470-471
Allport, F., 297
Allport, G., xi, 38, 85, 113-114, 119,
    120, 137, 138, 144, 145, 148,
    161, 168, 170-171, 173, 175-176,
    178, 180, 181, 182, 197, 200,
    201-202, 206, 245, 297, 298-299,
    324, 342-343, 345-347, 351, 395,
    396, 429, 431-432, 487-488
Andrews, G., 98, 110, 217-218, 223,
    272, 429
Aquinas, T., 536
Aristotle, 74, 117, 191, 259, 328, 360
Aron, R., 434, 444, 511
Arrow, K. J., 45, 47, 144
Asch, S. E., 164, 180, 181, 197, 209,
    297, 299
Ayer, A. J., 125
Ayers, C. E., 255

Bacon, F., 77
Bain, R., 96

Barton, A. H., 410
Bayliff, R. E., 52
Beard, C. A., 132, 241, 318-319, 375
Benedict, R., 40, 356
Bennett, J. W., 108, 306, 432, 471,
    492
Benson, L., 208
Bentham, J., 44, 45
Bergmann, G., 10, 95, 110, 113, 180,
    438
Berlin, I., 44
Bidney, D., 28, 40, 41, 84, 178, 239-
    240, 250-251, 252, 267, 304, 305,
    360-361, 377, 400, 402
Bierstedt, R., 21, 36, 39, 351-352, 354-
    355, 398
Black, M., 526
Blanshard, B., 18, 85, 86
Block, M. L. B., 381, 388
Boas, Franz, 305, 463, 493
Bonner, R., 138
Borgatta, E. F., 131
Boring, E. G., 11, 246
Born, M., 330
Bowers, A. M., 179
Bowers, R. V., 30, 104, 302
Brennan, J. G., 85, 86-87
Bridgman, P. W., 92-94, 112, 125,
    127-128, 266, 444
Brightman, E. S., 18, 85, 178

Brockunier, S. H., 44, 100, 106, 109, 116, 129, 142, 227-228, 263, 278, 279, 316, 317, 319, 375, 376-377, 378, 379, 381, 382, 411, 414, 416, 453, 465
Bronner, A. F., 179
Brown, J. F., 297, 439
Brown, L. G., 267
Brunswik, E., 272, 295, 296-297, 348-349
Buchler, J., 8, 181, 220, 234, 542
Burgess, J. W., 228, 317
Bury, J. P., 416
Bush, V., 130
Butterfield, H., 473
Byron, G. G., 544

Cairnes, J. E., 495
Calhoun, D., 28
Campbell, N. R., 324
Cantril, H., 396, 438
Carnap, R., 125, 281
Cassirer, E., 62, 85, 218
Catlin, G. E. G., 411
Cattell, R., 144, 486-487
Chapin, F. S., 178
Chinoy, E., 491-492
Churchman, C. W., 456-457
Clark, C., 408
Clark, E., 52
Clark, J. B., 256, 277, 408
Clark, J. M., 46, 47, 50, 140, 182, 257, 277, 364, 368, 369, 405, 408
Clough, S., 101, 142, 188, 262, 378
Coates, W. H., 132, 279
Cochran, T. C., 42, 317, 379, 382
Cohen, A. K., 204
Cohen, M. R., 54, 229, 231-232, 261, 280, 320, 323, 332, 375, 376, 377, 379, 382, 383, 411, 413, 414, 415, 458, 466-467, 479-480, 484-485, 505, 509-510
Collingwood, R. G., 106, 112, 262, 279, 433, 434, 474
Commons, J. H., 46, 257, 368, 369-371, 472
Comte, A., 288, 416

Conant, J. B., 130
Cooley, C. H., 23, 164, 247, 471
Copernicus, N., 244, 286, 293, 294, 392
Crutchfield, R., 297, 351
Cunningham, G. W., 219

Dalton, H., 294
Danto, R., 132, 210
Darwin, C., 286, 293, 294
Davis, A. K., 204
Davis, K., 207-208
Descartes, R., 72, 73, 74, 86, 329
Deutsch, M., 131, 179, 324, 397
Dewey, J., viii, 6, 7, 34, 67, 80, 113, 129, 172, 217, 221, 234-235, 283, 286, 374, 482-483, 502, 532
Dilthey, W., 124, 318, 356, 468, 474
Dingle, H., 324
Dobzhansky, T., 148
Dodd, S. C., 352, 398
Donagan, A., 411, 453-454, 504
Dray, W., 443, 444, 473, 504
Driscoll, J. M., 100, 108, 227, 240
Durkheim, E., 56, 203, 462

Easton, D., 12, 26, 28, 41, 52, 54, 84, 100, 108, 111, 116, 123, 141, 190-191, 232, 258, 259, 260, 278, 313, 314-315, 316, 371-372, 374, 409, 410-411, 499-500, 501, 502
Easton, L., 52, 53
Einstein, A., 9, 32, 52, 78, 81, 92, 125, 128, 185, 242, 243, 263, 270, 285, 286, 290, 293, 294, 319, 389, 392, 427
Elliott, W., 41, 191
Emerson, A. E., 22
Emerson, R. W., 67-68, 85
Eulau, H., 522
Evans-Pritchard, E. E., 105
Eysenck, H. J., 210

Feigl, H., 54, 125, 331, 336, 338
Festinger, L., 181
Firth, R., 203-204, 210, 306
Flewelling, R. T., 52

Fling, F. M., 201
Frank, L. K., 441
Frank, P., 330
Freud, S., 137, 157-159, 160, 179, 338
Friedman, M., 14, 100, 440, 458
Friedrich, C. J., 278, 500
Fromm, E., 52, 53, 159, 166, 545
Furfey, P. H., 39, 224

Garceau, O., 141, 182, 315, 372-373
Gardiner, P., 322, 382, 473
Gailbraith, J. K., 368
George, F. H., 430, 451
Gibson, J. J., 429
Gillin, J. P., 28, 276, 525
Goethe, J. W., von, 279
Goldenweiser, A., 307
Goldsmith, R. W., 464
Goldstein, K., 38, 52, 126, 200
Goldstein, L. J., 252, 306, 494-495
Good, C. V., 131, 235
Gordon, D. F., 99, 105, 404-405, 453
Gottschalk, L., 12, 43, 101, 116-117,
    131, 201, 278, 279, 282, 376,
    380, 413, 415, 433, 434, 442-443,
    466, 474, 508
Gouldner, A. W., 206-207
Greenberg, J. H., 252, 386
Grimes, B. E., 52
Grinker, R. R., 22, 136, 205
Gross, L., 52, 441, 445
Gruchy, A. G., 48, 54, 188, 240, 256,
    257, 268, 312-313, 368, 369, 404,
    407, 408

Haines, G., 228, 317, 416
Hall, C. S., 179
Hallowell, A. I., 139, 253, 267, 276,
    309, 360
Hamilton, W. H., 405
Hart, H., 121, 485, 489
Hass, M. R., 386
Hayek, F. A., 522
Healy, W., 179
Hebb, D. O., 274
Hegel, H. W. F., 259, 318, 380, 503
Heisenberg, W., 330

Heller, H., 409, 465
Hempel, C., viii, 95, 235, 291, 294,
    322, 393, 438-439, 441, 443, 444,
    446, 473, 479, 503, 504, 511
Herring, P., 12, 43, 141, 374, 502
Herskovits, M. J., 115, 186, 225, 357,
    401-402, 462, 492
Hilgard, E. R., 411
Hocking, W. E., 85, 178
Hook, S., 44, 338-339, 376, 382, 417,
    465, 508-509
Homan, P. T., 313
Horney, K., 159, 162
Hoselitz, B. F., 28, 520
Hull, C. L., 196, 197, 272, 295-297,
    345, 348-349, 395, 396
Hume, D., 76, 77, 78, 81, 329
Husserl, E., 243
Hutchinson, T. W., 403
Huxley, J. S., 40, 362-363
Hyneman, C S., 100, 108, 227, 240

Infeld, L., 9, 78, 125, 243, 270, 290,
    293, 294, 319
Israel, H. E., 126

James W., 67, 69, 518
Jennings, D. H., 52
Jevons, W. S., 115, 225, 256, 310,
    366, 404
Jung, K. G., 159-160, 179-180

Kant, I., 13, 38, 72, 78, 81, 82, 87,
    135, 220, 230, 243, 264, 285,
    329, 427, 438, 457, 533
Kantor, J., 118, 162, 217, 294, 475
Kaplan, A., 372
Kapp, K. W., 54, 123, 140, 193-194,
    277, 311, 367, 408
Kardiner, A., 179
Katona, G., 367
Kaufmann, F., 84, 235, 281
Keats, J., 8, 536
Kelly, G. A., 110, 167-168, 185, 272-
    273, 304
Kepler, J., 97, 233

Key, V. O., 12, 26, 42, 192, 260, 371, 372, 501
Keynes, J. M., 46, 255, 281, 367-368, 440
Klein, G. S., 14, 137, 144, 168-169, 182-183, 396, 520, 524
Kluckhohn, C., 11, 28, 33, 40, 52, 121, 143, 148, 166, 173, 178, 179, 181, 182, 202, 251, 303, 304, 305, 307, 309, 357-358, 401, 441, 463, 492, 493
Knight, F. H., 50, 406
Köhler, W., 33, 113, 178
Koppers, W., 493
Krech, D., 14, 137, 144, 197, 209, 297, 351, 396, 520, 524
Krikorian, V. H., 85
Kris, E., 180
Kroeber, A. L., 11, 39, 99, 115, 121, 225, 251, 253, 303, 304, 306, 355, 357-358, 361, 362, 386, 401, 441, 463, 471-472, 492, 493
Kuznets, S., 464

Lachman, S. J., 294, 324, 457
Lambert, W. W., 110, 273, 301
Lane, F. C., 99, 404, 406, 510
Lange, O., 115, 226, 255, 256, 310, 363-364, 402-403, 407, 495, 506
Laplace, P. S., 256, 292, 330-331, 355
Larrabee, H. A., 210, 234, 281
Larsen, O. N., 104
Lashley, K. S., 196, 209
Lasswell, D., 26, 41, 42, 187, 190, 258, 260, 315, 372
Lavine, T. Z., 85
Lazarsfeld, P. F., 14, 186, 287, 398, 410
Leibnitz, G., 73, 86
Leiserson, A., 100, 106, 116, 123, 130, 141, 227, 314, 315, 316, 409, 442, 453, 465
Lenzen, V. F., 27, 232, 427
Leonard, W. H., 52
Leontif, W., 226, 235
Lerner, D., 54, 411, 428
Lesser, A., 105, 492

Levin, H., 54
Levi-Strauss, C., 309
Levy, M. J., 204
Lewin, K., 120, 131, 156-157, 161, 179, 298, 300, 349-350, 397
Lewis, C. I., 52, 63, 234, 281
Lewis, O., 463-464
Lindzey, G., 127, 131, 138, 145, 168, 179, 295
Linton, R., 28, 178, 305, 361, 462, 493
Littman, R. A., 196, 197, 198
Locke, J., 16, 76
Loewenberg, B. J., 44, 100, 106, 109, 116, 124, 129, 131, 142, 188, 189, 227-228, 263, 278, 279, 316, 317, 319, 375, 376-377, 378, 379, 381, 382, 383, 411, 414, 416, 453, 465
Lovejoy, A. C., 7, 18
Lundberg, G. A., 11, 30, 32, 39, 52, 96, 98, 104, 120, 126, 178, 217, 224, 239, 249, 274, 275, 302-303, 352-353, 398, 440, 489, 490-491, 522
Lynd, R. S., 39, 53

MacCorquodale, K., 181
Machlup, F., 105, 111, 115, 268, 276, 310-311, 403, 404, 407, 452-453
MacIver, R. M., viii, 28, 39, 98, 158, 178, 182, 185, 189-190, 202-203, 233, 250, 259, 264, 274, 331, 334-339, 352, 353, 354, 369-370, 378, 379, 385, 398, 399, 400, 432, 445-446, 460, 468, 490, 492, 508, 525
MacIlwain, C. H., 54
Malinowski, B., 186, 203, 204, 305, 307, 356, 452, 463
Malthus, T. R., 496
Mandelbaum, M. H., viii, 84, 209, 220, 241, 264-266, 282, 319-320, 375, 381, 412
Mannheim, K., 56, 60, 61, 203
Margenau, H., 9, 10, 81, 86, 127, 128, 129, 232, 270-271, 427, 516-517

Marshall, A., 46, 111, 115, 122, 226, 255, 256, 310, 365-366, 404, 405, 464, 496-497
Martindale, D., 139
Marx, K., 44, 46, 56, 255, 318, 338, 380, 416, 503
Marx, M. H., 11, 104, 113, 119, 126, 223, 246, 272, 295, 394, 396, 439
Maslow, A. H., 38, 52, 53, 130, 396
McDougall, W., 162, 180, 297
McKeon, R., 543
McMaster, J. B., 317
Means, G. C., 46, 257, 312, 368
Meehl, P. E. 181
Mering, O. von, 527-530
Merriam, C. E., 145, 191, 315, 472, 501, 502
Merton, R. K., 14, 15, 84, 105, 114, 203, 204, 224, 289, 302, 314, 399, 400, 446, 452
Michels, R., 315, 499
Mill, J. S., 44, 46, 50, 77, 228, 465, 538, 539
Miller, J. G., 144, 523
Mills, C. W., 14, 287-288
Mills, F. C., 405
Mises, L. von, 111, 226, 277, 311, 495
Mises, R. von, 281
Mitchell, W. C., 46, 47, 54, 116, 257, 277, 313, 367, 368, 406
Montague, W. P., 64, 66, 71, 78, 85
Morgan, L., 267
Morris, C. W., 85, 234
Muller, H. J., 279, 417
Murdock, G. P., 99, 224, 252, 305-306, 356, 400, 492
Murphy, G., 28, 119-120, 131, 137, 144, 148, 165, 175, 182, 239, 347, 461
Murphy, L., 267
Murray, H., 28, 143, 148, 161, 166, 179, 180, 182, 183, 202, 350, 428

Nadel, S. F., 28, 105, 108, 111, 129, 247, 275, 356-357, 400-401, 432, 462-463
Naftalin, A., 28

Nagel, E., viii, 54, 56, 210, 229, 231-232, 264, 281, 323, 324, 376, 380, 384, 411, 415, 458, 476, 505, 511, 513, 521, 523
Nelson, B., 28, 416
Neuman, F., 260
Neurath, O., 337, 384-385
Nevins, A., 228, 442
Newcomb, T. M., 28, 104, 114, 120, 138, 152, 159, 162, 163-164, 202, 223-224, 247-248, 298-300, 350-351, 397, 438, 451-452, 459, 461, 489, 525
Newell, A., 144
Newton, I., 22, 255, 256, 257, 291-292, 293, 329, 332, 392, 439, 440, 499
Nichols, J. P., 414
Northrop, F. S. C., viii, 52, 54, 130, 222, 230, 235, 331, 426, 433, 440

Odegard, P. H., 42
Ogden, C. K., 85, 234
O'Kelley, L. T., 179, 180
Opler, M. E., 306, 357, 492
Oppenheim, P., 291, 294, 392, 439, 444, 479
Oppenheimer, R., 542-543

Page, C. H., 39
Papandreou, A., 28, 192
Pareto, V., 56
Parsons, T., viii, 12, 13, 21, 59, 104, 114, 133, 136, 140, 143, 147, 149, 150, 151, 161, 177, 178, 180, 186, 187, 192, 205-206, 213, 248-249, 252, 253, 271, 275, 286, 287, 288-289, 290, 301, 306, 310, 316, 353, 354, 356, 365, 392, 461, 462, 485-486, 524-525, 525-526
Pasteur, L., 294
Peirce, C. S., 67, 102, 110, 129
Pennock, J. R., 373
Perry, C., 191, 373, 500
Perry, R. B., 7
Peters, R. S., 126
Pigou, A. C., 46, 364

Planck, M., 92, 125, 128, 242, 243, 294, 329, 330-331
Plato, 27, 539
Polanyi, K., 140, 193, 255, 257
Popper, K., 443, 444, 473, 504
Pratt, C. C., 18, 96, 125-126
Pratt, J. B., 85
Ptolemy, C., 243, 392

Radcliffe-Brown, A. R., 204, 306
Randall, J. H., 228, 317, 416
Ranke, L. von, 317
Rapaport, D., 137, 160, 179
Rapoport, A., 445
Reder, M. W., 54
Redfield, R., 40, 276, 355-356, 402, 432
Reichenbach, H., 272, 281, 330, 439
Reitman, W. R., 521
Richards, I. A., 85, 234
Richardson, M., 475
Robbins, L., 44, 433
Romero, F., 178
Rose, A. M., 15, 111, 121, 131, 399, 441, 461, 462
Rosen, E., 196, 197, 198
Rosenberg, M., 14, 398
Rothwell, C. E., 37, 52
Rousseau, J. J., 540
Ruesch, J., 53, 161, 290
Ruggles, R., 188, 225-226, 235, 464-465
Russell, B., 52, 522

Sabine, G. H., 54
Salvemini, G., 282, 472-473
Samuelson, P. A., 54, 99, 188, 498
Sapir, E., 154, 219, 386
Sarbin, T. R., 181, 325
Sartre, J. P., 347
Say, J. B., 495
Scates, D. E., 131, 235
Schafer, R., 180
Scheerer, M., 198, 209, 385
Scheler, M., 56
Schiller, F., 67, 69
Schneider, D., 145

Schrag, C. C., 104
Schumpeter, E. B., 12, 403
Scitovsky, T., 45, 54, 47
Sears, R. R., 350
Senior, W. N., 256
Shakow, D., 160, 180
Sheldon, R. D., 149, 285, 289
Shepard, W. I., 258
Sherif, M., 297, 350
Shils, E., 114, 136, 149, 177, 178, 205, 286, 310
Sibley, M. E., 28
Simiand, F., 376
Simon, H. A., 144
Simpson, G., 15, 39, 301, 302, 522
Sjoberg, G., 14, 96, 98, 125
Skinner, B. F., 95, 344
Smith, A., 44, 45, 255, 364, 496
Smith, M. B., 28, 160, 179, 197, 209, 245, 246, 525
Smith, H., 541, 545
Sorokin, P. A., 11, 21, 224, 250, 301
Spence, K. W., 10, 110, 113, 198-199, 295, 344-345, 438
Spencer, H., 250, 288, 364, 399, 416, 503
Spencer, R. F., 105, 121
Spengler, J. J., 187
Spengler, O., 106, 318, 356, 380, 503
Spiegel, J. P., 28, 204
Spiethoff, A., 116, 226, 312, 366, 407, 472
Stabler, R., 475
Stevens, S. S., 125
Steward, J. S., 254, 306-307, 493-494
Stouffer, S. A., 114, 289
Strong, E. W., 142, 252, 322, 412, 435, 442, 467, 510
Sutton, F. X. 204

Tapp, E. J., 182, 376, 379, 383-384
Tax, S., 25, 53, 309
Teggart, F. J., 376, 381, 466
Thompson, L., 22, 309-310
Thompson, W. R., 274
Thorndike, E. L., 85
Timasheff, N. S., 352, 353-354

Tinbergen, J., 464
Titus, H. H., 85
Tolman, E. C., 28, 104, 137, 147, 169,
    180, 181, 183, 196, 245, 272,
    296-297, 333, 343-344, 345, 346,
    430-431
Toman, J. E. P., 22, 284
Toynbee, A., 106, 318
Troeltsch, E., 318
Tugwell, R. G., 46, 47, 54, 257, 368,
    496
Tylor, E. B., 355

Ulich, R., 543

Veblen, T., 46, 257

Waldo, D., 28, 54, 410, 499
Warner, W. L., 356
Washburn, S. L., 121
Watkins, J. W. N, 142
Watson, J. B., 95, 137, 162, 169, 196,
    246, 308, 338, 343, 347, 394-395,
    429, 431, 439, 451, 534
Weber, M., 48, 49, 54, 59, 84-85, 139,
    203, 271, 468-469, 524, 529
Weiss, P., 196

Werkmeister, W. H., viii, 6, 8, 9, 10,
    33, 49, 51, 61, 62, 85, 127, 128,
    218, 234, 241, 261, 271, 282, 322,
    331, 453, 457, 475, 507
White, L. A., 139, 251, 307-308, 309,
    358-360, 361
White, L., Jr., 177
White, L. D., 144
Whitehead, A. N., viii, 4, 17, 22, 178,
    188, 189, 219, 255, 257, 267, 291-
    293, 302, 332, 475, 541, 542, 546
Whorf, B. L., 356, 386, 401
Williamson, H. F., 464
Winch, P., 16, 17
Wirth, L., 84
Wissler, C., 306
Wolff, K. H., 84, 108, 306, 432, 471,
    492
Wood, L., 18
Woodworth, R. S., 210

Yuker, H., 247

Zetterberg, H. L., 110, 139, 397, 439,
    452, 453, 456-457, 462
Zilsel, E., 467, 506-507, 509
Znaniecki, F., 275, 432, 471

INDEX OF SUBJECTS

Adequacy, 389-394. See Coherence.

Allocation, 189-194, 254-260

Behavioral process, 21: temporal dimension of, 22-23, 184-189, 254-257, 261-266, 377-378; collective-individual dimension of, 24; sociocultural aspect of, 147; motivational aspect of, 157-177

Causality: as a principle of objective reference, 328; reconstructed conception of, 328-332; toward a definition of, 332-336; as multiple behavioral causation, 336-384; denial of, 329-332, 347-349, 352-353

Classification, 427. See Synoptic model

Coherence (consistency and adequacy) as a generic logical criterion for verifying explanatory and predictive hypotheses, 220-221, 389-394, 394-418, 449-454

Conceptual framework for orienting behavioral data, 133-134, 137-143; of synoptic model, 146-147, 147-194; as distinguished from theoretical framework, 135-136, 244

Consistency, 390, 449-454, 475. See Coherence and Deduction of implications

Constructed knowledge (epistemological dualism), 7-12, 80-83, 230-233

Culture, 150-151, 250-254, 355-363

Deduction of implications, 86, 450-451, 475. See Hypothetical-deductive method

Dogmatic authoritarianism, 58, 64-66

Empirical testing, 107, 389-391, 454: as experimental testing, 455-458; as statistical correlating, 271-272, 281, 456-457, 521-522; as controlled observation, 457-459; as experiential testing, 459-461; through comparative case analysis, 461-467; through introspective projection, 467-475

Empiricism: naïve sense impressionism, 58, 69-71; pure empiricism, 58, 75-78; scientific empiricism, 92-95, 330, 342, 523

Epistemological perspective, 13, 63, 213-233

Epistemological dualism (constructive knowledge), 7-12, 80-83, 230-233

Epistemology and methodology, 13-17

Epistemology and social-scientific inquiry, vii-x, 3-7, 18, 85, 223-229, 239-241, 514-515

Explanation and prediction, 437-447, 478-511

Factual data, 230-233

Faustian quest, 214-215

Functional-structural synchronization, 203-208

Hypothetical-deductive method for correlating diverse observational and verificative techniques, 220-222, 425-435; acknowledgment by social scientists, 223-229

Hypotheses: as classificatory constructs, 427-428; as explanatory constructs, 437-439; as predictive constructs, 439-446

Idiographic: See Nomothetic-idiographic synchronization

Induction: See Hypothetical-deductive method

Institutions, 152-153

Interdisciplinary integration with relative autonomy, 194-195, 522-527

Introspection, 427-435, 467-475, 532-533

Knowing, ways of, 63, 64-84, 220-222, 425-435

Knowledge: as highly probable, 109-112, 269-280, 451; as inferential, 7-12, 80-82; as operational, see Operationalism; as problem-centered vs. technique-centered, 117-125

Knowledge situation, 58: of reflective inquiry, 220-222

Law-like generalizations, 290-295, 295-324, 478-511

Linguistics, 386

Logical positivism, 92-95, 330, 342, 523

Meaning-Situation, 58, 61-63, 237-241: its derivation from the value-situation, 215; its determination of the knowledge-situation, 215-217; its postulational character, 217-220

Methodology and epistemology, 13-17

Molar-molecular distinction, 195-199, 347-350, 519-520

Motivation, 299: psychodynamic, 157-161; interpersonal, 161-166; conscious goal-seeking, 166-177, 181-183

Mysticism, 58, 66

Nature, 148-149

Nomothetic-idiographic synchronization, 199-203, 344-346, 369-371, 483-484, 507-511

Objectivity: as attitude of inquirer, 215, 490-491, 538-539; as referent of scientific constructs, 242-244, 290-294, 328; as epistemological objectivity, 218-220, 449-450, 515-522, 531

Observational techniques, 425, 427-428. See Introspection

Operationalism: narrower operationalism, 91-101; broader operationalism, 91, 101-128; uncritical non-operationalism, 64-71; critical non-operationalism, 71-78; operationism, 92-93

Personality, 154-157, 165-166, 178-179, 244-248, 342-351; psychological field of, 300-301

Pragmatism: naïve in knowledge-situation, 58, 67-69; critical in meaning-situation, 102, 215-220, 392-393

Prediction and explanation, 437-447, 478-511

Rationalism, 58, 72-75

Reflective inquiry, 58, 213-233

Relative self-determinism, 168-177: vs. indeterminism and radical determinism, 174-175, 328-342, 346-347, 358-363, 372-374, 383-384

Relativism, 55-84: radical, 55-57; situational, 57-62, 543-545

Relevancy, 391

Role, 152; and role behavior, 164-165, 299-300

Scepticism: negative, 51, 78-80; positive, 32, 80-83

Social-scientific inquiry and epistemology, viii-ix, 3-7, 223-229, 239-241, 514-515

Society, 151-153

Sociocultural evolution, 184-189, 254, 255-257, 262-263, 361-363, 368-371, 377-379, 381, 493-494

Sociology of knowledge, 51, 55-57, 60-61

Statistical correlations, 271-272, 281, 330-331, 338-339, 352, 456-457, 521-522

Structure: See Functional-structural synchronization

Subject matter of social-scientific disciplines: psychology, 25; sociology, 25; anthropology, 25; economics, 26; political science, 26; history, 26-27

Systematic conceptualizing, 112-117, 283-284, 286, 391-392, 478-479: vs. fragmentizing, 284-290; 295-323, 521-526

Technological determinism, 194, 358-360, 368-369

Temporal dimension of behavior, 22-23, 184-189, 254-257, 261-266, 377-378

Testing: See Empirical testing

Value judgments and behavioral inquiry, 5: evaluational complications for inquiry, 29-31, 481-483; value-motivation of inquiry, 31-33, 214-215; unreflective and reflective values as behavioral data, 33-35, 166-177; policy involvement by social scientists, 36-47; social-scientific and philosophical normative judgments, 48-54, 527-546

Variables of behavioral data: dependent variables, 147, 456; independent variables, 147-168, 456; intervening variable, 166-177, 467, 501-503, 532-533; problem of isolating, 480-481

Verification: See Coherence